core

JAVA™ 1.1

Volume II - Advanced Features

D0206424

THE SUNSOFT PRESS
JAVA SERIES

▼ **Core Java 1.1,** *Volume I - Fundamentals*
Cay S. Horstmann & Gary Cornell

▼ **Core Java 1.1,** *Volume II - Advanced Features*
Cay S. Horstmann & Gary Cornell

▼ **Graphic Java 1.1,** *Second Edition*
David M. Geary

▼ **Inside Java WorkShop 2.0,** *Second Edition*
Lynn Weaver

▼ **Instant Java,** *Second Edition*
John A. Pew

▼ **Java by Example,** *Second Edition*
Jerry R. Jackson & Alan L. McClellan

▼ **Jumping JavaScript**
Janice Winsor & Brian Freeman

▼ **Just Java 1.1 and Beyond,** *Third Edition*
Peter van der Linden

▼ **Not Just Java**
Peter van der Linden

core

JAVA™ 1.1

Volume II - Advanced Features

CAY S. HORSTMANN • GARY CORNELL

Sun Microsystems Press
A Prentice Hall Title

The publisher offers discounts on this book when ordered in bulk quantities.
For more information, contact Corporate Sales Department, Prentice Hall PTR ,
One Lake Street, Upper Saddle River, NJ 07458. Phone: 800-382-3419; FAX: 201- 236-7141.
E-mail: corpsales@prenhall.com.

Editorial/production supervision: *Navta Associates*
Cover design director: *Jerry Votta*
Cover designer: *Anthony Gemmellaro*
Cover illustration: *Karen Strelecki*
Manufacturing manager: *Alexis R. Heydt*
Marketing manager: *Stephen Solomon*
Acquisitions editor: *Gregory G. Doench*
Sun Microsystems Press publisher: *Rachel Borden*

10 9 8 7 6 5 4 3 2

ISBN 0-13-766965-8

Sun Microsystems Press
A Prentice Hall Title

Contents

Tables, Examples, and Figures

Figures

Preface

To the Reader

The book you have in your hands is the second part of the third edition of *Core Java*. The first edition appeared in early 1996, the second in late 1996. The first two editions appeared in a single volume, but the second edition was already 150 pages longer than the first, which was itself not a thin book. When we sat down to work on the third edition, it became clear to us that a one-volume treatment of all the features of Java that a serious programmer needs to know was no longer possible. Hence, we decided to break up the third edition into two volumes; the second volume is what you are looking at.

The first volume covered the essential features of the language; this volume covers the advanced topics that a Java programmer will need to know so that he or she will (we hope) be in a position to do commercial Java development. Thus, as with the first volume and the previous editions of this book, we still *are targeting programmers who want to put Java to work on real projects.*

Please note: If you are an experienced Java developer who is comfortable with the new event model and the other language features, such as inner classes, that were added to Java 1.1, *you need not have read the first volume* in order to benefit from this volume. (While we do refer to sections of the previous volume when appropriate and, of course, hope you will buy or have bought Volume 1, you can find the needed background material in any *comprehensive* introductory Java 1.1 book.)

Finally, when any book is being written, errors and inaccuracies are inevitable. We would very much like to hear about them. Of course, we would prefer to hear about them only once. For this reason, we have put up a Web page at http://www.horstmann.com with an FAQ, bug fixes, and workarounds. Strategically placed at the end of the Web page (to encourage you to read the previous reports) is a Java applet that you can use to report bugs or problems and to send suggestions for improvements to future editions.

About This Book

First, except for Chapter 1, which is a thorough discussion of input and output in Java 1.1, the remaining chapters in this book can almost certainly be read independently of each other—only occasional backtracking will be needed at most. We suggest reading Chapter 1 first and then turning to whatever topic interests you the most in the remaining chapters. Here are short descriptions of the various chapters.

Input/output in Java is handled through what Java calls *streams*, which are conceptually the same as the similarly named feature of C++. Streams let you deal in a uniform manner with the large number of possible ways of getting input from any source of data that can send out a sequence of bytes and then sending it to any destination that can also work with a sequence of bytes. In particular, we include detailed coverage of the new Reader and Writer classes in Java 1.1, which make it easy to deal with Unicode; and we include the new object serialization mechanism in Java 1.1, which makes saving the state of an object almost trivial.

Chapter 2 covers *multithreading*, which enables you to program tasks to be done in parallel. (A *thread* is a flow of control within a program.) We show you how to set up threads and how to make sure none of them get stuck. We put this knowledge to practical use by example, showing you the techniques needed to build timers and animations.

Chapter 3 covers one of the most exciting APIs in Java: the one for networking. Java makes it phenomenally easy to do sophisticated network programming. Not only do we cover this API in depth, we also discuss the important consequences of the applet security model for network programming.

Chapter 4 covers the *JDBC*, the Java database connectivity API. We show you how to write useful programs to handle realistic databases, using a core subset of the JDBC API. Please note that this is not a complete treatment of everything you can do with the rich JDBC API. (A complete treatment of the JDBC API would certainly require a book almost as long as this one.)

Chapter 5 covers *remote objects* and *Remote Method Invocation* (RMI). This API lets you work with Java objects that are distributed over a net or running in separate processes on a single machine. We also show you where the rallying cry of "objects everywhere" can realistically be used.

Chapter 6 covers some advanced features of the *Abstract Windowing Toolkit* (AWT) that seemed too specialized for coverage in Volume 1 but are, nonetheless, techniques that should be part of every Java programmer's toolkit. These features include the image manipulation API and the (partially implemented) cut-and-paste API. We actually take the cut-and-paste API one step further than JavaSoft itself did: We show you how to cut and paste Java objects between different Java programs via the system clipboard.

Chapter 7 shows you what you need to know about the new component API for Java—*JavaBeans*™. We show you what you need to know in order to write your own Java beans. (We do not cover the various builder environments that are

designed to manipulate beans, however.) The JavaBeans™ component technology is an extraordinarily important technology for the eventual success of Java because it can potentially bring the same ease of use to Java programming environments that ActiveX™ controls give to the millions of Visual Basic™ programmers out there. Of course, since these components are written in Java, they have the advantage over ActiveX controls in that they are immediately cross-platform and immediately capable of fitting into the sophisticated security model of Java.

In fact, Chapter 8 takes up that security model. Java was designed from the ground up to be secure, and this chapter takes you under the hood to see how this design is implemented. We show you how to write your own class loaders and security managers for special-purpose applications. Then, we take up the new security API that allows for such important features as signed classes.

Chapter 9 discusses a specialized feature that we feel can only grow in importance: internationalization. Java is one of the few languages designed from the start to handle Unicode. As a result, you can internationalize Java applications so that they not only cross platforms but cross country boundaries as well. For example, we show you how to write a retirement calculator applet that uses either English, German, or Chinese—depending on the locale of the *browser*.

Chapter 10 takes up *native methods,* which let you call methods written for a specific machine such as the Windows API. Obviously, this feature is controversial: Use native methods, and the cross-platform nature of Java vanishes. Nonetheless, every serious programmer writing Java applications for specific platforms needs to know these techniques. There will be times when you need to turn to the operating system's API for your target platform when you are writing a serious application. We illustrate this by showing you how to access the registry functions in Windows.

Appendix I contains instructions for installing the software and example code from the CD-ROM.

Conventions

As is common in many computer books, we use `courier type` to represent computer code.

There are many C++ notes that explain the difference between Java and this language. You can skip over them if you aren't interested in C++.

Notes are tagged with a "notepad" icon that looks like this.

Java comes with a large programming library or Application Programming Interface (API). When using an API call for the first time, we add a short summary description, tagged with an API icon. These descriptions are a bit more informal, but also a little more informative than those in the official on-line API documentation.

Programs whose source code is on the CD-ROM are listed as examples, for instance, **Example 15-8: WarehouseServer.java** refers to the corresponding code on the CD-ROM.

Acknowledgements

Cay's love, gratitude, and apologies go to his wife Hui-Chen and his children Tommy and Nina for their continuing support for this never-ending project. He also appreciates the support and understanding from Vincent Pluvinage and his colleagues at Preview Software.

Gary also wants to thank Cay's family. They were extraordinarily gracious as revisions came too rapidly and took far too long. He also wants to thank his friends and his co-workers for their patience as he too slowly extricated himself from the quagmire of his own overcommitments.

Next, we both want to thank Mary Lou Nohr for her great copyediting job. Her ability to mesh two conflicting writing styles and keep things consistent amazed us. David Geary, Blake Ragsdell, and Christopher Taylor provided us with very useful reviews. Next, we want to thank the people at Prentice Hall, especially our long-suffering editor Greg Doench, for coordinating this very complicated project. Rachel Borden and John Bortner, our publisher and publicist, respectively, at Sun Microsystems Press were always there to listen with a patient ear when we complained about yet another problem—and do their best to fix it. Nikki Wise and her team at Navta Associates, Inc., came through yet one more time for a project that was again on an impossible schedule. Finally, we want to thank Niko Mak (WinZip), Keith MacDonald (TextPad), and Bob Andreasen (HexWorkshop) for allowing us to include their shareware products on the CD.

CHAPTER

1

Input and Output

Applets would not normally be allowed to work with files on the user's system. Applications, of course, need to do this a lot. In this chapter we cover the methods for handling files and directories as well as the methods for actually writing and reading back information to and from files. This chapter also shows you the object serialization mechanism that is now in Java. This lets you store objects as easily as you can store text or numeric data.

Streams

Input/output techniques are not particularly exciting, but without the ability to read and write data, your applications and (occasionally) applets are severely limited. This chapter is about how to get input from any source of data that can send out a sequence of bytes and how to send output to any destination that can receive a sequence of bytes. These sources and destinations of byte sequences can be—and often are—files, but they can also be network connections and even blocks of memory. There is a nice payback to keeping this generality in mind: information stored in files and information retrieved from a network connection are handled in *essentially the same way*. (See Chapter 3 for information on how to work with networks.) Of course, while data is always *ultimately* stored in a series of bytes, it is often more convenient to think of it as having some higher-level structure such as being a sequence of characters or objects. We cover Java higher-level input/output facilities as well.

In Java, an object from which we can read a sequence of bytes is called an *input stream*. An object to which we can write a sequence of bytes is called an *output stream*. These are implemented in the abstract classes `InputStream` and `OutputStream`. Since byte-oriented streams are inconvenient for processing information stored in Unicode (recall Unicode uses two bytes per character),

there is a separate hierarchy of classes for processing Unicode characters that inherit from the abstract `Reader` and `Writer` superclasses. These classes have read and write operations that are based on 2-byte Unicode characters rather than on single-byte characters.

You saw abstract classes in Chapter 5 of Volume 1. Recall that the point of an abstract class is to provide a mechanism for factoring out the common behavior of classes to a higher level. This leads to cleaner code and makes the inheritance tree easier to understand. The same game is at work with input and output in Java.

As you will soon see, Java derives from these four abstract classes a zoo of concrete classes: you can visit almost any conceivable input/output creature in this zoo.

Reading and Writing Bytes

The `InputStream` class has an abstract method:

```
public abstract int read() throws IOException
```

This method reads one byte and returns the byte read, or –1 if it encounters the end of the input source. The designer of a concrete input stream class overrides this method in order to provide useful functionality. For example, in the `FileInputStream` class, this method reads one byte from a file. The `InputStream` class also has non-abstract methods to read an array of bytes or to skip a number of bytes. These methods call the abstract `read` method, so that subclasses only need to override one method.

Similarly, the `OutputStream` class defines the abstract method

```
public abstract void write(int b) throws IOException
```

which writes one byte to an output file.

Both the `read` and `write` methods can *block* a thread until the byte is actually read or written. This means if the byte cannot immediately be read from or written to (usually because of a busy network connection), Java suspends the thread containing this call. This gives other threads the chance to do useful work while the method is waiting for the stream to again become available. (We discuss threads in Chapter 2.)

The `available` method lets you check the number of bytes that are currently available for reading. This means a fragment like the following is unlikely to ever block:

```
int bytesAvailable = System.in.available();
if (bytesAvailable > 0)
{   byte [] data = new byte [bytesAvailable];
    System.in.read(data);
}
```

When you have finished reading or writing to a stream, close it, using the appropriately named `close` method, because streams use operating system resources that are in limited supply. If an application opens many streams without closing them, system resources may become depleted. Closing an output stream also *flushes* the buffer used for the output stream: any characters that were temporarily placed in a buffer so that they could be delivered as a larger packet are sent off. In particular, if you do not close a file, the last packet of bytes may never be delivered. You can also manually flush the output with the `flush` method.

Even if a stream class provides concrete methods to work with the raw `read` and `write` functions, Java programmers seldom use them. This is because you rarely need to read and write streams of bytes. The data that you are interested in probably contain numbers, strings, and objects.

Java gives you many stream classes derived from the basic `InputStream` and `OutputStream` classes that let you work with data in the forms that you usually use rather than at the low, byte level.

`java.io.InputStream`

- `abstract int read()`

  reads a byte of data and returns the byte read. The `read` method returns a –1 at the end of the stream.

- `int read(byte b[])`

  reads into an array of bytes and returns the number of bytes read. As before, the `read` method returns a –1 at the end of the stream.

- `int read(byte b[], int off, int len)`

  reads into an array of bytes. The `read` method returns the actual number of bytes read, or –1 at the end of the stream.

Parameters:		
	`b`	the array into which the data is read
	`off`	the offset into `b` where the first bytes should be placed
	`len`	the maximum number of bytes to read

- `long skip(long n)`

  skips n bytes in the input stream. It returns the actual number of bytes skipped (which may be less than n if the end of the stream was encountered).

- `int available()`

  returns the number of bytes available without blocking. (Recall that blocking means that the current thread loses its turn.)

- `void close()`

  closes the input stream.

- `void mark(int readlimit)`

  The `mark` method puts a marker at the current position in the input stream. (Not all streams support this feature.) If more than `readlimit` bytes have been read from the input stream, then the stream is allowed to forget the marker.

- `void reset()`

  returns to the last marker. Subsequent calls to `read` reread the bytes.

- `boolean markSupported()`

  returns `true` if the stream supports marking.

 `java.io.OutputStream`

- `public abstract void write(int b)`

  writes a byte of data.

- `public void write(byte b[])`

  writes all bytes in the array b.

- `public void write(byte b[], int off, int len)`

Parameters:	b	the array from which to write the data
	off	the offset into b to the first byte that will be written
	len	the number of bytes to write

- `public void close()`

  closes the output stream.

- `public void flush()`

  flushes the output stream, that is, sends any buffered data to its destination.

The Complete Stream Zoo

Unlike C, which gets by just fine with a single type FILE*, or VB, which has three file types, Java has a whole zoo of 58 (!) different stream types (see Figures 1-1 and 1-2). Library designers claim that there is a good reason to give users a wide choice of stream types: it is supposed to reduce programming errors. For example, in C, some people think it is a common mistake to send output to a file that was open only for reading. (Well, it is not that common, actually.) Naturally, if you do this, the output is ignored at run time. In Java and C++, the compiler catches that kind of mistake because an InputStream (Java) or istream (C++) has no methods for output.

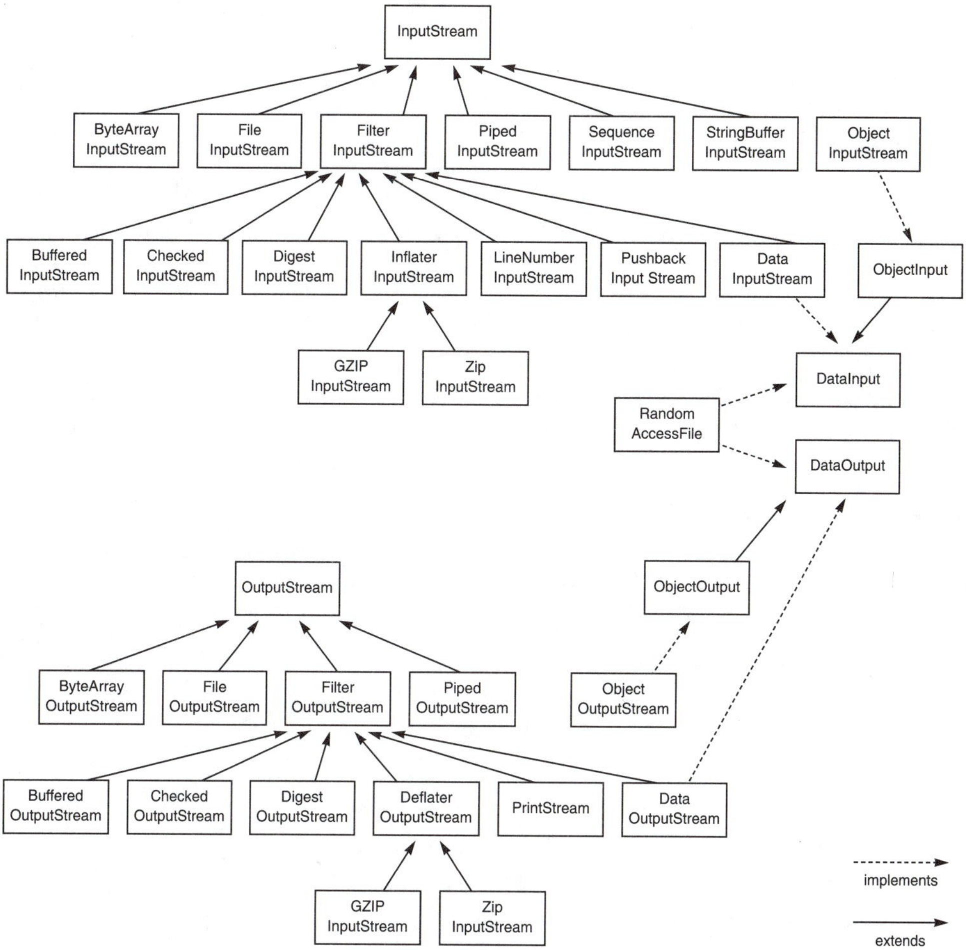

```
                              InputStream

ByteArray    File      Filter       Piped      Sequence    StringBuffer    Object
InputStream  InputStream InputStream InputStream InputStream InputStream   InputStream

Buffered   Checked    Digest     Inflater    LineNumber   Pushback    Data         ObjectInput
InputStream InputStream InputStream InputStream InputStream Input Stream InputStream

              GZIP        Zip
              InputStream InputStream
                                                                        DataInput
                                           Random
                                           AccessFile
                                                                        DataOutput

                                                           ObjectOutput

       OutputStream

ByteArray    File      Filter       Piped                  Object
OutputStream OutputStream OutputStream OutputStream        OutputStream

Buffered    Checked     Digest      Deflater    PrintStream    Data
OutputStream OutputStream OutputStream OutputStream            OutputStream

              GZIP        Zip
              InputStream InputStream
```

--------→ implements

————→ extends

Figure 1-1: Input and Output stream hierarchy

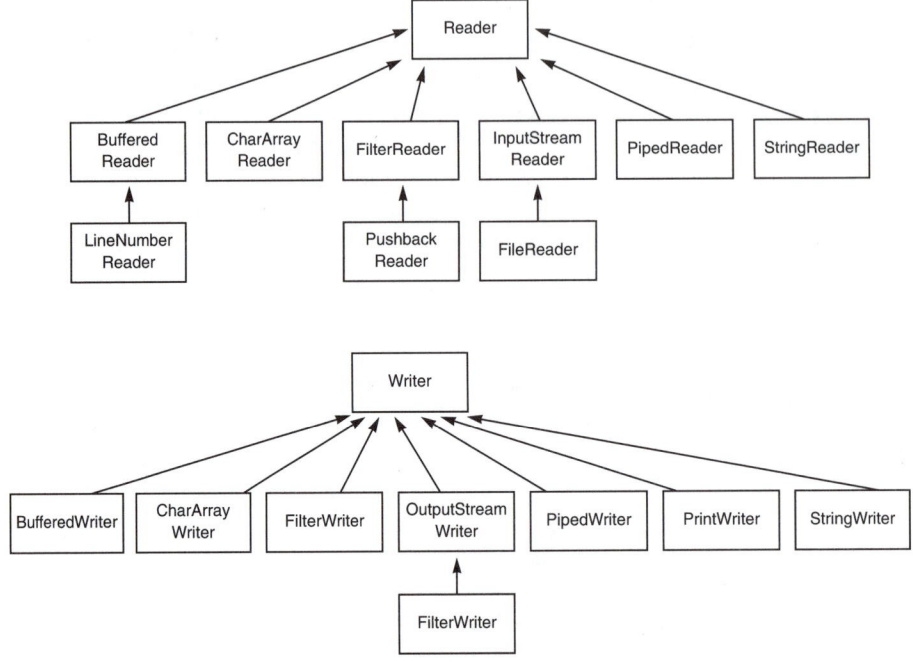

Figure 1-2: Reader and Writer hierarchy

(We would argue that, in C++ and even more so in Java, the main tool that the stream interface designers have against programming errors is intimidation. The sheer complexity of the stream libraries keeps programmers on their toes.)

C++ NOTE: C++ gives us more stream types than we want, such as `istream`, `ostream`, `iostream`, `ifstream`, `ofstream`, `fstream`, `istream_with_assign`, `istrstream`, and so on. The ANSI library takes away some of them and gives back others, such as `wistream`, to deal with wide characters, and `istringstream`, to handle string objects. But Java really goes overboard with streams and gives you the choice (or forces you to specify, depending on your outlook) of having buffering, lookahead, random access, text formatting, or binary data.

Let us divide the animals in the stream class zoo by how they are used. You have already seen the four abstract classes that are at the base of the zoo: `InputStream`, `OutputStream`, `Reader`, and `Writer`. You do not make objects of these types, but other functions can return them. For example, as you saw in Chapter 8 of Volume 1, the URL class has the method `openStream` that returns an `InputStream`. You then use this `InputStream` object to read from the URL. As

we mentioned before, the `InputStream` and `OutputStream` classes let you read and write only individual bytes and arrays of bytes; they have no methods to read and write strings and numbers. You need more capable child classes for this. For example, `DataInputStream` and `DataOutputStream` let you read and write all the basic Java types.

For Unicode text, on the other hand, as we mentioned before, you use classes that descend from `Reader` and `Writer`. The basic methods of the `Reader` and `Writer` classes are similar to the ones for `InputStream` and `OutputStream`.

```
public abstract int read() throws IOException
public abstract void write(int b) throws IOException
```

They work just as the comparable methods do in the `InputStream` and `OutputStream` classes except, of course, these methods return either a Unicode character (as an integer between 0 and 65535) or –1 when you have reached the end of the file.

Finally, there are streams that do useful stuff, for example, the `ZipInputStream` and `ZipOutputStream` that let you read and write files in the familiar ZIP compression format.

Mixing and Matching Stream Filters

`FileInputStream` and `FileOutputStream` give you input and output streams attached to a disk file. You give the name or full pathname of the file in the constructor. For example,

```
FileInputStream fin = new FileInputStream("employee.dat");
```

looks in the current directory for a file named `"employee.dat"`. You can also use a `File` object:

```
File f = new File("employee.dat")
FileInputStream fin = new FileInputStream(f);
```

Like the abstract `InputStream` and `OutputStream` classes, these classes only support reading and writing on the byte level. That is, we can only read bytes and byte arrays from the object `in`.

```
byte b = fin.read();
```

As we will see in the next section, if we just had a `DataInputStream`, then we could read numeric types:

```
DataInputStream din = . . .;
double s = din.readDouble();
```

But just as the `FileInputStream` has no methods to read numeric types, the `DataInputStream` has no method to get data from a file.

Java uses a clever mechanism to separate two kinds of responsibilities. Some streams (such as the FileInputStream and the input stream returned by the openStream method of the URL class) can retrieve bytes from files and other more exotic locations. Other streams (such as the DataInputStream and the PrintWriter) can assemble bytes into more useful data types. The Java programmer has to combine the two into what are often called *filtered streams* by feeding an existing stream to the constructor of another stream. For example, to be able to read numbers from a file, first create a FileInputStream and then pass it to the constructor of a DataInputStream.

```
FileInputStream fin = new FileInputStream("employee.dat");
DataInputStream din = new DataInputStream(fin);
double s = din.readDouble();
```

The data input stream does not correspond to a new disk file. It accesses the data from the file attached to the file input stream, but it has a more capable interface.

If you look at Figure 1-1 again, you can see the classes FilterInputStream and FilterOutputStream. You combine their child classes into a new filtered stream to construct the streams you want. For example, by default, streams are not buffered. That is, every call to read contacts the operating system to ask it to dole out yet another byte. If you want buffering *and* data input, you need to use the following rather monstrous sequence of constructors:

```
DataInputStream din = new DataInputStream
    (new BufferedInputStream
        (new FileInputStream("employee.dat")));
```

Notice that we put the DataInputStream *last* in the chain of constructors because we want to use the DataInputStream methods, and we want *them* to use the buffered read method.

Sometimes you need to keep track of the intermediate streams when chaining them together. For example, when reading input, you often need to peek at the next byte to see if it is the value that you expect. Java provides the PushbackInputStream for this purpose.

```
PushbackInputStream pbin = new PushbackInputStream
    (new BufferedInputStream
        (new FileInputStream("employee.dat")));
```

Now you can speculatively read the next byte

```
int b = pbin.read();
```

and throw it back if it wasn't what you wanted.

```
if (b != '<') pbin.unread(b);
```

But reading and unreading are the *only* methods that apply to the pushback input stream. If you want to look ahead and also read numbers, then you need both a pushback input stream and a data input stream reference.

```
DataInputStream din = new DataInputStream
    (pbin = new PushbackInputStream
        (new BufferedInputStream
        (new FileInputStream("employee.dat"))));
```

Of course, in the stream libraries of other programming languages, niceties such as buffering and lookahead are automatically taken care of, so it is a bit of a hassle in Java that one has to resort to stream filters in these cases. But you can also mix and match filter classes to construct truly useful sequences of streams. For example, you can read numbers from a compressed ZIP file by using the following sequence of streams (see Figure 1-3).

```
ZipInputStream zin = new ZipInputStream(new
FileInputStream("employee.zip"));
DataInputStream din = new DataInputStream(zin);
```

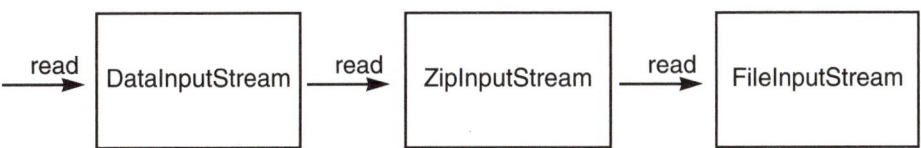

Figure 1-3: A sequence of filtered streams

(See the section on "ZIP file streams" later on in this chapter for more on Java's ability to handle ZIP files.)

All in all, apart from the rather monstrous constructors that are needed to layer streams, the ability to mix and match streams is a very useful feature of Java!

java.io.FileInputStream

- FileInputStream(String name)

  creates a new file input stream using the file whose pathname is specified by the name string.

- FileInputStream(File f)

  creates a new file input stream using the information encapsulated in the File object. (The File class is described at the end of this chapter.)

java.io.BufferedInputStream

- BufferedInputStream(InputStream in)

  creates a new buffered stream with a default buffer size. A buffered input stream reads characters from a stream without causing a device access every time. When the buffer is empty, a new block of data is read into the buffer.

- BufferedInputStream(InputStream in, int n)

  creates a new buffered stream with a user-defined buffer size.

java.io.BufferedOutputStream

- BufferedOutputStream(OutputStream out)

  creates a new buffered stream with a default buffer size. A buffered output stream collects characters to be written without causing a device access every time. When the buffer fills up, the data is written.

- BufferedOutputStream(OutputStream out, int n)

  creates a new buffered stream with a user-defined buffer size.

java.io.PushbackInputStream

- PushbackInputStream(InputStream in)

  constructs a stream with one-character lookahead.

- PushbackInputStream(InputStream in, int size)

  constructs a stream with a push-back buffer of specified size.

- void unread(int ch)

  pushes back a character, which is retrieved again by the next call to read. You can push back only one character at a time.

  Parameters: ch   the character to be read again

Data Streams

You often need to write the result of a computation or read one back. The data streams support methods for reading back all of the basic Java types. To write a number, character, Boolean value, or string, use one of the following methods:

```
writeChars
writeInt
writeShort
writeLong
writeFloat
writeDouble
writeChar
writeBoolean
writeUTF
```

For example, `writeInt` writes an integer as a 4-byte binary quantity, and `writeDouble` writes a `double` as an 8-byte binary quantity. The resulting output is not humanly readable—see the section on the `PrintWriter` class later in this chapter for text output of numbers.

NOTE: There are two different methods of storing integers and floating-point numbers in memory, depending on the platform you are using. Suppose, for example, you are working with a 4-byte quantity, like an `int` or a `float`. This can be stored in such a way that the first of the 4 bytes in memory holds the most significant byte (MSB) of the value, the so-called *big-endian* method, or it can hold the least significant byte (LSB) first, which is called, naturally enough, the *little-endian* method. For example, the SPARC uses big-endian; the Pentium, little-endian. This can lead to problems. For example, when saving a file using C or C++, the data is saved *exactly* as the processor stores it. That makes it challenging to move even the simplest data files from one platform to another. In Java, all values are written in the big-endian fashion, regardless of the processor. That makes Java data files platform independent.

The `writeUTF` method writes string data using Unicode Text Format (UTF). UTF format is as follows. A 7-bit ASCII value (that is, a 16-bit Unicode character with the top 9 bits zero) is written as one byte:

$$0a_6a_5a_4a_3a_2a_1a_0$$

A 16-bit Unicode character with the top 5 bits zero is written as a 2-byte sequence:

$$110a_{10}a_9a_8a_7a_6 \qquad 10a_5a_4a_3a_2a_1a_0$$

(The `writeUTF` method actually writes only the 11 lowest bits.)

All other Unicode characters are written as 3-byte sequences:

$$1110a_{15}a_{14}a_{13}a_{12} \qquad 10a_{11}a_{10}a_9a_8a_7a_6 \qquad 10a_5a_4a_3a_2a_1a_0$$

This is a useful format for text consisting mostly of ASCII characters, because ASCII characters still take only a single byte. On the other hand, it is not a good format for Asiatic languages, for which you are better off directly writing sequences of double-byte Unicode characters. Use the `writeChars` method for that purpose.

Note that the top bits of a UTF byte determine the nature of the byte in the encoding scheme.

0xxxxxxx : ASCII

10xxxxxx : Second or third byte

110xxxxx : First byte of 2-byte sequence

1110xxxx : First byte of 3-byte sequence

To read the data back in, use the following methods:

readInt	readDouble
readShort	readChar
readLong	readBoolean
readFloat	readUTF

NOTE: The binary data format is compact and platform independent. Except for the UTF strings, it is also suited to random access. The major drawback is that binary files are not readable by humans.

java.io.DataInput

- `boolean readBoolean()`

  reads in a Boolean value.

- `byte readByte()`

  reads an 8-bit byte.

- `char readChar()`

  reads a 16-bit Unicode character.

- `double readDouble()`

  reads a 64-bit double.

- `float readFloat()`

  reads a 32-bit float.

- `void readFully(byte b[])`

  reads bytes, blocks until all bytes are read.

  Parameters: b   the buffer into which the data is read

- `void readFully(byte b[], int off, int len)`

  reads bytes, blocking until all bytes are read.

Parameters:	b	the buffer into which the data is read
	off	the start offset of the data
	len	the maximum number of bytes read

- `int readInt()`

  reads a 32-bit integer.

- `String readLine()`

  reads in a line that has been terminated by a \n, \r, \r\n, or EOF. Returns a string containing all bytes in the line converted to Unicode characters.

- `long readLong()`

  reads a 64-bit long integer.

- `short readShort()`

  reads a 16-bit short integer.

- `String readUTF()`

  reads a string of characters in UTF format.

- `int skipBytes(int n)`

  skips bytes, blocks until all bytes are skipped.

Parameters:	n	the number of bytes to be skipped

java.io.DataOutput

- `void writeBoolean(boolean b)`

  writes a Boolean value.

- `void writeByte(byte b)`

  writes an 8-bit byte.

- `void writeChar(char c)`

  writes a 16-bit Unicode character.

- `void writeChars(string s)`

  writes a string as a sequence of characters.

- `void writeDouble(double d)`

  writes a 64-bit double.

- void writeFloat(float f)

  writes a 32-bit float.

- void writeInt(int i)

  writes a 32-bit integer.

- void writeLong(long l)

  writes a 64-bit long integer.

- void writeShort(short s)

  writes a 16-bit short integer.

- void writeUTF(String s)

  writes a string of characters in UTF format.

Random-Access File Streams

The RandomAccessFile stream class lets you find or write data anywhere in a file. Disk files are random access, but streams of data from a network are not. You open a random-access file either for reading only or for both reading and writing. You specify the option by using the string "r" (for read access) or "rw" (for read/write access) as the second argument in the constructor.

```
RandomAccessFile in = new RandomAccessFile("employee.dat", "r");
RandomAccessFile inOut
   = new RandomAccessFile("employee.dat", "rw");
```

A random-access file also has a *file pointer* setting that comes with it. The file pointer always indicates the position of the next record that will be read or written. The seek method sets the file pointer to an arbitrary byte position within the file. The argument to seek is a long integer between zero and the length of the file in bytes.

The getFilePointer method returns the current position of the file pointer.

To read from a random-access file, you use the same methods—such as readInt and readUTF—as for DataInputStream objects. That is no accident. These methods are actually defined in the DataInput interface that both DataInputStream and RandomAccessFile implement.

Similarly, to write a random-access file, you use the same writeInt and writeUTF methods as in the DataOutputStream class. These methods are defined in the DataOutput interface that is common to both classes.

The advantage of this setup is that you can write methods whose argument types are the DataInput and DataOutput *interfaces*.

```
class Employee
{   . . .
    read(DataInput in) { . . . }
    write(DataOutput out) { . . . }
}
```

Note that the read method can handle either a DataInputStream or a RandomAccessFile object because both of these classes implement the DataInput interface. The same is true for the write method.

java.io.RandomAccessFile

- RandomAccessFile(String name, String mode)

  Parameters: name   system-dependent file name

                              mode   "r" for reading only, or "rw" for reading and writing

- RandomAccessFile(File file, String mode)

  Parameters: file   a File object encapsulating a system-dependent file name. (The File class is described at the end of this chapter.)

                              mode   "r" for reading only, or "rw" for reading and writing

- long getFilePointer()

  returns the current location of the file pointer.

- void seek(long pos)

  sets the file pointer to pos bytes from the beginning of the file.

- public long length()

  returns the length of the file in bytes.

Text streams

In the last section, we discussed *binary* input and output. While binary I/O is fast and efficient, it is not easily readable by humans. In this section, we will focus on *text* I/O. For example, if the integer 1234 is saved in binary, it is written as the sequence of bytes 00 00 04 D2 (in hexadecimal notation). In text format, it is saved as the string "1234". But as you know, there is a problem. Java uses Unicode characters. That is, the character encoding for the string "1234" really is 00 31 00 32 00 33 00 34 (in hex). However, at the present time most environments where your Java programs will run use their own character encoding. This may be a single-byte, a double-byte, or a variable-byte scheme.

For example, under Windows, the string would need to be written in ASCII, as 31 32 33 34, without the extra zero bytes. If the Unicode encoding were written into a text file, then it would be quite unlikely that the resulting file will be humanly readable with the tools of the host environment. To overcome this problem, as we mentioned before, Java now has a set of stream filters that bridges the gap between Unicode encoded text and the character encoding used by the local operating system. All of these classes descend from the abstract Reader and Writer classes, and the names are reminiscent of the ones used for binary data. For example, the InputStreamReader class turns an input stream that reads bytes in a particular character encoding into a reader that emits Unicode characters. Similarly, the OutputStreamWriter class turns a stream of Unicode characters into a stream of bytes in a particular character encoding.

For example, here is how you make an input reader that reads keystrokes from the console and automatically converts them to Unicode.

```
InputStreamReader in = new InputStreamReader(System.in);
```

This input stream reader assumes the normal character encoding used by the host system. For example, under Windows, it uses the ISO 8859-1 encoding (also known as ISO Latin-1 or, among Windows programmers, as "ANSI code"). You can choose a different encoding by specifying it in the constructor for the InputStreamReader. This takes the form

```
InputStreamReader(InputStream, String)
```

where the string describes the encoding scheme that you want to use. For example,

```
InputStreamReader in = new InputStreamReader(new
    FileInputStream("kremlin.dat"), "8859_5");
```

Table 1-1 lists the currently supported encoding schemes.

Of course, there are many Unicode characters that cannot be represented by these encoding schemes. If those characters are part of the stream, they are displayed by a ? in the output.

Because it is so common to want to attach a reader or writer to a file, there is a pair of convenience classes, FileReader and FileWriter, for this purpose. For example, the writer definition

```
FileWriter out = new FileWriter("output.txt");
```

is equivalent to

```
OutputStreamWriter out = new OutputStreamReader(new
    FileOutputStream("output.txt"));
```

Writing text output

For text output, you want to use a `PrintWriter`. A print writer can print strings and numbers in text format. Just as a `DataOutputStream` has useful output methods but no destination, a `PrintWriter` must be combined with a destination writer.

```
PrintWriter out = new PrintWriter(new FileWriter("employee.txt"));
```

You can also combine a print writer with a destination (output) stream.

```
PrintWriter out = new PrintWriter(new
    FileOutputStream("employee.txt"));
```

The `PrintWriter(OutputStream)` constructor automatically adds an `OutputStreamWriter` to convert Unicode characters to bytes in the stream.

To write to a print writer, you use the same `print` and `println` methods that you used with `System.out`. You can use these methods to print numbers (`int`, `short`, `long`, `float`, `double`), characters, Boolean values, strings, and objects.

NOTE: Java veterans probably wonder whatever happened to the `PrintStream` class and to `System.out`. In Java 1.0, the `PrintStream` class simply truncated all Unicode characters to ASCII characters by dropping the top byte. Conversely, the `readLine` method of the `DataInputStream` turned ASCII to Unicode by setting the top byte to 0. Clearly, that was not a clean or portable approach, and it was fixed with the introduction of readers and writers in Java 1.1. For compatibility with existing code, `System.in`, `System.out`, and `System.err` are still streams, not readers and writers. But now the `PrintStream` class internally converts Unicode characters to the default host encoding in the same way as the `PrintWriter`. And all constructors for `PrintStream` are now deprecated—simply use `PrintWriter` instead. That means that new Java code has exactly two objects of type `PrintStream`, namely, `System.out` and `System.err`. These act exactly like print writers when you use the `print` and `println` methods, but unlike print writers, you can also send raw bytes to them with the `write(int)` and `write(byte[])` methods.

Table 1-1: Character encodings

8859_1	ISO Latin-1
8859_2	ISO Latin-2
8859_3	ISO Latin-3
8859_5	ISO Latin/Cyrillic
8859_6	ISO Latin/Arabic
8859_7	ISO Latin/Greek
8859_8	ISO Latin/Hebrew
8859_9	ISO Latin-5
Cp1250	Windows Eastern Europe / Latin-2
Cp1251	Windows Cyrillic
Cp1252	Windows Western Europe / Latin-1
Cp1253	Windows Greek
Cp1254	Windows Turkish
Cp1255	Windows Hebrew
Cp1256	Windows Arabic
Cp1257	Windows Baltic
Cp1258	Windows Vietnamese
Cp437	PC Original
Cp737	PC Greek
Cp775	PC Baltic
Cp850	PC Latin-1
Cp852	PC Latin-2
Cp855	PC Cyrillic
Cp857	PC Turkish
Cp860	PC Portuguese
Cp861	PC Icelandic
Cp862	PC Hebrew
Cp863	PC Canadian French
Cp864	PC Arabic
Cp865	PC Nordic
Cp866	PC Russian
Cp869	PC Modern Greek
Cp874	Windows Thai
EUCJIS	Japanese EUC
JIS	JIS
MacArabic	Macintosh Arabic
MacCentralEurope	Macintosh Latin-2
MacCroatian	Macintosh Croatian
MacCyrillic	Macintosh Cyrillic
MacDingbat	Macintosh Dingbat
MacGreek	Macintosh Greek
MacHebrew	Macintosh Hebrew
MacIceland	Macintosh Icelandic
MacRoman	Macintosh Roman
MacRomania	Macintosh Romania
MacSymbol	Macintosh Symbol
MacThai	Macintosh Thai
MacTurkish	Macintosh Turkish
MacUkraine	Macintosh Ukraine
SJIS	PC and Windows Japanese
UTF8	Standard UTF-8

For example, consider this code:

```
String name = "Harry Hacker";
double salary = 75000;
out.print(name);
out.print(' ');
out.println(salary);
```

This writes the characters

```
Harry Hacker 75000
```

to the stream `out`. The characters are then converted to bytes and end up in the file `employee.txt`.

As you know, the `println` method always prints a *line terminator*. This is the string obtained by the call `System.getProperty("line.separator")`, such as `"\n"` (Unix), `"\r\n"` (DOS) or `"\r"` (Macintosh). If the writer is set to *auto flush mode*, then all characters in the buffer are sent to their destination whenever `println` is called. (Print writers are always buffered.) By default, auto flushing is *not* enabled. You can enable or disable auto flushing by using the `PrintWriter(Writer, boolean)` constructor and passing the appropriate Boolean as the second argument.

```
PrintWriter out = new PrintWriter(new
    FileWriter("employee.txt"), true); // auto flush
```

The `print` methods don't throw exceptions. You can call the `checkError` method to see if something went wrong with the stream.

NOTE: You cannot write raw bytes to a `PrintWriter`. Print writers are designed for text output only.

`java.io.PrintStream`

- `void print(Object obj)`

  prints an object by printing the string resulting from `toString`.

  Parameters: `obj`   the object to be printed

- `void print(String s)`

  prints a Unicode string.

- `void println(String s)`

  prints a string followed by a line terminator. Flushes the stream if the stream is in autoflush mode.

- `void print(char s[])`

  prints an array of Unicode characters.

- `void print(char c)`

  prints a Unicode character.

- `void print(int i)`

  prints an integer in text format.

- `void print(long l)`

  prints a long integer in text format.

- `void print(float f)`

  prints a floating-point number in text format.

- `void print(double d)`

  prints a double-precision floating-point number in text format.

- `void print(boolean b)`

  prints a Boolean value in text format.

- `boolean checkError()`

  returns `true` if a formatting or output error occurred. Once the stream has encountered an error, it is tainted and all calls to `checkError` return `true`.

 `java.io.PrintWriter`

- `PrintWriter(Writer out)`

  Creates a new `PrintWriter`, without automatic line flushing.

Parameters:	out	a character-output writer

- `PrintWriter(Writer out, boolean autoFlush)`

  Creates a new `PrintWriter`.

Parameters:	out	a character-output writer
	autoFlush	if true, the `println()` methods will flush the output buffer

- `PrintWriter(OutputStream out)`

  Creates a new `PrintWriter`, without automatic line flushing, from an existing `OutputStream` by automatically creating the necessary intermediate `OutputStreamWriter`.

Parameters:	out	an output stream

- `PrintWriter(OutputStream out, boolean autoFlush)`

  Also creates a new `PrintWriter` from an existing `OutputStream` but allows you determine whether the writer autoflushes or not.

Parameters:	out	an output stream
	autoFlush	if true, the `println()` methods will flush the output buffer

Reading text input

As you know:

- To write data in binary format, you use a `DataOutputStream`.

- To write in text format, you use a `PrintWriter`.

Therefore, you might expect that there is an analog to the `DataInputStream` that lets you read data in text format. Unfortunately, Java does not provide such a class. (That is why we wrote our own `Console` class in Volume 1.) The only game in town for processing text input is the `BufferedReader` method—it has a method, `readLine`, that lets you read a line of text. You need to combine a buffered reader with an input source.

```
BufferedReader in = new BufferedReader(new
    FileReader("employee.txt"));
```

The `readLine` method returns `null` when no more input is available. A typical input loop, therefore, looks like this:

```
String s;
while ((s = in.readLine()) != null)
{ do something with s;
}
```

The `FileReader` class already converts bytes to Unicode characters. For other input sources, you need to use the `InputStreamReader`—unlike the `PrintWriter`, there is no automatic convenience method to bridge the gap between bytes and Unicode characters.

```
BufferedReader in2 = new BufferedReader(new
    InputStreamReader(System.in));
BufferedReader in3 = new BufferedReader(new
    InputStreamReader(url.openStream()));
```

To read numbers from text input, you need to read a string first and then convert it.

```
String s = in.readLine();
double x = new Double(s).doubleValue();
```

That works if there is a single number on each line. Otherwise, you must work harder and break up the input string. We will see an example of this later in this chapter.

TIP: Java now has `StringReader` and `StringWriter` classes that allow you to treat a string as if it were a data stream. This can be quite convenient if you want to parse both strings and data from a stream using the same code. The `StringWriter` classes, although more convenient, are not usually as efficient as using a `StringBuffer` class, however.

ZIP File Streams

ZIP files are archives that store one or more files in (usually) compressed format. Java 1.1 can handle both GZIP and ZIP format. (See RFC 1950, RFC 1951, and RFC 1952 at ftp://ds.internic.net/rfc/.) In this section we concentrate on the more familiar (but somewhat more complicated) ZIP format and leave the GZIP classes to you if you need them. (They work in much the same way.)

NOTE: The classes for handling ZIP files are in `java.util.zip` and not in `java.io`, so remember to add the necessary `import` statement. Although not part of `java.io`, the GZIP and ZIP classes do subclass `java.io.FilterInputStream` and `java.io.FilterOutputStream`. The `java.util.zip` packages also contain classes for computing CRC checksums. (CRC stands for cyclic redundancy check and is a method to generate a hashlike code that the receiver of a file can use to check the integrity of data transmission.)

Each ZIP file has a header with information such as the name of the file and the compression method that was used. In Java, you use a `ZipInputStream` to read a ZIP file. You then look at the entries. The `getNextEntry` method returns an object of type `ZipEntry` that describes the entry. The `read` method of the `ZipInputStream` is modified to return –1, not at the end of the ZIP file but at the end of the current entry. You must then call `closeEntry` to read the next entry. Here is a typical code sequence to read through a ZIP file:

```
ZipInputStream zin = new ZipInputStream
   (new FileInputStream(zipname));
ZipEntry entry;
while ((entry = zin.getNextEntry()) != null)
{  analyze entry;
   read the contents of zin;
   zin.closeEntry();
}
zin.close();
```

To read the contents of a ZIP entry, you will probably not want to use the raw `read` method; usually, you will use the methods of a more competent stream filter. For example, to read a text file inside a ZIP file, you can use the following loop:

```
BufferedReader in = new BufferedReader
    (new InputStreamReader(zin));
String s;
while ((s = in.readLine()) != null)
    do something with s;
```

The program in Example 1-1 lets you open a ZIP file. It then displays the files stored in the ZIP archive in the list box at the top of the screen. If you double-click on one of the files, the contents of the file are displayed in the text area, as shown in Figure 1-4.

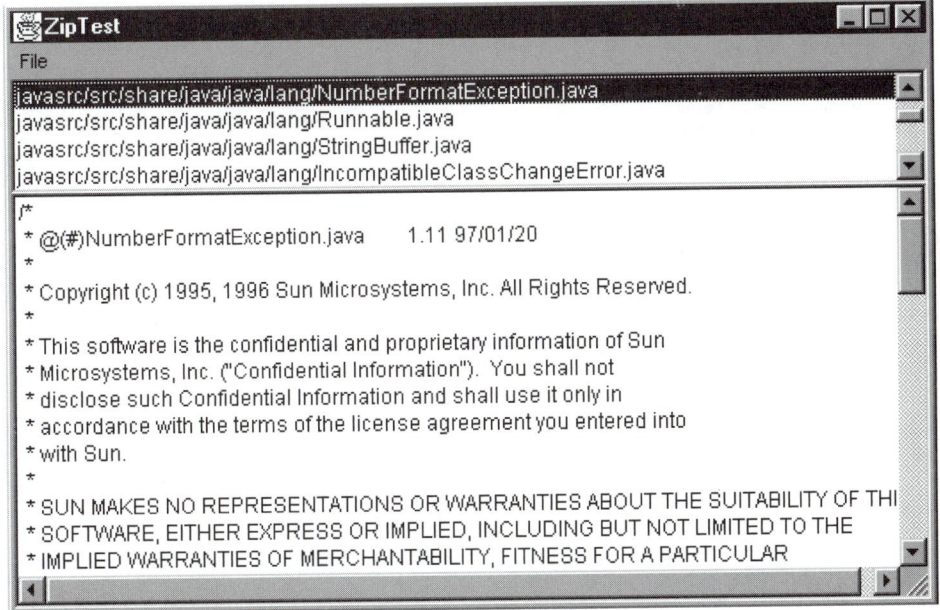

Figure 1-4: The ZipTest program

Example 1-1: ZipTest.java

```java
import java.awt.*;
import java.awt.event.*;
import java.io.*;
import java.util.*;
import java.util.zip.*;
import corejava.*;

public class ZipTest extends CloseableFrame
    implements ActionListener
{  public ZipTest()
   {  MenuBar mbar = new MenuBar();
      Menu m = new Menu("File");
      MenuItem m1 = new MenuItem("Open");
      m1.addActionListener(this);
      m.add(m1);
      MenuItem m2 = new MenuItem("Exit");
      m2.addActionListener(this);
      m.add(m2);
      mbar.add(m);
      setMenuBar(mbar);
      fileList.addActionListener(this);

      add(fileList, "North");
      add(fileText, "Center");
   }

   public void actionPerformed(ActionEvent evt)
   {  String arg = evt.getActionCommand();
      if (evt.getSource() == fileList)
      {  loadZipFile(arg);
      }
      else if (arg.equals("Open"))
      {  FileDialog d = new FileDialog(this,
            "Open zip file", FileDialog.LOAD);
         d.setFile("*.zip");
         d.setDirectory(lastDir);
         d.show();
         String f = d.getFile();
         lastDir = d.getDirectory();
         if (f != null)
         {  zipname = lastDir + f;
            scanZipFile();
         }
      }
      else if(arg.equals("Exit")) System.exit(0);
   }
```

```java
public void scanZipFile()
{   fileList.removeAll();
    try
    {   ZipInputStream zin = new ZipInputStream(new
            FileInputStream(zipname));
        ZipEntry entry;
        while ((entry = zin.getNextEntry()) != null)
        {   fileList.add(entry.getName());
            zin.closeEntry();
        }
        zin.close();
    }
    catch(IOException e) {}
}

public void loadZipFile(String name)
{   try
    {   ZipInputStream zin = new ZipInputStream(new
            FileInputStream(zipname));
        ZipEntry entry;
        fileText.setText("");
        while ((entry = zin.getNextEntry()) != null)
        {   if (entry.getName().equals(name))
            {   BufferedReader in = new BufferedReader(new
                    InputStreamReader(zin));
                String s;
                while ((s = in.readLine()) != null)
                    fileText.append(s + "\n");
            }
            zin.closeEntry();
        }
        zin.close();
    }
    catch(IOException e) {}
}

public static void main(String args[])
{   Frame f = new ZipTest();
    f.show();
}

private List fileList = new List();
private TextArea fileText = new TextArea();
private String lastDir = "";
private String zipname;
}
```

 NOTE: Java throws a `ZipException` when there is an error in reading a ZIP file. Normally this occurs when the ZIP file is corrupted.

To write a ZIP file, you open a `ZipOutputStream`. For each entry that you want to place into the ZIP file, you create a `ZipEntry` object. You pass the file name to the `ZipEntry` constructor; it sets the other parameters such as file date and decompression method automatically. You can override these settings if you like. Then, you call the `putNextEntry` method of the `ZipOutputStream` to begin writing a new file. Send the file data to the ZIP stream, and when you are done, call `closeEntry`. Repeat for all the files you want to store. Here is a code skeleton:

```
FileOutputStream fout = new FileOutputStream("test.zip");
   ZipOutputStream zout = new ZipOutputStream(fout);
for all files
{  ZipEntry ze = new ZipEntry(file name);
      zout.putNextEntry(ze);
   send data to ze;
   zout.closeEntry();
}
zout.close();
```

 NOTE: The files that are produced by the Java 1.1 `ZipOutputStream` methods are not proper ZIP archives. PKZip and WinZip 6.2 can extract the file names, but not the files themselves. WinZip 6.3 (which is in beta at the time that this book is written) "handles certain invalid zips more gracefully" and can handle ZIP files that are generated by the `ZipOutputStream` class. The same is true for JAR files (which were discussed in the applet chapter of Volume 1). JAR files are simply ZIP files with another entry, the so-called manifest.

ZIP streams are a good example of the power of the stream abstraction. Both the source and the destination of the ZIP data are completely flexible. You attach the most convenient reader to the ZIP file to read the data that is stored in compressed form, and that reader doesn't even realize that the data is being decompressed as it is being requested. And the source of the bytes in ZIP formats need not be a file—the ZIP data can come from a network connection. In fact, the JAR files that we discussed in Chapter 10 of Volume 1 are ZIP formatted files. Whenever the class loader of an applet reads a JAR file, it uses a `ZipInputStream` to read and decompress data from the network.

java.util.zip.ZipInputStream

- `ZipInputStream(InputStream in)`

  This constructor creates a `ZipInputStream` that allows you to inflate data from the given `InputStream`.

  Parameters   `in`   the underlying input stream

- `ZipEntry getNextEntry()`

  returns a `ZipEntry` object for the next entry or `null` if there are no more entries.

- `void closeEntry()`

  This method closes the current open entry in the ZIP file. You can then read the next entry using `getNextEntry()`.

java.util.zip.ZipOutputStream

- `ZipOutputStream(OutputStream out)`

  This constructor creates a `ZipOutputStream` that you use to write compressed data to the specified `OutputStream`.

  Parameters   `out`   the underlying output stream

- `putNextEntry(ZipEntry ze)`

  writes the information in the given `ZipEntry` to the stream and positions the stream for the data. The data can then be written to the stream using `write()`.

  Parameters   `ze`   the new entry

- `void closeEntry()`

  closes the currently open entry in the ZIP file. Use `putNextEntry()` to start the next entry.

- `void setLevel(int level)`

  sets the default compression level of subsequent `DEFLATED` entries. The default value is `Deflater.DEFAULT_COMPRESSION`. Throws an `IllegalArgumentException` if the level is not valid.

  Parameters   `level`   a compression level, from 0 (`NO_COMPRESSION`) to 9 (`BEST_COMPRESSION`)

- void setMethod(int method)

  sets the default compression method for this ZipOutputStream for any entries that do not specify a method.

Parameters	method	the compression method, either DEFLATED or STORED

 java.util.zip.ZipEntry

- ZipEntry(String name)

Parameters	name	the name of the entry

- long getCrc()

  returns the CRC32 checksum value for this ZipEntry.

- String getName()

  returns the name of this entry.

- long getSize()

  returns the uncompressed size of this entry, or −1 if the uncompressed size is not known.

- boolean isDirectory()

  returns a Boolean that indicates whether or not this entry is a directory.

- setMethod(int method)

Parameters	method	the compression method for the entry; must be either DEFLATED or STORED

- void setSize(long size)

  sets the size of this entry. Only required if the compression method is STORED.

Parameters:	size	the uncompressed size of this entry

- void setCrc(long crc)

  sets the CRC32 checksum of this entry. Use the CRC32 class to compute this checksum. Only required if the compression method is STORED.

Parameters:	crc	the checksum of this entry

`java.util.zip.ZipFile`

- `ZipFile(String name)`

  This constructor creates a `ZipFile` for reading from the given string.

Parameters	name	a string that contains the pathname of the file

- `ZipFile(File file)`

  This constructor creates a `ZipFile` for reading from the given `File` object.

Parameters	file	the file to read. The `File` class is described at the end of this chapter

- `Enumeration entries()`

  returns an `Enumeration` object that enumerates the `ZipEntry` objects that describe the entries of the `ZipFile`.

- `ZipEntry getEntry(String name)`

  returns the entry corresponding to the given name, or `null` if there is no such entry.

Parameters	name	the entry name

- `InputStream getInputStream(ZipEntry ze)`

  returns an `InputStream` for the given entry.

Parameters	ze	a `ZipEntry` in the ZIP file

- `String getName()`

  returns the path of this ZIP file.

Putting Streams to Use

In the next four sections, we will show you how to put some of the creatures in the stream zoo to good use. For these examples, we will assume you are working with the `Employee` class and some of its derived classes, such as `Manager`. (See Chapters 4 and 5 of Volume 1 for more on these example classes.) We will consider four separate scenarios for saving an array of employee records to a file and then reading them back into memory.

1. Saving data of the same type (`Employee`) in text format

2. Saving data of the same type in binary format

3. Saving and restoring polymorphic data (a mixture of `Employee` and `Manager` objects)

4. Saving and restoring data containing embedded references (managers with pointers to other employees)

Writing Delimited Output

In this section, you will learn how to store an array of `Employee` records in the time-honored *delimited* format. This means that each record is stored in a separate line. Instance fields are separated from each other by delimiters. We use a vertical bar (|) as our delimiter. (A colon (:) is another popular choice. Part of the fun is that everyone uses a different delimiter.) Naturally, we punt on the issue of what might happen if a | actually occurred in one of the strings we save.

NOTE: Especially on Unix systems, an amazing number of files are stored in exactly this format. We have seen entire employee databases with thousands of records in this format, queried with nothing more than the Unix awk, sort, and `join` utilities. (In the PC world, where excellent database programs are available at low cost, this kind of ad hoc storage is much less common.)

Here is a sample set of records:

```
Harry Hacker|35500|1989|10|1
Carl Cracker|75000|1987|12|15
Tony Tester|38000|1990|3|15
```

Writing records is simple. Since we write to a text file, we use the `PrintWriter` class. We simply write all fields, followed by either a | or, for the last field, a \n. Finally, in keeping with the idea that we want the *class* to be responsible for responding to messages, we add a method, `writeData`, to our `Employee` class.

```
public void writeData(PrintWriter os) throws IOException
{  Format.print(os, "%s|", name);
   Format.print(os, "%.14g|", salary);
   Format.print(os, "%d|", hireDay.getYear());
   Format.print(os, "%d|", hireDay.getMonth());
   Format.print(os, "%d\n", hireDay.getDay());
}
```

To read records, we read in a line at a time and separate the fields. This is the topic of the next section, in which we use a utility class supplied with Java to make our job easier.

String Tokenizers and Delimited Text

When reading a line of input, we get a single long string. We want to split it into individual strings. This means finding the | delimiters and then separating out the individual pieces, that is, the sequence of characters up to the next delimiter. (These are usually called *tokens*.) The `StringTokenizer` class in `java.util` is designed for exactly this purpose. It gives you an easy way to break up a large string that contains delimited text. The idea is that a string tokenizer object

attaches to a string. When you construct the tokenizer object, you specify which characters are the delimiters. For example, we need to use

```
StringTokenizer t = new StringTokenizer(line, "|");
```

You can specify multiple delimiters in the string. For example, to set up a string tokenizer that would let you search for any delimiter in the set

```
" \t\n\r"
```

use the following:

```
StringTokenizer t = new StringTokenizer(line, " \t\n\r");
```

(Notice that this means that any white space marks off the tokens.)

> NOTE: These four delimiters are used as the defaults if you construct a string tokenizer like this:
> ```
> StringTokenizer t = new StringTokenizer(line);
> ```

Once you have constructed a string tokenizer, you can use its methods to quickly extract the tokens from the string. The `nextToken` method returns the next unread token. The `hasMoreTokens` method returns `true` if more tokens are available.

> NOTE: In our case, we know how many tokens we have in every line of input. In general, you have to be a bit more careful: call `hasMoreTokens` before calling `nextToken` because the `nextToken` method throws an exception when no more tokens are available.

java.util.StringTokenizer

- `StringTokenizer(String str, String delim)`

  Parameters: `str`   the input string from which tokens are read

  `delim`   a string containing delimiter characters (any character in this string is a delimiter)

- `StringTokenizer(String str)`

  constructs a string tokenizer with the default delimiter set `" \t\n\r"`.

- `boolean hasMoreTokens()`

  returns `true` if more tokens exist.

- `String nextToken()`

  returns the next token; throws a `NoSuchElementException` if there are no more tokens.

- `String nextToken(String delim)`

  returns the next token, after switching to the new delimiter set. The new delimiter set is subsequently used.

- `int countTokens()`

  returns the number of tokens still in the string.

Reading Delimited Input

Reading in an `Employee` record is simple. We simply read in a line of input with the `readLine` method of the `BufferedReader` class. Here is the code needed to read one record in a string.

```
BufferedReader in
   = new BufferedReader(new FileReader("employee.dat"));
. . .
String line = in.readLine();
```

Next, we need to extract the individual tokens. When we do this, we end up with *strings,* so we need to convert them into numbers when appropriate. To do this, we turn to the `atoi` and `atof` methods from the `Format` class in our `corejava` package.

Just as with the `writeData` method, we add a `readData` method of the `Employee` class. When you call

```
e.readData(in);
```

this method overwrites the previous contents of `e`. Note that the method may throw an `IOException` if the `readLine` method throws that exception. There is nothing this method can do if an `IOException` occurs, so we just let it propagate up the chain.

Here is the code for this method:

```
public void readData(BufferedReader in) throws IOException
{  String line = in.readLine();
   if (line == null) return;
   StringTokenizer t = new StringTokenizer(line, "|");
   name = t.nextToken();
   salary = Format.atof(t.nextToken());
   int y = Format.atoi(t.nextToken());
   int m = Format.atoi(t.nextToken());
   int d = Format.atoi(t.nextToken());
   hireDay = new Day(y, m, d);
}
```

Finally, in the code for a program that tests these methods, the static method

```
void writeData(Employee[] e, PrintWriter out)
```

first writes the length of the array, then writes each record. The static method

```
readData(Employee[] BufferedReader in)
```

first reads in the length of the array, then reads in each record, as illustrated in Example 1-2.

Example 1-2: DataFileTest.java

```
import java.io.*;
import java.util.*;
import corejava.*;

public class DataFileTest
{   static void writeData(Employee[] e, PrintWriter os)
        throws IOException
    {   Format.print(os, "%d\n", e.length);
        int i;
        for (i = 0; i < e.length; i++)
            e[i].writeData(os);
    }

    static Employee[] readData(BufferedReader is)
        throws IOException
    {   int n = Format.atoi(is.readLine());
        Employee[] e = new Employee[n];
        int i;
        for (i = 0; i < n; i++)
        {   e[i] = new Employee();
            e[i].readData(is);
        }
        return e;
    }


    public static void main(String[] args)
    {   Employee[] staff = new Employee[3];

        staff[0] = new Employee("Harry Hacker", 35500,
            new Day(1989,10,1));
        staff[1] = new Employee("Carl Cracker", 75000,
            new Day(1987,12,15));
        staff[2] = new Employee("Tony Tester", 38000,
            new Day(1990,3,15));
        int i;
        for (i = 0; i < staff.length; i++)
            staff[i].raiseSalary(5.25);
```

```
      try
      {   PrintWriter os = new PrintWriter(new
              FileWriter("employee.dat"));
          writeData(staff, os);
          os.close();
      }
      catch(IOException e)
      {   System.out.print("Error: " + e);
          System.exit(1);
      }

      try
      {   BufferedReader is = new BufferedReader(new
              FileReader("employee.dat"));
          Employee[] in = readData(is);
          for (i = 0; i < in.length; i++) in[i].print();
          is.close();
      }
      catch(IOException e)
      {   System.out.print("Error: " + e);
          System.exit(1);
      }
   }
}

class Employee
{   public Employee(String n, double s, Day d)
    {   name = n;
        salary = s;
        hireDay = d;
    }
    public Employee() {}
    public void print()
    {   System.out.println(name + " " + salary
            + " " + hireYear());
    }
    public void raiseSalary(double byPercent)
    {   salary *= 1 + byPercent / 100;
    }
    public int hireYear()
    {   return hireDay.getYear();
    }
    public void writeData(PrintWriter os) throws IOException
    {   Format.print(os, "%s|", name);
        Format.print(os, "%.14g|", salary);
        Format.print(os, "%d|", hireDay.getYear());
        Format.print(os, "%d|", hireDay.getMonth());
        Format.print(os, "%d\n", hireDay.getDay());
    }
```

```
public void readData(BufferedReader is) throws IOException
{  String s = is.readLine();
   StringTokenizer t = new StringTokenizer(s, "|");
   name = t.nextToken();
   salary = Format.atof(t.nextToken());
   int y = Format.atoi(t.nextToken());
   int m = Format.atoi(t.nextToken());
   int d = Format.atoi(t.nextToken());
   hireDay = new Day(y, m, d);
}

private String name;
private double salary;
private Day hireDay;
}
```

Random-Access Streams

If you have a large number of employees, the storage technique used in the pre-ceding section suffers from one limitation: it is not possible to read a record in the middle of the file without first reading all records that come before it. In this section, we will make all records the same length. This lets us implement a ran-dom-access method of reading back the information—we can get at any record in the same amount of time.

We will store the numbers in the instance fields in our classes in a binary for-mat. This is done using the `writeInt` and `writeDouble` methods of the `DataOutput` interface. (This is the common interface of the `DataOutputStream` and the `RandomAccessFile` classes.)

However, since the size of each record must remain constant, we need to make all the strings the same size when we save them. The variable-size UTF format does not do this, and the rest of the Java library provides no convenient means for accomplishing this. We need to write a bit of code to implement two helper methods. We will call them `writeFixedString` and `readFixedString`. These methods read and write Unicode strings that always have the same length.

The `writeFixedString` method takes the parameter `size`. Then, it writes the specified number of characters, starting at the beginning of the string. (If there are too few characters, it pads the string using characters whose ASCII/Unicode values are zero.) Here is the code for the `writeFixedString` method:

```
static void writeFixedString
    (String s, int size, DataOutput out)
    throws IOException
{   int i;
    for (i = 0; i < size; i++)
    {   char ch = 0;
        if (i < s.length()) ch = s.charAt(i);
        out.writeChar(ch);
    }
}
```

The `readFixedString` method reads characters from the input stream until it has consumed `size` characters, or until it encounters a character with Unicode 0. Then, it should skip past the remaining zero characters in the input field.

For added efficiency, this method uses the `StringBuffer` class to read in a string. A `StringBuffer` is an auxiliary class that lets you preallocate a memory block of a given length. In our case, we know that the string is, at most, `size` bytes long. We make a string buffer in which we reserve `size` characters. Then we append the characters as we read them in.

NOTE: This is more efficient than reading in characters and appending them to an existing string. Every time you append characters to a string, Java needs to find new memory to hold the larger string: this is time consuming. Appending even more characters means the string needs to be relocated again and again. Using the `StringBuffer` class avoids this problem.

Once the string buffer holds the desired string, we need to convert it to an actual `String` object. This is done with the `String(StringBuffer b)` constructor. This constructor does not copy the characters in the string buffer. Instead, it freezes the buffer contents. If you later call a method that makes a modification to the `StringBuffer` object, the buffer object first gets a new copy of the characters and then modifies those.

```
static String readFixedString(int size, DataInput in)
    throws IOException
{   StringBuffer b = new StringBuffer(size);
    int i = 0;
    boolean more = true;
    while (more && i < size)
    {   char ch = in.readChar();
        i++;
        if (ch == 0) more = false;
        else b.append(ch);
    }
    in.skipBytes(2 * (size - i));
    return b.toString();
}
```

NOTE: These two functions are packaged inside the `DataIO` helper class.

To write a fixed-size record, we simply write all fields in binary.

```
public void writeData(DataOutput out) throws IOException
{  DataIO.writeFixedString(name, NAME_SIZE, out);
   out.writeDouble(salary);
   out.writeInt(hireDay.getYear());
   out.writeInt(hireDay.getMonth());
   out.writeInt(hireDay.getDay());
}
```

Reading the data back is just as simple.

```
public void readData(DataInput in) throws IOException
{  name = DataIO.readFixedString(NAME_SIZE, in);
   salary = in.readDouble();
   int y = in.readInt();
   int m = in.readInt();
   int d = in.readInt();
   hireDay = new Day(y, m, d);
}
```

In our example, each employee record is 100 bytes long because we specified that the name field would always be written using 40 characters. This gives us a breakdown as indicated in the following:

40 characters = 80 bytes for the name

1 `double` = 8 bytes

3 `int` = 12 bytes

As an example, suppose we want to position the file pointer to the third record. We can use the following version of the `seek` method:

```
long int n = 3;
int RECORD_SIZE = 100;
in.seek((n - 1) * RECORD_SIZE);
```

To determine the total number of bytes in a file, use the `length` method. The total number of records is the length divided by the size of each record.

```
long int nbytes = in.length(); // length in bytes
int nrecords = (int)(nbytes / RECORD_SIZE);
```

The test program shown in Example 1-3 writes three records into a data file and then reads them from the file in reverse order. To do this efficiently requires random access—we need to get at the third record first.

Example 1-3: RandomFileTest.java

```java
import java.io.*;
import corejava.*;

public class RandomFileTest
{  public static void main(String[] args)
   {  Employee[] staff = new Employee[3];

      staff[0] = new Employee("Harry Hacker", 35000,
         new Day(1989,10,1));
      staff[1] = new Employee("Carl Cracker", 75000,
         new Day(1987,12,15));
      staff[2] = new Employee("Tony Tester", 38000,
         new Day(1990,3,15));
      int i;
      try
      {  DataOutputStream out = new DataOutputStream(new
            FileOutputStream("employee.dat"));
         for (i = 0; i < staff.length; i++)
            staff[i].writeData(out);
         out.close();
      }
      catch(IOException e)
      {  System.out.print("Error: " + e);
         System.exit(1);
      }

      try
      {  RandomAccessFile in
            = new RandomAccessFile("employee.dat", "r");
         int n = (int)(in.length() / Employee.RECORD_SIZE);
         Employee[] newStaff = new Employee[n];

         for (i = n - 1; i >= 0; i--)
         {  newStaff[i] = new Employee();
            in.seek(i * Employee.RECORD_SIZE);
            newStaff[i].readData(in);
         }
         for (i = 0; i < newStaff.length; i++)
            newStaff[i].print();
      }
      catch(IOException e)
      {  System.out.print("Error: " + e);
         System.exit(1);
      }

   }
}
```

```
class Employee
{  public Employee(String n, double s, Day d)
   {  name = n;
      salary = s;
      hireDay = d;
   }
   public Employee() {}
   public void print()
   {  System.out.println(name + " " + salary
         + " " + hireYear());
   }
   public void raiseSalary(double byPercent)
   {  salary *= 1 + byPercent / 100;
   }
   public int hireYear()
   {  return hireDay.getYear();
   }
   public void writeData(DataOutput out) throws IOException
   {  DataIO.writeFixedString(name, NAME_SIZE, out);
      out.writeDouble(salary);
      out.writeInt(hireDay.getYear());
      out.writeInt(hireDay.getMonth());
      out.writeInt(hireDay.getDay());
   }

   public void readData(DataInput in) throws IOException
   {  name = DataIO.readFixedString(NAME_SIZE, in);
      salary = in.readDouble();
      int y = in.readInt();
      int m = in.readInt();
      int d = in.readInt();
      hireDay = new Day(y, m, d);
   }

   public static final int NAME_SIZE = 40;
   public static final int RECORD_SIZE
      = 2 * NAME_SIZE + 8 + 4 + 4 + 4;

   private String name;
   private double salary;
   private Day hireDay;
}

class DataIO
{  public static String readFixedString(int size,
      DataInput in) throws IOException
   {  StringBuffer b = new StringBuffer(size);
      int i = 0;
```

```
      boolean more = true;
      while (more && i < size)
      {   char ch = in.readChar();
          i++;
          if (ch == 0) more = false;
          else b.append(ch);
      }
      in.skipBytes(2 * (size - i));
      return b.toString();
   }

   public static void writeFixedString(String s, int size,
      DataOutput out) throws IOException
   {   int i;
      for (i = 0; i < size; i++)
      {   char ch = 0;
          if (i < s.length()) ch = s.charAt(i);
          out.writeChar(ch);
      }
   }
}
```

 `java.lang.StringBuffer`

- `StringBuffer()`

  constructs an empty string buffer.

- `StringBuffer(int length)`

  constructs an empty string buffer with the initial capacity `length`.

- `StringBuffer(String str)`

  constructs a string buffer with the initial contents `str`.

- `int length()`

  returns the number of characters of the buffer.

- `int capacity()`

  returns the current capacity, that is, the number of characters that can be
  contained in the buffer before it must be relocated.

- `void ensureCapacity(int m)`

  enlarges the buffer if the capacity is fewer than `m` characters.

- `void setLength(int n)`

  If `n` is less than the current length, characters at the end of the string are dis-
  carded. If `n` is larger than the current length, the buffer is padded with `'\0'`
  characters.

- `char charAt(int i)`

  returns the i'th character (i is between 0 and `length()-1`); throws a `StringIndexOutOfBoundsException` if the index is invalid.

- `void getChars(int from, int to, char a[], int offset)`

  copies characters from the string buffer into an array.

Parameters		
	`from`	the first character to copy
	`to`	the first character not to copy
	`a`	the array to copy into
	`offset`	the first position in `a` to copy into

- `void setCharAt(int i, char ch)`

  sets the i'th character to `ch`.

- `StringBuffer append(String str)`

  appends a string to the end of this buffer (the buffer may be relocated as a result); returns `this`.

- `StringBuffer append(char c)`

  appends a character to the end of this buffer (the buffer may be relocated as a result); returns `this`.

- `StringBuffer insert(int offset, String str)`

  inserts a string at position `offset` into this buffer (the buffer may be relocated as a result); returns `this`.

- `StringBuffer insert(int offset, char c)`

  inserts a character at position `offset` into this buffer (the buffer may be relocated as a result); returns `this`.

- `String toString()`

  returns a string pointing to the same data as the buffer contents. (No copy is made.)

`java.lang.String`

- `String(StringBuffer buffer)`

  makes a string pointing to the same data as the buffer contents. (No copy is made.)

Object Streams

Using a fixed-length record format is a good choice if you need to store data of the same type. However, objects that you create in an object-oriented program are rarely all of the same type. For example, you may have an array called `staff` that is nominally an array of `Employee` records but contains objects that are actually instances of a child class such as `Manager`.

If we want to save files that contain this kind of information, we must first save the type of each object and then the data that defines the current state of the object. When we read this information back from a file, we must

- Read the object type
- Create a blank object of that type
- Fill it with the data that we stored in the file

It is entirely possible to do this by hand, and the first edition of this book did exactly this. However, JavaSoft developed a powerful mechanism that allows this to be done with much less effort. As you will soon see, this mechanism, called *object serialization*, almost completely automates what was previously a very tedious process. (You will see later in this chapter where the term "serialization" comes from.)

Storing Objects of Variable Type

To save object data, you first need to open an `ObjectOutputStream` object:

```
ObjectOutputStream out = new ObjectOutputStream(new
    FileOutputStream("employee.dat"));
```

Now, to save an object, you simply use the `writeObject` method of the `ObjectOutputStream` class as in the following fragment:

```
Employee harry = new Employee("Harry Hacker",
    35000, new Day(1989, 10, 1));
Manager carl = new Manager("Carl Cracker",
    75000, new Day(1987, 12, 15));
out.writeObject(harry);
out.writeObject(carl);
```

To read the objects back in, first get an `ObjectInputStream` object:

```
ObjectInputStream in = new ObjectInputStream(new
    FileInputStream("employee.dat"));
```

Then, retrieve the objects in the same order in which they were written, using the `readObject` method.

```
Employee e1 = (Employee)in.readObject();
Employee e2 = (Employee)in.readObject();
```

When reading back objects, you must carefully keep track of the number of objects that were saved, their order, and their types. Each call to readObject reads in another object of the type Object. You, therefore, will need to cast it to its correct type.

If you don't need the exact type, or you don't remember it, then you can cast it to any superclass or even leave it as type Object. For example, e2 is an Employee object variable even though it actually refers to a Manager object. If you need to dynamically query the type of the object, you can use the getClass method that we described in Chapter 5 of Volume 1.

You can only write and read *objects,* not numbers. To write and read numbers, you use methods such as writeInt/readInt or writeDouble/readDouble. (The object stream classes implement the DataInput/DataOutput interfaces.) Of course, numbers inside objects (such as the salary field of an Employee object) are saved and restored automatically. (Recall that, in Java, strings and arrays are objects and can, therefore, be restored with the writeObject/readObject methods.)

There is, however, one change you need to make to any class that you want to save and restore in an object stream. The class must implement the Serializable interface:

```
class Employee implements Serializable { . . .}
```

The Serializable interface has no methods, so you don't need to change your classes in any way. In this regard, it is similar to the Cloneable interface that we also discussed in Chapter 5 of Volume 1. However, to make a class cloneable, you still had to override the clone method of the Object class. To make a class serializable, you do not need to do *anything* else. Why aren't all classes serializable by default? We will discuss this in the section "Security."

Example 1-4 is a test program that writes an array containing two employees and one manager to disk and then restores it. Once the information is restored, we give each employee a 100% raise, not because we are feeling generous, but because you can then easily distinguish employee and manager objects by their different raiseSalary actions. This should convince you that we did restore the correct type.

Example 1-4: ObjectFileTest.java

```java
import java.io.*;
import corejava.*;

class ObjectFileTest
{  public static void main(String[] args)
   {  try
      {  Employee[] staff = new Employee[3];

         staff[0] = new Employee("Harry Hacker", 35000,
            new Day(1989,10,1));
         staff[1] = new Manager("Carl Cracker", 75000,
            new Day(1987,12,15));
         staff[2] = new Employee("Tony Tester", 38000,
            new Day(1990,3,15));

         ObjectOutputStream out = new ObjectOutputStream(new
            FileOutputStream("test1.dat"));
         out.writeObject(staff);
         out.close();

         ObjectInputStream in =  new
            ObjectInputStream(new FileInputStream("test1.dat"));
         Employee[] newStaff = (Employee[])in.readObject();

         int i;
         for (i = 0; i < newStaff.length; i++)
            newStaff[i].raiseSalary(100);
         for (i = 0; i < newStaff.length; i++)
            newStaff[i].print();
      }
      catch(Exception e)
      {  System.out.print("Error: " + e);
         System.exit(1);
      }
   }
}

class Employee implements Serializable
{  public Employee(String n, double s, Day d)
   {  name = n;
      salary = s;
      hireDay = d;
   }

   public Employee() {}
```

```java
   public void print()
   {  System.out.println(name + " " + salary
         + " " + hireYear());
   }

   public void raiseSalary(double byPercent)
   {  salary *= 1 + byPercent / 100;
   }

   public int hireYear()
   {  return hireDay.getYear();
   }

   private String name;
   private double salary;
   private Day hireDay;
}

class Manager extends Employee
{  public Manager(String n, double s, Day d)
   {  super(n, s, d);
      secretaryName = "";
   }

   public Manager() {}

   public void raiseSalary(double byPercent)
   {  // add 1/2% bonus for every year of service
      Day today = new Day();
      double bonus = 0.5 * (today.getYear() - hireYear());
      super.raiseSalary(byPercent + bonus);
   }

   public void setSecretaryName(String n)
   {  secretaryName = n;
   }

   public String getSecretaryName()
   {  return secretaryName;
   }

   private String secretaryName;
}
```

java.io.ObjectOutputStream

- `ObjectOutputStream(OutputStream out)`

  creates an `ObjectOutputStream` so that you can write to the specified `OutputStream`.

- `void writeObject(Object obj)`

  writes the specified object to the `ObjectOutputStream`. The class of the object, the signature of the class, and the values of any field not marked as `transient` are written, as well as the non-static fields of the class and all of its supertypes.

- `ObjectInputStream(InputStream is)`

  creates an `ObjectInputStream` to read back object information from the specified `InputStream`.

- `Object readObject()`

  reads an object from the `ObjectInputStream`. In particular, this reads back the class of the object, the signature of the class, and the values of the non-transient and non-static fields of the class and all of its superclasses. It does deserializing to allow multiple object references to be recovered.

The Object Serialization File Format

Object serialization saves object data in a particular file format. Of course, you can use the `writeObject`/`readObject` methods without having to know the exact sequence of bytes that represents objects in a file. Nonetheless, we found studying the data format to be extremely helpful for gaining insight into the object streaming process. We did this by looking at hex dumps of various saved object files. However, the details are somewhat technical, so feel free to skip this section if you are not interested in the implementation.

Every file begins with the 2-byte "magic number"

    AC ED

followed by the version number of the object serialization format, which is currently

    00 05

(We will be using hexadecimal numbers throughout this section to denote bytes.) Then it contains a sequence of objects, in the order that they were saved.

String objects are saved as

    74

2-byte length

characters

For example, the string "Harry" is saved as

```
74
00 05
H a r r y
```

The Unicode characters of the string are saved in UTF format.

When saving an object, the class of that object must be saved as well. The class description contains

1. The name of the class

2. The *serial version unique ID*, which is a fingerprint of the data field types and method signatures

3. A set of flags describing the serialization method

4. A description of the data fields

Java gets the fingerprint by:

*   First, ordering descriptions of the class, superclass, interfaces, field types, and method signatures in a canonical way

*   Then, applying the so-called Secure Hash Algorithm (SHA) to that data

SHA is a very fast algorithm that gives a "fingerprint" to a larger block of information. This fingerprint is always a 20-byte data packet, regardless of the size of the original data. It is created by a clever sequence of bit operations on the data that makes it essentially 100% certain that the fingerprint will change if the information is altered in any way. SHA is a U.S. standard, recommended by the National Institute for Science and Technology (NIST). (For more details on SHA, see, for example, *Network and Internetwork Security,* by William Stallings [Prentice-Hall].) However, Java only uses the first 8 bytes of the SHA code as a class fingerprint. It is still very likely that the class fingerprint will change if the data fields or methods change in any way.

Java can then check the class fingerprint in order to protect us from the following scenario: An object is saved to a disk file. Later, the designer of the class makes a change, for example, by removing a data field. Then, the old disk file is read in again. Now the data layout on the disk no longer matches the data layout in memory. If the data were read back in its old form, it could corrupt memory. Java takes great care to make such memory corruption close to impossible. Hence, it checks, using the fingerprint, that the class definition has not changed when restoring an object. It does this by comparing the fingerprint on disk with the fingerprint of the current class.

NOTE: Technically, as long as the data layout of a class has not changed, it ought to be safe to read objects back in. But Java is conservative and checks that the methods have not changed either. (After all, the methods describe the meaning of the stored data.) Of course, in practice, classes do evolve and it may be necessary for a program to read in older versions of objects. We will discuss this in the section "Versioning Objects."

Here is how a class identifier is stored:

72

2-byte length of class name

class name

8-byte fingerprint

1-byte flag

2-byte count of data field descriptors

data field descriptors

78 (end marker)

superclass type (70 if none)

The flag byte is composed of three bit masks, defined in `java.io.ObjectStreamConstants`:

```
static final byte SC_WRITE_METHOD = 1;
    // class has writeObject method that writes additional data
static final byte SC_SERIALIZABLE = 2;
    // class implements Serializable interface
static final byte SC_EXTERNALIZABLE = 4;
    // class implements Externalizable interface
```

We will discuss the `Externalizable` interface later in this chapter; for now, all our example classes will implement the `Serializable` interface and have a flag value of 02.

Each data field descriptor has the format

1-byte type code
2-byte length of field name
field name
class name (if field is an object)

The type code is one of the following:

```
B       byte
C       char
D       double
```

```
F       float
I       int
J       long
L       object
S       short
Z       Boolean
[       array
```

When the type code is L, the field name is followed by the field type. Class and field name strings do not start with the string code 74, but field types do. Field types use a slightly different encoding of their names, namely, the format used by native methods. (See Chapter 10 for native methods.)

For example, the day field of the Day class is encoded as

```
I 00 03 d a y
```

Here is the complete class descriptor of the Day class:

```
72
00 0C c o r e j a v a . D a y
16 9A C1 B6 6E 7E C0 13
02
00 03
I 00 03 d a y
I 00 05 m o n t h
I 00 04 y e a r
78
70
```

These descriptors are fairly long. If the *same* class descriptor is needed again in the file, then an abbreviated form is used:

```
71 4-byte serial number
```

The serial number refers to the previous explicit class descriptor. We will discuss the numbering scheme later.

An object is stored as

```
73
class descriptor
object data
```

For example, here is how a Day object is stored:

73	new object
72 . . . 70	new class descriptor
00 00 00 01	integer 1
00 00 00 0A	integer 10
00 00 07 C5	integer 1989

As you can see, the data file contains enough information to restore the Day object.

Arrays are saved in the following format:

```
75
class descriptor
4-byte number of entries
entries
```

The array class name in the class descriptor is in the same format as that used by native methods (which is slightly different from the class name used by class names in other class descriptors). In this format, class names start with an L and end with a semicolon.

For example, here is an array of two Day objects.

75	array
72	class descriptor
00 0F	length
[L c o r e j a v a / D a y ;	class name
FE . . . 36 02	fingerprint and flag
00 00	no data fields
78	end marker
70	no superclass
00 00 00 02	number of entries
73	new object
72 . . . 70	new class
00 00 00 01	integer 1
00 00 00 0A	integer 10
00 00 07 C5	integer 1989
73	new object
71 00 7E 00 02	existing class + serial number
00 00 00 0F	integer 15
00 00 00 0C	integer 12
00 00 07 C3	integer 1987

Of course, studying these codes can be about as exciting as reading the average phone book. But it is still instructive to know that the object stream contains a detailed description of all the objects that it contains, with sufficient detail to be able to reconstruct both objects and arrays of objects.

The Problem of Saving Object References

We now know how to save objects that contain numbers, strings, or other simple objects (like the Day object in the Employee class). However, there is one important situation that we still need to consider. What happens when one object is shared by several objects as part of its state?

To illustrate the problem, let us make a slight modification to the Manager class. Rather than storing the name of the secretary, save a reference to a secretary object, which is an object of type Employee. (It would make sense to derive a class Secretary from Employee for this purpose, but we will not do that here.)

```
class Manager extends Employee
{   // previous code remains the same
    private Employee secretary;
}
```

This is a better approach to designing a realistic Manager class than simply using the name of the secretary—the Employee record for the secretary can now be accessed without having to search the staff array.

Having done this, you must keep in mind that the Manager object now contains a *reference* to the Employee object that describes the secretary, *not* a separate copy of the object.

In particular, two managers can share the same secretary, as is the case in Figure 1-5 and the following code:

```
harry = new Employee("Harry Hacker", . . .);
Manager carl = new Manager("Carl Cracker", . . .);
carl.setSecretary(harry);
Manager tony = new Manager("Tony Tester, . . .);
tony.setSecretary(harry);
```

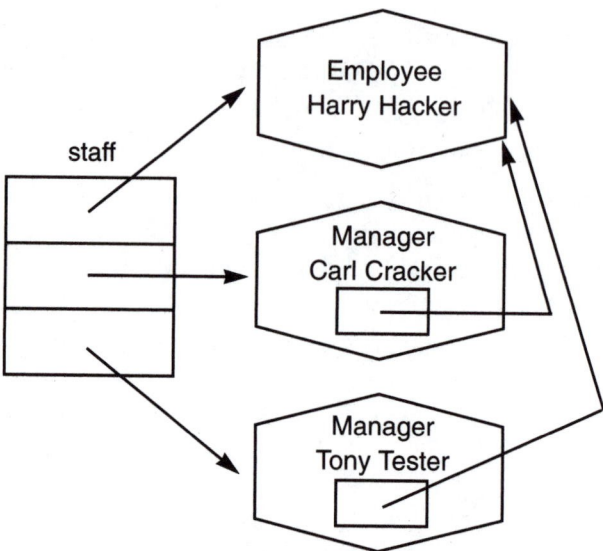

Figure 1-5: Two managers can share a mutual employee

Now suppose we write the employee data to disk. What we *don't* want is that the Manager saves its information according to the following logic:

- Save employee data

- Save secretary data

Then, the data for harry would be saved *three times*. When reloaded, the objects would have the configuration shown in Figure 1-6.

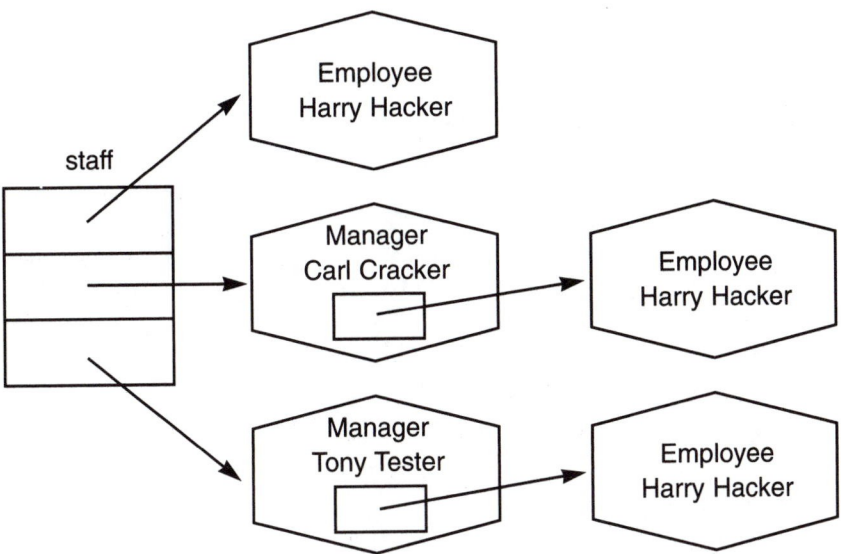

Figure 1-6: Here, Harry is saved three times

This is not what we want. Suppose the secretary gets a raise. We would not want to hunt for all other copies of that object and apply the raise as well. We want to save and restore only *one copy* of the secretary. To do this, we must copy and restore the original references to the objects. In other words, we want the object layout on disk to be exactly like the object layout in memory. This is called *persistence* in object-oriented circles.

Of course, we cannot save and restore the memory addresses for the secretary objects. When an object is reloaded, it will likely occupy a completely different memory address than it originally did.

Instead, Java uses a *serialization* approach. Hence, the name *object serialization* for this new mechanism. Remember:

- All objects that are saved to disk are given a serial number (1, 2, 3, and so on, as shown in Figure 1-7).

- When saving an object to disk, find out if the same object has already been stored.

- If it has been stored previously, just write "same as previously saved object with serial number *x*". If not, store all its data.

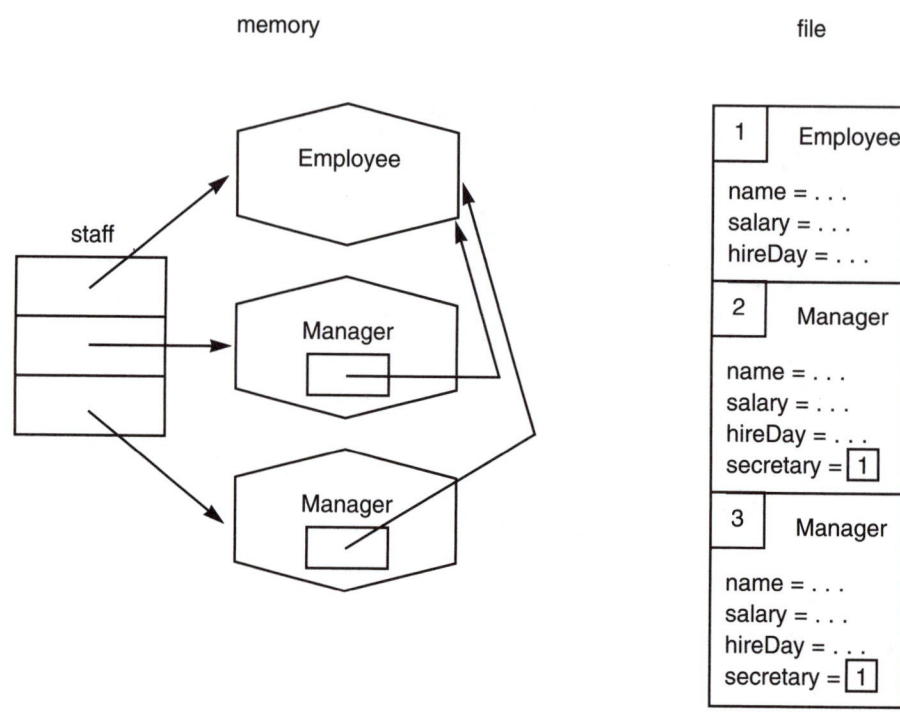

Figure 1-7: An example of object serialization

When reading back the objects, we simply reverse the procedure. For each object that we load, we note its sequence number and remember where we put it in memory. When we encounter the tag "same as previously saved object with serial number x", we look up where we put the object with serial number x and set the object reference to that memory address.

Note that the objects need not be saved in any particular order. Figure 1-8 shows what happens when a manager occurs first in the staff array.

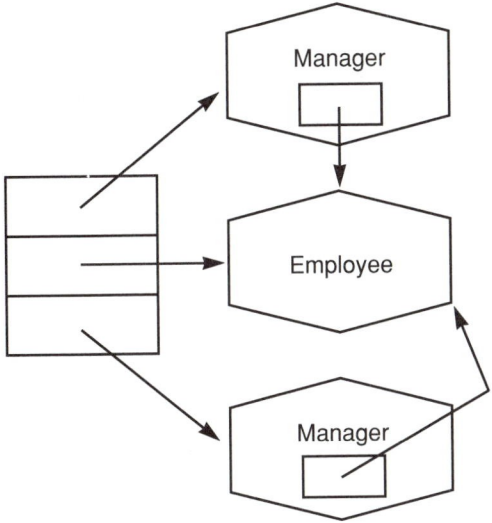

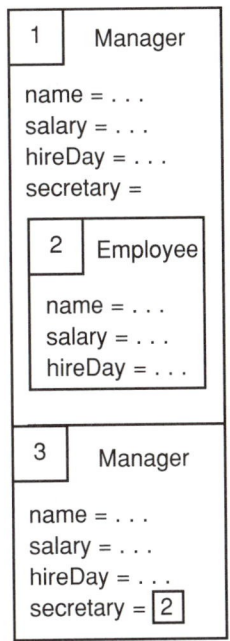

Figure 1-8: Objects saved in random order

All of this sounds confusing, and it is. Fortunately, when using object streams, it is also *completely automatic*. Object streams assign the serial numbers and keep track of duplicate objects. The exact numbering scheme is slightly different from that used in the figures—see the next section.

> NOTE: In this chapter, we use serialization to save a collection of objects to a disk file and retrieve it exactly as we stored it. Another very important application is the transmittal of a collection of objects across a network connection to another computer. Just as raw memory addresses are meaningless in a file, they are also meaningless when communicating with a different processor. Since serialization replaces memory addresses with serial numbers, it permits the transport of object collections from one machine to another. We will study that use of serialization in Chapter 5.

Example 1-5 is a program that saves and reloads a network of employee and manager objects (some of which share the same employee as a secretary). Note that the secretary object is unique after reloading—when `staff[0]` gets a raise, that is reflected in the secretary fields of the managers.

Example 1-5: ObjectRefTest.java

```java
import java.io.*;
import java.util.*;
import corejava.*;

class ObjectRefTest
{  public static void main(String[] args)
   {  try
      {
         Employee[] staff = new Employee[3];

         Employee harry = new Employee("Harry Hacker", 35000,
            new Day(1989,10,1));
         staff[0] = harry;
         staff[1] = new Manager("Carl Cracker", 75000,
            new Day(1987,12,15), harry);
         staff[2] = new Manager("Tony Tester", 38000,
            new Day(1990,3,15), harry);

         ObjectOutputStream out = new ObjectOutputStream(new
            FileOutputStream("test2.dat"));
         out.writeObject(staff);
         out.close();

         ObjectInputStream in =  new
            ObjectInputStream(new FileInputStream("test2.dat"));
         Employee[] newStaff = (Employee[])in.readObject();

         for (int i = 0; i < newStaff.length; i++)
            newStaff[i].raiseSalary(100);
         for (int i = 0; i < newStaff.length; i++)
            newStaff[i].print();
      }
      catch(Exception e)
      {  e.printStackTrace();
         System.exit(1);
      }
   }
}

class Employee implements Serializable
{  public Employee(String n, double s, Day d)
   {  name = n;
      salary = s;
      hireDay = d;
   }
```

```
    public Employee() {}

    public void raiseSalary(double byPercent)
    {   salary *= 1 + byPercent / 100;
    }

    public int hireYear()
    {   return hireDay.getYear();
    }

    public void print()
    {   System.out.println(name + " " + salary
            + " " + hireYear());
    }

    private String name;
    private double salary;
    private Day hireDay;
}

class Manager extends Employee
{   public Manager(String n, double s, Day d, Employee e)
    {   super(n, s, d);
        secretary = e;
    }

    public Manager() {}

    public void raiseSalary(double byPercent)
    {   // add 1/2% bonus for every year of service
        Day today = new Day();
        double bonus = 0.5 * (today.getYear() - hireYear());
        super.raiseSalary(byPercent + bonus);
    }

    public void print()
    {   super.print();
        System.out.print("Secretary: ");
        if (secretary != null) secretary.print();
    }

    private Employee secretary;
}
```

The Output Format for Object References

This section continues the discussion of the output format of object streams. If you skipped the discussion before, you should skip this section as well.

All objects (including arrays and strings) and all class descriptors are given serial numbers as they are saved in the output file. This process is referred to as *serialization* since every saved object is assigned a serial number. (The count starts at 00 7E 00 00.)

We already saw that a full class descriptor for any given class only occurs once. Subsequent descriptors refer to it. For example, in our previous example, the second reference to the Day class in the array of days was coded as

```
71 00 7E 00 02
```

The same mechanism is used for objects. If a reference to a previously saved object is written, it is saved in exactly the same way, that is, 71 followed by the serial number. It is always clear from the context whether the particular serial reference denotes a class descriptor or an object.

Finally, a null reference is stored as

```
 70
```

Here is the commented output of the ObjectRefTest program of the preceding section. If you like, run the program, look at a hex dump of its data file test2.dat, and compare it with the commented listing. The important lines towards the end of the output (in bold) show the reference to a previously saved object.

```
AC ED 00 05                           file header
75                                    array staff (serial #1)
    72                                new class Employee[] (serial #0)
        00 0B                         length
        [ L E m p l o y e e ;         class name
        FC BF 36 11 C5 91 11 C7 02    fingerprint and flags
        00 00                         number of data fields
        78                            end marker
        70                            no superclass
        00 00 00 03                   number of entries
    73                                new object harry (serial #5)
        72                            new class Employee (serial #2)
            00 08                     length
            E m p l o y e e           class name
            3E BB 06 E1 38 0F 90 C9 02  fingerprint and flags
            00 03                     number of data fields
```

```
    D 00  06  salary
    L 00  07  hireDay
       74 00  0E  Lcorejava/Day;          (serial #3)
    L 00  04  name
       74 00  12  Ljava/lang/String;      (serial #4)
    78                                     end marker
    70                                     no superclass
40  E1 17  00  00  00  00  00             8-byte double salary
73                                         new object harry.hireDay
                                           (serial #7)
    72                                     new class Day (serial #6)
       00 0C                               length
       c o r e j a v a . D a y
       16 9A  C1  B6  6E  7E  C0  13  02   fingerprint and flags
       00 03                               3 data fields
       I 00  03  day
       I 00  05  month
       I 00  04  year
       78                                  end marker
       70                                  no superclass
    00 00  00  01                          3 integers day, month, year
    00 00  00  0A
    00 00  07  C5
    74                                     string (serial #8)
       00 0C                               length
    H a r r y    H a c k e r
73                                         new object staff[1] (serial
                                           #11)
    72                                     new class Manager (serial #9)
       00 07                               length
    M a n a g e r                          class name
    B1 C5  48  6B  95  EE  BE  C2  02      fingerprint and flags
       00 01                               1 data field
    L 00  09  secretary
    74 00  0A  Employee;                   (serial #10)
    78                                     end marker
    71 00  7E  00  02                      existing base class
                                           Employee--use serial #2
40  F2 4F  80  00  00  00  00             8-byte double salary
73                                         new object staff[1].hireDay
                                           (serial #12)
```

71 00 7E 00 06	existing class **Day**--use serial #6
00 00 00 0F	3 integers day, month, year
00 00 00 0C	
00 00 07 C3	
74	string (serial #13)
00 0C	length
C a r l C r a c k e r	
71 00 7E 00 05	existing object **harry**--use serial #5
73	new object staff[2] (serial #14)
71 00 7E 00 09	existing class **Manager**-- use serial #9
40 E2 8E 00 00 00 00 00	8-byte double salary
73	new object staff[2].hireDay (serial #15)
71 00 7E 00 06	existing class **Day**--use serial #6
00 00 00 0F	3 integers day, month, year
00 00 00 03	
00 00 07 C6	
74	string (serial #16)
00 0B	length
T o n y T e s t e r	
71 00 7E 00 05	existing object **harry**--use serial #5

It is usually not important to know the exact file format (unless you are trying to create an evil effect by modifying the data—see the next section). What you should remember is this:

- The object stream output contains the types and data fields of all objects.

- Each object is assigned a serial number.

- Repeated occurrences of the same object are stored as references to that serial number.

Security

Even if you only glanced at the file format description of the preceding section, it should become obvious that a knowledgeable hacker can exploit this information and modify an object file so that invalid objects will be read in when you go to reload the file.

Consider, for example, the Day class in the corejava package. That class has been carefully designed so that all of its constructors check that the day, month, and year fields never represent an invalid date. For example, if you try to build a new Day(1996, 2, 31), no object is created and an IllegalArgumentException is thrown instead.

However, this safety guarantee can be subverted through serialization. When a Day object is read in from an object stream, it is possible—either through a device error or through malice—that the stream contains an invalid date. There is nothing that the serialization mechanism can do in this case—it has no under-standing of the constraints that define a legal date.

For that reason, Java's serialization mechanism provides a way for individual classes to add validation or any other desired action instead of the default behavior. A serializable class can define methods with the signature

```
private void readObject(ObjectInputStream in)
    throws IOException, ClassNotFoundException;
private void writeObject(ObjectOutputStream out)
    throws IOException;
```

Then, the data fields are no longer automatically serialized, and these methods are called instead.

For example, let us add validation to the Day class. We don't need to change the writing of Day objects, so we won't implement the writeObject method.

In the readObject method, we first need to read the object state that was writ-ten by the default write method, by calling the defaultReadObject method. This is a special method of the ObjectInputStream class that can only be called from within a readObject method of a serializable class.

```
class Day
{   . . .
    private void readObject(ObjectInputStream in)
        throws IOException, ClassNotFoundException
    {   in.defaultReadObject();
        if (!isValid()) throw new IOException("Invalid date");
    }
}
```

If the day, month, and year fields do not represent a valid date (for example, because someone modified the data file), then we throw an exception.

NOTE: Another way of protecting serialized data from tampering is authentication. As we will see in Chapter 8, a stream can save a *message digest* (such as the SHA fin-gerprint) to detect any corruption of the stream data.

Classes can also write additional information to the output stream by defining a `writeObject` method that first calls `defaultWriteObject` and then writes other data. Of course, the `readObject` method must then read the saved data—otherwise, the stream state will be out of synch with the object. Also, the `writeObject` and `readObject` can completely bypass the default storage of the object data by simply *not* calling the `defaultWriteObject` and `defaultReadObject` methods.

In any case, the `readObject` and `writeObject` methods only need to save and load their data fields. They should not concern themselves with superclass data or any other class information.

Rather than letting the serialization mechanism save and restore object data, a class can define its own mechanism. To do this, a class must implement the `Externalizable` interface. This in turn requires it to define two methods:

```
public void readExternal(ObjectInputStream in)
   throws IOException, ClassNotFoundException;
public void writeExternal(ObjectOutputStream out)
   throws IOException;
```

Unlike the `readObject` and `writeObject` methods that were described in the preceding section, these methods will be fully responsible for saving and restoring the entire object, *including the superclass data.* The serialization mechanism merely records the class of the object in the stream.

CAUTION: Unlike the `readObject` and `writeObject` methods, which are private and can only be called by the serialization mechanism, the `readExternal` and `writeExternal` methods are *public.* In particular, `readExternal` potentially permits modification of the state of an object.

Finally, there are certain data members that should never be serialized, for example, integer values that store file handles or handles of windows that are only meaningful to native methods. Such information is guaranteed to be useless when you reload an object at a later time or transport it to a different machine. In fact, improper values for such fields can actually cause native methods to crash. Java has an easy mechanism to prevent such fields from ever being serialized. Mark them with the keyword `transient`. Transient fields are always skipped when objects are serialized.

Beyond the possibility of data corruption, there is another potentially worrisome security aspect to serialization. Any code that can access a reference to a serializable object can:

- Write that object to a stream
- Then study the stream contents

and thereby know the values of all the data fields in the objects, *even the private ones*. After all, the serialization mechanism automatically saves all private data. Fortunately, this knowledge cannot be used to *modify* data. The `readObject` method does not overwrite an existing object but always creates a new object. Nevertheless, if you need to keep certain information safe from inspection via the serialization mechanism, you should take one of the following three steps:

1. Don't make the class serializable.

2. Mark the sensitive data fields as `transient`.

3. Do not use the default mechanism for saving and restoring objects. Instead, define `readObject/writeObject` or `readExternal/writeExternal` to encrypt the data.

Versioning

In the past sections, we showed you how to save relatively small collections of objects via an object stream. But those were just demonstration programs. With object streams, it helps to think big. Suppose you write a program that lets the user produce a document. This document contains paragraphs of text, tables, graphs, and so on. You can stream out the document object with a single call to `writeObject`, and the paragraph, table and graph objects are automatically streamed out as well. One user of your program can then give the output file to another user who also has a copy of your program, and that program loads the entire document with a single call to `readObject`.

This is very useful, but your program will inevitably change, and you will release a version 1.1. Can version 1.1 read the old files? Can the users who still use 1.0 read the files that the new version is now producing? Clearly, it would be desirable if object files could cope with the evolution of classes.

At first glance it seems that this would not be possible. When a class definition changes in any way, then its SHA fingerprint also changes and you know that Java will refuse to read in objects with different fingerprints. However, a class can indicate that it is *compatible* with an earlier version of itself. To do this, one must first obtain the fingerprint of the *earlier* version of the class. You use the standalone `serialver` program that is part of the JDK to obtain this number. For example, running

```
serialver corejava.Day
```

prints out

```
corejava.Day:    static final long serialVersionUID =
    1628827204529864723L;
```

If you start the `serialver` program with the `-show` option, then it brings up a graphical dialog box (see Figure 1-9).

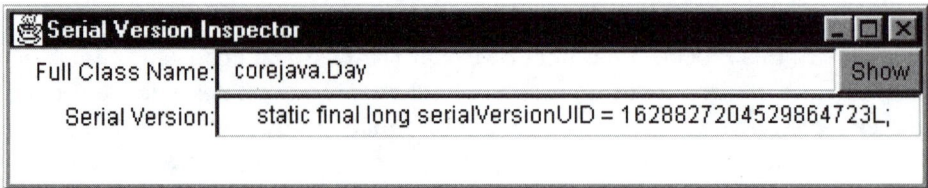

Figure 1-9: The graphical version of the `serialver` program

All *later* versions of the class must define the `serialVersionUID` constant to the same fingerprint as the original.

```
class Day // version 1.1
{  . . .
    static final long serialVersionUID = 1628827204529864723L;
}
```

When a class has a static data member named `serialVersionUID`, it will not compute the fingerprint manually but instead will use that value.

Once that static data member has been placed inside a class, the serialization system is now willing to read in different versions of objects of that class.

If only the methods of the class change, then there is no problem with reading the object new data. However, if data fields change, then you may have problems. For example, the old file object may have more or fewer data fields than the one in the program, or the types of the data fields may be different. In that case, Java makes an effort to convert the stream object to the current version of the class.

Java compares the data fields of the current version of the class with the data fields of the version in the stream. Of course, Java considers only the non-transient and non-static data fields. If two fields have matching names but different types, then Java makes no effort to convert one type to the other—the objects are incompatible. If the object in the stream has data fields that are not present in the current version, then Java ignores the data in the stream. If the current version has data fields that are not present in the streamed object, the added fields are set to their default (`null` for objects, zero for numbers).

Here is an example. Suppose we have saved a number of employee records on disk, using the original version (1.0) of the class. Now we change the `Employee` class to version 2.0 by adding a data field called `department`. Figure 1-10 shows what happens when a 1.0 object is read into a program that uses 2.0 objects. The

department field is set to `null`. Figure 1-11 shows the opposite scenario: a program using 1.0 objects reads a 2.0 object. The additional `department` field is ignored.

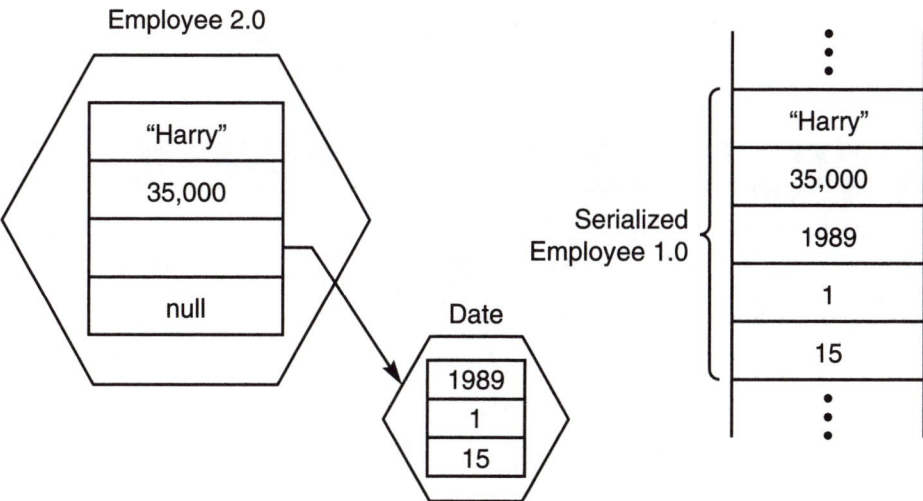

Figure 1-10: Reading an object with fewer data fields

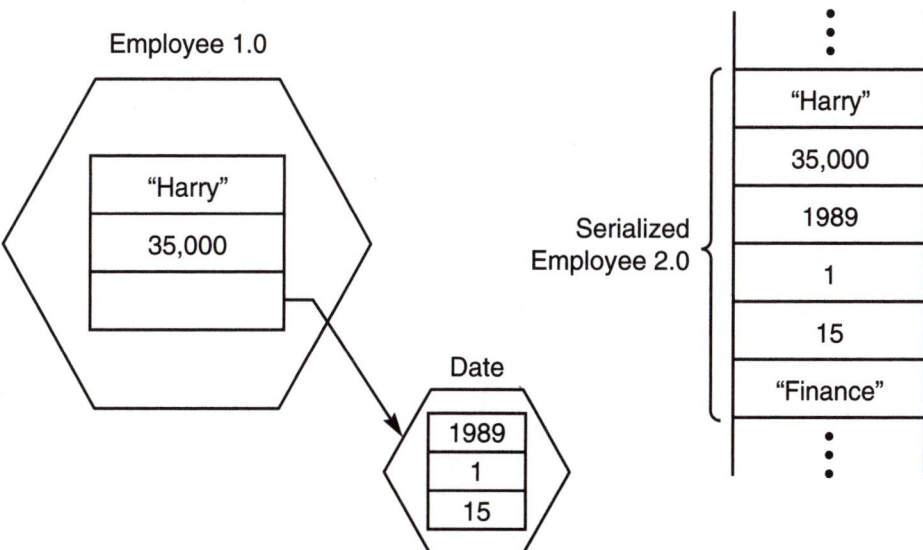

Figure 1-11: Reading an object with more data fields

Is this process safe? It depends. Dropping a data field seems harmless—the recipient still has all the data that it knew how to manipulate. Setting a data field to `null` may not be so safe. Many classes work hard to initialize all data fields in all constructors to non-null values, so that the methods don't have to be prepared to handle `null` data. It is up to the class designer to implement additional code in the `readObject` method to fix version incompatibilities or to make sure the methods are robust enough to handle `null` data.

Using serialization for cloning

There is one other amusing (and, occasionally, very useful) use for the new serialization mechanism: it gives you an easy way to clone an object *provided* the class is serializable. (Recall from Chapter 5 of Volume 1 that you need to do a bit of work in order to allow an object to be cloned.) As the following example program shows, to get `clone` for free, simply derive from the `SerialCloneable` class, and you are done.

```java
import java.io.*;
import corejava.*;

public class SerialCloneTest
{  public static void main(String[] args)
   {  Employee harry = new Employee("Harry Hacker", 35000,
         new Day(1989,10,1));
      Employee harry2 = (Employee)harry.clone();
      harry.raiseSalary(100);
      harry.print();
      harry2.print();
   }
}

class SerialCloneable implements Cloneable, Serializable
{  public Object clone()
   {  try
      {  ByteArrayOutputStream bout = new
            ByteArrayOutputStream();
         ObjectOutputStream out = new ObjectOutputStream(bout);
         out.writeObject(this);
         out.close();
         ByteArrayInputStream bin = new
            ByteArrayInputStream(bout.toByteArray());
         ObjectInputStream in = new ObjectInputStream(bin);
         Object ret = in.readObject();
         in.close();
         return ret;
      } catch(Exception e)
```

```
            {   return null;
            }
        }
    }
}

class Employee extends SerialCloneable
{   public Employee(String n, double s, Day d)
    {   name = n;
        salary = s;
        hireDay = d;
    }
    public Employee() {}

    public void print()
    {   System.out.println(name + " " + salary + " " +
            hireYear());
    }

    public void raiseSalary(double byPercent)
    {   salary *= 1 + byPercent / 100;
    }

    public int hireYear()
    {   return hireDay.getYear();
    }

    private String name;
    private double salary;
    private Day hireDay;
}
```

File Management

We have learned how to read and write data from a file. However, there is more to file management than reading and writing. The File class encapsulates the functionality that you will need to work with the file system on the user's machine. For example, you use the File class to find out when a file was last modified or to remove or rename the file. In other words, the stream classes are concerned with the contents of the file, whereas the File class is concerned with the storage of the file on a disk.

NOTE: As is so often the case in Java, the File class takes the least common denominator approach. For example, under Windows, you can find out if a file is write protected, but you cannot find out if it is a system or hidden file without using a native method (see Chapter 10).

The simplest constructor for a `File` object takes a (full) file name. If you don't supply a pathname, then Java uses the current directory. For example:

```
File foo = new File("test.txt");
```

gives you a handle on a file with this name in the current directory. (The current directory is the directory in which the program is running.) A call to this constructor *does not create a file with this name if it doesn't exist.* Actually, creating a file from a `File` object is done with one of the stream class constructors. In fact, once you have a `File` object, the `exists` method in the `File` class tells you whether a file exists with that name. For example, the following trial program would almost certainly print "false" on anyone's machine and yet it can print out a pathname to this nonexistent file.

```
import java.io.*;

public class test
{   public static void main(String args[])
    {   File foo = new File( "sajkdfshds");
        System.out.println(foo.getAbsolutePath());
        System.out.println(foo.exists());
    }
}
```

There are two other constructors for `File` objects:

```
File(String path, String name)
```

which creates a `File` object with the given name in the directory specified by the `path` parameter. (If the `path` parameter is `null`, this constructor then creates a `File` object using the current directory.)

Finally, you can use an existing `File` object in the constructor:

```
File(File dir, String name)
```

where the `File` object represents a directory and, as before, if `dir` is null, the constructor creates a `File` object in the current directory.

Next, along with the `exists` method that you have already seen, there are `isDirectory` and `isFile` methods to tell you whether the file object represents a file or a directory. If the file object represents a directory, use `list()` to get an array of the file names in that directory. The program in Example 1-6 uses all these methods to print out the directory substructure of whatever path is entered on the command line. (It would be easy enough to change this into a utility class that returns a vector of the subdirectories for further processing.)

Example 1-6: FindDirectories.java

```java
import java.io.*;

public class FindDirectories
{   public static void main(String args[])
    {   if (args.length == 0) args = new String[] { ".." };

        try
        {   File pathName = new File(args[0]);
            String[] fileNames = pathName.list();

            for (int i = 0; i<fileNames.length; i++)
            {   File tf = new File(pathName.getPath(),
                    fileNames[i]);
                if (tf.isDirectory())
                {   System.out.println(tf.getCanonicalPath());
                    main(new String [] { tf.getPath() });
                }
            }
        }
        catch(IOException e)
        {   System.out.println("Error: " + e);
        }
    }
}
```

Rather than listing all files in a directory, you can use a `FileNameFilter` object as a parameter to the `list` method to narrow down the list. These objects are simply instances of a class that satisfies the `FilenameFilter` interface.

NOTE: You may recall from Volume 1 that a `FilenameFilter` is supposed to be used to limit the choices shown in a file dialog box; however, that feature is not implemented in Java 1.1.

All a class needs to do to implement the `FilenameFilter` interface is define a method called `accept()`. Here is an example of a simple `FilenameFilter` class that only allows files with a specified extension:

```java
import java.io.*;
public class ExtensionFilter implements FilenameFilter
{   private String extension;
    public ExtensionFilter(String ext)
    {   extension = "." + ext;
    }
    public boolean accept(File dir, String name)
    {   return name.endsWith(extension);
    }
}
```

When writing portable programs, it is a challenge to specify file names with subdirectories. As it turns out, you can use a forward slash (the Unix and Mac separator) as the directory separator in Windows as well, but other operating systems might not permit this, so we don't recommend that.

TIP: If you do use forward slashes as a directory separator in Windows, the `getAbsolutePath` method returns a file name that contains forward slashes, which will look strange to Windows users. Instead, use the `getCanonicalPath` method—it replaces the forward slashes with backslashes.

It is much better to use the information about the current directory separator that the `File` class stores in a static instance field called `separatorChar`. (In a Windows environment, this is a backslash (\), while in a Unix or Macintosh environment, it is a forward slash (/)). For example:

```
File foo = new File("Documents" + File.separatorChar + "data.txt")
```

Of course, if you use the second alternate version of the `File` constructor,

```
File foo = new File("Documents", "data.txt")
```

then Java will supply the correct separator.

The API notes that follow give you what we think are the most important remaining methods of the `File` class; their use should be straightforward.

`java.io.File`

- `boolean canRead()`

  indicates whether the file can be read by the current application.

- `boolean canWrite()`

  indicates whether the file is writable or read only.

- `boolean delete()`

  tries to delete the file; returns `true` if the file was deleted; `false` otherwise.

- `boolean exists()`

  `true` if the file or directory exists; `false` otherwise.

- `String getAbsolutePath()`

  returns a string that contains the absolute pathname. Tip: Use `getCanonicalPath` instead.

- `String getCanonicalPath()`

  returns a string that contains the canonical pathname. In particular, redundant "." directories are removed, the correct directory separator is used, and the capitalization preferred by the underlying file system is obtained.

- `String getName()`

  returns a string that contains the file name of the `File` object (does not include path information).

- `String getParent()`

  returns a string that contains the parent directory of the file, or `null` if you are at the root.

- `String getPath()`

  returns a string that contains the pathname of the file.

- `boolean isDirectory()`

  returns `true` if the `File` represents a directory; `false` otherwise.

- `boolean isFile()`

  returns `true` if the `File` object represents a file as opposed to a directory or a device.

- `long lastModified()`

  returns the time the file was last modified, or 0 if the file does not exist.

- `long length()`

  returns the length of the file in bytes, or 0 if the file does not exist.

- `String[] list()`

  returns an array of strings that contain the names of the files and directories contained by this `File` object, or null if this `File` was not representing a directory.

- `String[] list(FilenameFilter filter)`

  returns an array of the names of the files and directories contained by this `File` that satisfy the filter, or `null` if none exist.

  Parameters: `filter`   the `FilenameFilter` object to use

- `boolean mkdir()`

  makes a subdirectory off the directory represented by the `File` object. Returns `true` if the directory was successfully created; `false` otherwise.

- `boolean mkdirs()`

  unlike `mkdir`, creates the parent directories if necessary.

- `boolean renameTo(File dest)`

  returns `true` if the name was changed; `false` otherwise.

  Parameters: dest   a `File` object that specifies the new name

`java.io.FilenameFilter`

- `boolean accept(File dir, String name)`

  returns `true` if the file matches the filter criterion.

  Parameters: dir   a `File` object representing the directory that contains the file

                                     name   the name of the file

CHAPTER 2

Multithreading

You are probably familiar with *multitasking:* the ability to have more than one program working at what seems like the same time. For example, you can print while editing or sending a fax. Of course, unless you have a multiple-processor machine, what is really going on is that the operating system is doling out resources to each program, giving the impression of simultaneity. This is possible because while the user may think he or she is keeping the computer busy by, for example, entering data, most of the CPU's time will be idle. (A fast typist takes around ½₀ of a second per character typed, after all.)

Multitasking can be done in two ways, depending on whether the operating system insists that a program let go or whether the program must cooperate in letting go. The former is called *preemptive multitasking;* the latter is called *cooperative* (or, simply, nonpreemptive multitasking). Windows 3.1 is a cooperative multitasking system, and Windows NT (and Windows 95 for 32-bit programs) is preemptive. (Although harder to implement, preemptive multitasking is much more effective. With cooperative multitasking, a badly behaved program can hog everything.)

Multithreaded programs extend the idea of multitasking by taking it one level lower: individual programs will appear to do multiple tasks at the same time. (Each task is usually called a *thread*—which is short for thread of control. Programs that can run more than thread at once are said to be *multithreaded.*) Think of each thread as running in a separate context: contexts make it seem as though each thread has its own CPU—with registers, memory, and its own code.

So what is the difference between multiple *processes* and multiple *threads?* The essential difference is that while each process has a complete set of its own variables, threads share the same data segment. This sounds somewhat risky, and indeed it can be, as you will see later in this chapter. But it takes much less over-

head to create and destroy individual threads than it does to launch new processes, which is why all modern operating systems support multithreading. Moreover, cross-process communication, even when permitted, is much slower than cross-thread communication.

Multithreading is extremely useful in practice: for example, a browser should be able to deal with multiple hosts or to open an e-mail window or to view another page while downloading data. Java itself uses a thread to do garbage collection in the background—thus saving you the trouble of managing memory! This chapter shows you how to add multithreading capability to your Java applications and applets.

NOTE: In many programming languages, you have to use an external thread package to do multithreaded programming. Java has multithreading built into the language, which makes your job much easier.

What Are Threads?

Let us start by looking at a Java program that does not use multiple threads and that, as a consequence, makes it difficult for the user to perform several tasks with that program. After we dissect it, we will then show you how easy it is to have this program run separate threads. This program animates a bouncing ball by continually moving the ball, finding out if it bounces against a wall, and then redrawing it. (See Figure 2-1.)

As soon as you click on the Start button, the program launches a ball from the upper-left corner of the screen and begins bouncing. The handler of the Start button calls the method bounce() of the Ball class, which contains a loop running through 1,000 moves. After each move, we call the static sleep method of the Thread class to pause the ball for 5 milliseconds.

```
class Ball
{   . . .
    public void bounce()
    {   draw();
        for (int i = 1; i <= 1000; i++)
        {   move();
            try { Thread.sleep(5); }
            catch(InterruptedException e) {}
        }
    }
}
```

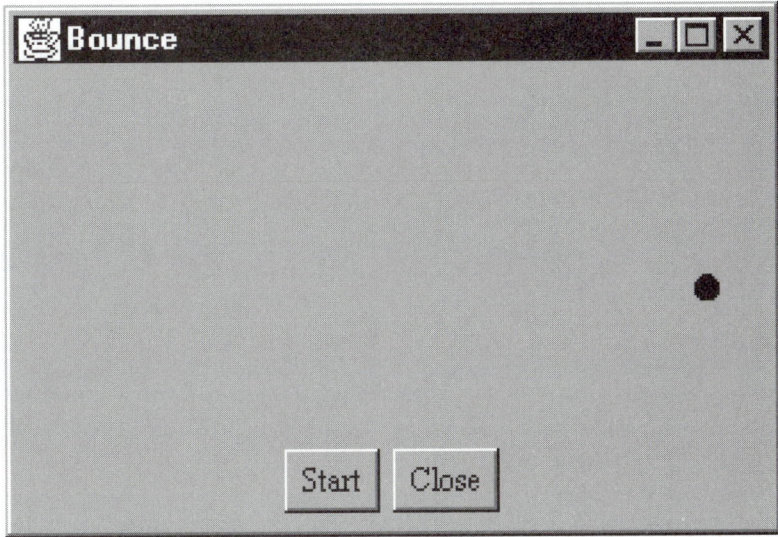

Figure 2-1: Using a thread to animate a bouncing ball

If you run the program, you can see that the ball bounces around nicely, but it completely takes over the application. If you become tired of the bouncing ball before it has finished its 1,000 bounces and click on the Close button, the ball continues bouncing anyway. You cannot interact with the program until the ball has finished bouncing.

This is not a good situation in theory or in practice, and it is becoming more and more of a problem as networks become more central. After all, when you are reading data over a network connection, it is all too common to be stuck in a time-consuming task that you would *really* like to interrupt. For example, suppose you download a large image and decide, after seeing a piece of it, that you do not need or want to see the rest; you certainly would like to be able to click on a Stop or Back button to interrupt the loading process. In the next section, we will show you how to keep the user in control by running crucial parts of the code in a separate *thread*.

Example 2-1 is the entire code for the program.

Example 2-1: Bounce.java

```java
import java.awt.*;
import java.awt.event.*;
import corejava.*;

public class Bounce extends CloseableFrame
{  public Bounce()
   {  canvas = new Canvas();
      add(canvas, "Center");
      Panel p = new Panel();
      addButton(p, "Start",
         new ActionListener()
         {  public void actionPerformed(ActionEvent evt)
            {  Ball b = new Ball(canvas);
               b.bounce();
            }
         });

      addButton(p, "Close",
         new ActionListener()
         {  public void actionPerformed(ActionEvent evt)
            {  System.exit(0);
            }
         });
       add(p, "South");
   }

   public void addButton(Container c, String title,
      ActionListener a)
   {  Button b = new Button(title);
      c.add(b);
      b.addActionListener(a);
   }


   public static void main(String[] args)
   {  Frame f = new Bounce();
      f.show();
   }

   private Canvas canvas;
}

class Ball
{  public Ball(Canvas c) { box = c; }

   public void draw()
```

```
  {  Graphics g = box.getGraphics();
     g.fillOval(x, y, XSIZE, YSIZE);
     g.dispose();
  }

  public void move()
  {  Graphics g = box.getGraphics();
     g.setXORMode(box.getBackground());
     g.fillOval(x, y, XSIZE, YSIZE);
     x += dx;
     y += dy;
     Dimension d = box.getSize();
     if (x < 0)
     { x = 0; dx = -dx; }
     if (x + XSIZE >= d.width)
     { x = d.width - XSIZE; dx = -dx; }
     if (y < 0)
     { y = 0; dy = -dy; }
     if (y + YSIZE >= d.height)
     { y = d.height - YSIZE; dy = -dy; }
     g.fillOval(x, y, XSIZE, YSIZE);
     g.dispose();
  }

  public void bounce()
  {  draw();
     for (int i = 1; i <= 1000; i++)
     {  move();
        try { Thread.sleep(5); }
        catch(InterruptedException e) {}
     }
  }

  private Canvas box;
  private static final int XSIZE = 10;
  private static final int YSIZE = 10;
  private int x = 0;
  private int y = 0;
  private int dx = 2;
  private int dy = 2;
}
```

Using Threads to Give Other Tasks a Chance

We will make our bouncing-ball program more responsive by running the code
that moves the ball in a separate thread.

NOTE: Since most computers do not have multiple processors, Java uses a mechanism in which each thread gets a chance to run for a little while, and then it activates another thread. It also relies on the host operating system to provide the thread scheduling package.

In our next program, we use *two* threads: one for the bouncing ball and another for the *main thread* that takes care of the user interface. Because each thread gets a chance to run, the main thread has the opportunity to notice when you click on the Close button while the ball is bouncing. It can then process the "close" action.

There is a simple process for running code in a separate thread in Java: place the code into the run method of a class derived from Thread.

To make our bouncing-ball program into a separate thread, we need only derive Ball from Thread and rename the bounce method run, as in the following code:

```
class Ball extends Thread
{   . . .
    public void run()
    {   draw();
        for (int i = 1; i <= 1000; i++)
        {   move();
            try { sleep(5); }
            catch(InterruptedException e) {}
        }
    }
}
```

You may have noticed that we are catching an exception called InterruptedException. Methods like sleep and wait throw this exception when your thread is interrupted because another thread has called the interrupt method. Interrupting a thread is a very drastic way of getting the thread's attention and should not normally be used. In our programs, we never call interrupt, so we supply no exception handler for it.

Running and Starting Threads

When you construct an object derived from Thread, Java does not automatically call the run method.

```
Ball b = new Ball(. . .); // won't run yet
```

You should call the start method in your object to actually start a thread.

```
b.start();
```

NOTE: Do *not* call the `run` method directly—`start` will call it when the thread is set up and ready to go.

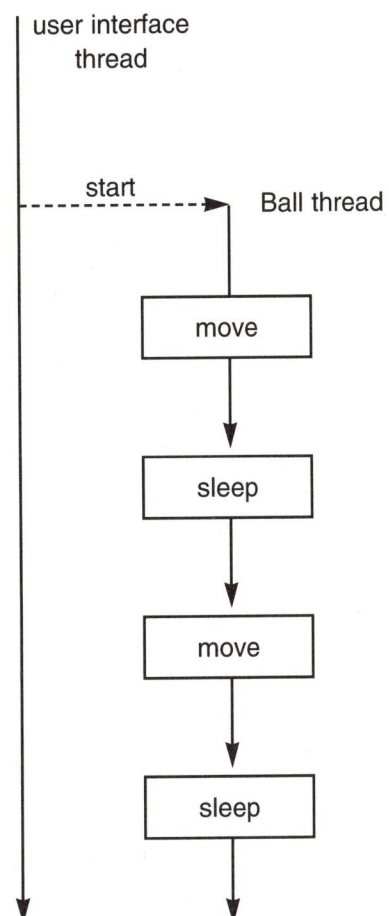

In Java, a thread needs to tell the other threads when it is idle, so the other threads can grab the chance to execute the code in their `run` procedures. (See Figure 2-2.) The usual way to do this is through the `sleep` method (`sleep` is a static method in `Thread`). The `run` method of the `Ball` class uses the call to `sleep(5)` to indicate that the thread will be idle for the next 5 milliseconds. After 5 milliseconds, it will start up again, but in the meantime, other threads have a chance to get work done.

From a design point of view, it seems strange to have the class `Ball` extend the class `Thread`. A ball is an object that moves on the screen and bounces off the corners. Does the is–a rule for inheritance apply here? Is a ball a thread? Not really. Here, we are using inheritance strictly for technical reasons. To get a thread you can control, you need a thread object with a `run` method. We might as well add that `run` method to the class whose methods and instance fields the `run` method uses. Therefore, we make `Ball` a child class of `Thread`.

The complete code is shown in Example 2-2.

Figure 2-2: The UI and ball threads

Example 2-2: BounceThread.java

```
import corejava.*;
import java.awt.*;
import java.awt.event.*;

public class BounceThread extends CloseableFrame
{  public BounceThread()
   {  canvas = new Canvas();
```

```
        add(canvas, "Center");
        Panel p = new Panel();
        addButton(p, "Start",
            new ActionListener()
            {  public void actionPerformed(ActionEvent evt)
                {  Ball b = new Ball(canvas);
                   b.start();
                }
            });

        addButton(p, "Close",
            new ActionListener()
            {  public void actionPerformed(ActionEvent evt)
                {  canvas.setVisible(false);
                   System.exit(0);
                }
            });
        add(p, "South");
    }

    public void addButton(Container c, String title,
        ActionListener a)
    {  Button b = new Button(title);
       c.add(b);
       b.addActionListener(a);
    }


    public static void main(String[] args)
    {  Frame f = new BounceThread();
       f.show();
    }

    private Canvas canvas;
}

class Ball extends Thread
{  public Ball(Canvas c) { box = c; }

    public void draw()
    {  Graphics g = box.getGraphics();
       g.fillOval(x, y, XSIZE, YSIZE);
       g.dispose();
    }

    public void move()
    {  if (!box.isVisible()) return;
       Graphics g = box.getGraphics();
       g.setXORMode(box.getBackground());
```

```java
        g.fillOval(x, y, XSIZE, YSIZE);
        x += dx;
        y += dy;
        Dimension d = box.getSize();
        if (x < 0)
        { x = 0; dx = -dx; }
        if (x + XSIZE >= d.width)
        { x = d.width - XSIZE; dx = -dx; }
        if (y < 0)
        { y = 0; dy = -dy; }
        if (y + YSIZE >= d.height)
        { y = d.height - YSIZE; dy = -dy; }
        g.fillOval(x, y, XSIZE, YSIZE);
        g.dispose();
    }

    public void run()
    {   draw();
        for (int i = 1; i <= 1000; i++)
        {   move();
            try { Thread.sleep(5); } catch(InterruptedException e) {}
        }
    }

    private Canvas box;
    private static final int XSIZE = 10;
    private static final int YSIZE = 10;
    private int x = 0;
    private int y = 0;
    private int dx = 2;
    private int dy = 2;
}
```

`java.lang.Thread`

- `Thread()`

  constructs a new thread. The thread must have a `run` method. You must `start` the thread to activate its `run` function.

- `void run()`

  You must override this function and add the code that you want to have executed in the thread.

- `void start()`

  starts this thread. This will cause the `run()` method to be called. This method will return immediately. The new thread runs concurrently.

- `static void sleep(long millis)`

  puts the currently executing thread to sleep for the specified number of milliseconds. Note that this is a static method.

- `void interrupt()`

  sends an interrupt request to a thread.

- `static boolean interrupted()`

  asks whether or not the current thread has been interrupted. Note that this is a static method.

Running Multiple Threads

Run the program in the preceding section. Now, click on the Start button again while a ball is running. Click on it a few more times. You will see a whole bunch of balls bouncing away as captured in Figure 2-3. Each of them will move 1,000 times until it comes to its final resting place.

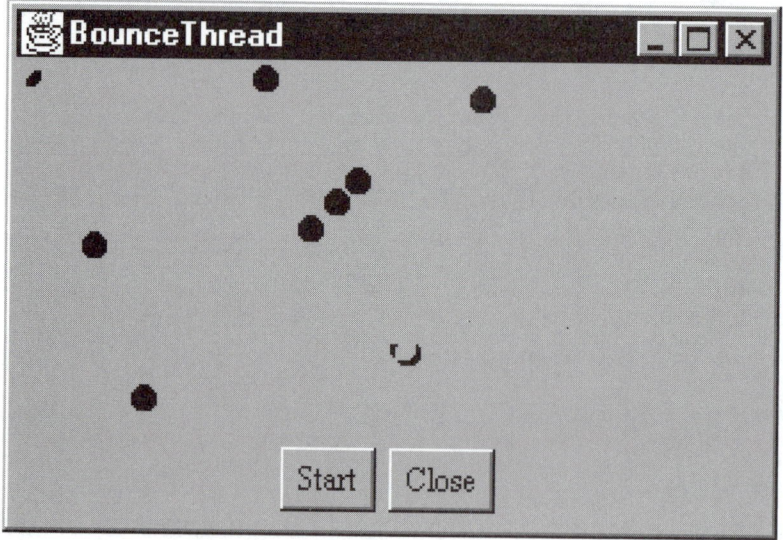

Figure 2-3: Multiple threads

This is a great advantage of the Java thread architecture. It is very easy to create any number of autonomous objects that appear to run in parallel.

You can enumerate the currently running threads—see the API note in the "Thread Groups" section.

Thread Properties

Thread States

Threads can be in one of four states:

* new
* runnable
* blocked
* dead

Each of these states is explained as follows:

New threads

When you create a thread with the `new` operator—for example, `new Ball()`—the thread is not yet running. This means that it is in the *new* state. When a thread is in the new state, Java has not started executing code inside of it. A certain amount of bookkeeping needs to be done before a thread can run. Doing the bookkeeping and determining the needed memory allocation are the tasks of the `start` method.

Runnable threads

Once you invoke the `start` method, the thread is *runnable.* A runnable thread may not yet be running. It is up to the operating system to give it time to do so. When the code inside the thread begins executing, the thread is *running.* (The Java documentation does not call this a separate state, though. A running thread is still in the runnable state.)

How this happens is up to the operating system. The thread package in Java needs to work with the underlying operating system. Only the operating system can provide the CPU cycles. The so-called *green threads* package that is used by Java 1.x on Solaris, for example, keeps a running thread active until a higher-priority thread awakes and takes control. Other thread systems (such as Windows 95 and Windows NT) give each runnable thread a slice of time to perform its task. When that slice of time is exhausted, the operating system gives another thread an opportunity to work. This approach is more sophisticated and makes better use of the multithreading capabilities of Java. Future releases of Java on Solaris are expected to allow use of the native Solaris threads, which also perform time-slicing.

NOTE: As we write this, Sun has released an early version of the native thread package for Solaris. Check out `http://java.sun.com/products/jdk/1.1/index.html#techpacks`.

Always keep in mind that a runnable thread may or may not be running at any given time. See Figure 2-4. (This is why the state is called "runnable" and not "running.")

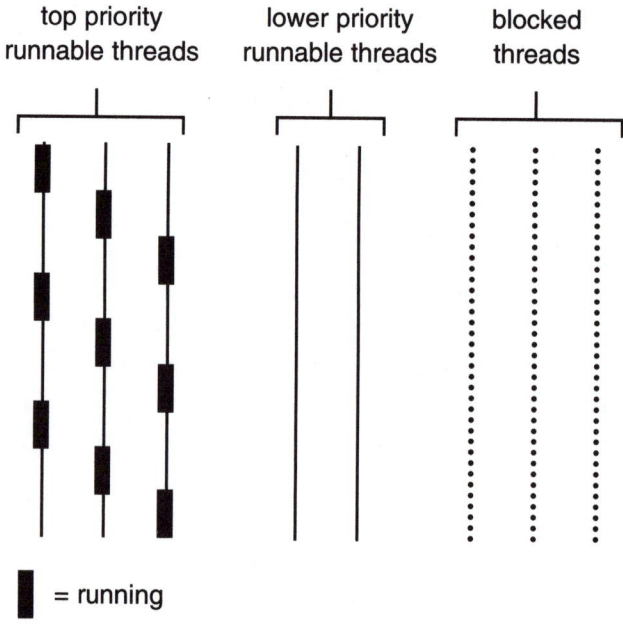

Figure 2-4: Time-slicing on a single CPU

Blocked threads

A thread enters the *blocked* state when one of the following four actions occurs:

1. Someone calls the `sleep()` method of the thread.

2. Someone calls the `suspend()` method of the thread.

3. The thread calls the `wait()` method.

4. The thread calls an operation that is *blocking on input/output,* that is, an operation that will not return to its caller until input and output operations are complete.

Figure 2-5 shows the states that a thread can have and the possible transitions from one state to another. When a thread is blocked (or, of course, when it dies), another thread is scheduled to run. When a blocked thread is reactivated (for example, because it has slept the required number of milliseconds or because the I/O it waited for is complete), the scheduler checks to see if it has a higher

priority than the currently running thread. If so, it *preempts* the current thread and starts running the blocked thread again. (On a machine with multiple processors, each processor runs a separate thread.)

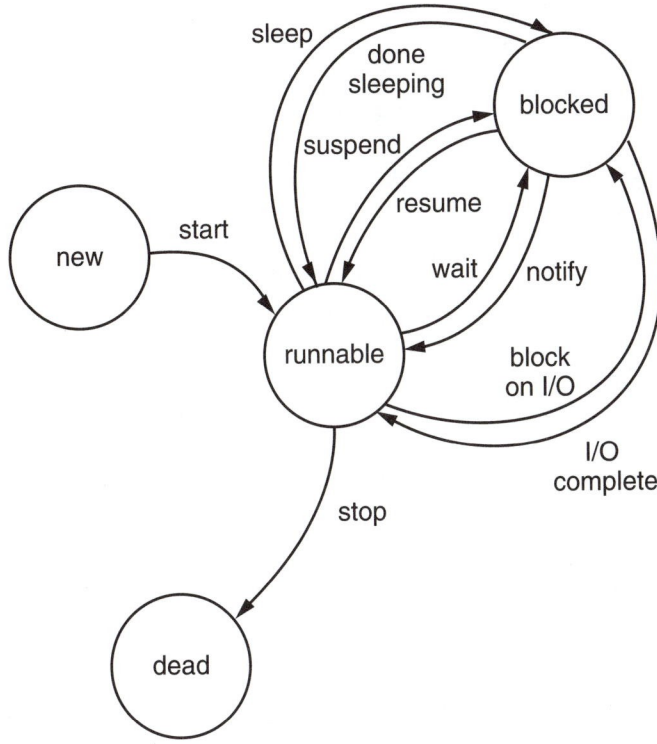

Figure 2-5: Thread states

For example, the run method of the Ball thread puts itself to sleep for 5 milliseconds after it has completed a move.

```
class Ball extends Thread
{   . . .
    public void run()
    {   draw();
        for (int i = 1; i <= 1000; i++)
        {   move();
            try { sleep(5); }
            catch(InterruptedException e) {}
        }
    }
}
```

This gives other threads (in our case, other balls and the main thread) the chance to run. If the computer has multiple processors, then more than one thread has a chance to run at the same time.

Moving Out of a Blocked State

The thread must move out of the blocked state and back into the runnable state, using the opposite of the route that put it into the blocked state.

1. If a thread has been put to sleep, the specified number of milliseconds must expire.

2. If a thread has been suspended, then someone must call its `resume` method.

3. If a thread called `wait`, then the owner of the monitor on whose availability the thread is waiting must call `notify` or `notifyAll`. (We cover monitors later in this chapter.)

4. If a thread is waiting for the completion of an input or output operation, then the operation must have finished.

> NOTE: You cannot activate a blocked thread unless you use the same route that blocked it in the first place.

For example, if a thread is blocked on input and you call its `resume` method, it stays blocked.

If you invoke a method on a thread that is incompatible with its state, then Java throws an `IllegalThreadStateException`. For example, this happens when you call `suspend` on a thread that is not currently runnable.

Dead Threads

A thread is dead for one of two reasons:

- It dies a natural death because the `run` method exits.
- It is killed because someone invoked its `stop` method.

If you stop a thread, it does not immediately die. Technically, the `stop` method throws an object of type `ThreadDeath` to the thread object. Once the thread passes a `ThreadDeath` object to its `Thread` base class, the thread truly dies. `ThreadDeath` is a child class of `Error`, not `Exception`, so you do not have to catch it. In most circumstances, you would not want to catch this. The exceptions are in the rare situations when you must do some clean-up prior to the thread being permanently put to rest.

NOTE: If you do catch `ThreadDeath`, be sure to rethrow it in order to make the thread actually die.

Finding Out the State of a Thread

To find out whether a thread is currently runnable or blocked, use the `isAlive` method. This method returns `false` if the thread is still new and not yet runnable or if the thread is dead.

NOTE: You cannot find out if a thread is actually running, nor can you differentiate between a thread that has not yet become runnable and one that has already died.

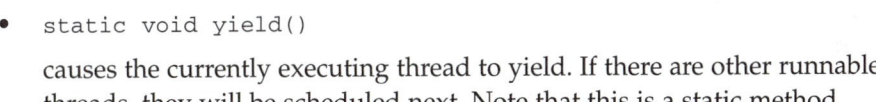

`java.lang.Thread`

* `boolean isAlive()`

  returns `true` if the thread has started and has not been stopped.

* `static void yield()`

  causes the currently executing thread to yield. If there are other runnable threads, they will be scheduled next. Note that this is a static method.

* `void suspend()`

  suspends this thread's execution.

* `void resume()`

  resumes this thread. This method is only valid after `suspend()` has been invoked.

* `void stop()`

  kills the thread.

* `void join()`

  waits for the specified thread to cease to be "alive."

* `void join(long millis)`

  waits for the specified thread to cease to be "alive" or for the specified amount of milliseconds to have passed.

  Parameters   `millis`   the number of milliseconds

Thread Priorities

Every thread in Java has a *priority*. By default, a thread inherits the priority of its parent thread. You can increase or decrease the priority of any thread with the setPriority method. You can set the priority to any value between MIN_PRIORITY (defined as 1 in the Thread class) and MAX_PRIORITY (defined as 10). NORM_PRIORITY is defined as 5.

Whenever the thread-scheduler has a chance to pick a new thread, it picks the *highest priority thread that is currently runnable.* The highest-priority runnable thread keeps running until:

*   It yields by calling the yield method, or

*   It ceases to be runnable (either by dying or by entering the blocked state), or

*   It is replaced by a higher-priority thread that has become runnable (because it has slept long enough, because its I/O operation is complete, or because someone called resume or notify).

Then, the scheduler selects a new thread to run. The highest-priority remaining thread is picked among those that are runnable.

What happens if there is more than one thread with the same priority? Each thread at that priority gets a turn in round-robin fashion. In other words, a thread is not scheduled again for execution until all other threads with the same priority have been scheduled at least once.

Consider the following test program, which modifies the previous program to run the threads of one kind of balls (displayed in red) with a higher priority than the other threads. (Set by the line in bold below.)

If you click on the Start button, five threads are launched at the normal priority, animating five black balls. If you click on the Express button, then you launch five red balls whose thread runs at a higher priority than the regular balls.

```
class BounceExpress
{  public BounceExpress()
   {  Panel p = new Panel();
      addButton(p, "Start",
         new ActionListener()
         {  public void actionPerformed(ActionEvent evt)
            {  for (int i = 0; i < 5; i++)
               {  Ball b = new Ball(canvas, Color.black);
                  b.setPriority(Thread.NORM_PRIORITY);
                  b.start();
               }
            }
         });
```

```
addButton(p, "Express",
   new ActionListener()
   {  public void actionPerformed(ActionEvent evt)
      {  for (int i = 0; i < 5; i++)
         {  Ball b = new Ball(canvas, Color.red);
            b.setPriority(Thread.NORM_PRIORITY + 2);
            b.start();
         }
      }
   });
      . . .
   }
}
```

Try it out. Launch a set of regular balls and a set of express balls. You will notice that the express balls seem to run faster. This is solely a result of their higher priority, *not* because the red balls run at a higher speed. The code to move the express balls is the same as that of the regular balls.

Here is why this demonstration works: 5 milliseconds after an express thread goes to sleep, the scheduler wakes it. Now:

- The scheduler again evaluates the priorities of all the runnable threads.

- It finds that the express threads have the highest priority.

One of the express balls gets another turn right away. This can be the one that just woke up, or perhaps it is another express thread—you have no way of knowing. The express threads take turns, and only when they are all asleep does the scheduler give the lower-priority threads a chance to run. See Figure 2-6 and Example 2-3.

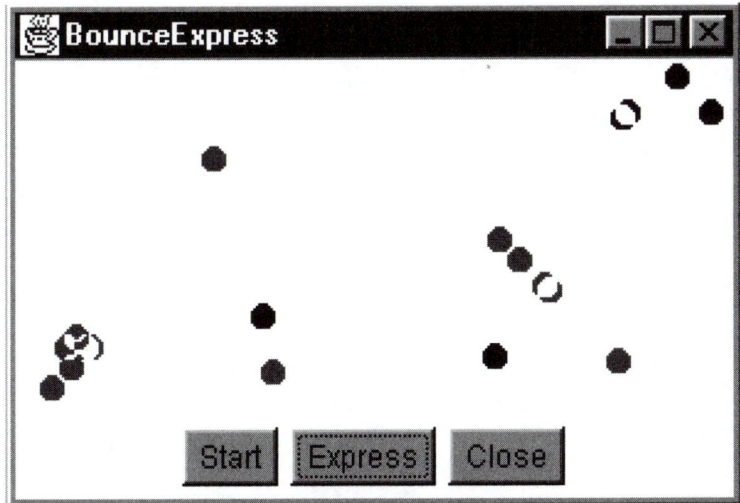

Figure 2-6: Threads with different priorities

Example 2-3: BounceExpress.java

```java
import java.awt.*;
import java.awt.event.*;
import corejava.*;

public class BounceExpress extends CloseableFrame
{  public BounceExpress()
   {  canvas = new Canvas();
      add(canvas, "Center");
      Panel p = new Panel();
      addButton(p, "Start",
         new ActionListener()
         {  public void actionPerformed(ActionEvent evt)
            {  for (int i = 0; i < 5; i++)
               {  Ball b = new Ball(canvas, Color.black);
                  b.setPriority(Thread.NORM_PRIORITY);
                  b.start();
               }
            }
         });

      addButton(p, "Express",
         new ActionListener()
         {  public void actionPerformed(ActionEvent evt)
            {  for (int i = 0; i < 5; i++)
               {  Ball b = new Ball(canvas, Color.red);
                  b.setPriority(Thread.NORM_PRIORITY + 2);
                  b.start();
               }
            }
         });

      addButton(p, "Close",
         new ActionListener()
         {  public void actionPerformed(ActionEvent evt)
            {  canvas.setVisible(false);
               System.exit(0);
            }
         });
      add(p, "South");
   }

   public void addButton(Container c, String title,
      ActionListener a)
   {  Button b = new Button(title);
      c.add(b);
      b.addActionListener(a);
   }
```

```
   public static void main(String[] args)
   {  Frame f = new BounceExpress();
      f.show();
   }

   private Canvas canvas;
}

class Ball extends Thread
{  public Ball(Canvas c, Color co) { box = c; color = co; }

   public void draw()
   {  Graphics g = box.getGraphics();
      g.setColor(color);
      g.fillOval(x, y, XSIZE, YSIZE);
      g.dispose();
   }

   public void move()
   {  if (!box.isVisible()) return;
      Graphics g = box.getGraphics();
      g.setColor(color);
      g.setXORMode(box.getBackground());
      g.fillOval(x, y, XSIZE, YSIZE);
      x += dx;
      y += dy;
      Dimension d = box.getSize();
      if (x < 0)
      { x = 0; dx = -dx; }
      if (x + XSIZE >= d.width)
      { x = d.width - XSIZE; dx = -dx; }
      if (y < 0)
      { y = 0; dy = -dy; }
      if (y + YSIZE >= d.height)
      { y = d.height - YSIZE; dy = -dy; }
      g.fillOval(x, y, XSIZE, YSIZE);
      g.dispose();
   }

   public void run()
   {  draw();
      for (int i = 1; i <= 1000; i++)
      {  move();
         try { Thread.sleep(5); }
         catch(InterruptedException e) {}
      }
   }
```

```
private Canvas box;
private static final int XSIZE = 10;
private static final int YSIZE = 10;
private int x = 0;
private int y = 0;
private int dx = 2;
private int dy = 2;
private Color color;
}
```

`java.lang.Thread`

- `void setPriority(int newPriority)`

  sets the priority of this thread. Must be between `Thread.MIN_PRIORITY` and `Thread.MAX_PRIORITY`. Use `Thread.NORM_PRIORITY` for normal priority.

- `static int MIN_PRIORITY`

  is the minimum priority that a `Thread` can have. The minimum priority value is 1.

- `static int NORM_PRIORITY`

  is the default priority to a `Thread`. The default priority is equal to 5.

- `static int MAX_PRIORITY`

  is the maximum priority that a `Thread` can have. The maximum priority value is 10.

Cooperating and Selfish Threads

Our ball threads were well behaved and cooperated with each other. They did this by using the `sleep` function to wait their turns. The `sleep` function blocks the thread and gives the other threads a chance to be scheduled. Even if a thread does not want to put itself to sleep for any amount of time, it can call `yield()` whenever it does not mind being interrupted. A thread should always call `yield` or `sleep` when it is executing a long loop, to ensure that it is not monopolizing the system. A thread that does not follow this rule is called *selfish*.

The following program shows what happens when a thread contains a *tight loop*, a loop in which it carries out a lot of work without giving other threads a chance. When you click on the Selfish button, a blue ball is launched whose `run` method contains a tight loop.

```
class SelfishBall extends Ball
{   . . .
    public void run()
    {   draw();
        for (int i = 1; i <= 1000; i++)
        {   move();
            long t = System.currentTimeMillis();
            while (System.currentTimeMillis() < t + 5)
                ;
        }
    }
}
```

The `run` procedure will last about 5 seconds before it returns, ending the thread. In the meantime, it never calls `yield` or `sleep`.

What actually happens when you run this program depends on your operating system. For example, when you run this program under Solaris with the "green thread" package as opposed to the "native thread" package, you will find that the selfish ball indeed hogs the whole application. Try closing the program or launching another ball; you will have a hard time getting even a mouse-click into the application. However, when you run the same program under Windows 95 or NT, nothing untoward happens. The blue ball can run in parallel with other balls.

The reason is that the underlying thread package in Windows performs *time-slicing*. It periodically interrupts threads in midstream, even if they are not cooperating. When (even a selfish) thread is interrupted, Windows activates another thread—picked among the top-priority-level runnable threads. The green threads implementation used by Java 1.x on Solaris does not perform time-slicing, but the new native thread package does. If you *know* that your program will execute on a machine whose operating system performs time-slicing, then you do not need to worry about making your threads polite. But the point of Internet computing is that you generally *do not know* the environments of the people who will use your program. You should, therefore, plan for the worst and put calls to `yield` or `sleep` in every loop.

See Example 2-4 for the complete source code.

Example 2-4: BounceSelfish.java

```java
import java.awt.*;
import java.awt.event.*;
import java.util.*;
import corejava.*;

public class BounceSelfish extends CloseableFrame
{  public BounceSelfish()
   {  canvas = new Canvas();
      add(canvas, "Center");
      Panel p = new Panel();
      addButton(p, "Start",
         new ActionListener()
         {  public void actionPerformed(ActionEvent evt)
            {  Ball b = new Ball(canvas, Color.black);
               b.setPriority(Thread.NORM_PRIORITY);
               b.start();
            }
         });

      addButton(p, "Express",
         new ActionListener()
         {  public void actionPerformed(ActionEvent evt)
            {  Ball b = new Ball(canvas, Color.red);
               b.setPriority(Thread.NORM_PRIORITY + 2);
               b.start();
            }
         });

      addButton(p, "Selfish",
         new ActionListener()
         {  public void actionPerformed(ActionEvent evt)
            {  Ball b = new SelfishBall(canvas, Color.blue);
               b.setPriority(Thread.NORM_PRIORITY + 2);
               b.start();
            }
         });

      addButton(p, "Close",
         new ActionListener()
         {  public void actionPerformed(ActionEvent evt)
            {  canvas.setVisible(false);
               System.exit(0);
            }
         });
      add(p, "South");
   }
```

```
    public void addButton(Container c, String title,
        ActionListener a)
    {   Button b = new Button(title);
        c.add(b);
        b.addActionListener(a);
    }


    public static void main(String[] args)
    {   Frame f = new BounceSelfish();
        f.show();
    }

    private Canvas canvas;
}

class Ball extends Thread
{   public Ball(Canvas c, Color co) { box = c; color = co; }

    public void draw()
    {   Graphics g = box.getGraphics();
        g.setColor(color);
        g.fillOval(x, y, XSIZE, YSIZE);
        g.dispose();
    }

    public void move()
    {   if (!box.isVisible()) return;
        Graphics g = box.getGraphics();
        g.setColor(color);
        g.setXORMode(box.getBackground());
        g.fillOval(x, y, XSIZE, YSIZE);
        x += dx;
        y += dy;
        Dimension d = box.getSize();
        if (x < 0)
        { x = 0; dx = -dx; }
        if (x + XSIZE >= d.width)
        { x = d.width - XSIZE; dx = -dx; }
        if (y < 0)
        { y = 0; dy = -dy; }
        if (y + YSIZE >= d.height)
        { y = d.height - YSIZE; dy = -dy; }
        g.fillOval(x, y, XSIZE, YSIZE);
        g.dispose();
    }
```

```java
public void run()
{   draw();
    for (int i = 1; i <= 1000; i++)
    {   move();
        try { Thread.sleep(5); } catch(InterruptedException e) {}
    }
}

private Canvas box;
private static final int XSIZE = 10;
private static final int YSIZE = 10;
private int x = 0;
private int y = 0;
private int dx = 2;
private int dy = 2;
private Color color;
}

class SelfishBall extends Ball
{   public SelfishBall(Canvas c, Color co) { super(c, co); }

    public void run()
    {   draw();
        for (int i = 1; i <= 1000; i++)
        {   move();
            long t = System.currentTimeMillis();
            while (System.currentTimeMillis() < t + 5)
                ;
        }
    }
}
```

Thread Groups

Some programs contain quite a few threads. It then becomes useful to categorize them by functionality. For example, consider an Internet browser. If many threads are trying to acquire images from a server and the user clicks on a Stop button to interrupt the loading of the current page, then it is handy to have a way of killing all of these threads simultaneously. Java lets you construct what it calls a *thread group* in order to allow you to simultaneously work with a group of threads.

You construct a thread group with the constructor:

```java
ThreadGroup g = new ThreadGroup(string)
```

The string identifies the group and must be unique. For example:

```
class ImageLoader extends ThreadGroup
{  public ImageLoader(String name, ThreadGroup g)
   {  super(g, "Loading " + name);
        . . .
   }
}
```

To find out whether any threads of a particular group are still runnable, use the `activeCount` method.

```
if (g.activeCount() == 0)
{  // all threads in the group g have stopped
}
```

To kill all threads in a thread group, simply call `stop` on the group object.

```
g.stop(); // stops all threads in g
```

Thread groups can have child subgroups. By default, a newly created thread group becomes a child of the current thread group. But you can also explicitly name the parent group in the constructor (see the API notes). Methods such as `activeCount` and `stop` refer to all threads in their group and all child groups.

---

java.lang.ThreadGroup

- `ThreadGroup(String name)`

  creates a new `ThreadGroup`. Its parent will be the thread group of the current thread.

Parameters:	name	the name of the new thread group

- `ThreadGroup(ThreadGroup parent, String name)`

  creates a new `ThreadGroup`.

Parameters:	parent	the parent thread group of the new thread group
	name	the name of the new thread group

- `int activeCount()`

  returns an upper bound for the number of active threads in the thread group.

- `int enumerate(Thread list[])`

  gets references to every active thread in this thread group. You can use the `activeCount()` method to get an upper bound for the array; this method returns the number of threads put into the array.

Parameters:	`list`	an array to be filled with the thread references

- `ThreadGroup getParent()`

  gets the parent of this thread group.

- `void resume()`

  resumes all threads in this thread group and all of its child groups.

- `void stop()`

  stops all threads in this thread group and all of its child groups.

- `void suspend()`

  suspends all threads in this thread group and all of its child groups.

`java.lang.Thread`

- `ThreadGroup getThreadGroup()`

  returns the thread group of this thread.

Synchronization

So far, we have not used threads that share the data segment. More precisely, a running thread can access any object to which it has a reference. Since it is possible for two threads to simultaneously have access to the same object, they can interfere with each other. For example, a thread might be trying to read a file that another thread is writing to. What happens if two threads have access to the same object and each calls a method that modifies the state of the object? As you might imagine, the threads step on each other's toes, leading to corrupted objects. This is usually called the *synchronization problem.*

Thread Communication Without Synchronization

To solve the synchronization problem, you must learn how to *synchronize* access to shared objects. In this section, you'll see what happens if you do not do this. In the next section, you'll see how to synchronize object access in Java.

In the next test program, we simulate a bank with 10 accounts. We randomly generate transactions that move money between these accounts. There are 10 threads, one for each account. Each transaction moves a random amount of

money from the account serviced by the thread to another random account.

The simulation code is straightforward. We have the class Bank with the method transfer. This method transfers some amount of money from one account to another. If the source account does not have enough money in it, then the thread calling the transfer method is put to sleep for a short time so that other threads have a chance to transfer some money into this account.

Here is the code for the transfer method of the Bank class.

```
public void transfer(int from, int to, int amount)
{   while (accounts[from] < amount)
    // wait for another thread to add more money
    {   try {  Thread.sleep(5); }
        catch(InterruptedException e) {}
    }

    accounts[from] -= amount;
    accounts[to] += amount;
    ntransacts++;
    if (ntransacts % 5000 == 0) test();
}
```

Each thread generates a random transaction, calls transfer on the bank object, and then puts itself to sleep. Here is the code for the run method of the thread class.

```
public void run()
{   while (true)
    {   int to = (int)(Bank.NACCOUNTS  * Math.random());
        if (to == from) to = (to + 1) % Bank.NACCOUNTS;
        int amount = (int)(Bank.INITIAL_BALANCE * Math.random());
        bank.transfer(from, to, amount);
        try { sleep(1); } catch(InterruptedException e) {}
    }
}
```

When this simulation runs, we do not know how much money is in any one bank account at any time. But we do know that the total amount of money in all the accounts should remain unchanged since all we do is move money from one account to another.

Every 5,000 transactions, the transfer method calls a test method that recomputes the total and prints it out.

This program never finishes. Just press CTRL+C to kill the program.

Here is a typical printout:

```
Transactions:0 Sum: 100000
Transactions:5000 Sum: 100000
Transactions:10000 Sum: 100000
Transactions:15000 Sum: 99840
Transactions:20000 Sum: 98079
Transactions:25000 Sum: 98079
Transactions:30000 Sum: 98079
Transactions:35000 Sum: 98079
Transactions:40000 Sum: 98079
Transactions:45000 Sum: 98079
Transactions:50000 Sum: 98079
Transactions:55000 Sum: 98079
Transactions:60000 Sum: 98079
Transactions:65000 Sum: 95925
Transactions:70000 Sum: 95925
Transactions:75000 Sum: 95925
```

As you can see, something is very wrong. For several thousand transactions, the bank balance remains at $100,000, which is the correct total for 10 accounts of $10,000 each. But after some time, the balance changes slightly. This situation does not inspire confidence, and we would probably not want to deposit our hard-earned money into this bank.

Example 2-5 provides the complete source code. See if you can spot the problem with the code. We will unravel the mystery in the next section.

Example 2-5: UnsynchBankTest.java

```java
class UnsynchBankTest
{  public static void main(String[] args)
   {  Bank b = new Bank();
      int i;
      for (i = 1; i <= Bank.NACCOUNTS; i++)
         new TransactionSource(b, i).start();
   }
}

class Bank
{  public Bank()
   {  accounts = new long[NACCOUNTS];
      int i;
      for (i = 0; i < NACCOUNTS; i++)
         accounts[i] = INITIAL_BALANCE;
      ntransacts = 0;
      test();
   }
```

```java
    public void transfer(int from, int to, int amount)
    {  while (accounts[from] < amount)
       {  try {  Thread.sleep(5); }
          catch(InterruptedException e) {}
       }

       accounts[from] -= amount;
       accounts[to] += amount;
       ntransacts++;
       if (ntransacts % 5000 == 0) test();
    }

    public void test()
    {  int i;
       long sum = 0;

       for (i = 0; i < NACCOUNTS; i++) sum += accounts[i];
       System.out.println("Transactions:" + ntransacts
          + " Sum: " + sum);
    }

    public static final int INITIAL_BALANCE = 10000;
    public static final int NACCOUNTS = 10;
    private long[] accounts;
    private int ntransacts;
}

class TransactionSource extends Thread
{  public TransactionSource(Bank b, int i)
    {  from = i - 1;
       bank = b;
    }

    public void run()
    {  while (true)
       {  int to = (int)(Bank.NACCOUNTS * Math.random());
          if (to == from) to = (to + 1) % Bank.NACCOUNTS;
          int amount = (int)(Bank.INITIAL_BALANCE
             * Math.random());
          bank.transfer(from, to, amount);
          try { sleep(1); } catch(InterruptedException e) {}
       }
    }

    private Bank bank;
    private int from;
}
```

Synchronizing Access to Shared Resources

In the previous section, we ran a program in which several threads updated bank account balances. After a few thousand transactions, errors crept in and some amount of money was either lost or spontaneously created. This problem occurs when two threads are simultaneously trying to update an account. Suppose two threads simultaneously carry out the instruction:

```
accounts[to] += amount;
```

The problem is that these are not *atomic* operations. The instruction might be processed as follows:

1.   Load `accounts[to]` into a register.

2.   Add `amount`.

3.   Move the result back to `accounts[to]`.

Now, suppose the first thread executes Steps 1 and 2, and then it is interrupted. Suppose the second thread awakens and updates the same entry in the `account` array. Then, the first thread awakens and completes its Step 3.

That action wipes out the modification of the other thread. As a result, the total is no longer correct. (See Figure 2-7.)

Our test program detects this corruption. (Of course, there is a slight chance of false alarms if the thread is interrupted as it is performing the tests!)

NOTE: You can actually peek at the Java bytecodes that execute each statement in our class. Run the command

```
javap -c -v Bank
```

to decompile the `Bank.class` file. (You need to unzip `\java\lib\classes.zip` for this to work.) For example, the line

```
accounts[to] += amount;
```

is translated into the following bytecodes.

```
aload_0
getfield #16 <Field Bank.accounts [J>
iload_1
dup2
laload
iload_3
i2l
lsub
lastore
```

What these codes mean does not matter. The point is that the increment command is made up of several instructions, and the thread executing them can be interrupted at the point of any instruction.

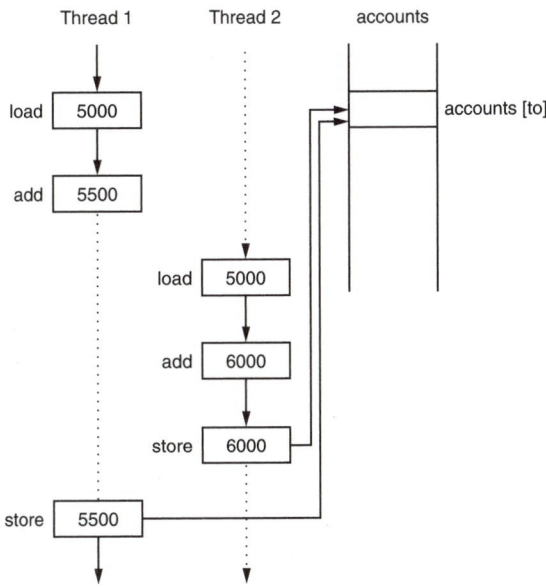

Figure 2-7: Simultaneous access by two threads

What is the chance of this happening? It is fairly common when the operating system performs time-slicing on threads. Our test program shows a corruption of the buffer every few thousand entries under Windows 95. When a thread system, such as the green threads on Solaris, does not perform time-slicing on threads, corruption is less frequent. (To simulate the behavior on Solaris with green threads, run another higher-priority thread that occasionally wakes up. When it goes to sleep, another transaction thread is scheduled.)

Of course, as Java programmers, we must cope with the worst possible scenario and must assume that threads will be frequently interrupted.

We must have some way of ensuring that once a thread has begun inserting an element into the buffer, it can complete the operation without being interrupted. Most programming environments force the programmer to fuss with so-called semaphores and critical sections to gain uninterrupted access to a resource—the fiddling is painful and the process is error prone. Java has a nicer mechanism, inspired by the *monitors* invented by Tony Hoare.

You simply tag any operation shared by multiple threads as `synchronized`, like this:

```
public synchronized void transfer(int from, int to,
    int amount)
{   . . .
    accounts[from] -= amount;
    accounts[to] += amount;
    ntransacts++;
    if (ntransacts % 5000 == 0) test();
    . . .
}
```

When one thread calls a synchronized method, Java guarantees that the method will finish before another thread can execute any synchronized method on the same object. When one thread calls `transfer` and then another thread also calls `transfer`, the second thread cannot continue. Instead, it is deactivated and must wait for the first thread to finish executing the `transfer` method.

When you create an object with one or more synchronized methods, Java sets up a queue of all the threads waiting to be "let inside" the object. This is shown in Figure 2-8. Whenever one thread has completed its work with the object, the highest-priority thread in the waiting queue gets the next turn.

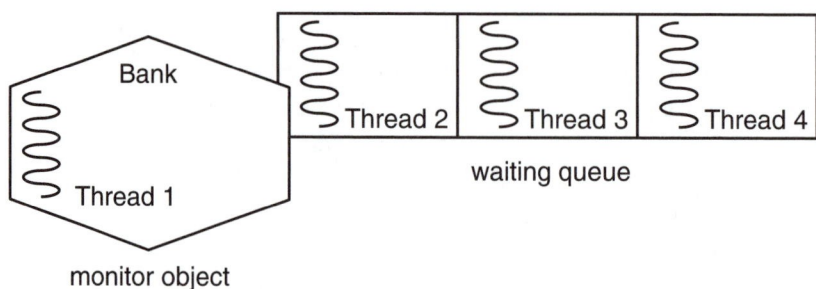

Figure 2-8: A monitor

An object that can block threads and notify them when it becomes available is called a *monitor*. In Java, any object with one or more synchronized methods is a monitor.

In our simulation of the bank, we do not want to transfer money out of an account that does not have the funds to cover it. Note that we cannot use code like:

```
if (bank.getBalance(from) >= amount)
    bank.transfer(from, to, amount);
```

It is entirely possible that the current thread will be interrupted between the successful outcome of the test and the call to `transfer`. By the time the thread is running again, the account balance may have fallen below `amount`. We must make sure that the thread cannot be interrupted between the test and the insertion. You ensure this by putting the test inside a synchronized version of the `transfer` method:

```
public synchronized void transfer(int from, int to,
   int amount)
{   while (accounts[from] < amount)
   {   // wait
   }
   // transfer funds
}
```

Now, what do we do when there is not enough money in the account? We wait until some other thread has added funds. But this thread has just gained exclusive access to the bank object, so no other thread has a chance to make a deposit. A second feature of synchronized methods takes care of this situation. You use the `wait` method in the thread class.

When a thread calls `wait` inside a synchronized method, that thread is deactivated, and Java puts it in the waiting queue for that object. This lets in another thread that can, hopefully, change the account balance. Java awakens the original threads again when another method calls the `notifyAll` method. This is the signal that the state of the bank object has changed and that waiting threads should be given another chance to inspect the object state. In our buffer example, we will call `notifyAll` when we have finished with the funds transfer.

This notification gives the waiting threads the chance to run again. A thread that was waiting for a higher balance then gets a chance to check the balance again. If the balance is sufficient, the thread performs the transfer. If not, it calls `wait` again.

It is important that the `notifyAll` function is called by some thread—otherwise, the threads that called `wait` will wait forever. The waiting threads are *not* automatically reactivated when no other thread is working on the object.

TIP: If your multithreaded program gets stuck, double-check that every `wait` is matched by a `notifyAll`. There is also a method `notify` that is less useful. It randomly awakens *one* thread, and if that thread can't proceed, then the system can deadlock. Unless you are certain that *all* waiting threads can proceed, you should use `notifyAll`, not `notify`.

Here is the code for the `transfer` method that uses synchronized methods. Notice the calls to `wait` and `notifyAll`.

```
public synchronized void transfer(int from, int to, int
    amount)
{   while (accounts[from] < amount)
    {   try { wait(); } catch(InterruptedException e) {}
    }
    accounts[from] -= amount;
    accounts[to] += amount;
    ntransacts++;
    if (ntransacts % 5000 == 0) test();
    notifyAll();
}
```

If you run the sample program with the synchronized version of the `transfer` method, you will notice that nothing ever goes wrong. The total balance stays at $100,000 forever. (Again, you need to press CTRL+C to terminate the program.)

You will also notice that the program in Example 2-6 runs a bit slower—this is the price you pay for the added bookkeeping involved in the synchronization mechanism.

Example 2-6: SynchBankTest.java

```
class SynchBankTest
{   public static void main(String[] args)
    {   Bank b = new Bank();
        int i;
        for (i = 1; i <= Bank.NACCOUNTS; i++)
            new TransactionSource(b, i).start();
    }
}


class Bank
{   public Bank()
    {   accounts = new long[NACCOUNTS];
        int i;
        for (i = 0; i < NACCOUNTS; i++)
            accounts[i] = INITIAL_BALANCE;
        ntransacts = 0;
        test();
    }

    public synchronized void transfer(int from, int to,
        int amount)
    {   while (accounts[from] < amount)
        {   try { wait(); } catch(InterruptedException e) {}
        }
```

```
        accounts[from] -= amount;
        accounts[to] += amount;
        ntransacts++;
        if (ntransacts % 5000 == 0) test();
        notifyAll();
    }

    public void test()
    {   int i;
        long sum = 0;

        for (i = 0; i < NACCOUNTS; i++) sum += accounts[i];
        System.out.println("Transactions:" + ntransacts
            + " Sum: " + sum);
    }

    public static final int INITIAL_BALANCE = 10000;
    public static final int NACCOUNTS = 10;

    private long[] accounts;
    private int ntransacts;
}

class TransactionSource extends Thread
{   public TransactionSource(Bank b, int i)
    {   from = i - 1;
        bank = b;
    }

    public void run()
    {   while (true)
        {   int to = (int)(Bank.NACCOUNTS * Math.random());
            if (to == from) to = (to + 1) % Bank.NACCOUNTS;
            int amount = (int)(Bank.INITIAL_BALANCE
                * Math.random());
            bank.transfer(from, to, amount);
            try { sleep(1); } catch(InterruptedException e) {}
        }
    }

    private Bank bank;
    private int from;
}
```

Here is a summary of how the synchronization mechanism works.

1. If a class has one or more synchronized methods, each object of the class gets a queue that holds all threads waiting to execute one of the synchronized methods.

2. There are two ways for a thread to get onto this queue: either by calling the method while another thread is using the object or by calling `wait` while using the object.

3. When a synchronized method call returns or when a method calls `wait`, another thread gets access to the object.

4. As always, the scheduler chooses the highest-priority thread among those in the queue.

5. If a thread was put in the queue by a call to `wait`, it must be "unfrozen" by a call to `notifyAll` or `notify` before it can be scheduled for execution again.

The scheduling rules are undeniably complex, but it is actually quite simple to put them into practice. Just follow these three rules:

1. If two or more threads modify an object, declare the methods that carry out the modifications as synchronized.

2. If a thread must wait for the state of an object to change, it should wait inside the object, not outside, by entering a synchronized method and calling `wait`.

3. Whenever a method changes the state of an object, it should call `notifyAll`. That gives the waiting threads a chance to see if circumstances have changed.

java.lang.Object

*   `void notifyAll()`

    notifies the threads waiting on this monitor object that the state of the object has changed. This method can only be called from within a synchronized method. The method throws an `IllegalMonitorStateException` if the current thread is not the owner of the object's monitor.

*   `void notify()`

    notifies one randomly selected thread waiting on this monitor object that the state of the object has changed. This method can only be called from within a synchronized method. The method throws an

`IllegalMonitorStateException` if the current thread is not the owner of the object's monitor.

- `void wait()`

  causes a thread to wait until it is notified. This method can only be called from within a synchronized method. It throws an `IllegalMonitorStateException` if the current thread is not the owner of the object's monitor.

Deadlocks

The synchronization feature in Java is convenient and powerful, but it cannot solve all problems that might arise in multithreading. Consider the following situation:

Account 1: $2,000

Account 2: $3,000

Thread 1: Transfer $3,000 from Account 1 to Account 2

Thread 2: Transfer $4,000 from Account 2 to Account 1

As Figure 2-9 indicates, Threads 1 and 2 are clearly blocked. Neither can proceed since the balances in Accounts 1 and 2 are insufficient.

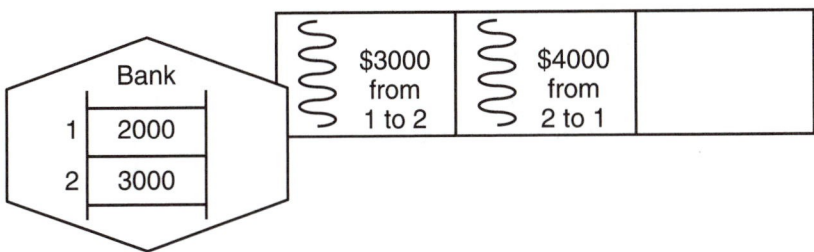

Figure 2-9: A deadlock situation

Is it possible that all 10 threads are blocked because each is waiting for more money? Such a situation is called a *deadlock*.

In our program, a deadlock could not occur for a simple reason. Each transfer amount is for, at most, $10,000. Since there are 10 accounts and a total of $100,000 in them, at least one of the accounts must have more than $10,000 at any time. The thread moving money out of that account can, therefore, proceed.

But if you change the `run` method of the threads to remove the $10,000 transaction limit, deadlocks can occur quickly. (Another way to create a deadlock is to make the `i`'th thread responsible for putting money into the `i`'th account, rather

than for taking it out of the i'th account. In this case, there is a small chance that all threads will gang up on one account, each trying to remove more money from it than it contains.)

Here is another situation in which a deadlock can occur easily: Change the notifyAll method to notify in the SynchBankTest program. You will find that the program hangs quickly. Unlike notifyAll, which notifies all threads that are waiting for added funds, the notify method activates only one thread. If that thread can't proceed, all threads can be blocked. Consider the following sample scenario of a developing deadlock.

Account 1: $19,000

All other accounts: $9,000 each

Thread 1: Transfer $9,500 to from Account 1 to Account 2

All other threads: Transfer $9,100 from their account to another account

Clearly, all threads but Thread 1 are blocked since there isn't enough money in their accounts.

Thread 1 proceeds. Afterward, we have the following situation:

Account 1: $9,500

Account 2: $18,500

All other accounts: $9,000 each

Then, Thread 1 calls notify. The notify method picks a thread at random. Suppose it picks Thread 3. That thread is awakened, finds that there isn't enough money in its account, and calls wait again. But Thread 1 is still running. A new random transaction is generated, say,

Thread 1: Transfer $9,600 to from Account 1 to Account 2

Now, Thread 1 also calls wait, and *all* threads are blocked. The system has deadlocked.

There is nothing that Java can do to avoid or break these deadlocks. You must design your threads to ensure that a deadlock situation cannot occur. Analyze your program and ensure that every thread awaiting an object will eventually be activated. For example, in the preceding scenario, calling notifyAll instead of notify avoids the deadlock.

Thread synchronization and deadlock avoidance are difficult subjects, and we refer the interested reader to the book *Programming with Threads* by Steve Kleiman, Devang Shah, and Bart Smaalders [Sunsoft Press/Prentice-Hall, 1996].

Using Pipes for Communication between Threads

Sometimes, the communication pattern between threads is very simple. One thread, the so-called *producer*, generates a stream of bytes. Another thread, the so-called *consumer*, reads and processes that byte stream. If no bytes are available for reading, the consumer thread blocks. If the producer generates data much more quickly than the consumer can handle it, then the write operation of the producer thread blocks. Java has a convenient set of classes, PipedInputStream and PipedOutputStream, to implement this communication pattern. (There is another pair of classes, PipedReader and PipedWriter, if the producer thread generates a stream of Unicode characters instead of bytes.)

The principal reason to use pipes is to keep each thread simple. The producer thread simply sends its results to a stream and forgets about them. The consumer simply reads the data from a stream, without having to care where it comes from. By using pipes, multiple threads can be connected with each other.

Example 2-7 is a program that shows off piped streams. We have a producer thread that emits random numbers at random times, a filter thread that reads the input numbers and continuously computes the average of the data, and a consumer thread that prints out the answers. (You'll need to use Ctrl+C to stop this program.) Figure 2-10 shows the threads and the pipes that connect them. Unix users will recognize these pipe streams as the equivalent of pipes connecting processes in Unix.

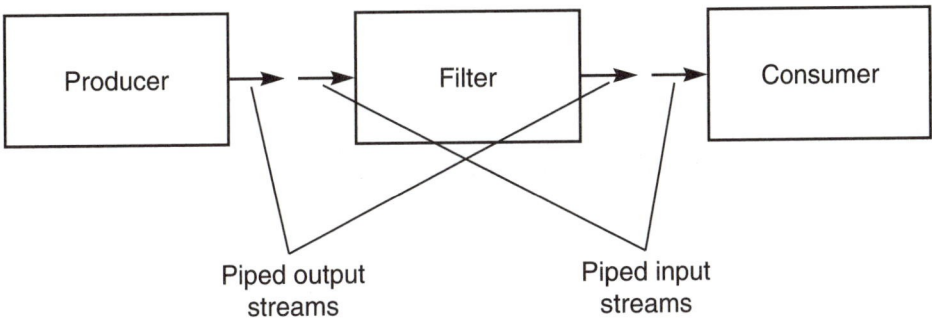

Figure 2-10: A sequence of pipes

Example 2-7: PipeTest.java

```java
import java.util.*;
import java.io.*;

public class PipeTest
{   public static void main(String args[])
    {   try
        {   /* set up pipes */
            PipedOutputStream pout1 = new PipedOutputStream();
            PipedInputStream pin1 = new PipedInputStream(pout1);

            PipedOutputStream pout2 = new PipedOutputStream();
            PipedInputStream pin2 = new PipedInputStream(pout2);

            /* construct threads */

            Producer prod = new Producer(pout1);
            Filter filt = new Filter(pin1, pout2);
            Consumer cons = new Consumer(pin2);

            /* start threads */

            prod.start();
            filt.start();
            cons.start();
        }
        catch (IOException e){}
    }
}

class Producer extends Thread
{   public Producer(OutputStream os)
    {   out = new DataOutputStream(os);
    }

    public void run()
    {   for(;;)
        {   try
            {   double num = rand.nextDouble();
                out.writeDouble(num);
                out.flush();
                sleep(Math.abs(rand.nextInt() % 1000));
            }
            catch(Exception e)
            {   System.out.println("Error: " + e);
            }
        }
    }
```

```
    private DataOutputStream out;
    private Random rand = new Random();
}

class Filter extends Thread
{   public Filter(InputStream is, OutputStream os)
    {   in = new DataInputStream(is);
        out = new DataOutputStream(os);
    }

    public void run()
    {   for (;;)
        {   try
            {   double x = in.readDouble();
                total += x;
                count++;
                if (count != 0) out.writeDouble(total / count);
            }
            catch(IOException e)
            {   System.out.println("Error: " + e);
            }
        }
    }

    private DataInputStream in;
    private DataOutputStream out;
    private double total = 0;
    private int count = 0;
}

class Consumer extends Thread
{   public Consumer(InputStream is)
    {    in = new DataInputStream(is);
    }

    public void run()
    {   for(;;)
        {   try
            {   double avg = in.readDouble();
                if (Math.abs(avg - old_avg) > 0.01)
                {   System.out.println("Current average is " + avg);
                    old_avg = avg;
                }
            }
            catch(IOException e)
            {   System.out.println("Error: " + e);
            }
        }
    }
```

```
    private double old_avg = 0;
    private DataInputStream in;
}
```

java.io.PipedInputStream

- `PipedInputStream()`

  creates a new piped input stream that is not yet connected to a piped output stream.

- `PipedInputStream(PipedOutputStream out)`

  creates a new piped input stream that reads its data from a piped output stream.

  Parameters: out   the source of the data

- `void connect(PipedOutputStream out)`

  attaches a piped output stream from which the data will be read.

  Parameters: out   the source of the data

java.io.PipedOutputStream

- `PipedOutputStream()`

  creates a new piped output stream that is not yet connected to a piped input stream.

- `PipedOutputStream(PipedInputStream in)`

  creates a new piped output stream that writes its data to a piped input stream.

  Parameters: in   the destination of the data

- `void connect(PipedInputStream in)`

  attaches a piped input stream to which the data will be written.

  Parameters: in   the destination of the data

Timers

In many programming environments, you can set up timers. A timer alerts your program elements at regular intervals. For example, to display a clock in a window, the clock object must be notified once every second.

Java does not have a built-in timer class, but it is easy enough to build one using threads. In this section, we describe how to do that. You can use this timer class in your own code.

Our timer runs in its own thread, so it must extend `Thread`. In its `run` method, it goes to sleep for the specified interval, then notifies its target.

```
class Timer extends Thread
{   .  .  .
   public void run()
      {  while (true)
         {   try { sleep(interval); }
             catch(InterruptedException e) {}
             // notify target
         }
      }

   private int interval;
}
```

There is a slight problem with writing a general-purpose timer class. The timer holds an object reference to the target, and it is supposed to notify the object whenever the time interval has elapsed. In C or C++ programming, the timer object would hold a pointer to a function, and it would call that function periodically. For safety reasons, Java does not make it easy to use method pointers. (As we have seen in Chapter 5 of Volume 1, the reflection mechanism provides method pointers, but they are slow and tedious to use.)

We showed you in Chapter 5 of Volume 1 how to overcome this problem by making a special interface for the callback. In our case, the interface is called `Timed` and the callback is called `tick`. Thus, an object that wants to receive timer ticks must implement the `Timed` interface. The action to be repeated in regular intervals must be put into the `tick` method.

Figure 2-11 shows six different clocks.

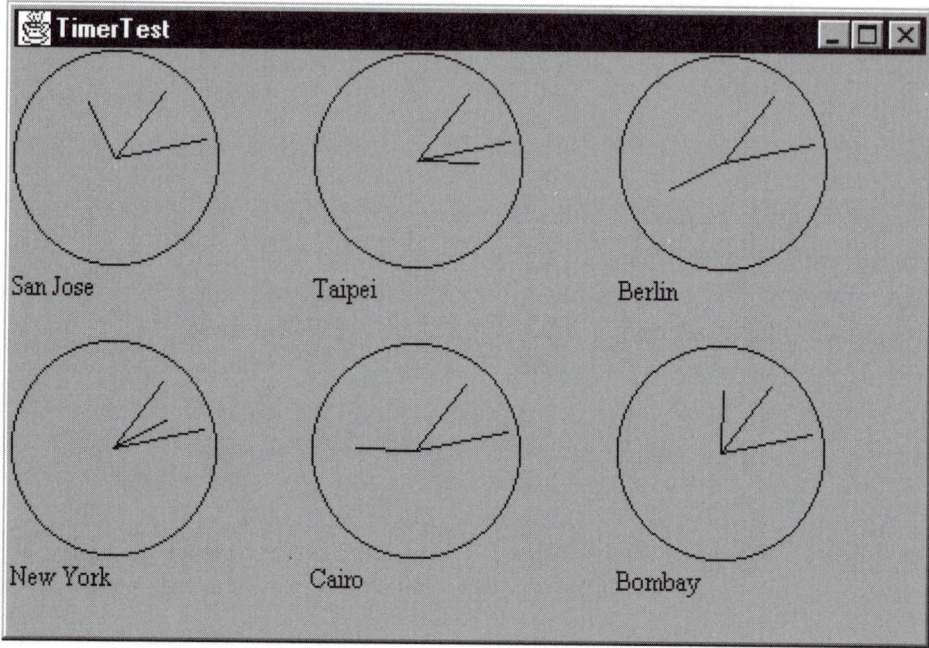

Figure 2-11: Clock threads

Each clock is an instance of the ClockCanvas class, which implements Timed. The tick method of the Clock class redraws the clock.

```
class ClockCanvas extends Canvas implements Timed
{   . . .
    public void tick(Timer t)
    {   GregorianCalendar d = new GregorianCalendar();
        seconds = (d.get(Calendar.HOUR) - LOCAL + offset)
            * 60 * 60 + d.get(Calendar.MINUTE) * 60
            + d.get(Calendar.SECOND);
        repaint();
    }
}
```

Note that the tick method does not actually get the time from the timer object t. The timer ticks come only *approximately* once a second. For an accurate clock display, we still need to get the system time.

Example 2-8 is the complete code.

Example 2-8: TimerTest.java

```java
import java.awt.*;
import java.util.*;
import corejava.*;

public class TimerTest extends CloseableFrame
{  public TimerTest()
   {  setTitle("TimerTest");
      setLayout(new GridLayout(2, 3));
      add(new ClockCanvas("San Jose", 16));
      add(new ClockCanvas("Taipei", 8));
      add(new ClockCanvas("Berlin", 1));
      add(new ClockCanvas("New York", 19));
      add(new ClockCanvas("Cairo", 2));
      add(new ClockCanvas("Bombay", 5));
   }

   public static void main(String[] args)
   {  Frame f = new TimerTest();
      f.setSize(450, 300);
      f.show();
   }
}

interface Timed
{  public void tick(Timer t);
}

class Timer extends Thread
{  public Timer(Timed t, int i)
   {  target = t; interval = i;
      setDaemon(true);
   }

   public void run()
   {  while (true)
      {  try { sleep(interval); }
         catch(InterruptedException e) {}
         target.tick(this);
      }
   }

   private Timed target;
   private int interval;
}
```

```
class ClockCanvas extends Canvas implements Timed
{  public ClockCanvas(String c, int off)
   {  city = c; offset = off;
      new Timer(this, 1000).start();
      setSize(125, 125);
   }

   public void paint(Graphics g)
   {  g.drawOval(0, 0, 100, 100);
      double hourAngle = 2 * Math.PI
         * (seconds - 3 * 60 * 60) / (12 * 60 * 60);
      double minuteAngle = 2 * Math.PI
         * (seconds - 15 * 60) / (60 * 60);
      double secondAngle = 2 * Math.PI
         * (seconds - 15) / 60;
      g.drawLine(50, 50, 50 + (int)(30
         * Math.cos(hourAngle)),
         50 + (int)(30 * Math.sin(hourAngle)));
      g.drawLine(50, 50, 50 + (int)(40
         * Math.cos(minuteAngle)),
         50 + (int)(40 * Math.sin(minuteAngle)));
      g.drawLine(50, 50, 50 + (int)(45
         * Math.cos(secondAngle)),
         50 + (int)(45 * Math.sin(secondAngle)));
      g.drawString(city, 0, 115);
   }

   public void tick(Timer t)
   {  GregorianCalendar d = new GregorianCalendar();
      seconds = (d.get(Calendar.HOUR) - LOCAL + offset)
         * 60 * 60 + d.get(Calendar.MINUTE) * 60
         + d.get(Calendar.SECOND);
      repaint();
   }

   private int seconds = 0;
   private String city;
   private int offset;
   private final int LOCAL = 16;
}
```

Daemon Threads

If you look carefully into the constructor of the timer class above, you will note
the method call that looks like this:

```
setDaemon(true);
```

This method call makes the timer thread a *daemon thread*. There is nothing demonic about it. A daemon is simply a thread that has no other role in life than to serve others. When only daemon threads remain, then the program exits. There is no point in keeping the program running if all remaining threads are daemons.

In a graphical application, the timer class threads do not affect when the program ends. It stays alive until the user closes the application. (The user-interface thread is not a daemon thread.) But when you use the timer class in a text application, you need not worry about stopping the timer threads. When the non-timer threads have finished their `run` methods, the application automatically terminates.

`java.lang.Thread`

* `void setDaemon(boolean on)`

    marks this thread as a daemon thread or a user thread. When there are only daemon threads left running in the system, Java exits. This method must be called before the thread is started.

Animation

In the previous sections, you learned what is required to split a program into multiple concurrent tasks. Each task needs to be placed into a `run` method of a class that extends `Thread`. But what if we want to add the `run` method to a class that already extends another class? This occurs most often when we want to add multithreading to an applet. An applet class already inherits from `Applet`, and, in Java, we cannot inherit from two parent classes, so we need to use an interface. The necessary interface is built into Java. It is called `Runnable`. We take up this important interface next.

The Runnable Interface

Whenever you need to use multithreading in a class that is already derived from a class other than `Thread`, make the class implement the `Runnable` interface. As though you had derived from `Thread`, put the code that needs to run in the `run` method. For example,

```
class Animation extends Applet implements Runnable
{   . . .
    public void run()
    {   // thread action goes here
    }
}
```

You still need to make a thread object to launch the thread. Give that thread a reference to the `Runnable` object in its constructor. The thread then calls the `run` method of that object.

This call is most commonly made in the `start` method of an applet, as in the following example:

```
class Animation extends Applet implements Runnable
{   . . .
    public void start()
    {   if (runner == null)
        {   runner = new Thread(this);
            runner.start();
        }
    }
    . . .
    private Thread runner;
}
```

In this case, the `this` argument to the `Thread` constructor specifies that the object whose `run` function should be called when the thread executes is an instance of the `Animation` object.

Wouldn't it be easier if we just defined another class from `Thread` and launched it in the applet?

```
class AnimationThread extends Thread
{   public void run()
    {   // thread action goes here
    }
}

class Animation extends Applet
{   . . .
    public void start()
    {   if (runner == null)
        {   runner = new AnimationThread();
            runner.start();
        }
    }
    . . .
    private Thread runner;
}
```

Indeed, this would be clean and simple. However, if the `run` method must have access to an applet's private data, then it makes sense to keep the `run` method with the applet and use the `Runnable` interface instead.

`java.lang.Thread`

- `Thread(Runnable target)`

  constructs a new thread that calls the `run()` method of the specified target.

`java.lang.Runnable`

- `void run()`

  You must override this method and place in the thread the code that you want to have executed.

Loading and Displaying Frames

In this section, we dissect one of the most common uses for threads in Java applets: animation. An animation sequence displays images, giving the viewer the illusion of motion. Each of the images in the sequence is called a *frame*. Of course, the frames must be rendered ahead of time—today's personal computers do not have the horsepower to compute the drawing fast enough for real-time animation.

You can put each frame in a separate file or put all frames into one file. We do the latter. It makes the process of loading the image much easier. In our example, we use a file with 36 images of a rotating globe. Figure 2-12, courtesy of Silviu Marghescu of the University of Maryland, shows the first few frames.

The animation applet must first acquire all the frames. Then, it shows each of them, in turn, for a fixed time. You know from Chapter 6 of Volume 1 how to load an image file. When you call `getImage`, the image is not actually loaded. Instead, the first time you access the image data with `prepareImage`, a separate thread is spawned to start the loading process. Loading an image can be very slow, especially if it has many frames or is located across the network. The thread acquiring the image periodically calls the `imageUpdate` method of the applet. Eventually, the `ALLBITS` flag of the `infoflags` parameter is set, and the image is complete.

Figure 2-12: This file has 36 images of a globe

Once the image is loaded, we render one frame at a time. To draw the i'th frame, we make a method call as follows:

```
g.drawImage(image, 0, - i * imageHeight / imageCount, null);
```

Figure 2-13 shows the *negative* offset of the *y*-coordinate. This offset causes the first frame to be well above the origin of the canvas. The top of the i'th frame becomes the top of the canvas.

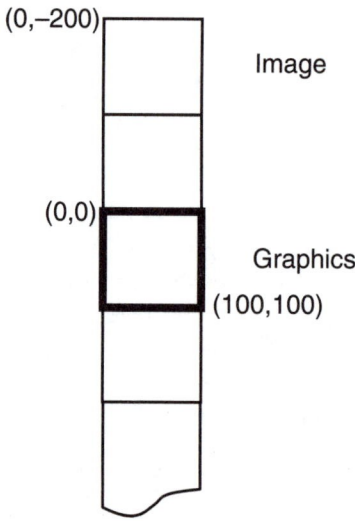

Figure 2-13: Picking a frame from a strip of frames

After a delay, we increment i and draw the next frame.

Using a Thread to Control the Animation

Our applet will have a single thread.

```
class Animation implements Runnable
{   .  .  .
    Thread runner = null;
}
```

You will see such a thread variable in many Java applets. Often, it is called kicker, and we once saw killer as the variable name. We think runner makes more sense, though.

First and foremost, we will use this thread to:

• Start the animation when the user is watching the applet.

• Stop the animation when the user has switched to a different page in the browser.

We do these tasks by creating the thread in the `start` method of the applet and by destroying it in the `stop` method. You can do this with the following code, which you will find in many applets.

```
class Animation implements Runnable
{   public void start()
    {   if (runner == null)
        {   runner = new Thread(this);
            runner.start();
        }
    }
    public void stop()
    {   if (runner != null && runner.isAlive())
            runner.stop();
        runner = null;
    }


    . . .

}
```

Note the method call:

```
runner = new Thread(this);
```

This call creates a thread that calls the `run` function of this applet.

Here is the `run` method. If the image is not yet loaded, the `loadImage` function is called to load it. Otherwise, the `run` function loops, painting the screen and sleeping when it can.

```
class Animation implements Runnable
{   public void run()
    {   loadImage();
        while (runner != null)
        {   repaint();
            try { Thread.sleep(200); }
            catch (InterruptedException e) {}
        }
    }


    . . .

}
```

The `loadImage` method of the `Animation` class (in the listing at the end of this section) is interesting. It is a synchronized method (that is, it is capable of *blocking* the current thread). When the thread enters the `loadImage` procedure, it creates the `image` object and then checks whether the image is already loaded. It does this by looking at the `loaded` instance variable of the `Animation` class. The first time around, that flag is certainly `false`, and the runner thread is suspended.

Whenever the image-loading thread has acquired another scan line of the image, it calls the `imageUpdate` method. (See Figure 2-14). Once the image is complete, it sets the `loaded` flag to `true` *and calls* `notify()`! This awakens the runner thread that was pending in the `loadImage` method.

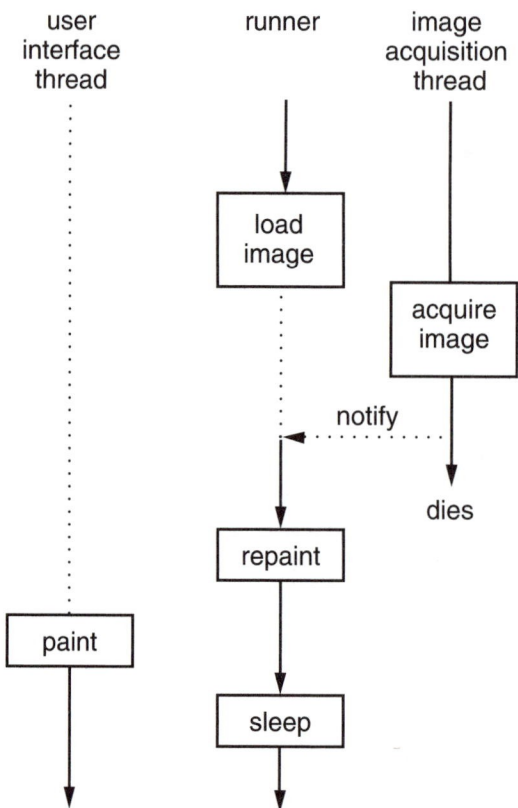

Figure 2-14: Threads in the image loading process

This description explains how the applet suppresses animation while image-loading is still in progress. If you do not implement this interlocking mechanism, partially loaded frames will be drawn, which looks quite unsightly.

TIP: If you load multiple images and audio files, monitoring their loading progress becomes tedious. The `MediaTracker` class does this for you automatically. In this example, we chose to do it by hand to show you what goes on behind the scenes.

Finally, we implement another method of stopping and restarting the animation. When you click with the mouse on the applet window, the animation stops. When you click again, it restarts. This behavior is implemented in the `toggleAnimation` method.

```java
public class Animation extends Applet implements Runnable
{  public void init()
   {  addMouseListener(new MouseAdapter()
         {  public void mouseClicked(MouseEvent evt)
            {  toggleAnimation();
            }
         });

      . . .

   }

   public void toggleAnimation()
   {  if (loaded)
      {  if (runner != null && runner.isAlive())
         {  if (stopped)
            {  showStatus("Click to stop");
               runner.resume();
            }
            else
            {  showStatus("Click to restart");
               runner.suspend();
            }
            stopped = !stopped;
         }
         else
         {  stopped = false;
            current = 0;
            runner = new Thread(this);
            runner.start();
         }
      }
   }
   . . .
}
```

Figure 2-15 shows the state-transition diagram of the runner thread.

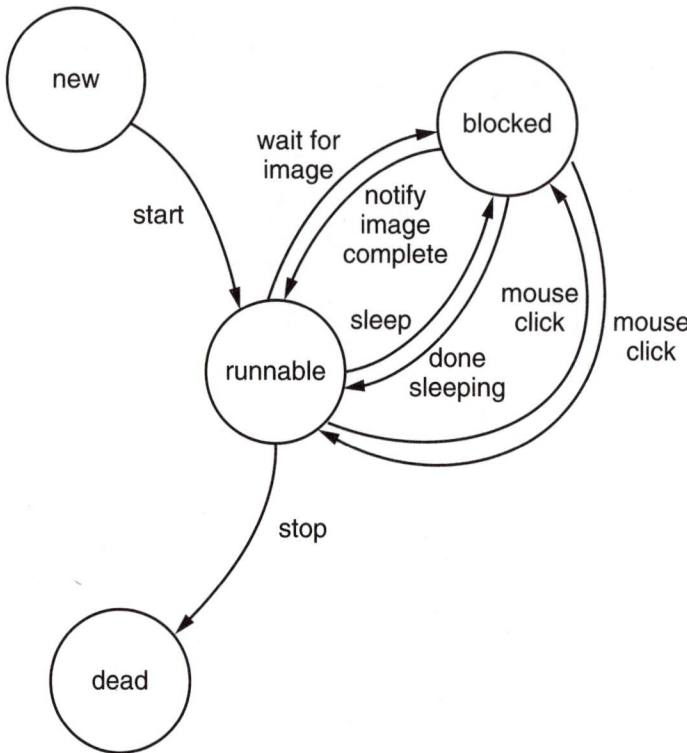

Figure 2-15: State diagram for runner thread

The applet reads the name of the image and the number of frames in the strip from the PARAM section in the HTML file (on the CD-ROM as well).

```
<html>
<title>Animation Applet</title>
<body>
<applet code=Animation.class width=100 height=100>
<param name=imagename value="globe.gif">
<param name=imagecount value="36">
</applet>
</body>
</html>
```

Example 2-9 is the code of the applet. Have a close look at the interplay between the run, loadImage, paint, and imageUpdate methods.

Example 2-9: Animation.java

```
import java.awt.*;
import java.awt.image.*;
import java.awt.event.*;
import java.applet.*;
import java.net.*;

public class Animation extends Applet implements Runnable
{  public void start()
   {  if (runner == null)
      {  runner = new Thread(this);
         runner.start();
      }
   }

   public void stop()
   {  if (runner != null && runner.isAlive())
         runner.stop();
      runner = null;
   }

   public void init()
   {  addMouseListener(new MouseAdapter()
         {  public void mouseClicked(MouseEvent evt)
            {  toggleAnimation();
            }
         });

      try
      {  imageName = getParameter("imagename");
         if (imageName == null) imageName = "";

         imageCount = 1;
         String param = getParameter("imagecount");
         if (param != null)
            imageCount = Integer.parseInt(param);
      }
      catch (Exception e)
      {  showStatus("Error: " + e);
      }
   }

   public synchronized void loadImage()
   {  if (loaded) return;
      try
         {  URL url = new URL(getDocumentBase(), imageName);
            showStatus("Loading " + imageName);
```

```
            image = getImage(url);
            prepareImage(image, this);
        }
        catch(Exception e)
        {   showStatus("Error: " + e);
        }

    while (!loaded)
        try { wait(); } catch (InterruptedException e) {}
    resize(imageWidth, imageHeight / imageCount);
}

public void run()
{   loadImage();
    while (runner != null)
    {   repaint();
        try { Thread.sleep(200); }
        catch (InterruptedException e) {}
        current = (current + 1) % imageCount;
    }
}

public void paint(Graphics g)
{   if (!loaded) return;

    g.drawImage(image, 0, - (imageHeight / imageCount)
        * current, null);
}

public void update(Graphics g)
{   paint(g);
}

public void toggleAnimation()
{   if (loaded)
    {   if (runner != null && runner.isAlive())
        {   if (stopped)
            {   showStatus("Click to stop");
                runner.resume();
            }
            else
            {   showStatus("Click to restart");
                runner.suspend();
            }
            stopped = !stopped;
        }
        else
        {   stopped = false;
```

```
            current = 0;
            runner = new Thread(this);
            runner.start();
        }
    }
}

public synchronized boolean imageUpdate(Image img,
    int infoflags, int x, int y, int width, int height)
{   if ((infoflags & ImageObserver.ALLBITS) != 0)
    {   // image is complete
        imageWidth = image.getWidth(null);
        imageHeight = image.getHeight(null);
        showStatus("Click to stop");
        loaded = true;
        notify();
        return false;
    }
    return true; // want more info
}

private Image image;
private int imageCount;
private int imageWidth = 0;
private int imageHeight = 0;
private String imageName;
private Thread runner = null;
private int current = 0;
private boolean loaded = false;
private boolean stopped = false;
}
```

This animation applet is simplified in order to show you what goes on behind the scenes. If you are interested only in how to put a moving image on your Web page, look instead at the `Animator` applet in the demo section of the JDK. That applet has many more options than ours, and it lets you add sound.

CHAPTER 3

- Connecting to a Server
- Implementing Servers
- Retrieving Information from a Remote Site
- Sending Information to the Server
- Harvesting Information from the Web

Networking

J ava is supposed to become the premier tool for connecting computers over the Internet and corporate Intranets. In this realm, Java mostly lives up to the hype. If you are used to programming network connections in C or C++, you will be pleasantly surprised at how easy it is to program them in Java. For example, as you saw in the applet chapter in Volume 1, it is easy to open a URL (uniform resource locator) on the Net: simply pass the URL to the `showDocument` method in the `AppletContext` class.

We begin this chapter by talking a little bit about basic networking. Then, we move on to reviewing and extending the information that was briefly presented in the applet chapter in Volume 1. The rest of the chapter moves on to the intricacies of doing sophisticated work on the Net with Java. For example, we show you how to do common gateway interface (CGI) programming on the server, using a Java application. In particular, we show you how to use a combination of a Java applet and a Java CGI application to harvest information on the Internet.

In the first part of this chapter, we assume that you have no network programming experience. If you have written TCP/IP programs before, and ports and sockets are no mystery to you, you should breeze through the sample code. Toward the end of this chapter, the code becomes complex and is geared more toward those with some experience in network programming.

Connecting to a Server

Before writing our first network program, let's learn about a great debugging tool for network programming that you already have, namely, telnet. Unix systems always come with telnet; Windows 95 and NT also come with a simple tel-

net program. However, it is optional, and you may not have installed it when you installed the operating system. Just look for TELNET.EXE in the \Windows directory. If you don't find it, run Setup again.

You may have used telnet to connect to a remote computer and to check your e-mail, but you can use it to communicate with other services provided by Net hosts as well. Here is an example of what you can do:

1. Start telnet.

2. In the host field, type time-A.timefreq.bldrdoc.gov.

3. In the port field, type 13. (It doesn't matter what terminal type you choose.)

See Figure 3-1.

If you have a command-line version of telnet, type

```
telnet time-A.timefreq.bldrdoc.gov 13
```

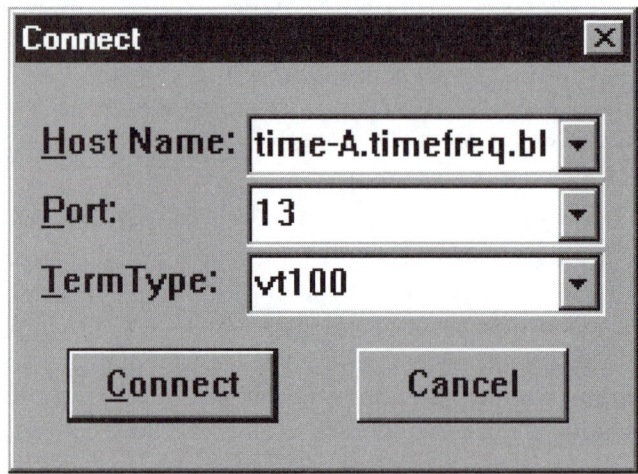

Figure 3-1: The Telnet Connect dialog box

As Figure 3-2 shows, you should get back a line like this:

```
50692 97-09-01 21:43:15 50 0 0  50.0 UTC(NIST) *
```

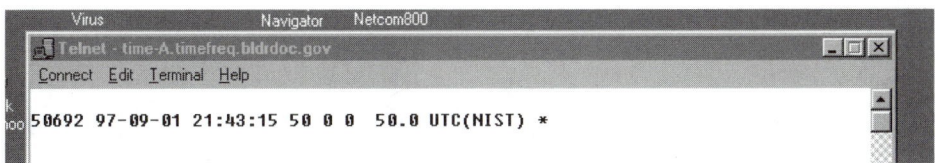

Figure 3-2: Output of the "Time of day" service

What is going on? You have connected to the "time of day" service that most
Unix machines constantly run. The particular server that you connected to is
operated by the National Institute of Standards and Technology in Boulder,
Colorado, and gives the measurement of a Cesium atomic clock. (Of course, the
reported time is not completely accurate due to network delays.) By convention,
the "time of day" service is always attached to "port" number 13.

NOTE: In network parlance, a port is not a physical device, but an abstraction to
facilitate communication between a server and a client.

What is happening is that the server software is continuously running on the
remote machine, waiting for any network traffic that wants to chat with port 13.
When the operating system on the remote computer gets a network package
that contains a request to connect to port number 13, it wakes up the listening
process and establishes the connection.

The connection stays up until it is terminated by one of the parties.

When you began the telnet session with `time-A.timefreq.bldrdoc.gov` at
port 13, an unrelated piece of network software knew enough to convert the
string `time-A.timefreq.bldrdoc.gov` to its correct Internet address,
132.163.135.130. The software then sent a connection request to that computer,
asking for a connection to port 13. Once the connection was established, the
remote program sent back a line of data and then closed the connection. In general, of course, clients and servers engage in a more extensive dialog before one
or the other closes the connection.

Here is another experiment, along the same lines, that is a bit more interesting.
First, turn on the local key echo. (In Windows 95, this is done from the
Terminal | Preferences dialog box in the Windows telnet program.) Then, do the
following:

1. Connect to `java.sun.com` on port 80.

2. Type the following, *exactly as it appears, without pressing backspace.*

   ```
   GET / HTTP/1.0
   ```

3. Now, press the ENTER key *two times.*

Figure 3-3 shows the response. It should look eerily familiar—you got a page of HTML-formatted text, namely, the `new.html` Web page.

This is *exactly* the same process that your Web browser goes through to get a Web page.

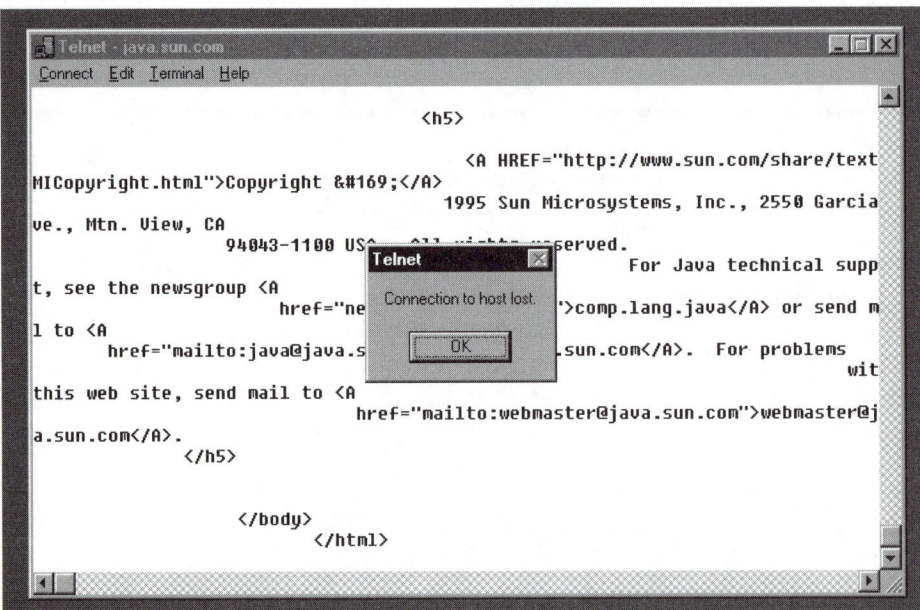

Figure 3-3: Using telnet to access an HTTP port

Our first network program in Example 3-1 will do the same thing we did using telnet—connect to a port and print out what it finds.

Example 3-1: SocketTest.java

```java
import java.io.*;
import java.net.*;

class SocketTest
{  public static void main(String[] args)
   {  try
      {  Socket t = new Socket("time-A.timefreq.bldrdoc.gov", 13);

         BufferedReader is = new BufferedReader
            (new InputStreamReader(t.getInputStream()));
         boolean more = true;
         while (more)
         {  String str = is.readLine();
            if (str == null) more = false;
            else
               System.out.println(str);
         }

      }
      catch(IOException e)
      { System.out.println("Error" + e); }
   }
}
```

This program is extremely simple, but before we analyze the two key lines, note that we are importing the `java.net` class (most of Java's networking capability can be found in this package) and catching any input/output errors because the code is encased in a `try`/`catch` block. (Since there are many things that can go wrong with a network connection, most of the network-related methods threaten to throw I/O errors. You must catch them for the code to compile.)

As for the code itself, the key lines are as follows:

```java
Socket t = new Socket("time-A.timefreq.bldrdoc.gov", 13);
BufferedReader is = new BufferedReader
   new InputStreamReader(t.getInputStream()));
```

The first line opens a *socket,* which is an abstraction for the network software that enables communication out of and into this program. We pass the remote address and the port number to the socket constructor. If the connection fails, then an `UnknownHostException` is thrown. If there is another problem, then an `IOException` occurs. Since `UnknownHostException` is derived from `IOException` and this is a sample program, we just catch the base class.

Once the socket is open, the `getInputStream` method in `java.net.Socket` returns an `InputStream` object that you can use just like any other file. (See Chapter 1.) Once you have grabbed the stream, this program simply

1. Reads all characters sent by the server using `readLine`.

2. Prints each line out to standard output.

This process continues until the stream is finished and the server disconnects. You know this happens when the `readLine` method returns a `null` string.

Plainly, the `Socket` class is pleasant and easy to use in Java. Java hides the complexities of establishing a networking connection and sending data across and, essentially, gives you the same programming interface you would use to work with a file.

NOTE: In this book, we cover only the TCP networking protocol. TCP establishes a reliable connection between two computers. Java also supports the so-called UDP protocol, which can be used to send packets (also called *datagrams*) with much less overhead than that for TCP. The drawback is that the packets can be delivered in random order or even be dropped altogether. It is up to the recipient to put the packets in order and to request retransmission of missing packets. UDP is most suited for applications where missing packets can be tolerated, for example, in audio or video streams or for continuous measurements. To learn more about UDP programming in Java, see, for example, *Java Network Programming* by Elliotte Harold (O'Reilly, 1997).

java.net.Socket

*   `Socket(String host, int port)`

    creates a socket and connects it to a port on a remote host.

Parameters:	host	the host name
	port	the port number

*   `synchronized void close()`

    closes the socket.

*   `InputStream getInputStream()`

    gets the input stream to read from the socket.

*   `OutputStream getOutputStream()`

    gets an output stream to write to this socket.

- ```
  void setSoTimeout(int timeout)
  ```

  Parameters   `timeout`   the timeout in milliseconds (0 for
  infinite timeout)

  Read requests on the `InputStream` associated with this `Socket` will block
  for only this amount of time. If the timeout expires, then an
  `InterruptedIOException` is raised.

Implementing Servers

Now that we have implemented a basic network client that receives data from
the Net, let's implement a simple server that can send information out to the
Net. Once you start the server program, it waits for some client to attach to its
port. We chose port number 8189, which is not used by any of the standard services. The `ServerSocket` class is used to establish a socket. In our case, the command

```
ServerSocket s = new ServerSocket(8189);
```

establishes a server that monitors port 8189. The command

```
Socket incoming = s.accept();
```

tells Java to wait indefinitely until a client connects to that port. Once someone
connects to this port by sending the correct request over the Net, this method
returns a `Socket` object that represents the connection that was made. You can
use this object to get an input reader and an output writer from that socket, as is
done in the following code:

```
BufferedReader in = new BufferedReader
   (new InputStreamReader(incoming.getInputStream()));
PrintWriter out = new PrintWriter
   (incoming.getOutputStream(), true /* autoFlush */);
```

Everything that the server sends to the output stream becomes the input of the
client program, and all the output from the client program ends up in our input
stream.

In all of the examples in this chapter, we will transmit *text* through sockets. We,
therefore, turn the streams into readers and writers. Then, we can use the
`readLine` method (defined in `BufferedReader`, but not in `InputStream`) and
the `print` method (defined in `PrintStream`, but not in `OutputStream`). If we
wanted to transmit *binary data*, we would turn the streams into
`DataInputStream` and `DataOutputStreams`. To transmit *serialized objects*, we
would use `ObjectInputStream` and `ObjectOutputStreams` instead.

Let's send the client a greeting:

```
out.println("Hello! Enter BYE to exit.");
```
```

When you use telnet to connect to this server program at port 8189, you will see the above greeting on the terminal screen.

In this simple server, we just read the client input, a line at a time, and echo it. This demonstrates that the program gets the client's input. An actual server would obviously compute and return an answer that depended on the input.

```
String str = in.readLine();
if (str != null)
{  out.println("Echo: " + str);
    if (str.trim().equals("BYE")) done = true;
}
else done = true;
```

In the end, we close the incoming socket.

```
incoming.close();
```

That is all there is to it. Every server program, such as an http Web server, continues performing this loop:

1.   It gets a command from the client ("get me this information") through an incoming data stream.

2.   It somehow fetches the information.

3.   It sends the information to the client through the outgoing data stream.

Example 3-2 is the complete program.

Example 3-2: EchoServer.java

```
import java.io.*;
import java.net.*;

public class EchoServer
{  public static void main(String[] args )
    {  try
        {  ServerSocket s = new ServerSocket(8189);
            Socket incoming = s.accept( );
            BufferedReader in = new BufferedReader
                (new InputStreamReader(incoming.getInputStream()));
            PrintWriter out = new PrintWriter
                (incoming.getOutputStream(), true /* autoFlush */);

            out.println( "Hello! Enter BYE to exit." );
```

```
        boolean done = false;
        while (!done)
        {   String str = in.readLine();
            if (str == null) done = true;
            else
            {   out.println("Echo: " + str);

                if (str.trim().equals("BYE"))
                    done = true;
            }
        }
        incoming.close();
    }
    catch (Exception e)
    {   System.out.println(e);
    }
  }
}
```

To try it out, you need to compile and run the program. Then, use telnet to connect to the following server and port:

> Server: 127.0.0.1
>
> Port: 8189

The IP address 127.0.0.1 is a special address, called the *local loopback address*, that denotes the local machine. Since you are running the echo server locally, that is where you want to connect.

NOTE: If you are using a dial-up connection, you need to have it running for this experiment. Even though you are only talking to your local machine, the network software must be loaded.

Actually, anyone in the world can access your echo server, provided it is running and they know your IP address and the magic port number.

When you connect to the port, you will get the message shown in Figure 3-4:

```
Hello! Enter BYE to exit.
```

Type anything and watch the input echo on your screen. Type BYE (all uppercase letters) to disconnect. The server program will terminate as well.

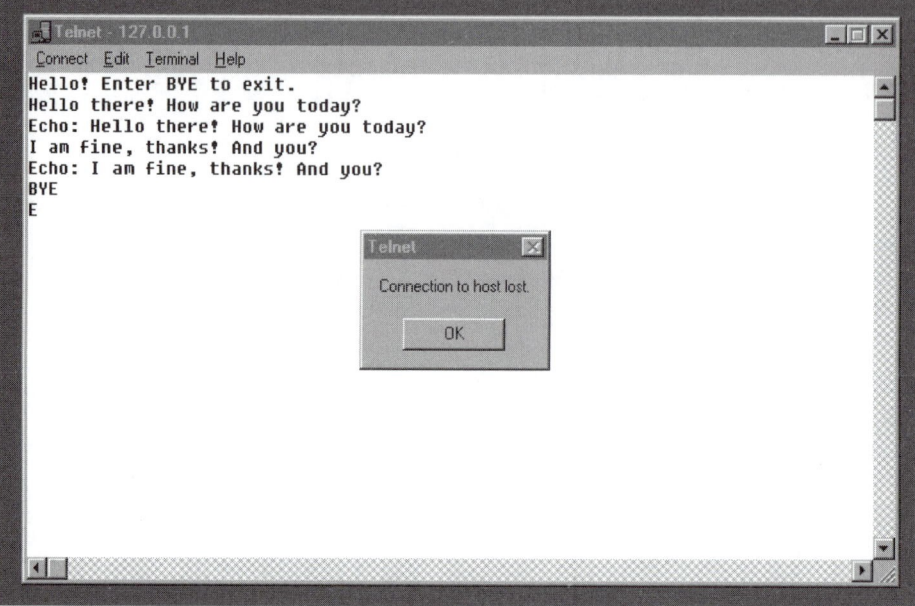

Figure 3-4: Accessing an echo server

Serving Multiple Clients

There is one problem with the simple server in the preceding example. Suppose we want to allow multiple clients to connect to our server at the same time. Typically, a server runs constantly on a server computer, and clients from all over the Internet may want to use the server at the same time. Rejecting multiple connections allows any one client to monopolize the service by connecting to it for a long time. We can do much better through the magic of threads.

Every time we know Java has established a new socket connection, that is, when the call to accept was successful, we will launch a new thread to take care of the connection between the server and *that* client. The main program will just go back and wait for the next connection. For this to happen, the main loop of the server should look like this:

```
while (true)
{  Socket incoming = s.accept();
   Thread t = new ThreadedEchoHandler(incoming);
   t.start();
}
```

The `ThreadedEchoHandler` class derives from `Thread` and contains the communication loop with the client in its `run` method.

```
class ThreadedEchoHandler extends Thread
{   . . .
    public void run()
    {   try
        {   BufferedReader in = new BufferedReader
                (new InputStreamReader(incoming.getInputStream()));
            PrintWriter out = new PrintWriter
                (incoming.getOutputStream(), true /* autoFlush */);

            out.println( "Hello! Enter BYE to exit." );

            boolean done = false;
            while (!done)
            {   String str = in.readLine();
                if (str == null) done = true;
                else
                {   out.println("Echo (" + counter + "): " + str);
                    if (str.trim().equals("BYE"))
                        done = true;
                }
            }
            incoming.close();
        }
        catch(Exception e)
        {   System.out.println(e);
        }
    }
}
```

Because each connection starts a new thread, multiple clients can connect to the server at the same time. You can easily check out this fact. Compile and run the server program (Example 3-3). Open several telnet windows as we have in Figure 3-5. You can communicate through all of them simultaneously. The server program never dies. Use CTRL+C to kill it.

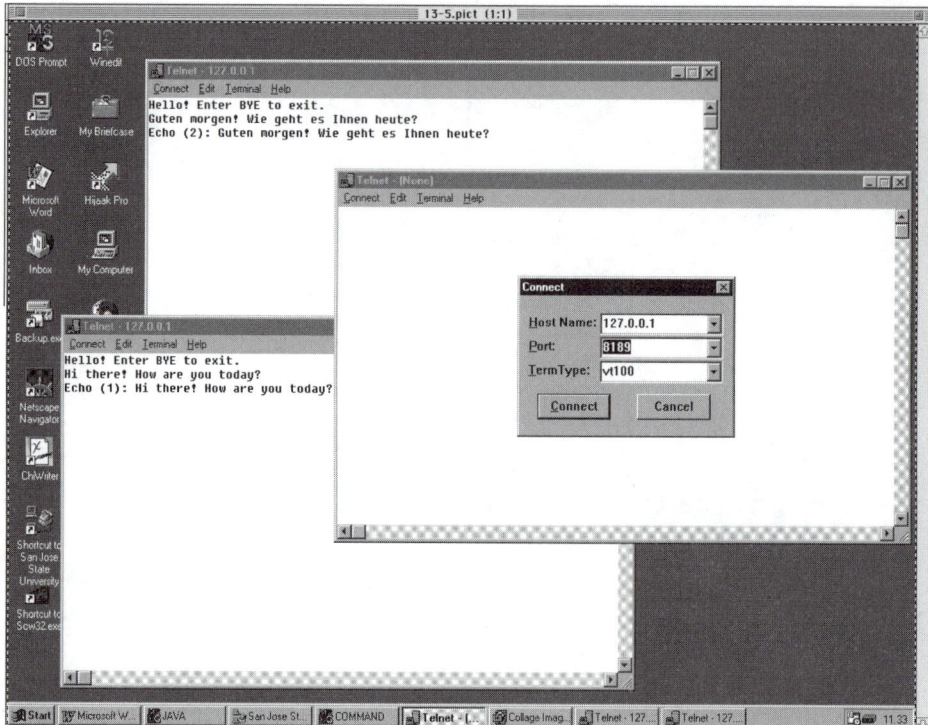

Figure 3-5: Simultaneous access to the threaded Echo server

Example 3-3: ThreadedEchoServer.java

```java
import java.io.*;
import java.net.*;

public class ThreadedEchoServer
{  public static void main(String[] args )
   {  int i = 1;
      try
      {  ServerSocket s = new ServerSocket(8189);

         for (;;)
         {  Socket incoming = s.accept( );
            System.out.println("Spawning " + i);
            new ThreadedEchoHandler(incoming, i).start();
            i++;
         }
      }
```

```
      catch (Exception e)
      {  System.out.println(e);
      }
   }
}

class ThreadedEchoHandler extends Thread
{  public ThreadedEchoHandler(Socket i, int c)
   {  incoming = i; counter = c; }

   public void run()
   {  try
      {  BufferedReader in = new BufferedReader
            (new InputStreamReader(incoming.getInputStream()));
         PrintWriter out = new PrintWriter
            (incoming.getOutputStream(), true /* autoFlush */);

         out.println( "Hello! Enter BYE to exit." );

         boolean done = false;
         while (!done)
         {  String str = in.readLine();
            if (str == null) done = true;
            else
            {  out.println("Echo (" + counter + "): " + str);

               if (str.trim().equals("BYE"))
                  done = true;
            }
         }
         incoming.close();
      }
      catch (Exception e)
      {  System.out.println(e);
      }
   }

   private Socket incoming;
   private int counter;
}
```

---

java.net.ServerSocket

- `ServerSocket(int port) throws IOException`

  creates a server socket that monitors a port.

  Parameters: port   the port number

- `Socket accept() throws IOException`

  waits for a connection. This method will block (that is, idle) the current thread until the connection is made. The method returns a `Socket` object through which the program can communicate with the connecting client.

- `void close() throws IOException`

  closes the server socket.

Retrieving Information from a Remote Site

In this section, we want to use as an example an applet that takes orders from visitors to a Web page. Since this is meant as an illustration, this applet is a simplified form of what would be used in a commercial setting. It is certainly not enough to convince any actual customers to fork over their money.

The key point is that you will always want to make applets flexible. For example, you will want to be able to change the prices or the goods offered at a moment's notice—without having to reprogram the applet. The obvious (and probably easiest) way to do this is to store the data in a file. Whenever you want to change the goods and prices, just update that file. The applet and the HTML code for the Web page can stay the same.

When the client visits your Web page, the browser downloads the HTML page and the applet code from your server. The applet then runs on the client's computer. First, the applet downloads the data file containing the price list. Let's suppose that the data is stored in a file called `prices.dat`, in the same directory as the HTML page. The applet then needs to open the URL, which is accomplished in the following code:

```
URL url = new URL(getDocumentBase(), "prices.dat");
```

This constructor creates a URL for the file `prices.dat`, relative to the URL returned by `getDocumentBase`. As you saw in the applet chapter in Volume 1, this method returns the URL of the Web page that contained the applet—it is the one given by the `APPLET` tag in the HTML file.

TIP: It is a good idea to use relative URLs. Then, if you move your files, you do not need to recompile the Java code.

The other important method you need is showDocument, which we also discussed in the applet chapter in Volume 1. This method yields an InputStream object. Using this stream object, we can easily read the contents of the file.

```
InputStream in = url.openStream();
```

In our case, the price list is formatted in the Properties data format, like this:

```
#Price list
#Wed Feb 07 21:04:53   1996
Toaster=19.95;
Blender=59.95;
Microwave+oven=179.95;
Citrus+press=19.95;
Espresso+maker=199.95;
Rice+cooker=29.95;
Waffle+iron=39.95;
Bread+machine=119.95;
```

See the chapter on "Data Structures" in Volume 1 for more information on the Properties class. For now, recall that it is simply a dictionary that can load and save its contents to a disk file. Note that we use + signs instead of spaces in the data file. The load method of the Properties class does not like spaces. We later replace the + signs with spaces, using code like this:

```
prices.get(itemName).replace('+', ' ');
```

As long as none of the product names contain a +, we can get away with this technique.

You would probably find this format limiting in a real-life applet, but it is handy for this toy example since we can now read the data into the Properties object with a single statement.

```
prices.load(in);
```

This example shows one method with which your applet can get information from the server: by reading in a file. There is no limit on the structure of the file—it can be a text or binary file of any convenient format. Obviously, using a file for data storage is better than building the data right into the applet. It keeps the applet small and flexible.

The information flow in the price list applet is shown in Figure 3-6.

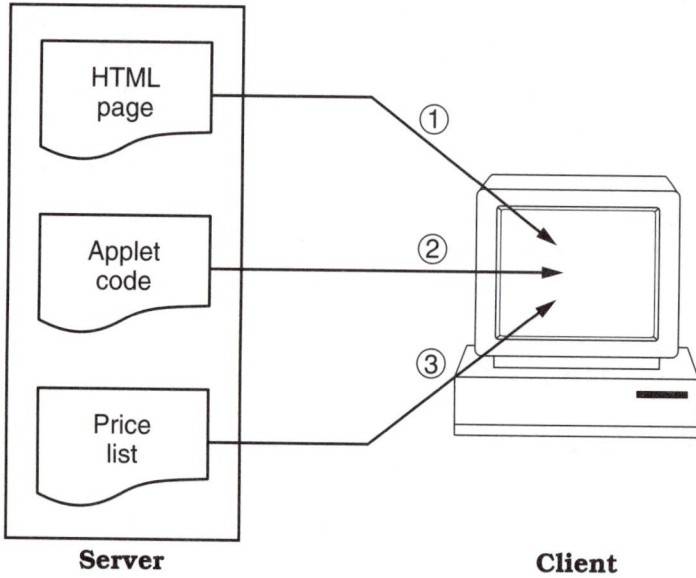

Figure 3-6: Information flow in the price list applet

If the data set is large, it may not make sense to send the entire file to the client site. Instead, the applet should find out what information the client needs and ask for just that information, as in Figure 3-7. You will see later in this chapter how to implement such a query. The code for the price list applet is presented in Example 3-4.

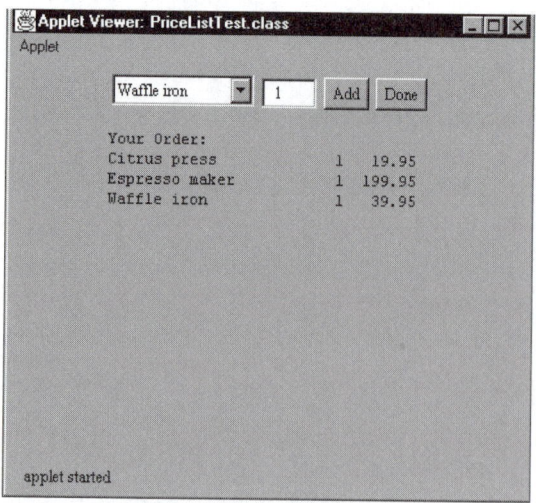

Figure 3-7: Price list applet

Example 3-4: PriceListTest.java

```java
import java.awt.*;
import java.awt.event.*;
import java.applet.*;
import java.util.*;
import java.net.*;
import corejava.*;

public class PriceListTest extends Applet
    implements ActionListener
{  public void init()
    {  setLayout(new BorderLayout());
        Panel p = new Panel();
        p.setLayout(new FlowLayout());
        name = new Choice();

        try
        {  URL url = new URL(getDocumentBase(), "prices.dat");
            prices.load(url.openStream());
        } catch(Exception e) {}

        Enumeration e = prices.propertyNames();
        while (e.hasMoreElements())
            name.addItem(((String)e.nextElement())
                .replace('+', ' '));
        quantity = new IntTextField(1, 4);
        p.add(name);
        p.add(quantity);
        addButton(p, "Add");
        addButton(p, "Done");
        add(p, "North");
        add(canvas = new PurchaseOrderCanvas(), "Center");
        canvas.setSize(250, 150);
        canvas.redraw(a);
    }

    public void addButton(Container c, String name)
    {  Button b = new Button(name);
        b.addActionListener(this);
        c.add(b);
    }

    public void actionPerformed(ActionEvent evt)
    {  String arg = evt.getActionCommand();
        if (arg.equals("Add"))
        {  if (quantity.isValid())
            {  String itemName = name.getSelectedItem();
```

```
                    a.addElement(new Item(itemName,
                        quantity.getValue(),
                        Format.atof((String)prices.get(itemName
                        .replace(' ', '+'))))));
                }
            }
            else if (arg.equals("Done"))
            {   a.addElement(new Item("State Tax", 1, 0.00));
                a.addElement(new Item("Shipping", 1, 5.00));
                a.trimToSize();
            }
            canvas.redraw(a);
        }

    private Vector a = new Vector();
    private Choice name;
    private IntTextField quantity;
    private PurchaseOrderCanvas canvas;
    private int m = 1;
    private Properties prices = new Properties();
}

class Item
{   public Item(String n, int q, double u)
    {   name = n;
        quantity = q;
        unitPrice = u;
    }

    public String toString()
    {   return new Format("%-20s").form(name)
            + new Format("%6d").form(quantity)
            + new Format("%8.2f").form(unitPrice);
    }

    private String name;
    private int quantity;
    private double unitPrice;
}

class PurchaseOrderCanvas extends Canvas
{   public void redraw(Vector new_a)
    {   a = new_a;
        repaint();
    }

    public void paint(Graphics g)
    {   Font f = new Font("Monospaced", Font.PLAIN, 12);
```

```
    g.setFont(f);
    FontMetrics fm = g.getFontMetrics(f);
    int height = fm.getHeight();
    int x = 80;
    int y = 0;
    int i = 0;
    y += height;
    g.drawString("Your Order: ", x, y);
    for (i = 0; i < a.size(); i++)
    {  y += height;
        g.drawString(a.elementAt(i).toString(), x, y);
    }
    }

    private Vector a;
}
```

Sending Information to the Server

Let us now complete the order-taking applet. Once the customer has specified the order, the information must be returned to the server. To return information, we need to enhance the applet to enable it to get the name and address of the customer. In a realistic application, we would also concern ourselves with billing information (such as a credit card number), but we will ignore that for now. Figure 3-8 shows the complete order screen.

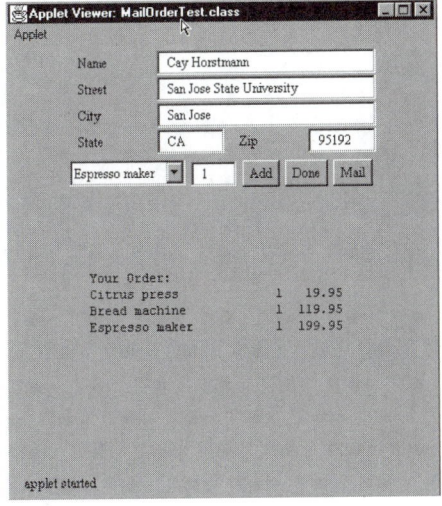

Figure 3-8: MailOrder test applet

When the user clicks on the Mail button, the ordering information (name, address, and items ordered) must be sent off to the server. The applet makes contact with the server, opens a stream, and sends the information through that stream.

To make contact with the server, a special server process can continually monitor an agreed-upon port, such as port 8189 in the preceding example. The applet then connects to that port and sends the ordering information. The server program on the host computer must connect to a database and enter the order.

Another alternative is for the applet to connect to a service that already runs on the server. For example, the applet can make a socket connection to port 25, the sendmail daemon. Then, it sends a mail header (in the format expected by the sendmail daemon, which is easy to generate), followed by the ordering information. The order arrives by e-mail. This looks like an attractive idea for a simple ordering application that processes only a couple of orders every day. And it is easy to do; here's how:

1. Open a socket to your host.

    ```
    Socket s = new Socket("www.corejava.com", 25); // 25 is SMTP
    PrintWriter out = new PrintWriter(s.getOutputStream());
    ```

2. Send the following information to the print stream:

    ```
    HELO sending host
    MAIL FROM: sender
    RCPT TO: recipient
    DATA
    mail message
    (any number of lines)
    .
    QUIT
    ```

Since the applet cannot determine the sending host and the sender name, you need placeholders for this information. The sendmail program does not check this information. (Keep this in mind the next time you get an e-mail message from president@whitehouse.gov inviting you to a black-tie affair on the front lawn. Anyone can telnet into any sendmail host and create a fake message.)

We will not pursue this route in our program because if you get more than a handful of orders, you probably do not want them to clutter up a mailbox. More importantly, many system administrators disable the sendmail port on Web servers because it serves no useful function and is potentially a security risk. As we will see later in this chapter, an applet can establish a socket connection only to the server on which it resides. If that server does not monitor the sendmail port, you cannot use this port to send data from the applet to the server.

The third route from your applet to the server is the CGI. It is the topic of the next section.

CGI Scripts

Even before Java came along, there was a mechanism to send information from a Web browser to the host. A person would fill out a *form*, like the one in Figure 3-9.

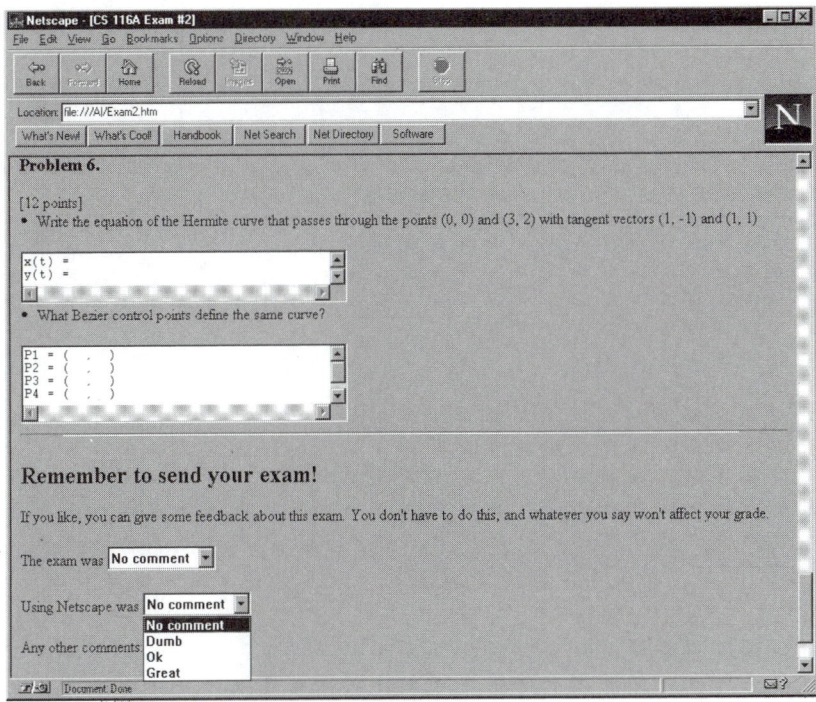

Figure 3-9: An HTML form

When the user clicks on the Submit button, the text in the text fields and the settings of the check boxes and radio buttons are sent back to the server to be processed by a so-called CGI script. (The CGI script to use is usually specified in the ACTION attribute of the FORM tag.)

The CGI script is a program that resides on the server computer. There are usually many CGI scripts on a server, conventionally residing in the `cgi-bin` directory. The http daemon on the server launches the CGI script and feeds it the form data. The CGI script processes the form data and sends another HTML page back to the browser. This sequence is illustrated in Figure 3-10. That page

can contain new information (for example, in an information-search program) or just an acknowledgment. The Web browser then displays the response page.

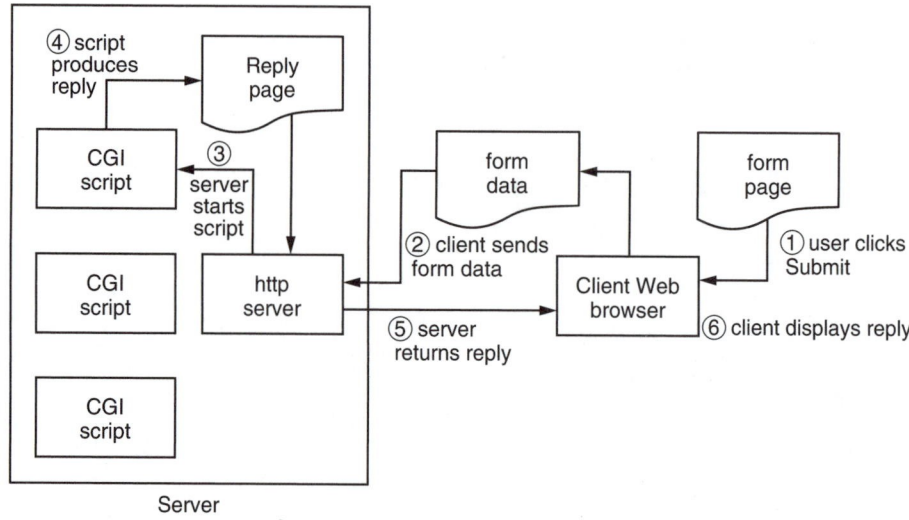

Server

Figure 3-10: Data flow during execution of a CGI script

CGI programs are commonly written in Perl, but they can be written in any language that can read from standard input and write to standard output. In particular, they can be written in Java. (Of course, a CGI script written in Java is not an applet. It is an *application* running on the http server, and you need to have some way for the server to run Java class files.) The CGI application will need to be launched by the http server whenever a client submits a query asking that that script be used as the processing agent.) For example, here is about the simplest Java program that could be used for CGI—yet another version of "Hello world."

```
public class HelloWorld
{  public static void main(String[] args)
   {  System.out.println("Content-type: text/html\n\n");
      System.out.println("<html>");
      System.out.println("<head><title>Hello</title> </head>");
      System.out.println("<body>");
      System.out.println("Hello, World.");
      System.out.println("</body>");
      System.out.println("</html>");
   }
}
```

> NOTE: We will not discuss how to design HTML forms that interact with CGI. A good reference for that topic is *HTML The Definitive Guide* (2nd edition) by Musciano and Kennedy, (O'Reilly, 1997). Our interest lies in the interface between CGI and Java applets, not in HTML forms.

> NOTE: CGI is often a good mechanism to use because it is well established and system administrators are familiar with it. It does have the disadvantage of having to fork a new process rather than a new thread for each request. Furthermore, it is difficult to control the security of those scripts, and this difficulty is an issue for ISPs that allow their customers to run CGI scripts. You might want to check out the new Java servlet package that would replace multiple CGI processes by Java "servlets" running in separate threads. Just like applets, the security privileges of servlets can be tightly controlled.

Anyway, if you are like most of us, you do not have your own, personal http server. To run programs on a server, you need to work with a system administrator or service provider, who will most likely have only CGI in place. Obviously, there would be some advantages if there were a way for an applet to use the CGI mechanism that is already present in the browser. Unfortunately, the standard Java library does not provide such a communication path. We need to invoke a CGI script manually, in the same way that a Web browser would. We connect to the http port (port 80) of the server.

```
Socket s = new Socket("www.corejava.com", 80);
```

(Of course, you will need to change the domain `corejava.com` to another domain name in your programs.)

As always, we get streams for input and output.

```
BufferedReader in = new BufferedReader
    (new InputStreamReader(s.getInputStream()));
PrintWriter out = new PrintWriter(s.getOutputStream());
```

There are two methods with which to send information to the CGI program. They are called the GET method and the POST method. In the GET method, we send the following string through the `out` stream to ask the http daemon to process a specific script.

```
GET scriptname?parameters
```

The string must be followed by a blank line.

For example, suppose we wanted to ask the script `priceinfo`, located in the `cgi-bin` subdirectory, about the price of an item. Then, we would print the following command to the `out` stream:

```
out.print("GET /cgi-bin/priceinfo?Toaster\n\n");
```

The `priceinfo` script would receive the information following the ? as a command-line parameter (`args[0]` in Java). You can send more than one argument to the command line, but you must separate the arguments by + signs, not spaces. For example, when you send the query

```
out.print("GET /cgi-bin/priceinfo?Toaster+oven\n\n");
```

the script receives two command-line arguments, `args[0]` as `"Toaster"` and `args[1]` as `"oven."` You are supposed to encode all non-alphanumeric characters, except + and & by using a %, followed by a two-digit hexadecimal number. For example, to transmit the book title *Mastering C++*, you use `Mastering+C%2b%2b`, since the hexadecimal number 2b (or decimal 43) is the ASCII code of the + character. This encoding keeps any intermediate programs from messing with spaces and interpreting other special characters. This encoding scheme is called *URL encoding*.

With the GET method, the CGI script gets no further input.

The POST method works the other way around. The CGI script gets no command-line arguments, but it gets all its input from standard input. The applet must send the information for the CGI script through the `out` stream. The applet first sends a header, then the data. The first line of the header must be

```
Content-type: type
```

where *type* is usually one of the following:

```
text/plain
text/html
application/octet-stream
application/x-www-form-urlencoded
```

The content type must be followed by the line

```
Content-length: length
```

for example,

```
Content-length: 1024
```

The end of the header is indicated by a blank line. Then, the data portion follows. The http daemon strips off the header and routes the data portion to the server script.

Here is how you might ask about the price of the toaster oven if your script uses the POST method:

```
String sdata = "Toaster oven"
os.print("POST /cgi-bin/priceinfo\n");
os.print("Content-type: plain/text\n");
os.print("Content-length: " + sdata.length() + "\n\n");
os.print(sdata);
os.flush();
```

As a response to either a GET or a POST query, the script on the server sends a reply to standard output. The first part of the reply is, again, a header. The http daemon strips off the header and routes the data portion to the client socket. Your program captures it by reading from the in stream. If the information arrives in text format, it can be captured with the following code:

```
String rdata = "";
String line;
while ((line = in.readLine()) != null)
    rdata += line + "\n";
```

The format of the data is completely up to you and the server. Unless you need to use an existing script designed to interact with Web pages, there is no requirement to use the rather complex form used for encoding input to the script, or even to use HTML for the reply. In fact, using ASCII text or binary data is usually more convenient. In the case of the price-information script, the price information can be sent back either in ASCII or as binary data that can be read with the readDouble method.

Completing the MailOrder Applet

In a realistic situation, the order-taking applet would send the order information to a CGI script that routes it to a database. The major database vendors have CGI-to-database interfaces, but they are, at this point, neither standardized nor freely available (that is, they cost big bucks). For this reason, our sample script simply mails the received data to orders@corejava.com.

For this purpose, we use a CGI script that passes the received data to the send-mail program. Most Web service providers provide such a script for their users, tailored for usage with HTML forms. If your provider doesn't, you can use the CGI script of Example 3-5, written in Java.

Example 3-5: MailTo.java

```
import java.io.*;

public class MailTo
{   public static void main(String[] args)
    {   try
        {   String line;
            BufferedReader in = new BufferedReader
                (new InputStreamReader(System.in));
            String recipient = in.readLine();
            Runtime rt = Runtime.getRuntime();
            Process p = rt.exec
                ("/usr/lib/sendmail " + recipient);
            PrintWriter out = new PrintWriter
                (p.getOutputStream(), true /* autoFlush */);
```

```
        while ((line = in.readLine()) != null
                && !line.equals("."))
            out.println(line);
        out.close();
        }
        catch (Exception e)
        {   System.out.println("Error " + e);
        }
    }
}
```

Example 3-6 is the CGI script in Perl, in case your system administrator will not let you run a Java program on the server.

Example 3-6: mailto.pl

```perl
#!/usr/bin/perl

# This should match the mail program on your system.
$mailprog = '/usr/lib/sendmail';

# first line of input is recipient

print "Content-type: text/plain\n\n";

$recipient=<STDIN>;

# Now send mail to $recipient
if (open (MAIL, "|$mailprog $recipient"))
{

while (($input = <STDIN>) && $input ne ".\n" && $input ne ".\r\n")
{   print MAIL $input;
}

close (MAIL);
print "OK\n"

}
else
{
print "ERROR\n"
}
```

Finally, Example 3-7 is the complete applet that runs on the client's computer. When you click on the Send button, the address and order information are made into one long string and sent to the CGI script, using the POST method.

Example 3-7: MailOrderTest.java

```
import java.awt.*;
import java.awt.event.*;
import java.applet.*;
import java.util.*;
import java.net.*;
import java.io.*;
import corejava.*;

public class MailOrderTest extends Applet
    implements ActionListener
{   public void init()
    {   Panel p = new Panel();
        p.setLayout(new FlowLayout());
        name = new Choice();
        try
        {   URL url = new URL(getDocumentBase(), "prices.dat");
            prices.load(url.openStream());
        } catch(Exception e) { showStatus("Error " + e); }

        Enumeration e = prices.propertyNames();
        while (e.hasMoreElements())
            name.addItem(((String)e.nextElement()).replace('+',
                ' '));
        quantity = new IntTextField(1, 4);
        p.add(name);
        p.add(quantity);
        addButton(p, "Add");
        addButton(p, "Done");
        addButton(p, "Send");
        Panel p2 = new Panel();
        p2.setLayout(new GridLayout(2, 1));
        p2.add(addressDialog());
        p2.add(p);

        add(p2, "North");
        add(canvas = new PurchaseOrderCanvas(), "Center");
        canvas.setSize(250, 150);
        canvas.redraw(a);
    }

    public void addButton(Container c, String name)
    {   Button b = new Button(name);
        b.addActionListener(this);
        c.add(b);
    }
```

```java
private Panel addressDialog()
{  Panel p = new Panel();
   GridBagLayout gbl = new GridBagLayout();
   p.setLayout(gbl);

   GridBagConstraints gbc = new GridBagConstraints();
   gbc.fill = GridBagConstraints.BOTH;
   gbc.weightx = 100;
   gbc.weighty = 100;
   add(p, new Label("Name"), gbc, 0, 0, 1, 1);
   add(p, nameField, gbc, 1, 0, 3, 1);
   add(p, new Label("Street"), gbc, 0, 1, 1, 1);
   add(p, streetField, gbc, 1, 1, 3, 1);
   add(p, new Label("City"), gbc, 0, 2, 1, 1);
   add(p, cityField, gbc, 1, 2, 3, 1);
   add(p, new Label("State"), gbc, 0, 3, 1, 1);
   add(p, stateField, gbc, 1, 3, 1, 1);
   add(p, new Label("Zip"), gbc, 2, 3, 1, 1);
   add(p, zipField, gbc, 3, 3, 1, 1);

   return p;
}

public void add(Container p, Component c,
   GridBagConstraints gbc,
   int x, int y, int w, int h)
{  gbc.gridx = x;
   gbc.gridy = y;
   gbc.gridwidth = w;
   gbc.gridheight = h;
   p.add(c, gbc);
}


public void actionPerformed(ActionEvent evt)
{  String arg = evt.getActionCommand();
   if (arg.equals("Add"))
   {  if (quantity.isValid())
      {  String itemName = name.getSelectedItem();
         a.addElement(new Item(itemName,
            quantity.getValue(),
            Format.atof((String)
               prices.get(itemName.replace(' ', '+')))));
      }
   }
   else if (arg.equals("Done"))
   {  a.addElement(new Item("State Tax", 1, 0.00));
      a.addElement(new Item("Shipping", 1, 5.00));
```

```java
         a.trimToSize();
      }
      else if (arg.equals("Send"))
      {   int i;
         String data;
         data = nameField.getText() + "\n"
             + streetField.getText() + "\n"
             + cityField.getText() + " "
             + stateField.getText() + " "
             + zipField.getText() + "\n\n";
         for (i = 0; i < a.size(); i++)
             data += a.elementAt(i).toString() + "\n";
         mailOrder(data);
         a = new Vector();
      }
      canvas.redraw(a);
   }

   public void mailOrder(String sdata)
   {   String home = "www.horstmann.com";
      String script = "/cgi-bin/mailto.cgi";
      String recipient = "orders@corejava.com";
      int port = 80;
      Socket s = null;

      try
      {   s = new Socket(home, port);

         PrintWriter out
             = new PrintWriter(s.getOutputStream());
         BufferedReader in = new BufferedReader
             (new InputStreamReader(s.getInputStream()));
         /* the first line of the data is the recipient address
            and the data is terminated by a .
         */
         sdata = recipient + "\r\n"
             + "Subject: Order\r\n"
             + sdata
             + ".\r\n";
         out.print("POST " + script
             + " HTTP/1.0\r\n"
             + "Content-type: "
             + "application/x-www-form-urlencoded\r\n"
             + "Content-length: "
             + sdata.length() + "\r\n\r\n");
         out.print(sdata);
         out.flush();
```

```
            String rdata = "";
            String line;
            while ((line = in.readLine()) != null)
                rdata += line + "|";
            showStatus(rdata);
            s.close();
        }
        catch (Exception e)
        {   showStatus("Error " + e);
            if (s != null)
            {   try
                {   s.close();
                }
                catch (IOException ex) {}
            }
        }
    }

    private Vector a = new Vector();
    private Choice name;
    private IntTextField quantity;
    private PurchaseOrderCanvas canvas;
    private Properties prices = new Properties();
    private TextField nameField = new TextField();
    private TextField streetField = new TextField();
    private TextField cityField = new TextField();
    private TextField stateField = new TextField();
    private TextField zipField = new TextField();
}

class Item
{   Item(String n, int q, double u)
    {   name = n;
        quantity = q;
        unitPrice = u;
    }

    public String toString()
    {   return new Format("%-20s").form(name)
            + new Format("%6d").form(quantity)
            + new Format("%8.2f").form(unitPrice);
    }

    private String name;
    private int quantity;
    private double unitPrice;
}
```

```
class PurchaseOrderCanvas extends Canvas
{   public void redraw(Vector new_a)
    {   a = new_a;
        repaint();
    }

    public void paint(Graphics g)
    {   Font f = new Font("Monospaced", Font:PLAIN, 12);
        g.setFont(f);
        FontMetrics fm = g.getFontMetrics(f);
        int height = fm.getHeight();
        int x = 0;
        int y = 0;
        int i = 0;
        y += height;
        g.drawString("Your Order: ", x, y);
        for (i = 0; i < a.size(); i++)
        {   y += height;
            g.drawString(a.elementAt(i).toString(), x, y);
        }
    }

    private Vector a;
}
```

Harvesting Information from the Web

The last example showed you how to read data that accompanies an applet stored on a server. In this section, we show you how to read and process data that is available anywhere on the Internet. The Internet contains a wealth of information both interesting and not: it is the lack of guidance through this mass of information that is the major complaint of most Web users. One major promise of Java is that it may help to bring order to this chaos: you can use Java to retrieve information and present it to the user in an appealing format.

There are many possible uses. Here are a few that come to mind:

- An applet can look at all the Web pages the user has specified as interesting and find which have recently changed.

- An applet can visit the Web pages of all scheduled airlines to find out which is running a special.

- Applets can gather and display recent stock quotes, monetary exchange rates, and other financial information.

- Applets can search FAQs, press releases, articles, and so on, and return text that contains certain keywords.

Much of the information on the Net is in HTML format, the *lingua franca* of the World Wide Web. While HTML is not difficult to parse, it is tedious enough that we will develop an applet that instead fetches information in plain ASCII text. This approach allows us to focus on the networking mechanisms instead of on HTML parsing.

The *gopher* service presents plain text information. If you grew up in the days of the World Wide Web, you may never have seen gopher. It looks much plainer than the Web. There are no fonts. Everything is a directory of links (Figure 3-11), plain text (Figure 3-12), or a solitary picture.

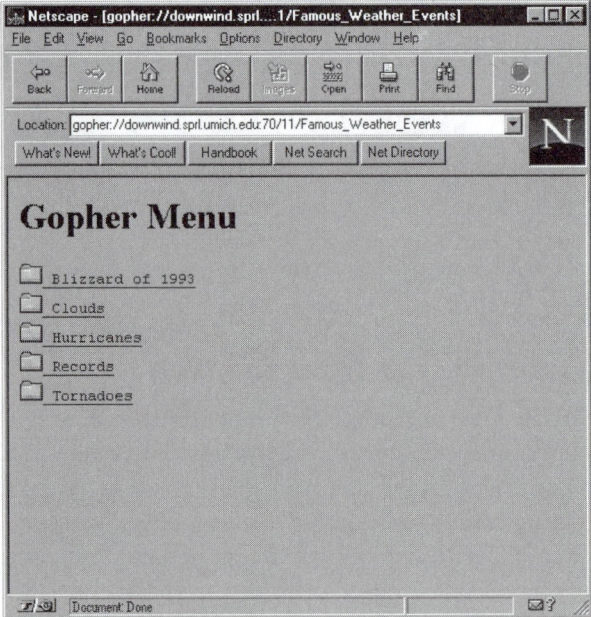

Figure 3-11: Directory of links using the gopher service

Nowadays, gopher is no longer fashionable, but it is still a good workhorse for information storage, and many information providers still support it. For example, the University of Michigan has a gopher site for weather reports at

```
gopher://downwind.sprl.umich.edu.
```

Go to the subdirectory:

```
Weather_Text/U.S._City_Forecasts.
```

Then, select a state subdirectory, then a city subdirectory. You will get an up-to-date weather report like that shown in Figure 3-13.

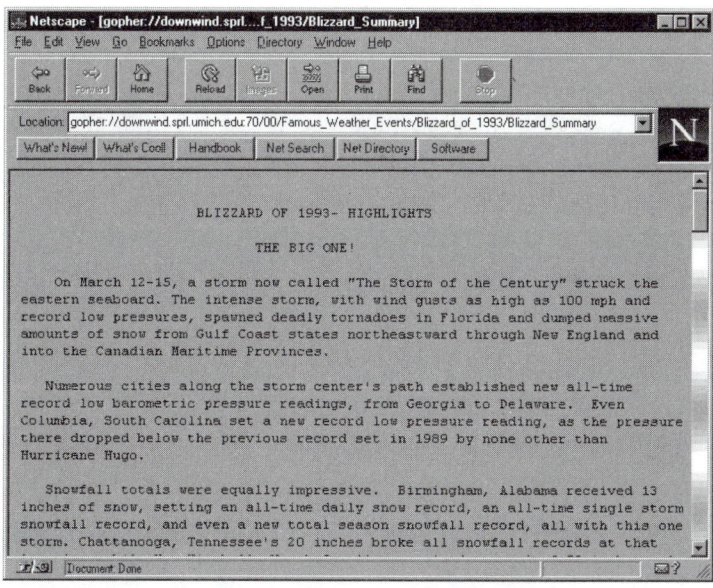

Figure 3-12: Text screen using the gopher service

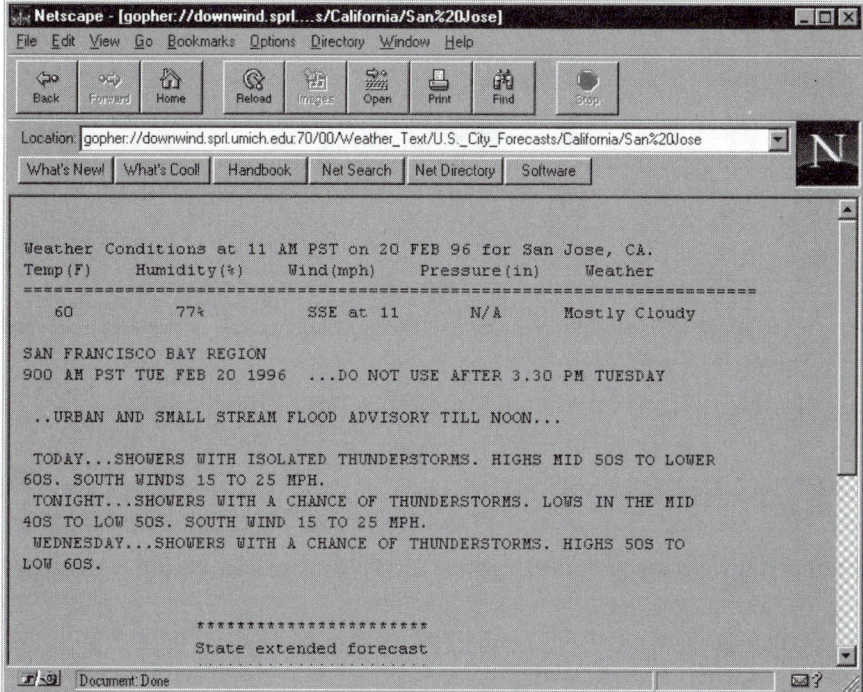

Figure 3-13: The weather forecast with gopher

We will build an applet that wraps a friendlier user interface around this information. The list box on the left contains the list of all states. You double-click on a state. Then, the applet shows a list of cities in the list box on the right. When you double-click on a city, the text window in Figure 3-14 fills with the weather report.

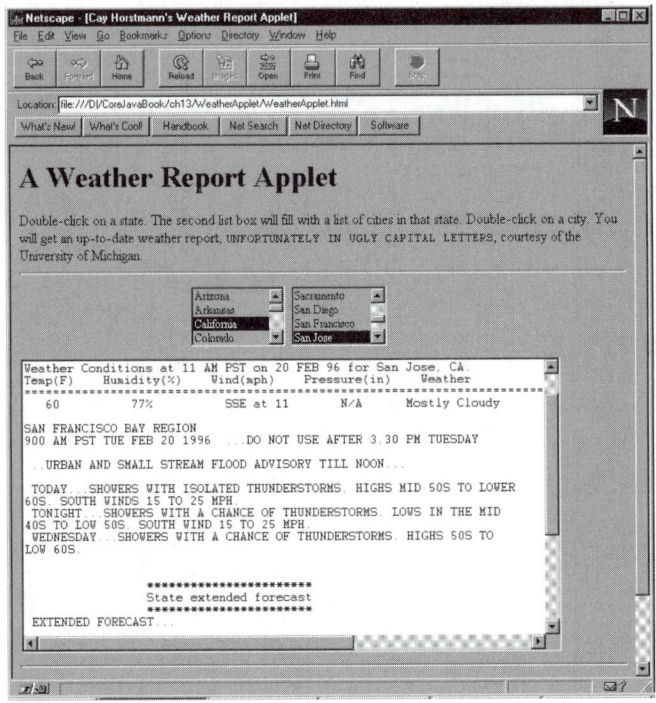

Figure 3-14: The weather report applet

Connecting to a Gopher Site

The next step to get our applet running is to connect to the University of Michigan gopher site. Unfortunately, the obvious method does not work.

If you try

```
URL url = new URL("gopher://downwind.sprl.umich.edu");
```

you will get a `MalformedURLException`. Actually, there is nothing malformed about this URL. The current release of Java does not implement the gopher protocol (the Sun programmers probably just ran out of time). Gopher is an easy protocol, and we will implement it manually, which will be a good learning experience, anyway.

By convention, the gopher service uses port number 70. When a client connects to the gopher port, the client simply sends the desired path of the directory. The server sends back the content of that directory, which is either another directory or a text file.

Try it out: Use telnet to connect to port 70 of a host running the gopher service, such as `downwind.sprl.umich.edu`. Then type `/`. You will get a listing of the root directory. Then the server disconnects automatically. You need to reconnect to get more information. The http server that serves Web pages works the same way. The browser can retrieve one piece of information; then, it must reconnect to get more data.

We can easily program this reconnection in Java.

```
Socket s = new Socket("downwind.sprl.umich.edu", 70);
BufferedReader in = new BufferedReader
   (new InputStreamReader(s.getInputStream()));
PrintWriter out = new PrintWriter(s.getOutputStream());
out.println("/");
String rdata = "";
String line;
while ((line = in.readLine()) != null)
   rdata += line + "\n";
```

Here is a sample listing of the gopher directory:

```
0Information         0/info.txt      turkey.acme.com    70
1Software            1/software      turkey.acme.com    70
8Stock_information                   scrooge.acme.com   3000
1Movies              1/movie_text    turkey.acme.com    70
```

The listing has a special structure. There are four columns: one for the title, one for the file, one for the host address, and one for the port number. Lines starting with 0 denote links to text files. Lines starting with 1 denote links to other directories. Lines starting with 8 denote links to other gopher sites.

In our weather applet, we use the following strategy: When the user clicks on a state, say, California, we connect to the gopher site and request the directory

```
/Weather_Text/U.S._City_Forecasts/California
```

That directory contains subdirectories for the cities in California for which a weather report is available. The applet reads that file through the stream obtained from the socket. It parses the directory information by stripping off the 1 denoting a directory. Then, it fills a list box with the values that it obtained.

```
String query = "/Weather_Text/U.S._City_Forecasts" + "/" +
   state;
out.println(query);
String line;
while ((line = in.readLine()) != null)
```

```
{ int i = line.indexOf("O/", 1); // start of second column
   if (i >= 0)
   {   String t = line.substring(1, i).trim();
       city.addItem(t); // add to list box
   }
}
```

Finally, when the user of the applet clicks on the city, we connect again to the server, append the name of the city, and ask for a path, such as:

```
/Weather_Text/U.S._City_Forecasts/California/San+Jose
```

We read and display the resulting text file, which is our weather report.

```
String query = "/Weather_Text/U.S._City_Forecasts" + "/" +
   state + "/" + city;
out.println(query);
String line;
while ((line = in.readLine()) != null)
{   weather.appendText(line + "\n");
}
```

Example 3-8 gives the full source code.

Example 3-8: WeatherApplet.java

```
import java.net.*;
import java.io.*;
import java.awt.*;
import java.awt.event.*;
import java.applet.*;

public class WeatherApplet extends Applet
   implements ActionListener
{  public void init()
   {   setLayout(new BorderLayout());

      state = new List(4, false);
      city = new List(4, false);
      state.addItem("Alabama");
      state.addItem("Alaska");
      state.addItem("Arizona");
      state.addItem("Arkansas");
      state.addItem("California");
      state.addItem("Colorado");
      state.addItem("Connecticut");
      state.addItem("Delaware");
      state.addItem("Florida");
      state.addItem("Georgia");
      state.addItem("Hawaii");
      state.addItem("Idaho");
      state.addItem("Illinois");
      state.addItem("Indiana");
```

```
        state.addItem("Iowa");
        state.addItem("Kansas");
        state.addItem("Kentucky");
        state.addItem("Lousisiana");
        state.addItem("Maine");
        state.addItem("Maryland");
        state.addItem("Massachusetts");
        state.addItem("Michigan");
        state.addItem("Minnesota");
        state.addItem("Mississippi");
        state.addItem("Missouri");
        state.addItem("Montana");
        state.addItem("Nebraska");
        state.addItem("Nevada");
        state.addItem("New_Hampshire");
        state.addItem("New_Jersey");
        state.addItem("New_Mexico");
        state.addItem("New_York");
        state.addItem("North_Carolina");
        state.addItem("North_Dakota");
        state.addItem("Ohio");
        state.addItem("Oklahoma");
        state.addItem("Oregon");
        state.addItem("Pennsylvania");
        state.addItem("Rhode_Island");
        state.addItem("South_Carolina");
        state.addItem("South_Dakota");
        state.addItem("Tennessee");
        state.addItem("Texas");
        state.addItem("Utah");
        state.addItem("Vermont");
        state.addItem("Virginia");
        state.addItem("Washington");
        state.addItem("West_Virginia");
        state.addItem("Wisconsin");
        state.addItem("Wyoming");

        Panel p = new Panel();
        p.add(state);
        p.add(city);
        state.addActionListener(this);
        city.addActionListener(this);

        add(p, "North");
        weather = new TextArea();
        weather.setFont(new Font("Monospaced", Font.PLAIN, 12));
        weather.setText("Double-click on a state!");
        add(weather, "Center");
    }
```

```java
public void actionPerformed(ActionEvent evt)
{   if (evt.getSource().equals(state))
    {   showStatus("Please wait...getting list of cities");
        weather.setText("");
        getCities(state.getSelectedItem());
        showStatus("Double-click on a city!");
    }
    else if (evt.getSource().equals(city))
    {   showStatus
            ("Please wait...getting weather information");
        weather.setText("");
        getWeather(state.getSelectedItem(),
            city.getSelectedItem());
        showStatus("Double-click on a state or city!");
    }
}

public void getCities(String state)
{   try
    {   String query = "gopher://downwind.sprl.umich.edu"
            + "/Weather_Text/U.S._City_Forecasts/" + state;
        URL s = new URL(server + script + "?" + query);
        BufferedReader in = new BufferedReader
            (new InputStreamReader(s.openStream()));

        city.removeAll();
        int ch;
        boolean more = true;
        while (more)
        {   String str = in.readLine();
            if (str != null)
            {   int i = str.indexOf('0', 1);
                if (i >= 0)
                {   String t = str.substring(1, i).trim();
                    city.addItem(t);
                }
            }
            else more = false;
        }
    }
    catch(IOException e)
    {   showStatus("Error " + e);
    }
}
```

```java
public void getWeather(String state, String city)
{   String r = new String();
    try
    {   String query = "gopher://downwind.sprl.umich.edu"
            + "/Weather_Text/U.S._City_Forecasts/" + state
            + "/" + replaceAll(city, " ", "%20");
        URL s = new URL(server + script + "?" + query);
        BufferedReader in = new BufferedReader
            (new InputStreamReader(s.openStream()));

        boolean more = true;
        while (more)
        {   String str = in.readLine();
            if (str != null)
                weather.append(str + "\n");
            else more = false;
        }
    }
    catch(IOException e)
    {   showStatus("Error " + e);
    }
}

private static String replaceAll(String s, String t,
    String u)
{   String r = "";
    int pos = 0;
    int nextpos;
    while ((nextpos = s.indexOf(t, pos)) >= 0)
    {   r = r + s.substring(pos, nextpos) + u;
        pos = nextpos + t.length();
    }
    r = r + s.substring(pos);
    return r;
}

private String server = "http://www.horstmann.com";
private String script = "/corejava/proxysvr.cgi";
private TextArea weather;
private List city;
private List state;
}
```

- `URL(String spec)`

  creates a `URL` object from an unparsed absolute URL string.

  Parameters: `spec`   the URL string to parse

- `String getHost()`

  returns the host name (for instance, `"java.sun.com"`).

- `String getFile()`

  gets the name of the file to be requested (for instance, `"new.html"`).

- `int getPort()`

  gets the port number. Returns -1 if the port is not set.

- `String getProtocol()`

  gets the protocol name (for instance, `"http"`).

- `InputStream openStream()`

  opens an input stream.

Applet Security

When running the weather report applet locally with appletviewer, the applet works as described. However, if you put the applet on your Web page and have others try to read it with Netscape, it will not work. When they click on a state, the city list box never fills up. This result occurs because of a security restriction in Netscape. You can test this phenomenon locally on your machine. When you load the applet into Netscape 4.0 or Internet Explorer, it will not work. (Netscape 3.0 doesn't apply this security restriction to applets loaded with the `File|Open File` command, so the applet will work when loaded locally with Netscape 3.0.)

Web browsers allow an applet to read and write data only on the host that serves the applet. Applets can connect only to sockets on the computer from which the applet came. This rule is often described as "applets can only phone home."

At first, this restriction seems to make no sense. If you try, you will find that you can use Netscape to browse the gopher URL. (Netscape has no problem with gopher; it is only the Java library that cannot handle the protocol.) So why does Netscape deny the applet what the ambient browser can see? To understand the rationale, it helps to visualize the three hosts involved, as shown in Figure 3-15:

- The originating host—your computer that delivers the Web page and Java applet to clients

- The local host—the user's machine that runs your applet

- The third-party data repository that your applet would like to see

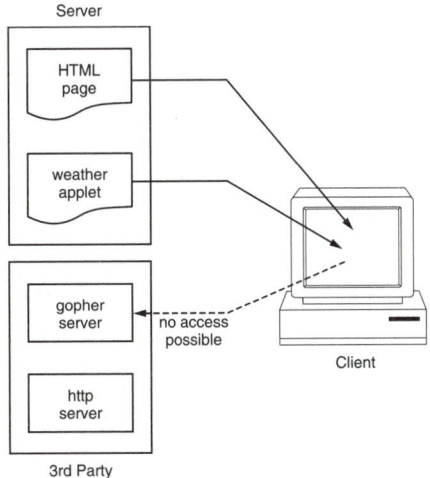

Figure 3-15: Applet security disallows connection to 3rd party

The Netscape security rule says that the applet can read and write data only on
the originating host. Certainly it makes sense that the applet cannot write to the
local host. If it could, it might be able to plant viruses or alter important files.
After all, the applet starts running immediately when the user stumbles upon
our Web page, and the user must be protected from damage by malicious or
incompetent applets.

It also makes sense that the applet cannot read from the local host. Otherwise, it
might browse the files on the local computer for sensitive information, such as
credit card numbers, open a socket connection to the applet host, and write the
information back. You might open a great-looking Web page, interact with an
applet that does something fun or useful, and be completely unaware of what
that applet does in other threads. Netscape denies your applet all access to the
files on your computer.

DILBERT reprinted by permission of United Feature Syndicate, Inc.

But why can't the applet read other files from the Web? Isn't the Web a wealth of publicly available information, made available for everyone to read? If you browse the Web from home, through a service provider, this is indeed the situation. But it is quite different when you do your Web surfing in your office (searching only for work-relevant information, of course). Many companies have their computer sitting behind a firewall.

A firewall is a computer that filters traffic going into and out of the corporate network. This computer will deny attempts to access services with less than stellar security histories. For example, there are known security holes in protocols such as anonymous ftp. The firewall might simply disallow anonymous ftp requests or shunt them off to an isolated ftp server. It might also deny a request to access the mail port on all machines except the mail server. Depending on the security philosophy, the firewall (shown in Figure 3-16) can also apply filtering rules to the traffic between the corporate network and the Internet, but that is much more difficult.

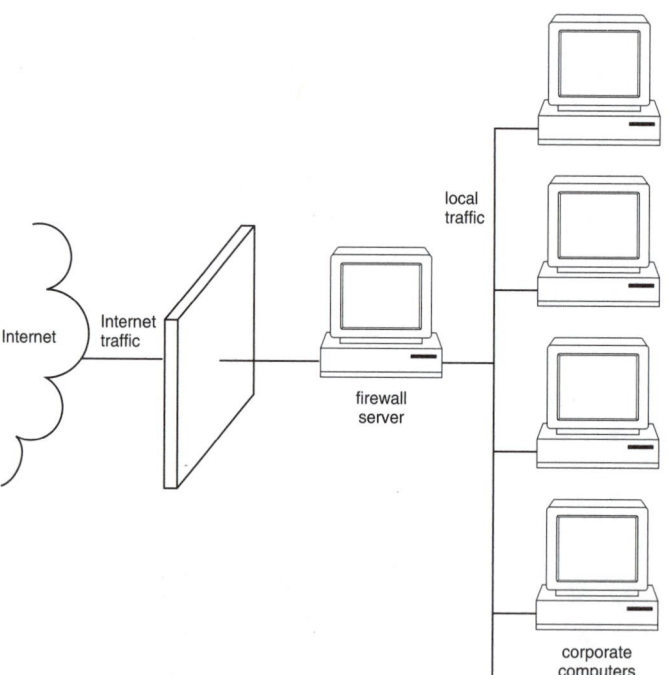

Figure 3-16: A firewall provides security

(If you are interested in this topic, turn to *Firewalls and Internet Security* by William R. Cheswick and Steven M. Bellovin [Addison-Wesley, 1994].)

Having a firewall allows a company to use the Web to distribute internal information that is of interest to employees but should not be accessible outside the company. The company simply sets up a Web server, tells the address only to its employees, and programs the firewall to deny any access requests to that server from the outside. The employees can then browse the internal information with the same Web tools they already know and use.

If an employee visits your Web page, the applet is downloaded into the computer behind the firewall and starts running there. If it were able to read all the Web pages that the ambient browser can read, it would have access to the corporate information. Then, it could open a connection to the host from which it came and send all that private information back. That is obviously insecure. Since Netscape has no idea which Web pages are public and which are confidential, it disallows access to all of them.

That is too bad—you simply cannot write an applet that goes out on the Web, grabs information, processes and formats it, and presents it to the applet user. For example, our weather report applet does not want to write any information back to its host. Why doesn't Netscape let the applet strike a deal? If the applet promises not to write anywhere, it ought to be able to read from everywhere. That way, it would just be a harvester and processor, showing an ephemeral result on the user's screen.

The trouble is that Netscape cannot distinguish *read* from *write* requests. When you ask to open a stream on a URL, this is obviously a read request. Well, maybe not. The URL might be of the form

```
http://www.rogue.com/cgi-bin/cracker.pl?Garys+password+is+Sicily
```

Here, the culprit is the CGI mechanism. It is designed to take arbitrary arguments and process them. The script that handles the CGI request can, and often does, store the request data. It is easy to hide information in a CGI query text. (A data stream that contains hidden information is called a *covert channel* in security circles.)

So, should Netscape disallow all CGI queries and allow access only to plain Web pages? The solution is not that simple. Netscape has no way of knowing that the server to which it connects on port 80 (the http port) is actually a standard http server. It might be just a shell that saves all requests to a file and returns an HTML page: "Sorry, the information you requested is not available." Then, the applet could transmit information by pretending to read from the URL

```
http://www.rogue.com/Garys/password/is/Sicily
```

Since Netscape cannot distinguish read from write requests, it must disallow them both.

To summarize: Applets run on the computer browsing your Web page, but they can access files and sockets only on the computer serving the Web page.

Proxy Servers

How, then, can you distribute an applet that harvests information for your users? You could make a Web page that shows the applet in action with fake data, stored on your server. (This is exactly the approach that Sun takes with their stock-ticker sample applet.) You could then provide a button with which the user downloads the applet. Users would need to load it as a local applet into Netscape or run it from the applet viewer.

That approach will probably greatly limit the attractiveness of your applet. Many people will be too lazy to download and install the applet locally if they did not first get to use it a few times with real data on your Web page.

Fortunately, there is a way to feed the applet real data: install a proxy server on your HTML server. That proxy server is a service, usually installed as a CGI script, that grabs requested information from the Web and sends it to whoever requested it. For example, if you request the URL

```
gopher://downwind.sprl.umich.edu/Weather_Text/U.S._City
    _Forecasts/California/San+Jose
```

from the proxy server, you get the weather report page back through the output channel of the CGI request.

Scripts for this purpose must exist, but we could not find one, so we wrote our own in Java. The idea of the script is simple: it tests whether or not the script is a gopher script. If so, it handles it manually. Otherwise, the script uses the standard Java mechanism to open a URL. It opens the stream, reads the information line by line, and sends it to standard output.

NOTE: The compiled Java application needs to be installed in the `cgi-bin` directory on the Web server. That requires the permission of the system administrator, of course. (If your system administrator does not trust Java or know how to deal with it, try using the Perl script with the same functionality as explained in the sidebar later in this chapter.)

Example 3-9 lists the full code.

Example 3-9: ProxySvr.java

```java
import java.io.*;
import java.net.*;
import corejava.*;

public class ProxySvr
{   public static String urlDecode(String in)
    {   StringBuffer out = new StringBuffer(in.length());
        int i = 0;
```

```
    while (i < in.length())
    {   char ch = in.charAt(i);
        i++;
        if (ch == '+') ch = ' ';
        else if (ch == '%')
        {   ch = (char)(Format.atoi("0x"
                + in.substring(i, i + 2)));
            i++;
        }
        out.append(ch);
    }
    return new String(out);
}

public static void main(String[] args)
{   try
    {   String urlname = urlDecode(args[0]);
        DataInputStream is = null;
        try
        {   URL url = new URL(urlname);
            is = new DataInputStream(url.openStream());
        }
        catch (MalformedURLException e)
        {   // 1.0 release doesn't know Gopher
            int pos = urlname.indexOf("://");

            String protocol = urlname.substring(0, pos);
            if (!protocol.equals("gopher")) throw e;
            pos += 3;
            int pos2 = urlname.indexOf("/", pos);
            if (pos2 < 0) throw e;
            String host = urlname.substring(pos, pos2);
            String file = urlname.substring(pos2);

            Socket t = new Socket(host, 70);
            PrintStream os
                = new PrintStream(t.getOutputStream());

            is = new DataInputStream(t.getInputStream());
            os.print(file + "\r\n");
        }

        System.out.print("Content-type: text/html\n\n");
        boolean more = true;
        while (more)
        {   String str = is.readLine();
            if (str == null) more = false;
            else System.out.println(str);
        }
    }
    catch(Exception e) { System.out.println("Error" + e); }
}
}
```

Most of the code in the `ProxySvr` class should be straightforward. (See Figure 3-17.) The `urlDecode` method does the following:

1. Changes the + signs to spaces

2. Strips out the % sign and formats the digits following it in the correct form

The `main` method assumes that the first argument is the name of the URL. It decodes it by a call to the `urlDecode` method. Then, it tries to open the URL and get a data stream. If we get the `MalformedURLException`, we find out if we are using the gopher protocol by searching for the text before the `'//'`. If we don't detect the string `'gopher'`, we rethrow the exception. Otherwise, we open a new socket for the gopher site and collect the needed information.

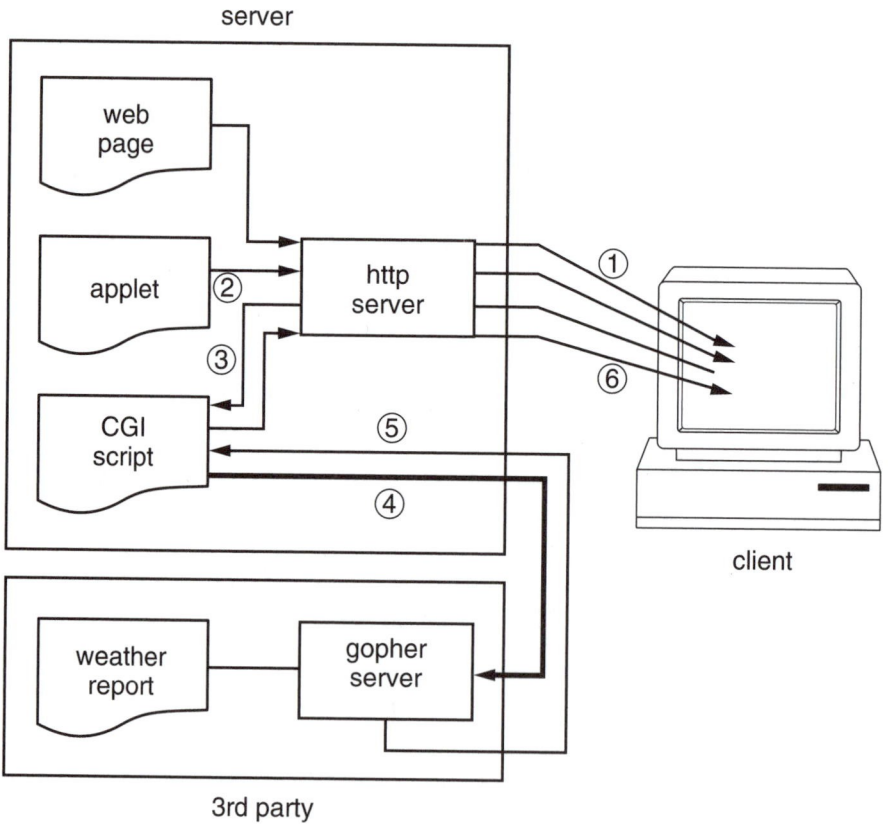

Figure 3-17: Data flow in the weather report applet

In our specific case, the `WeatherApplet` requests the information from the proxy server on its local host, which goes out to the University of Michigan, gets the data, and feeds it back.

This looks like a lot of trouble, but we have avoided any security risk. Now the applet can access all data that is publicly available from our host but none of the private data behind the firewall.

Instead, the monkey is on *our* back. By installing the `proxysvr` script on our `cgi-bin` directory, other users at our site could write applets that allow the downloading of our confidential files. Mercifully, in the case of our computer science department server, that was not a problem.

Note that your applet cannot use our proxy server—it can only access services on its host. If you want to write applications like this one, you need to install this script, or a similar mechanism, on your host.

Does it make sense to have the server merely grab the information and reflect it to the applet? In this case, it does, but in general, it might make sense for the server to cache it, thus improving performance when there are multiple requests, or even to preprocess the information.

In our case, caching was not useful because weather reports change frequently. And we had a difficult enough time installing a simple reflector on the server's `cgi-bin` directory. Had the script done some real processing, it would have taken longer to have it audited against security risks.

Comparing Java, C, and Perl for CGI Scripts

CGI scripts can be written in any language that can read from standard input and write to standard output. We first wrote the proxy server script in C because we did not realize that Perl can connect to sockets and because Java is not installed in the http server we used.

The Perl and C codes are listed in Examples 3-10 and 3-11. As you can see, the C code is much longer than the corresponding Java code. Even the most elementary operations (for example, reading a line of input) must be programmed in gory detail in C. Most of the code is completely routine. We modified a sample program from *Unix Network Programming*, by W. Richard Stevens (Prentice-Hall, 1990). It wasn't difficult to write the program, only tedious.

The Perl code is much shorter, but, as you can see by glancing at it, is completely unreadable to the uninitiated, with its charming variable names like $! and $|. Consider, for example, the statement

```
$url =~ s/%([a-fA-F0-9][a-fA-F0-9])/pack("C", hex($1))/eg;
```

This means "replace all strings of the form '% followed by two hex digits' by the corresponding hex value." (No, we didn't come up with that ourselves. We copied it from another script.) The remainder of the program is a modification of an example from *Programming Perl,* by Larry Wall and Randal L. Schwarz, (O'Reilly, 1991). We don't pretend to understand the details, but it works.

Neither C nor Perl can automatically handle URLs. Both programs split the URL into service, host, and file. They handle only gopher and http at the standard port numbers, 70 and 80. They open the connection and send the name of the requested file (gopher) or GET followed by the file name (http). Then, they grab the output, a line at a time, and send it to standard output.

As a result of this experiment, we can heartily recommend Java as a great language for writing CGI scripts. The network programming interface and string handling beats the daylights out of C, and the Java code is more readable and more easily maintained than the equivalent Perl code. (Of course, there is one added complication: Java class files may not be executable on your platform. If they are not, you will need some sort of shell script to execute the class file.

Example 3-10: proxysvr.c

```c
#include <netdb.h>
#include <sys/types.h>
#include <sys/socket.h>
#include <netinet/in.h>
#include <arpa/inet.h>
#include <stdio.h>
#include <string.h>
#include <stdlib.h>

#define MAXLINE 512
#define MAXNAME 128
#define HTTP 80
#define GOPHER 70

unsigned writen(fd, vptr, n)
int fd;
char* vptr;
unsigned n;
{   unsigned nleft;
    unsigned nwritten;
    char* ptr;

    ptr = (char*)vptr;
    nleft = n;
    while (nleft > 0)
    {   if ((nwritten = write(fd, ptr, nleft)) <= 0)
            return nwritten;
```

```
        nleft -= nwritten;
        ptr += nwritten;
    }
    return n - nleft;
}

unsigned readline(fd, vptr, maxlen)
int fd;
char* vptr;
int maxlen;
{   unsigned n;
    unsigned rc;
    char* ptr;
    char c;

    ptr = vptr;
    for (n = 1; n < maxlen; n++)
    {   if ((rc = read(fd, &c, 1)) == 1)
        {   *ptr++ = c;
            if (c == '\n')
            {   *ptr = 0;
                return n;
            }
        }
        else if (rc == 0)
        {   if (n == 1) return 0;
            else
            {   *ptr = 0;
                return n;
            }
        }
        else
            return -1;
    }
    *ptr = 0;
    return n;
}

void error(msg)
char* msg;
{   fputs(msg, stderr);
    fputc('\n', stderr);
    exit(1);
}

void url_decode(in, out, outlen)
char* in;
char* out;
```

```c
int outlen;
{   int i = 0;
    int j = 0;
    while (in[i] != '\0' && j < outlen - 1)
    {   if (in[i] == '+') out[j] = ' ';
        else if (in[i] == '%')
        {   int ch;
            sscanf(in + i + 1, "%x", &ch);
            out[j] = ch;
            i += 2;
        }
        else out[j] = in[i];
        i++;
        j++;
    }
    out[j] = 0;
}

int main(argc, argv)
int argc;
char** argv;
{   int sockfd;
    struct sockaddr_in serv_addr;
    int i;
    int n;
    char* name;
    struct hostent* hostptr;
    char url[MAXLINE + 1];
    char sendline[MAXLINE + 1];
    char recvline[MAXLINE + 1];
    char server_name[MAXNAME];
    char file_name[MAXLINE];
    char service_name[MAXNAME];
    int port;
    int service = 0;
    char* p;
    char* q;

    url_decode(argv[1], url, sizeof(url));

    p = strstr(url, "://");
    if (p == NULL)
        error("Sorry--can only recognize service://server/file");
    strncpy(service_name, url, p - url);
    service_name[p - url] = 0;
    if (strcmp(service_name, "http") == 0)
        service = HTTP;
    else if (strcmp(service_name, "gopher") == 0)
```

```
      service = GOPHER;
   else
      error("Sorry--can only recognize http and gopher");
   p += 3;
   q = strchr(p, '/');
   if (q == NULL)
      error("Sorry--can only recognize service://server/file");
   strncpy(server_name, p, q - p);
   server_name[q - p] = '\0';
   strncpy(file_name, q, sizeof(file_name) - 1);
   file_name[sizeof(file_name) - 1] = '\0';
   port = service;

   if ((sockfd = socket(PF_INET, SOCK_STREAM, 0)) < 0)
      error("Can't open stream socket");

   bzero((char*)&serv_addr, sizeof(serv_addr));
   serv_addr.sin_family = AF_INET;
   hostptr = gethostbyname(server_name);
   if (hostptr == 0) error("Can't find host");
   name = inet_ntoa(*(struct in_addr*)*hostptr->h_addr_list);
   serv_addr.sin_addr.s_addr = inet_addr(name);
   serv_addr.sin_port = htons(port);

   if (connect(sockfd, (struct sockaddr*)&serv_addr,
      sizeof(serv_addr)) < 0)
      error("Can't connect to server");

   sendline[sizeof(sendline) - 1] = 0;
   if (service == GOPHER)
      strncpy(sendline, file_name, sizeof(sendline) - 1);
   else if (service == HTTP)
   {  strcpy(sendline, "GET ");
      strncat(sendline, file_name, sizeof(sendline) - 1
         - strlen(sendline));
   }
   strncat(sendline, "\r\n", sizeof(sendline) - 1
      - strlen(sendline));

   n = strlen(sendline);
   if (writen(sockfd, sendline, n) != n)
      error("Write error on socket");

   fputs("Content-type: text/html\n\n", stdout);

   do
   {  n = readline(sockfd, recvline, MAXLINE);
      if (n < 0)
```

```
            error("Read error on socket");
        else if (n > 0)
        {   recvline[n] = 0;
            fputs(recvline, stdout);
        }
    } while (n > 0);

    return 0;
}
```

Example 3-11: proxysvr.pl

```
($url) = @ARGV;

$url =~ tr/+/ /;
$url =~ s/%([a-fA-F0-9][a-fA-F0-9])/pack("C", hex($1))/eg;

$pos = index($url, "://");

if ($pos < 0)
{   die "Sorry--can only recognize service://server/file";
}

$service_name = substr($url, 0, $pos);

if ($service_name eq "http")
{   $port = 80;
}
elsif ($service_name eq "gopher")
{   $port = 70;
}
else
{   die "Sorry--can only recognize http and gopher";
}

$pos += 3;
$pos2 = index($url, "/", $pos);
if ($pos2 < 0)
{   die "Sorry--can only recognize service://server/file";
}

$server_name = substr($url, $pos, $pos2 - $pos);
$file_name = substr($url, $pos2);
$AF_INET = 2;
$SOCK_STREAM =1;

$sockaddr = 'S n a4 x8';
```

```
($name, $aliases, $proto) = getprotobyname ('tcp');
($name,$aliases,$type,$len,$thataddr)
    = gethostbyname($server_name);
$that = pack($sockaddr, $AF_INET, $port, $thataddr);

if (!socket (S, $AF_INET, $SOCK_STREAM, $proto))
{  die $!;
}

if (!connect (S, $that))
{  die $!;
}

select(S); $|=1; select(STDOUT);

if ($service_name eq "http")
{  $command = "GET ".$file_name;
}
elsif ($service_name eq "gopher")
{   $command = $file_name;
}

print S $command."\r\n";

print "Content-type: text/html\n\n";
while (<S>)
{  print;
}
```

NOTE: The current interface between client- and server-side computing is still quite immature. Just as Sun is working on a seamless database connectivity interface, it and other vendors are working to make the interaction between applets and their host more standardized and convenient. When this happens, information-harvesting applets will become ubiquitous. They will perform computation, formatting, and presentation locally and will interact with servers that perform data retrieval and caching.

CHAPTER

4

- Structured Query Language

- Installing JDBC

- Basic JDBC Programming Concepts

- Populating a Database

- Executing Queries

- Metadata

Database Connectivity: JDBC

I n the summer of 1996, Sun released the first version of the JDBC (Java database connectivity) kit. This package lets Java programmers connect to a database, query it, or update it, using the industry standard query language. We think this is one of the most important developments in Java programming. It is not just that databases are among the most common use of hardware and software today. After all, there are a lot of products running after this market; so why do we think Java has the potential to make a big splash? The reason we think that Java and JDBC have an essential advantage over other database programming environments is this:

- Programs developed with Java and the JDBC are platform independent and vendor independent.

The same Java database program can run on a PC, a workstation, or a Java-powered terminal ("network computer"). You can move your data from one database to another, for example, from Microsoft SQL Server to Oracle, and the same program can still read your data. This is in sharp contrast to the database programming typically done on personal computers today. It is all too common that one writes database applications in a proprietary database language, using a database management system that is available only from a single vendor. The result is that you can run the resulting application only on one or two platforms. We believe that *because of their universality,* Java and JDBC will eventually replace proprietary database languages, such as Borland's PAL, or the various incompatible BASIC derivatives used by vendors such as Powersoft, Oracle, and Microsoft for accessing databases.

Having said this, we still must caution you that the JDK offers no tools for database programming with Java. We are only beginning to see the form designers,

query builders, and report generators that database developers have come to expect. Similarly, there are only beginning to appear the kinds of database controls that you find for Visual Basic or Delphi. However, we are confident that many more tools will be released in the near future. Judging from the C++ marketplace, it is likely that all "corporate" or "professional" versions of Java development environments will ship with database integration tools (such as the currently available Visual Café and JBuilder Professional and Enterprise editions).

In this chapter, we:

- Explain some of the ideas behind JDBC—the "Java database connectivity API"

- Give you enough details and examples so that you can get started in actually using JDBC

The first part of this chapter gives you an overview of how JDBC is put together. The last part gives you example code that illustrates the major JDBC features.

NOTE: Over the years, many technologies were invented to make database access more efficient and failsafe. Standard databases support indexes, triggers, stored procedures, and transaction management. JDBC supports all these features, but we do not discuss them in this chapter. One could write an entire book on advanced database programming in Java, and (many) such books are or will be written. The material in this chapter will give you enough information to effectively deal with a departmental database in Java and to make it easy to go further with the JDBC if you want to.

The Design of JDBC

From the start, the people at JavaSoft were aware of the potential Java showed for working with databases. They began working on extending Java to deal with SQL access to databases roughly as soon as the JDK went into beta testing. (They started working in November 1995.) What they first hoped to do was to extend Java so that it could talk to any random database, using only "pure" Java. It didn't take them very long to realize that this is an impossible task: there are simply too many databases out there, utilizing too many protocols. Moreover, while database vendors were all in favor of JavaSoft providing a standard network protocol for database access, they were only in favor of it if JavaSoft decided to use *their* network protocol.

What all the database vendors and tool vendors *did* agree on was that it would be useful if JavaSoft provided a purely Java API for SQL access *along* with a

device manager to allow third-party drivers to connect to specific databases. Database vendors could provide their own drivers to plug into the driver manager. There would then be a simple mechanism for registering third-party drivers with the device manager—the point being that all they needed to do was follow the requirements laid out in the device manager API.

After a fairly long period of public discussion, the API for database access became the JDBC API, and the rules for writing device drives were encapsulated in the JDBC driver API. (The JDBC driver API is of interest only to database vendors and database tool providers; we don't cover it here.)

This protocol follows the very successful model of Microsoft's ODBC, which provided a C-programming language interface to *structured query language* (SQL), which is the standard for accessing relational databases. Both the JDBC and ODBC, in turn, are based on the X/Open SQL call-level interface specification. In the end, the idea behind the JDBC is the same as with ODBC: Programs written using the JDBC API would talk to the JDBC driver manager, which, in turn, would use the drivers that were plugged into it at that moment to talk to the actual database.

NOTE: A list of JDBC drivers currently available can be found at:
    http://splash.javasoft.com/jdbc/jdbc.drivers.html

More precisely, the JDBC consists of two layers. The top layer is the JDBC API. This API communicates with the JDBC manager driver API, sending it the various SQL statements. The manager should (transparently to the programmer) communicate with the various third-party drivers that actually connect to the database and return the information from the query or perform the action specified by the query.

NOTE: The JDBC specification will actually allow you to pass any string to the underlying driver. The driver can pass this string to the database. This feature allows you to use specialized versions of SQL that may be supported by the driver and its associated database.

All this means the Java/JDBC layer is all that most programmers will ever have to deal with. Figure 4-1 illustrates what happens.

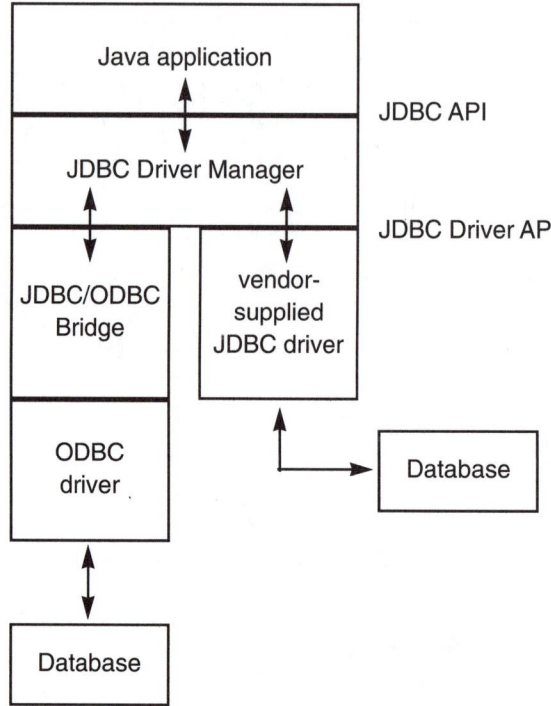

Figure 4-1: JDBC-to-database communication path

In summary, the ultimate goal of the JDBC is to make possible the following:

- Programmers can write applications in Java to access any database, using standard SQL statements—or even specialized extensions of SQL—while still following Java language conventions. (JavaSoft insists that all JDBC drivers support at least the entry-level version of SQL 92.)

- Database vendors and database tool vendors can supply the low-level drivers. Thus, they can optimize their drivers for their specific situation.

NOTE: If you are curious as to why JavaSoft just didn't adopt the ODBC model, their response, as given at the JavaOne Conference in May 1996, was:

- ODBC is hard to learn.
- ODBC has a few commands with lots of complex options. The Java style is to have simple and intuitive methods, but to have lots of them.
- ODBC relies on the multiple use of `void*` pointers and other C features that are not natural in Java.
- It was felt to be too hard to map ODBC to Java because of the frequent use of multiple pointers and pointer indirection.

Typical Uses of the JDBC

Just as one can use Java for both applications and applets, one can use the JDBC-enhanced version of Java in both applications and applets. When that version is used in an applet, all the normal security restrictions apply. The JDBC continues to assume that all Java applets are untrusted.

In particular, applets that use JDBC would only be able to open a database connection from the server from which they are downloaded. They can make neither explicit nor implicit use of local information. Although the JDBC extensions of the Java security model allow one to download a JDBC driver and register it with JDBC device manager on the server, that driver can be used only for connections from the same server the applet came from. That means the Web server and the database server must be the same machine, which is not a typical setup. Of course, the Web server can have a proxy service that routes database traffic to another machine. When signed Java applets become possible, this restriction could be loosened. To summarize: You can use JDBC with applets, but you must manage the server carefully.

Applications, on the other hand, have complete freedom. They can give the application total access to files and remote servers. We envision that JDBC applications will be very common.

Finally, there is a third possible use for the JDBC-enhanced version of Java. This possibility is somewhat speculative, and we do not give any examples of it here. But the thinking at JavaSoft is that this will be an important area in the future, so we want to briefly mention it. The idea is sometimes referred to as the "three tier model," meaning that a Java application (or applet) calls on a middleware layer that in turn accesses the data. This approach would work best with RMI (see Chapter 5) or an object request broker for the communication between the client and the middle layer, with JDBC between the middle tier and a back-end database. Especially through the use of better compilation techniques (just-in-time compilers and native compilers), Java is becoming fast enough that it can be used to write the middleware layer. (You might want to check out `www.weblogic.com` to see more on one company's implementation of this idea.)

Structured Query Language

JDBC is an interface to SQL, which is the interface to essentially all modern relational databases. Desktop databases usually have a graphical user interface that lets users manipulate the data directly, but server-based databases are accessed purely through SQL. Most desktop databases have an SQL interface as well, but it often does not support the full range of ANSI SQL92 features, the current standard for SQL.

The JDBC package can be thought of as nothing more than an application programming interface (API) for communicating SQL statements to databases. We will give a short introduction to SQL in this section. If you have never seen SQL before, you may not find this material sufficient. If so, you should turn to one of the many books on the topic. (One online book service lists 123 books on SQL, ranging from the expected *SQL for Dummies* to one titled (we kid you not) *SQL for Smarties*—which is actually not a bad book.) We recommend *Client/Server Databases,* by James Martin and Joe Leben [Prentice-Hall, 1995], or the venerable and opinionated book *A Guide to the SQL Standard,* by C.J. Date [Addison-Wesley, 1996].

A modern relational database can be thought of as a bunch of named tables with rows and columns that can be joined on certain common columns. The rows contain the actual data (these are usually called *records*). The column headers in each table correspond to the field names.

Figure 4-2 shows a sample table that contains a set of books on HTML that is adopted from a useful, essentially complete, list of HTML books maintained by Cye H. Waldman at `http://wwwiz.com/books/`.

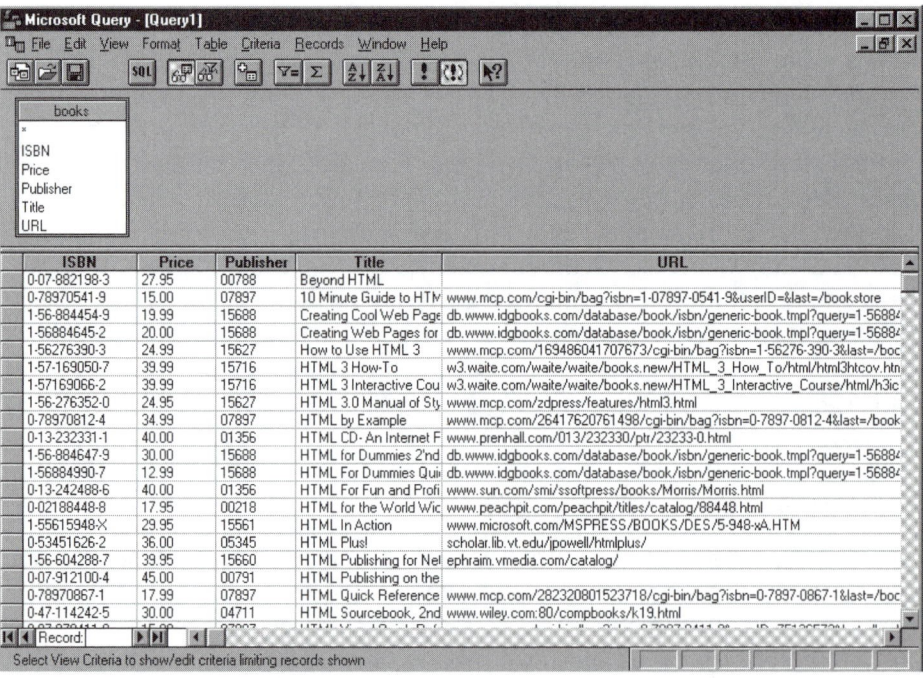

Figure 4-2: Sample table containing the HTML books

Figure 4-3 shows the result of linking this table with a table of publishers. Both the book table and the publisher table contain a numerical code for the publisher. The publisher table contains the publisher's name and Web page URL. When we link both tables on the publisher code, we obtain a *query result*. Each row in the result contains the information about a book, together with the publisher name and Web page URL. Note that the publisher names and URLs are duplicated across several rows since we have several rows with the same publisher.

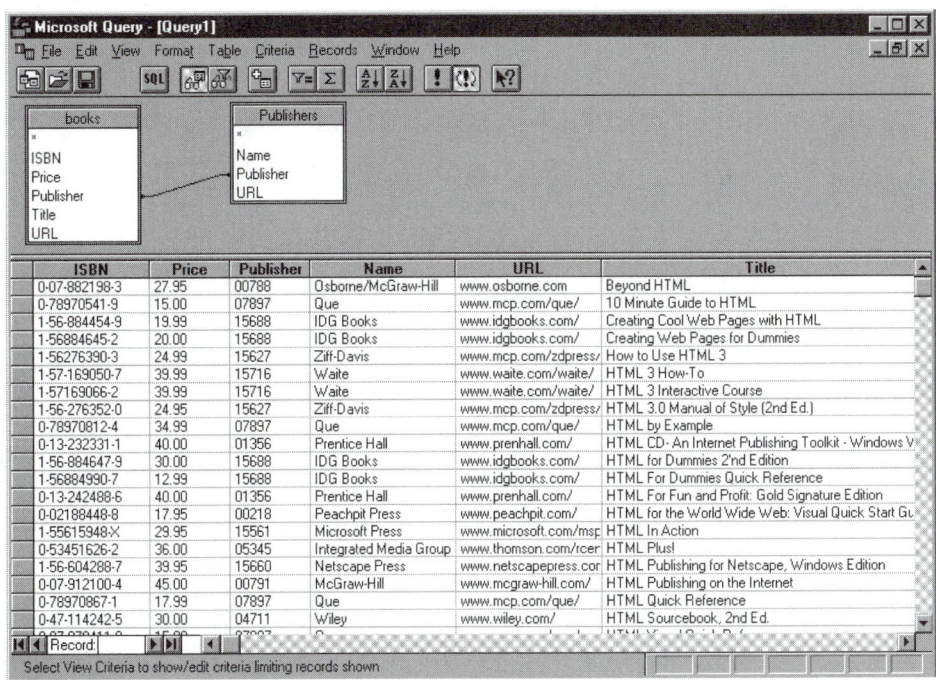

Figure 4-3: Two tables linked together

The benefit of using a relational database and the linking strategy for queries is to avoid unnecessary duplication of data in the database tables. For example, a native database design might have had columns for the publisher name and URL right in the book table. But then the database itself, and not just the query result, would have many duplicates of these entries. If a publisher's Web address changed, *all* entries would need to be updated. Clearly, this is somewhat error prone. In the relational model, we distribute data into multiple tables such that no information is ever unnecessarily duplicated. For example, each publisher URL is contained only once in the publisher table. If the information needs to be combined, then the tables are joined.

In this example, we used the Microsoft Query tool to inspect and link the tables. Microsoft Query is a part of Microsoft Office, so if you have Office, you already have a copy. Many other vendors have similar tools. Microsoft Query is a graphical tool that lets us express queries in a simple form by connecting column names and filling information into forms. Such tools are often called *query by example* (QBE) tools. In contrast, a query that uses SQL is written out in text, using the SQL syntax. For example:

```
SELECT Books.ISBN, Books.Price, Books.Title,
    Books.Publisher_Id,    Publishers.Name, Publishers.URL
FROM Books, Publishers
WHERE Books.Publisher_Id = Publishers.Publisher_Id
```

This is a complex query. In the remainder of this section, we will learn how to write such queries. If you are already familiar with SQL, just skip this section.

By convention, SQL keywords are written in all caps, although this is not necessary.

The SELECT operation is quite flexible. You can simply select all elements in the Books table with the following query:

```
SELECT * FROM Books
```

The FROM statement is required in every SQL SELECT statement. The FROM clause tells the database which tables to examine to find the data.

You can choose the columns that you want.

```
SELECT ISBN, Price, Title,
FROM Books
```

You can restrict the rows in the answer with the WHERE clause.

```
SELECT ISBN, Price, Title,
FROM Books
WHERE Price <= 29.95
```

Be careful with the "equals" comparison. SQL uses = and <>, not == or != , as in Java, for equality testing.

The WHERE clause can also use pattern matching, using the LIKE operator. The wildcard characters are not the usual * and ?, however. Use a % for zero or more characters and an underscore for a single character. For example:

```
SELECT ISBN, Price, Title,
FROM Books
WHERE Title NOT LIKE '%HTML%'
```

Note that strings are enclosed in single quotes, not double quotes. A single quote inside a string is denoted as a pair of single quotes. For example,

```
SELECT Title,
FROM Books
WHERE Books.Title LIKE '%''%'
```

reports all titles that contain a single quote.

You can select data from multiple tables.

```
SELECT * FROM Books, Publishers
```

Without a WHERE clause, this query is not very interesting. It lists *all combinations* of rows from both tables. In our case, where Books has 37 rows and Publishers has 18 rows, the result is a table with 37×18 entries and lots of duplications. We really want to constrain the query to say that we are only interested in *matching* books with their publishers.

```
SELECT * FROM Books, Publishers
WHERE Books.Publisher_Id = Publishers.Publisher_Id
```

This query result has 37 rows, one for each book, since each book has a publisher in the Publisher table.

Whenever you have multiple tables in a query, the same column name can occur in two different places. That happened in our example. There is a publisher code column called Publisher_Id in both the Books and the Publishers table. To resolve ambiguities, you must prefix each column name with the name of the table to which it belongs, such as Books.Publisher_Id.

Now you have seen all SQL constructs that were used in the query at the beginning of this section:

```
SELECT Books.ISBN, Books.Price, Books.Title,
    Books.Publisher_Id,    Publishers.Name, Publishers.URL
FROM Books, Publishers
WHERE Books.Publisher_Id = Publishers.Publisher_Id
```

SQL can be used to change the data inside a database as well, by using so-called *action queries* (i.e., queries that move or change data). For example, suppose you want to reduce by $5.00 the current price of all books that do not have HTML 3 in their title.

```
UPDATE Books
SET Price = Price - 5.00
WHERE Title NOT LIKE '%HTML 3%'
```

Similarly, you can change several fields at the same time by separating the SET clauses with commas. There are many other SQL keywords you can use in an action query. Probably the most important besides UPDATE is DELETE, which allows the query to delete those records that satisfy certain criteria. Finally, SQL comes with built-in functions for taking averages, finding maximums and minimums in a column, and a lot more. Consult a book on SQL for more information.

Of course, before you can query and modify data, you must have a place to store data and you must have the data. There are two SQL statements you need for this purpose. The CREATE TABLE command makes a new table. You specify the name and data type for each column. For example,

```
CREATE TABLE Books
(  Title CHAR(60),
   ISBN CHAR(13),
   Publisher_Id CHAR(5),
   URL CHAR(80),
   Price DECIMAL(6,2)
)
```

Table 4-1 shows the most common SQL data types.

Table 4-1: SQL Data Types

Data Types	Description
INTEGER or INT	typically, a 32-bit integer
SMALLINT	typically, a 16-bit integer
NUMERIC(m,n), DECIMAL(m,n) or DEC(m,n)	fixed-point decimal number with m total digits and n digits after the decimal point
FLOAT(n)	a floating-point number with n binary digits of precision
REAL	typically, a 32-bit floating point number
DOUBLE	typically, a 64-bit floating point number
CHARACTER(n) or CHAR(n)	fixed-length string of length n
VARCHAR(n)	variable-length strings of maximum length n
DATE	calendar date, implementation dependent
TIME	time of day, implementation dependent
TIMESTAMP	date and time of day, implementation dependent

Again, we are not discussing in this book many of the clauses you can add to the CREATE TABLE command that deal with database information, such as keys and constraints.

Typically, to insert values into a table, you use the INSERT statement:

```
INSERT INTO Books
VALUES ('Beyond HTML', '0-07-882198-3', '00788', '', 27.95)
```

You need a separate INSERT statement for every row being inserted in the table unless you embed a SELECT statement inside an INSERT statement. (Consult an SQL book for examples of how to embed a statement.)

Installing JDBC

If you install the software from the CD-ROM, you will already have the JDBC package installed. You can also obtain the newest JDBC version from Sun and combine it with your existing Java installation. Be sure that the version numbers are compatible, and carefully follow the installation directions.

Of course, you need a database program that is compatible with JDBC. You will also need to create a database for your experimental use. We assume you will call this database COREJAVA. Create a new database, or have your database administrator create one with the appropriate permissions. You need to be able to create, update, and drop tables.

Some database vendors already have JDBC drivers, so you may be able to install one, following your vendor's directions. For those databases that do not have a JDBC driver, you need to go a different route. Since ODBC drivers exist for most databases, JavaSoft decided to write (with the help of Intersolv) a JDBC-to-ODBC bridge. To make a connection between such a database and Java, you need to install the database's ODBC driver and the JDBC-to-ODBC bridge.

NOTE: As of this writing, the JDBC to ODBC bridge works only with Solaris and Windows 95/NT. Versions for other platforms are expected to be available at a later date. The bridge does not work with Microsoft J++ 1.x—the Microsoft virtual machine uses a nonstandard native calling convention that is not compatible with the native bridge code.

The JDBC-to-ODBC bridge has the advantage of letting people use the JDBC immediately. It has the disadvantage of requiring yet another layer between the database and the JDBC, although in most cases, performance will be acceptable. Most major vendors have announced plans to come out with native drivers that plug directly into the JDBC driver manager that will give you access to the most popular databases. (For example, Weblogic, which was alluded to earlier, has a few native drivers available.) We suggest you contact your database vendor to find out if (more likely, when) a native JDBC driver will be available for your database. But for experimentation and in most other cases, the bridge works just fine. In this chapter, we developed the examples by using the bridge and a) Microsoft SQL server running on NT Workstation 4.0, b) Microsoft Access running on Windows 95, and c) Borland Interbase running on Windows 95.

If your database doesn't have direct JDBC support, you need to install the ODBC driver for your database. Directions for this vary widely, so consult your database administrator or, if all else fails, the vendor documentation.

> NOTE: Some databases support SQL through a proprietary mechanism, not JDBC. For example, Borland has a BDE engine and Microsoft has a Jet engine that give somewhat better performance than ODBC for local databases. These mechanisms are not compatible with Java. If you are looking in vain for ODBC drivers, you may not have installed or purchased the correct driver.

You then need to make your experimental database into an ODBC data source. In Windows, use the ODBC control in the control panel. Click on Add. You will see a list of available ODBC drivers. Click on the one that contains your new database. Fill out the resulting dialog box with the name of the database and the location of the server. When you are done, you should see your database listed as a data source. (If you create your test database with Microsoft Access, then you need to close the Access database before you can establish an ODBC connection to it.)

If you have Microsoft Query, use it to test your configuration. Start the Query program and make a new query. You will see a list of all data sources. If you see COREJAVA, then your setup is correct. Of course, there are no tables in the database yet. We will see how to use Java to create tables in the next section.

If you have never installed a client/server database before, you may find that setting up the database and the ODBC driver is somewhat complex and that it can be difficult to diagnose the cause for failure. It may be best to seek expert help if your setup is not working correctly. When working with Microsoft SQL Server, we found it to be a real lifesaver to have a book on server and database administration such as *Microsoft BackOffice Administrator Survival Guide*, by Arthur Knowles [Sams Publications, 1996]. The same is undoubtedly true on other platforms as well.

Basic JDBC Programming Concepts

Programming with the JDBC classes is, by design, not very different from programming with the usual Java classes: you build objects from the JDBC core classes, extending them by inheritance if need be. This section takes you through the details.

Database URLs

When connecting to a database, you must specify the data source and you may need to specify additional parameters. For example, network protocol drivers may need a port, and ODBC drivers may need various attributes.

As you might expect, JDBC uses a syntax similar to ordinary Net URLs to describe data sources. Here is an example of the syntax you need:

```
jdbc:odbc:corejava
```

This command would access an ODBC data source named `corejava`, using the JDBC-ODBC bridge. The general syntax is:

```
jdbc:subprotocol name:other_stuff
```

where a subprotocol is the specific driver used by JDBC to connect to the database.

NOTE: JavaSoft has said that it will act as a temporary registry for JDBC subprotocol names. To reserve a subprotocol name, send a message to `jdbc@wombat.eng.sun.com`.

The format for the `other_stuff` parameter depends on the subprotocol used. JavaSoft recommends that if you are using a network address as part of the `other_stuff` parameter, you use the standard URL naming convention of `//hostname:port/other`. For example:

```
jdbc:odbc://whitehouse.gov:5000/Cat;PWD=Hillary
```

would connect to Cat database on port 5000 of whitehouse.gov, using the ODBC attribute value of PWD set to "Hillary."

Making the Connection

The `DriverManager` is the class responsible for loading database drivers and creating a new database connection. You need to load the driver manager code so that your program can use it. For example, to load the JDBC-to-ODBC bridge driver, you use the command

```
Class.forName("sun.jdbc.odbc.JdbcOdbcDriver");
    // force loading of driver
```

If you have a driver from another vendor, then find out the class name of that driver and load it instead.

For practical programming, you need not be particularly interested in the details of driver management. After loading the driver, you can just open a database connection with the following code:

```
String url = "jdbc:odbc:corejava";
String user = "Cay";
String password = "wombat";
Connection con = DriverManager.getConnection(url,
    user, password);
```

The JDBC manager will try to find a driver than can use the protocol specified in the database URL by iterating through the available drivers currently registered with the device manager.

The connection object you get via a call to `getConnection` lets you use JDBC drives to manage SQL queries. You can execute queries and action statements, commit, or roll back transactions.

Querying with JDBC

To make a query, you first create a `Statement` object. The `Connection` object that you obtained from the call to `DriverManager.getConnection` can create statement objects.

```
Statement stmt = con.createStatement();
```

You can then execute a query simply by using the `executeQuery` object of the `Statement` class and supplying the SQL command for the query as a string. Note that you can use the same `Statement` object for multiple, unrelated queries.

Of course, you are interested in the result of the query. The `executeQuery` object returns an object of type `ResultSet` that you use to walk through the result a row at a time.

```
ResultSet rs = stmt.executeQuery("SELECT * FROM Books")
```

The basic loop for analyzing a result set looks like this:

```
while (rs.next())
{   look at a row of the result set
}
```

When inspecting an individual row, you will want to know the contents of each column. A large number of accessor methods give you this information.

```
String isbn = rs.getString(1);
float price = rs.getDouble("Price");
```

There are accessors for every Java *type*, such as `getString` and `getDouble`. Each accessor has two forms, one that takes a numeric argument and one that takes a string argument. When you supply a numeric argument, you refer to the column with that number. For example, `rs.getString(1)` returns the value of the first column in the current row. (Unlike array indexes, database column numbers start at 1.) When you supply a string argument, you refer to the column in the result set with that name. For example, `rs.getDouble("Price")` returns the

value of the column with name `Price`. Using the numeric argument is a bit more efficient, but the string arguments make the code easier to read and maintain.

Java will make reasonable type conversions when the type of the `get` method doesn't match the type of the column. For example, the call `rs.getString("Price")` yields the price as a string.

NOTE: SQL data types and Java data types are not exactly the same. See Table 4-2 for a listing of the basic SQL data types and their Java equivalents.

Table 4-2: SQL data types and their corresponding Java types

SQL data type	Java data type
`INTEGER` or `INT`	`int`
`SMALLINT`	`short`
`NUMERIC(m,n)`, `DECIMAL(m,n)` or `DEC(m,n)`	`java.sql.Numeric`
`FLOAT(n)`	`double`
`REAL`	`float`
`DOUBLE`	`double`
`CHARACTER(n)` or `CHAR(n)`	`String`
`VARCHAR(n)`	`String`
`DATE`	`java.sql.Date`
`TIME`	`java.sql.Time`
`TIMESTAMP`	`java.sql.Timestamp`

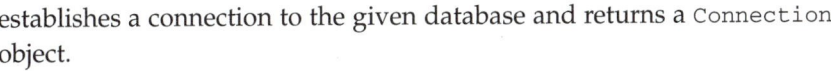

`java.sql.DriverManager`

- `static Connection getConnection(String url, String user, String password)`

  establishes a connection to the given database and returns a `Connection` object.

Parameters:	url	the URL for the database
	user	the database logon ID
	password	the database logon password

java.sql.Connection

- `Statement createStatement()`

  creates a statement object that can be used to execute SQL queries and updates without parameters.

- `void close()`

  immediately closes the current connection.

interface java.sql.Statement

- `ResultSet executeQuery(String sql)`

  executes the SQL statement given in the string and returns a `ResultSet` to view the query result.

  Parameters: sql   the SQL query

- `int executeUpdate(String sql)`

  executes the SQL INSERT, UPDATE, or DELETE statement specified by the string. Also used to execute DDL (Data Definition Language) statements. Returns the number of records affected.

  Parameters: sql   the SQL statement

- `void cancel()`

  cancels a JDBC statement that is being executed by another thread.

java.sql.ResultSet

- `boolean next()`

  makes the current row in the result set move forward by one. Returns `false` after the last row. Note that you must call this method to advance to the first row.

- `Xxx getXxx(int columnNumber)`

- `Xxx getXxx(String columnName)`

  (*Xxx* is a type such as int, `double`, String, Date, etc.)

return the value of the column with column index c or with column names, converted to the specified type. Not all type conversions are legal. See the JDBC documentation for details.

- `int findColumn(String columnName)`

  gives the column index associated with a column name.

- `void close()`

  immediately closes the current result set.

SQLException

Most JDBC methods throw this exception, and you must be prepared to catch it. The following methods give more information about the exceptions.

- `String getSQLState()`

  gets the SQLState formatted, using the X/Open standard.

- `int getErrorCode()`

  gets the vendor-specific exception code.

- `SQLException getNextException()`

  gets the exception chained to this one. It may contain more information about the error.

Populating a Database

We now want to write our first, real, JDBC program. Of course, it would be nice if we could execute some of the fancy queries that we discussed earlier. Unfortunately, we have a problem: right now, there is no data in the database. And you won't find a database file on the CD-ROM that you can simply copy onto your hard disk for the database program to read, because no database file format lets you interchange SQL relational databases from one vendor to another. SQL does not have anything to do with files. It is a language to issue queries and updates to a database. How the database executes these statements most efficiently and what file formats it uses toward that goal is entirely up to the *implementation* of the database. Database vendors try very hard to come up with clever strategies for query optimization and data storage, and different vendors arrive at different mechanisms. Thus, while SQL statements are portable, the underlying data representation is not.

To get around our problem, we provide you with a small set of data in a series of text files. The first program we give reads such a text file and creates a table whose column headings match the first line of the text file and whose column

types match the second line. The remaining lines of the input file are the data, and we insert the lines into the table. Of course, we use SQL statements and JDBC to create the table and insert the data.

At the end of this section, you can see the code for the program that reads a text file and populates a database table. Even if you are not interested in looking at the implementation, you must run this program if you want to execute the more interesting examples in the next two sections. Run the program as follows:

```
java MakeDB Books.txt
java MakeDB Authors.txt
java MakeDB Publishers.txt
java MakeDB BooksAuthors.txt
```

The following steps provide an overview of the program.

1. Connect to the database.

2. If there is no command line, then ask for the input file.

3. Extract the table name from the file by removing the extension of the input file (e.g., `Books.txt` is stored in the table `Books`).

4. Read in the column names, using the `readLine` method that reads a line and splits it into an array of tokens. This is done using the `StringTokenizer` class that you saw in Chapter 1.

5. Read in the column types.

6. Use the `createTable` method to make a string command of the form:

    ```
    CREATE TABLE Name ( Column1 Type1, Column2 Type2, ... )
    ```

7. Pass this string to the `executeUpdate` method:

    ```
    stmt.executeUpdate(command);
    ```

    Here, we use `executeUpdate`, not `executeQuery`, because this statement has no result. (It is a DDL SQL statement.)

8. For each line in the input file, execute an `INSERT` statement, using the `insertInto` method. The only complications are that strings must be surrounded by single quotes and that single quotes inside strings must be duplicated.

9. After all elements have been inserted, run a `SELECT * FROM Name` query, using the `showTable` method to show the result. This method shows that the data has been successfully inserted.

Example 4-1 provides the code for these steps.

Example 4-1: MakeDB.java

```java
import java.net.*;
import java.sql.*;
import java.io.*;
import java.util.*;

class MakeDB
{  public static void main (String args[])
   {  try
      {  Class.forName("sun.jdbc.odbc.JdbcOdbcDriver");
         // force loading of driver
         String url = "jdbc:odbc:corejava";
         String user = "Cay";
         String password = "password";
         Connection con = DriverManager.getConnection(url,
            user, password);
         Statement stmt = con.createStatement();

         String fileName = "";
         if (args.length > 0)
            fileName = args[0];
         else
         {  System.out.println("Enter filename: ");
            fileName = new BufferedReader
               (new InputStreamReader(System.in)).readLine();
         }

         int i = 0;
         while (i < fileName.length()
            && (Character.isLowerCase(fileName.charAt(i))
            || Character.isUpperCase(fileName.charAt(i))))
            i++;
         String tableName = fileName.substring(0, i);

         BufferedReader in = new BufferedReader(new
            FileReader(fileName));
         String[] columnNames = readLine(in);
         String[] columnTypes = readLine(in);
         createTable(stmt, tableName, columnNames,
            columnTypes);
         boolean done = false;
         while (!done)
         {  String[] values = readLine(in);
            if (values.length == 0) done = true;
            else insertInto(stmt, tableName,
               columnTypes, values);
         }
```

```
        showTable(stmt, tableName, columnNames.length);
        stmt.close();
        con.close();
     }
     catch (SQLException ex)
     {   System.out.println ("SQLException:");
         while (ex != null)
         {   System.out.println ("SQLState: "
                 + ex.getSQLState());
             System.out.println ("Message:   "
                 + ex.getMessage());
             System.out.println ("Vendor:    "
                 + ex.getErrorCode());
             ex = ex.getNextException();
             System.out.println ("");
         }
     }
     catch (java.lang.Exception ex)
     {   System.out.println("Exception: " + ex);
         ex.printStackTrace ();
     }
  }

  private static String[] readLine(BufferedReader in)
     throws IOException
  {   String line = in.readLine();
      Vector result = new Vector();
      if (line != null)
      {   StringTokenizer t = new StringTokenizer(line, "|");
          while (t.hasMoreTokens())
              result.addElement(t.nextToken().trim());
      }
      String[] retval = new String[result.size()];
      result.copyInto(retval);
      return retval;
  }

  private static void createTable(Statement stmt,
     String tableName, String[] columnNames,
     String[] columnTypes) throws SQLException
  {   String command = "CREATE TABLE " + tableName + "(\n";
      String primary = "";
      for (int i = 0; i < columnNames.length; i++)
      {   if (i > 0) command += ",\n";
          String columnName = columnNames[i];
          if (columnName.charAt(0) == '*')
          {   if (primary.length() > 0) primary += ", ";
              columnName = columnName.substring(1,
```

```
                columnName.length());
            primary += columnName;
        }
        command += columnName + " " + columnTypes[i];
    }
    if (primary.length() > 0)
        command += "\nPRIMARY KEY (" + primary + ")";
    command += ")\n";
    stmt.executeUpdate(command);
}

private static void insertInto(Statement stmt,
    String tableName, String[] columnTypes, String[] values)
        throws SQLException
{   String command = "INSERT INTO " + tableName
        + " VALUES (";
    for (int i = 0; i < columnTypes.length; i++)
    {   if (i > 0) command += ", ";
        String columnType = columnTypes[i].toUpperCase();
        String value = "";
        if (i < values.length) value = values[i];
        if (columnType.startsWith("CHAR")
            || columnType.startsWith("VARCHAR"))
        {   int from = 0;
            int to = 0;
            command += "'";
            while ((to = value.indexOf('\'', from)) >= 0)
            {   command += value.substring(from, to) + "''";
                from = to + 1;
            }
            command += value.substring(from) + "'";
        }
        else command += value;
    }
    command += ")";
    stmt.executeUpdate(command);
}

private static void showTable(Statement stmt,
    String tableName, int numCols) throws SQLException
{   String query = "SELECT * FROM " + tableName;
    ResultSet rs = stmt.executeQuery(query);
    while (rs.next())
    {   for (int i = 1; i <= numCols; i++)
        {   if (i > 1) System.out.print("|");
            System.out.print(rs.getString(i));
        }
```

```
        System.out.println("");
    }
    rs.close();
  }
}
```

Executing Queries

In this section, we will write a program that executes queries against the `book` database. For this program to work, you must have populated the `corejava` database with tables, as described in the preceding section. Figure 4-4 shows the query application.

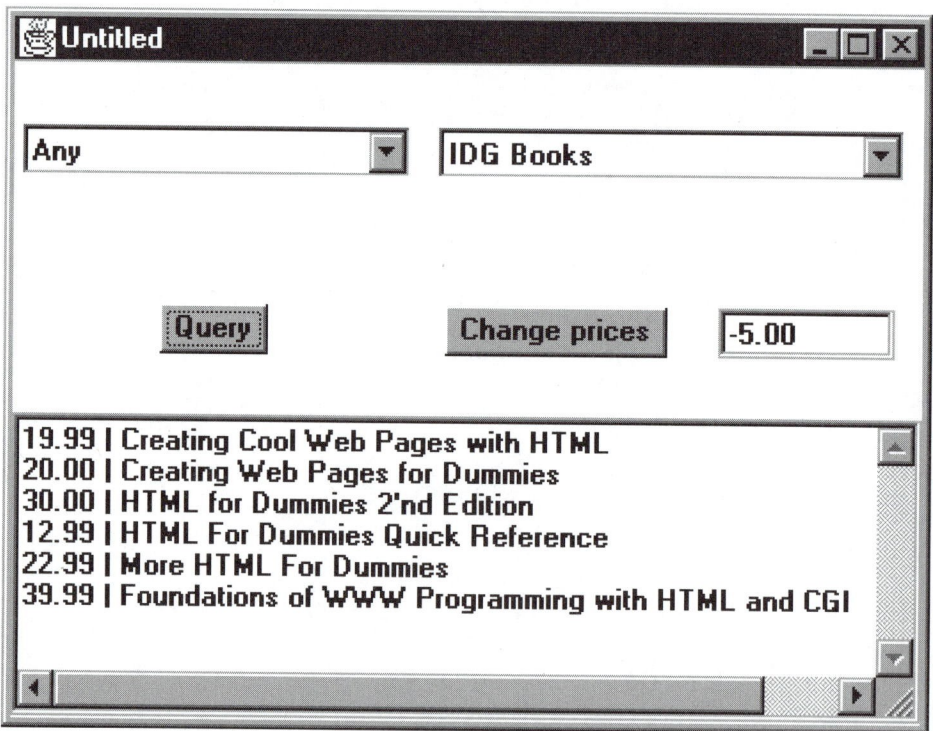

Figure 4-4: The QueryDB application

You can select the author and the publisher or leave either of them as Any. Click on Query; all books matching your selection will be displayed in the text box.

You can also change the data in the database. Select a publisher and type an amount into the textbox next to the Change prices button. When you click on the button, all prices of that publisher are adjusted by the amount you entered, and the text area contains a message indicating how many records were changed. However, to minimize unintended changes to the database, you can't change all prices at once. The author field is ignored when you change prices. After a price change, you may want to run a query to verify the new prices.

In this program, we use one new feature, *prepared statements*. Consider the query for all books by a particular publisher, independent of the author. The SQL query is

```
SELECT Books.Price, Books.Title
FROM Books, Publishers
WHERE Books.Publisher_Id = Publishers.Publisher_Id
AND Publishers.Name = the name from the list box
```

Rather than build a separate query command every time the user launches such a query, we can *prepare* a query with a host variable and use it many times, each time filling in a different string for the variable. That technique gives us a performance benefit. Whenever the database executes a query, it first computes a strategy of how to efficiently execute the query. By preparing the query and reusing it, that planning step is done only once. (The reason you do not *always* want to prepare a query is that the optimal strategy may change as your data changes. You have to balance the expense of optimization versus the expense of querying your data less efficiently.)

Each host variable in a prepared query is indicated with a ?. If there is more than one variable, then you must keep track of the positions of the ? when setting the values. For example, our prepared query becomes

```
String publisherQuery =
    "SELECT Books.Price, Books.Title " +
    "FROM Books, Publishers " +
    "WHERE Books.Publisher_Id = Publishers.Publisher_Id " +
    "AND Publishers.Name = ?";
PreparedStatement publisherQueryStmt
    = con.prepareStatement(publisherQuery);
```

Before executing the prepared statement, we must bind the host variables to actual values with a `set` method. As with the `ResultSet` `get` methods, there are different `set` methods for the various types. Here, we want to set a string.

```
publisherQueryStmt.setString(1, publisher);
```

The first argument is the host variable that we want to set. The position 1 denotes the first ?. The second argument is the value that we want to assign to the host variable.

If you reuse a prepared query that you have already executed and the query has more than one host variable, all host variables stay bound as you set them unless you change them with a `set` method. That means you only need to call `set` on those host variables that change from one query to the next.

Once all variables have been bound to values, you can execute the query

```
ResultSet rs = publisherQueryStmt.executeQuery();
```

You process the result set in the usual way. Here, we add the information to the text area result.

```
result.setText("");
while (rs.next())
    result.appendText(rs.getString(1) + " | " +
        rs.getString(2) + "\n");
rs.close();
```

There are a total of four prepared queries in this program, one each for the cases shown in Table 4-3.

Table 4-3: Selected queries

Author	Publisher
any	any
any	specified
specified	any
specified	specified

The price update feature is implemented as a simple UPDATE statement. For variety, we did not choose to make a prepared statement in this case. Note that we call `executeUpdate`, not `executeQuery`, since the UPDATE statement does not return a result set and we don't need one. The return value of `executeUpdate` is the count of changed rows. We display the count in the text area.

```
String updateStatement = "UPDATE Books ...";
int r = stmt.executeUpdate(updateStatement);
result.setText(r + " records updated");
```

The following steps provide an overview of the program.

1. Arrange the components in the frame, using a grid bag layout (see Chapter 7 in Volume 1).

2. Populate the author and publisher text boxes by running two queries that return all author and publisher names in the database.

3. When the user selects Query, find which of the four query types needs to be executed. If this is the first time this query type is executed, then the prepared statement variable is `null`, and the prepared statement is constructed. Then, the values are bound to the query and the query is executed.

   The queries involving authors are more complex. Because a book can have multiple authors, the `BooksAuthors` table gives the correspondence between authors and books. For example, the book with ISBN number 1-56-604288-7 has two authors with codes `HARR` and `KIDD`. The `BooksAuthors` table has the rows

   ```
   1-56-604288-7 | HARR | 1
   1-56-604288-7 | KIDD | 2
   ```

   to indicate this fact. The third column lists the order of the authors. (We can't just use the position of the records in the table. There is no fixed row ordering in a relational table.) Thus, the query has to snake (join) itself from the `Books` table to the `BooksAuthors` table, then to the `Authors` table to compare the author name with the one selected by the user.

   ```
   SELECT Books.Price, Books.Title
   FROM Books, Publishers, BooksAuthors, Authors
   WHERE Books.Publisher_Id = Publishers.Publisher_Id
   AND Publishers.Name = ?
   AND Books.ISBN = BooksAuthors.ISBN
   AND BooksAuthors.Author = Authors.Author
   AND Authors.Name = ?
   ```

4. The results of the query are displayed in the results text box.

5. When the user selects Change price, then the update query is constructed and executed. The query is quite complex because the `WHERE` clause of the `UPDATE` statement needs the publisher *code* and we know only the publisher *name*. This problem is solved with a nested subquery:

   ```
   UPDATE Books
   SET Price = Price + price change
   WHERE Books.Publisher_Id =
       (SELECT Publisher_Id
       FROM Publishers
       WHERE Name = publisher name)
   ```

NOTE: Nested subqueries are explained in most books on SQL, including the book by Martin and Leben mentioned earlier.

6. We initialize the connection and statement objects in the constructor. We hang on to them for the life of the program. Just before the program exits, we call the `dispose` method, and Java closes these objects.

```
class QueryDB extends Frame
{   QueryDB()
    {   con = DriverManager.getConnection(url, user,
        password);
        stmt = con.createStatement();
        . . .
    }
    . . .
    void dispose()
    {   stmt.close();
        con.close();
    }
    . . .
    Connection con;
    Statement stmt;
}
```

Example 4-2 is the complete program code.

Example 4-2: QueryDB.java

```
import java.net.*;
import java.sql.*;
import java.awt.*;
import java.awt.event.*;
import java.util.*;
import corejava.*;

public class QueryDB extends CloseableFrame
    implements ActionListener
{   public QueryDB()
    {   setLayout(new GridBagLayout());
        GridBagConstraints gbc = new GridBagConstraints();
        authors = new Choice();
        authors.addItem("Any");
        publishers = new Choice();
        publishers.addItem("Any");
        result = new TextArea(4, 50);
        result.setEditable(false);
        priceChange = new TextField(8);
        priceChange.setText("-5.00");

        try
        {   Class.forName("sun.jdbc.odbc.JdbcOdbcDriver");
            // force loading of driver
```

```
        String url = "jdbc:odbc:corejava";
        String user = "Cay";
        String password = "password";
        con = DriverManager.getConnection(url, user,
            password);
        stmt = con.createStatement();

        String query = "SELECT Name FROM Authors";
        ResultSet rs = stmt.executeQuery(query);
        while (rs.next())
            authors.addItem(rs.getString(1));

        query = "SELECT Name FROM Publishers";
        rs = stmt.executeQuery(query);
        while (rs.next())
            publishers.addItem(rs.getString(1));
    }
    catch(Exception e)
    {   result.setText("Error " + e);
    }

    gbc.fill = GridBagConstraints.NONE;
    gbc.weightx = 100;
    gbc.weighty = 100;
    add(authors, gbc, 0, 0, 2, 1);
    add(publishers, gbc, 2, 0, 2, 1);
    gbc.fill = GridBagConstraints.NONE;
    Button queryButton = new Button("Query");
    add(queryButton, gbc, 0, 1, 1, 1);
    queryButton.addActionListener(this);
    Button changeButton = new Button("Change prices");
    add(changeButton, gbc, 2, 1, 1, 1);
    changeButton.addActionListener(this);
    add(priceChange, gbc, 3, 1, 1, 1);
    gbc.fill = GridBagConstraints.BOTH;
    add(result, gbc, 0, 2, 4, 1);
}

private void add(Component c, GridBagConstraints gbc,
    int x, int y, int w, int h)
{   gbc.gridx = x;
    gbc.gridy = y;
    gbc.gridwidth = w;
    gbc.gridheight = h;
    add(c, gbc);
}
```

```java
public void actionPerformed(ActionEvent evt)
{  String arg = evt.getActionCommand();
   if (arg.equals("Query"))
   {  ResultSet rs = null;
      try
      {  String author = authors.getSelectedItem();
         String publisher = publishers.getSelectedItem();
         if (!author.equals("Any")
            && !publisher.equals("Any"))
         {  if (authorPublisherQueryStmt == null)
            {  String authorPublisherQuery =
"SELECT Books.Price, Books.Title " +
"FROM Books, BooksAuthors, Authors, Publishers " +
"WHERE Authors.Author_Id = BooksAuthors.Author_Id AND " +
"BooksAuthors.ISBN = Books.ISBN AND " +
"Books.Publisher_Id = Publishers.Publisher_Id AND " +
"Authors.Name = ? AND " +
"Publishers.Name = ?";
               authorPublisherQueryStmt =
                  con.prepareStatement(authorPublisherQuery);
            }
            authorPublisherQueryStmt.setString(1, author);
            authorPublisherQueryStmt.setString(2, publisher);
            rs = authorPublisherQueryStmt.executeQuery();
         }
         else if (!author.equals("Any")
            && publisher.equals("Any"))
         {  if (authorQueryStmt == null)
            {  String authorQuery =
"SELECT Books.Price, Books.Title " +
"FROM Books, BooksAuthors, Authors " +
"WHERE Authors.Author_Id = BooksAuthors.Author_Id AND " +
"BooksAuthors.ISBN = Books.ISBN AND " +
"Authors.Name = ?";
               authorQueryStmt
                  = con.prepareStatement(authorQuery);
            }
            authorQueryStmt.setString(1, author);
            rs = authorQueryStmt.executeQuery();
         }
         else if (author.equals("Any")
            && !publisher.equals("Any"))
         {  if (publisherQueryStmt == null)
            {  String publisherQuery =
"SELECT Books.Price, Books.Title " +
"FROM Books, Publishers " +
"WHERE Books.Publisher_Id = Publishers.Publisher_Id AND " +
"Publishers.Name = ?";
```

```
                    publisherQueryStmt
                       = con.prepareStatement(publisherQuery);
                 }
                 publisherQueryStmt.setString(1, publisher);
                 rs = publisherQueryStmt.executeQuery();
             }
             else
             {   if (allQueryStmt == null)
                 {   String allQuery =
"SELECT Books.Price, Books.Title FROM Books";
                     allQueryStmt
                        = con.prepareStatement(allQuery);
                 }
                 rs = allQueryStmt.executeQuery();
             }

             result.setText("");
             while (rs.next())
                 result.append(rs.getString(1)
                    + " | " + rs.getString(2) + "\n");
             rs.close();
           }
           catch(Exception e)
           {   result.setText("Error " + e);
           }
        }
        else if (arg.equals("Change prices"))
        {   String publisher = publishers.getSelectedItem();
            if (publisher.equals("Any"))
               result.setText
                   ("I am sorry, but I cannot do that.");
            else
               try
               {   String updateStatement =
"UPDATE Books " +
"SET Price = Price + " + priceChange.getText() +
" WHERE Books.Publisher_Id = " +
"(SELECT Publisher_Id FROM Publishers WHERE Name = '" +
    publisher + "')";
                   int r = stmt.executeUpdate(updateStatement);
                   result.setText(r + " records updated.");
               }
               catch(Exception e)
               {   result.setText("Error " + e);
               }
        }
    }
```

```
        public void dispose()
        {   try
            {   stmt.close();
                con.close();
            }
            catch(SQLException e) {}
        }

        public static void main (String args[])
        {   Frame f = new QueryDB();
            f.setSize(400, 300);
            f.show();
        }

        private Choice authors;
        private Choice publishers;
        private TextField priceChange;
        private TextArea result;
        private Connection con;
        private Statement stmt;
        private PreparedStatement authorQueryStmt;
        private PreparedStatement authorPublisherQueryStmt;
        private PreparedStatement publisherQueryStmt;
        private PreparedStatement allQueryStmt;
    }
```

java.sql.Connection

- PreparedStatement prepareStatement(String sql)

  returns a PreparedStatement object containing the precompiled statement. The string sql contains an SQL statement that may contain one or more ? parameter placeholders.

java.sql.PreparedStatement

- void set*XXX*(int n, *XXX* x)

  (*XXX* is a type such as int, double, String, Date, etc.)

  sets the value of the nth parameter to x.

- void clearParameters()

  clears all current parameters in the prepared statement.

- ResultSet executeQuery()

  executes a prepared SQL query and returns a ResultSet object.

- `int executeUpdate()`

  executes the prepared SQL INSERT, UPDATE, or DELETE statement represented by the `PreparedStatement` object. Returns the number of rows affected or 0 for DDL statements.

Metadata

In the last two sections, you saw how to populate, query, and update database tables. However, JDBC can give you additional information about the *structure* of a database and its tables. For example, you can get a list of the tables in a particular database or the column names and types of a table. This information is not useful when you are implementing a particular database. After all, if you design the tables, you know the tables and their structure. Structural information is, however, extremely useful for programmers who write tools that work with any database.

In this section, we will show you how to write such a simple tool. This tool lets you browse all tables in a database.

The choice box on top displays all tables in the database. Select one of them, and the center of the frame is filled with the field names of that table and the values of the first record, as shown in Figure 4-5. Click on Next to scroll through the records in the table.

Figure 4-5: The ViewDB application

We fully expect tool vendors to develop much more sophisticated versions of programs like this one. For example, it then clearly would be possible to let the user edit the values or add new ones, and then update the database. We developed this program mostly to show you how such tools can be built.

In SQL, data that describes the database or one of its parts is called *metadata* (to distinguish it from the actual data that is stored in the database). JDBC reports to us two kinds of metadata: about a database and about a result set.

To find out more about the database, you need to request an object of type `DatabaseMetaData` from the database connection.

```
DatabaseMetaData md = con.getMetaData();
```

Databases are complex, and the SQL standard leaves plenty of room for variability. There are well over a hundred methods in the `DatabaseMetaData` class to inquire about the database, including calls with exotic names such as

```
md.supportsCatalogsInPrivilegeDefinitions()
```

and

```
md.nullPlusNonNullIsNull()
```

Clearly, these are geared toward advanced users with special needs, in particular, those who need to write highly portable code. In this section, we will study only one method that lets you list all tables in a database, and we won't even look at all *its* options. The call

```
ResultSet rs = md.getTables(null, null, null, new String[]
  { "TABLE" })
```

returns a result set that contains information about all tables in the database. (See the API note for other parameters to this method.)

Each row in the result set contains information about the table. We only care about the third entry, the name of the table. (Again, see the API note for the other columns.) Thus, `rs.getString(3)` is the table name. Here is the code that populates the choice box.

```
while (rs.next())
    tableNames.addItem(rs.getString(3));
rs.close();
```

The more interesting metadata is reported about result sets. Whenever you have a result set from a query, you can inquire about the number of columns and each column's name, type, and field width.

We will make use of this information to make a label for each name and a text field of sufficient size for each value.

```
ResultSet rs = stmt.executeQuery("SELECT * FROM " + tableName);
ResultSetMetaData rsmd = rs.getMetaData();
for (int i = 1; i <= rsmd.getColumnCount(); i++)
{   String columnName = rsmd.getColumnLabel(i);
    int columnWidth = rsmd.getColumnDisplaySize(i);
    Label l = new Label(columnName);
    TextField tf = new TextField(columnWidth);
    . . .
}
```

The following steps provide a brief overview of the program.

1. Have the border layout put the table name choice component on the top, the table values in the center, and the Next button on the bottom.

2. Connect to the database. Get the table names and fill them into the choice component.

3. When the user selects a table, make a query to see all its values. Get the metadata. Throw out the old components from the center panel. Create a grid bag layout of labels and text boxes. Store the text boxes in a vector. Call the `pack` method to have the window resize itself to exactly hold the newly added components. Then, call `showNextRow` to show the first row.

4. The `showNextRow` method is called to show the first record, and is also called whenever the Next button is clicked. It gets the next row from the table and fills the column values into the text boxes. When at the end of the table, the result set is closed.

Example 4-3 is the program.

Example 4-3: ViewDB.java

```
import java.net.*;
import java.sql.*;
import java.awt.*;
import java.awt.event.*;
import java.util.*;
import corejava.*;

public class ViewDB extends CloseableFrame
    implements ActionListener, ItemListener
{  public ViewDB()
    {  tableNames = new Choice();
       tableNames.addItemListener(this);
       dataPanel = new Panel();
       add(dataPanel, "Center");
       Panel p = new Panel();
       Button nextButton = new Button("Next");
       p.add(nextButton);
       nextButton.addActionListener(this);
       add(p, "South");
       fields = new Vector();

       try
       {  Class.forName("sun.jdbc.odbc.JdbcOdbcDriver");
              // force loading of driver
          String url = "jdbc:odbc:corejava";
          String user = "Cay";
```

```java
                String password = "password";
                con = DriverManager.getConnection(url, user,
                    password);
                stmt = con.createStatement();
                md = con.getMetaData();
                ResultSet mrs = md.getTables(null, null, null,
                    new String[] { "TABLE" });
                while (mrs.next())
                    tableNames.addItem(mrs.getString(3));
                mrs.close();
            }
        catch(Exception e)
        {   System.out.println("Error " + e);
        }

        add(tableNames, "North");
    }

    private void add(Container p, Component c,
        GridBagConstraints gbc, int x, int y, int w, int h)
    {   gbc.gridx = x;
        gbc.gridy = y;
        gbc.gridwidth = w;
        gbc.gridheight = h;
        p.add(c, gbc);
    }

    public void itemStateChanged(ItemEvent evt)
    {   if (evt.getStateChange() == ItemEvent.SELECTED)
        {   remove(dataPanel);
            dataPanel = new Panel();
            fields.removeAllElements();
            dataPanel.setLayout(new GridBagLayout());
            GridBagConstraints gbc = new GridBagConstraints();
            gbc.fill = GridBagConstraints.NONE;
            gbc.anchor = GridBagConstraints.WEST;
            gbc.weightx = 100;
            gbc.weighty = 100;

            try
            {   String tableName = (String)evt.getItem();
                if (rs != null) rs.close();
                rs = stmt.executeQuery("SELECT * FROM "
                    + tableName);
                ResultSetMetaData rsmd = rs.getMetaData();
                for (int i = 1; i <= rsmd.getColumnCount(); i++)
                {   String columnName = rsmd.getColumnLabel(i);
                    int columnWidth = rsmd.getColumnDisplaySize(i);
```

```
                TextField tb = new TextField(columnWidth);
                fields.addElement(tb);
                add(dataPanel, new Label(columnName),
                    gbc, 0, i - 1, 1, 1);
                add(dataPanel, tb, gbc, 1, i - 1, 1, 1);
            }
        }
        catch(Exception e)
        {   System.out.println("Error " + e);
        }
        add(dataPanel, "Center");
        doLayout();
        pack();

        showNextRow();
    }
}

public void actionPerformed(ActionEvent evt)
{   if (evt.getActionCommand().equals("Next"))
    {   showNextRow();
    }
}

public void showNextRow()
{   if (rs == null) return;
    {   try
        {   if (rs.next())
            {   for (int i = 1; i <= fields.size(); i++)
                {   String field = rs.getString(i);
                    TextField tb
                        = (TextField)fields.elementAt(i - 1);
                    tb.setText(field);
                }
            }
            else
            {   rs.close();
                rs = null;
            }
        }
        catch(Exception e)
        {   System.out.println("Error " + e);
        }
    }
}

public static void main (String args[])
{   Frame f = new ViewDB();
```

```
        f.show();
    }

    private Panel dataPanel;
    private Choice tableNames;
    private Vector fields;

    private Connection con;
    private Statement stmt;
    private DatabaseMetaData md;
    private ResultSet rs;
}
```

java.sql.Connection

- DatabaseMetaData getMetaData()

returns the metadata for the connection as a DataBaseMetaData object.

java.sql.DatabaseMetaData

- ResultSet getTables(String catalog, String schemaPattern, String tableNamePattern, String types[])

gets a description of all tables in a catalog that match the schema and table name patterns and the type criteria. (A *schema* describes a group of related tables and access permissions. A *catalog* describes a related group of schemas. These concepts are important for structuring large databases.)

Parameters: catalog

schema Pattern

table Name Pattern

types []

The catalog and schema parameters can be " " to retrieve those tables without a catalog or schema, or null to return tables regardless of catalog or schema.

The types array contains the names of the table types to include. Typical types are TABLE, VIEW, SYSTEM TABLE, GLOBAL TEMPORARY, LOCAL TEMPORARY, ALIAS, and SYNONYM. If types is null, then tables of all types are returned.

The result set has five columns, all of which are of type String, as shown in Table 4-4.

Table 4-4: Five columns of the result set

1	TABLE_CAT	table catalog (may be null)
2	TABLE_SCHEM	table schema (may be null)
3	TABLE_NAME	table name
4	TABLE_TYPE	table type
5	REMARKS	comment on the table

`java.sql.ResultSet`

- `resultSetMetaData getMetaData()`

  gives you the metadata associated with the current `ResultSet` columns.

`interface java.sql.ResultSetMetaData`

- `int getColumnCount()`

  returns the number of columns in the current `ResultSet` object.

- `int getColumnDisplaySize(int column)`

  tells you the usual maximum width of the column specified by the index parameter.

  Parameters: column   the column number

- `String getColumnLabel(int column)`

  gives you the suggested title for the column.

  Parameters: column   the column number

- `String getColumnName(int column)`

  gives the column name associated with the column index specified.

  Parameters: column   the column number

CHAPTER

5

- Remote Method Invocations
- Setting Up Remote Method Invocation
- Parameter Passing in Remote Methods
- Using RMI with Applets

Remote Objects

P eriodically, the programming community starts thinking of "objects everywhere" as the solution to all its problems. The idea is to have a happy family of collaborating objects that can be located anywhere. These objects are, of course, supposed to communicate through standard protocols across a network. For example, you'll have an object on the client where the user can fill in a request for data. The client object sends a message to an object on the server which it turns (somehow), gets the information, and sends it back to the client. Like most bandwagons in programming, this plan contains a fair amount of hype that can obscure the utility of the concept. This chapter:

- Explains the models that make interobject communication possible

- Explains situations where distributed objects can be useful

- Shows you how to use remote objects and the associated *remote method invocation* (RMI) for communicating between two machines running Java Virtual Machines

Introduction to Remote Objects: The Roles of Client and Server

Let's go back to that idea of locally collecting information on a client computer and sending the information across the Net to a server. We are supposing that a user on a local machine will fill out an information request form. The form gets sent to the vendor's server, and the server processes the request and will, in turn, want to send back product information the client can view, as shown in Figure 5-1.

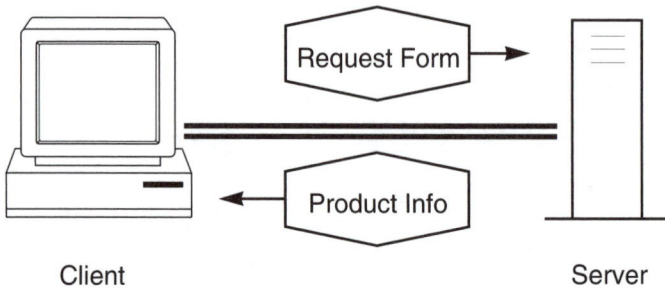

Client　　　　　　　　　　　　　　　　Server

Figure 5-1: Transmitting objects between client and server

You have seen two ways to transmit information:

- Use a socket connection to send byte streams between the customer and the vendor computers.

- Use JDBC to make database queries and updates.

Both ways work well in certain situations. For example, a socket connection is great if you just need to send raw data across the Net. JDBC is useful if the information that you are sending fits into the relational database's table model. Keep in mind that both of these models essentially send a stream of *bytes* across the Net. In both these cases, there is a significant coding hassle: the programmer has to come up with appropriate ways of coding the data and specifying the transmission protocols for sending the data. Of course, when you are connecting to a database with JDBC, all the details of communication protocols are taken care of in advance. But relational databases are not very effective for storing information that doesn't fit into a "rows and columns" database structure. In particular, they are not very good at storing collections of objects of different types, such as a mixture of employees, managers, and contractors. Also, as you have seen, these kinds of heterogeneous object collections are very important in object-oriented programming.

What would go into a possible solution? Well, keeping in mind that object sending messages to one another is the central tenet of OOP, we could try to find a way to have objects lying on different machines send messages to each other. Let's assume that the client object was written in Java so that it can theoretically run anywhere. For the server objects, there are two obvious possibilities:

- The server object was *not* written in Java (either because it is a legacy object or because somebody hasn't joined the appropriate bandwagon).

- The server object *was* written in Java.

The first situation requires us to have a way for objects to talk to each other *regardless* of what language they were originally written in. If you think about it, you will agree with us that even the theoretical possibility of this is an amazing achievement. How can what is ultimately a sequence of bytes written in an arbitrary language, that we may have no knowledge of, tell us what services it offers, what messages it responds to? Of course, getting this to work in practice isn't easy, but the idea is elegant. The "common object request broker architecture," or CORBA standard, by the Object Management Group or OMG (www.omg.org) defines a common mechanism for data interchange and service discovery.

The fundamental idea is that we delegate the task of finding out this information and activating any services requested to a so-called *Object Request Broker* (or ORB). You can think of an ORB as a kind of universal translator for interobject communication. Objects don't talk directly to each other. They always use an object broker to bargain between them. ORBs are located across the network, and it is important that they can communicate with each other. Most (but not all) ORBs follow the specification set up by the OMG for inter-ORB communication. This specification is called the Internet inter-ORB Protocol or IIOP.

NOTE: Microsoft avoids the use of an explicit ORB in its common object model (COM). One corollary of this practice is that only objects built in a certain way on Windows 95 and NT platforms can talk to each other. (You can use many languages to build COM objects, however.) CORBA, on the other hand, is truly a cross-language and cross-platform architecture for interobject communication.

CORBA is completely language neutral. Client and server programs can be written in C++, Java, or any other language with a CORBA binding. You use an *Interface Definition Language* (or IDL) to specify the signatures of the messages and the types of the data your objects can send and understand. (IDL specifications look a lot like Java interfaces; in fact, you can think of them as defining interfaces that the communicating objects must support. One nice feature of this model is you can supply an IDL specification for an existing legacy object and then access its services through the ORB even if it was written long before the first ORB arrived.)

NOTE: Sun wants Java objects to be able to talk to objects written in other languages, of course, so it supplies a Java-IDL interface and a tool called `idltojava` that compiles IDL files to Java source code. Information on the Java-IDL interface is, as we write this, at `http://java.sun.com/products/jdk/idl/index.html`.

There are quite a few people who believe that CORBA will become very important very soon and that Java is an excellent language for implementing CORBA clients and servers. Upcoming versions of Netscape browsers and servers will ship with IIOP-compliant ORBs and a Java toolkit for CORBA programming. However, frankly speaking, the interoperability between ORBs has not been fully tested at this point. And there is little agreement on how to best write Java code for CORBA. Netscape uses a mechanism that is quite interesting, but it is completely different from the Java-IDL mechanism developed by Sun Microsystems. While CORBA may be interesting tomorrow, the Remote Method Invocation (RMI) mechanism, invented by JavaSoft for Java-to-Java communication, is available today, and it works. For that reason, we will discuss RMI in this chapter. RMI is useful only for communication between Java objects, and it does not currently use a standard transmission protocol such as IIOP. But the basic concepts of distributed computing are similar for RMI and CORBA, which means that you will benefit from understanding RMI, no matter what the eventual fate of RMI and CORBA is.

Remote Method Invocations

Java implements remote objects by supplying a transport layer that handles the data encoding and the transmission and call protocols. That way, you need not worry about managing streams of bytes. You can write code that sends messages to Java objects of *any* type. Thus, you are not limited to the rigid structure of a database as you would be if you stuck with JDBC.

There is another major benefit to remote objects in Java: Not only can you transport objects across a network, but you can invoke method calls on objects that reside on another computer *without* having to move those objects to the machine making the method call. Such method calls are called *remote method invocations* (RMI). For example, the client seeking product information can query a Warehouse object on the server. It calls a remote method, find, which has one parameter: the request form object. The find method returns an object to the client: the product information object. (See Figure 5-2.)

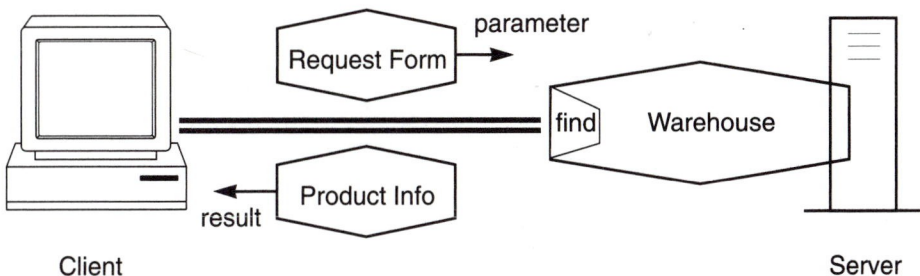

Figure 5-2: Invoking a remote method on a server object

For remote method invocation (RMI), code on the client computer calls a method of a server object. It is important to remember that the client/server terminology applies only to a single method call. The computer running the Java code that calls the remote method is the client for *that* call, and the computer hosting the object that processes the call is the server for *that* call. It is entirely possible that the roles are reversed somewhere down the road. The server of a previous call can itself become the client when it invokes a remote method on an object residing on another computer.

Stubs and Skeletons

When client code wants to invoke a remote method on a remote object, it actually calls a regular Java method that is encapsulated in a surrogate object called a *stub*. The stub resides on the client machine, not on the server. The stub packages as a block of bytes the parameters used in the remote method. This packaging uses a device-independent encoding for each parameter. For example, numbers are always sent in big-endian format. Strings and objects are a little trickier since object references point to memory locations on the client. These memory locations will not make sense on the server. The stub, when it has an object reference to send across, uses the object serialization mechanism of Java to eliminate any explicit object references. (See Chapter 1.) The process of encoding the parameters into a format suitable for transporting them between objects running in different processes or across the Net is called *parameter marshalling*.

To sum up: the stub method on the client builds an information block that consists of:

- An identifier of the remote object to be used

- An operation number, describing the method to be called

- The marshalled parameters

The stub then sends this information to the server. On the server side, a *skeleton* object makes sense out of the information contained in the packet and passes that information to the actual object executing the remote method. Specifically, the skeleton performs five actions for every remote method call:

- It unmarshals the parameters.

- It calls the desired method on the real remote object that lies on the server.

- It captures the return value or exception of the call on the server.

- It marshals that value.

- It sends a package consisting of the value in the marshalled form back to the stub on the client.

The stub unmarshals the return value or exception from the server. This value becomes the return value of the remote method call. Or, if the remote method threw an exception, the stub rethrows it in the process space of the caller. Figure 5-3 shows the information flow of a remote method invocation.

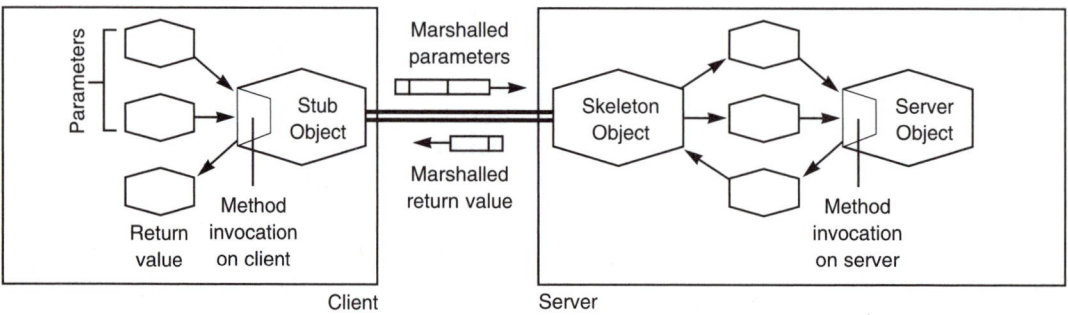

Figure 5-3: Stub and skeleton objects

This is obviously a complex process, but the good news is that it is completely automatic and, to a large extent, transparent for the Java programmer. Moreover, the designers of the Java remote object architecture tried hard to give remote objects the same "look and feel" as local objects. Nevertheless, there are important differences between local and remote objects, as you will see later in this chapter.

Remote objects are garbage collected automatically, just as local objects are. However, the current distributed collector uses reference counting and cannot detect cycles of unreferenced objects. Cycles must be explicitly broken by the programmer.

The syntax for a remote method call is the same as for a local call. If `centralWarehouse` is a stub object for a central warehouse object on a remote (currently, the client) machine and `getQuantity` is the method you want to invoke remotely, then a typical call looks like this:

```
centralWarehouse.getQuantity("SuperSucker 100 Vacuum Cleaner");
```

The client code always uses object variables whose type is an *interface* to access remote objects. For example, associated to this call would be an interface:

```
interface Warehouse
{   public int getQuantity(String)
        throws RemoteException;
    . . .
}
```

and an object declaration for a variable that will implement the interface:

```
Warehouse centralWarehouse;
```

Of course, interfaces are abstract entities that only spell out what methods can be called along with their signatures. Variables whose type is an interface must always be bound to an actual object of some type. In the case of remote objects, this is a *stub class*. The client program does not actually know the type of those objects. The stub classes and the associated objects are created automatically.

While the Java designers did a good job of hiding many details of remote method invocation from the Java programmer, a number of techniques and caveats still must be mastered. Those programming tasks are the topic of the rest of this chapter.

Dynamic Class Loading

When you pass a remote object to another Java program, either as a parameter or return value of a remote method, then that program must be able to deal with the associated stub object. That is, it must have the Java code for the stub class. The stub methods don't do a lot of interesting work. They just marshal and unmarshal the parameters and then connect this information with the server. Of course, they do all this work transparently to the programmer.

Furthermore, the classes for parameters, return values, and exception objects may need to be loaded as well. This loading can be more complex than you might think. For example, you may declare a remote method with a certain return type that is known to the client, but the method actually returns an object of a derived class that is not known to the client. The class loader will then load that derived class.

While unglamorous, the stub classes must be available to the running client program. One obvious way to make these classes available is to put them on the local file system. If they aren't there, then Java is quite willing to load them from another place. It does this by a process similar to what is used when running applets in a browser.

With an applet, a browser loads the applet class and checks the bytecodes for validity. The loading of the applet class from a remote location is the job of a *class loader*. The applet class loader is quite restrictive. It will load classes only from the same machine that served the Web page containing the applet. The stub class loader can be configured to permit more activities. For example, you can allow it to search for stub code on other network locations. This search is particularly useful for distributed Java programs where a number of processors that are cooperating to perform a difficult computation will all want to fetch the same stubs from a central location.

The class loader determines where the classes may be loaded from. The *security manager* determines what these classes can do when they run. You have seen in Chapter 10 of Volume 1 and Chapter 3 of this volume that the applet security manager won't let classes read and write local files or make socket connections to third parties. The stub security manager is even more restrictive than the applet security manager. Since it governs the behavior only of stub code, the stub security manager prevents all activities except those that stubs must be able to carry out. This is a safety mechanism that protects the program from viruses in stub code. For specialized applications, Java programmers can substitute their own class loaders and security managers, but those provided by the RMI system suffice for normal usage. (See Chapter 8 for more on class loaders.)

Setting Up Remote Method Invocation

Running even the simplest remote object example requires quite a bit more setup than does running a standalone Java program or applet. You must run Java programs on both the server and client computers. The necessary object information must be separated into client-side interfaces and server-side implementations. There is also a special query mechanism that allows the client to locate objects on the server.

To get started with the actual coding, we walk through each of these requirements, using a simple example. In our first example, we generate a couple of objects of a type `Product` on the server computer. The client computer will run a Java program that locates and queries these objects.

> NOTE: You can try out this example on a single computer or on a pair of networked computers. The code on the CD is set up to run on a single computer. To run the server code remotely, set the URL of the server in the client code and recompile. We indicate where make these changes.
>
> You also must distribute the class files between the client and the server. The server program classes, together with the interface, stub, and skeleton classes, must be on the server. The client program, together with the interface and stub classes, must be on the client.

Even if you run this code on a single computer, you must have network services available. In particular, be sure that you have TCP/IP running. This is always the case on a machine running Unix and will also be true on any machine that is permanently connected to the Internet. If your computer doesn't have a network card, you can use the dialup networking feature under Windows 95 to set up a TCP/IP connection. (Consult the Windows 95 documentation to see how to set up the connection.)

Interfaces and Implementations

Your client program needs to manipulate server objects, but it doesn't actually have copies of them. The objects themselves reside on the server. The client code must still know what it can do with those objects. Their capabilities are expressed in an interface that is shared between the client and server and so resides simultaneously on both machines.

```
interface Product // shared by client and server
    extends Remote
{   public String getDescription() throws RemoteException;
}
```

Just as in this example, *all* interfaces for remote objects must extend the `Remote` interface defined in the `java.rmi` package. All the methods in those interfaces must also declare that they will throw a `RemoteException`. The reason for the declaration is that remote method calls are inherently less reliable than local calls—it is always possible that a remote call will fail. For example, the server or the network connection may be temporarily unavailable, or there may be a network problem. Your client code must be prepared to deal with these possibilities. For these reasons, Java forces you to catch the `RemoteException` with *every* remote method call and to specify the appropriate action to take when the call does not succeed. The client accesses the server object through a stub that implements this interface.

```
Product p = ...;
    // see below how the client gets a stub
    // reference to a remote object
String d = p.getDescription();
System.out.println(d);
```

In the next section, you will see ways the client can obtain a reference to this kind of remote object.

Next, on the server side, you must implement the class that actually carries out the methods advertised in the remote interface.

```
public class ProductImpl // server
    extends UnicastRemoteObject
    implements Product
{  public ProductImpl(String d) throws RemoteException
      { descr = d; }
    public String getDescription()
    {  return "I am a " + descr + ". Buy me!";
    }
    private String descr;
}
```

This class has a single method, getDescription, that can be called from the remote client. It is a server class because it extends UnicastRemoteObject, which is a concrete Java class that makes objects remotely accessible.

NOTE: When you use RMI (or any distributed object mechanism, for that matter), there is a somewhat bewildering set of classes to master. In this chapter, we use a uniform naming convention for all of our examples that, hopefully, makes it easier to recognize the purpose of each class. (See Table 5-1.) You can avoid the "server" classes by putting the server methods into the main method of the "implementation" classes.

Table 5-1: Naming Conventions for RMI classes

no suffix (e.g., Product)	A remote interface
Impl suffix (e.g., ProductImpl)	A server class implementing that interface
Server suffix (e.g., ProductServer)	A server program that creates server objects
Client suffix (e.g., ProductClient)	A client program that calls remote methods
_Stub suffix (e.g., ProductImpl_Stub)	A stub class that is automatically generated by the rmic program
_Skel suffix (e.g., ProductImpl_Skel)	A skeleton class that is automatically generated by the rmic program

Actually, all server classes must extend the class RemoteServer from the java.rmi.server package. But RemoteServer is an abstract class that defines only the basic mechanisms for the communication between server objects and their remote stubs. The UnicastRemoteObject class that comes with RMI extends the RemoteServer abstract class and is concrete—so you can use it without writing any code. The "path of least resistance" for a server class is to derive from UnicastRemoteObject, and all server classes in this chapter will do so. Figure 5-4 shows the inheritance relationship between these classes.

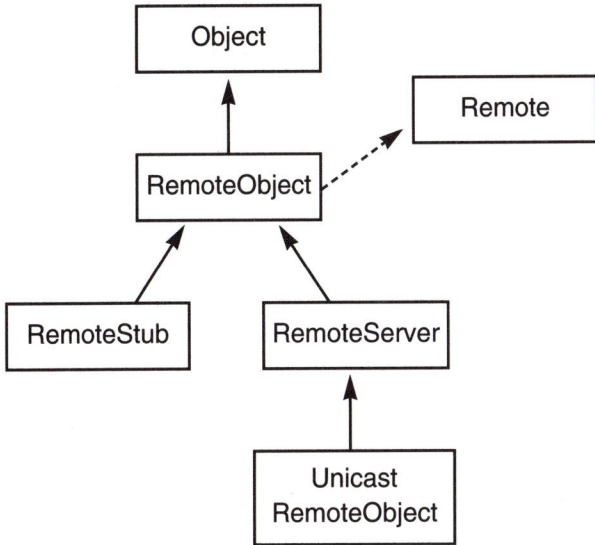

Figure 5-4: Inheritance diagram

A UnicastRemoteObject object resides on a server. It must be alive when a service is requested, and reachable through the TCP/IP protocol. This is the class that we will be extending for all the server classes in this book and is the only server class available in the current version of the RMI package. Sun or third-party vendors may, in the future, design other classes for use by servers for RMI. For example, Sun is talking about a MulticastRemoteObject class for objects that are replicated over multiple servers. Other possibilities are for objects that are activated on demand or ones that can use other communications protocols, such as UDP.

Creating Server Objects

For a client to access a remote object that exists on the server, there must be a mechanism to obtain a remote reference that can access the remote object. There

are a number of methods for the client code to gain access to a server object. The most common method is to call a remote method whose return value is a server object. When a server object is returned to the client as a method result, the RMI mechanism automatically sends back a remote reference, not the actual object. There is, however, a chicken-and-egg problem here. The *first* server object needs to be located some other way. That object typically has plenty of methods to return other objects. The Sun RMI library provides a *bootstrap registry service* to locate the first server object.

The server registers objects with the bootstrap registry service, and the client retrieves stubs to those objects. You register a server object by giving the bootstrap registry service a reference to the object and a *name*. The name is a string that is (hopefully) unique.

```
// server
ProductImpl p1 = new ProductImpl("Blackwell Toaster");
Naming.bind("toaster", p1);
```

The client code gets a stub to access that server object by specifying the server name and the object name in a URL-style format:

```
// client
String url = "rmi://";
    // change to rmi://www.yourserver.com/
    // if server runs remotely on www.yourserver.com
Product c1 = (Product)Naming.lookup(url + "toaster");
```

NOTE: Because it is notoriously difficult to keep names unique in a global registry, you should not use this technique as the general method for locating objects on the server. Instead, there should be relatively few named server objects registered with the bootstrap service. In our example, we temporarily violate this rule and register relatively trivial objects to show you the mechanics for registering and locating objects.

However, we aren't quite ready to register any objects, yet. Because the bootstrap registry service must be available, it also must stay active for the duration. So, under Windows 95 or NT, you execute the statement

```
start rmiregistry
```

at a DOS prompt or from the Run dialog box. (The `start` command is a Windows command that starts a program in a new window.)

Under Unix, use:

```
rmiregistry &
```

> TIP: You must set the desired class path *before* starting the registry service because new command windows inherit the class path of the command window in which they start. Otherwise, the registry won't find the stub classes.

Next, generate skeletons and stubs for the `ProductImpl` class. Recall that skeletons and stubs are on the server-level and client-level classes and that RMI uses those classes to marshal (encode and send) the parameters and marshal the results of method calls across the network. The Java programmer never uses those classes directly. Moreover, they need *not* be written by hand. The `rmic` tool generates them automatically, as in the following example.

```
rmic ProductImpl
```

This call to the `rmic` tool generates two class files named `ProductImpl_Skel.class` and `ProductImpl_Stub.class`. If your class is in a package, you must call `rmic` with the full package name.

> NOTE: Remember to first compile the Java source file with `javac` before running `rmic`. If you are generating stubs and skeletons for a class in a package, you must give `rmic` the full package name.

All server and client programs that use RMI should install a security manager to control the code of any skeletons and stubs that are dynamically loaded from a network location. Java provides such a security manager, the `RMISecurityManager`. You install it with the instruction

```
System.setSecurityManager(new RMISecurityManager());
```

> NOTE: In this case, we do not actually need dynamic class loading. All the classes are available in the local file system. Nevertheless, Java insists that a security manager be in place. For applets, there is already a security manager that makes sure that the applet code does not do any harm. When you are dealing with applications, be aware there is no default security manager, so you always need to set a security manager when using RMI.

Example 5-1 shows a complete program that registers two `Product` objects under the names `toaster` and `microwave`.

Example 5-1: ProductServer.java

```
import java.rmi.*;
import java.rmi.server.*;
import sun.applet.*;

public class ProductServer
{  public static void main(String args[])
   {  System.setSecurityManager(new RMISecurityManager());

      try
      {  ProductImpl p1 = new ProductImpl("Blackwell Toaster");
         ProductImpl p2 = new ProductImpl("ZapXpress Microwave
            Oven");

         Naming.rebind("toaster", p1);
         Naming.rebind("microwave", p2);
      }
      catch(Exception e)
      {  System.out.println("Error: " + e);
      }
   }
}
```

Once you compile this program, you run it as a separate process. Under Windows, use the command:

```
start java ProductServer
```

Under Unix, use the command

```
java ProductServer &
```

If you run the server program as

```
java ProductServer
```

then the program will never exit normally. This seems strange—after all, the program just creates two objects and registers them. Actually, the main function does exit immediately after registration, as you would expect. But, when you create an object of a class that extends UnicastRemoteObject, Java starts a separate thread that keeps the program alive indefinitely. Thus, the program stays around in order to allow clients to connect to it.

Before writing the client program, let's verify that we succeeded in registering the remote objects. The `Naming` class has a method `list` that returns a list of all currently registered names. Example 5-2 shows a simple program that lists the names in the registry.

Example 5-2: ShowBindings.java

```java
import java.rmi.*;
import java.rmi.server.*;

public class ShowBindings
{  public static void main(String[] args)
   {  System.setSecurityManager(new RMISecurityManager());
      try
      {  String[] bindings = Naming.list("");
         for (int i = 0; i < bindings.length; i++)
            System.out.println(bindings[i]);
      }
      catch(Exception e)
      {  System.out.println("Error: " + e);
      }
   }
}
```

In our case, its output is

```
rmi:/toaster
rmi:/microwave
```

The Client Side

Now, we can write the client program that asks each newly registered product object to print its description. See Example 5-3.

Example 5-3: ProductClient.java

```java
import java.rmi.*;
import java.rmi.server.*;

public class ProductClient
{  public static void main(String[] args)
    {  System.setSecurityManager(new RMISecurityManager());
        String url = "rmi:///";
            // change to "rmi://www.yourserver.com/"
            // when server runs on remote machine
            // www.yourserver.com
        try
        {  Product c1 = (Product)Naming.lookup(url + "toaster");
            Product c2 = (Product)Naming.lookup(url + "microwave");
            System.out.println(c1.getDescription());
            System.out.println(c2.getDescription());
        }
        catch(Exception e)
        {  System.out.println("Error: " + e);
        }
        System.exit(0);
    }
}
```

You run this program on the client, in the usual way:

```
java ProductClient
```

The program simply prints

```
I am a Blackwell Toaster. Buy me!
I am a ZapXpress Microwave Oven. Buy me!
```

This output doesn't seem all that impressive, but consider what goes on behind the scenes when Java executes the call to the `getDescription` method. The client program has a reference to a stub object that it obtained from the `lookup` method. It calls the `getDescription` method, which sends a network message to the skeleton object on the server side. The skeleton object invokes the `getDescription` method on the `ProductImpl` object located on the server. That method computes a string. The string is returned to the skeleton, sent across the network, received by the stub, and returned as the result. See Figure 5-5.

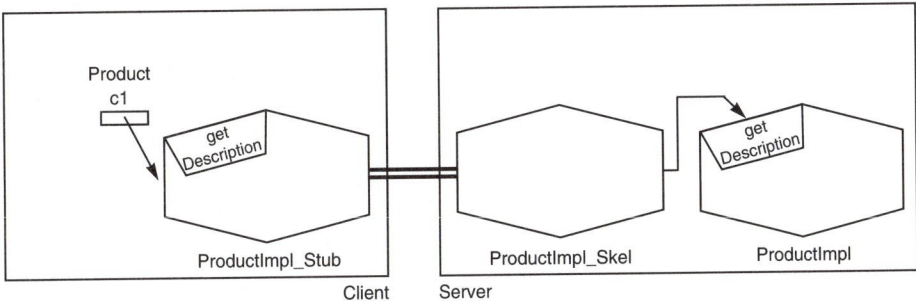

Client   Server

Figure 5-5: Calling a remote method

Summary of Steps for Setting up RMI

Here is a summary of the steps you need to take to get remote method invocation working:

1. Place the interface class extending `Remote` on the server and the client.

2, Place the implementation class extending `RemoteObject` on the server.

3. Generate stubs and skeletons on the server by running `rmic`. Copy the stubs to the client.

4. Start the bootstrap registry service on the server.

5. Start a program that creates and registers objects of the implementation class on the server.

6. Run a program that looks up server objects and invokes remote methods on the client.

`java.rmi.server.Naming`

- `static Remote lookup(String url)`

  returns the remote object for the URL. Throws the `NotBound` exception if the name is not currently bound.

- `static void bind(String name, Remote obj)`

  binds name to the remote object `obj`. Throws an `AlreadyBoundException` if the object is already bound.

- `static void unbind(String name)`

  unbinds the name. Throws the `NotBound` exception if the name is not currently bound.

- `static void rebind(String name, Remote obj)`

  binds `name` to the remote object `obj`. Replaces any existing binding.

- `static String[] list(String url)`

  returns an array of strings of the URLs in the registry located at the given URL. The array contains a snapshot of the names present in the registry.

Parameter Passing in Remote Methods

You often want to pass parameters to remote objects. This section explains some of the techniques for doing so—along with some of the pitfalls.

Passing Nonremote Objects

When Java passes a remote object from the server to the client, the client receives a stub. Using the stub, it can manipulate the server object by invoking remote methods. The object, however, stays on the server. It is also possible to pass and return *any* objects via a remote method call, not just those that implement the `Remote` interface. For example, the `getDescription` method of the preceding section returned a `String` object. That string was created on the server and had to be transported to the client. Since `String` does not implement the `Remote` interface, the client cannot return a string stub object. Instead, the client gets a *copy* of the string. Then, after the call, the client has its own `String` object to work with. This means that there is no need for any further connection to any object on the server to deal with that string.

Whenever an object that is not a remote object needs to be transported from one Java Virtual Machine to another, the Java Virtual Machine makes a copy and sends that copy across the network connection. This technique is very different from parameter passing in a local method. When you pass objects into a local method or return them as method results, only object *references* are passed. However, object references are memory addresses of objects in the local Java Virtual Machine. This information is meaningless to a different Java Virtual Machine.

It is not difficult to imagine how a copy of a string can be transported across a network. Java can also make copies of more complex objects, provided they are *serializable*. RMI uses the serialization mechanism described in Chapter 1 to send objects across a network connection. This means that Java will only be able to copy the information in any classes that implement *Serializable*. The following program shows the copying of parameters and return values in action. This program is a simple application that lets a user shop for a gift. On the client, the user runs a program that gathers information about the gift recipient, in this case, age, sex, and hobbies (see Figure 5-6).

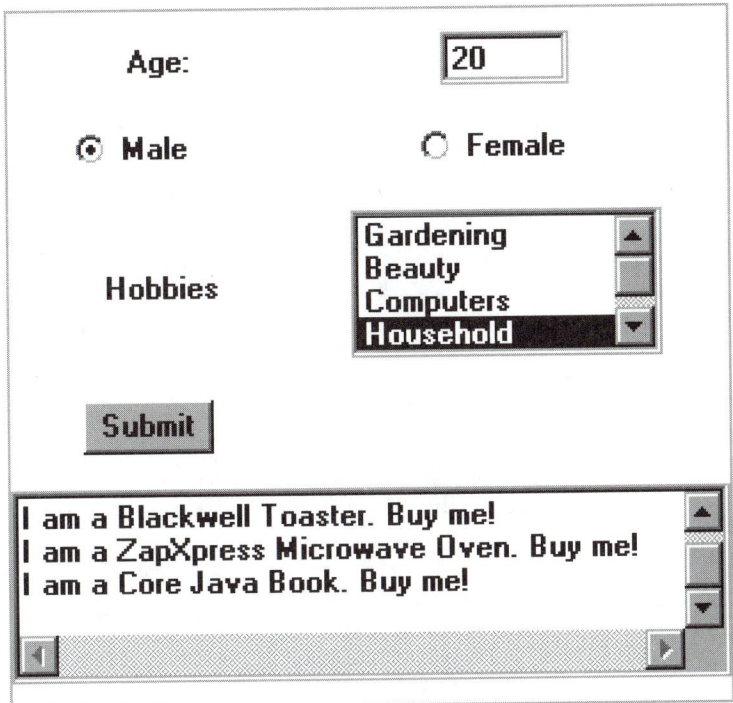

Figure 5-6: Obtaining product suggestions from the server

An object of type `Customer` is then sent to the server. Since `Customer` is not a remote object, a copy of the object is made on the server. The server program sends back a vector of products. The vector contains those products that match the customer profile, and it always contains that one item that will delight anyone, namely, a copy of the book *Core Java*. Again, `Vector` is not a remote class, so the vector is copied from the server back to its client. As described in Chapter 1, the serialization mechanism makes copies of all objects that are referenced inside a copied object. In our case, it makes a copy of all vector entries as well. We added an extra complexity: the entries are actually remote `Product` objects. Thus, the recipient gets a copy of the vector, filled with stub objects to the products on the server (see Figure 5-7).

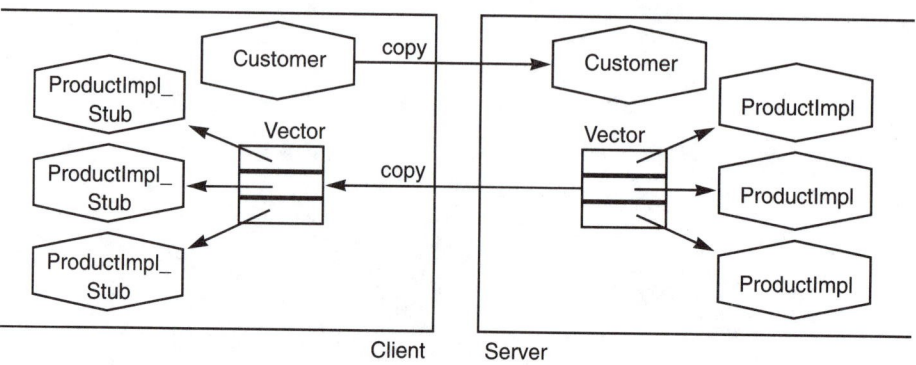

Figure 5-7: Copying local parameter and result objects

To summarize, remote objects are passed across the network as stubs. Non-remote objects are copied. All of this is automatic and requires no programmer intervention.

Whenever code calls a remote method, the stub makes a package that contains copies of all parameter values and sends it to the server, using the object serialization mechanism to marshal the parameters. The server skeleton unmarshals them. Naturally, the process can be quite slow—especially when the parameter objects are large.

Let's look at the complete program. First, we have the interfaces for the product and warehouse services, as shown in Examples 5-4 and 5-5.

Example 5-4: Product.java

```
import java.rmi.*;
import java.awt.*;

public interface Product
    extends Remote
{   String getDescription()
        throws RemoteException;

    static final int MALE = 1;
    static final int FEMALE = 2;
    static final int BOTH = MALE + FEMALE;
}
```

Example 5-5: Warehouse.java

```
import java.rmi.*;
import java.util.*;

public interface Warehouse
    extends Remote
{   public Vector find(Customer c)
        throws RemoteException;
}
```

Example 5-6 shows the implementation for the product service. Products store a description, an age range, the gender targeted (male, female, or both), and the matching hobby. Note that this class implements the getDescription method advertised in the Product interface, and it also implements another method, match, which is not a part of that interface. The match method is an example of a *local method*, a method that can be called only from the local program, not remotely. Since the match method is local, it need not be prepared to throw a RemoteException.

Example 5-6: ProductImpl.java

```
import java.rmi.*;
import java.rmi.server.*;

public class ProductImpl
    extends UnicastRemoteObject
    implements Product
{   public ProductImpl(String n, int s, int age1, int age2, String h)
        throws RemoteException
    {   name = n;
        ageLow = age1;
        ageHigh = age2;
        sex = s;
        hobby = h;
    }

    public boolean match(Customer c) // local method
    {   if (c.getAge() < ageLow || c.getAge() > ageHigh)
            return false;
        if (!c.hasHobby(hobby)) return false;
        if ((sex & c.getSex()) == 0) return false;
        return true;
    }
```

```java
    public String getDescription()
        throws RemoteException
    {   return "I am a " + name + ". Buy me!";
    }

    private String name;
    private int ageLow;
    private int ageHigh;
    private int sex;
    private String hobby;
}
```

Example 5-7: Customer.java

```java
import java.io.*;

public class Customer implements Serializable
{   public Customer(int theAge, int theSex, String[] theHobbies)
    {   age = theAge;
        sex = theSex;
        hobbies = theHobbies;
    }

    public int getAge() { return age; }

    public int getSex() { return sex; }

    public boolean hasHobby(String aHobby)
    {   if (aHobby == "") return true;
        for (int i = 0; i < hobbies.length; i++)
            if (hobbies[i].equals(aHobby)) return true;

        return false;
    }

    public void reset()
    {   age = 0;
        sex = 0;
        hobbies = null;
    }

    public String toString()
    {   String result = "Age: " + age + " Sex: ";
        if (sex == Product.MALE) result += "Male";
        if (sex == Product.FEMALE) result += "Female";
        result += " Hobbies: ";
        for (int i = 0; i < hobbies.length; i++)
            result += hobbies[i] + " ";
```

```
      return result;
   }

   private int age;
   private int sex;
   private String[] hobbies;
}
```

Example 5-8 shows the implementation for the warehouse service. Like the ProductImpl class, the WarehouseImpl class has local and remote methods. The add method is local; it is used by the server to add products to the warehouse. The find method is remote; it is used to find items in the warehouse.

To illustrate that the Customer object is actually copied, the find method of the WarehouseImpl class actually clears the customer object it receives. When the remote method returns, the WarehouseClient displays the customer object that it sent to the server. As you will see, that object has not changed. The server cleared only *its copy*. In this case, the clear operation serves no useful purpose except to demonstrate that local objects are copied when they are passed as parameters.

Example 5-8: WarehouseImpl.java

```
import java.rmi.*;
import java.util.*;
import java.rmi.server.*;


public class WarehouseImpl
   extends UnicastRemoteObject
   implements Warehouse
{  public WarehouseImpl()
      throws RemoteException
   {  products = new Vector();
   }

   public synchronized void add(ProductImpl p) // local method
   {  products.addElement(p);
   }

   public synchronized Vector find(Customer c)
      throws RemoteException
   {  Vector result = new Vector();
      for (int i = 0; i < products.size(); i++)
      {  ProductImpl p = (ProductImpl)products.elementAt(i);
         if (p.match(c)) result.addElement(p);
      }
```

```
            result.addElement(new ProductImpl("Core Java Book",
               0, 200, Product.BOTH, ""));
            c.reset();
            return result;
         }


      private Vector products;
   }
```

In general, the methods of server classes such as `ProductImpl` and `WarehouseImpl` should be synchronized. Then, it is possible for multiple client stubs to make simultaneous calls to a server object, even if some of the methods change the state of the server. (See Chapter 2 for more details on synchronized methods.) In Example 5-8, we synchronize the methods of the `WarehouseImpl` class because it is conceivable that the local `add` and the remote `find` methods are called simultaneously. We don't synchronize the methods of the `ProductImpl` class because the product server objects don't change their state. Example 5-9 shows the server program that creates a warehouse object and registers it with the bootstrap registry service.

Example 5-9: WarehouseServer.java

```
import java.rmi.*;
import java.rmi.server.*;

public class WarehouseServer
{  public static void main(String args[])
   {  System.setSecurityManager(new RMISecurityManager());
      try
      {  WarehouseImpl w = new WarehouseImpl();
         fillWarehouse(w);
         Naming.rebind("central_warehouse", w);
      }
      catch(Exception e)
      {  System.out.println("Error: " + e);
      }
   }

   public static void fillWarehouse(WarehouseImpl w)
      throws RemoteException
   {  w.add(new ProductImpl("Blackwell Toaster", Product.BOTH,
         18, 200, "Household"));
```

```
     w.add(new ProductImpl("ZapXpress Microwave Oven",
        Product.BOTH,
        18, 200, "Household"));
     w.add(new ProductImpl("Jimbo After Shave", Product.MALE,
        18, 200, "Beauty"));
     w.add(new ProductImpl("Handy Hand Grenade", Product.MALE,
        20, 60, "Gardening"));
     w.add(new ProductImpl("DirtDigger Steam Shovel",
        Product.MALE,
        20, 60, "Gardening"));
     w.add(new ProductImpl("U238 Weed Killer", Product.BOTH,
        20, 200, "Gardening"));
     w.add(new ProductImpl("Van Hope Cosmetic Set",
        Product.FEMALE,
        15, 45, "Beauty"));
     w.add(new ProductImpl("Persistent Java Fragrance",
        Product.FEMALE,
        15, 45, "Beauty"));
     w.add(new ProductImpl("Rabid Rodent Computer Mouse",
        Product.BOTH,
        6, 40, "Computers"));
     w.add(new ProductImpl("Learn Bad Java Habits in 21 Days
        Book", Product.BOTH,
        20, 200, "Computers"));
     w.add(new ProductImpl("My first Espresso Maker",
        Product.FEMALE,
        6, 10, "Household"));
     w.add(new ProductImpl("JavaJungle Eau de Cologne",
        Product.FEMALE,
        20, 200, "Beauty"));
     w.add(new ProductImpl("Fast/Wide SCSI Coffee Maker",
        Product.MALE,
        20, 50, "Computers"));
     w.add(new ProductImpl("ClueLess Network Computer",
        Product.BOTH,
        6, 200, "Computers"));
   }
}
```

NOTE: Remember that you must start the registry and the server program and keep both running before you start the client.

Example 5-10 shows the code for the client. When the user clicks on the Submit button, a new customer object is generated and passed to the remote `find` method. Then, the customer record is displayed in the text area (to prove that the `clear` call in the server did not affect it). Finally, the product descriptions of the returned products in the vector are added to the text area. Note that each `getDescription` call is again a remote method invocation.

Example 5-10: WarehouseClient.java

```java
import java.awt.*;
import java.awt.event.*;
import java.rmi.*;
import java.rmi.server.*;
import java.util.*;
import corejava.*;

public class WarehouseClient extends CloseableFrame
    implements ActionListener
{   public WarehouseClient()
    {   setLayout(new GridBagLayout());

        GridBagConstraints gbc = new GridBagConstraints();
        gbc.fill = GridBagConstraints.NONE;
        gbc.weightx = 100;
        gbc.weighty = 100;
        add(new Label("Age:"), gbc, 0, 0, 1, 1);
        add(age = new IntTextField(0, 4), gbc, 1, 0, 1, 1);
        CheckboxGroup cbg = new CheckboxGroup();
        add(male = new Checkbox("Male", cbg, true), gbc, 0, 1, 1,
            1);
        add(female = new Checkbox("Female", cbg, true), gbc, 1, 1,
            1, 1);
        add(new Label("Hobbies"), gbc, 0, 2, 1, 1);
        hobbies = new List(4, true);
        hobbies.addItem("Gardening");
        hobbies.addItem("Beauty");
        hobbies.addItem("Computers");
        hobbies.addItem("Household");
        hobbies.addItem("Sports");
        add(hobbies, gbc, 1, 2, 1, 1);
        Button submitButton = new Button("Submit");
        add(submitButton, gbc, 0, 3, 2, 1);
        submitButton.addActionListener(this);
        result = new TextArea(4, 40);
        result.setEditable(false);
        add(result, gbc, 0, 4, 2, 1);
```

```
    System.setSecurityManager(new RMISecurityManager());
    String url = "rmi:///";
        // change to "rmi://www.yourserver.com/"
        // when server runs on remote machine
        // www.yourserver.com
    try
    {   centralWarehouse =
        (Warehouse)Naming.lookup("central_warehouse");
    }
    catch(Exception e)
    {   System.out.println("Error: Can't connect to warehouse. "
        + e);
    }
}

private void add(Component c, GridBagConstraints gbc,
    int x, int y, int w, int h)
{   gbc.gridx = x;
    gbc.gridy = y;
    gbc.gridwidth = w;
    gbc.gridheight = h;
    add(c, gbc);
}

public void actionPerformed(ActionEvent evt)
{   String arg = evt.getActionCommand();
    if (arg.equals("Submit"))
    {   if (age.isValid())
        {   Customer c = new Customer(age.getValue(),
                (male.getState() ? Product.MALE : 0)
                + (female.getState() ? Product.FEMALE : 0),
                hobbies.getSelectedItems());
            String t = c + "\n";
            try
            {   Vector result = centralWarehouse.find(c);
                for (int i = 0; i < result.size(); i++)
                {   Product p = (Product)result.elementAt(i);
                    t += p.getDescription() + "\n";
                }
            }
            catch(Exception e)
            {   t = "Error: " + e;
            }
            result.setText(t);
        }
    }
}
```

```
public static void main(String[] args)
{  Frame f = new WarehouseClient();
   f.setSize(300, 300);
   f.show();
}

private Warehouse centralWarehouse;
private IntTextField age;
private Checkbox male;
private Checkbox female;
private List hobbies;
private TextArea result;
}
```

Passing Remote Objects

Passing remote objects from the server to the client is simple. The client receives a stub object, then saves it in an object variable whose type is the same as the remote interface. The client can now access the actual object on the server through the variable. The client can copy this variable in its own local machine—all those copies are simply references to the same stub. It is important to note that only the *remote interfaces* can be accessed through the stub. A remote interface is any interface extending `Remote`. All local methods are inaccessible through the stub. (A local method is any method that is not defined in a remote interface.) Local methods can run only on the virtual machine containing the actual object.

Next, stubs are generated only from classes that implement a remote interface, and only the methods specified in the interfaces are provided in the stub classes. If a derived class doesn't implement a remote interface but a base class does and an object of the derived class is passed to a remote method, only the base class methods are accessible. To understand this better, consider the following example. We derive a class `BookImpl` from `ProductImpl`:

```
class BookImpl extends ProductImpl
{  public BookImpl(String title, String theISBN,
      int sex, int age1, int age2, String hobby)
   {  super(title + " Book", sex, age1, age2, hobby);
      ISBN = theISBN;
   }
   public String getStockCode() { return ISBN; }
   String ISBN;
}
```

Now, suppose we pass a book object to a remote method, either as a parameter or as a return value. The recipient obtains a stub object. But that stub is not a

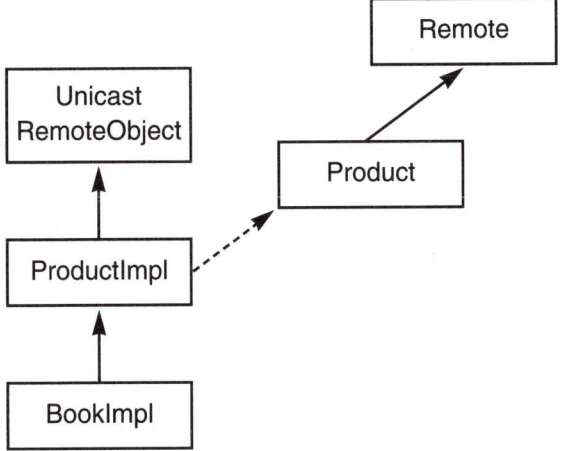

Figure 5-8: Only the `ProductImpl` methods are remote

book stub. Instead, it is a stub to the base class `ProductImpl` since only that class implements a remote interface (see Figure 5-8). Thus, in this case, the `getStockCode` method isn't available remotely.

A remote class can implement multiple interfaces. For example, the `BookImpl` class can implement a second interface in addition to `Product`. Here, we define a remote interface `StockUnit` and have the `BookImpl` class implement it.

```
interface StockUnit extends Remote
{  public String getStockCode() throws RemoteException;
}

class BookImpl extends ProductImpl implements StockUnit
{  public BookImpl(String title, String theISBN,
      int sex, int age1, int age2, String hobby)
      throws RemoteException
   {  super(title + " Book", sex, age1, age2, hobby);
      ISBN = theISBN;
   }
   public String getStockCode() throws RemoteException
   { return ISBN; }

   private String ISBN;
}
```

Figure 5-9 shows the inheritance diagram.

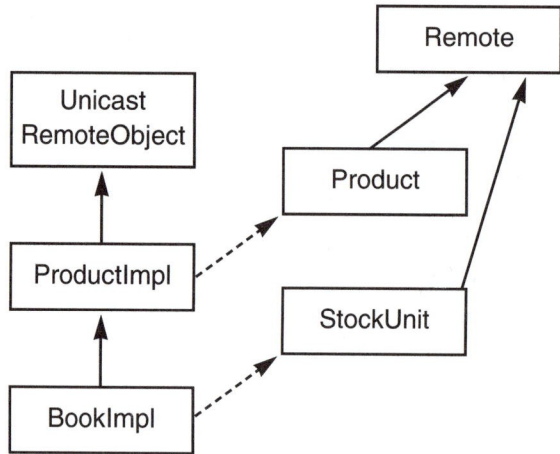

Figure 5-9: BookImpl has additional remote methods

Now, when Java passes a book object to a remote method, the recipient obtains a stub that has access to the remote methods in both the `Product` and the `StockUnit` class. In fact, you can use the `instanceof` operator to find out whether a particular remote object implements an interface. Here is a typical situation where you will use this feature. Suppose you receive a remote object through a variable of type `Product`.

```
Vector result = centralWarehouse.find(c);
for (int i = 0; i < result.size(); i++)
{   Product p = (Product)result.elementAt(i);
    . . .
}
```

Now, the remote object may or may not be a book. We'd like to use `instanceof` to find out whether it is or not. But we can't test

```
if (p instanceof BookImpl) // wrong
{   BookImpl b = (BookImpl)p;
    . . .
}
```

The object p refers to a stub object, and `BookImpl` is the class of the server object. We could cast the stub object to a `BookImpl_Stub`,

```
if (p instanceof BookImpl_Stub)
{   BookImpl_Stub b = (BookImpl_Stub)p; // not useful
    . . .
}
```

but that would not do us much good. The stubs are generated mechanically by the `rmic` program for internal use by the RMI mechanism, and clients should not have to think about them. Instead, we cast to the second interface:

```
if (p instanceof StockUnit)
{   StockUnit s = (StockUnit)p;
    String c = s.getStockCode();
    . . .
}
```

This code tests whether the stub object to which `p` refers implements the `StockUnit` interface. If so, it calls the `getStockCode` remote method of that interface.

To summarize:

- If an object belonging to a class that implements a remote interface is passed to a remote method, the remote method receives a stub object.

- You can cast that stub object to any of the remote interfaces that the implementation class implements.

- You can call all remote methods defined in those interfaces, but you cannot call any local methods through the stub.

Using Remote Objects in Hash Tables

As we saw in Chapter 11 of Volume 1, objects inserted in a hash table must override the `equals` and `hashCode` methods. Both methods are needed to find an object in a hash table. First, Java computes the hash code to find the appropriate bucket. Then, each object in that bucket is compared with the object to be matched, using the `equals` method. However, there is a problem when trying to compare remote objects. To find out if two remote objects have the same contents, the call to `equals` would need to contact the servers containing the objects and compare their contents. And that call could fail. But the `equals` method in the class `Object` is not declared to throw a `RemoteException`, whereas all methods in a remote interface must throw that exception. Since a subclass method cannot throw more exceptions than the superclass method it replaces, you cannot define an `equals` method in a remote interface. The same holds for `hashCode`.

Instead, you must rely on the redefinitions of the `equals` and `hashCode` methods in the `RemoteObject` class that is the base class for all stub and server objects. These methods do not look at the object contents, just at the location of the server objects. Two stubs that refer to the same server object are found to be equal by the `equals` method. Two stubs that refer to different server objects are never equal, even if those objects have identical contents. Similarly, the hash code is computed only from the object identifier. Stubs that refer to different

server objects will likely have different hash codes, even if the server objects have identical contents.

This limitation refers only to stubs. You can redefine `equals` or `hashCode` for the server object classes. Those methods are called when you are inserting server objects in a hash table on the server, but they are never called when you are comparing or hashing stubs. To clarify the difference between client and server behavior, look at the inheritance diagram in Figure 5-10.

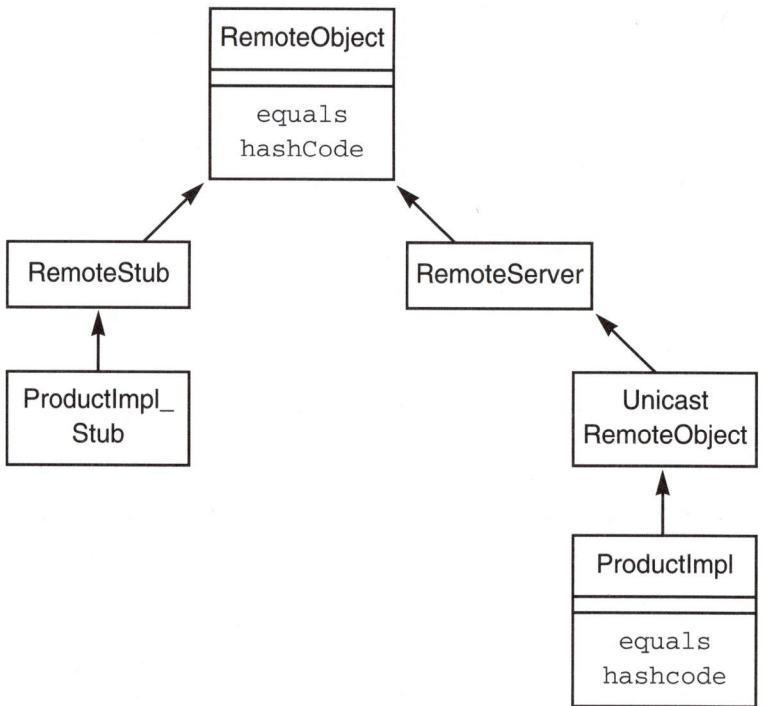

Figure 5-10: Inheritance of `equals` and `hashCode` methods

The `RemoteObject` class is the base for *both* stub and server classes. On the stub side, you cannot override the `equals` and `hashCode` methods because the stubs are mechanically generated. On the server side, you can override the methods for the implementation classes, but they are only used locally on the server. If you do override these methods, implementation and stub objects are no longer considered identical.

To summarize: You can use stub objects in hash tables, but you must remember that equality testing and hashing do not take the contents of the remote objects into account.

Cloning Remote Objects

Stubs do not have a `clone` method, so you cannot clone a remote object by invoking `clone` on the stub. The reason is again somewhat technical. If `clone` were to make a remote call to tell the server to clone the implementation object, then the `clone` method would need to throw a `RemoteException`. But the `clone` method in the `Object` superclass promised never to throw any exception except `CloneNotSupportedException`. That is the same limitation that you encountered in the previous section, when you saw that `equals` and `hashCode` don't look up the remote object value at all but just compare stub references. But it makes no sense for `clone` to make another clone of a stub—if you wanted to have another reference to the remote object, you could just copy the stub variable. Therefore, `clone` is simply not defined for stubs.

If you want to clone a remote object, you must write another method, say, `remoteClone`. Place it into the interface that defines the remote object services. Of course, that method may throw a `RemoteException`. In the implementation class, simply define `remoteClone` to call `clone` and return the cloned implementation object.

```
interface Product extends Remote
{   public Object remoteClone()
      throws RemoteException, CloneNotSupportedException;
      . . .
}

class ProductImpl extends UnicastRemoteObject
      implements Product
{   public Object remoteClone()
      throws CloneNotSupportedException
      { return clone(); }
      . . .
}
```

Inappropriate Remote Parameters

Suppose we enhance our shopping application by having the application show a picture of each gift. Can we simply add the remote method

```
void paint(Graphics g) throws RemoteException
```

to the `Product` interface? Unfortunately, this code cannot work, and it is important you understand why. The problem is that the `Graphics` class does not implement remote interfaces. Therefore, a copy of an object of type `Graphics` would need to be passed to the remote object, and you can't do this. Why? Well, `Graphics` is an abstract class, and `Graphics` objects are returned via a call to the `getGraphics` method of the `Component` class. This call, in turn, can happen only

when you have some subclass that implements a graphics context on a particular platform. Those objects, in turn, need to interact with the native graphics code, and to do so, they must store pointers to the memory blocks that are needed by the native graphics methods. Java, of course, has no pointers, so this information is stored as integers in the graphics object and is only cast back to pointers in the native peer methods. Now, first of all, the target machine may be a different platform. For example, if the client runs Windows and the server runs X11, then the server does not have the native methods available to render Windows graphics. But even if the server and the client have the same graphics system, the pointer values would not be valid on the server. Therefore, it makes no sense to copy a graphics object. For that reason, the Graphics class is not serializeable and so cannot be sent via RMI.

Instead, if the server wants to send an image to the client, it has to come up with some other mechanism for transporting the data across the network. As it turns out, this data transport is actually difficult to do for images. The Image class is just as device dependent as the Graphics class. We could send the image data as a sequence of bytes in JPEG format, but there is no method in the AWT package to turn a block of JPEG data into an image. (Currently, this can be done only by using unpublished classes in the sun.awt.image package.) Another alternative is to send an array of integers representing the pixels via a call to the PixelGrabber class and do the translation yourself—you will see this technique in Chapter 7. In the next section, we show how to solve this problem in a more mundane way: by sending a URL to the client and using a method of the Applet class that can read an image from a URL.

Using RMI with Applets

There are a number of special concerns when running RMI with applets. Applets have their own security manager since they run inside a browser. Thus, we do not use the RMISecurityManager on the client side.

We must take care where to place the stub and server files. Consider a browser that opens a Web page with an APPLET tag. The browser loads the class file referenced in that tag and all other class files as they are needed during execution. The class files are loaded from the same host that contains the Web page. Because of applet security restrictions, the applet can make network connections only to its originating host. Therefore, the server objects must reside on the same host as the Web page. That is, the same host must store

- Web page
- Applet code

- Stub code

- Skeletons and server objects

- Bootstrap registry

Here is a sample applet that further extends our shopping program. Just like the preceding application, the applet gets the customer information and then recommends matching purchases. When the user clicks on one of the suggestions, the applet displays an image of the item. As we mentioned previously, it is not easy to send an image from the server to the client because images are stored in a format that depends on the local graphics system. Instead, the server simply sends the client a string with the image file name, and we use the `getImage` method of the `Applet` class to obtain the image (see Figure 5-11).

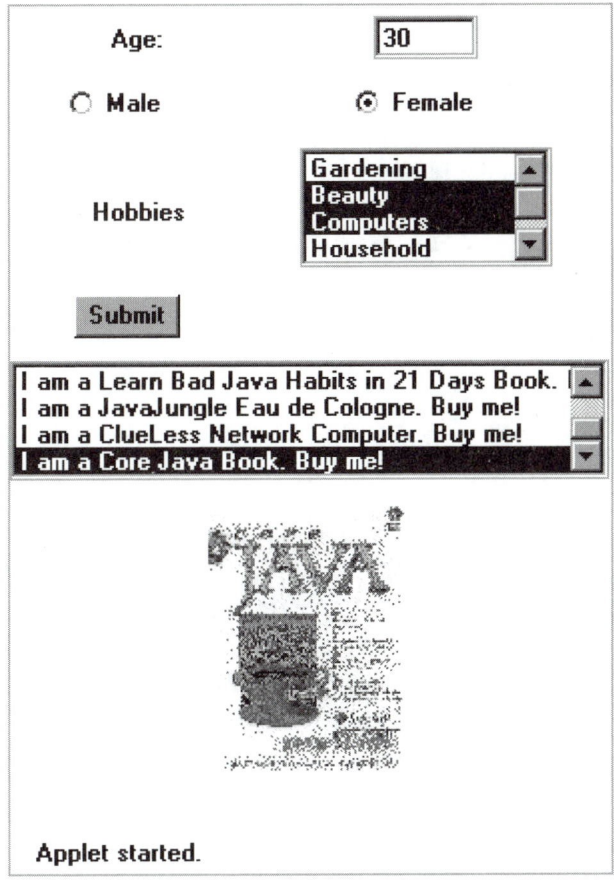

Figure 5-11: The warehouse applet

Here is how you must distribute the code for this kind of situation:

- `java.rmi.registry.RegistryImpl`—Anywhere on host; the registry must be running before applet starts
- `WarehouseServer`—Anywhere on host; must be running before the applet starts
- `WarehouseImpl`—Skeletons; can be anywhere on the host as long as `WarehouseServer` can find it
- `WarehouseApplet`—Directory referenced in `APPLET` tag
- `Stubs`—Must be in the same directory as `WarehouseApplet`

Do not try this code with a browser that does not support the RMI features of Java 1.1. The code will not work and may even crash browsers that are not ready for RMI applets. The applet works fine with the JDK applet viewer.

Example 5-11 shows the code for the applet. Note that the applet does not install a security manager and that it looks for the bootstrap registry on the same host that contains the applet.

Example 5-11: WarehouseApplet.java

```java
import java.awt.*;
import java.awt.event.*;
import java.applet.*;
import java.rmi.*;
import java.rmi.server.*;
import java.util.*;
import corejava.*;

public class WarehouseApplet extends Applet
   implements ActionListener, ItemListener
{  public void init()
   {  setLayout(new GridBagLayout());

      GridBagConstraints gbc = new GridBagConstraints();
      gbc.fill = GridBagConstraints.NONE;
      gbc.weightx = 100;
      gbc.weighty = 100;
      add(new Label("Age:"), gbc, 0, 0, 1, 1);
      add(age = new IntTextField(0, 4), gbc, 1, 0, 1, 1);
      CheckboxGroup cbg = new CheckboxGroup();
      add(male = new Checkbox("Male", cbg, true), gbc, 0, 1, 1,
         1);
```

```
        add(female = new Checkbox("Female", cbg, true), gbc, 1, 1,
            1, 1);
        add(new Label("Hobbies"), gbc, 0, 2, 1, 1);
        hobbies = new List(4, true);
        hobbies.addItem("Gardening");
        hobbies.addItem("Beauty");
        hobbies.addItem("Computers");
        hobbies.addItem("Household");
        hobbies.addItem("Sports");
        add(hobbies, gbc, 1, 2, 1, 1);
        Button submitButton = new Button("Submit");
        add(submitButton, gbc, 0, 3, 2, 1);
        submitButton.addActionListener(this);
        descriptions = new List(4, false);
        gbc.fill = GridBagConstraints.HORIZONTAL;
        add(descriptions, gbc, 0, 4, 2, 1);
        descriptions.addItemListener(this);
        gbc.fill = GridBagConstraints.NONE;
        canvas = new Canvas();
        canvas.setSize(150, 150);
        add(canvas, gbc, 0, 5, 2, 1);

        String url = getCodeBase().getHost();
        if (url.equals("default")) url = "";
        url = "rmi://" + url;
        try
        {   centralWarehouse = (Warehouse)Naming.lookup(url +
                "/central_warehouse");
        }
        catch(Exception e)
        {   showStatus("Error: Can't connect to warehouse. " + e);
        }
    }

    private void add(Component c, GridBagConstraints gbc,
        int x, int y, int w, int h)
    {   gbc.gridx = x;
        gbc.gridy = y;
        gbc.gridwidth = w;
        gbc.gridheight = h;
        add(c, gbc);
    }

    public void actionPerformed(ActionEvent evt)
    {   if (evt.getActionCommand().equals("Submit"))
        {   if (age.isValid())
            {   Customer c = new Customer(age.getValue(),
                    (male.getState() ? Product.MALE : 0)
                    + (female.getState() ? Product.FEMALE : 0),
                    hobbies.getSelectedItems());
```

```
            try
            {   products = centralWarehouse.find(c);
                descriptions.removeAll();
                for (int i = 0; i < products.size(); i++)
                {   Product p = (Product)products.elementAt(i);
                    descriptions.addItem(p.getDescription());
                }
            }
            catch(Exception e)
            {   System.out.println("Error: " + e);
            }
        }
    }
}

public void itemStateChanged(ItemEvent evt)
{   if (evt.getStateChange() == ItemEvent.SELECTED)
    {   int index = descriptions.getSelectedIndex();
        if (index < 0) return;
        try
        {   Product p = (Product)products.elementAt(index);
            productImage = getImage(getCodeBase(),
                p.getImageFile());
            repaint();
        }
        catch(Exception e)
        {   System.out.println("Error: " + e);
        }
    }
}

public void paint(Graphics g)
{   if (productImage == null) return;
    Graphics cg = canvas.getGraphics();
    cg.clearRect(0, 0, canvas.getSize().width,
        canvas.getSize().height);
    cg.drawImage(productImage, 0, 0, this);
    cg.dispose();
}

private Warehouse centralWarehouse;
private IntTextField age;
private Checkbox male;
private Checkbox female;
private List hobbies;
private List descriptions;
private Vector products;
private Canvas canvas;
private Image productImage;
}
```

The server sets the file names when it populates the database.

Example 5-12: WarehouseServer.java

```java
import java.rmi.*;
import java.rmi.server.*;

public class WarehouseServer
{  public static void main(String args[])
    {  System.setSecurityManager(new RMISecurityManager());
        try
        {  WarehouseImpl w = new WarehouseImpl();
            fillWarehouse(w);
            Naming.rebind("central_warehouse", w);
        }
        catch(Exception e)
        {  System.out.println("Error: " + e);
        }
    }

    public static void fillWarehouse(WarehouseImpl w)
        throws RemoteException
    {  w.add(new ProductImpl("Blackwell Toaster", Product.BOTH,
            18, 200, "Household", "toaster.jpg"));
        w.add(new ProductImpl("Jimbo After Shave", Product.MALE,
            18, 200, "Beauty", "shave.jpg"));
        w.add(new ProductImpl("U238 Weed Killer", Product.BOTH,
            20, 200, "Gardening", "weed.jpg"));
        w.add(new ProductImpl("Rabid Rodent Computer Mouse",
            Product.BOTH,
            6, 40, "Computers", "rodent.jpg"));
        w.add(new ProductImpl("Learn Bad Java Habits in 21 Days
            Book", Product.BOTH,
            20, 200, "Computers", "book.jpg"));
        w.add(new ProductImpl("JavaJungle Eau de Cologne",
            Product.FEMALE,
            20, 200, "Beauty", "cologne.jpg"));
        w.add(new ProductImpl("Fast/Wide SCSI Coffee Maker",
            Product.MALE,
            20, 50, "Computers", "coffee.jpg"));
        w.add(new ProductImpl("ClueLess Network Computer",
            Product.BOTH,
            6, 200, "Computers", "computer.jpg"));
        w.add(new ProductImpl("Digging Dinosaur", Product.BOTH,
            6, 200, "Gardening", "dino.jpg"));
        w.add(new ProductImpl("Fantastic Fan", Product.BOTH,
            6, 200, "Household", "fan.jpg"));
        w.add(new ProductImpl("Japanese Cat", Product.BOTH,
            6, 200, "Gardening", "cat.jpg"));
        w.add(new ProductImpl("Ms. Frizzle Curling Iron",
            Product.FEMALE,
            6, 200, "Beauty", "curl.jpg"));
    }
}
```

CHAPTER

6

- An Overview of Java's Image Manipulation

- The Java Color Models

- Image Filters

- Memory Image Sources

- Pixel Grabbing

- Data Transfer

Advanced AWT

I f all you are doing is scanning in images or downloading existing images from the net, you rarely need to get under the hood of an image. Ultimately, however, an image is an array of bits describing the pixels; Java, like most languages with sophisticated image handling, has methods both for converting an image to an array of pixels and for converting an array of pixels back to an image. This capability lets you:

- Build up images via a mathematical formula. (It is certainly quicker to send a formula for building an image across the net than it is to send a large image. Fractals like the ubiquitous Mandelbrot set are good examples of this.)

- Write conversion routines that let you move images from one Java program to another, or even to programs written in other languages.

- Easily modify the image pixel by pixel. (For example, you might want to make it brighter or to sharpen it in some way.)

This chapter shows you the techniques that you need in order to do this kind of pixel-by-pixel manipulation. We first show you the image filtering classes built into Java. You can use one of these image filters to modify an existing image fairly effortlessly, and you can build your own image filters for more sophisticated image editing. Then, we move on to the methods for building up an image from an array of pixels, including a nifty new way to do animations that was added to Java 1.1.

We end this chapter by taking up Java's new Cut and Paste feature. Note that although "Cut and Paste" is prominently mentioned as a major addition to Java 1.1, in practice the implementation is yet one more reminder that you are dealing with the "Java development kit"—some assembly is definitely required. The off-the-shelf JDK implements only the simplest case of transferring strings, curiously omitting the capability to transfer Java objects between different Java programs. In the last section of this book, we show you how to remedy this omission for serializable Java objects—while we all await JavaSoft's official solution for the general case in the next version of Java.

NOTE: This (relatively) short chapter can in no way substitute for such specialized books as David Geary's *Graphic Java 1.1* (also from Sunsoft/Prentice Hall) or the very comprehensive and useful book by John Zukowski, *Java AWT Reference* (O'Reilly, 1997). We advise people needing more specialized techniques than those covered here to consult one of these two books. Also note that we do *not* cover the various Java class libraries that extend the basic AWT and that are still in development. Both the Java Foundation classes (JFC—sometimes called the "Swing Set" from the Sun/IBM/Netscape alliance) and the "Application Foundation Classes" (AFC from Microsoft) promise to revolutionize the GUI end of the AWT by adding the kind of components that users have grown to expect. In either case, using them will not be much different than using the existing AWT components, as described in Volume 1.

An Overview of Java's Image Manipulation

As you saw in Chapter 7 of Volume 1, the basic AWT toolkit can load graphics files in the standard GIF and JPEG format. (Java 1.1 can also transparently handle animated GIF files, the so-called GIF89a specification—calling `drawImage` will start the animation.) To manipulate these images or to write the code that will allow images of other types to be used in Java programs, you need to understand the basic Java imaging classes and interfaces, as shown in Figure 6-1.

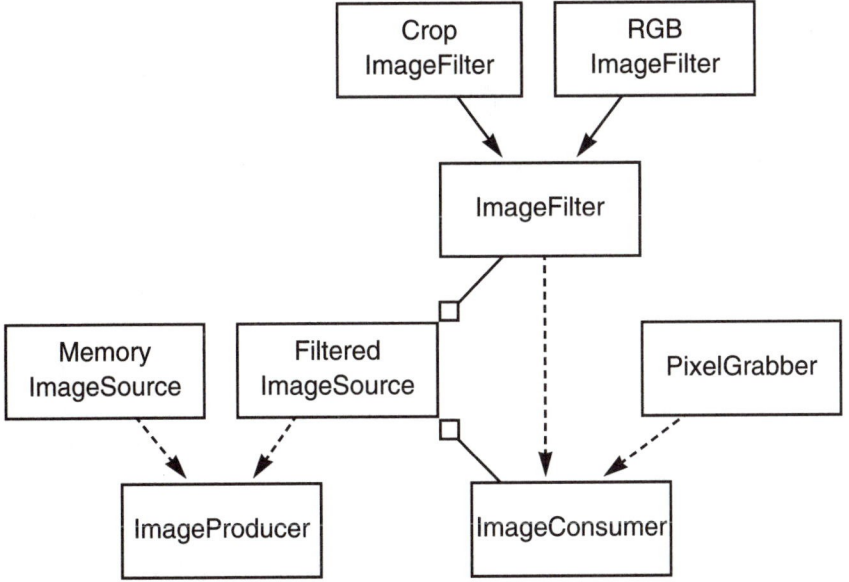

Figure 6-1: The image manipulation classes and interfaces

From the figure, you can deduce the following:

- Any object that implements Java's `ImageProducer` interface can produce the data for an image.

- Any object that implements the `ImageConsumer` interface can take the data from an image producer.

- You can place any object that implements the `ImageFilter` interface between an image producer and an image consumer in order to modify the image. Use `FilteredImageSource` objects for the communication between producer, filter, and consumer.

Of course, as you will soon see, Java comes with filter classes, and you can also design your own. For example, a specialized image filter might try to "sharpen" or "bleach" the image produced by the image producer.

NOTE: For monitoring the asynchronous loading of images, an object that implements `ImageObserver` must be involved. See Chapter 7 of Volume 1 for more on image observers.

The Java Color Models

Before you can go deeper with the image manipulation process, you need to understand the various ways Java can handle color for individual pixels. Java uses subclasses of an abstract class called `ColorModel` to hold color information. The default color model is encapsulated in a subclass called `DirectColorModel`. This model uses a single integer to describe each pixel, thus allowing 32 bits for the color model. The bits are divided into four bytes: three for the familiar red, green, blue and the fourth byte for the "alpha," which defines the transparency of the pixel. If the alpha byte is 0, then the pixel is transparent and the background shines clearly through. If the alpha byte is 255, then the pixel is opaque. Using 24 bits for the color information allows the standard "true" color model (16,777,216 colors) to be used. Keep in mind that while the AWT will make its best approximation to the color of a pixel if the target system doesn't support high color, it does require at least 256-color support.

The other common situation that you may find yourself in is one where video memory is at a premium and high color is not needed. For this situation Java allows you to use an *indexed color model*, which gives you a palette of a small number of colors to work with—16 or 256 colors are typical. With an indexed color model, the colors are not themselves limited—only the number of colors that you can display on the screen at any one time is limited. As the API notes indicate, most of the constructors that build images can use an indexed color model in addition to the default color model. (For those who are familiar with the internals of video cards, standard VGA on a PC uses an indexed color model.) The constructors of the `IndexColorModel` class take arrays of bytes to specify the red, green, and blue values for each of the colors that you want to use.

java.awt.image.ColorModel

- `ColorModel getRGBdefault()`

  returns the default `ColorModel` (which specifies color values in the format `0xAARRGGBB`).

- `int getAlpha(int pixel)`

  returns the alpha component of pixel for a color model as a value between 0 and 255. A value of 0 means the pixel is transparent; 255 means the pixel is opaque. Values between 0 and 255 specify varying degrees of transparency.

- `int getRed(int pixel)`

- `int getGreen(int pixel)`

- `int getBlue(int pixel)`

  return the redness, greenness, or blueness of a pixel on a scale of 0 to 255, with 255 being the maximum intensity for that color.

- `int getRGB(int pixel)`

  returns the color of the pixel in the default RGB color model (in the format `0xAARRGGBB`). This operation simply returns `pixel` in the default color model, but in other color models (such as the `IndexColorModel`), it looks up the actual color.

`java.awt.image.ColorModel.IndexColorModel`

- `IndexColorModel(int bits, int size, byte[] r, byte[] g, byte[] b)`

- `IndexColorModel(int bits, int size, byte[] r, byte[] g, byte[] b, byte[] a)`

  construct an `IndexColorModel` from the given arrays of red, green, blue, and alpha components. All of the arrays must have at least `size` entries.

Parameters:	bits	the number of bits per pixel
	size	the size of the component arrays
	r	the red color components
	g	the green color components
	b	the blue color components
	a	the alpha components

- `IndexColorModel (int bits, int size, byte colorMap[], int start, boolean hasalpha, int transparent)`

Parameters	bits	the number of bits per pixel
	size	the number of elements in the color map
	colorMap	the array to hold the color map; the array contains consecutive (r, g, b) or (r, g, b, a) values
	start	where to start looking in the `colorMap` array (usually 0)
	hasAlpha	`true` if `colorMap` has alpha (transparency) components

`transparent`	the location of the transparent pixel in the map. An `IndexColorMap` can have one designated, completely transparent pixel (with alpha value of zero, irrespective of the setting in the `colorMap` array). If there is no designated transparent pixel, this parameter should be –1.

Image Filters

Suppose you have an image object, for example, as the return value of the `getImage` method of the `Toolkit` class.

```
Image img = Toolkit.getDefaultToolkit().getImage("myfile.gif");
```

As you saw in Chapter 7 of Volume 1, an `Image` object does not contain the actual pixels of the image; it just knows where to find these pixels. The image is acquired only when the image pixels are actually needed. You can display an image object with the `drawImage` method of the `Graphics` class, but if you want to modify the image, you need an `ImageProducer`. Actually, `ImageProducer` is an interface, so you need an object of a class implementing that interface.

However, the class `Image` does not implement the `ImageProducer` interface. To obtain an object that can produce the pixels of the image (which is of some unknown class that implements the `ImageProducer` interface), you call the `getSource` method of the `Image` class:

```
ImageProducer prod = img.getSource();
```

Now, you are ready to apply an image filter. Image filters are objects of classes that extend `ImageFilter`. The base class `ImageFilter` implements the `ImageConsumer` interface. Typical filtering operations are to crop, blur, sharpen, or brighten the image. Each filtering operation requires a filter object of a particular `ImageFilter` subclass. You pass the image producer and the filter object to the constructor of `FilteredImageSource`, which is yet another class implementing `ImageProducer`.

```
ImageProducer filteredProd = new FilteredImageSource(prod,
    filter);
```

Of course, you can now apply a second filter.

```
ImageProducer filteredProd2 = new
    FilteredImageSource(filteredProd, filter2);
```

When you are done, you need to turn the result back into an image. The `Toolkit` class has a method `createImage` that turns an image producer back into an image.

```
Image filtered =
    Toolkit.getDefaultToolkit().createImage(filteredProd2);
```

There is also a `createImage` method in the `Component` class. If the call to `createImage` is contained in a method of a class derived from a component such as `Frame` or `Canvas`, you can simply call

```
Image filtered = createImage(filteredProd2);
// inside Component subclass
```

`java.awt.Image`

- `ImageProducer getSource()`

  returns an image producer that produces pixels from the image.

`java.awt.image.FilteredImageSource`

- `FilteredImageSource(ImageProducer original,`
  `ImageFilter filter)`

Parameters	original	the source of the original image
	filter	the filter to use

`java.awt.Toolkit`

- `Image createImage(ImageProducer producer)`

  creates an image from the pixels that are produced by the image producer.

`java.awt.Component`

- `Image createImage(ImageProducer producer)`

  creates an image from the pixels that are produced by the image producer.

CropImageFilter

Java 1.1 supplies a few image filters, and it is usually a simple, albeit tedious, task to roll your own. Let's first take up the supplied filter for getting a rectangular piece of an existing image ("cropping" in publishers' jargon). It is, therefore, called the `CropImageFilter`.

You do not need to subclass this class. Its constructor is:

```
CropImageFilter(int x, int y, int width, int height)
```

This constructor specifies the (rectangular) part of the old image to use for the new image. The x, y parameters specify the top left corner for the cropped image, and the width and height parameters specify how large and image to crop. If the (x, y) coordinates are outside the original image area, you end up with nothing in the cropped image. If you ask for too large a width and height relative to the starting coordinates x and y, you get a black region in the excess area. Example 6-1 puts the crop filter to use. The `getFilteredImage` method has as parameters the image file name and the percentage of the image to be retained. It then loads and filters the image. You can select a different file name from the File menu option. Use the scrollbar at the bottom of the screen to change the crop factor. Figure 6-2 shows an example of a cropped image.

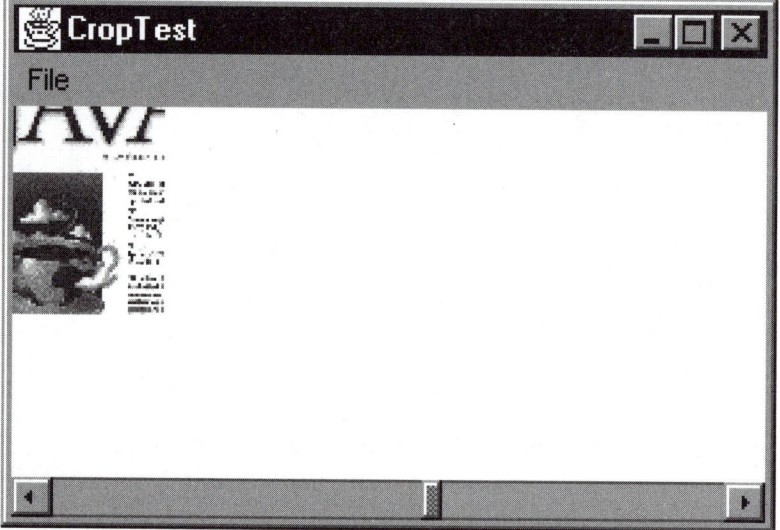

Figure 6-2: The crop filter

Example 6-1: CropTest.java

```java
import java.awt.*;
import java.awt.event.*;
import java.awt.image.*;
import corejava.*;

public class CropTest extends CloseableFrame
   implements ActionListener, AdjustmentListener
{  public CropTest()
    {  MenuBar mbar = new MenuBar();
```

```
    Menu m = new Menu("File");
    MenuItem m1 = new MenuItem("Open");
    m1.addActionListener(this);
    m.add(m1);
    MenuItem m2 = new MenuItem("Exit");
    m2.addActionListener(this);
    m.add(m2);
    mbar.add(m);
    setMenuBar(mbar);

    scroller = new Scrollbar(Scrollbar.HORIZONTAL, 0, 0,
        0, 100);
    scroller.setValue(50);
    scroller.setBlockIncrement(10);
    scroller.addAdjustmentListener(this);
    add(scroller, "South");
}

public double getScrollValue()
{   return (double)scroller.getValue()
        / scroller.getMaximum();
}

public void adjustmentValueChanged(AdjustmentEvent evt)
{   getFilteredImage(getScrollValue(), fileName);
}

public void actionPerformed(ActionEvent evt)
{   String arg = evt.getActionCommand();
    if (arg.equals("Open"))
    {   FileDialog d = new FileDialog(this,
            "Open file", FileDialog.LOAD);
        d.setDirectory(lastDir);
        d.show();
        String f = d.getFile();
        lastDir = d.getDirectory();
        if (f != null)
        {   fileName = lastDir + f;
            getFilteredImage(getScrollValue(), fileName);
        }
    }
    else if(arg.equals("Exit")) System.exit(0);
}

public void getFilteredImage(double d, String file)
{   Toolkit tk = Toolkit.getDefaultToolkit();
    orig = tk.getImage(file);
    MediaTracker mt = new MediaTracker(this);
```

```
            mt.addImage(orig, 0);
            try
            {   mt.waitForAll();
                int w = orig.getWidth(this);
                int h = orig.getHeight(this);
                int neww = (int)(d * w);
                int newh = (int)(d * h);
                ImageProducer prod = orig.getSource();
                ImageFilter filter = new CropImageFilter
                    ((w - neww) / 2, (h - newh) / 2, neww, newh);
                ImageProducer filteredProd
                    = new FilteredImageSource(prod, filter);
                filtered = tk.createImage(filteredProd);
                repaint();
            }
            catch (InterruptedException e)
            {   e.printStackTrace();
            }
        }

    public void paint(Graphics g)
    {   g.translate(getInsets().left, getInsets().top);
        if (filtered != null)
            g.drawImage(filtered, 0, 0, this);
    }

    public static void main(String[] args)
    {   Frame f = new CropTest();
        f.setVisible(true);
    }

    private Image orig;
    private Image filtered;
    private String fileName = "";
    private String lastDir = "";
    private Scrollbar scroller;
}
```

`java.awt.image.CropImageFilter`

- `CropImageFilter(int x, int y, int width, int height)`

  The x and y coordinates specify the top left corner for the cropped image;
  the width and height parameters specify the width and height of the
  cropped image.

RGBImageFilter

The most common image filters used in the AWT are subclasses of the abstract class RGBImageFilter. Subclasses of RGBImageFilter classes give you filters that let you modify individual pixels based on their current color and transparency. To build a subclass of RGBImageFilter, simply override the filterRGB method. For example, the following filter can make more or less of the background show through by changing the alpha portion of the pixel.

TIP: If the filtering you build is based only on the old pixel's color, the AWT can optimize the filtering process for images that use an IndexColorModel. All it has to do is filter the image's color map rather than each pixel. To filter the image's color map, set the canFilterIndexColorModel instance field in your class to true. (The default is false.)

```
class TransparentImageFilter extends RGBImageFilter
{   public TransparentImageFilter(double d)
        throws IllegalArgumentException
    {   if ((d < 0.0) || (d > 1.0))
            throw new IllegalArgumentException();
        level = d;
        canFilterIndexColorModel = true;
    }

    public int filterRGB(int x, int y, int argb)
    {   int alpha = (argb >> 24) & 0xFF;
        alpha = (int)(alpha * level);
        return ((argb & 0x00FFFFFF) | (alpha << 24));
    }

    private double level;
}
```

Example 6-2 shows how to use this RGB image filter. You can select a file with the File menu option. Use the scrollbar at the bottom of the screen to change the transparency level. When the slider is all the way to the left, the yellow background color hides the image. When the slider is all the way to the right, the image covers the background. At other settings, the background shines through to varying degrees (see Figure 6-3).

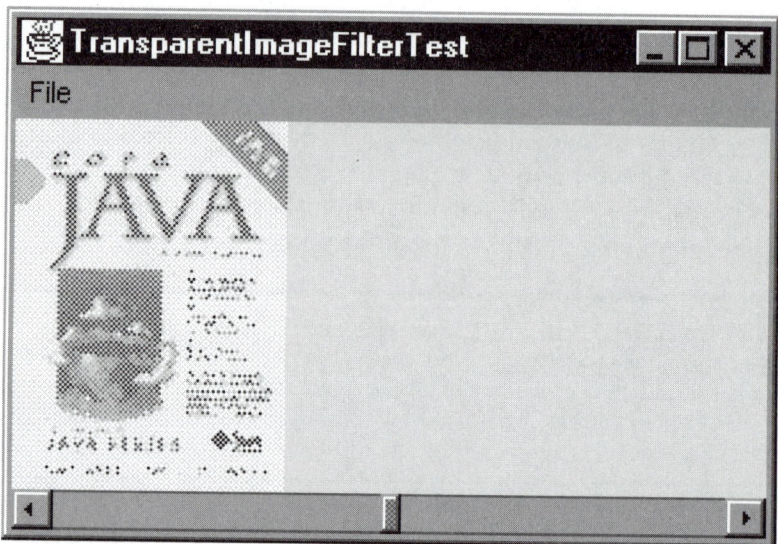

Figure 6-3: The transparent filter

Example 6-2: TransparentImageFilterTest.java

```java
import java.awt.*;
import java.awt.event.*;
import java.awt.image.*;
import corejava.*;

public class TransparentImageFilterTest extends CloseableFrame
    implements ActionListener, AdjustmentListener
{   public TransparentImageFilterTest()
    {   MenuBar mbar = new MenuBar();
        Menu m = new Menu("File");
        MenuItem m1 = new MenuItem("Open");
        m1.addActionListener(this);
        m.add(m1);
        MenuItem m2 = new MenuItem("Exit");
        m2.addActionListener(this);
        m.add(m2);
        mbar.add(m);
        setMenuBar(mbar);

        scroller = new Scrollbar(Scrollbar.HORIZONTAL, 0, 0,
            0, 100);
        scroller.setValue(50);
        scroller.setBlockIncrement(10);
        scroller.addAdjustmentListener(this);
        add(scroller, "South");
```

```
      setBackground(Color.yellow);
   }

   public double getScrollValue()
   {  return (double)scroller.getValue() / scroller.getMaximum();
   }

   public void adjustmentValueChanged(AdjustmentEvent evt)
   {  getFilteredImage(getScrollValue(), fileName);
   }

   public void actionPerformed(ActionEvent evt)
   {  String arg = evt.getActionCommand();
      if (arg.equals("Open"))
      {  FileDialog d = new FileDialog(this,
            "Open file", FileDialog.LOAD);
         d.setDirectory(lastDir);
         d.show();
         String f = d.getFile();
         lastDir = d.getDirectory();
         if (f != null)
         {  fileName = lastDir + f;
            getFilteredImage(getScrollValue(), fileName);
         }
      }
      else if(arg.equals("Exit")) System.exit(0);
   }

   public void getFilteredImage(double d, String file)
   {  Toolkit tk = Toolkit.getDefaultToolkit();
      orig = tk.getImage(file);
      ImageProducer prod = orig.getSource();
      ImageFilter filter = new TransparentImageFilter(d);
      ImageProducer filteredProd
         = new FilteredImageSource(prod, filter);
      filtered = tk.createImage(filteredProd);
      repaint();
   }

   public void paint(Graphics g)
   {  g.translate(getInsets().left, getInsets().top);
      if (filtered != null)
         g.drawImage(filtered, 0, 0, this);
   }
```

```
    public static void main(String[] args)
    {   Frame f = new TransparentImageFilterTest();
        f.show();
    }

    private Image orig;
    private Image filtered;
    private String fileName = "";
    private String lastDir = "";
    private Scrollbar scroller;
}

class TransparentImageFilter extends RGBImageFilter
{   public TransparentImageFilter(double d)
        throws IllegalArgumentException
    {   if ((d < 0.0) || (d > 1.0))
            throw new IllegalArgumentException();
        level = d;
        canFilterIndexColorModel = true;
    }

    public int filterRGB(int x, int y, int argb)
    {   int alpha = (argb >> 24) & 0xFF;
        alpha = (int)(alpha * level);
        return ((argb & 0x00FFFFFF) | (alpha << 24));
    }

    private double level;
}
```

java.awt.image.RGBImageFilter

- `int filterRGB (int x, int y, int argb)`

returns the new color value for the pixel.

Parameters	`x, y`	the coordinates of the pixel
	`argb`	the color value at the position

Obviously, RGB filters are about the simplest kinds of filters to create since you are working with one pixel at a time. More complex filters such as sharpening or blurring filters typically look at the value of the original and (at least) the eight pixels that typically surround the pixel you want to modify. You build one of these more sophisticated image filters by subclassing the `ImageFilter` class. The reason to use filters (rather than directly manipulating arrays of pixels) is to enable *incremental rendering*. Since the image can come from a slow network

source, it is desirable if the filter processes pixels whenever they are available and passes them on to the image consumer as soon as possible. That way, parts of the image can be displayed as soon as the pixels are downloaded and processed. In contrast, if all pixels of an image need to be available before the image processing starts, then the user viewing the processed image may have to wait a long time before seeing the result.

Unfortunately, writing a good image filter is quite complex. Here is the basic process.

The filter is called repeatedly by the image producer. First, the producer calls the `setDimensions`, `setHints`, and `setColorModel` methods to tell the filter about the image size and pixel delivery. Then, the producer keeps calling `setPixels` to deliver pixels to the filter. Finally, the producer calls `imageComplete` to signal completion.

The `setHints` method tells the filter how the pixels will be delivered. The options are:

- `COMPLETESCANLINES`—The pixels will be delivered in complete scan lines; that is, each time `setPixels` is called, one or more complete scan lines are delivered.

- `RANDOMPIXELORDER`—The pixels will be delivered in a random order. This happens, for example, for interlaced GIF files.

- `TOPDOWNLEFTRIGHT`—The pixels will be delivered from the top to the bottom, and each delivery contains either complete scan lines or a part of a single scan line, with scan line parts delivered left to right.

- `SINGLEPASS`—The pixels will be delivered in a single pass. This flag is `false`, for example, for a progressively rendered JPEG, in which a better representation follows an initial approximate representation. When this flag is `true`, each pixel is delivered exactly once.

`SINGLEFRAME`—The image consists of a single frame. This flag is `false` for an animated GIF.

A filter that wants to support incremental rendering has to implement two separate strategies for processing the image. If the image is delivered in random order (for example, an interlaced GIF), then the image filter must first store all incoming pixels in an array and perform the processing when its `imageComplete` method is called. However, if the image is delivered in a more regular fashion, then the image filter should process the available pixels immediately.

To further complicate matters, there are two separate `setPixels` methods:

```
void setPixels(int x, int y, int w, int h,
    ColorModel model, int[] pixels, int off, int scansize)
```

and

```
void setPixels(int x, int y, int w, int h,
    ColorModel model, byte[] pixels, int off, int scansize)
```

One of them delivers the pixels in an `int[]` array; the other, in a `byte[]` array. Either one may be called by the image producer, depending on whether pixels are represented as integers (for example, in the default color model) or as bytes (in an indexed color model with, at most, 256 colors).

Finally, note that *each call* to `setPixels` can use a different color model! Before pixels are delivered, the image producer may call the `setColorModel` method to inform the filter which color model is likely to be used by most or all calls to `setPixels`, but there is no guarantee that all calls to `setPixels` use that color model. That means that you must translate the incoming pixels to the default color model. Or, if you are really ambitious, you can keep the pixels in the color model that was set by the `setColorModel` and hope that it does not change—usually it will not. But if it does change, you must immediately translate all cached pixels to the default color model and use the default color model from then on.

Before any pixels are sent, the `setDimensions` method of the filter is called with the width and height of the image. You can use that information to allocate buffers to hold the pixels.

The image filter needs to tell its consumer about the image that it is about to produce. That is, it must make the following calls to the consumer object:

```
setDimensions
setHints
setColorModel
setPixels
imageComplete
```

The methods of the `ImageFilter` base class automatically notify the image consumer. In your derived class, you should, therefore, pass these calls on to `super`. For example, if the filtered image has the same size as the original, then you notify the superclass, which then notifies the consumer.

```
class MyFilter extends ImageFilter
{  public void setDimensions(int w, int h)
   {  width = w; height = h;
      super.setDimensions(w, h);
   }
   . . .
}
```

However, you will probably call `super.setPixels` with some delay, when you have the actual pixels available, or in the `imageComplete` method, when all source pixels are acquired.

Example 6-3 shows an image filter in action. This filter blurs an image (see Figure 6-4). It does this as follows: For each pixel, we compute the *average* color values of the pixel and its eight neighboring pixels. Depending on a blur factor, we then replace the pixel with a weighted average of the original pixel and the computed average. If the blur factor is zero, the original pixel is kept, and the result is the original sharp image. If the blur factor is one, then the original image is replaced by the average, and the result is a blurred image. As with the preceding two programs, you can read in new images with the File menu option and adjust the blur factor with the scrollbar.

The implementation of this filter follows the general plan that was just described. Before the pixel delivery starts, the `setDimensions`, `setHints`, and `setColorModel` methods are called. We remember the width and height so that we can later allocate buffers of the appropriate size, and we tell the `ImageFilter` superclass to notify the consumer that the output image has the same size as the input image. We ignore the color model and ask the superclass to tell the consumer that the output image will have the default color model.

If the hints indicate that the input image is delivered in a single pass, in complete scan lines, and top to bottom, then we render the output incrementally. That decision is recorded in the Boolean variable `incremental`. Otherwise, we buffer the entire input in the `bufferPixels` array. For incremental rendering, we remember three scan lines at a time in the `inPixels` array. We can then compute the blur of the middle scan line. That computation is handled in the `emitFilteredScanLine` method.

The `setPixels` method feeds the pixels either to the `bufferPixels` or to the `inPixels` array, depending on the incremental rendering status. When the output is rendered incrementally, we call the `emitFilteredScanLine` method each time a new scan line has been acquired. Otherwise, we emit all output scan lines in the `imageComplete` method.

Note that, in both cases, the output image is rendered in a single pass, in complete scan lines, and top to bottom. In the `setHints` method, we ask the `ImageFilter` superclass to give the consumer that happy news.

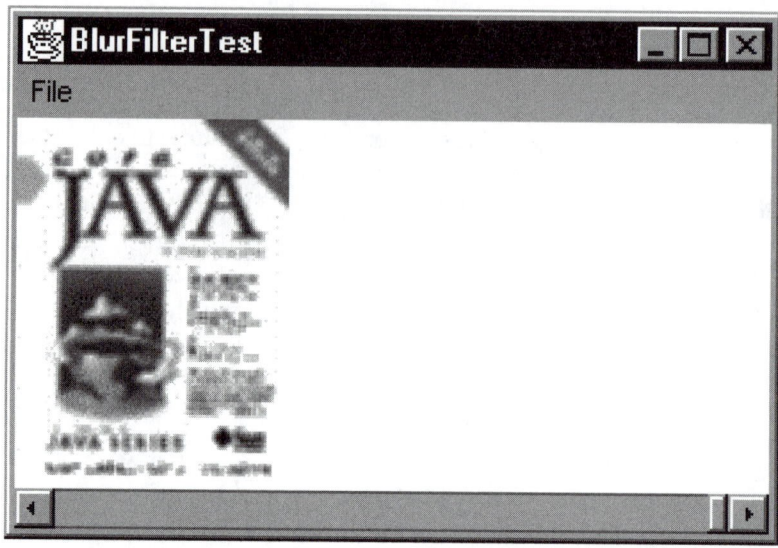

Figure 6-4: The blur filter

Example 6-3: BlurFilterTest.java

```
import java.awt.*;
import java.awt.event.*;
import java.awt.image.*;
import corejava.*;

public class BlurFilterTest extends CloseableFrame
    implements ActionListener, AdjustmentListener
{   public BlurFilterTest()
    {   MenuBar mbar = new MenuBar();
        Menu m = new Menu("File");
        MenuItem m1 = new MenuItem("Open");
        m1.addActionListener(this);
        m.add(m1);
        MenuItem m2 = new MenuItem("Exit");
        m2.addActionListener(this);
        m.add(m2);
        mbar.add(m);
        setMenuBar(mbar);

        scroller = new Scrollbar(Scrollbar.HORIZONTAL, 0, 0,
            0, 100);
        scroller.setValue(50);
        scroller.setBlockIncrement(10);
        scroller.addAdjustmentListener(this);
```

```
        add(scroller, "South");
    }

    public double getScrollValue()
    {   return (double)scroller.getValue()
            / scroller.getMaximum();
    }

    public void adjustmentValueChanged(AdjustmentEvent evt)
    {   getFilteredImage(getScrollValue(), fileName);
    }

    public void actionPerformed(ActionEvent evt)
    {   String arg = evt.getActionCommand();
        if (arg.equals("Open"))
        {   FileDialog d = new FileDialog(this,
                "Open file", FileDialog.LOAD);
            d.setDirectory(lastDir);
            d.show();
            String f = d.getFile();
            lastDir = d.getDirectory();
            if (f != null)
            {   fileName = lastDir + f;
                getFilteredImage(getScrollValue(), fileName);
            }
        }
        else if(arg.equals("Exit")) System.exit(0);
    }

    public void getFilteredImage(double d, String file)
    {   Toolkit tk = Toolkit.getDefaultToolkit();
        orig = tk.getImage(file);
        ImageProducer prod = orig.getSource();
        ImageFilter filter = new BlurFilter(d);
        ImageProducer filteredProd
            = new FilteredImageSource(prod, filter);
        filtered = tk.createImage(filteredProd);
        repaint();
    }

    public void paint(Graphics g)
    {   g.translate(getInsets().left, getInsets().top);
        if (filtered != null)
            g.drawImage(filtered, 0, 0, this);
    }

    public static void main(String[] args)
    {   Frame f = new BlurFilterTest();
```

```
        f.show();
    }

    private Image orig;
    private Image filtered;
    private String fileName = "";
    private String lastDir = "";
    private Scrollbar scroller;
}

class BlurFilter extends ImageFilter
{   public BlurFilter(double d)
        throws IllegalArgumentException
    {   if ((d < 0.0) || (d > 1.0))
            throw new IllegalArgumentException();
        level = d;
    }

    public void setPixels(int x, int y, int w, int h,
        ColorModel model, byte pixels[],
        int off, int scansize)
    {
        if (incremental)
        {   for (int i = 0; i < h; i++)
            {   emitFilteredScanLine();
                for (int j = 0; j < w; j++)
                {
                    inPixels[2][j]
                        = model.getRGB(0xFF & pixels[i * scansize
                            + j + off]);
                }
            }
        }
        else
        {   if (bufferPixels == null)
                bufferPixels = new int[width * height];
            for (int i = 0; i < h; i++)
                for (int j = 0; j < w; j++)
                    bufferPixels[(i + y) * width + j + x]
                        = model.getRGB(pixels[i * scansize
                            + j + off]);
        }
    }

    public void setPixels(int x, int y, int w, int h,
        ColorModel model, int pixels[],
        int off, int scansize)
    {   if (incremental)
```

```java
    {   for (int i = 0; i < h; i++)
        {   emitFilteredScanLine();
            for (int j = 0; j < w; j++)
                inPixels[2][j]
                    = model.getRGB(pixels[i * scansize
                        + j + off]);
        }
    }
    else
    {   if (bufferPixels == null)
            bufferPixels = new int[width * height];
        for (int i = 0; i < h; i++)
            for (int j = 0; j < w; j++)
                bufferPixels[(i + y) * width + j + x]
                    = model.getRGB(pixels[i * scansize
                        + j + off]);
    }
}

public void imageComplete(int status)
{   if (status == ImageConsumer.STATICIMAGEDONE
        || status == ImageConsumer.SINGLEFRAMEDONE)
    {   if (!incremental)
        {   for (int i = 0; i < height; i++)
            {   emitFilteredScanLine();
                for (int j = 0; j < width; j++)
                {   inPixels[2][j]
                        = bufferPixels[i * width + j];
                }
            }
        }
        emitFilteredScanLine();
        emitFilteredScanLine();
    }
    super.imageComplete(status);
}

public void emitFilteredScanLine()
{   if (inPixels == null)
    {   inPixels = new int[3][width];
        outPixels = new int[width];
        yout = -2;
    }
    if (yout >= 0)
    {   for (int i = 0; i < width; i++)
        {   int count = 0;
            int asum = 0;
            int rsum = 0;
```

```
                    int gsum = 0;
                    int bsum = 0;
                    for (int y = -1; y <= 1; y++)
                       for (int x = -1; x <= 1; x++)
                          if (0 <= yout + y && yout + y < height
                             && 0 <= i + x && i + x < width)
                          {  count++;
                             int p = inPixels[1 + y][i + x];
                             asum += (p >> 24) & 0xFF;
                             rsum += (p >> 16) & 0xFF;
                             gsum += (p >> 8)  & 0xFF;
                             bsum += p         & 0xFF;
                          }

                 int p = inPixels[1][i];
                 int a = (int)((level * asum) / count
                    + (1 - level) * ((p >> 24) & 0xFF));
                 int r = (int)((level * rsum) / count
                    + (1 - level) * ((p >> 16) & 0xFF));
                 int g = (int)((level * gsum) / count
                    + (1 - level) * ((p >> 8) & 0xFF));
                 int b = (int)((level * bsum) / count
                    + (1 - level) * (p & 0xFF));

                 outPixels[i] = (a << 24) | (r << 16)
                    | (g << 8) | b;
              }
           super.setPixels(0, yout, width, 1,
              ColorModel.getRGBdefault(), outPixels, 0, width);
        }
        int[] temp = inPixels[0];
        inPixels[0] = inPixels[1];
        inPixels[1] = inPixels[2];
        inPixels[2] = temp;
        yout++;
   }

   public void setColorModel(ColorModel model)
   {  super.setColorModel(ColorModel.getRGBdefault());
   }

   public void setDimensions(int w, int h)
   {  width = w; height = h;
      super.setDimensions(w, h);
   }

   public void setHints(int h)
   {  incremental = (h & ImageConsumer.TOPDOWNLEFTRIGHT) != 0
```

```
            && (h & ImageConsumer.COMPLETESCANLINES) != 0
            && (h & ImageConsumer.SINGLEPASS) != 0;
      super.setHints(ImageConsumer.TOPDOWNLEFTRIGHT |
         ImageConsumer.COMPLETESCANLINES);
   }

   private boolean incremental = false;
   private int width;
   private int height;
   private double level;
   private int yout;
   private int[] bufferPixels;
   private int[][] inPixels;
   private int[] outPixels;
}
```

---

java.awt.image.ImageFilter

- void setDimensions(int width, int height)

  notifies the image filter of the width and height of the image to be filtered.

- void setColorModel(ColorModel model)

  notifies the image filter of the color model to be used for most or all pixel deliveries.

- void setHints(int hints)

  notifies the image filter of the order in which pixels will be delivered.

Parameters	hints	may contain the following flags: COMPLETESCANLINES, RANDOMPIXELORDER, TOPDOWNLEFTRIGHT, SINGLEPASS, SINGLEFRAME

- void setPixels(int x, int y, int w, int h,
     ColorModel model, int[] pixels, int off, int scansize)
- void setPixels(int x, int y, int w, int h,
     ColorModel model, byte[] pixels, int off, int scansize)

  deliver a rectangular area of pixels to the image filter.

Parameters	x, y	the top left pixel in the source image
	w, h	the width and height of the area
	model	the color model used for these pixels

	`pixels`	the pixels, as an array of `byte` or `int`
	`off`	the offset of the first pixel to be used in the `pixels` array
	`scansize`	the width of a scan line in the source image

- `void imageComplete(int status)`

  notifies the image filter that pixel delivery is complete.

  Parameters   `status`   one of the following:

  > `IMAGEERROR`: an error was detected during the image creation process

  > `IMAGEABORTED`: the image creation process was aborted

  > `SINGLEFRAMEDONE`: one frame is done but there are more frames to come

  > `STATICIMAGEDONE`: all pixels are delivered

Memory Image Sources

As you have seen, image filters can be quite complex. Unless you require incremental rendering, it is usually easier to work with arrays of pixels. Where do these arrays come from? They can come from actual images, or they can be made from scratch, from mathematical formulas, or just by specifying each pixel manually. In any case, you edit an image by the following process:

1. Obtain an array of pixels.

2. Transform the array.

3. Convert the array back into an image.

The last step of this process is carried out by the `MemoryImageSource` class.

The `MemoryImageSource` class produces an image from an array of integers. A `MemoryImageSource` object is an `ImageProducer`. Therefore, you can obtain an image with the `createImage` method in the `Component` or `Toolkit` class. Alternatively, the `MemoryImageSource` can become the input of an image filter.

The simplest constructor for a `MemoryImageSource` object is:

```
MemoryImageSource(int width, int height, int[] pixels,
    int offset, int scansize)
```

This constructor creates an image of size width × height, using the information in the array of pixels interpreted according to the default color model. The offset parameter tells the constructor where to start. (For example, use 0 to start with the beginning of the array.) Finally, the scansize parameter is the number of pixels per line (and therefore is usually equal to the width parameter).

The simplest use of the MemoryImageSource class is to build up an icon directly from an array of pixels. The program in Example 6-4 does just that, drawing a purple letter "C" and a cyan letter "J" whose pixels have been specified directly. For example:

```
0xFFFF00FF
```

means a pixel that is opaque and purple, since the opaque, red, and blue values are all set to 255. We scale the image by a factor of 10 so that you can see the individual pixels clearly. Figure 6-5 shows the output of the program.

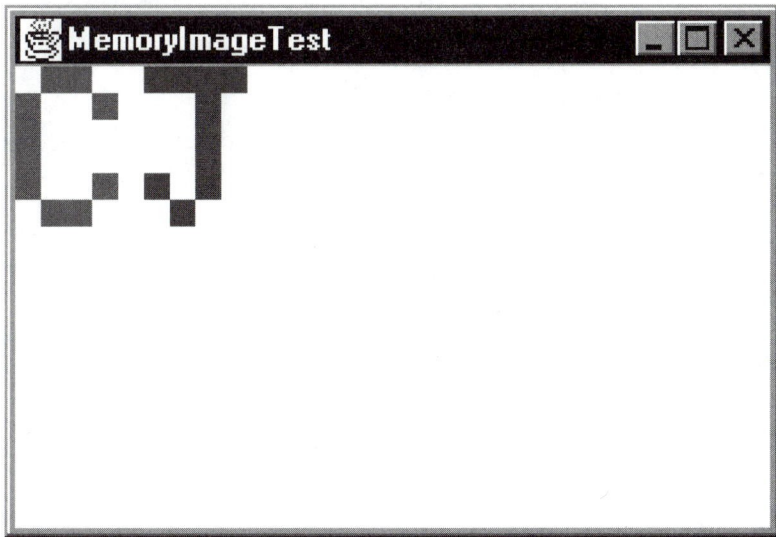

Figure 6-5: Constructing an image from individual pixels

Example 6-4: MemoryImageTest.java

```java
import java.awt.*;
import java.awt.image.*;
import corejava.*;

public class MemoryImageTest extends CloseableFrame
{   public void paint (Graphics g)
    {   g.translate(getInsets().left, getInsets().top);
        if (memImage == null)
            memImage=createImage(new MemoryImageSource(9, 6,
                pixArray, 0, 9));
        g.drawImage(memImage, 0, 0, 90, 60, this);
        // scale 9 x 6 image to 90 x 60
    }

    public static void main (String[] args)
    {   Frame f = new MemoryImageTest();
        f.show();
    }

    private int[] pixArray =
    {   0, 0xFFFF00FF, 0xFFFF00FF, 0, 0,
        0xFF007F7F, 0xFF007F7F, 0xFF007F7F, 0xFF007F7F,
        0xFFFF00FF, 0, 0, 0xFFFF00FF, 0,
        0, 0, 0xFF007F7F, 0,
        0xFFFF00FF, 0, 0, 0, 0,
        0, 0, 0xFF007F7F, 0,
        0xFFFF00FF, 0, 0, 0, 0,
        0, 0, 0xFF007F7F, 0,
        0xFFFF00FF, 0, 0, 0xFFFF00FF, 0,
        0xFF007F7F, 0, 0xFF007F7F, 0,
        0, 0xFFFF00FF, 0xFFFF00FF, 0, 0,
        0, 0xFF007F7F, 0, 0
    };


    private Image memImage;
}
```

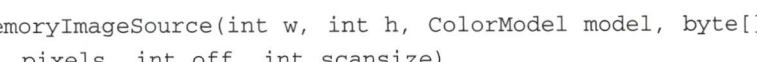

`java.awt.image.MemoryImageSource`

- `MemoryImageSource(int w, int h, int[] pixels, int off, int scansize)`

  `MemoryImageSource(int w, int h, ColorModel model, byte[] pixels, int off, int scansize)`

- `MemoryImageSource(int w, int h, ColorModel model, int[] pixels, int off, int scansize)`

  create a new memory image source from an array of pixels. The pixel at location (x, y) in the image is given by the array entry:

  `pixels[y * scansize + x + off]`.

Parameters	`w`	the width of the image being created, in pixels
	`h`	the height of the image
	`model`	the color model that describes the color representation used in the pixel data; if you omit this parameter, the `MemoryImageSource` uses the default RGB color model
	`pixels`	the array of pixel information to be converted to the image; may be either a `byte` array or an `int` array, depending on the color model used
	`off`	the first pixel used in the array (usually 0)
	`scansize`	the number of pixels per line (usually equal to `w`)

A Formula-based Example: A Black-and-White Mandelbrot Set

Obviously, building a larger image by translating the image pixel by pixel directly into an array would be rather unpleasant. (It wouldn't be hard to build an icon editor program to do this, of course. Ultimately, all non-vector-based paint programs are working on a pixel-by-pixel level.) Usually, however, you build up the `MemoryImageSource` mathematically via some formula. In this section, we bow to tradition and do a Mandelbrot set, as shown in Figure 6-6. To keep the code down to its essentials, we stick to black and white only.

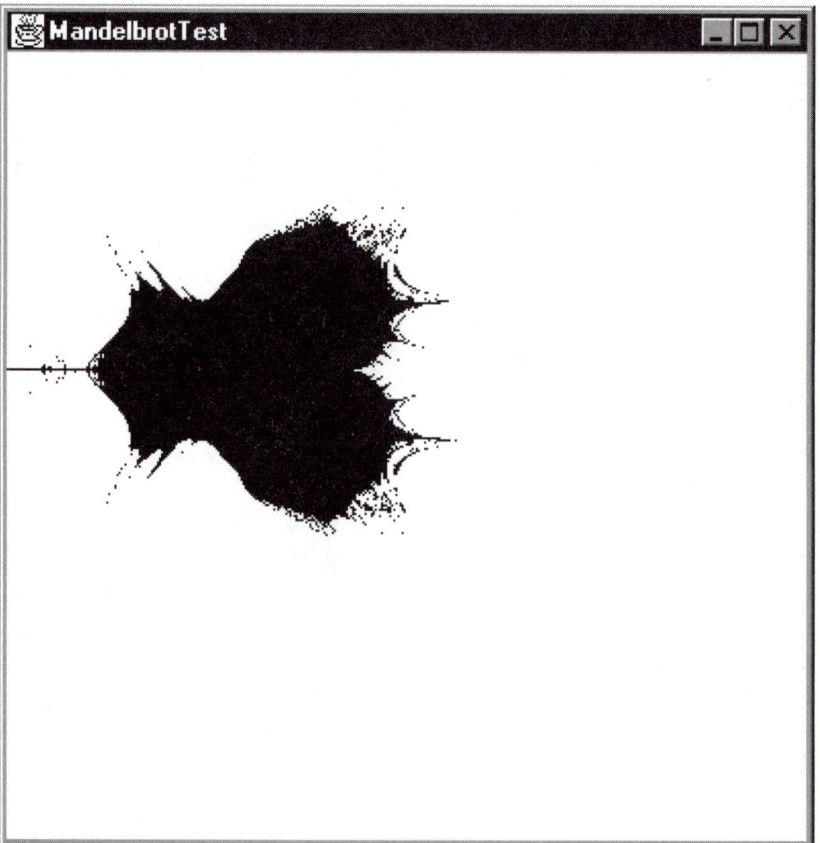

Figure 6-6: A Mandelbrot set

The idea of the Mandelbrot set is that you use an iterative process to transform points according to a formula that comes ultimately from the mathematics of complex numbers. For the simplest Mandelbrot set, you iterate:

```
xValue = (xValue * xValue) - (yValue * yValue) + xCoord;
yValue = (2 * xValue * yValue) + yCoord;
```

and check whether the point "escapes to infinity"[1]. The idea of the following code is that we place a 0xFFFFFFFF in the pixel array if the point (x,y) "escapes to infinity." We build up the array point by point in a routine we call pixArray, which returns an array of integers. Example 6-5 shows the code.

---

[1] We omit the mathematics behind this equation and the test for "escaping to infinity." For more on the mathematics of fractals, there are hundreds of books out there; one that is quite thick and comprehensive is: *Chaos and Fractals: New Frontiers of Science* by Heinz-Otto Peitgen, Hartmut Jurgens, and Dietmar Saupe (Springer Verlag, 1992).

Example 6-5: MandelbrotTest.java

```
import java.awt.*;
import java.awt.image.*;
import corejava.*;

public class MandelbrotTest extends CloseableFrame
{  public static void main (String[] args)
   {  Frame f = new MandelbrotTest(300, 300, 2.0, 2.0);
      f.setSize(400,400);
      f.show();
   }

   public MandelbrotTest(int h, int w, double x, double y)
   {  width = w;
      height = h;
      xSize = x;
      ySize = y;
      xOffset = (2.0 * xSize) / width;
      yOffset = (2.0 * ySize) / height;
      memImage = createImage(new MemoryImageSource(width,
         height, pixArray(), 0, width));
   }

   public void update(Graphics g)
   // to avoid flicker--see vol. 1 ch. 7
   {  paint(g);
   }

   public void paint(Graphics g)
   {  g.translate(getInsets().left, getInsets().top);
      g.drawImage(memImage, 0, 0, null);
   }

   public int[] pixArray()
   {  int[] pixels = new int[height * width];
      for (int i = 0; i < height; i++)
         for (int j = 0; j < width; j++)
            if (escapesToInfinity(i, j))
               pixels[i * width + j] = 0xFF000000;
            else
               pixels[i * width + j] = 0xFFFFFFFF;
      return pixels;
   }

   private boolean escapesToInfinity(int row, int col)
   {  double xCoord = - xSize + col * xOffset;
      double yCoord = - ySize + row * yOffset;
```

```
        double xValue = 0.0;
        double yValue = 0.0;
        int iterations = 0;
        while (iterations < MAX_ITERATIONS)
        {  xValue = (xValue * xValue)
                - (yValue * yValue) + xCoord;
            yValue = (2 * xValue * yValue) + yCoord;
            if (xValue > 2 || yValue > 2) break;
            iterations++;
        }
        return iterations == MAX_ITERATIONS;
    }

    private Image memImage;
    private int width;
    private int height;
    private double xSize;
    private double ySize;
    private double xOffset;
    private double yOffset;
    private int MAX_ITERATIONS = 16;
}
```

Memory Source Animations

One nice feature added to the `MemoryImageSource` class in Java 1.1 is the ability to use the class to do animations. To do an animation, you simply:

1.   Construct a `MemoryImageSource` from an array of pixels.

2.   Call `setAnimated(true)`.

3.   Attach one or more image consumers to the `MemoryImageSource`.

4.   Repeat the following for each image consumer:

     a.   Update the contents of the pixel array.

     b.   Call `newPixels`.

     c.   Repaint the image.

     d.   Sleep for a short time.

The following "poor man's morphing" program uses the animation feature in `MemoryImageSource`. The program works like this: We start with an original image and a final image that are of the same size. In our example, the original image is a purple square and the final image is a blue-green circle (see Figure 6-7).

We interpolate between the original pixel and the final pixel via the standard
formula

```
intermediateValue = (1 - t) * initialValue + t * finalValue
```

so that at time t = 0 we use the original value and at time t = 1 we use the final
value. This interpolation needs to be carried out separately for the red, green,
and blue color values.

The animation is placed into a separate thread that keeps going back and forth
between the original and final image. As you can see, the animation works well,
and it is very easy to program. But the interpolation does not give a Hollywood-
like morphing effect. For a really good morphing effect, one must work harder
and actually gradually transform the shapes, not just interpolate the pixel
colors.

Example 6-6 shows the animation program.

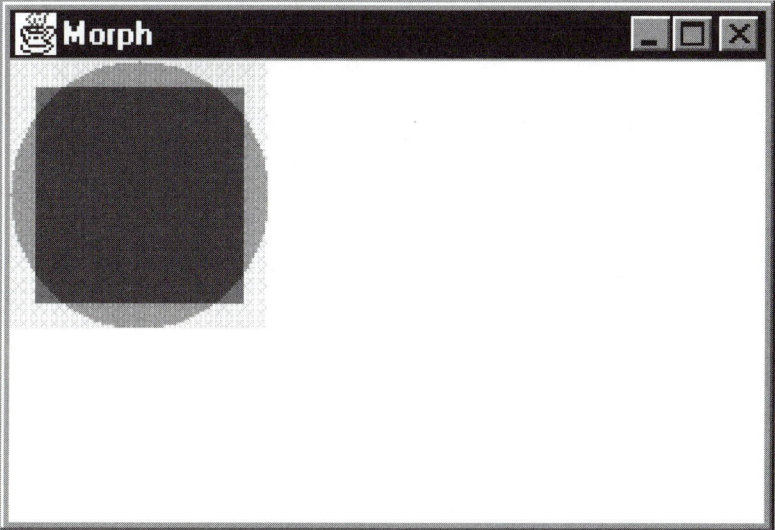

Figure 6-7: The morphing program

Example 6-6: Morph.java

```
import java.util.*;
import java.awt.*;
import java.awt.image.*;
import java.net.*;
import corejava.*;
```

```java
public class Morph extends CloseableFrame implements Runnable
{  public Morph()
   {  originalPixels = new int[SIZE * SIZE];
      for (int x = 0; x < SIZE; x++)
         for (int y = 0; y < SIZE; y++)
            if (inSquare(x, y))
               originalPixels[y * SIZE + x] = 0xFFFF00FF;
            else
               originalPixels[y * SIZE + x] = 0xFFFFFFFF;

      finalPixels = new int[SIZE * SIZE];
      for (int x = 0; x < SIZE; x++)
         for (int y = 0; y < SIZE; y++)
            if (inCircle(x, y))
               finalPixels[y * SIZE + x] = 0xFF007F7F;
            else
               finalPixels[y * SIZE + x] = 0xFFFFFFFF;

      anim = new Thread(this);
      anim.start();
   }

   private boolean inSquare(int x, int y)
   {  return SIZE / 10 <= x && x <= SIZE * 9 / 10
         && SIZE / 10 <= y && y <= SIZE * 9 / 10;
   }

   private boolean inCircle(int x, int y)
   {  double dx = x - SIZE / 2;
      double dy = y - SIZE / 2;
      return (dx * dx) / (SIZE * SIZE / 4) +
         (dy * dy) / (SIZE * SIZE / 4) <= 1;
   }

   public static void main(String[] args)
   {  Frame f = new Morph();
      f.show();
   }

   public void run()
   {  intermediatePixels = new int[SIZE * SIZE];
      System.arraycopy(originalPixels, 0,
         intermediatePixels, 0, SIZE * SIZE);
      MemoryImageSource mis
         = new MemoryImageSource(SIZE, SIZE,
            intermediatePixels, 0, SIZE);
      mis.setAnimated(true);
      theImage = createImage(mis);
```

```
        repaint();
        try
        {   double t = 0;
            int direction = 1;
            while (true)
            {   t = t + direction * 0.05;
                if (t <= 0 || t >= 1) direction *= -1;
                interpolatePixels(t);
                mis.newPixels();
                repaint();
                anim.sleep(100);
            }
        }
        catch(InterruptedException e){}
    }

    public void paint(Graphics g)
    {   g.translate(getInsets().left, getInsets().top);
        g.drawImage(theImage, 0, 0, SIZE, SIZE, null);
    }

    public void update(Graphics g)
    {   paint(g);
    }

    private void interpolatePixels(double t)
    {   for(int i = 0; i < SIZE * SIZE; i++)
        {   int p = originalPixels[i];
            int q = finalPixels[i];

            int r = (int)((1 - t) * (p & 0xFF0000)
                + t * (q  & 0xFF0000)) & 0xFF0000;
            int g = (int)((1 - t) * (p & 0xFF00)
                + t * (q & 0xFF00)) & 0xFF00;
            int b = (int)((1 - t) * (p & 0xFF)
                + t * (q & 0xFF));

            intermediatePixels[i] = 0xFF000000 | r | g | b;
        }
    }

    private Image theImage;
    private int[] originalPixels;
    private int[] finalPixels;
    private int[] intermediatePixels;
    private Thread anim;
    private static final int SIZE = 100;
}
```

 `java.awt.image.MemoryImageSource`

- `setAnimated(boolean animated)`

  determines whether animation will occur (`animated=true`). (The default is `false`.) You should call this method right after you call the `MemoryImageSource` constructor.

- `void setFullBufferUpdates(boolean fullBuffers)`

  If `fullBuffers` is `true`, then the `MemoryImageSource` sends all of an image's data to the consumers whenever it receives new data (by a call to `newPixels()`). If `fullBuffers` is `false` (the default), the `MemoryImageSource` sends only the changed portion of the image. The `setFullBufferUpdates()` method should also be called right after the `MemoryImageSource` constructor is called.

- `void newPixels()`

- `void newPixels(int x, int y, int w, int h)`

  notify the consumers attached to the `MemoryImageSource` that the contents of the pixel array have changed. The `MemoryImageSource` constructor does not make a copy of the pixel array that specifies the initial pixels; it just retains the location of that array. You can change the contents of the pixel array and call `newPixels` to make the change visible.

  The second method specifies the rectangular area (with starting point (x,y), width w and height h) that has been changed. If full buffer updates have not been requested, only the pixels in this area will be sent to the attached image consumers.

- `void newPixels(byte[] pixels, ColorModel model, int off, int scansize)`

- `void newPixels(int[] pixels, ColorModel model, int off, int scansize)`

  switch to a new pixel array and notify the consumers attached to the `MemoryImageSource`.

Parameters	`pixels`	the new array of image information
	`model`	the color model for the pixels
	`off`	the beginning of the data in the array (usually 0)
	`scansize`	the number of pixels per line

Pixel Grabbing

As we already mentioned, the `ImageFilter` classes are useful for incremental filtering, but they can be difficult to implement. It is usually much easier to manipulate the image after it has been loaded into an array of pixels. In the preceding section, you saw how to create such an array from scratch. In this section, you will see how a `PixelGrabber` can grab the pixels of an existing image and put them into an array.

The most convenient way to grab the pixels of an image is as follows:

1. Use the constructor

   ```
   PixelGrabber(image, 0, 0, -1, -1, true)
   ```

   Then, all pixels of the image will grabbed. The last parameter indicates all pixels should be converted to the default color model.

2. Call the `grabPixels` method and check that it returns `true`.

3. Obtain the dimensions of the grabbed image with the `getWidth` and `getHeight` methods.

4. Call `getPixels` to get the pixel array. You need to cast the return value to `int[]`. (If you don't convert pixels to the default color model and the color model of the image is an index color model with, at most, 256 colors, then the method returns a `byte[]` array instead. For that reason, the return type of `getPixels` is declared as an `Object`, and you must cast it to the appropriate array type.)

5. Access individual pixels. The pixel with coordinates (x,y) is stored in `pixels[y * width + x]`.

The code for this sequence looks like this:

```
try
{   PixelGrabber grabber = new PixelGrabber(image, 0, 0, -1, -1,
        true)
    if (grabber.grabPixels())
    {   int width = grabber.getWidth()
        int height = grabber.getHeight();
        int[] pixels = (int[])grabber.getPixels();
        for (int x = 0; x < width; x++)
            for (int y = 0; y < height; y++)
                do something with pixels[y * width + x];
    }
}
catch(InterruptedException e) {}
```

In Example 6-7, we will *transpose* an image, that is, flip the x- and y-coordinates of every pixel (see Figure 6-8). To achieve this, we grab the pixels of an image, compute the transposed pixels, and use the `MemoryImageSource` class of the preceding section to turn the transposed pixels back into an image.

In this case, there is no benefit to incremental rendering because all pixels must be available before the transformed image can be computed. Therefore, it makes sense to use the pixel grabber instead of an incremental filter.

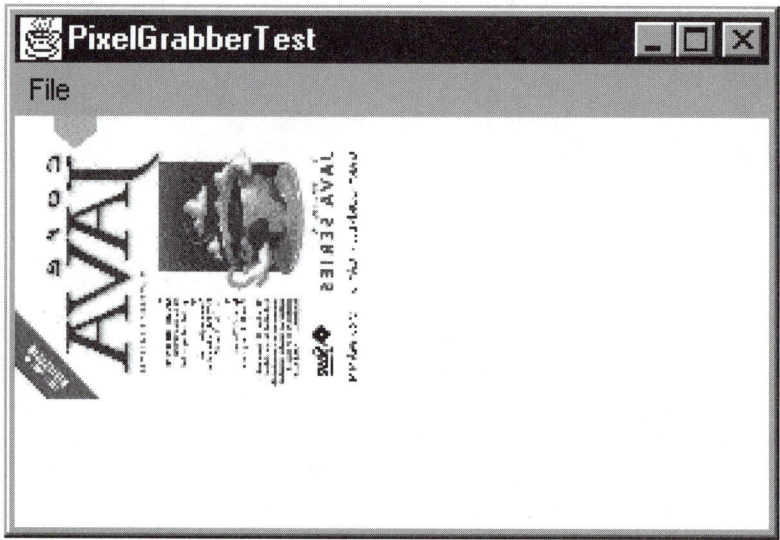

Figure 6-8: Transposing the pixels of an image

Example 6-7: PixelGrabberTest.java

```java
import java.awt.*;
import java.awt.event.*;
import java.awt.image.*;
import corejava.*;

public class PixelGrabberTest extends CloseableFrame
    implements ActionListener
{   public PixelGrabberTest()
    {   MenuBar mbar = new MenuBar();
        Menu m = new Menu("File");
        MenuItem m1 = new MenuItem("Open");
        m1.addActionListener(this);
        m.add(m1);
        MenuItem m2 = new MenuItem("Exit");
```

```java
        m2.addActionListener(this);
        m.add(m2);
        mbar.add(m);
        setMenuBar(mbar);
    }

    public void actionPerformed(ActionEvent evt)
    {   String arg = evt.getActionCommand();
        if (arg.equals("Open"))
        {   FileDialog d = new FileDialog(this,
                "Open file", FileDialog.LOAD);
            d.setDirectory(lastDir);
            d.show();
            String f = d.getFile();
            lastDir = d.getDirectory();
            if (f != null)
            {   fileName = lastDir + f;
                transposeImage(fileName);
            }
        }
        else if(arg.equals("Exit")) System.exit(0);
    }

    public void transposeImage(String f)
    {   Image image = Toolkit.getDefaultToolkit().getImage(f);
        PixelGrabber grabber
            = new PixelGrabber(image, 0, 0, -1, -1, true);
        try
        {   if (grabber.grabPixels())
            {   width = grabber.getWidth();
                height = grabber.getHeight();
                int[] pixels = (int[])grabber.getPixels();
                int[] transposedPixels = new int[height * width];
                for (int x = 0; x < width; x++)
                    for (int y = 0; y < height; y++)
                        transposedPixels[x * height + y]
                            = pixels[y * width + x];
                transposedImage = createImage(new
                    MemoryImageSource(height, width,
                        transposedPixels, 0, height));
                repaint();
            }
        }
        catch(InterruptedException e) {}
    }

    public void paint (Graphics g)
    {   g.translate(getInsets().left, getInsets().top);
```

```
        if (transposedImage != null)
            g.drawImage(transposedImage, 0, 0,
                height, width, this);
    }

    public static void main (String[] args)
    {   Frame f = new PixelGrabberTest();
        f.show();
    }

    private Image transposedImage;
    private int width;
    private int height;
    private String fileName = "";
    private String lastDir = "";
}
```

java.awt.image.PixelGrabber

- PixelGrabber(Image image, int x, int y, int width, int height, boolean forceRGB)

This is the best version of the constructor to use because you don't have to supply an array to store the pixels first. (Other versions require you to pre-allocate the array.)

Parameters	image	the image to convert
	x, y	where to start grabbing
	width, height	The size of the image to grab; setting width or height to –1 tells the PixelGrabber to take the width and height from the image itself
	forceRGB	If true, converts the pixels of the image to the default RGB model; if false, *and* if all pixels are supplied with the same color model by the image producer, then the original color model is preserved

- boolean grabPixels()

- boolean grabPixels(long ms)

start a synchronized grabbing process. The first version won't return until all the data was grabbed. The second version won't return until all pixels

have been grabbed or until `ms` milliseconds have passed. Both return `true` if all pixels were grabbed; otherwise, both return `false`. Throw an `InterruptedException` if another thread interrupts this one while it was waiting for pixel data.

- `void startGrabbing()`

  asynchronously starts grabbing the pixels. (Use with the `getStatus()` method that is described next.)

- `int getStatus()`

  determines whether an asynchronous pixel grabbing (via `startGrabbing()`) was successful. If the return value has the `ImageObserver` flags `ALLBITS` or `FRAMEBITS` set, then the grabbing was successful. If the `ABORT` or `ERROR` flags are set, it wasn't.

- `void abortGrabbing()`

  aborts the grabbing process.

- `int getWidth()`
- `int getHeight()`

  return the width or height of the image data.

- `Object getPixels()`

  returns an `int[]` or `byte[]` array that contains the pixels. The return type depends on the color model. You need to cast it to the appropriate type of array.

Data Transfer

One of the most powerful and convenient user interface mechanisms of graphical user interface environments (such as Windows and X Window System) is *cut and paste*. You select some data in one program and cut or copy it to the clipboard. Then, you select another program and paste the clipboard contents into that application. Using the clipboard, you can transfer text, images, or other data from one document to another, or, of course, from one place in a document to another place in the same document. Cut and paste is so natural that most computer users never think about it.

However, in Java 1.0, there was no support for cut and paste. You could not cut and paste between Java applications. For example, if you have a browser written in Java (such as HotJava), then you could not copy text and images from a Web page and transfer them into a Java-based word processor.

Actually, there is one form of cut and paste that was always supported: you can cut and paste text in text fields and text areas as long as the peer classes that implement the text edit components can communicate with the system clipboard.

Even though the clipboard is conceptually simple, implementing clipboard services is actually harder than you might think. Suppose you copy text from a word processor into the clipboard. If you paste that text into another word processor, then you expect that the fonts and formatting will stay intact. That is, the text in the clipboard needs to retain the formatting information. But if you paste the text into a plain text field, then you expect that just the characters are pasted in, without additional formatting codes.

The situation is even more complicated for graphics. Many graphics programs produce images that can be scaled to different sizes without quality loss. These images are made up of elements such as lines, circles, text, and so on, that can be scaled to different sizes. Other graphics programs treat images as collections of pixels. These images cannot be scaled without introducing "jaggies." Suppose a scalable image, say, a flowchart, is copied onto the clipboard. Then, it is pasted into another program. If the target program is a bitmap editor, then the image should be pasted as a bitmap. If the target program is a word processor, it would be better to paste the image as a graphics metafile—a file format that retains the geometric elements of the image.

The system clipboard of a graphical user interface environment can hold the clipboard data in multiple formats, and the program that provides the data must negotiate the data format with the program that consumes the data.

Furthermore, individual programs usually have their own local clipboards. When you cut and paste text inside a word processor, then the word processor saves the data in its own format in a local clipboard. There is no universal standard for exchanging formatted text. When text is pasted onto the system clipboard, some formatting information is usually lost. While this loss is tolerable for text interchange from one word processor to another, it does not suffice for moving data within one word processor. Program users have the legitimate expectation that no information is lost when they move information from one place in a document to another place in the same document. To achieve perfect information transfer within a program, a local clipboard is required whenever that information is richer than the data that can be stored in the clipboard.

The system clipboard implementations of Microsoft Windows, OS/2 and the Macintosh are similar, but, of course, there are slight differences. And the X Windows clipboard mechanism is much more limited—cutting and pasting of anything but plain text is only sporadically supported. These differences are a major challenge for Java programs. A Java program is supposed to run unmodi-

fied on many platforms. As so often, Java must cater to the lowest common denominator, and again, as so often, that lowest common denominator is the X Window system. Since the X Window system has no standard method for storing formatted text or graphics on the clipboard, Java programs are currently limited to storing only plain text on the system clipboard. You will learn in this chapter how a Java program can place text onto the system clipboard and how to retrieve text that was placed there by another program.

However, when copying data from one Java program to another, you can overcome the plain text limitation. Consider how attachments are sent by e-mail. E-mail messages can hold only text, and some mail gateways are quite restrictive about the maximum length of each text line. But e-mail systems have learned to cope with these limitations. Attachments, which can consist of binary data, are transferred in MIME (Multipurpose Internet Mail Extensions) format.

NOTE: For an HTML version of the RFC (Request for Comment) that defines the MIME format, see, for example, `http://www.oac.uci.edu/indiv/ehood/MIME`.

MIME-compliant mailers know how to encode attachments into plain text and how to decode the MIME format and present the attachments to the user. Of course, if you use an ancient mail reader (such as the original Unix `mail` program), then the attachments will simply show up as strange-looking text.

It is possible to use the same approach to transfer data from one MIME-aware Java program to another by placing encoded data onto the clipboard. Of course, it makes no sense to paste that text into a non-Java program. But if the target Java program can understand the header that describes the encoding format, then it can decode the information. Currently, Java has no support for this transfer method. But since Java does use MIME data types to describe data formats, we found it reasonable to encode clipboard data in MIME format as well. We give you a sample program that shows how you can easily exchange arbitrary serializable objects between Java applications through the system clipboard by using this approach. Perhaps a later version of Java will officially use a similar mechanism for data transfer between Java programs.

Finally, Java supports a local clipboard that you can use to store arbitrary Java objects. Naturally, this is not nearly as difficult as transferring data between programs. Why can't you simply store the clipboard data in a global variable? The Java mechanism also supports format negotiation. (In Java, the data formats are called *flavors*.)

Table 6-1 summarizes the data transfer capabilities of the new clipboard mechanism.

Table 6-1: Capabilities of the Java data transfer mechanism

Transfer	Format
Between Java and native program	Plain text
Between two MIME-aware Java programs	Text-encoded data
Within one Java program	Any object

Classes and Interfaces for Data Transfer

Data transfer in Java is implemented in a package called `java.awt.datatransfer` that has three classes, two interfaces, and a new checked exception class. Table 6-2 contains brief descriptions of the parts of this package.

Table 6-2: Classes in the `java.awt.datatransfer` package

`Transferable` interface	Objects that can be transferred must implement this interface.
`Clipboard` class	A class that encapsulates a clipboard. Transferable objects are the only items that can be put on or taken off a clipboard. The system clipboard is a concrete example of a `Clipboard`.
`ClipboardOwner` interface	A class that wants to be able to copy data to a clipboard must implement this interface.
`DataFlavor` class	A way of identifying the type (or "flavor") of the data that was placed on a clipboard.
`StringSelection` class	The only concrete class that Java 1.1 supplies that implements `Transferable` and, as a convenience, `ClipboardOwner`. Used to transfer text strings.
`UnsupportedFlavorException`	Thrown by a `Transferable` when it can't give you data in that flavor.

Transferring Text

The best way to get comfortable with the data transfer classes is to start with the simplest (and, therefore, only) supported situation for Java 1.1: transferring text to and from the system clipboard. The idea of the following program is simple. First we get a reference to the system clipboard:

```
Clipboard sysClipboard =
    Toolkit.getDefaultToolkit().getSystemClipboard();
```

For strings to be transferred to the clipboard, they need to be wrapped into `StringSelection` objects. The constructor takes the text you want to transfer. The actual transfer is done by a call to `setContents`, which takes a `StringSelection` object and a `ClipBoardOwner` as parameters.

The second parameter is used as the target of the `lostOwnership` callback when the contents of the clipboard change. This callback is necessary to support "delayed formatting" of complex data. If data is simple (such as a string), then it is simply placed on the clipboard and the class that placed it there moves on to do the next thing. However, if a class wants to place complex data that can be formatted in multiple flavors onto the clipboard, then it may not actually want to prepare all the flavors, since there is a good chance that most of them are never needed. However, then it needs to hold on to all information that is needed to create the flavors later when they are requested. The `lostOwnership` callback can release that information since it is no longer needed when a different item is placed onto the clipboard. If no callback is needed, you can simply set the second parameter of `setContents` to `null`.

```
private void copyIt()
{   String text = textArea.getSelectedText();
    StringSelection selection = new StringSelection(text);
    sysClipboard.setContents(selection, null);
}
```

Finally, to get the contents, we first need to get a `Transferable` by a call to `getContents()`. Once we have the `Transferable`, we use its `getTransferData` method to actually pick up the information. This method has to be encased in a try/catch block because of the possibility of throwing an `UnsupportedFlavorException`.

```
private void pasteIt()
{   String text;
    Transferable selection = sysClipboard.getContents(this);
    {   try
        {   text = (String)(selection.getTransferData
                (DataFlavor.stringFlavor));
            int start = textArea.getSelectionStart();
            int end = textArea.getSelectionEnd();
            textArea.replaceRange(text, start, end);
        }
        catch(Exception e) {}
    }
}
```

Example 6-8 is a program that demonstrates cutting and pasting between a Java application and the system clipboard. Figure 6-9 shows a screen shot. If you select an area of text in the text area and click on Copy, then the selected text is copied to the system clipboard. As Figure 6-10 shows, the copied text does indeed get stored on the system clipboard. When you subsequently click on the Paste button, the contents of the clipboard (which may come from a non-Java program) are pasted at the cursor position.

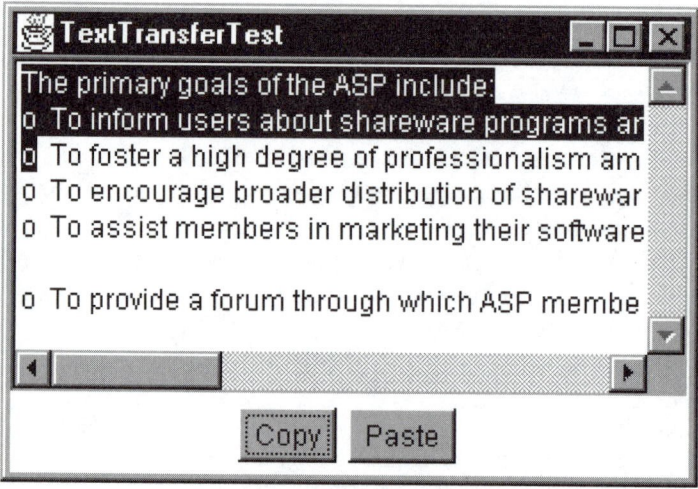

Figure 6-9: The `TextTransferTest` program

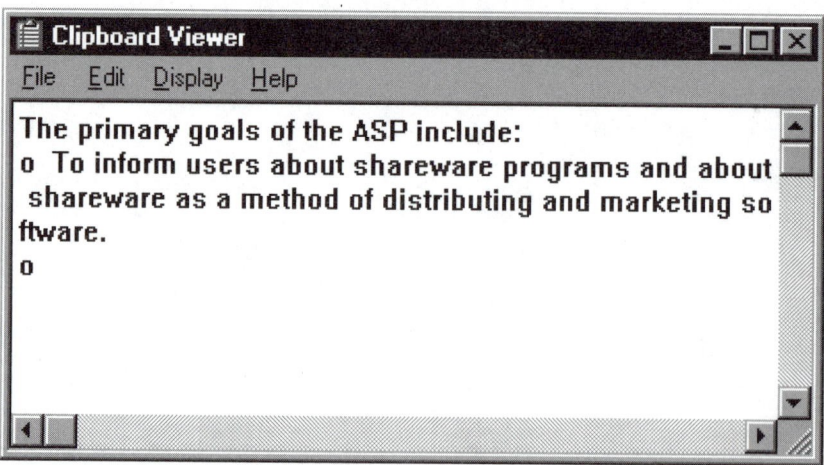

Figure 6-10: The Windows clipboard viewer after a copy

Example 6-8: TextTransferTest.java

```java
import java.io.*;
import java.awt.*;
import java.awt.datatransfer.*;
import java.awt.event.*;
import corejava.*;


public class TextTransferTest
    extends CloseableFrame implements ActionListener
{  public TextTransferTest()
   {  add (textArea, "Center");
      Panel p = new Panel();
      Button copy = new Button ("Copy");
      p.add(copy);
      copy.addActionListener(this);
      Button paste = new Button ("Paste");
      p.add (paste);
      paste.addActionListener(this);
      add (p, "South");
      sysClipboard
         = Toolkit.getDefaultToolkit().getSystemClipboard();
   }

   public void actionPerformed(ActionEvent evt)
   {  String arg = evt.getActionCommand();
      if (arg.equals("Copy")) copyIt();
      else if (arg.equals("Paste")) pasteIt();
   }

   private void copyIt()
   {  String text = textArea.getSelectedText();
      if (text.equals("")) text = textArea.getText();
      StringSelection selection = new StringSelection(text);
      sysClipboard.setContents(selection, null);
   }

   private void pasteIt()
   {  String text;
      Transferable selection = sysClipboard.getContents(this);
      {  try
         {  text = (String)(selection.getTransferData
               (DataFlavor.stringFlavor));
            int start = textArea.getSelectionStart();
            int end = textArea.getSelectionEnd();
            textArea.replaceRange(text, start, end);
         }
```

```
        catch(Exception e)
        {}
    }
}

public static void main(String[] args)
{   Frame f = new TextTransferTest();
    f.show();
}

private TextArea textArea = new TextArea();
private Clipboard sysClipboard;
}
```

java.awt.Toolkit

• `Clipboard getSystemClipboard()`

gets the system clipboard.

java.awt.datatransfer.Clipboard

• `Transferable getContents(Object requester)`

gets the clipboard contents.

Parameters	requester	the object requesting the clipboard contents

• `void setContents(Transferable contents, ClipboardOwner owner)`

puts contents on the clipboard.

Parameters	contents	the `Transferable` encapsulating the contents
	owner	the object to be notified (via its `lostOwnership` method) when new information is placed on the clipboard

`java.awt.datatransfer.Clipboard`

- void lostOwnership(Clipboard clipboard, Transferable contents)
  notifies this object that it is no longer the owner of the contents of the clipboard.

Parameters	clipboard	the clipboard onto which the contents were placed
	contents	the item that this owner had placed onto the clipboard

Building a Transferable

Objects that you want to transfer via the clipboard must implement the `Transferable` interface. The `StringSelection` class is currently the only class in the Java standard library that implements the `Transferable` interface. We will first build an `ImageSelection` class that can be used to transfer images through the local clipboard. Finally, we will build up the machinery to construct a `Transferable` for serializable Java objects.

The Transferable Interface and Data Flavors

The `Transferable` interface has three methods, two of which help you discover what flavors the transferred object supports. These methods let you find out whether data stored on a clipboard is useable by a specific part of the program that can handle data only of a certain type. For example, if you had a bitmap image on the clipboard, it could be delivered either as an object of type `Image` or as a GIF file. In this case, the `Clipboard` object would report that it comes in two flavors. Flavors are represented by instances of the `DataFlavor` class.

You can find out all data flavors that a transferable object supports:

```
DataFlavor[] flavors = transferable.getTransferDataFlavors()
```

Or, you can test whether a particular flavor is supported.

```
DataFlavor flavor = . . .;
if (transferable.isDataFlavorSupported(flavor)) { . . . }
```

Finally, there is a method to actually transfer the data.

```
Object data = transferable.getTransferData(flavor);
```

Of course, this is where all the real work will need to be done. This method will need to look at the flavor and return an object that contains the transfer data formatted according to the flavor. The method throws an `UnsupportedFlavorException` if the flavor is not supported.

Currently, the `DataFlavor` class has two constructors. Objects can be constructed with two names, a human-readable name (such as `"GIF Bitmap"`) and a MIME type name (such as `"image/gif"`). For example,

```
DataFlavor gifFlavor
    = new DataFlavor("image/gif", "GIF Bitmap");
```

When data of this type is retrieved, the `Transferable` object must yield an `InputStream` object from which the data can be read.

```
InputStream in
    = (InputStream)transferable.getTransferData(gifFlavor);
```

It is then up to the application to turn the stream into an image object.

Of course, it is more convenient to retrieve Java objects directly from the clipboard. Since Java objects do not yet have a standard MIME type, JavaSoft has created one:

```
application/x-java-serialized-object; class=classname
```

(The `x-` prefix indicates that this is an experimental name, not one that is sanctioned by IANA, the organization that assigns standard MIME type names.) For example, the content type of an `Image` object would be:

```
application/x-java-serialized-object; class=java.awt.Image
```

Such a data flavor is constructed as

```
DataFlavor imageFlavor
    = new DataFlavor(java.awt.Image.class, "AWT Image");
```

This flavor can be retrieved easily:

```
Image img = (Image)transferable.getTransferData(imageFlavor);
```

java.awt.datatransfer.DataFlavor

- `DataFlavor(String mimeType, String humanPresentableName)`

  creates a data flavor that describes stream data in a format described by a MIME type.

Parameters	mimeType	a MIME type string
	humanPresentableName	a more readable version of the name

- `DataFlavor(Class class, String humanPresentableName)`

  creates a data flavor that describes a Java class.

Parameter	`class`	the class that is retrieved from the `Transferable`
	`humanPresentableName`	a readable version of the name

- `String getMimeType()`

  returns the MIME type string for this data flavor.

- `String getHumanPresentableName()`

  returns the human-presentable name for the data format of this data flavor.

- `Class getRepresentationClass()`

  returns a `Class` object that represents the class of the object that a `Transferable` will return when called with this data flavor.

`java.awt.datatransfer.Transferable`

- `DataFlavor[] getTransferDataFlavors()`

  returns an array of the supported flavors.

- `boolean isDataFlavorSupported(DataFlavor flavor)`

  returns `true` if the specified flavor is one of the supported data flavors; `false` otherwise.

- `Object getTransferData(DataFlavor flavor)`

  returns the data, formatted in the requested flavor. Throws an `UnsupportedFlavorException` if the flavor requested is not supported.

Building an Image Transferable

Let us put the information of the preceding section to work and design a transferable image class. Right now, we only want to transfer images inside a single Java program; that is, we will just use a local clipboard.

Here's what you need to do:

1. Define a class `ImageSelection` that implements the `Transferable` interface.

    ```
    class ImageSelection implements Transferable { . . . };
    ```

2. Define the single supported flavor as a class flavor for the class `java.awt.image`, with a human-presentable name of `"AWT Image"`. Construct a static object `imageFlavor` to represent that flavor.

```
public static final DataFlavor imageFlavor
    = new DataFlavor(java.awt.Image.class, "AWT Image");
```

3. Make the `getTransferDataFlavors` method return an array with the single entry, `imageFlavor` of type `DataFlavor`.

```
private static DataFlavor[] flavors = { imageFlavor };
public DataFlavor[] getTransferDataFlavors()
{   return flavors;
}
```

4. Have the `isDataFlavorSupported` check whether the requested flavor is equal to the `imageFlavor` object.

```
public boolean isDataFlavorSupported(DataFlavor flavor)
{   return flavor.equals(imageFlavor);
}
```

5. Have the `ImageSelection` constructor accept and store an object of type `Image`.

```
public ImageSelection(Image image)
{   theImage = image;
}
private Image theImage;
```

6. Return a reference to the stored `Image` object as the value of `getTransferData`.

```
public synchronized Object getTransferData
    (DataFlavor flavor)
    throws UnsupportedFlavorException
{   if(flavor.equals(imageFlavor))
    {   return theImage;
    }
    else
    {   throw new UnsupportedFlavorException(flavor);
    }
}
```

See Example 6-9 for the complete source code.

Of course, all this is a bit underwhelming. The ImageSelection class is simply a wrapper for Image objects. This class, to be more interesting, would need to be able to deliver its contents in more than one way, for example, as an Image object and a GIF file. Then, you would see some real work in the getTransferData method. It would look like this:

```
public synchronized Object getTransferData
    (DataFlavor flavor)
    throws UnsupportedFlavorException
{   if(flavor.equals(imageFlavor))
    {   return theImage;
    }
    else if(flavor.equals(gifFlavor))
    {   byte[] gifBytes = . . .; // translate image to GIF
            format
        return new ByteArrayInputStream(gifBytes);
    }
    else
    {   throw new UnsupportedFlavorException(flavor);
    }
}
```

We will not do work that here, since it is a bit tedious to compute the GIF format of an image.

Using the ImageSelection Class

The program of Example 6-9 creates two windows. You can load an image file into each window, or you can copy and paste between the windows, with the "Edit | Copy" and "Edit | Paste" menu options (see Figure 6-11). Coding the copy and paste operations using the ImageSelection class is not much different than using the StringSelection class.

```
private void copyIt()
{   ImageSelection selection = new ImageSelection(theImage);
    localClipboard.setContents(selection, null);
}

private void pasteIt()
{   Transferable selection
        = localClipboard.getContents(this);
    try
    {   theImage = (Image)selection.getTransferData
            (ImageSelection.imageFlavor);
        repaint();
    }
    catch(Exception e) {}
}
```

In this case, `selection` is an `ImageSelection` instance. We obviously also need to cast the return value of `getTransferData` to an `Image` this time rather than to a string, and use a call to `repaint()` rather than adding the result to the text area. Note that we are using a local clipboard rather than the system clipboard. It is constructed as

```
static Clipboard localClipboard = new Clipboard("local");
```

We cannot use the system clipboard because, at this time, Java can transfer only text into the system clipboard.

Example 6-9 shows the full code for the example.

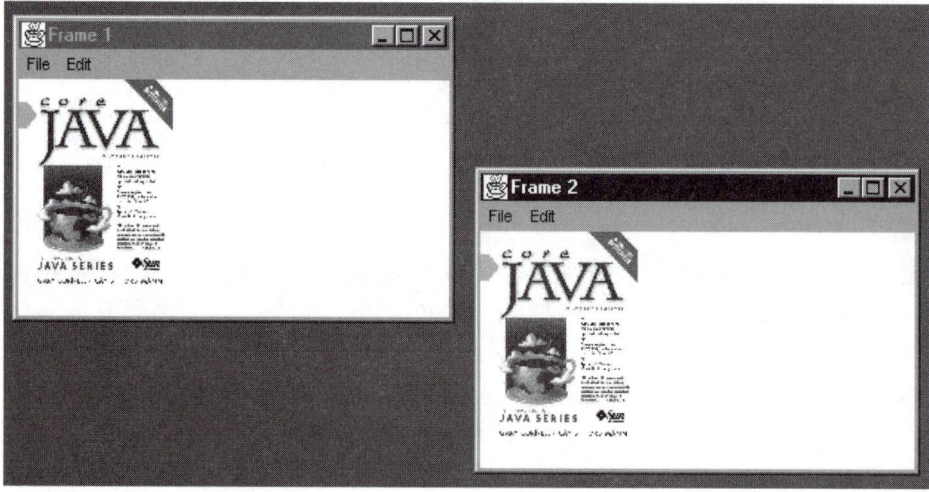

Figure 6-11: The `ImageTransferTest` program

Example 6-9: ImageTransferTest.java

```
import java.awt.*;
import java.awt.image.*;
import java.awt.event.*;
import java.awt.datatransfer.*;
import corejava.*;

public class ImageTransferTest extends CloseableFrame
    implements ActionListener
{  public ImageTransferTest()
   {  MenuBar mbar = new MenuBar();
      Menu m = new Menu("File");
      MenuItem m1 = new MenuItem("Open");
      m1.addActionListener(this);
```

```
        m.add(m1);
        MenuItem m2 = new MenuItem("Exit");
        m2.addActionListener(this);
        m.add(m2);
        mbar.add(m);
        m = new Menu("Edit");
        MenuItem m3 = new MenuItem("Copy");
        m3.addActionListener(this);
        m.add(m3);
        MenuItem m4 = new MenuItem("Paste");
        m4.addActionListener(this);
        m.add(m4);
        mbar.add(m);
        setMenuBar(mbar);
    }

    public void actionPerformed(ActionEvent evt)
    {   String arg = evt.getActionCommand();
        if (arg.equals("Open"))
        {   FileDialog d = new FileDialog(this,
                "Open file", FileDialog.LOAD);
            d.setDirectory(lastDir);
            d.show();
            String f = d.getFile();
            lastDir = d.getDirectory();
            if (f != null)
            {   theImage = Toolkit.getDefaultToolkit().getImage
                    (lastDir + f);
                repaint();
            }
        }
        else if(arg.equals("Exit")) System.exit(0);
        else if (arg.equals("Copy")) copyIt();
        else if (arg.equals("Paste")) pasteIt();
    }

    public void paint(Graphics g)
    {   g.translate(getInsets().left, getInsets().top);
        if(theImage != null)
            g.drawImage(theImage, 0, 0, this);
    }

    private void copyIt()
    {   ImageSelection selection = new ImageSelection(theImage);
        localClipboard.setContents(selection, null);
    }
```

```
    private void pasteIt()
    {   Transferable selection
            = localClipboard.getContents(this);
        try
        {   theImage = (Image)selection.getTransferData
                (ImageSelection.imageFlavor);
            repaint();
        }
        catch(Exception e) {}
    }

    public static void main(String [] args)
    {   Frame f1 = new ImageTransferTest();
        Frame f2 = new ImageTransferTest();
        f1.setTitle("Frame 1");
        f2.setTitle("Frame 2");
        f2.setLocation(300, 100);
        f1.show();
        f2.show();
    }

    private static Clipboard localClipboard
        = new Clipboard("local");
    private Image theImage;
    private String lastDir = "";
}

class ImageSelection implements Transferable
{   public ImageSelection(Image image)
    {   theImage = image;
    }

    public DataFlavor[] getTransferDataFlavors()
    {   return flavors;
    }

    public boolean isDataFlavorSupported(DataFlavor flavor)
    {   return flavor.equals(imageFlavor);
    }

    public synchronized Object getTransferData
        (DataFlavor flavor)
        throws UnsupportedFlavorException
    {   if(flavor.equals(imageFlavor))
        {   return theImage;
        }
        else
        {   throw new UnsupportedFlavorException(flavor);
        }
    }
```

```
    public static final DataFlavor imageFlavor
        = new DataFlavor(java.awt.Image.class, "AWT Image");

    private static DataFlavor[] flavors = { imageFlavor };
    private Image theImage;
}
```

Transferring Java Objects via the System Clipboard

Now, suppose you want to paste the images by using the *system* clipboard rather than a private clipboard. This capability would have the nice consequence that the image would persist and so you could paste images between different Java programs even if the original program was over. (This is better than using RMI: RMI certainly allows you to transfer images between Java programs, *but* RMI requires both programs to be running at the same time.)

Unfortunately, if you try to place a `Transferable` other than a `StringSelection` on the system clipboard, you will find that nothing happens. The system clipboard doesn't have a clue how to store a Java object, and it simply ignores the request. The result is you can't get the object back off the system clipboard because it never really got there in the first place!

In this section, we show you how to overcome this limitation by encoding objects into text strings and placing those text strings onto the system clipboard. This method works for any *serializable* Java object. We choose the following simple text encoding:

```
Content-type: application/x-java-serialized-object
Content-length: length

serialized object data in BASE64 encoding
```

For example,

```
Content-type: application/x-java-serialized-object
Content-length: 80311

rO0ABXNyAAZCaXRtYXA8A5/mgeUpsAIAA0kABmhlaWdodEkABXdpZHRoOWwAGcG14ZWxzdAACW014
cAAAAIwAAABqdXIAAltJTbpgJnbqsqUCAAB4cAAAOfj////////////////////////////////
. . .
```

The BASE64 encoding is a commonly used method to encode binary data as printable characters. The exact encoding scheme is not important. You can find a description in the MIME RFC, and the code in Example 6-10 contains classes to carry out the encoding and decoding.

Because the system clipboard class can put only text onto the clipboard, we designed a special `MimeClipboard` class. This class delegates storage and retrieval requests to another clipboard, typically the system clipboard, and it handles the data encoding and decoding.

```
class MimeClipboard extends Clipboard
{  public MimeClipboard(Clipboard cb)
   {  . . .
      clip = cb;
   }

   public synchronized void setContents(Transferable contents,
      ClipboardOwner owner)
   {  encode data and put on clip
   }

   public synchronized Transferable getContents
      (Object requestor)
   {  get data from clip and decode
   }

   private Clipboard clip;
}
```

We also use a transfer wrapper `SerializableSelection` for serializable objects—it is exactly analogous to the `ImageSelection` class of the preceding section. When a `Transferable` object is placed onto a `MimeClipboard`, the following happens:

1. If the `Transferable` object is a `StringSelection`, then it is simply put on the clipboard.

2. Otherwise, if the `Transferable` is of the type `SerializableSelection`, then the object is serialized into a sequence of bytes. The serialized bytes are encoded in BASE64, the MIME header is added, and the resulting string is placed on the clipboard.

```
public synchronized void setContents(Transferable
   contents, ClipboardOwner owner)
{  if (contents instanceof SerializableSelection)
   {  try
      {  DataFlavor flavor
            = SerializableSelection.serializableFlavor;
         Serializable obj = (Serializable)
            contents.getTransferData(flavor);
         String enc = encode(obj);
         String header = "Content-type: "
            + flavor.getMimeType()
```

```
            + "\nContent-length: "
            + enc.length() + "\n\n";
        StringSelection selection
            = new StringSelection(header + enc);
        clip.setContents(selection, owner);
      }
      catch(UnsupportedFlavorException e) {}
      catch(IOException e) {}
    }
    else clip.setContents(contents, owner);
  }
```

When a `Transferable` object is read from the clipboard, these steps are reversed.

1. The `StringSelection` is obtained from the system clipboard.

2. If the string doesn't start with `Content-type`, then the string selection object is returned. (A more sophisticated implementation should be able to handle the various content types and return data other than Java serialized objects as input streams.)

3. Otherwise, the BASE64 data is converted to binary and read as object stream data. The resulting object is wrapped into a `SerializableSelection` transfer object, which is returned.

```
    public synchronized Transferable getContents
        (Object requestor)
    {   Transferable contents = clip.getContents(requestor);

        if (contents instanceof StringSelection)
        {   String data = (String)contents.getTransferData
                (DataFlavor.stringFlavor);

            if (!data.startsWith("Content-type: "))
                return contents;
            int start = . . .; // skip three newlines
            Serializable obj = decode(data, start);
            SerializableSelection selection
                = new SerializableSelection(obj);
            return selection;
        }
        else return contents;
    }
```

You use this clipboard just like any other clipboard:

```
Clipboard mimeClipboard
      = new MimeClipboard
         (Toolkit.getDefaultToolkit().getSystemClipboard());
   . . .
private void copyIt()
{  SerializableSelection selection
      = new SerializableSelection(theBitmap);
   mimeClipboard.setContents(selection, null);
}
```

To encode an object, we serialize it to a stream. The `Base64OutputStream` class encodes all bytes written to it into BASE64. We layer an `ObjectOutputStream` on top of it. Here is the code from the `encode` method.

```
StringBuffer sbuf = new StringBuffer();
Base64OutputStream bout
   = new Base64OutputStream(sbuf);
ObjectOutputStream out
   = new ObjectOutputStream(bout);
out.writeObject(obj);
out.flush();
return sbuf.toString();
```

To decode, we follow the same approach. A `Base64InputStream` has its `read` method defined to turn BASE64 characters into bytes, and an `ObjectInputStream` reads the serialized object data from that stream. Here is the code from the `decode` method.

```
Base64InputStream bin
   = new Base64InputStream(s, start);
ObjectInputStream in
   = new ObjectInputStream(bin);
Object obj = in.readObject();
return (Serializable)obj;
```

When this technique is put to work for transfering images, there is a minor technical setback: the `Image` class does not implement `Serializable`. To overcome this problem, we designed a serializable class `Bitmap` that holds the pixels of an image in the default color map. A bitmap can be constructed from an image, and the `getImage` method can construct an equivalent image from a bitmap object. This construction happens with the `PixelGrabber` and `MemoryImageSource` classes that you saw earlier in this chapter.

```
class Bitmap implements Serializable
{   public Bitmap(Image img)
    {   try
        {   PixelGrabber pg
                = new PixelGrabber(img, 0, 0, -1, -1, true);
            if (pg.grabPixels())
            {   width = pg.getWidth();
                height = pg.getHeight();
                pixels = (int[])pg.getPixels();
            }
        }
        catch(InterruptedException e) {}
    }

    public Image getImage()
    {   return Toolkit.getDefaultToolkit().createImage(new
            MemoryImageSource(width, height, pixels, 0, width));
    }

    private int width;
    private int height;
    private int[] pixels;
}
```

Remember from Chapter 1 that we need not actually write any methods for seri-alization and deserialization. Java will automatically serialize the `width` and `height` fields and the array of pixels.

Now we have all the pieces together to write a program that can copy an image to the system clipboard. The program in Example 6-10 does just that. Run the program, load an image, and copy it into the clipboard. Then, close the program and run it again. Select Edit | Paste and watch how the image transferred into the new instance of the program. Or run several copies of the program, as in Figure 6-12, and copy and paste between them.

If you use the clipboard viewer or if you simply select Paste in your word processor, you can see the MIME encoding of the clipboard data (see Figure 6-13). However, what you cannot do is have the bitmap in the clipboard pasted as an image into your word processor. The system clipboard does not know that the data is actually an image, and it does not understand the encoding. For the same reason, you cannot select an image in your Web browser, copy it into the clipboard, and paste it into our example program. As mentioned previously, it is currently not possible to transfer anything other than text between a Java pro-gram and a non-Java application.

Figure 6-12: Data is copied between two instances of the
MimeClipboardTest program

Figure 6-13: The clipboard contents after an image is copied

Example 6-10: MimeClipboardTest.java

```
import java.io.*;
import java.awt.*;
import java.awt.image.*;
import java.awt.event.*;
import java.awt.datatransfer.*;
import corejava.*;

public class MimeClipboardTest extends CloseableFrame
    implements ActionListener
{   public MimeClipboardTest()
    {   MenuBar mbar = new MenuBar();
        Menu m = new Menu("File");
        MenuItem m1 = new MenuItem("Open");
        m1.addActionListener(this);
        m.add(m1);
        MenuItem m2 = new MenuItem("Exit");
        m2.addActionListener(this);
        m.add(m2);
        mbar.add(m);
        m = new Menu("Edit");
        MenuItem m3 = new MenuItem("Copy");
        m3.addActionListener(this);
        m.add(m3);
        MenuItem m4 = new MenuItem("Paste");
        m4.addActionListener(this);
        m.add(m4);
        mbar.add(m);
        setMenuBar(mbar);
    }

    public void actionPerformed(ActionEvent evt)
    {   String arg = evt.getActionCommand();
        if (arg.equals("Open"))
        {   FileDialog d = new FileDialog(this,
                "Open file", FileDialog.LOAD);
            d.setDirectory(lastDir);
            d.show();
            String f = d.getFile();
            lastDir = d.getDirectory();
            if (f != null)
            {   theImage = Toolkit.getDefaultToolkit().getImage
                    (lastDir + f);
                theBitmap = new Bitmap(theImage);
                repaint();
            }
        }
        else if(arg.equals("Exit")) System.exit(0);
        else if (arg.equals("Copy")) copyIt();
        else if (arg.equals("Paste")) pasteIt();
    }
```

```
    public void paint(Graphics g)
    {   g.translate(getInsets().left, getInsets().top);
        if(theImage != null)
            g.drawImage(theImage, 0, 0, this);
    }

    private void copyIt()
    {   SerializableSelection selection
            = new SerializableSelection(theBitmap);
        mimeClipboard.setContents(selection, null);
    }

    private void pasteIt()
    {   Transferable selection
            = mimeClipboard.getContents(this);
        try
        {   theBitmap = (Bitmap)selection.getTransferData
                (SerializableSelection.serializableFlavor);
            theImage = theBitmap.getImage();
            repaint();
        }
        catch(Exception e) {}
    }

    public static void main(String [] args)
    {   Frame f = new MimeClipboardTest();
        f.show();
    }

    private static Clipboard mimeClipboard
        = new MimeClipboard
            (Toolkit.getDefaultToolkit().getSystemClipboard());
    private Bitmap theBitmap;
    private Image theImage;
    private String lastDir = "";
}

class Bitmap implements Serializable
{   public Bitmap(Image img)
    {   try
        {   PixelGrabber pg
                = new PixelGrabber(img, 0, 0, -1, -1, true);
            if (pg.grabPixels())
            {   width = pg.getWidth();
                height = pg.getHeight();
                pixels = (int [])pg.getPixels();
            }
        }
        catch(InterruptedException e) {}
    }
```

```java
    public Image getImage()
    {  return Toolkit.getDefaultToolkit().createImage(new
           MemoryImageSource(width, height, pixels, 0, width));
    }

    private int width;
    private int height;
    private int[] pixels;
}

class SerializableSelection implements Transferable
{  public SerializableSelection(Serializable object)
   {  theObject = object;
   }

   public boolean isDataFlavorSupported(DataFlavor flavor)
   {  return flavor.equals(serializableFlavor);
   }

   public synchronized Object getTransferData
       (DataFlavor flavor)
       throws UnsupportedFlavorException
   {  if(flavor.equals(serializableFlavor))
      {  return theObject;
      }
      else
      {  throw new UnsupportedFlavorException(flavor);
      }
   }

   public DataFlavor[] getTransferDataFlavors()
   {  return flavors;
   }

   public static final DataFlavor serializableFlavor
       = new DataFlavor(java.io.Serializable.class,
       "Serializable Object");

   private static DataFlavor[] flavors
       = { serializableFlavor };

   private Serializable theObject;
}

class MimeClipboard extends Clipboard
{  public MimeClipboard(Clipboard cb)
   {  super("MIME/" + cb.getName());
      clip = cb;
   }
```

```java
public synchronized void setContents(Transferable contents,
    ClipboardOwner owner)
{   if (contents instanceof SerializableSelection)
    {   try
        {   DataFlavor flavor
                = SerializableSelection.serializableFlavor;
            Serializable obj = (Serializable)
                contents.getTransferData(flavor);
            String enc = encode(obj);
            String header = "Content-type: "
                + flavor.getMimeType()
                + "\nContent-length: "
                + enc.length() + "\n\n";
            StringSelection selection
                = new StringSelection(header + enc);
            clip.setContents(selection, owner);
        }
        catch(UnsupportedFlavorException e)
        {}
        catch(IOException e)
        {}
    }
    else clip.setContents(contents, owner);
}

public synchronized Transferable getContents
    (Object requestor)
{   Transferable contents = clip.getContents(requestor);

    if (contents instanceof StringSelection)
    {   String data = null;
        try
        {   data = (String)contents.getTransferData
                (DataFlavor.stringFlavor);
        }
        catch(UnsupportedFlavorException e)
        { return contents; }
        catch(IOException e)
        { return contents; }

        if (!data.startsWith("Content-type: "))
            return contents;
        int start = -1;
        // skip three newlines
        for (int i = 0; i < 3; i++)
        {   start = data.indexOf('\n', start + 1);
            if (start < 0) return contents;
        }
        Serializable obj = decode(data, start);
        SerializableSelection selection
            = new SerializableSelection(obj);
        return selection;
    }
    else return contents;
}
```

```java
    private static String encode(Serializable obj)
    {  try
       {  StringBuffer sbuf = new StringBuffer();
          Base64OutputStream bout
             = new Base64OutputStream(sbuf);
          ObjectOutputStream out
             = new ObjectOutputStream(bout);
          out.writeObject(obj);
          out.flush();
          return sbuf.toString();
       }
       catch(Exception e)
       {  return "";
       }
    }

    private static Serializable decode(String s, int start)
    {  try
       {  Base64InputStream bin
             = new Base64InputStream(s, start);
          ObjectInputStream in
             = new ObjectInputStream(bin);
          Object obj = in.readObject();
          return (Serializable)obj;
       }
       catch(Exception e)
       {  return null;
       }
    }

    private Clipboard clip;
}

/* BASE64 encoding encodes 3 bytes into 4 characters.
   |11111122|22223333|33444444|
   Each set of 6 bits is encoded according to the
   toBase64 map. If the number of input bytes is not
   a multiple of 3, then the last group of 4 characters
   is padded with one or two = signs. Each output line
   is at most 76 characters.
*/

class Base64OutputStream extends OutputStream
{  public Base64OutputStream(StringBuffer sb)
   {  sbuf = sb;
   }

   public void write(int c) throws IOException
   {  inbuf[i] = c;
      i++;
      if (i == 3)
      {  sbuf.append(toBase64[(inbuf[0] & 0xFC) >> 2]);
         sbuf.append(toBase64[((inbuf[0] & 0x03) << 4) |
```

```
                ((inbuf[1] & 0xF0) >> 4)]);
        sbuf.append(toBase64[((inbuf[1] & 0x0F) << 2) |
            ((inbuf[2]` & 0xC0) >> 6)]);
        sbuf.append(toBase64[inbuf[2] & 0x3F]);
        col += 4;
        i = 0;
        if (col >= 76)
        {  sbuf.append('\n');
           col = 0;
        }
      }
   }

   public void flush()
   {  if (i == 1)
      {  sbuf.append(toBase64[(inbuf[0] & 0xFC) >> 2]);
         sbuf.append(toBase64[(inbuf[0] & 0x03) << 4]);
         sbuf.append('=');
         sbuf.append('=');
      }
      else if (i == 2)
      {  sbuf.append(toBase64[(inbuf[0] & 0xFC) >> 2]);
         sbuf.append(toBase64[((inbuf[0] & 0x03) << 4) |
            ((inbuf[1] & 0xF0) >> 4)]);
         sbuf.append(toBase64[(inbuf[1] & 0x0F) << 2]);
         sbuf.append('=');
      }
      sbuf.append('\n');
   }

   private static char[] toBase64 =
   {  'A', 'B', 'C', 'D', 'E', 'F', 'G', 'H',
      'I', 'J', 'K', 'L', 'M', 'N', 'O', 'P',
      'Q', 'R', 'S', 'T', 'U', 'V', 'W', 'X',
      'Y', 'Z', 'a', 'b', 'c', 'd', 'e', 'f',
      'g', 'h', 'i', 'j', 'k', 'l', 'm', 'n',
      'o', 'p', 'q', 'r', 's', 't', 'u', 'v',
      'w', 'x', 'y', 'z', '0', '1', '2', '3',
      '4', '5', '6', '7', '8', '9', '+', '/'
   };

   StringBuffer sbuf;
   int col = 0;
   int i = 0;
   int[] inbuf = new int[3];
}

class Base64InputStream extends InputStream
{  public Base64InputStream(String s, int start)
   {  str = s;
      pos = start;
      i = 0;
   }
```

```java
public int read()
{  while (pos < str.length() &&
        Character.isWhitespace(str.charAt(pos)))
   {  pos++;
   }
   if (pos >= str.length()) return -1;
   if (i == 0)
   {  int ch1 = str.charAt(pos) & 0x7F;
      int ch2 = str.charAt(pos + 1) & 0x7F;
      i++;
      return (fromBase64[ch1] << 2)
         | (fromBase64[ch2] >> 4);
   }
   else if (i == 1)
   {  int ch1 = str.charAt(pos + 1) & 0x7F;
      int ch2 = str.charAt(pos + 2) & 0x7F;
      if (ch2 == '=') return -1;
      i++;
      return ((fromBase64[ch1] & 0x0F) << 4)
         | (fromBase64[ch2] >> 2);
   }
   else
   {  int ch1 = str.charAt(pos + 2) & 0x7F;
      int ch2 = str.charAt(pos + 3) & 0x7F;
      if (ch2 == '=') return -1;
      i = 0;
      pos += 4;
      return ((fromBase64[ch1] & 0x03) << 6)
         | fromBase64[ch2];
   }
}

private static int[] fromBase64 =
{  -1, -1, -1, -1, -1, -1, -1, -1,
   -1, -1, -1, -1, -1, -1, -1, -1,
   -1, -1, -1, -1, -1, -1, -1, -1,
   -1, -1, -1, -1, -1, -1, -1, -1,
   -1, -1, -1, -1, -1, -1, -1, -1,
   -1, -1, -1, 62, -1, -1, -1, 63,
   52, 53, 54, 55, 56, 57, 58, 59,
   60, 61, -1, -1, -1, -1, -1, -1,
   -1,  0,  1,  2,  3,  4,  5,  6,
    7,  8,  9, 10, 11, 12, 13, 14,
   15, 16, 17, 18, 19, 20, 21, 22,
   23, 24, 25, -1, -1, -1, -1, -1,
   -1, 26, 27, 28, 29, 30, 31, 32,
   33, 34, 35, 36, 37, 38, 39, 40,
   41, 42, 43, 44, 45, 46, 47, 48,
   49, 50, 51, -1, -1, -1, -1, -1
};

String str;
int pos;
int i;
}
```

CHAPTER 7

Java Beans

The official JavaSoft definition of a bean is:

"A Java Bean is a reusable software component that can be manipulated visually in a builder tool."

This chapter explains what you need to know about beans in order to *build* them. We do not cover any of the various builder environments, such as SunSoft's Java WorkShop, Borland's JBuilder, IBM's VisualAge, or Symantec's Visual Café, that are designed to help you use beans in order to produce applications or applets more efficiently.

NOTE: Beans should eventually also be scriptable in tools such as Netscape's Visual JavaScript (`http://www.netscape.com/download/`). Unfortunately, these kinds of tools which use simple scripting languages to control beans are at an even earlier stage in their development than the Java builder tools currently available

Why Beans?

Programmers coming from a Windows background (specifically, Visual Basic or Delphi) will immediately know why beans are so important. Programmers coming from an environment where the tradition is to "roll your own" for everything may not understand at once. Our experience is that even more is true: Programmers who do not come from a Visual Basic or Delphi background often find it hard to believe that Visual Basic is the most successful example of reusable objects in the programming universe. For example, the market for reusable Visual Basic and Delphi components last year was more than

$400,000,000—far more than the market for Java tools and Java-based products. One reason for Visual Basic's popularity becomes clear if you consider how you build a Visual Basic application. For those who have never worked with Visual Basic, here, in a nutshell, is how you do it:

- You build the interface by dropping components (called controls) in Visual Basic onto a form window.

- When you are done "drawing" the interface, the containing window and the controls (such as command buttons, text boxes, file dialog boxes, or any one of the more than 3,000 or so other controls that are out there) automatically recognize user actions such as mouse movements and button clicks.

Only after you finish designing the interface does anything like traditional programming occur. The way this works is that Visual Basic objects generally have:

- Properties of the object such as height or width that you can set at design time or run time. You can set them at design time without any programming, often in a rather user friendly fashion.

- Methods to perform actions that you code with at run time.

- Events that the controls can respond to. You write code in an event procedure associated to the event (calling the methods of the components as needed).

For example, in Chapter 2 of Volume 1, we wrote a program that would display an image on a form. It took a little over a page of code. Here's what you would do in Visual Basic to create a program with pretty much the same functionality.

1. Add two controls to a window: an *Image* control for displaying graphics and a *Common Dialog* control for selecting a file.

2. Set the *Filter* properties of the CommonDialog control so that only files that the Image control can handle will show up. This is done in what VB calls the Properties window, as shown in Figure 7-1.

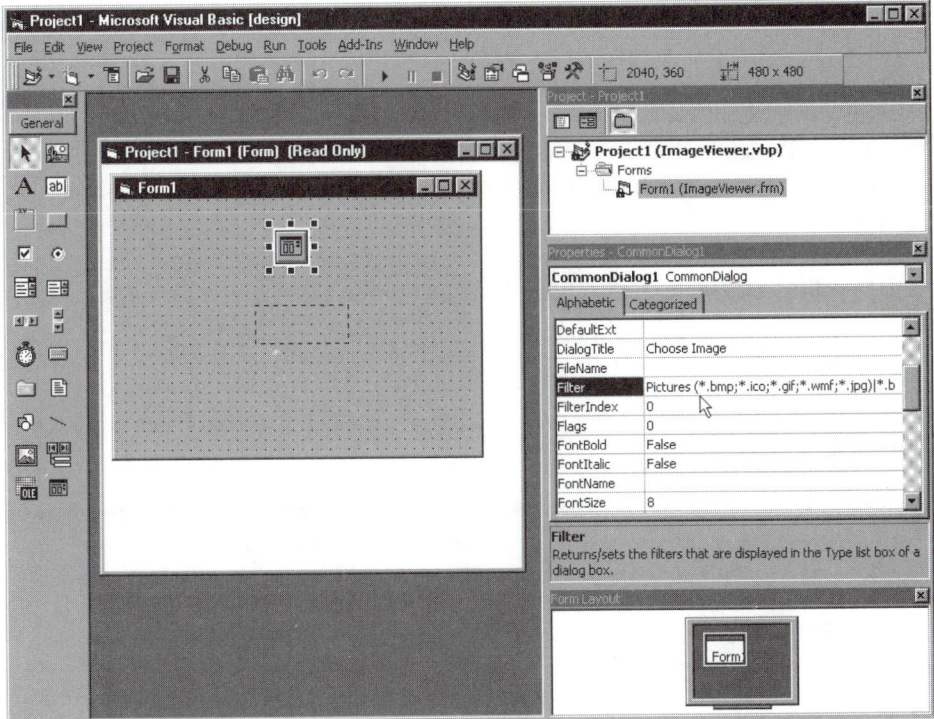

Figure 7-1: The Properties window in VB for an image application

Now, we need to write the three lines of VB code that will be activated when the project first starts running. This corresponds to an event called the `Form_Load`, so the code goes in the `Form_Load` event procedure. The following code pops up the File dialog box—but only files with the right extension are shown because of how we set the Filter property. After the user selects an image file, the code then tells the Image control to display it. All the code you need for this sequence looks like this:

```
Private Sub Form_Load()
  On Error Resume Next
  CommonDialog1.ShowOpen
  Image1.Picture = LoadPicture(CommonDialog1.FileName)
End Sub
```

That's it. These three lines of code give essentially the same functionality as the 45 or so lines of Java code. Of course, in Visual Basic, you do have to locate and then drop down the components, and you have to set properties. But it is a lot easier to learn how to do that than it is to write code.

The point is that right now Java is still a tool used only by top-notch, object-oriented programmers. And, realistically, even such programmers are unlikely to be as productive as a good Visual Basic programmer is for a small- to medium-sized GUI-intensive application. Note that we do not want to imply that Visual Basic is a good solution for every problem. It is clearly optimized for a particular kinds of problems—UI-intensive Windows programs. In contrast, Java will always have a much wider range of uses. And the good news is that with the advent of JavaBeans, some of the benefits of Visual Basic-style application building are on the horizon for Java. We predict that in the near future:

1. Beans with the same functionality as the most common Visual Basic controls will become readily available.

2. Java Builder tools will become as easy to use as the Visual Basic environment is today.

NOTE: Of course, once you have built a bean, you have the nice bonus that you will be able to use it everywhere. You can even, through the magic of the JavaSoft "Beans to ActiveX Bridge," use them in Visual Basic and Delphi (`http://www.javasoft.com/beans/bridge`).

The Bean-Writing Process

Most of the rest of this chapter shows you the techniques that you will use to write beans. Before we go into details, we give an overview of the process. First, we want to stress that writing a bean is not technically difficult—there are only a few new classes and interfaces for you to master. In fact, no new techniques are involved. (For example, to make a bean persistent, simply make sure it implements the `Serializable` interface.)

In particular, the simplest kind of bean is really nothing more than a Java class that follows some fairly strict naming conventions for its event listeners and its methods. Example 7-1 shows the code for an ImageViewer Bean that could give a Java-based builder environment the same functionality as the Visual Basic Image control that we mentioned in the previous section. (Except, of course, this bean can handle only GIF or JPEGs because of limitations in the Java Image class; compare the class to the Visual Basic Image control.)

Example 7-1: ImageViewerBean.java

```
import java.awt.*;

public class ImageViewerBean extends Component
{  public void setFileName(String f)
   {  fileName = f;
      image = Toolkit.getDefaultToolkit().getImage(fileName);
      setSize(getPreferredSize());
      repaint();
   }

   public String getFileName()
   {  return fileName;
   }

   public void paint(Graphics g)
   {  if (image == null)
      {  Dimension d = getSize();
         g.drawRect(0, 0, d.width, d.height);
      }
      else
         g.drawImage(image, 0, 0, this);
   }

   public Dimension getPreferredSize()
   {  if (image == null)
         return new Dimension(MINSIZE, MINSIZE);
      return new Dimension(image.getWidth(null),
         image.getHeight(null));
   }

   private static final int MINSIZE = 50;
   private Image image = null;
   private String fileName = "";
}
```

When you look at this code, notice that it really doesn't look any different from any other well-designed Java class. For example, all mutator methods begin with set, all accessor methods begin with get. (As you will soon see, using a standard naming convention is one way builder tools can get information about the properties and events your bean supports.)

In general, the properties of your bean will usually be the part of its internal state that can be programmed. In particular, just as with any well-designed class, you should only expose private data fields through accessor and mutator methods. When you do this using the standard naming convention that we will

describe shortly, then these methods become the properties of your bean. Events that your bean supports are simply any event handling code that follows the Java 1.1 event model. If these are custom events, you'll need to follow the requirements for adding custom event listeners to a class (see Chapter 8 of Volume 1 or the `TimerBean` example below for examples). Finally, the methods of your bean are any public methods that are not associated to a property or an event.

VB NOTE: Unfortunately, the JavaSoft people decided not to introduce a Property or Event keyword like VB5 has. You simply use `setX` and `getX` for a property named X and trust to Java to realize that they are properties. (See the section on "Design Patterns" a little later on in this chapter.)

The real problems come from what you need to do to make beans reusable by a large class of users. In particular, if you are interested in developing beans for commercial use (either for in-house use or for sale to other programmers), you need to keep two (possibly conflicting) points in mind.

- First: Beans may need to be usable by less than expert programmers. Such people will access the functionality of your bean either with a scripting language or with a visual design tool that uses essentially no programming language at all. (The connect-the-dots approach to application development seems to be growing more popular.)

  If the users of your beans want to script them by using JavaScript or VBScript on a Web page, your beans must be full featured enough to be worthwhile, while not being too complex for a naïve user to understand. For example, based on the Visual Basic component market, your naïve users will tend to think of:

  - Properties as things that describe what a bean is

  - Methods as describing what your bean can do

  - Events as being what actions the bean is aware of and can respond to

- Second: A full-featured bean that can be used by either a naïve user or a professional developer often turns out to be quite tedious to code—useful components must deal with the complexity of the real world. Of course, that is why people can charge hundreds of dollars for a professional component, such as a full-featured chart control. For example, the prototypical VB chart control has

- 60 properties
- 47 events
- 14 methods
- 178 pages of documentation

  Obviously, a chart control is about as full featured a control as one can imagine, but even a bean as simple as an Integer text field turns out to be not quite so simple to code as one might first imagine.

  Consider, for example, what should happen as the user types digits into the text field. Should the new numbers be *immediately* reported to the listeners? On the one hand, this approach is attractive because it gives instant feedback to the user of your bean. But many applications restrict the range for valid entries, and partial entries that can go into an eventual valid entry might not themselves be valid. This restriction is particularly important for beans because the bean specification allows a listener for a property change in your bean to veto an invalid input, as you will shortly see.

  For example, suppose a listener vetoed all odd numbers. If a user tried to enter 256, the input 25 would be vetoed, and the user could never get past the veto. So, in this case, incremental update is a bad idea because the incremental value would be vetoed even though the eventual entry would not have been. In cases like this, your bean should report the value to listeners only when the user has finished entering the number, that is, when the user presses ENTER or if the text field loses focus.

  If you are writing a program for a single application, then you will simply choose one behavior or the other. But if you are building a bean, you aren't programming for yourself but for a wide audience of users with different needs. Therefore, it would be best to add a property called something like `incrementalUpdate` and implement both behaviors, depending on the value of that property. Add a few more options like this, and even a simple `IntTextBean` will end up with a dozen properties.

Fortunately, you need to master only a small number of concepts to write beans with a rich set of behavior. The example beans in this chapter, while not trivial, are kept simple enough to illustrate the necessary concepts.

TIP: You will find full-featured beans available for sale from many programming products stores, bundled with Java development environments, or for free at sites such as www.gamelan.com. Also, all the AWT components in Java 1.1 are beans, but, more importantly, all the components in the JFC ("swing set") are beans. Using the swing set components as a base class for your own beans gives you a great starting point. These components are quite a bit slicker and more sophisticated than the simple AWT controls that are supplied with Java 1.1. As we write this, the swing set is in beta, but it is freely available after you register (also free) at the Java Developer connection (developer.javasoft.com).

The BDK and the BeanBox

Before we get into the mechanics of writing beans, we want you to see how you might use or test them. (The ImageViewerBean is a perfectly usable bean, but outside a builder environment it can't show off any of its special features. In particular, the only way to use it in an ordinary Java program would be to write a class that instantiates it and calls the setFileName method.) So, the question is how can we show off the power of this simple bean? This question, in turn, leads to the question of what bean builder tool to use. Our current opinion is that no bean environment that we are familiar with seems mature enough to recommend unconditionally. Instead, we use the least common denominator environment, the so-called BeanBox, that is part of JavaSoft's Bean Developer Kit (or BDK). The BeanBox is not very full featured and is certainly flaky at times, but it is available on many platforms and it lets you test simple beans. Moreover, if you get your bean working in the BeanBox, then it should work in other development environments without any changes.

NOTE: At this time, the BDK installation is separate from the JDK installation. You may need to obtain it from the Java Web site (java.sun.com). Be sure that you have installed it before going any further.

Using the BeanBox

By default, the BDK is installed into a directory bdk. The BeanBox is automatically installed into a subdirectory called BeanBox. This directory has a batch file (run.bat) to start up the BeanBox under Windows and a shell script (run.sh) for Unix systems. When you start up the BeanBox, you'll see a message box that looks like Figure 7-2. (As you will soon see, JAR files are how beans are packaged for use.)

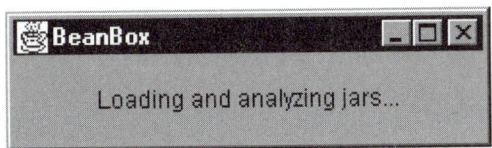

Figure 7-2: The Analyzing Jars message box

The actual BeanBox consists of three independently resizable and movable windows, as shown in Figure 7-3. The Toolbox lists all the beans that the BeanBox knows about. The default installation of the BDK comes with 16 beans. (See below for how to add new beans to the BeanBox.) As you can see in Figure 7-3, some beans have associated icons that show up in the left side of the Toolbox as well. The window marked BeanBox is where you will drop the beans and where you will (try to) connect them so that events in one trigger actions in another. The window marked Properties - BeanBox is where you control the properties of your beans. This is a vital part of component-based development tools since setting properties at design time is how you set the initial state of a component.

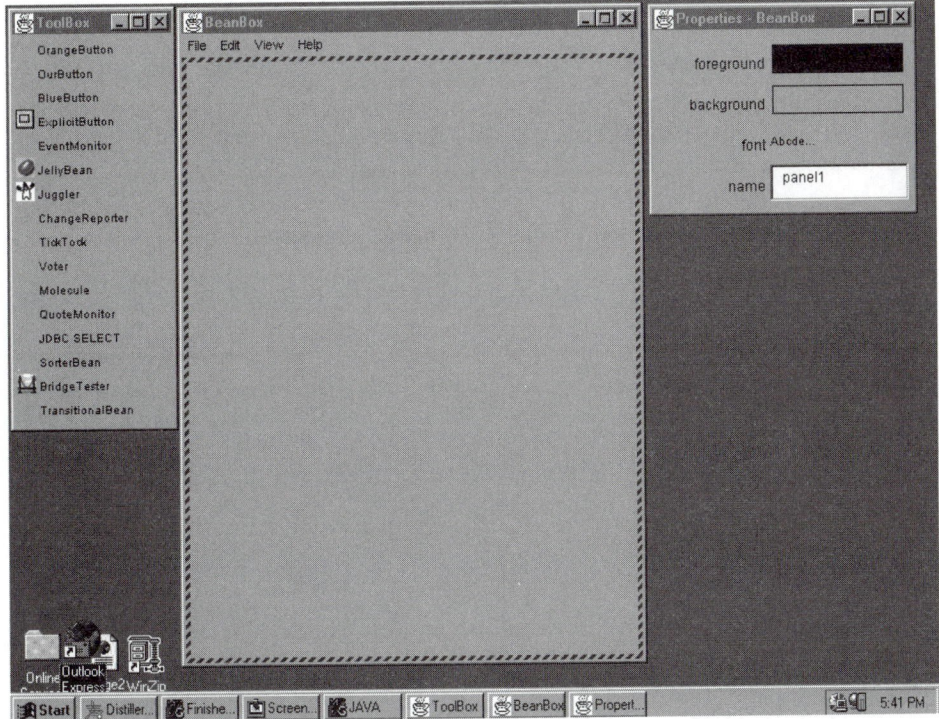

Figure 7-3: The parts of the BeanBox

For example, you can reset the *name* property of the Panel used for the BeanBox by simply typing in the text box in the window marked Properties-BeanBox. (This type of window for setting the properties of a bean in the BeanBox is often called a *Property Sheet*.) Changing the name property is simple—you just edit a string in a text field. But properties don't have to be strings; they can be values of any Java type. To make it possible for users to set values for properties of any type, builder tools access specialized *property editors*. (Property editors either come with the builder or are supplied by the bean developer. You'll see how to write your own property editors later in this chapter.)

To see a simple property editor at work, try to reset the background color of the BeanBox window as follows:

1. Click in the box marked background in the Property Sheet. This brings up a property editor for editing objects of type *Color*, as shown in Figure 7-4.

2. Choose a new color either by entering new hex digits in the first box or by making a selection via the choice box in the editor.

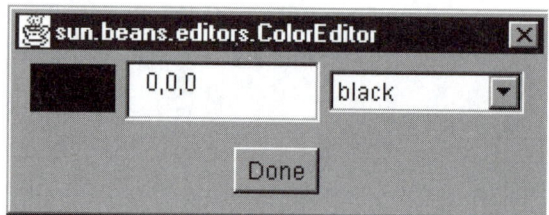

Figure 7-4: Using a property editor to set properties

Notice that you'll immediately see the change to the background color.

VB NOTE: What JavaSoft calls a Property Sheet is analogous to the Properties window; what VB calls a Property Sheet is analogous to what JavaSoft calls a *customizer* (see the section on them below).

Using a Bean in the BeanBox

Using a bean that the BeanBox knows about is not hard:

1. Select the bean in the Toolbox. (The cursor will become a crosshair).

2. Click on the spot in the BeanBox window where you want the bean to go.

The user interface is not very clever. It neither gives you a clue as to which bean you selected nor lets you cancel the operation once you start it. Once you have a

bean in the BeanBox window, click in it to select it. A hatched border indicates that the bean is selected (see Figure 7-5—the bottom button is the one selected).

Figure 7-5: A selected bean versus an unselected bean

You can move selected beans around the BeanBox window by:

1. Moving the mouse cursor to the boundary. (You may have to try various spots—you'll know you are at the right place when the cursor changes to a four-headed arrow, as shown in Figure 7-6.)

2. Dragging the bean to the new location.

Figure 7-6: A bean ready for moving

Similarly, you can resize most beans by moving the cursor to one of the corners (it will change to a two-sided arrow) and dragging the boundary of the bean to be the size that you want.

TIP: To remove a bean that you inadvertently placed on the BeanBox window:
1. Select the bean.
2. Choose Edit | Cut.

Building a Simple Application in the BeanBox

We explain in the section on Introspection near the end of this chapter how builder tools such as the BeanBox can know what properties a bean supports or what events it triggers. For now though, we simply want to show you that it all works. For this, we will follow tradition and hook up Start and Stop buttons to the juggling, tooth-shaped character shown in the Juggler bean. Here are the steps to follow (see Figure 7-7 for what the results might look like):

1. Add two "Explicit" beans to the BeanBox window.

2. Set the Label property of one to Start and the other to Stop.

3. Add the Juggler bean to the BeanBox. (Notice that it immediately starts juggling.)

Figure 7-7: The BeanBox window for our Stop/Start Juggler application

Since the Juggler is already annoyingly juggling, let's hook up the Stop button first.

1. Select the Stop button.

2. Choose Edit | Events | button push (see Figure 7-8). Choose the `actionPerformed` event from this submenu.

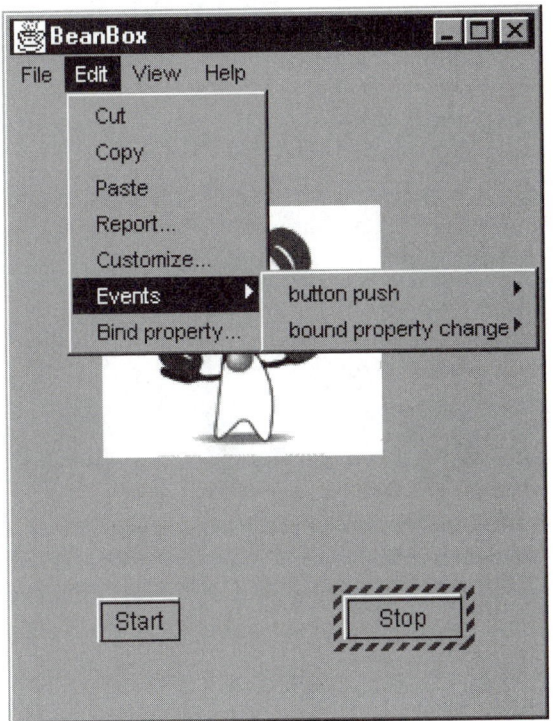

Figure 7-8: The possible events for the Stop Button window for our Stop/Start Juggler application

Now, when you move the mouse cursor on the BeanBox window, you'll see a red line growing from the Stop button. (See Figure 7-9.)

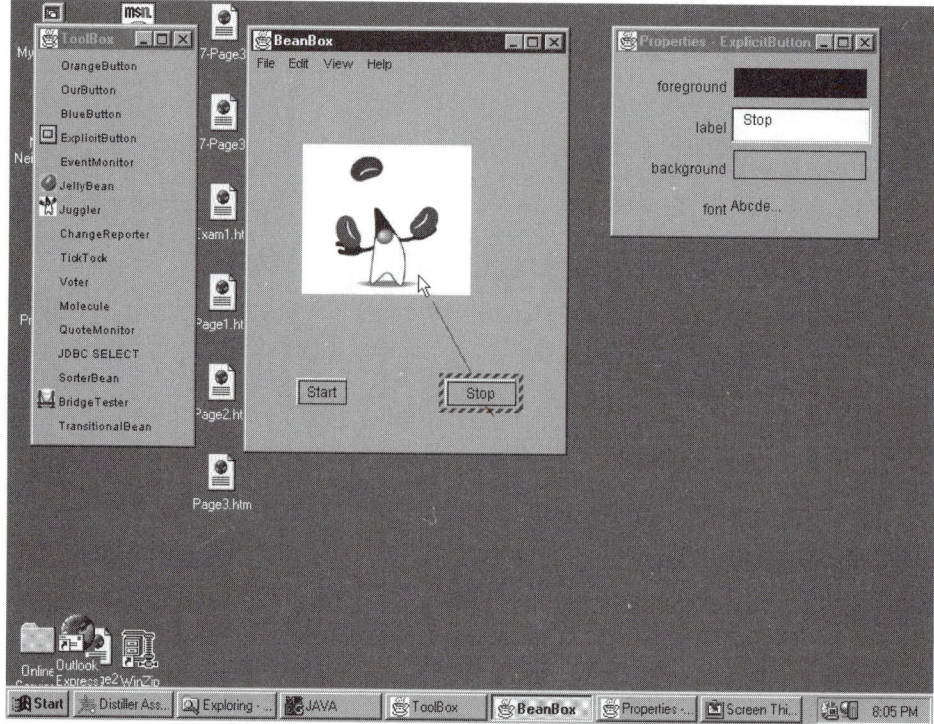

Figure 7-9: The marker for an event hookup

Now, choose the Juggler bean. You'll see a window like that shown in Figure 7-10 where you can select the method you want to hook up to the `actionPerformed` event.

We wanted to stop the juggling, so just choose `stopJuggling` in the dialog box shown in Figure 7-10. After you click on OK, the BeanBox will generate the needed adapter code. (Look inside the `tmp\sunw\beanbox` directory below where the BeanBox is stored.)

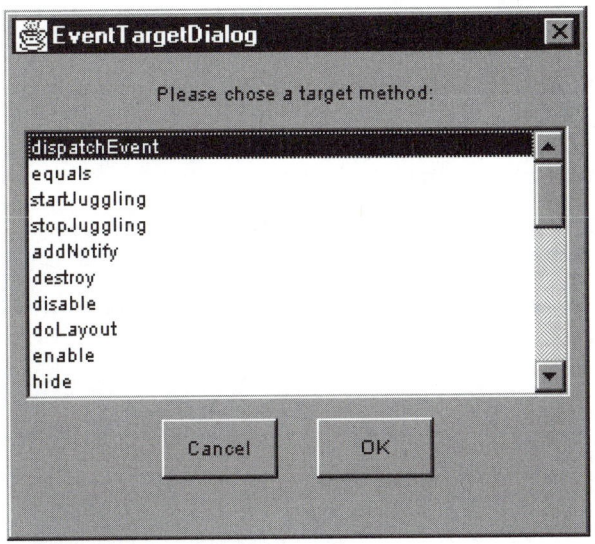

Figure 7-10: The target method dialog

Here is what the code looks like:

```
// Automatically generated event hookup file.

package tmp.sunw.beanbox;
import sunw.demo.juggler.Juggler;
import java.awt.event.ActionListener;
import java.awt.event.ActionEvent;

public class ___Hookup_146ca316c4 implements
java.awt.event.ActionListener, java.io.Serializable {

    public void setTarget(sunw.demo.juggler.Juggler t) {
        target = t;
    }

    public void actionPerformed(java.awt.event.ActionEvent
            arg0) {
        target.stopJuggling(arg0);
    }

    private sunw.demo.juggler.Juggler target;
}
```

Notice that the adapter class is given an absurd name, but the key is that the `actionPerformed` method calls the `stopJuggling` method of the `Juggler` class. Once you have called this class, clicking the Stop button really does stop the Juggler.

Saving and Restoring the State of the BeanBox

As you might expect, the BeanBox uses object serialization (Chapter 1) to save the state of your BeanBox.

> NOTE: It is essential that a builder tool be able to save the state of a bean (such as the current property settings), so design your beans so that their current state is serializable (see Chapter 1).

To save the state of an application that you are testing in the BeanBox, choose File I Save and fill in the File dialog box as desired. To restore the state of the BeanBox, make sure the BeanBox is clear of any beans (choose File I Clear). then choose File I Open to reload the previous application.

Building an Applet from the BeanBox

If you finish hooking up the Start button to the Juggler as well, you might want to see this application in a Browser, like HotJava or Internet Explorer 4, that has the Java 1.1 event model enabled. This is how it is supposed to work:

1.   Choose File I Make Applet.

2.   In the Dialog Box (Figure 7-11) that pops up, you can give the JAR file a new name or simply accept the default choice.

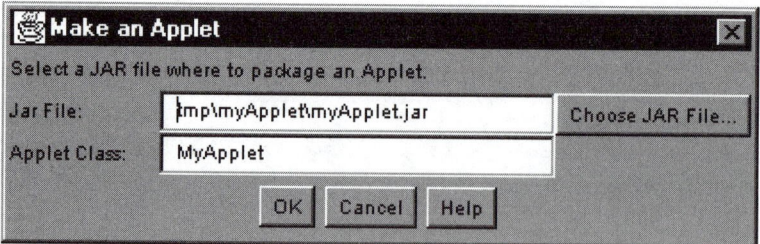

Figure 7-11: The applet creation dialog

That's it. The BeanBox will generate the needed HTML code (`myApplet.HTML` is the default name). You can load the HTML file in your favorite Java 1.1 event-enabled browser or the applet viewer (see Figure 7-12).

Figure 7-12: The connected beans as an applet in the applet viewer

Adding Beans to the Toolbox

The first step in making any bean usable (whether in the BeanBox or any builder tool) is to package all class files that are used by the bean code into a JAR file. (See Chapter 10 of Volume 1 for more on JAR files). Unlike the JAR files for an applet that you saw previously, a JAR file for a bean needs a manifest file that specifies which class files in the archive are beans and should be included in the Toolbox. For example, here is the manifest file `ImageViewerBean.mf` for the ImageViewerBean:

```
Name: ImageViewerBean.class
Java-Bean: True
```

If your bean contains multiple class files, you do not need to mention them in the manifest unless they are also beans that you want to have displayed in the Toolbox.

To make the JAR file, follow these steps:

1. Edit the manifest file.

2. Gather all needed class files in a directory.

3. Run the `jar` tool as follows:

   ```
   jar cfm JarFile ManifestFile *.class
   ```

   For example,

   ```
   jar cfm ImageViewerBean.jar ImageViewerBean.mf *.class
   ```

You can also add other items, such as GIF files, to the JAR file.

TIP: If you prefer to build a make file to create the needed jar file, look at the `demo` directory below the `bdk` directory for some sample make (`.mk`) files.

Finally, to make the BeanBox's Toolbox aware of your JAR file that contains the bean, copy the JAR file to the `jars` subdirectory of the BDK or choose File | Load Jar in the BeanBox window.

Building an Image Viewer Application via Beans

We now have shown you enough BeanBox techniques so that you can use the two Java beans on the CD that give you the equivalent of the Visual Basic ImageViewer program. To see these beans at work, add the `ImageViewerBean` and the `FileNameBean` JAR files to the BeanBox by choosing File | LoadJar, or by copying the JAR file to the `jars` subdirectory of the `bdk` directory.

NOTE: You have already seen the code for the `ImageViewerBean`. The code for the `FileNameBean` is a lot more sophisticated. We'll analyze it in depth later in this chapter. For now, all you have to know is that clicking on the ellipsis will open a standard File Open dialog box where you can enter the name of the file.

If you add the `ImageViewerBean`, then, as you can see from Figure 7-13, you can choose a file name for a GIF or JPEG file. Once you do so, the `ImageViewerBean` automatically displays the bean.

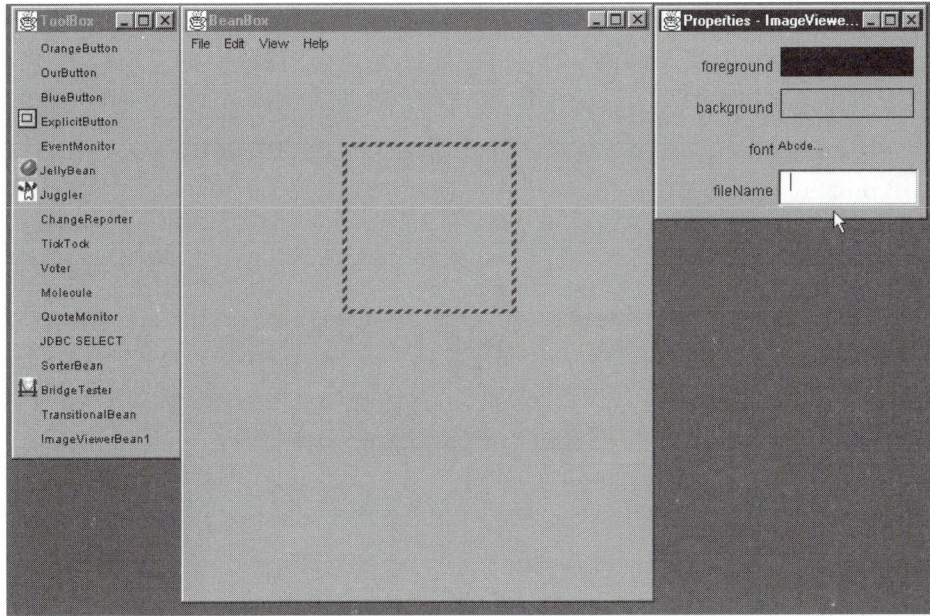

Figure 7-13: The `ImageViewerBean` at work

To imitate the functionality of the Visual Basic program, we don't want to hook up events, as we did for the juggler. Instead, we link together the respective `fileName` properties of the beans. The idea is that a change in the `fileName` property of the `FileNameBean` is immediately reflected in the current value of the `fileName` property of `ImageViewerBean`. (Of course, this actually happens through a `propertyChange` event; we discuss these kinds of events a little later in this chapter.) This name change, in turn, results in the `ImageViewerBean` immediately displaying the right image—exactly as the VB program did.

NOTE: We describe the way it is supposed to work in the BeanBox. Be sure to use the most updated version of the BeanBox. Some older versions do not update the image, some versions do not update the Property Sheet, and, unfortunately, some do neither.

To hook up the properties in the respective beans:

1. Select the `FileNameBean`.

2. Choose Edit | Bind Property.

3. In the resulting dialog box that pops up (Figure 7-14), choose the `filename` property.

4. Click on OK.

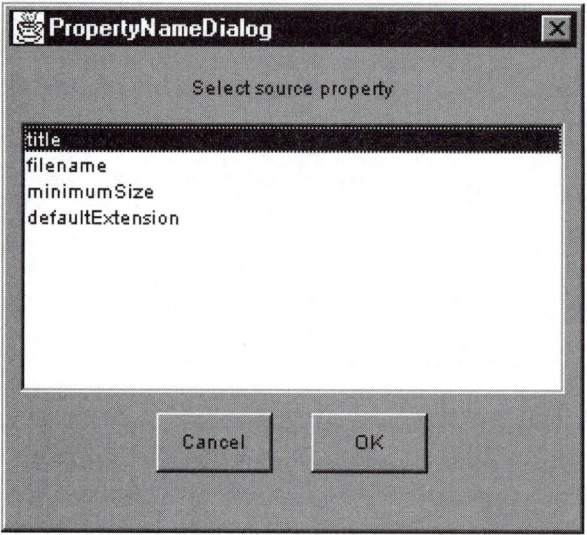

Figure 7-14: The Bind PropertyNameDialog box for the `FileNameBean`

Now, the magic red line should appear, and you stretch it to reach the `ImageViewerBean`.

NOTE: You can't see the `ImageViewerBean` when you are trying to bind the properties of the `FileNameBean` to it. Rest assured, though, it is still there—you can see the red line stop increasing in size when it hits the `ImageViewerBean`—even if the BeanBox is behaving badly by not showing it to you. We could have overcome this problem by setting the background color of the bean to, say, pink, but this is an issue only for the BeanBox. Other bean-building environments would show the outlines of the beans.

Click when the magic line reaches to the `ImageViewerBean`. The BeanBox will then pop up another dialog box (see Figure 7-15).

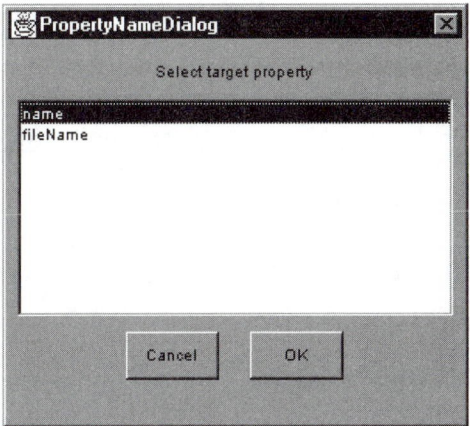

Figure 7-15: The PropertyNameDialog box for the ImageViewerBean

At this point, the two fileName properties are hooked up, so you can use the FileNameBean to update the image by clicking on the ellipsis and choosing the name of a GIF or JPEG file (see Figure 7-16).

Figure 7-16: The result of hooking up the fileName properties

"Design Patterns" for Bean Properties and Events

First, we want to stress there is *no* cosmic base beans class that you extend to build your beans. Visual beans obviously have to extend from `Component` or a subclass of `Component`, but nonvisual beans can simply extend implicitly from `Object`. Remember, a bean is simply *any* class that can be manipulated in a visual design tool. The design tool does not look at the base class to determine the bean nature of a class, but it analyzes the names of its methods. To enable this analysis, the method names for beans must follow a certain pattern.

NOTE: There is a `java.beans.Beans` class, but all methods in it are static. Extending it would, therefore, be rather pointless, even though you will see it done occasionally, supposedly for greater "clarity." Clearly, since a bean can't both extend `Beans` and `Component`, this approach can't work for visual beans. In fact, the `Beans` class contains methods that are designed to be called by builder tools, for example, to check whether the bean is being used at design time or run time.

Other languages for visual design environments, such as Visual Basic and Delphi, have special keywords such as "Property" and "Event "to express these concepts directly. The designers of Java decided not to add keywords to the language in order to support visual programming. Therefore, they needed an alternative so that a builder tool could analyze a bean to learn its properties or events. The first method they suggest that builder tools should use is based on the bean writer using a standard naming pattern for properties and events. If you use a standard naming pattern for your properties and events, then the builder tool can use the powerful reflection mechanism added to Java 1.1 (see Chapter 5 of Volume 1) to understand what properties and events the bean is supposed to expose.

NOTE: Although the JavaBeans documentation calls this standard naming practice "Design patterns," these are really only naming conventions and have nothing to do with the term as used in OOP theory books.

The naming convention to use for properties so that a builder tool can use reflection to discover them automatically is simple:

- Any pair of methods

    ```
    X getPropertyName()
    void setPropertyName(X x)
    ```

    corresponds to a read/write property of type *X*.

For example, in our `ImageViewerBean`, there is only one `read/write` property (for the file name to be viewed), with the following methods:

```
public void setFileName(String f)
public String getFileName()
```

Note that if you have a `get` method but not an associated `set` method, you define a read-only property.

Be careful with the capitalization pattern you use for your method names. JavaSoft decided that the name of the property in our example would be f̲ileName, with a lowercase f, even though the `get` and `set` methods contain an uppercase F (getF̲ileName, setF̲ileName). The bean analyzer performs a process called *decapitalization* to derive the property name. (That is, the first character after `get` or `set` is converted to lower case.) The JavaBeans designers felt that this process would result in method and property names that are more natural to Java programmers.

NOTE: The `get` and `set` methods you create can do more than simply get and set a private data field. Like any Java method, they can carry out arbitrary actions. For example, notice that the `setFileName` method of the `ImageViewerBean` class not only sets the value of the `fileName` data field, but it also opens the file, loads the image, and displays the image.

VB NOTE: In VB, properties also come from `get` and `set` methods. (Delphi uses `read` and `write`.) But, as we already mentioned, in both these languages there is a Property keyword, which allows the the compiler to not have to second-guess the programmer's intentions by analyzing method names. And using a keyword in those languages has another advantage: Using a property name on the left-hand side of an assignment automatically calls the `set` method. Using a property name in an expression automatically calls the `get` method. For example, in VB you can write

```
imageBean.fileName = "corejava.gif"
```

instead of

```
imageBean.setFileName("corejava.gif");
```

There is one exception to the `get`/`set` naming pattern. Properties that have Boolean values should use a naming convention as in the following examples:

```
public bool isPropertyName()
public void setPropertyName(boolean b)
```

For example, an animation might have a property `running`, with two methods

```
public boolean isRunning()
public void setRunning(boolean b)
```

The `setRunning` method would start and stop the animation. The `isRunning` method would report its current status. (The juggler bean does not have such a property, however.)

For events, the naming conventions are even simpler. A bean builder environment will infer that your bean generates events when you supply methods to add and remove event listeners. For example, suppose your bean generates events of type *EventName*Event. (All events must end in `Event`.) Then, the listener interface must be called *EventName*Listener, and the methods to add and remove a listener must be called

```
public void addEventNameListener(EventNameListener e)
public void removeEventNameListener(EventNameListener e)
```

If you look at the code for the `ImageViewerBean`, you'll see that it has no events to expose. Later, we will see a timer bean that generates `TimerEvent` objects and has the following methods to manage event listeners:

```
public void addTimerListener(TimerListener e)
public void removeTimerListener(TimerListener e)
```

Writing Bean Properties

A sophisticated bean will have lots of different kinds of properties that it should expose in a builder tool for a user to set at design time or get at run time. It can also trigger both standard and custom events. Properties can be as simple as the file name property that you saw in the `ImageViewerBean` and the `FileNameBean` or as sophisticated as a color value or even an array of data points—we encounter both of these cases later in this chapter. Obviously, the more sophisticated a property, the more important it is that you give your users a friendly way to set it. Later in this chapter, we show you beans that exhibit all the various ways of letting users *set* properties. These examples should provide reasonable models on which you can make property settings for your own beans user friendly. Before we do that, though, you should first be familiar with the kinds of properties beans can support. The next few sections give examples of custom beans that show off the possible kinds of properties.

Getting your properties of your beans right is probably the most complex part of building a bean because the model is quite rich. The beans specification (`http://java.sun.com/beans/`) allows four types of properties, which we illustrate by various examples.

Simple Properties

A simple property is one that takes a single value such as a string or a number. The `fileName` property of the ImageViewer is an example of a simple property. Simple properties are easy to program: just use the `set`/`get` naming convention we indicated earlier. For example, if you look at the code in Example 7-1, you can see that all it took to implement a simple string property is:

```
public void setFileName(String f)
{   fileName = f;
    image = Toolkit.getDefaultToolkit().getImage(fileName);
    setSize(getPreferredSize());
    repaint();
}

public String getFileName()
{   return fileName;
}
```

Notice that, as far as the JavaBeans specification is concerned, we also have a read-only property of this bean because we have a method with this signature inside the class:

```
public Dimension getPreferredSize()
```

without a corresponding `setPreferredSize` method. You would not normally be able to see read-only properties at design time in a Property Sheet.

TIP: In the version of the BeanBox we are working with, you have to initialize private data members explicitly to non-`null` values, or the BeanBox simply won't display them, leaving you to wonder whether you misspelled something. For example,

```
public String getProp() { return prop; }
public void setProp(String p) { prop = p; )
 . . .
private String prop = "";
    // if not set, BeanBox won't display prop
```

Problems such as this one make programming beans decidedly unpleasant. If you make any mistake at all, a part of your bean will silently fail, and you have no idea what the problem is or whether you just ran up against a limitation of the BeanBox. Of course, if you use a bean development environment, more of the routine code is generated automatically and there is less room for error.

Indexed Properties

An indexed property is one that gets or sets an array. A chart bean (see below) would certainly use an indexed property for the data points. With an indexed property, you supply two pairs of get and set methods: one for the array and one for individual entries. They must follow the pattern

```
X[] getPropertyName()
void setPropertyName(X[] x)
X getPropertyName(int i)
void setPropertyName(int i, X x)
```

Here's an example of the indexed property we use in the chart bean that you will see later in this chapter.

```
public double[] getValues() { return values; }
public void setValues(double[] v) { values = v; }
public double getValues(int i) { return values[i]; }
public void setValues(int i, double v) { values[i] = v; }
    . . .
private double[] values;
```

The get/set functions that set individual array entries can assume that i is within the legal range. Builder tools will not call them with an index that is less than 0 or larger than the length of the array. In particular, the

```
setPropertyName(int i, X[] x)
```

method cannot be used to *grow* the array. To grow the array, you must manually build a new array and then pass it to this method:

```
setPropertyName(X[] x)
```

As a practical matter, however, the get and set methods can still be called programmatically, not just by the builder environment. Therefore, it is best to add some error checking, after all. For example, here is the code that we really use in the ChartBean class:

```
public double getValues(int i)
{   if (0 <= i && i < values.length) return values[i];
    return 0;
}

public void setValues(int i, double value)
{   if (0 <= i && i < values.length) values[i] = value;
}
```

> NOTE: As we write this, the BeanBox's Property Sheet does not support indexed prop-
> erties. That is, they don't show up on the Property Sheet, and you can't set them in
> the builder. You will see later in this chapter how to overcome this limitation by supply-
> ing a property editor for arrays.

Bound Properties

Bound properties tell interested listeners that their value has changed. For
example, the `fileName` property in the `FileNameBean` is a bound property.
When the file name changes, then the `ImageViewerBean` is automatically notified and it loads the new file. To implement a bound property, you must implement two mechanisms.

1. Whenever the value of the property changes, you must fire a
    `PropertyChange` event to all registered listeners. This change can occur
    when the `set` method is called or when the program user carries out an
    action, such as editing text or selecting a file.

2. To enable interested listeners to register themselves, the bean has to imple-
    ment the following two methods:

    ```
    void addPropertyChangeListener(PropertyChangeListener l)
    void removePropertyChangeListener(PropertyChangeListener l)
    ```

The `java.beans` package has a convenience class, called
`PropertyChangeSupport`, that manages the listeners for you. To use this convenience class, your bean must have a data field of this class that looks like this:

```
private PropertyChangeSupport pcs = new
    PropertyChangeSupport(this);
```

You delegate the task of adding and removing property change listeners to that
object.

```
public void addPropertyChangeListener(PropertyChangeListener l)
{   pcs.addPropertyChangeListener(l);
}

public void removePropertyChangeListener(PropertyChangeListener
    l)
{   pcs.removePropertyChangeListener(l);
}
```

Whenever the value of the property changes, use the `firePropertyChange`
method of the `PropertyChangeSupport` object to deliver an event to all the registered listeners. That method has three parameters: the name of the property,
the old value, and the new value. For example,

```
pcs.firePropertyChange("fileName", oldValue, newValue);
```

The values must be objects. If the property type is not an object, then you must use an object wrapper. For example,

```
pcs.firePropertyChange("running", new Boolean(false), new
    Boolean(true));
```

Other beans that want to be notified when the property value changes must implement the `PropertyChangeListener` interface. That interface contains only one method:

```
void propertyChange(PropertyChangeEvent evt)
```

The code in the `propertyChange` method is triggered whenever the property value changes, provided, of course, that you have added the recipient to the property change listeners of the bean that generates the event. The `PropertyChangeEvent` object encapsulates the old and new value of the property, obtainable via

```
Object oldVal = evt.getOldValue();
Object newVal = evt.getNewValue();
```

If the property type is not a class type, then the returned objects are the usual wrapper types. For example, if a `boolean` property is changed, then an `Integer` is returned and you need to retrieve the `boolean` value with the `booleanValue` method.

Thus, a listening object must follow this model:

```
class Listener
{   public Listener()
    {   bean.addPropertyChangeListener(this);
    }
    void propertyChange(PropertyChangeEvent evt)
    {   Object newVal = evt.getNewValue();
        . . .
    }
    . . .
}
```

Now, you may be wondering how the `ImageViewerBean` got notified when the file name in the `FileNameBean` changed. After all, there is no listener method in the `ImageViewerBean` source code. In this case, the BeanBox registered itself as a property change listener to the `FileNameBean`, and *it* called the `setFileName` method of the `ImageViewerBean` in its `propertyChange` listener method.

Here's the full code for the `FileNameBean`:

Example 7-2: FileNameBean.java

```java
import java.awt.*;
import java.awt.event.*;
import java.beans.*;

public class FileNameBean extends Panel
    implements ActionListener
{  public FileNameBean()
   {  setLayout(new GridBagLayout());
      GridBagConstraints gbc = new GridBagConstraints();
      gbc.weightx = 100;
      gbc.weighty = 100;
      gbc.anchor = GridBagConstraints.WEST;
      gbc.fill = GridBagConstraints.HORIZONTAL;
      add(nameField, gbc, 0, 0, 1, 1);
      dialogButton.addActionListener(this);
      nameField.setEditable(false);
      gbc.weightx = 0;
      gbc.anchor = GridBagConstraints.EAST;
      gbc.fill = GridBagConstraints.NONE;
      add(dialogButton, gbc, 1, 0, 1, 1);
   }

   public void add(Component c, GridBagConstraints gbc,
      int x, int y, int w, int h)
   {  gbc.gridx = x;
      gbc.gridy = y;
      gbc.gridwidth = w;
      gbc.gridheight = h;
      add(c, gbc);
   }

   public void actionPerformed(ActionEvent evt)
   {  if (evt.getSource() == dialogButton)
         showFileDialog();
   }

   public void showFileDialog()
   {  if (fileDialog == null)
      {  Container c = getParent();
         while (c != null && !(c instanceof Frame))
         {  c = c.getParent();
         }

         if (c != null)
            fileDialog = new FileDialog((Frame)c, title);
      }
      if (fileDialog == null) return;
```

```
      fileDialog.setFile(defaultExtension);
      fileDialog.setDirectory(lastDir);
      fileDialog.show();
      String f = fileDialog.getFile();
      lastDir = fileDialog.getDirectory();
      if (f != null)
      {  setFileName(lastDir + f);
      }
   }

   public void setFileName(String newValue)
   {  String oldValue = nameField.getText();
      pcs.firePropertyChange("fileName", oldValue, newValue);
      nameField.setText(newValue);
   }

   public String getFileName() { return nameField.getText(); }

   public Dimension getMinimumSize()
   {  return new Dimension(XMINSIZE, YMINSIZE);
   }

   public void addPropertyChangeListener
      (PropertyChangeListener l)
   {  pcs.addPropertyChangeListener(l);
   }

   public void removePropertyChangeListener
      (PropertyChangeListener l)
   {  pcs.removePropertyChangeListener(l);
   }

   public String getDefaultExtension()
   {  return defaultExtension;
   }

   public void setDefaultExtension(String s)
   {  defaultExtension = s;
   }

   public String getTitle() { return title; }
   public void setTitle(String s) { title = s; }

   private static final int XMINSIZE = 100;
   private static final int YMINSIZE = 20;
   private Button dialogButton = new Button("...");
   private TextField nameField = new TextField("");
   private FileDialog fileDialog;
```

```
    private int mode = FileDialog.LOAD;
    private String defaultExtension = "*.*";
    private String title = "";
    private String lastDir = "";
    private PropertyChangeSupport pcs
        = new PropertyChangeSupport(this);
}
```

`java.beans.PropertyChangeListener`

- `void propertyChange(PropertyChangeEvent evt)`

  is called when a property change event is fired.

  Parameters   evt   the property change event

`java.beans.PropertyChangeSupport`

- `PropertyChangeSupport(Object sourceBean)`

  constructs the (convenience) `PropertyChangeSupport` object.

  Parameters   sourcebean   the bean that is the source of the
                                              property change (usually `this`)

- `void addPropertyChangeListener(PropertyChangeListener listener)`

  registers an interested listener for the bound property.

  Parameters   listener   the bean that wants to be notified of
                                              a change in the bound property

- `void removePropertyChangeListener(PropertyChangeListener listener)`

  removes a previously registered interested listener for the bound property.

  Parameters   listener   the bean to be removed from the list
                                              of listeners

- `void firePropertyChange(String propertyName, Object oldValue, Object newValue)`

  sends the (convenience) `PropertyChangeEvent` to registered listeners.

  Parameters   propertyName   the name of the property

                        oldValue   the old value

                        newValue   the new value

- PropertyChangeEvent(Object source, String propertyName, Object oldValue, Object newValue)

  constructs a new PropertyChangeEvent object.

Parameters	Object	the bean source for the property
	propertyName	the name of the property
	oldValue	the old value
	newValue	the new value

- Object getNewValue()

  returns the new value of the property.

- Object getOldValue();

  returns the previous value of the property.

- String getPropertyName()

  returns the name of the property.

Constrained Properties

A constrained property is the most interesting of the properties (and, therefore, the most painful to implement). The idea is that these are properties of your bean such that certain state changes can be "vetoed" by the various users of your bean. For example, consider a text field to enter a number, implemented as a bean IntTextBean. The consumer of that number may have restrictions on the value; for example, perhaps the number should be between 0 and 255. Such a restriction would be easy to implement: add a minValue and maxValue to the IntTextBean. However, the restriction may be more complex than that. Perhaps the number should be even. Or it may depend on another number that also changes. In that case, no simple property of the IntTextBean is able to distinguish good user inputs from bad ones. Instead, the bean must notify its consumers of the new value and give the consumers the chance to *veto* the change. A property that can be vetoed is called a *constrained* property.

We will put this concept to use with a *range bean* (see Figure 7-17). This bean contains two IntTextBean fields to specify the lower and the upper bound of a range. (You might use such a bean in a print dialog where the user can specify the range of pages to be printed.) If the user enters a to value that is less than the current from value (or a from value that is greater than the current to value), then the RangeBean vetoes the change.

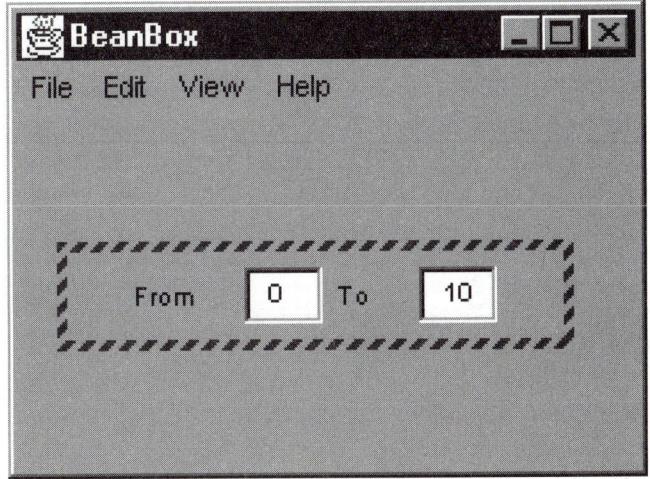

Figure 7-17: The range bean

In this example, the `IntTextBean` is the producer of the vetoable event, and the `RangeBean` is the consumer that (occasionally) issues a veto.

To build a constrained (vetoable) property, your bean must have the following two methods to let it register `VetoableChangeListener` objects:

```
void addVetoableChangeListener(VetoableChangeListener
    listener);
void removeVetoableChangeListener(VetoableChangeListener
    listener);
```

Just as there is a convenience class to manage property change listeners, there is a convenience class, called `VetoableChangeSupport`, that manages vetoable change listeners. Your bean should contain an object of this class.

```
private VetoableChangeSupport vcs
    = new VetoableChangeSupport(this);
```

Adding and removing listeners should be delegated to this object. For example:

```
public void addVetoableChangeListener(VetoableChangeListener l)
{   vcs.addVetoableChangeListener(l);
}
public void removeVetoableChangeListener(VetoableChangeListener
    l)
{   vcs.removeVetoableChangeListener(l);
}
```

Constrained properties should also be bound. That is, you need to have methods to add `PropertyChangeListener` objects in addition to `VetoableChangeListeners`. You saw how to implement those methods in the preceding section.

An object that is able to veto changes will then need to implement not only the `PropertyChangeListener` interface but the `VetoableChangeListener` interface as well. That interface contains one method:

```
void vetoableChange(PropertyChangeEvent evt)
    throws PropertyVetoException
```

This method receives a `PropertyChangeEvent` object, from which it can retrieve the current value and the proposed new value with the `getOldValue` and `getNewValue` methods.

Notice that the `vetoableChange` method throws an exception. A listener indicates its disapproval with the proposed change by throwing a `PropertyVetoException`. This exception forces the bean that produced the event to abandon the new value.

To see how to implement the `VetoableChangeInterface`, look at the code for the `RangeBean` class. It implements the needed method with the following code:

```
public void vetoableChange(PropertyChangeEvent evt)
    throws PropertyVetoException
{   int v = ((Integer)evt.getNewValue()).intValue();
    if (evt.getSource() == from && v > to.getValue())
        throw new PropertyVetoException("from > to", evt);
    if (evt.getSource() == to && v < from.getValue())
        throw new PropertyVetoException("to < from", evt);
}
```

To update a constrained property value:

1. Notify all vetoable listeners that a change is about to occur. (Use the `fireVetoableChange` method of the `VetoableChangeSupport` class.)

2. If none of the vetoable listeners has thrown a `PropertyVetoException`, then update the value of the property.

3. Notify all property listeners that a change has occurred.

Here is a typical example from the `IntTextBean` code:

```
public void setValue(int v) throws PropertyVetoException
{   Integer oldValue = new Integer(getValue());
    Integer newValue = new Integer(v);
    vcs.fireVetoableChange("value", oldValue, newValue);
    // survived, therefore no veto
    value = v;
    setText("" + v);
    pcs.firePropertyChange("value", oldValue, newValue);
}
```

It is important that you don't change the property value until all the registered vetoable change listeners have agreed with the proposed change. Conversely, a vetoable change listener should never assume that a change that it agrees with is actually happening until it receives a second notification through the `propertyChange` method.

Example 7-3 shows the code for the integer text bean that allows its values to be vetoed—it is based on the `IntTextField` class from Volume 1. Example 7-4 shows the code for the `RangeBean`. A range bean contains two `IntTextBean` objects and vetoes the change if it would result in an invalid range. Try typing in a lower bound that is greater than the upper bound, and you will not succeed. Then, try the following: In the property inspector, set the `from` property value to a value that is greater than the `to` property value. You will see a veto dialog box, as shown in Figure 7-18. This dialog is displayed by the BeanBox. Here is what happens:

1. You type a value into the edit field for the `from` property.

2. The BeanBox calls the `setFrom` method of the `RangeBean` class.

3. The `setFrom` method calls the `setValue` method of the `IntTextBean` class.

4. The `setValue` method notifies its vetoable listeners, in our case, the `RangeBean`.

5. The `vetoableChange` method of the `RangeBean` class throws a `PropertyVetoException`.

6. The `setValue` method of the `IntTextBean` class does not catch the exception, and the value is not updated.

7. The BeanBox captures the exception and displays the veto dialog box.

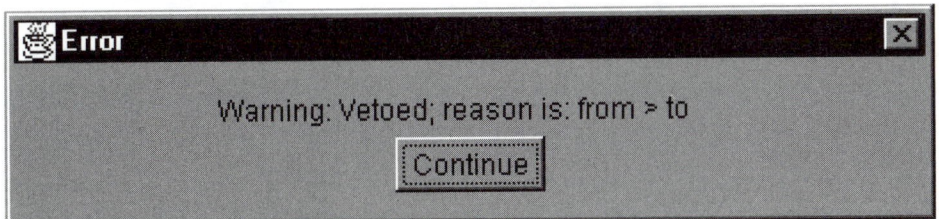

Figure 7-18: A property change veto dialog box

Example 7-3: IntTextBean.java

```java
import java.awt.*;
import java.awt.event.*;
import java.beans.*;
import java.io.*;

public class IntTextBean extends TextField
    implements Serializable
{  public IntTextBean()
   {  setText("0");

      addKeyListener(new KeyAdapter()
      {  public void keyTyped(KeyEvent evt)
         {  char ch = evt.getKeyChar();
            if (!('0' <= ch && ch <= '9'
                  || ch == '-'
                  || Character.isISOControl(ch)))
               evt.consume();
            else
               lastCaretPosition = getCaretPosition();
         }
         public void keyPressed(KeyEvent evt)
         {  if (evt.getKeyCode() == KeyEvent.VK_ENTER)
            {  editComplete();
            }
         }
      });

      addFocusListener(new FocusAdapter()
      {  public void focusLost(FocusEvent evt)
         {  if (!evt.isTemporary())
            {  editComplete();
            }
         }
      });

      addTextListener(new TextListener()
      {  public void textValueChanged(TextEvent evt)
         {  checkFieldValue();
         }
      });
   }

   public void editComplete()
   {  Integer oldValue = new Integer(value);
      Integer newValue = new Integer(getFieldValue());
      try
```

```
      {   vcs.fireVetoableChange("value", oldValue, newValue);
          // survived, therefore no veto
          value = getFieldValue();
          pcs.firePropertyChange("value", oldValue, newValue);
      }
      catch(PropertyVetoException e)
      {   // someone didn't like it
          // back to the drawing board...
          requestFocus();
      }
  }

  public boolean checkFieldValue()
  {   String lastValue = getText();
      try
      {   Integer.parseInt(getText().trim() + "0");
          return true;
      }
      catch(NumberFormatException e)
      {   setText(lastValue);
          setCaretPosition(lastCaretPosition);
          return false;
      }
  }

  public int getFieldValue()
  {   if (checkFieldValue())
          return Integer.parseInt(getText().trim());
      else
          return 0;
  }

  public int getValue()
  {   return value;
  }


  public void setValue(int v) throws PropertyVetoException
  {   Integer oldValue = new Integer(getValue());
      Integer newValue = new Integer(v);
      vcs.fireVetoableChange("value", oldValue, newValue);
      // survived, therefore no veto
      value = v;
      setText("" + v);
      pcs.firePropertyChange("value", oldValue, newValue);
  }
```

```
    public void addPropertyChangeListener
        (PropertyChangeListener l)
    {   pcs.addPropertyChangeListener(l);
    }

    public void removePropertyChangeListener
        (PropertyChangeListener l)
    {   pcs.removePropertyChangeListener(l);
    }

    public void addVetoableChangeListener
        (VetoableChangeListener l)
    {   vcs.addVetoableChangeListener(l);
    }

    public void removeVetoableChangeListener
        (VetoableChangeListener l)
    {   vcs.removeVetoableChangeListener(l);
    }

    public Dimension getMinimumSize()
    {   return new Dimension(XMINSIZE, YMINSIZE);
    }

    private static final int XMINSIZE = 50;
    private static final int YMINSIZE = 20;
    private PropertyChangeSupport pcs
        = new PropertyChangeSupport(this);

    private VetoableChangeSupport vcs
        = new VetoableChangeSupport(this);

    private int value = 0;

    int lastCaretPosition;
}
```

Example 7-4: RangeBean.java

```
import java.awt.*;
import java.beans.*;
import java.io.*;

public class RangeBean extends Panel
    implements VetoableChangeListener, Serializable
{   public RangeBean()
    {   add(new Label("From"));
        add(from);
```

```
    add(new Label("To"));
    add(to);

    from.addVetoableChangeListener(this);
    to.addVetoableChangeListener(this);
}

public void vetoableChange(PropertyChangeEvent evt)
    throws PropertyVetoException
{   int v = ((Integer)evt.getNewValue()).intValue();
    if (evt.getSource() == from && v > to.getValue())
        throw new PropertyVetoException("from > to", evt);
    if (evt.getSource() == to && v < from.getValue())
        throw new PropertyVetoException("to < from", evt);
}

public int getFrom() { return from.getValue(); }
public int getTo() { return to.getValue(); }

public void setFrom(int v) throws PropertyVetoException
{   from.setValue(v);
}

public void setTo(int v) throws PropertyVetoException
{   to.setValue(v);
}

private IntTextBean from = new IntTextBean();
private IntTextBean to = new IntTextBean();
}
```

Finally, when you build a constrained property into your bean, keep in mind that you have no control over how property change events are sent to the interested beans. This means that one bean can accept the change, think it's great, and decide to use the new value. But, when the AWT gets around to sending the same PropertyChange event to another bean component, that second bean component can veto it. Unless you make your constrained properties bound, you will have no way to notify the happy user of the new value that it can't use it anymore. For this reason, we strongly suggest that all your constrained properties be bound.

java.beans.VetoableChangeListener

- void vetoableChange(PropertyChangeEvent evt)

  is called when a property is about to be changed. It should throw a PropertyVetoException if the change is not acceptable.

  Parameters   evt   the event object describing the property change

java.beans.VetoableChangeSupport

- VetoableChangeSupport(Object sourceBean)

  constructs the (convenience) VetoableChangeSupport object.

  Parameters   sourcebean   the bean that is the source of the vetoable change (usually this)

- void addVetoableChangeListener(VetoableChangeListener listener)

  registers an interested listener for the constrained property.

  Parameters   listener   the bean that wants to have a chance to veto the constrained property

- removeVetoableChangeListener(VetoableChangeListener listener)

  removes a previously registered interested listener for the constrained property.

  Parameters   listener   the bean to be removed from the list of listeners

- void fireVetoableChange(String propertyName, Object oldValue, Object newValue)

  sends a (convenience) PropertyChangeEvent to registered listeners prior to updating the property value.

  Parameters   propertyName   the name of the property

            oldValue   the current value

            newValue   the proposed new value

java.beans.PropertyVetoException

- PropertyVetoException(String s, PropertyChangeEvent evt)

  creates a new PropertyVetoException.

Parameters	s	a string that describes the reason for the veto
	evt	the PropertyChangeEvent for the constrained property you want to veto

- PropertyChangeEvent getPropertyChangeEvent()

  returns the PropertyChangeEvent used to construct the exception.

Adding Custom Bean Events

When you add a bound or constrained property to a bean, you also enable the bean to fire events whenever the value of that property changes. However, there are other events that a bean can send out, for example,

- When the program user has clicked on a control within the bean

- When new information is available

- Or simply, when some amount of time has elapsed

Unlike the PropertyChangeEvent events, these events belong to custom classes and need to be captured by custom listeners.

Here is how to write a bean that generates custom events. (Please consult Chapter 8 of Volume 1 for more details on Java's event-handling mechanism.) Be sure to follow the first two steps precisely, or the introspection mechanism will not recognize that you are trying to define a custom event.

1. Write a class *Custom*Event that extends EventObject. (The event name must end in Event in order for a builder to use the naming patterns to find it.)

2. Write an interface *Custom*Listener with a single notification method. That notification method can have any name, but it must have a single parameter of type *Custom*Event and return type void.

3.   Supply the following two methods in the bean:

```
public void addCustomListener(CustomListener e)
public void removeCustomListener(CustomListener e)
```

PITFALL: If your event class doesn't extend `EventObject`, chances are that your code will compile just fine because none of the methods of the `EventObject` class are actually needed, and none of the various other methods ever try to cast the event objects to the `EventObject` class. However, your bean will mysteriously fail—the introspection mechanism will not recognize the events.

To implement the methods needed for adding, removing, and delivering custom events, you can no longer rely on convenience classes that automatically manage the event listeners. Instead, you need to collect all the event listeners, for example, in a `Vector`. Moreover, when delivering the event, you also need to call the notification method for all the collected listeners. This call can lead to a synchronization problem—it is possible that one thread tries to add or remove a listener at the same time that another thread is handling an event delivery to it. For that reason, synchronize access to the collection of listeners. The following code shows how you can provide the needed synchronization:

```
public synchronized void addCustomListener
    (CustomListener l)
{   listeners.addElement(l);
}

public synchronized void removeCustomListener
    (CustomListener l)
{   listeners.removeElement(l);
}

public void fireCustomEvent(CustomEvent evt)
{   Vector currentListeners = null;
    synchronized(this)
    {   currentListeners = (Vector)listeners.clone();
    }
    for (int i = 0; i < currentListeners.size(); i++)
    {   CustomListener listener
            = (CustomListener)currentListeners.elementAt(i);
        listener.notifyMethod(evt);
    }
}
. . .
private Vector timerListeners = new Vector();
```

The code for the synchronization is a bit tricky. Why don't we just make `fireCustomEvent` into a `synchronized` method as well? Then, we could be sure that no listeners were added or removed as the events were fired. However, that opens us up to the potential for deadlocks because, in some cases, the `notifyMethod` might call `addCustomListener` or `removeCustomListener`. Since it is not called in a separate thread, that call would give rise to a deadlock. Therefore, we first clone the vector. Only the block of code that performs the cloning is synchronized. Of course, now only the listeners that have been registered at the outset of the delivery process are notified. And if one listener is removed before the delivery process is completed, that listener is still called. This in turn means that there is no absolute guarantee that event deliveries will cease immediately when a listener removes itself from an event source.

Now, let's apply this technique to implementing a `TimerBean`. This bean should send `TimerEvent` objects to its listeners. (This is a modification of the `Timer` class from Chapter 2.) Timer events are generated at regular intervals (measured in milliseconds), set by the `interval` property, provided that the `running` property is set to `true`. Examples 7-5–7-7 show the code for the following:

- The `TimerEvent` class, the custom event that is generated by this bean

- The `TimerListener` class with a notification method that we called `timeElapsed`

- The `TimerBean` with methods `addTimerListener` and `removeTimerListener`

Here is how you can test the bean. Drop a timer bean into the BeanBox. (This is an *invisible bean* with no `paint` method—it is just displayed as a string "TimerBean" by the BeanBox.) Then, drop an `EventMonitor` bean into the BeanBox. Select the `TimerBean` and choose Edit | Events from the BeanBox menu. Note that there is a submenu `timer` with a child menu `timeElapsed`. These menus show that the introspection method has correctly identified the custom event. Select the `timeElapsed` method. Then, a red line appears. Connect it to the `EventMonitor`. A dialog asks you which method should be called when the event notification occurs. Choose the only method available, `initiateEventSourceMonitoring`. Now, select the `TimerBean` once again. In the property sheet, set the `running` property to `true` and watch the text area in the `EventMonitor` bean. Once every second, a notification message is displayed (see Figure 7-19).

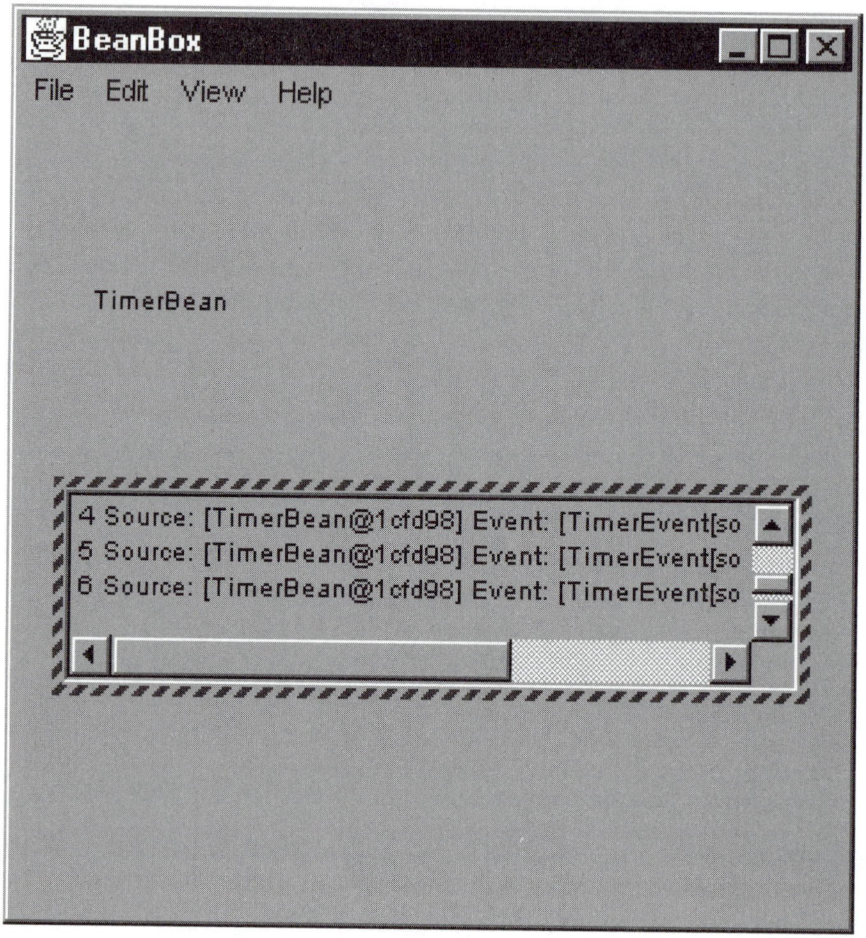

![BeanBox window with menu File Edit View Help, showing TimerBean label and a monitor panel displaying: 4 Source: [TimerBean@1cfd98] Event: [TimerEvent[so, 5 Source: [TimerBean@1cfd98] Event: [TimerEvent[so, 6 Source: [TimerBean@1cfd98] Event: [TimerEvent[so]

Figure 7-19: The BeanBox monitors a custom event

Here's the complete code for the TimerBean:

Example 7-5: TimerBean.java

```
import java.awt.*;
import java.util.*;
import java.io.*;

public class TimerBean implements Runnable, Serializable
{  public int getInterval() { return interval; }
   public void setInterval(int i) { interval = i; }

   public boolean isRunning() { return runner != null; }
   public void setRunning(boolean b)
```

```
{   if (b && runner == null)
    {   runner = new Thread(this);
        runner.start();
    }
    else if (!b && runner != null)
    {   runner.stop();
        runner = null;
    }
}

public synchronized void addTimerListener
    (TimerListener l)
{   timerListeners.addElement(l);
}

public synchronized void removeTimerListener
    (TimerListener l)
{   timerListeners.removeElement(l);
}

public void fireTimerEvent(TimerEvent evt)
{   Vector currentListeners = null;
    synchronized(this)
    {   currentListeners = (Vector)timerListeners.clone();
    }
    for (int i = 0; i < currentListeners.size(); i++)
    {   TimerListener listener
            = (TimerListener)currentListeners.elementAt(i);
        listener.timeElapsed(evt);
    }
}

public void run()
{   if (interval <= 0) return;
    while (true)
    {   try { Thread.sleep(interval); }
        catch(InterruptedException e) {}
        fireTimerEvent(new TimerEvent(this));
    }
}

private int interval = 1000;
private Vector timerListeners = new Vector();
private Thread runner;
}
```

Example 7-6: TimerListener.java

```
import java.util.*;

public interface TimerListener extends EventListener
{  public void timeElapsed(TimerEvent evt);
}
```

Example 7-7: TimerEvent.java

```
import java.util.*;

public class TimerEvent extends EventObject
{  public TimerEvent(Object source)
   {  super(source);
      now = new Date();
   }

   public Date getDate() { return now; }

   private Date now;
}
```

Property Editors

If you add an integer or string property to a bean, then that property is automatically displayed in the bean's Property Sheet. But what happens if you add a property whose values cannot easily be edited in a text field, for example, a Day or a Color? Then, you need to provide a separate component which the user can use to specify the property value. Such components are called *property editors*. For example, a property editor for a Day object might be a calendar that lets the user scroll through the months and pick a date. A property editor for a Color object would let the user select the red, green, and blue components of the color.

Actually, the BeanBox already has a property editor for colors—you saw it in Figure 7-4. And, of course, there are property editors for basic types such as String (a text field) and boolean (a choice list with values true and false). These property editors are registered with the *property editor manager*. You can add property editors to the manager with the static registerEditor method of the PropertyEditorManager class. You supply the class to which the editor applies and the class of the editor.

```
PropertyEditorManager.registerEditor(Day.class,
   CalendarSelector.class);
```

You can use the `findEditor` method in the `PropertyEditorManager` class to check whether a property editor exists for a given type in your builder tool. That method does the following:

1. It looks first to see which property editors are already registered with it. (These will be the editors supplied by the builder tool and the editors that you supplied by calling `registerEditor`.)

2. Then, it looks for a class whose name consists of the name of the type plus the word `Editor`.

3. If neither lookup succeeds, then it returns `null`.

For example, a `CalendarSelector` class would be used to edit a `Day` property.

The BeanBox also uses the `findEditor` method to locate an editor for each type it displays in a Property Sheet. But before looking for a generic editor, it checks whether you requested a specific editor in the *bean info* of your bean. The bean info is a collection of miscellaneous information about your bean. For example, if you have a property whose type is `int` or `String`, but whose legal values are restricted in some way, you may not want to use the general-purpose property editor that is supplied by the BeanBox. Instead, you can supply a specific editor for a particular property by naming it in the bean info.

The process for supplying a specific propery editor is slightly involved. First, you create a bean info class to accompany your bean. The name of the class must be the name of the bean, followed by the word `BeanInfo`. That class must implement the `BeanInfo` interface, an interface with eight methods. It is simplest to extend the `SimpleBeanInfo` class instead. This convenience class has do-nothing implementations for the eight methods. For example,

```
// bean info class for ChartBean
class ChartBeanBeanInfo
    extends SimpleBeanInfo
{ . . . }
```

To request a specific editor for a particular bean, you override the `getPropertyDescriptors` method. That method returns an array of `PropertyDescriptor` objects. You create one object for each property that should be displayed on a property editor, *even those for which you just want the default editor.*

You construct a `PropertyDescriptor` by supplying the name of the property and the class of the bean that contains it.

```
PropertyDescriptor pd1
    = new PropertyDescriptor("title", ChartBean.class);
```

To request a specific editor for the property, you call the
`setPropertyEditorClass` method of the `PropertyDescriptor` class.

```
PropertyDescriptor pd2
    = new PropertyDescriptor("titlePosition", ChartBean.class);
pd2.setPropertyEditorClass(TitlePositionEditor.class);
```

Next, you build an array of descriptors for properties of your bean.
For example, the chart bean that we discuss in this section has four properties:

- A `String` property, `title`

- An `int` property, `titlePosition`

- A `double[]` property, `values`

- A `boolean` property, `inverse`

Figure 7-20 shows the chart bean. You can see the title on the top. Its position
can be set to left, center, or right. The `values` property specifies the graph values. If the `inverse` property is true, then the background is colored and the bars
of the chart are white. Example 7-8 lists the code for the chart bean; the bean is
simply a modification of the chart applet in Volume 1, Chapter 10.

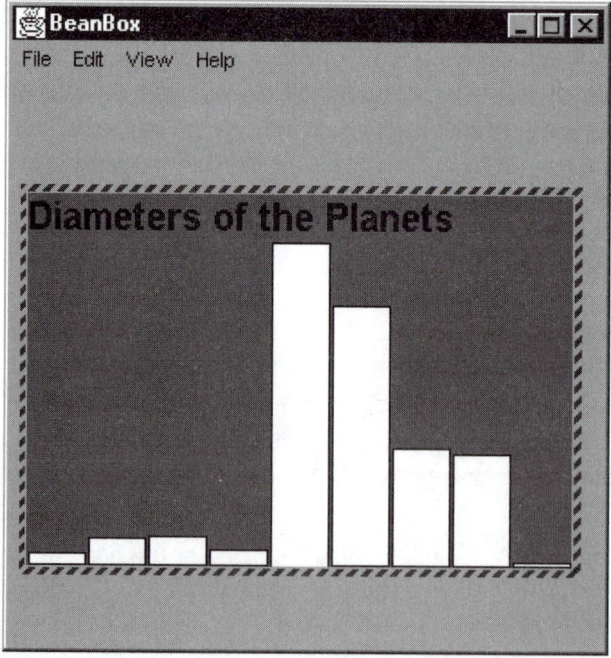

Figure 7-20: The chart bean

The code in Example 7-8 shows the `ChartBeanBeanInfo` class that specifies the property editors for these properties. It achieves the following:

1. In the `static` block, the `DoubleArrayEditor` is registered as an editor for any `double[]` array, both in this bean and in other beans.

2. The `getPropertyDescriptors` method returns a descriptor for each property. The `title` and `values` properties are used with the default editors, that is, the string editor that comes with the BeanBox and the `DoubleArrayEditor` that was registered in the `static` block.

3. The `titlePosition` and `inverse` properties use special editors of type `TitlePositionEditor` and `InverseEditor`, respectively.

Figure 7-21 shows the resulting property sheet. You'll see in the following sections how to implement these kinds of editors.

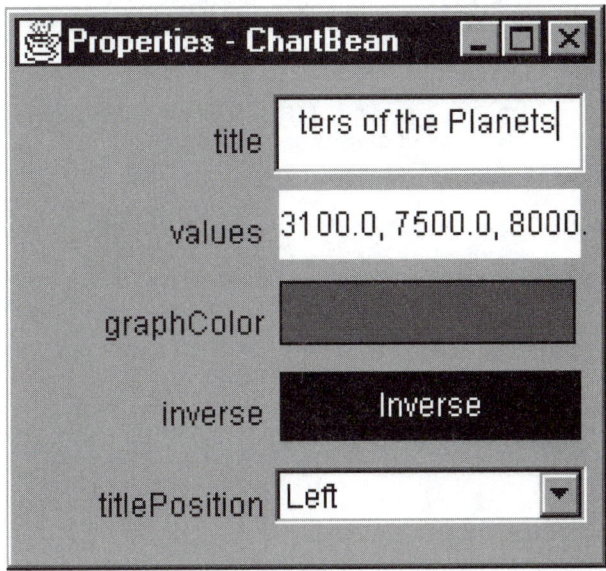

Figure 7-21: The property sheet for the chart bean

Example 7-8: ChartBean.java

```java
import java.awt.*;
import java.util.*;
import java.beans.*;
import java.io.*;

public class ChartBean extends Component
    implements Serializable
```

```
{  public void paint(Graphics g)
   {  if (values == null || values.length == 0) return;
      int i;
      double minValue = 0;
      double maxValue = 0;
      for (i = 0; i < values.length; i++)
      {  if (minValue > getValues(i)) minValue = getValues(i);
         if (maxValue < getValues(i)) maxValue = getValues(i);
      }
      if (maxValue == minValue) return;

      Dimension d = getSize();
      int clientWidth = d.width;
      int clientHeight = d.height;
      int barWidth = clientWidth / values.length;

      g.setColor(inverse ? color : Color.white);
      g.fillRect(0, 0, clientWidth, clientHeight);
      g.setColor(Color.black);

      Font titleFont = new Font("SansSerif", Font.BOLD, 20);
      FontMetrics titleFontMetrics
         = g.getFontMetrics(titleFont);

      int titleWidth = titleFontMetrics.stringWidth(title);
      int y = titleFontMetrics.getAscent();
      int x;
      if (titlePosition == LEFT)
         x = 0;
      else if (titlePosition == CENTER)
         x = (clientWidth - titleWidth) / 2;
      else
         x = clientWidth - titleWidth;

      g.setFont(titleFont);
      g.drawString(title, x, y);

      int top = titleFontMetrics.getHeight();
      double scale = (clientHeight - top)
         / (maxValue - minValue);
      y = clientHeight;

      for (i = 0; i < values.length; i++)
      {  int x1 = i * barWidth + 1;
         int y1 = top;
         int height = (int)(getValues(i) * scale);
         if (getValues(i) >= 0)
            y1 += (int)((maxValue - getValues(i)) * scale);
         else
         {  y1 += (int)(maxValue * scale);
```

```
            height = -height;
        }

        g.setColor(inverse ? Color.white : color);
        g.fillRect(x1, y1, barWidth - 2, height);
        g.setColor(Color.black);
        g.drawRect(x1, y1, barWidth - 2, height);
    }
}
public void setTitle(String t) { title = t; }
public String getTitle() { return title; }


public double[] getValues() { return values; }

public void setValues(double[] v) { values = v; }

public double getValues(int i)
{  if (0 <= i && i < values.length) return values[i];
   return 0;
}

public void setValues(int i, double value)
{  if (0 <= i && i < values.length) values[i] = value;
}

public boolean isInverse()
{  return inverse;
}

public void setTitlePosition(int p) { titlePosition = p; }

public int getTitlePosition()
{  return titlePosition;
}

public void setInverse(boolean b) { inverse = b; }

public Dimension getMinimumSize()
{  return new Dimension(MINSIZE, MINSIZE);
}

public void setGraphColor(Color c) { color = c; }
public Color getGraphColor() { return color; }

private static final int LEFT = 0;
private static final int CENTER = 1;
private static final int RIGHT = 2;
```

```
private static final int MINSIZE = 50;
private double[] values = { 1, 2, 3 };
private String title = "Title";
private int titlePosition = CENTER;
private boolean inverse;
private Color color = Color.red;
}
```

Example 7-9: ChartBeanBeanInfo.java

```
import java.beans.*;

public class ChartBeanBeanInfo extends SimpleBeanInfo
{  public PropertyDescriptor[] getPropertyDescriptors()
   {  try
      {  PropertyDescriptor titlePositionDescriptor
            = new PropertyDescriptor("titlePosition",
               ChartBean.class);
         titlePositionDescriptor.setPropertyEditorClass
            (TitlePositionEditor.class);
         PropertyDescriptor inverseDescriptor
            = new PropertyDescriptor("inverse",
               ChartBean.class);
         inverseDescriptor.setPropertyEditorClass
            (InverseEditor.class);

         return new PropertyDescriptor[]
         {  new PropertyDescriptor("title",
               ChartBean.class),
            titlePositionDescriptor,
            new PropertyDescriptor("values",
               ChartBean.class),
            new PropertyDescriptor("graphColor",
               ChartBean.class),
            inverseDescriptor
         };
      }
      catch(IntrospectionException e)
      {  System.out.println("Error: " + e);
         return null;
      }
   }

   static
   {  PropertyEditorManager.registerEditor(double[].class,
         DoubleArrayEditor.class);
   }
}
```

`java.beans.PropertyEditorManager`

- `static PropertyEditor findEditor(Class type)`

  returns a property editor for the given type, or `null` if none is registered.

Parameters	`targetType`	`Class` object for the type to be edited such, as `Class.Color`

- `static void registerEditor(Class type, Class editorClass)`

  registers an editor class to edit values of the given type.

Parameters	`targetType`	the `Class` object for the type to be edited
	`editorClass`	the `Class` object for the `editor` class (`null` will unregister the current editor)

`java.beans.PropertyDescriptor`

- `PropertyDescriptor(String name, Class beanClass)`

  constructs a `PropertyDescriptor` object.

Parameters	`name`	the name of the property
	`beanClass`	the class of the bean to which the property belongs

- `void setPropertyEditorClass(Class editorClass)`

  sets the class of the property editor to be used with this property.

`java.beans.BeanInfo`

- `PropertyDescriptor[] getPropertyDescriptors()`

  returns a descriptor for each property that should be displayed in the Property Sheet for the bean.

Writing a Property Editor

Before we begin showing you how to write a property editor, we want to point out that while each property editor works with a value of one specific type, it can nonetheless be quite elaborate. For example, a color property editor (which edits an object of type `Color`) could use sliders or a palette (or both) to allow the user to edit the color in a more congenial way.

Next, any property editor you write must implement the `PropertyEditor` interface, an interface with 12 methods. As with the `BeanInfo` interface, you will not want to do this directly. Instead, it is far more convenient to extend the convenience `PropertyEditorSupport` class that is supplied with Java. This support class comes with methods to add and remove property change listeners, and with default versions of all other methods of the `PropertyEditor` interface. For example, our editor for editing the title position of a chart in our chart bean starts out like this:

```
// property editor class for title position
class TitlePositionEditor
    extends PropertyEditorSupport
{ . . . }
```

Note that if a property editor class has a constructor, it must also supply a constructor without arguments.

Finally, before we get into the mechanics of actually writing a property editor, we want to point out that the editor is under the control of the builder, not the bean. The builder adheres to the following procedure to display the current value of the property:

1. It instantiates property editors for each property of the bean.

2. It asks the *bean* to tell it the current value of the property.

3. It then asks the *property editor* to display the value.

The property editor can either use text-based or graphically based methods to actually display the value. We discuss these methods next.

Simple Property Editors

Simple property editors work with text strings. You override the `setAsText` and `getAsText` methods. For example, our chart bean has a property that lets you set where the title should be displayed: Left, Center, or Right. These choices are implemented as integer constants.

```
private static final int LEFT = 0;
private static final int CENTER = 1;
private static final int RIGHT = 2;
```

But of course, we don't want them to appear as numbers 0, 1, 2 in the text field—unless we are competing for the User Interface Hall of Horrors. Instead, we define a property editor whose `getAsText` method returns the value as a string. The method calls the `getValue` method of the `PropertyEditor` to find the value of the property. Since this is a generic method, the value is returned as

an `Object`. If the property type is a basic type, we need to return a `wrapper` object. In our case, the property type is `int` and the call to `getValue` returns an `Integer`.

```
class TitlePositionEditor
   extends PropertyEditorSupport
{  public String getAsText()
   {  int p = ((Integer)getValue()).intValue();
      if (0 <= i && i < options.length) return options[i];
      return "";
   }
   . . .
   private String[] options = { "Left", "Center", "Right" };
}
```

Now, the text field displays one of these fields. When the user edits the text field, this triggers a call to the `setAsText` method to update the property value by invoking the `setValue` method. It, too, is a generic method whose parameter is of type `Object`. To set the value of a numeric type, we need to pass a `wrapper` object.

```
public void setAsText(String s)
{  for (int i = 0; i < options.length; i++)
   {  if (options[i].equals(s))
      {  setValue(new Integer(i));
         return;
      }
   }
}
```

Actually, this property editor is not a good choice for the `titlePosition` property, unless, of course, we are also competing for the User Interface Hall of Shame. The user may not know what the legal choices are. It would be better to display them in a Choice box (see Figure 7-22). The `PropertyEditorSupport` class gives a simple method to use a Choice box in a property editor. We simply write a `getTags` method that returns an array of strings.

```
public String[] getTags() { return options; }
```

The default `getTags` method returns `null`. By returning a non-null value, we indicate a choice field instead of a text field.

We still need to supply the `getAsText` and `setAsText` methods. The `getTags` method simply specifies the values to be displayed in the `Choice` field. The `getAsText`/`setAsText` methods translate between the strings and the data type of the property (which may be a string, an `int`, or a completely different type).

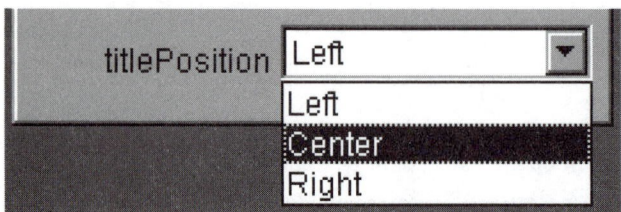

Figure 7-22: The TitlePositionEditor at work

Example 7-10 lists the complete code for the property editor (see Example 7-8 for the code for the actual bean).

Example 7-10: TitlePositionEditor.java

```java
import java.beans.*;

public class TitlePositionEditor
   extends PropertyEditorSupport
{  public String getAsText()
   {  int value = ((Integer)getValue()).intValue();
      return options[value];
   }

   public void setAsText(String s)
   {  for (int i = 0; i < options.length; i++)
      {  if (options[i].equals(s))
         {  setValue(new Integer(i));
            return;
         }
      }
   }

   public String[] getTags() { return options; }

   private String[] options = { "Left", "Center", "Right" };
}
```

`java.beans.PropertyEditorSupport`

• `Object getValue()`

returns the current value of the property. Basic types are wrapped into object wrappers.

- ```
  void setValue(Object newValue)
  ```

  sets the property to a new value. Basic types must be wrapped into object wrappers.

  Parameters   `newValue`   the new value of the object; should be a newly created object that the property can own

- ```
  String getAsText()
  ```

  override this method to return a string representation of the current value of the property. The default returns `null` to indicate that the property cannot be represented as a string.

- ```
  void setAsText(String text)
  ```

  override this method to set the property to a new value that is obtained by parsing the text. May throw an `IllegalArgumentException` if the text does not represent a legal value or if this property cannot be represented as a string.

- ```
  String[] getTags()
  ```

  override this method to return an array of all possible string representations of the property values so they can be displayed in a Choice box. The default returns `null` to indicate that there is not a finite set of string values.

GUI-Based Property Editors

More sophisticated property types can't be edited as text. Instead, they are represented in two ways. The property sheet contains a small area (which otherwise would hold a text box or choice field) onto which the property editor will draw a graphical representation of the current value. When the user clicks on that area, a custom editor dialog box pops up (see Figure 7-23). The dialog box contains a component to edit the property values, supplied by the property editor, and a button labeled Done at the bottom, supplied by the BeanBox.

Figure 7-23: A custom editor dialog

To build a GUI-based property editor:

1. Tell the builder tool that you will paint the value and not use a string.

2. "Paint" the value the user enters onto the GUI.

3. Tell the builder tool that you will be using a GUI-based property editor.

4. Build the GUI.

5. Write the code to validate what the user tries to enter as the value.

For the first step, you override the `getAsText` method in the `PropertyEditor` interface to return `null` and the `isPaintable` method to return `true`.

```
public String getAsText()
{   return null;
}
public boolean isPaintable()
{   return true;
}
```

Then, you implement the `paintValue` procedure. It receives a `Graphics` handle and the coordinates of the rectangle inside which you can paint. Note that this rectangle is typically small, so you can't have a very elaborate representation. To graphically represent the `inverse` property, we draw the string `"Inverse"` in white letters with a black background or the string `"Normal"` in black letters with a white background:

```
public void paintValue(Graphics g, Rectangle box)
{   boolean isInverse = ((Boolean)getValue()).booleanValue();
    String s = isInverse ? "Inverse" : "Normal";
    g.setColor(isInverse ? Color.black : Color.white);
    g.fillRect(box.x, box.y, box.width, box.height);
    g.setColor(isInverse ? Color.white : Color.black);
    FontMetrics fm = g.getFontMetrics();
    int w = fm.stringWidth(s);
    int x = box.x;
    if (w < box.width) x += (box.width - w) / 2;
    int y = box.y + (box.height - fm.getHeight()) / 2
        + fm.getAscent();
    g.drawString(s, x, y);
}
```

Of course, this graphical representation is not editable. The user must click on it to pop up a custom editor.

You indicate that you will have a custom editor by overriding the `supportsCustomEditor` in the `PropertyEditor` interface to return `true`:

```
public boolean supportsCustomEditor()
{   return true;
}
```

Now, you write the AWT code that builds up the component that will hold the custom editor. You will need to build a separate custom editor class for every property. For example, associated to our `InverseEditor` class is an `InverseEditorPanel` class (see Example 7-9) that describes a GUI with two radio buttons to toggle between normal and inverse mode. That code is straight-forward AWT code. However, the GUI actions must update the property values. We did this as follows:

1. Have the custom editor constructor receive a reference to the property editor object and store it in a variable `editor`.

2. To read the property value, we have the custom editor call `editor.getValue()`.

3. To set the object value, we have the custom editor call `editor.setValue(newValue)` followed by `editor.firePropertyChange()`.

Next, the `getCustomEditor` method of the `PropertyEditor` interface constructs and returns an object of the custom editor class.

```
public Component getCustomEditor()
{   return new InverseEditorPanel(this);
}
```

Example 7-11 shows the complete code for the `InverseEditor`.

The other custom editor that we built for the chart bean class lets you edit a `double[]` array. Recall that the BeanBox cannot edit array properties at all. We developed this custom editor to fill this obvious gap. That custom editor is a little involved. Figure 7-24 shows the custom editor in action. All array values are shown in the list box, prefixed by their array index. Clicking on an array value places it into the text field above it, and you can edit it. You can also resize the array. The code for the `DoubleArrayPanel` class that implements the GUI is listed in Example 7-14.

The code for the property editor class (shown in Example 7-13) is almost identical to that of the `InverseEditor`, except that we simply paint a string consisting of the first few array values, followed by . . ., in the `paintValue` method. And, of course, we return a different custom editor in the `getCustomEditor` method. These examples complete the code for the chart bean.

NOTE: Unfortunately, we have to *paint* the array values. It would be more convenient to return a string with the `getAsText` method. However, then the BeanBox assumes that you can edit that text, and it won't pop up a custom editor if you click on it, even if the `getCustomEditor` method is defined.

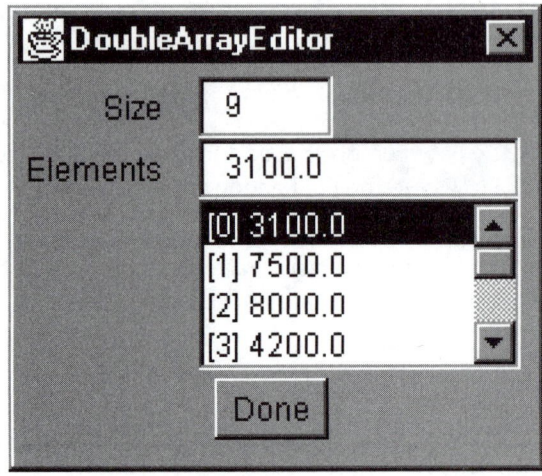

Figure 7-24: The custom editor dialog for editing an array

Example 7-11: InverseEditor.java

```java
import java.awt.*;
import java.beans.*;

public class InverseEditor extends PropertyEditorSupport
{  public Component getCustomEditor()
   {  return new InverseEditorPanel(this);
   }

   public boolean supportsCustomEditor()
   {  return true;
   }

   public boolean isPaintable()
   {  return true;
   }

   public void paintValue(Graphics g, Rectangle box)
   {  boolean isInverse = ((Boolean)getValue()).booleanValue();
      String s = isInverse ? "Inverse" : "Normal";
      g.setColor(isInverse ? Color.black : Color.white);
      g.fillRect(box.x, box.y, box.width, box.height);
      g.setColor(isInverse ? Color.white : Color.black);
      FontMetrics fm = g.getFontMetrics();
      int w = fm.stringWidth(s);
      int x = box.x;
      if (w < box.width) x += (box.width - w) / 2;
```

```
        int y = box.y + (box.height - fm.getHeight()) / 2
            + fm.getAscent();
        g.drawString(s, x, y);
    }

    public String getAsText()
    {   return null;
    }
}
```

Example 7-12: InverseEditorPanel.java

```
import java.awt.*;
import java.awt.event.*;
import java.text.*;
import java.lang.reflect.*;
import java.beans.*;

public class InverseEditorPanel extends Panel
    implements ItemListener
{   public InverseEditorPanel(PropertyEditorSupport ed)
    {   editor = ed;
        CheckboxGroup g = new CheckboxGroup();
        boolean isInverse
            = ((Boolean)editor.getValue()).booleanValue();
        normal = new Checkbox("Normal", g, !isInverse);
        inverse = new Checkbox("Inverse", g, isInverse);

        normal.addItemListener(this);
        inverse.addItemListener(this);
        add(normal);
        add(inverse);
    }

    public void itemStateChanged(ItemEvent evt)
    {   if (evt.getStateChange() == ItemEvent.SELECTED)
        {   editor.setValue(new Boolean(inverse.getState()));
        editor.firePropertyChange();
        }
    }

    private Checkbox normal;
    private Checkbox inverse;
    PropertyEditorSupport editor;
}
```

Example 7-13: DoubleArrayEditor.java

```java
import java.awt.*;
import java.beans.*;

public class DoubleArrayEditor extends PropertyEditorSupport
{  public Component getCustomEditor()
   {  return new DoubleArrayEditorPanel(this);
   }

   public boolean supportsCustomEditor()
   {  return true;
   }

   public boolean isPaintable()
   {  return true;
   }

   public void paintValue(Graphics g, Rectangle box)
   {  double[] values = (double[]) getValue();
      String s = "";
      for (int i = 0; i < 3; i++)
      {  if (values.length > i) s = s + values[i];
         if (values.length > i + 1) s = s + ", ";
      }
      if (values.length > 3) s += "...";

      g.setColor(Color.white);
      g.fillRect(box.x, box.y, box.width, box.height);
      g.setColor(Color.black);
      FontMetrics fm = g.getFontMetrics();
      int w = fm.stringWidth(s);
      int x = box.x;
      if (w < box.width) x += (box.width - w) / 2;
      int y = box.y + (box.height - fm.getHeight()) / 2
         + fm.getAscent();
      g.drawString(s, x, y);
   }

   public String getAsText()
   {  return null;
   }
}
```

Example 7-14: DoubleArrayEditorPanel.java

```java
import java.awt.*;
import java.awt.event.*;
import java.text.*;
import java.lang.reflect.*;
import java.beans.*;

public class DoubleArrayEditorPanel extends Panel
   implements ItemListener
{  public DoubleArrayEditorPanel(PropertyEditorSupport ed)
   {  editor = ed;
      setArray((double[])ed.getValue());
      setLayout(new GridBagLayout());
      GridBagConstraints gbc = new GridBagConstraints();
      gbc.weightx = 0;
      gbc.weighty = 0;
      gbc.fill = GridBagConstraints.NONE;
      gbc.anchor = GridBagConstraints.EAST;
      add(new Label("Size"), gbc, 0, 0, 1, 1);
      add(new Label("Elements"), gbc, 0, 1, 1, 1);
      gbc.weightx = 100;
      gbc.anchor = GridBagConstraints.WEST;
      add(sizeField, gbc, 1, 0, 1, 1);
      gbc.fill = GridBagConstraints.HORIZONTAL;
      add(valueField, gbc, 1, 1, 1, 1);
      gbc.weighty = 100;
      gbc.fill = GridBagConstraints.BOTH;
      add(elementList, gbc, 1, 2, 1, 1);
      gbc.fill = GridBagConstraints.NONE;

      elementList.addItemListener(this);
      sizeField.addKeyListener(new KeyAdapter()
         {  public void keyPressed(KeyEvent evt)
            {  if (evt.getKeyCode() == KeyEvent.VK_ENTER)
               {  resizeArray();
               }
            }
         });
      sizeField.addFocusListener(new FocusAdapter()
         {  public void focusLost(FocusEvent evt)
            {  if (!evt.isTemporary())
               {  resizeArray();
               }
            }
         });
      valueField.addKeyListener(new KeyAdapter()
         {  public void keyPressed(KeyEvent evt)
```

```java
            {   if (evt.getKeyCode() == KeyEvent.VK_ENTER)
                {   changeValue();
                }
            }
        });
    valueField.addFocusListener(new FocusAdapter()
        {   public void focusLost(FocusEvent evt)
            {   if (!evt.isTemporary())
                {   changeValue();
                }
            }
        });
}

public void add(Component c, GridBagConstraints gbc,
    int x, int y, int w, int h)
{   gbc.gridx = x;
    gbc.gridy = y;
    gbc.gridwidth = w;
    gbc.gridheight = h;
    add(c, gbc);
}

public void resizeArray()
{   fmt.setParseIntegerOnly(true);
    int s = 0;
    try
    {   s = fmt.parse(sizeField.getText()).intValue();
        if (s < 0)
            throw new ParseException("Out of bounds", 0);
    }
    catch(ParseException e)
    {   sizeField.requestFocus();
        return;
    }
    if (s == theArray.length) return;
    setArray((double[])arrayGrow(theArray, s));
    editor.setValue(theArray);
    editor.firePropertyChange();
}

public void changeValue()
{   double v = 0;
    fmt.setParseIntegerOnly(false);
    try
    {   v = fmt.parse(valueField.getText()).doubleValue();
    }
    catch(ParseException e)
```

```
   {  valueField.requestFocus();
      return;
   }
   setArray(currentIndex, v);
   editor.firePropertyChange();
}

public void itemStateChanged(ItemEvent evt)
{  if (evt.getStateChange() == ItemEvent.SELECTED)
   {  int i = elementList.getSelectedIndex();
      valueField.setText("" + theArray[i]);
      currentIndex = i;
   }
}

static Object arrayGrow(Object a, int newLength)
{  Class cl = a.getClass();
   if (!cl.isArray()) return null;
   Class componentType = a.getClass().getComponentType();
   int length = Array.getLength(a);

   Object newArray = Array.newInstance(componentType,
      newLength);
   System.arraycopy(a, 0, newArray, 0,
      Math.min(length, newLength));
   return newArray;
}

public double[] getArray()
{  return (double[])theArray.clone();
}

public void setArray(double[] v)
{  if (v == null) theArray = new double[0];
   else theArray = v;
   sizeField.setText("" + theArray.length);
   elementList.removeAll();
   for (int i = 0; i < theArray.length; i++)
      elementList.add("[" + i + "] " + theArray[i]);
   if (theArray.length > 0)
   {  valueField.setText("" + theArray[0]);
      elementList.select(0);
      currentIndex = 0;
   }
   else
      valueField.setText("");
}
```

```
public double getArray(int i)
{   if (0 <= i && i < theArray.length) return theArray[i];
    return 0;
}

public void setArray(int i, double value)
{   if (0 <= i && i < theArray.length)
    {   theArray[i] = value;
        elementList.replaceItem("[" + i + "] " + value, i);
        int previous = elementList.getSelectedIndex();
        elementList.select(i);
        valueField.setText("" + value);
        elementList.select(previous);
    }
}

private PropertyEditorSupport editor;
private double[] theArray;
private int currentIndex = 0;
private NumberFormat fmt = NumberFormat.getNumberInstance();
private TextField sizeField = new TextField(4);
private TextField valueField = new TextField(12);
private List elementList = new List();
}
```

Summing Up

For every property editor you write, you have to choose one of three ways to display and edit the property value:

1. As a text string (define `getAsText` and `setAsText`)

2. As a choice field (define `getAsText`, `setAsText`, and `getTags`)

3. Graphically, by painting it (define `isPaintable`, `paintValue`, `supportsCustomEditor`, and `getCustomEditor`)

You saw examples of all three cases in the chart bean.

Finally, some property editors might want to support a method called `getJavaInitializationString`. With this method, you can give the builder tool the Java code that sets a property to allow automatic code generation. We did not show you an example for this method.

`java.beans.PropertyEditorSupport`

- `boolean isPaintable()`

  override this method to return `true` if the class uses the `paintValue` method to display the property.

- `void paintValue(Graphics g, Rectangle box)`

  override this method to represent the value by drawing into a graphics context in the specified place on the component used for the property sheet.

  | *Parameters* | g | the graphics object to draw onto |
  | | box | a rectangle object that represents where on the Property Sheet component to draw the value. |

- `boolean supportsCustomEditor()`

  override this method to return `true` if the property editor has a custom editor.

- `Component getCustomEditor()`

  override this method to return the component that contains a customized GUI for editing the property value.

- `String getJavaInitializationString()`

  override this method to return a Java code string that can be used to enerate code that initializes the property value. Examples are `"0"`, `"new Color(64, 64, 64)"`.

Going Beyond "Design Patterns"—Building a `BeanInfo` Class

You have already seen that if you use the standard naming conventions for the members of your bean, then a builder tool can use reflection to determine the properties, events, and methods of your bean. This process makes it simple to get started with bean programming but is rather limiting in the end. As your beans become in any way complex, there *will* be features of your bean that naming patterns and reflection will simply not reveal. (Not to mention that using English naming patterns as the basis for all GUI builders in all languages for all times seems to be rather against the spirit of Java's internationalization support.)

Luckily, the JavaBeans specification allows a far more flexible and powerful mechanism for storing information about your bean for use by a builder. As with many features of beans, the mechanism is simple in theory but can be tedious to carry out in practice. The idea is that you can again use an object that implements the `BeanInfo` interface. (Recall that we used one small feature of the `BeanInfo` class when we supplied property editors for the chart bean class.)

When you implement this interface to describe your bean, a builder tool will look to the methods from the BeanInfo interface to tell it (potentially quite detailed) information about the properties, events, and methods your bean supports. The BeanInfo is supposed to free you from the tyranny of naming patterns. Somewhat ironically, the beans specification does require that you use a naming pattern to associate a BeanInfo object to the bean. You specify the name of the bean info class by adding BeanInfo to the name of the bean. For example, the bean info class associated to the class ChartBean *must* be named ChartBeanBeanInfo. The bean info class must be part of the same package as the bean itself.

NOTE: Any descriptions you supply in the bean info associated to your bean override any information that the builder might obtain by reflecting on the member names. Moreover, if you supply information about a feature set (such as the properties that your bean supports), you must then provide information about *all* the properties in the associated bean info. This, of course, gives you a way to have members of your bean that are not exposed in a builder environment yet are still public.

As you already saw, you won't normally write from scratch a class that implements the BeanInfo interface. Instead, you will probably turn again to the SimpleBeanInfo convenience class that has empty implementations (returning null) for all the methods in the BeanInfo interface. This practice is certainly convenient—just override the methods you really want to change. Moreover, this convenience class includes a useful method called loadImage that you can use to load an image (such as an icon—see below) for your bean. We use this class for all our examples of BeanInfo classes. For example, our ChartBeanBeanInfo class starts out:

```
public class ChartBeanBeanInfo extends SimpleBeanInfo
```

NOTE: That the methods in the SimpleBeanInfo class return null is actually quite important. This is exactly how the builder tool knows how to use naming patterns to find out the members of that feature set. A non-null return value turns off the reflective search.

For a taste of what you can do with the bean info mechanism, let's start with an easy-to-use, but most useful, method in the BeanInfo interface: the getIcon method that lets you give your bean a custom icon. (After all, builder tools will usually want to have an icon for the bean for some sort of palette. In the BeanBox, the icon shows up to the left of the bean name in its Toolbox—see Figure 7-3.) Actually, you can specify separate icon bitmaps. The BeanInfo interface has four constants that cover the standard sizes.

```
ICON_COLOR_16x16
ICON_COLOR_32x32
ICON_MONO_16x16
ICON_MONO_32x32
```

Here is an example of how you might use the `loadImage` convenience method in the `SimpleBeanInfo` class to add an icon to a class:

```
public Image getIcon(int iconType)
{   String name = "";
    if (iconType == BeanInfo.ICON_COLOR_16x16)
        name = "COLOR_16x16";
    else if (iconType == BeanInfo.ICON_COLOR_32x32)
        name = "COLOR_32x32";
    else if (iconType == BeanInfo.ICON_MONO_16x16)
        name = "MONO_16x16";
    else if (iconType == BeanInfo.ICON_MONO_32x32)
        name = "MONO_32x32";
    else return null;
    return loadImage("ChartBean_" + name + ".gif");
}
```

where we have cleverly named (as you can see in the CH7 directory) the image files to be

```
ChartBean_COLOR_16x16.gif
ChartBean_COLOR_32x32.gif
```

and so on.

NOTE: In the present version of Java, icons must be GIFs. JavaSoft says that in the future, other formats may be supported. Also note that JavaSoft recommends you provide at the very least a 16x16 color GIF for your bean. It is also best if the GIF images are transparent so the background can shine through.

FeatureDescriptor *Objects*

The key to using any of the more advanced features of the `BeanInfo` class is the `FeatureDescriptor` class and its various subclasses. As its name suggests, a `FeatureDescriptor` object provides information about a feature. Examples of features are properties, events, methods, and so on. More precisely, the `FeatureDescriptor` class is the base class for all descriptors, and it factors out the common operations that you need to deal with when trying to describe any feature. (For example, the name of the feature is obtained via a method in it called, naturally enough, `getName`. Since this method is in the base class, it works for all feature descriptors, no matter what they describe.) Here are the subclasses of the `FeatureDescriptor` class:

- `BeanDescriptor`

- `EventSetDescriptor`

- `MethodDescriptor`

- `ParameterDescriptor`

- `PropertyDescriptor` (with a further subclass— `IndexedPropertyDescriptor`)

These classes all work basically the same. You create a descriptor object for each member you are trying to describe, and you collect all descriptors of a feature set in an array and return it as the return value of one of the `BeanInfo` methods.

For example, to turn off reflection for event sets, you'll return an array of `EventSetDescriptor` objects in your bean info class:

```
class MyBeanBeanInfo extends SimpleBeanInfo
{  public EventSetDescriptor[] getEventSetDescriptors()
   {  . . .
   }
   . . .
}
```

Next, you'll construct all the various `EventSetDescriptor` objects that will go into this array. Generally, all the constructors for the various kinds of `FeatureDescriptor` objects work in the same way. In particular, for events, the most common constructor takes:

- The class of the bean that has the event

- The base name of the event

- The class of the `EventListener` interface that corresponds to the event

- The methods in the specified `EventListener` interface that are triggered by the event

Other constructors let you specify the methods of the bean that should be used to add and remove `EventListener` objects.

A good example of all this can be found in the `BeanInfo` class associated to the `ExplicitButtonBean` that ships with the BDK. Let's analyze the code that creates the needed event descriptors for this bean. The `ExplicitButtonBean` fires two events: when the button is pushed and when the state of the button has changed. Here's how you build these two `EventSetDescriptor` objects associated to these two events:

```
EventSetDescriptor push = new EventSetDescriptor(beanClass,
    "actionPerformed",
    java.awt.event.ActionListener.class,
    "actionPerformed");

EventSetDescriptor changed = new EventSetDescriptor(beanClass,
    "propertyChange",
    java.beans.PropertyChangeListener.class,
    "propertyChange");
```

The next step is to set the various display names for the events for the
EventSetDescriptor. In the code for the ExplicitButton in the BeanInfo
class, this is done via

```
push.setDisplayName("button push");
changed.setDisplayName("bound property change");
```

Actually, it is a little more messy to code the creation of the needed
EventSetDescriptor objects than the above fragments indicate because *all* constructors for feature descriptor objects can throw an IntrospectionException.
So, you actually have to build the array of descriptors in a try/catch block, as
the following code indicates:

```
public EventSetDescriptor[] getEventSetDescriptors()
{  try
   {   EventSetDescriptor push = new
           EventSetDescriptor(beanClass,
               "actionPerformed",
               java.awt.event.ActionListener.class,
               "actionPerformed");

       EventSetDescriptor changed = new
           EventSetDescriptor(beanClass,
               "propertyChange",
               java.beans.PropertyChangeListener.class,
               "propertyChange");

       push.setDisplayName("button push");
       changed.setDisplayName("bound property change");

       return new EventSetDescriptor[] { push, changed };
   } catch (IntrospectionException e)
   {   throw new Error(e.toString());
   }
}
```

Why was this particular event set descriptor needed? The event descriptors
differ from the standard naming pattern in two ways.

- The listener classes are not the name of the bean + `Listener`.

- The display names are not the same as the event names.

To summarize: When any feature of your bean differs from the standard naming pattern, you must do the following:

- Create feature descriptors for *all* features in that set (events, properties, methods).

- Return an array of the descriptors in the appropriate `BeanInfo` method.

interface java.beans.BeanInfo

- `EventSetDescriptor[] getEventSetDescriptors()`

- `MethodDescriptor[] getMethodDescriptors()`

- `PropertyDescriptor[] getPropertyDescriptors()`

  return an array of the specified descriptor objects. A return of `null` signals the builder to use the naming conventions and reflection to find the member. The `getPropertyDescriptors` method returns a mixture of plain and indexed property descriptors. Use `instanceof` to check if a specific `PropertyDescriptor` is an `IndexedPropertyDescriptor`.

- `Image getIcon(int iconType)`

  returns an image object that can be used to represent the bean in toolboxes, toolbars, etc. (There are four constants, as described earlier, for the standard types of icons.)

Parameters	`iconType`	the type of icon to use (16×16 color, 32×32 color, etc.)

- `int getDefaultEventIndex()`

- `int getDefaultPropertyIndex()`

  A bean may have a default event or property. Both of these methods return the array index that specifies which element of the descriptor array to use as that default member, or –1 if no default exists. A bean builder environment may visually enhance the default feature, for example, by placing it first in a list of features or by displaying its name in boldface.

- `BeanInfo[] getAdditionalBeanInfo()`

  returns an array of `BeanInfo` objects or `null`. Use this method when you want some information about your bean to come from `BeanInfo` classes for other beans. (For example, you might use this method if your bean aggregated lots of other beans.) The current `BeanInfo` class rules in case of conflict.

`java.beans.SimpleBeanInfo`

- `Image loadImage(String resourceName)`

  returns an image object file associated to the resource. Currently only GIFs are supported.

Parameters	`resourceName`	a path name (taken relative to the directory containing the current class)

`class java.beans.FeatureDescriptor`

- `String getName()`

  returns the name used in the bean's code for the member.

- `void setName(String name)`

  sets the programmatic name for the feature.

Parameters	`name`	the name of the feature

- `String getDisplayName()`

  returns a localized display name for the feature. The default value is the value returned by `getName`. However, currently there is no explicit support for supplying feature names in multiple locales.

- `void setDisplayName(String displayName)`

  sets the localized display name for the feature.

Parameters	`displayName`	the name to use

- `String getShortDescription()`

  returns a localized string that a builder tool can use to provide a short description for this feature. The default value is the return value of `getDisplayName`.

- `void setShortDescription(String text)`

  sets the descriptive string (short—usually less than 40 characters) that describes the feature.

Parameters	`text`	the localized short description to associate with this feature

- `void setValue(String attributeName, Object value)`

  associates a named attribute to this feature.

Parameters	`attributeName`	the name of the attribute whose value you are setting

- `Object getValue(String attributeName)`

  gets the value of the feature with the given name.

Parameters	`attributeName`	the name for the attribute to be retrieved

- `Enumeration attributeNames()`

  returns an enumeration object that contains names of any attributes registered with `setValue`.

- `void setExpert(boolean b)`

  lets you supply an expert flag that a builder can use to determine whether to hide the feature from a naïve user. (Not every builder is likely to support this feature.)

Parameters	`b`	`true` if you intend that this feature be used only by experts

- `boolean isExpert()`

  returns `true` if this feature is marked for use by experts.

- `void setHidden(boolean b)`

  marks a feature for use only by the builder.

Parameters	`b`	`true` if you want to hide this feature

- `boolean isHidden()`

  returns `true` if the user of the builder shouldn't see this feature but the builder tool needs to be aware of it.

java.beans.EventSetDescriptor

- `EventSetDescriptor(Class sourceClass, String eventSetName, Class listener, String listenerMethod)`

  constructs an `EventSetDescriptor`. This constructor assumes that you follow the standard pattern for the names of the event class and the names of the methods to add and remove event listeners. Throws an `IntrospectionException` if an error occurred during introspection.

Parameters	`sourceClass`	the class firing the event
	`eventSetName`	the name of the event
	`listener`	the listener interface to which these events get delivered
	`listenerMethod`	the method triggered when the event gets delivered to a listener

- `EventSetDescriptor(Class sourceClass, String eventSetName, Class listener, String[] listenerMethods, String addListenerMethod, String removeListenerMethod)`

  is the most general constructor for an `EventSetDescriptor`. Throws an `IntrospectionException` if an error occurred during introspection.

Parameters	`sourceClass`	the class firing the event
	`eventSetName`	the name of the event
	`listener`	the listener interface to which these events get delivered
	`listenerMethods`	the methods of the listener interface triggered when the event gets delivered to a listener
	`addListenerMethod`	the method to add a listener to the bean
	`removeListenerMethod`	the method to remove a listener from the bean

- `Method getAddListenerMethod()`

  returns the method used to register the listener.

- `Method getRemoveListenerMethod()`

  returns the method used to remove a registered listener for the event.

- `Method[] getListenerMethods()`
- `MethodDescriptor[] getListenerMethodDescriptors()`

  return an array of `Method` objects or `MethodDescriptor` objects for the methods triggered in the listener interface.

- `Class getListenerType()`

  returns a `Class` object for the target listener interface associated to the event.

- `void setUnicast(boolean b)`

  is set to `true` if this event can be propagated to only one listener.

- `boolean isUnicast()`

  is set to `true` if the event set is unicast (default is `false`).

 java.beans.PropertyDescriptor

- `PropertyDescriptor(String propertyName, Class beanClass)`
- `PropertyDescriptor(String propertyName, Class beanClass, String getMethod, String setMethod)`

  construct a `PropertyDescriptor` object. The methods throw an `IntrospectionException` if an error occurred during introspection. The first constructor assumes that you follow the standard convention for the names of the `get` and `set` methods.

Parameters	propertyName	the name of the property
	beanClass	the `Class` object for the bean being described
	getMethod	the name of the `get` method
	setMethod	the name of the `set` method

- `Class getPropertyType()`

  returns a `Class` object for the property type.

- `Method getReadMethod()`

  returns the `get` method.

- `Method getWriteMethod()`

  returns the `set` method.

- `void setBound(boolean b)`

  is set to `true` if this property fires a `PropertyChangeEvent` when its value is changed.

- `boolean isBound()`

  returns `true` if this is a bound property.

- `void setConstrained(boolean b)`

  is set to `true` if this property fires a `VetoableChangeEvent` before its value is changed.

- `boolean isConstrained()`

  returns `true` if this is a constrained property.

`java.beans.IndexedPropertyDescriptor`

- `IndexedPropertyDescriptor(String propertyName, Class beanClass)`

- `IndexedPropertyDescriptor(String propertyName, Class beanClass, String getMethod, String setMethod, String indexedGetMethod, String indexedSetMethod)`

  construct an `IndexedPropertyDescriptor` for the index property. The methods throw an `IntrospectionException` if an error occurred during introspection. The first constructor assumes that you follow the standard convention for the names of the `get` and `set` methods.

Parameters		
	propertyName	the name of the property
	beanClass	the `Class` object for the bean being described
	getMethod	the name of the `get` method
	setMethod	the name of the `set` method
	indexedGetMethod	the name of the indexed `get` method
	indexedSetMethod	the name of the indexed `set` method

- `Class getIndexedPropertyType()`

  returns the Java `Class` that describes the type of the indexed values of the property, that is, the return type of the indexed `get` method.

- `Method getIndexedReadMethod()`

  returns the indexed `get` method.

- `Method getIndexedWriteMethod()`

  returns the indexed `set` method.

java.beans.MethodDescriptor

- MethodDescriptor(Method method)

- MethodDescriptor(Method method, ParameterDescriptor
  parameterDescriptors[])

  construct a method descriptor for the given method with the associated
  parameters; throw an IntrospectionException if an error occurred during
  introspection.

  Parameters method   method object

          parameterDescriptors an array of parameter descrip-
                      tors that describe the parame-
                      ters for the method

- Method getMethod()

  returns the method object for that method.

- ParameterDescriptor[] getParameterDescriptors()

  returns an array of parameter descriptor objects for the methods
  parameters.

java.beans.ParameterDescriptor

- ParameterDescriptor()

  creates a new parameter descriptor object. Parameter descriptors carry no
  information beyond that stored in the FeatureDescriptor superclass.

Customizers

A property editor, no matter how sophisticated, is responsible for allowing the
user to set one property at a time. Especially if certain properties of a bean relate
to each other, it may be more user friendly to give users a way to edit multiple
properties at the same time. To enable this feature, you supply a *customizer*
instead of (or in addition to) multiple property editors.

In the example program for this section, we develop a customizer for the chart
bean. The customizer lets you set several properties of the chart bean at once,
and it lets you specify a file from which to read the data points for the chart.
Figure 7-25 shows you one card of the customizer for the ChartBean.

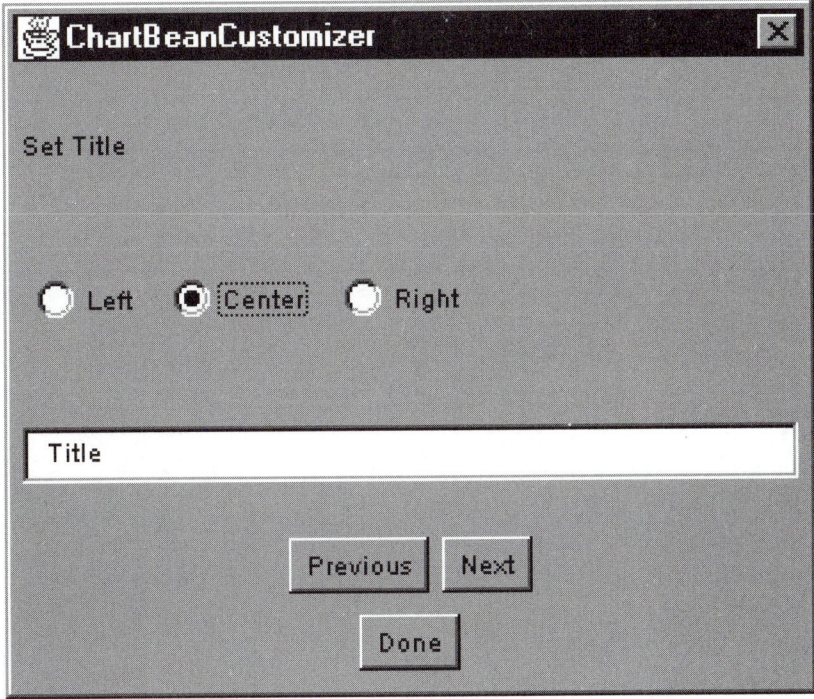

Figure 7-25: The customizer for the ChartBean

To add a customizer to your bean, you *must* supply a `BeanInfo` class and override the `getBeanDescriptor` method, as shown in the following example:

```
public BeanDescriptor getBeanDescriptor()
{   return new BeanDescriptor(ChartBean.class,
       ChartBeanCustomizer.class);
   }
```

The general procedure for your customizers follows the same model:

- Override the `getBeanDescriptor` method by returning a new `BeanDescriptor` object for your bean.

- Specify the customizer class as the second parameter of the constructor for the `BeanDescriptor` object.

Note that you need not follow any naming pattern for the customizer class. The builder can locate it by

- Finding the associated `BeanInfo` class

- Invoking its `getBeanDescriptor` method

- Calling the `getCustomizerClass` method

(Nevertheless, it is customary to name the customizer as *BeanName*Customizer.)

Example 7-15 has the code for the ChartBeanBeanInfo class that references the ChartBeanCustomizer. You will see in the next section how that customizer is implemented.

Example 7-15: ChartBeanBeanInfo.java

```java
import java.beans.*;

public class ChartBeanBeanInfo extends SimpleBeanInfo
{  public PropertyDescriptor[] getPropertyDescriptors()
   {  try
      {  PropertyDescriptor titlePositionDescriptor
            = new PropertyDescriptor("titlePosition",
               ChartBean.class);
         titlePositionDescriptor.setPropertyEditorClass
            (TitlePositionEditor.class);
         PropertyDescriptor inverseDescriptor
            = new PropertyDescriptor("inverse",
               ChartBean.class);
         inverseDescriptor.setPropertyEditorClass
            (InverseEditor.class);

         return new PropertyDescriptor[]
         {  new PropertyDescriptor("title",
               ChartBean.class),
            titlePositionDescriptor,
            new PropertyDescriptor("values",
               ChartBean.class),
            new PropertyDescriptor("graphColor",
               ChartBean.class),
            inverseDescriptor
         };
      }
      catch(IntrospectionException e)
      {  System.out.println("Error: " + e);
         return null;
      }
   }

   static
   {  PropertyEditorManager.registerEditor(double[].class,
         DoubleArrayEditor.class);
   }
}
```

- `BeanDescriptor getBeanDescriptor()`

    returns a `BeanDescriptor` object that describes features of the bean.

- `BeanDescriptor(Class beanClass, Class customizerClass)`

    constructs a `BeanDescriptor` object for a bean that has a customizer.

    | *Parameters* | `beanClass` | the `Class` object for the bean |
    | | `customizerClass` | the `Class` object for the bean's customizer |

- `Class getBeanClass()`

    returns the `Class` object that defines the bean.

- `Class getCustomizerClass()`

    returns the `Class` object that defines the bean's customizer.

Writing a Customizer Class

Any customizer class you write must implement the `Customizer` interface. There are only three methods in this interface:

- The `setObject` method, which takes a parameter that specifies the bean being customized

- The `addPropertyChangeListener` and `removePropertyChangeListener` methods, which manage the collection of listeners that are notified when a property is changed in the customizer

JavaSoft suggests that the target bean's visual appearance should be updated by broadcasting a `PropertyChangeEvent` whenever the user changes any of the property values, not just when the user is at the end of the customization process.

Unlike property editors, customizers are not automatically displayed. In the BeanBox, you must select Edit|Customize to pop up the customizer of a bean. At that point, the BeanBox will call the `setObject` method of the customizer that takes the bean being customized as a parameter. Notice that your customizer is thus created before it is actually linked to an instance of your bean. Therefore, you cannot assume any information about the state of a bean in the customizer, and you must provide a constructor without arguments.

There are three parts to writing a customizer class:

- Building the visual interface

- Initializing the customizer in the `setObject` method

- Updating the bean by firing property change events when the user changes properties in the interface

By definition, a customizer class is visual. It must, therefore, extend `Component` or a subclass of `Component`, such as `Panel`. Since customizers typically present the user with many options, it is often handy to use a "wizard" interface, in which the possible settings are presented as a sequence of cards in a logical order, with buttons labeled "Next" and "Previous" to navigate between the individual cards. You use a `CardLayout` to flip through the cards.

We use this wizard approach for the customizer of our chart bean. The customizer gathers the information in three cards, in the following order:

1. Data points (which are read in from a file)

2. Graph color and inverse mode

3. Title and title position

Of course, developing this kind of user interface can be tedious to code—our example devotes over 100 lines just to set it up in the constructor. However, this task requires only the usual AWT programming skills, and we won't dwell on the details here. (See Chapters 7–9 of Volume 1 for more information.)

There is one trick that is worth keeping in mind. You often need to edit property values in a customizer. Rather than implementing a new interface for setting the property value of a particular class, you can simply locate an existing property editor and add it to your user interface! For example, in our `ChartBean` customizer, we need to set the graph color. Since we know that the BDK has a perfectly good property editor for colors, we locate it as follows:

```
PropertyEditor colorEditor
    = PropertEditorManager.findEditor(Color.Class);
```

We then call `getCustomEditor` to get the component that contains the user interface for setting the colors and add it to one of the cards.

```
add(card, colorEditor.getCustomEditor(), . . .);
```

Once we have all components laid out, we initialize their values by using the `setObject` method. The `setObject` method is called when the customizer is displayed. Its parameter is the bean that is being customized. To proceed, we store that bean reference—we'll need it later to notify the bean of property changes. Then, we initialize each user interface component. Here is a part of the

`setObject` method of the chart bean customizer that does this initialization:

```
public void setObject(Object obj)
{  bean = (ChartBean)obj;
   titleField.setText(bean.getTitle());
   colorEditor.setValue(bean.getGraphColor());
      . . .
}
```

Finally, we hook up event handlers to track the user's activities. Whenever the user changes the value of a component, the component fires an event that our customizer must handle. The event handler must update the value of the property in the bean and must also fire a `PropertyChangeEvent` so that other listeners (such as the Property Sheet) can be updated. Let us follow that process with a couple of user interface elements in the chart bean customizer.

First, we implement property support listeners in the usual way, with a `PropertyChangeSupport` object:

```
public void addPropertyChangeListener
      (PropertyChangeListener l)
{  pcs.addPropertyChangeListener(l);
}
public void removePropertyChangeListener
      (PropertyChangeListener l)
{  pcs.removePropertyChangeListener(l);
}
private PropertyChangeSupport pcs
      = new PropertyChangeSupport(this);
```

When the user types a new title, we want to update the `title` property. We attach a `TextListener` to the text field into which the user types the title.

```
titleField.addTextListener(new TextListener()
{  public void textValueChanged(TextEvent evt)
   {  setTitle(titleField.getText());
   }
});
```

The `textValueChanged` method calls the `setTitle` method of the customizer. That method calls the bean to update the property value and then fires a property change event. (This update is necessary only for properties that are not bound.) Here is the code for the `setTitle` method:

```
public void setTitle(String newValue)
{  String oldValue = bean.getTitle();
   bean.setTitle(newValue);
   pcs.firePropertyChange("title", oldValue, newValue);
}
```

When the color value changes in the color property editor, we want to update the graph color of the bean. We track the color changes by attaching a listener to the property editor. Perhaps confusingly, that editor also sends out property change events.

```
colorEditor.addPropertyChangeListener
    (new PropertyChangeListener()
{   public void propertyChange(PropertyChangeEvent
        evt)
    {   setGraphColor((Color)colorEditor.getValue());
    }
});
```

Whenever the color value of the color property editor changes, we call the setGraphColor method of the customizer. That method updates the graphColor property of the bean and fires a different property change event that is associated with the graphColor property.

```
public void setValues(double[] newValue)
{   double[] oldValue = bean.getValues();
    bean.setValues(newValue);
    pcs.firePropertyChange("graphColor", oldValue, newValue);
}
```

Example 7-16 provides the full code of the chart bean customizer.

This particular customizer just set properties of the bean. In general, customizers can call any methods of the bean, whether or not they are property setters. That is, customizers are more general than property editors. (Some beans may have features that are not exposed as properties and that can be edited only through the customizer.)

Example 7-16: ChartBeanCustomizer.java

```
import java.awt.*;
import java.awt.event.*;
import java.beans.*;
import java.io.*;
import java.text.*;
import java.util.*;

public class ChartBeanCustomizer extends Panel
    implements Customizer
{   public ChartBeanCustomizer()
    {   Panel p;
        setLayout(new BorderLayout());

        final Panel cardPanel = new Panel();
        final CardLayout cardLayout = new CardLayout();
        cardPanel.setLayout(cardLayout);
```

```
Panel card = new Panel();
card.setLayout(new BorderLayout());

TextArea fileInfo = new TextArea(
   "You can read data values for the chart\n"
   + "from a text file. The file must contain one\n"
   + "data value in each line.",
   3, 50, TextArea.SCROLLBARS_NONE);
fileInfo.setEditable(false);
card.add(fileInfo, "Center");

Button loadButton = new Button("Load");
loadButton.addActionListener(new ActionListener()
   {  public void actionPerformed(ActionEvent evt)
      {  loadFile();
      }
   });
p = new Panel();
p.add(loadButton);
card.add(p, "South");
cardPanel.add(card, "0");

add(cardPanel, "Center");

card = new Panel();
card.setLayout(new GridBagLayout());

CheckboxGroup g = new CheckboxGroup();
normal = new Checkbox("Normal", g, true);
inverse = new Checkbox("Inverse", g, false);

p = new Panel();
p.add(normal);
p.add(inverse);
normal.addItemListener(new ItemListener()
   {  public void itemStateChanged(ItemEvent evt)
      {  if (evt.getStateChange() == ItemEvent.SELECTED)
            setInverse(false);
      }
   });

inverse.addItemListener(new ItemListener()
   {  public void itemStateChanged(ItemEvent evt)
      {  if (evt.getStateChange() == ItemEvent.SELECTED)
            setInverse(true);
      }
   });
```

```
colorEditor
   = PropertyEditorManager.findEditor(Color.class);
colorEditor.addPropertyChangeListener
   (new PropertyChangeListener()
   {  public void propertyChange(PropertyChangeEvent
         evt)
      {  setGraphColor((Color)colorEditor.getValue());
      }
   });

GridBagConstraints gbc = new GridBagConstraints();
gbc.weightx = 100;
gbc.weighty = 100;
gbc.fill = GridBagConstraints.NONE;
gbc.anchor = GridBagConstraints.WEST;

add(card, new Label("Set Color"), gbc, 0, 0, 1, 1);
add(card, p, gbc, 0, 1, 1, 1);
add(card, colorEditor.getCustomEditor(),
   gbc, 0, 2, 1, 1);
cardPanel.add(card, "1");

card = new Panel();
card.setLayout(new GridBagLayout());

positionGroup = new CheckboxGroup();
position = new Checkbox[3];
position[0] = new Checkbox("Left", g, false);
position[1] = new Checkbox("Center", g, true);
position[2] = new Checkbox("Right", g, false);

p = new Panel();
for (int i = 0; i < position.length; i++)
{  final int value = i;
   p.add(position[i]);
   position[i].addItemListener(new ItemListener()
      {  public void itemStateChanged(ItemEvent evt)
         {  if (evt.getStateChange()
               == ItemEvent.SELECTED)
               setTitlePosition(value);
         }
      });
}

titleField = new TextField();
titleField.addTextListener(new TextListener()
   {  public void textValueChanged(TextEvent evt)
      {  setTitle(titleField.getText());
```

```
            }
        });

    add(card, new Label("Set Title"), gbc, 0, 0, 1, 1);
    add(card, p, gbc, 0, 1, 1, 1);
    gbc.fill = GridBagConstraints.HORIZONTAL;
    add(card, titleField, gbc, 0, 2, 1, 1);
    cardPanel.add(card, "2");

    p = new Panel();
    Button nextButton = new Button("Next");
    Button previousButton = new Button("Previous");
    nextButton.addActionListener(new ActionListener()
        {  public void actionPerformed(ActionEvent evt)
            {  cardLayout.next(cardPanel);
            }
        });
    previousButton.addActionListener(new ActionListener()
        {  public void actionPerformed(ActionEvent evt)
            {  cardLayout.previous(cardPanel);
            }
        });
    p.add(previousButton);
    p.add(nextButton);
    add(p, "South");
}

public static void add(Container t,
    Component c, GridBagConstraints gbc,
    int x, int y, int w, int h)
{  gbc.gridx = x;
    gbc.gridy = y;
    gbc.gridwidth = w;
    gbc.gridheight = h;
    t.add(c, gbc);
}

public void loadFile()
{  Container c = getParent();
    while (c != null && !(c instanceof Frame))
        c = c.getParent();
    FileDialog dlg = new FileDialog((Frame)c,
            "Open data file", FileDialog.LOAD);
    dlg.show();
    String filename = dlg.getFile();
    if (filename != null)
    {  filename = dlg.getDirectory() + filename;
        NumberFormat fmt = NumberFormat.getNumberInstance();
```

```
        try
        {   Vector v = new Vector();
            BufferedReader in
                = new BufferedReader(new FileReader(filename));
            String line;
            while ((line = in.readLine()) != null)
                v.addElement(fmt.parse(line));
            double[] d = new double[v.size()];
            for (int i = 0; i < d.length; i++)
                d[i] = ((Number)v.elementAt(i)).doubleValue();
            setValues(d);
        }
        catch(IOException e) {}
        catch(ParseException e) {}
    }
}

public void setTitle(String newValue)
{   String oldValue = bean.getTitle();
    bean.setTitle(newValue);
    pcs.firePropertyChange("title", oldValue, newValue);
}

public void setTitlePosition(int i)
{   Integer oldValue = new Integer(bean.getTitlePosition());
    Integer newValue = new Integer(i);
    bean.setTitlePosition(i);
    pcs.firePropertyChange("title", oldValue, newValue);
}

public void setInverse(boolean b)
{   Boolean oldValue = new Boolean(bean.isInverse());
    Boolean newValue = new Boolean(b);
    bean.setInverse(b);
    pcs.firePropertyChange("inverse", oldValue, newValue);
}

public void setValues(double[] newValue)
{   double[] oldValue = bean.getValues();
    bean.setValues(newValue);
    pcs.firePropertyChange("inverse", oldValue, newValue);
}

public void setGraphColor(Color newValue)
{   Color oldValue = bean.getGraphColor();
    bean.setGraphColor(newValue);
    pcs.firePropertyChange("inverse", oldValue, newValue);
}
```

```
public Dimension getPreferredSize()
{   return new Dimension(300, 200);
}

public void setObject(Object obj)
{   bean = (ChartBean)obj;

    normal.setState(!bean.isInverse());
    inverse.setState(bean.isInverse());

    titleField.setText(bean.getTitle());

    positionGroup.setSelectedCheckbox
        (position[bean.getTitlePosition()]);

    colorEditor.setValue(bean.getGraphColor());
}

public void addPropertyChangeListener
    (PropertyChangeListener l)
{   pcs.addPropertyChangeListener(l);
}

public void removePropertyChangeListener
    (PropertyChangeListener l)
{   pcs.removePropertyChangeListener(l);
}

ChartBean bean;
PropertyChangeSupport pcs = new PropertyChangeSupport(this);
PropertyEditor colorEditor;

Checkbox normal;
Checkbox inverse;
Checkbox[] position;
CheckboxGroup positionGroup;
TextField titleField;
}
```

`interface java.beans.Customizer`

- `void setObject(Object bean)`

  specifies the bean to customize.

Advanced Use of Introspection

From the point of view of the Java beans specification, introspection is simply the process by which a builder tool finds out which properties, methods, and events a Java bean supports. Introspection is carried out in two ways:

- By searching for classes and methods that follow certain naming patters

- By querying the `BeanInfo` of a class

Normally, introspection is an activity that is reserved for bean environments. The bean environment uses introspection to learn about beans, but the beans themselves don't need to carry out introspection. However, there are some cases when one bean needs to use introspection to analyze other beans. A good example is when you want to tightly couple two beans on a form in a builder tool. Consider, for example, a spin bean, a small control element with two buttons, to increase or decrease a value (see Figure 7-26).

Figure 7-26: The spin bean

A spin bean by itself is not useful. It needs to be coupled with another bean. For example, a spin bean can to be coupled to an integer text field. Each time the user clicks on one of the buttons of the spin bean, the integer value is incremented or decremented. We will call the coupled bean the *buddy* of the spin bean. The buddy does not have to be an `IntTextBean`. It can be any other bean with an integer property.

You use the customizer of the spin bean to attach the buddy (see Figure 7-27).

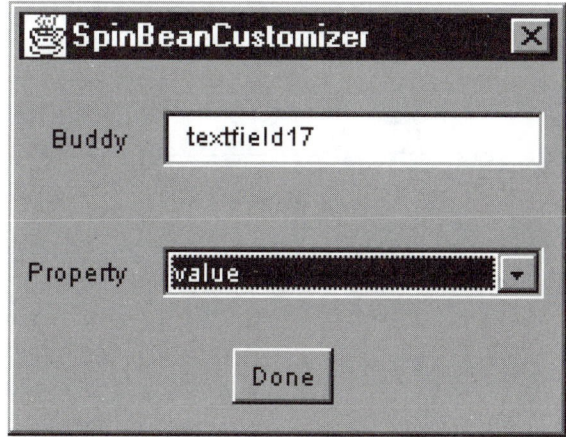

Figure 7-27: The customizer of the SpinBean

Here is how you can try it out:

1. Add the SpinBean and an IntTextBean on the form.

2. Click on the IntTextBean and look at the value of the name property in the Property Sheet. The name will be something like textfield12. Remember the name, or copy it into the clipboard.

3. Pop up the customizer of the spin bean by selecting it and selecting Edit I Customize from the menu.

4. Type or paste the name of the IntTextBean into the buddy text field.

5. Watch how all the int properties in the choice box are automatically filled in (see Figure 7-28).

6. Select value and Done.

7. Then, click on + and - and watch the integer text field value increase and decrease (see Figure 7-28).

Figure 7-28: The SpinBean coupled with an IntTextBean

It looks easy, but there were two challenges to implementing this customization.

1. How do you find all properties whose values are of type int of a bean?

2. How do you program the getting and setting of a property if you know it by name only at run time?

We use introspection (that is, the Reflection API) to solve both of these problems. To analyze the properties of a bean, first get the bean info by calling the static getBeanInfo method of the Introspector class.

```
BeanInfo info
    = Introspector.getBeanInfo(buddy.getClass());
```

Once we have the bean info, we can obtain an array of property descriptors:

```
PropertyDescriptor[] props = info.getPropertyDescriptors();
```

In the spin bean customizer, the next step is to loop through this array, picking out all properties of type int and adding them to a choice field.

```
for (int i = 0; i < props.length; i++)
{   if (props[i].getPropertyType().equals(int.class))
    {   propChoice.add(props[i].getName());
    }
}
```

This code shows how you can find out about the properties of a bean.

Next, we need to be able to get and set the property that the user selected. We obtain the get and set methods by calls to getReadMethod and getWriteMethod:

```
Method getMethod = prop.getReadMethod();
Method setMethod = prop.getWriteMethod();
```

(Why is it called getReadMethod? Probably because getGetMethod sounds too silly.)

Now, we invoke the methods to get a value, increment it, and set it. This process again uses the Reflection API—see, for example, Chapter 5 of Volume 1. Note that we must use an Integer wrapper around the int value.

```
int value = ((Integer)getMethod.invoke(buddy,
    null)).intValue();
value += increment;
setMethod.invoke(buddy,
    new Object[] { new Integer(value) });
```

Could we have avoided reflection if we had demanded that the buddy have methods getValue and setValue? No. You can only call

```
int value = buddy.getValue();
```

when the compiler knows that buddy is an object of a type that has a getValue method. But buddy can be of any type—there is no type hierarchy for beans. Whenever one bean is coupled with another arbitrary bean, then you need to use introspection and reflection.

Finally, we should point out that the code we use is more complicated than it might be. This complexity arises because the current JavaBean specification gives no way for *beans in the same project in a builder to know about each other*.

NOTE: The next version of beans, the so-called Glasgow specification, does allow this mutual knowledge. You can obtain the specification from http://java.sun.com/beans/index.html.

In our case, it would have been nice if the customizer of the spin bean simply enumerated all other beans on the form instead of forcing the BeanBox user to cut and paste the name of the buddy. The problem is that with the current beans specification, it is very difficult to enumerate all other beans on a form in a builder like the BeanBox. In the BeanBox, for example, you can't simply call

```
Component[] siblings = getParent().getComponents()
```

to get all the siblings of the spin bean. The reason you can't do this is that, unfortunately, the BeanBox surrounds every bean by a panel within a panel. (We suspect that is done to detect mouse clicks that select the bean and to draw the outline around a selected bean.) So, in the BeanBox, we'd have to write

```
Component[] siblings
    = getParent().getParent().getParent().getComponents()
```

However, there is no guarantee that this solution would work in another builder environment—since those environments might be smart enough not to need all these extra panels.

In fact, even when the name of a bean is known, it is not easy to locate the bean object. Fortunately, you can locate the object in a way that is independent of the design environment, by the following algorithm:

1. Find the top-level parent by calling `getParent` until the parent is `null`:

    ```
    Container parent = bean.getParent();
    while (parent.getParent() != null)
        parent = parent.getParent();
    ```

2. Look through all children of that top-level parent. Since the children can themselves be containers, the child containers must be searched recursively.

    ```
    public static Component findBuddy(Container parent, String
        name)
    {   Component[] children = parent.getComponents();
        for (int i = 0; i < children.length; i++)
        {   if (children[i].getName().equals(name))
                return children[i];
            if (children[i] instanceof Container)
            {   Component ret = findBuddy((Container)children[i],
                    name);
                if (ret != null) return ret;
            }
        }
        return null;
    }
    ```

We also wanted to program the spin bean to move next to its buddy. In principle, this should not be hard—get the location of the buddy and call `setLocation` to move the spin bean next to it. But `setLocation` moves the spin bean only within its container, which is, in the case of the BeanBox, a panel. We really would need to move the two nested panels as well. Since these panels are not present in other builder environments, we gave up.

Another possible user interface would have been to have the user drag the buddy bean on top of the spin bean. Unfortunately, though, a bean gets no event notification when another bean is dropped onto it in the current specification, so it is hard to develop good design interfaces for container beans until the Glasgow specification is implemented.

Examples 7-17 through 7-19 contain the full code for the `SpinBean`, including the needed bean info class to hook in the customizer.

Example 7-17: SpinBean.java

```
import java.awt.*;
import java.awt.event.*;
import java.beans.*;
import java.lang.reflect.*;
import java.io.*;

public class SpinBean extends Panel
    implements ActionListener, Serializable
{   public SpinBean()
    {   setLayout(new GridLayout(1, 2));
        Button plusButton = new Button("+");
        Button minusButton = new Button("-");
        add(plusButton);
        add(minusButton);
        plusButton.addActionListener(this);
        minusButton.addActionListener(this);
    }

    public void setBuddy(Component b, PropertyDescriptor p)
    {   buddy = b;
        prop = p;
    }

    public void actionPerformed(ActionEvent evt)
    {   if (buddy == null) return;
        if (prop == null) return;
        String arg = evt.getActionCommand();
        int increment = 0;
        if (arg.equals("+")) increment = 1;
        else if (arg.equals("-")) increment = -1;
        else return;
        Method readMethod = prop.getReadMethod();
        Method writeMethod = prop.getWriteMethod();
        try
        {   int value = ((Integer)readMethod.invoke(buddy,
                null)).intValue();
            value += increment;
            writeMethod.invoke(buddy,
                new Object[] { new Integer(value) });
        }
        catch(Exception e) {}
    }

    public Dimension getPreferredSize()
    {   return new Dimension(MINSIZE, MINSIZE);
    }

    String buddyName = "";
```

```java
    private static final int MINSIZE = 20;
    private Component buddy = null;
    private PropertyDescriptor prop = null;
}
```

Example 7-18: SpinBeanCustomizer.java

```java
import java.awt.*;
import java.awt.event.*;
import java.beans.*;
import java.io.*;
import java.text.*;
import java.util.*;

public class SpinBeanCustomizer extends Panel
    implements Customizer, ItemListener, TextListener
{   public SpinBeanCustomizer()
    {   setLayout(new GridBagLayout());
        GridBagConstraints gbc = new GridBagConstraints();
        gbc.weightx = 0;
        gbc.weighty = 100;
        gbc.fill = GridBagConstraints.NONE;
        gbc.anchor = GridBagConstraints.EAST;
        add(new Label("Buddy"), gbc, 0, 0, 1, 1);
        add(new Label("Property"), gbc, 0, 1, 1, 1);
        gbc.weightx = 100;
        gbc.anchor = GridBagConstraints.WEST;
        gbc.fill = GridBagConstraints.HORIZONTAL;
        add(buddyTextField, gbc, 1, 0, 1, 1);
        add(propChoice, gbc, 1, 1, 1, 1);

        buddyTextField.addTextListener(this);
        propChoice.addItemListener(this);
    }

    public void add(Component c, GridBagConstraints gbc,
        int x, int y, int w, int h)
    {   gbc.gridx = x;
        gbc.gridy = y;
        gbc.gridwidth = w;
        gbc.gridheight = h;
        add(c, gbc);
    }

    public void textValueChanged(TextEvent evt)
    {   findBuddyMethods();
    }
```

```java
public void findBuddyMethods()
{   propChoice.removeAll();

    Container parent = bean.getParent();
    while (parent.getParent() != null)
        parent = parent.getParent();

    buddy = findBuddy(parent, buddyTextField.getText());
    if (buddy == null)
    {   return;
    }

    try
    {   BeanInfo info
            = Introspector.getBeanInfo(buddy.getClass());
        props = info.getPropertyDescriptors();
        int j = 0;
        for (int i = 0; i < props.length; i++)
        {   if (props[i].getPropertyType().equals(int.class))
            {   propChoice.add(props[i].getName());
                props[j++] = props[i];
            }
        }
    }
    catch(IntrospectionException e){}
}

public static Component findBuddy(Container parent,
    String name)
{   Component[] children = parent.getComponents();
    for (int i = 0; i < children.length; i++)
    {   if (children[i].getName().equals(name))
            return children[i];
        if (children[i] instanceof Container)
        {   Component ret
                = findBuddy((Container)children[i], name);
            if (ret != null) return ret;
        }
    }
    return null;
}

public void itemStateChanged(ItemEvent evt)
{   if (evt.getStateChange() == ItemEvent.SELECTED)
    {   bean.setBuddy(buddy,
            props[propChoice.getSelectedIndex()]);
    }
}
```

```
    public Dimension getPreferredSize()
    {   return new Dimension(200, 100);
    }

    public void setObject(Object obj)
    {   bean = (SpinBean)obj;
    }

    public void addPropertyChangeListener
        (PropertyChangeListener l)
    {   support.addPropertyChangeListener(l);
    }

    public void removePropertyChangeListener
        (PropertyChangeListener l)
    {   support.removePropertyChangeListener(l);
    }

    SpinBean bean;
    PropertyChangeSupport support
        = new PropertyChangeSupport(this);
    TextField buddyTextField = new TextField();
    Choice propChoice = new Choice();
    Component buddy;
    PropertyDescriptor[] props;
}
```

Example 7-19: SpinBeanBeanInfo.java

```
import java.awt.*;
import java.beans.*;

public class SpinBeanBeanInfo extends SimpleBeanInfo
{   public BeanDescriptor getBeanDescriptor()
    {   return new BeanDescriptor(SpinBean.class,
            SpinBeanCustomizer.class);
    }
}
```

`java.beans.Introspector`

- `String decapitalize(String name)`

  converts a string to Java's naming convention. `SillyMethod` becomes `sillyMethod`, for example. (When there are two consecutive capitals, nothing happens.)

- `BeanInfo getBeanInfo(Class beanClass)`

  gets the `BeanInfo` class associated to the bean or creates one on the fly, using the naming convention discussed earlier in this chapter; throws an `IntrospectionException` if the introspection fails.

CHAPTER 8

- Class Loaders

- Security Managers

- The Java Security Package

- Authentication

- The Java Authentication Framework

- Code Signing

- Encryption

Security

Although Java is growing into a first-rate, general-purpose program language as its class libraries mature, that is not the reason for all the hype that surrounds it. We think it is fair to say that the excitement derives from the possibility of delivering executable content (applets) over the Internet (see Chapter 10 of Volume 1, for example). Obviously, delivering executable code is practical only when the recipients are sure that the applets can't go rogue. For this reason, security was and is a major concern of both the designers and the users of Java. This means that unlike other languages and systems, where security was implemented as an afterthought or a reaction to break-ins, security mechanisms are an integral part of Java.

Three mechanisms in Java help ensure safety:

- Language design features (bounds checking on arrays, legal type conversions only, no pointer arithmetic, and so on).

- A "sandbox" mechanism that controls what the code can do (such as file access).

- Code signing—Code authors can use standard cryptographic algorithms to embed a "certificate" into a Java class. Then, the users of the code can determine exactly who created the code and whether the code has been altered after it was signed.

The Java Virtual Machine checks for bad pointers, invalid array offsets, and so on. The other steps require controlling what goes *to* the Java Virtual Machine.

This chapter shows you how class files are loaded into the virtual machine and checked for integrity. More importantly, we show you how to control what goes to the virtual machine by building your own *class loader*. For maximum security,

both the default mechanism for loading class and a custom class loader need to work with a *security manager* class that controls what actions code can perform. (All browsers have a security manager that controls what actions applets can perform; these security managers may or may not be configurable.) You'll see how to write your own *security manager* class next. *Security manager* classes can be quite flexible; for example, you'll see in this chapter how to make one that can control what *applications* can do. Finally, you'll see the cryptographic algorithms supplied in the `java.security` package, which allow for, among other things, code signing.

Class Loaders

A Java compiler converts source into the machine language of a hypothetical machine, called, naturally enough, the Java Virtual Machine. This intermediate code is stored in a class file with a `.class` extension. Class files contain the code for all the methods of one class. These class files need to be interpreted by a program that can translate the instruction set of the Java Virtual Machine into the machine language of the target machine. Note that the Java interpreter loads only those class files that are needed for the execution of a program. Here are the steps to run `MyProgram.class`.

1. The Java interpreter has a mechanism to load class files; it uses this to load the `MyProgram` class file.

2. The Java interpreter then executes the `main` method in `MyProgram` (which is static, so no instance of a class needs to be created).

3. If the `main` method requires additional classes, these are loaded next.

4. Also, whenever a class has data fields or superclasses of a particular type, these class files are loaded. (The process of loading all the classes that a given class depends on is called *resolving* the class.)

Of course, the default mechanism built into a Java interpreter or JIT knows about the CLASSPATH environment variable, how to locate classes in ZIP and JAR files, and so on. Methods loaded through this mechanism are called *system classes*.

The default mechanism is the least secure mechanism for loading classes. Since these are Java programs, you still get checks for things like null pointers or array bounds checking but you won't get checks on much more. If you need more control, you should replace the default mechanism for loading classes with what is called a *class loader*. The most common example of a class loader is the applet class loader. The applet class loader knows how to load class files across a network and how to authenticate signed JAR files. The applet class

loader will also set up separate name spaces so that classes loaded from one host don't conflict with classes from other hosts.

A custom class loader like the applet class loader replaces the built-in mechanism for locating and loading class files. It lets you carry out specialized security checks before you pass the bytecodes to the virtual machine. As you might expect, Java programmers can write their own class loaders. For example, you can write a class loader that can refuse to load a class that has not been marked as "paid for". The next few sections show you how.

Writing Your Own Class Loader

A class loader is an implementation of the abstract class `ClassLoader`. The `loadClass` method in this class determines how to load the top-level class. Once a class is loaded through class loader, all other classes that it references are also loaded through that class loader.

To write your own class loader, you simply override the method

```
loadClass(String className, bool resolve)
```

(All other methods of the `ClassLoader` class are final.)

Your implementation of this method must:

1. Check whether this class loader has already loaded this class. For this purpose, your class loader needs to keep a record of the classes that it has previously loaded.

2. If it is a new class, you need to check whether it is a system class.

    Otherwise, load the bytecodes for the class from the local file system or from some other source.

3. Call the `defineClass` method of the `ClassLoader` base class to present the bytecodes to the virtual machine.

If the `resolve` flag is set, you must call the `resolveClass` method of the `ClassLoader` base class. Your class loader will be called again to load any other classes that this class refers to. (Your `loadClass` method might be called with `resolve` set to `false` if the virtual machine merely attempts to find out if a class exists, but every class must be fully resolved before you can create an instance or call a method.)

Usually, a class loader uses a hash table to store the references to the already loaded classes. The following code example shows the framework of the `loadClass` method of a typical class loader.

```
public class TypicalClassLoader extends ClassLoader
{  protected synchronized Class loadClass(String name, boolean
      resolve)
      throws ClassNotFoundException
   {  // check if class already loaded
      Class cl = (Class)classes.get(name);

      if (cl == null) // new class
      {  try
         {  // check if system class
            return findSystemClass(name);
         }
         catch (ClassNotFoundException e) {}
         catch (NoClassDefFoundError e) {}

         // load class bytes--details depend on class loader

         byte[] classBytes = loadClassBytes(name);
         if (classBytes == null) throw new
            ClassNotFoundException(name);

         cl = defineClass(name, classBytes, 0,
            classBytes.length);
         if (cl == null) throw new ClassNotFoundException(name);

         classes.put(name, cl); // remember class
      }

      if (resolve) resolveClass(cl);

      return cl;
   }

   private byte[] loadClassBytes(String name)
   {  . . .
   }


   private Hashtable classes = new Hashtable();
}
```

In the program of Example 8-1, we implement a class loader that loads encrypted class files. The program asks the user for the name of the first class to load (that is, the class containing main) and the decryption key. It then uses a special class loader to load the specified class and calls the main method. The class loader decrypts the specified class and all nonsystem classes that are refer- enced by it. For simplicity, we will ignore 2,000 years of progress in the field of

cryptography and use the venerable Caesar cipher for encrypting the class files—so that we can safely export this book.[1]

Our version of the Caesar cipher has as a key a number between 1 and 255. To decrypt, simply add that key to every byte and reduce modulo 256. The Caesar.java program of Example 8-2 carries out the encryption. To decrypt, the code simply subtracts the key. The decryption occurs in the class loader. We give the encrypted class files an extension .caesar to distinguish them from the regular class files. On the CD-ROM for this book, you will find a file, Calculator.caesar, encrypted (for historical reasons) with a key value of 3. You cannot load it via the regular Java interpreter, but you can run it by using the custom class loader defined in our ClassLoaderTest program.

Encrypting class files has a number of practical uses (provided, of course, that you use a cipher stronger than the Caesar cipher). Without the decryption key, the class files are useless. They can neither be executed by a standard Java interpreter nor readily disassembled.

This means that you can use a custom class loader to authenticate the user of the class or to ensure that a program has been paid for before it will be allowed to run. Of course, encryption is only one application of a custom class loader. You can use other types of class loaders to solve other problems, such as walling off part of your file system. We believe that the ability to control the class loading process via a custom class loader is one of the great advantages of the Java Virtual Machine.

Example 8-1: ClassLoaderTest.java

```
import java.util.*;
import java.io.*;
import java.lang.reflect.*;
import java.awt.*;
import java.awt.event.*;
import corejava.*;

public class ClassLoaderTest
    extends CloseableFrame
    implements ActionListener
{   public ClassLoaderTest()
    {   setLayout(new GridBagLayout());
        GridBagConstraints gbc = new GridBagConstraints();
```

[1] See, for example, David Kahn's wonderful book *The Code Breakers*, [Macmillan, NY, 1967 p. 84] where he refers to Suetonious as a source. Kahn says that Caesar shifted the 24 letters of the Roman alphabet by 3 letters. Strong encryption methods are tightly controlled by the U.S. Government, though the laws are currently in flux.

```java
        gbc.fill = GridBagConstraints.NONE;
        gbc.anchor = GridBagConstraints.EAST;
        add(new Label("Class"), gbc, 0, 0, 1, 1);
        add(new Label("Key"), gbc, 0, 1, 1, 1);
        gbc.anchor = GridBagConstraints.WEST;
        add(nameField, gbc, 1, 0, 1, 1);
        add(keyField, gbc, 1, 1, 1, 1);
        gbc.anchor = GridBagConstraints.CENTER;
        Button loadButton = new Button("Load");
        add(loadButton, gbc, 0, 2, 2, 1);
        loadButton.addActionListener(this);
    }

    public void add(Component c, GridBagConstraints gbc,
        int x, int y, int w, int h)
    {   gbc.gridx = x;
        gbc.gridy = y;
        gbc.gridwidth = w;
        gbc.gridheight = h;
        add(c, gbc);
    }

    public void actionPerformed(ActionEvent evt)
    {   try
        {   ClassLoader loader
                = new CryptoClassLoader(keyField.getValue());
            Class c = loader.loadClass(nameField.getText());
            String[] cargs = new String[] {};
            Method m = c.getMethod("main",
                new Class[] { cargs.getClass() });
            m.invoke(null, new Object[] { cargs });
            setVisible(false);
        }
        catch (Exception e)
        {   System.out.println(e);
        }
    }

    public static void main(String[] args)
    {   Frame f = new ClassLoaderTest();
        f.setSize(300, 200);
        f.show();
    }

    private IntTextField keyField = new IntTextField(3, 4);
    private TextField nameField = new TextField(30);
}
```

```
class CryptoClassLoader extends ClassLoader
{  public CryptoClassLoader(int k)
   {  key = k;
   }

   protected synchronized Class loadClass(String name,
      boolean resolve) throws ClassNotFoundException
   {  // check if class already loaded
      Class cl = (Class)classes.get(name);

      if (cl == null) // new class
      {  try
         {  // check if system class
            return findSystemClass(name);
         }
         catch (ClassNotFoundException e) {}
         catch (NoClassDefFoundError e) {}

         // load class bytes--details depend on class loader

         byte[] classBytes = loadClassBytes(name);
         if (classBytes == null)
            throw new ClassNotFoundException(name);

         cl = defineClass(name, classBytes,
            0, classBytes.length);
         if (cl == null)
            throw new ClassNotFoundException(name);

         classes.put(name, cl); // remember class
      }

      if (resolve) resolveClass(cl);

      return cl;
   }

   private byte[] loadClassBytes(String name)
   {  String cname = name.replace('.', '/') + ".class";
      FileInputStream in = null;
      try
      {  in = new FileInputStream(cname);
         ByteArrayOutputStream buffer
            = new ByteArrayOutputStream();
         int ch;
         while ((ch = in.read()) != -1)
            buffer.write(ch);
         return buffer.toByteArray();
```

```
      }
      catch (IOException e)
      {  if (in != null)
         {  try { in.close(); } catch (IOException e2) {}
         }
         return null;
      }
   }

   private Hashtable classes = new Hashtable();
   private int key;
}
```

Example 8-2: Caesar.java

```
import java.io.*;

public class Caesar
{  public static void main(String[] args)
   {  if (args.length != 3)
      {  System.out.println("USAGE: java Caesar in out key");
         return;
      }

      try
      {  FileInputStream in = new FileInputStream(args[0]);
         FileOutputStream out = new FileOutputStream(args[1]);
         int key = Integer.parseInt(args[2]);
         int ch;
         while ((ch = in.read()) != -1)
         {  byte c = (byte)(ch + key);
            out.write(c);
         }
         in.close();
         out.close();
      }
      catch(IOException e)
      {  System.out.println("Error: " + e);
      }
   }
}
```

`java.lang.ClassLoader`

- `Class defineClass(String name, byte data[],`
  `int offset, int length)`

  adds a new class to the virtual machine.

Parameters:	name	the name of the class. Use . as package name separator, and don't use a .class suffix
	data	an array holding the bytecodes of the class
	offset	the start of the bytecodes in the array
	length	the length of the bytecodes in the array

- `void loadClass(String name, boolean resolve)`

  is implemented by a class extending `ClassLoader`. It obtains the bytecodes for the class and then calls `defineClass` and, if the `resolve` flag is `true`, `resolveClass`. The class loader should implement a cache to ensure that previously loaded classes are not loaded again.

Parameters:	name	the name of the class. Use . as package name separator, and don't use a .class suffix
	resolve	true if the resolveClass method needs to be called after the class is loaded

- `void resolveClass(Class c)`

  should be called by `loadClass` if the `resolve` flag is `true`. It keeps loading dependent classes until all the classes that the class refers to either directly or indirectly are fully known to the virtual machine. Once the class is resolved, the virtual machine can create objects of the class and call class methods.

Parameters:	c	the class to be resolved

- `Class findSystemClass(String name)`

  finds the system class with the specified name and loads it, if necessary. A system class is a class loaded from the local file system in a platform-dependent way, using the value of the `CLASSPATH` environment variable. System classes have no class loader.

Parameters:	name	the name of the class. Use . as package name separator, and don't use a .class suffix

Verifying Your New Class

When your class loader (or the default class loading mechanism) presents the bytecodes of a newly loaded Java class to the virtual machine, these bytecodes are first inspected by a *verifier*. The verifier checks that the instructions cannot perform actions that are obviously damaging.

Actually, there are three possible verification levels:

1. Verify all loaded classes.

2. Skip verification for system classes and verify only classes loaded with a class loader (the default).

3. Do not verify classes.

The verification level is a startup option of the virtual machine—it cannot be changed after the virtual machine has been launched. When starting the Java interpreter, you can specify one of three options, -verify, -verifyremote (the default), and -noverify. For example,

```
java -verify Hello
```

Here are some of the checks that the verifier carries out:

- That variables are initialized before they are used

- That method calls match the types of object references

- That rules for accessing private data and methods are not violated

- That local variable accesses fall within the run-time stack

- That the run-time stack does not overflow

If any of these checks fails, then the class is considered corrupted and will not be loaded.

This strict verification is an important security consideration. Accidental errors, such as uninitialized variables, can easily wreak havoc if they are not caught. More importantly, in the wide open world of the Internet, you must be protected against malicious programmers who create evil effects on purpose. For example, by modifying values on the run-time stack or by writing to the private data fields of system objects, a program can break through the security system of a browser.

However, you may wonder why there is a special verifier to check all these features. After all, the Java compiler would never allow you to generate a class file in which an uninitialized variable is used or in which a private data field is accessed from another class. Indeed, a class file generated by a Java compiler always passes verification. But the bytecode format used in the class files is well

documented, and it is an easy matter for someone with some experience in assembly programming and a hex editor to manually produce a class file that contains valid but unsafe instructions for the Java Virtual Machine. Once again, keep in mind that the verifier is always guarding against maliciously altered class files, not just checking the class files produced by a Java compiler.

Here's an example of how to construct such an altered class file. We start with the program VerifierTest.java of Example 8-3. This is a simple program that calls a function and displays the function result. The program can be run both as a console program and as an applet. The fun method itself just computes 1 + 2:

```
static int fun()
{   int m;
    int n;
    m = 1;
    n = 2;
    int r = m + n;
    return r;
}
```

As an experiment, try to compile the following modification of this program:

```
static int fun()
{   int m = 1;
    int n;
    m = 1;
    m = 2;
    int r = m + n;
    return r;
}
```

In this case, n is not initialized, and it could have any random value. Of course, the Java compiler detects that problem and refuses to compile the program. To create a bad class file, we have to work a little harder. First, run the javap program to find out how the compiler translates the fun method. The command

```
javap -c VerifierTest
```

shows the bytecodes in the class file in mnemonic form.

```
Method int fun()
   0 iconst_1
   1 istore_0
   2 iconst_2
   3 istore_1
   4 iload_0
   5 iload_1
   6 iadd
   7 istore_2
```

```
8 iload_2
9 ireturn
```

We will use a hex editor to change instruction 3 from `istore_1` to `istore_0`. That is, local variable 0 (which is m) is initialized twice, and local variable 1 (which is n) is not initialized at all. We need to know the hexadecimal values for these instructions. These are readily available from *The Java Virtual Machine* by Tim Lindholm and Frank Yellin [Addison-Wesley, 1997].

```
0 iconst_1 04
1 istore_0 3B
2 iconst_2 05
3 istore_1 3C
4 iload_0  1A
5 iload_1  1B
6 iadd     60
7 istore_2 3D
8 iload_2  1C
9 ireturn  AC
```

We will use Hex Workshop (which is included in the companion CD-ROM for this book), our favorite hex editor, to carry out the modification. In Figure 8-1, you see the class file `VerifierTest.class` loaded into Hex Workshop, with the bytecodes of the `fun` method highlighted.

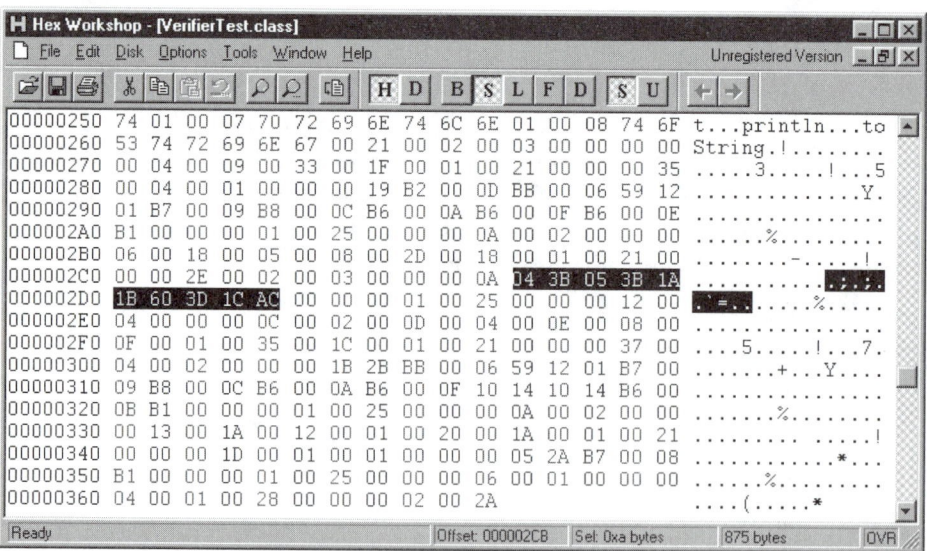

Figure 8-1: Modifying bytecodes with a hex editor

We simply change 3C to 3B and save the class file. (If you don't want to run the hex editor yourself, you can find the edited `VerifierTest.class` on the CD-ROM. Just make sure not to compile the `VerifierTest` source file again.)

Now, when this class file is executed, the result is surprising. The `fun` method returns a seemingly random value. This is actually 2 plus the value that happened to be stored in the variable `n`, which never was initialized. Here is a typical result:

```
1 + 2 = 15102330
```

This result shows that a class loaded as a system class does not go through the bytecode verifier. You can force verification by using the `-verify` option when invoking the Java interpreter:

```
java -verify VerifierTest
```

Then, the Java interpreter will refuse to load the class, giving the somewhat confusing error message "Can't find class VerifierTest."

However, to demonstrate how the Java interpreter verifies classes that are loaded by a class loader, let us use the class loader of the previous section.

1. Copy `VerifierTest.class` to `VerifierTest.caesar`.

2. Start the `ClassLoaderTest` program.

3. Load the `VerifierTest` class file with a key of 0.

You will see that the call to `resolveClass` throws an exception. This result indicates that the virtual machine has run the verifier and that the bad class file has been rejected.

To see how browsers handle verification, we wrote this program to run either as an application or an applet. Load the applet into a browser, using a file URL:

```
file:///C|/CoreJavaBook/v2ch8/VerifierTest/VerifierTest.html
```

Then, you see an error message displayed indicating that verification has failed (see Figure 8-2).

Example 8-3: VerifierTest.java

```java
import java.security.*;
import java.io.*;
import corejava.*;

public class CipherTest
{  public static void main(String[] args) throws Exception
   {  Security.addProvider(new CoreJavaProvider());
```

```java
KeyGenerator keyGen
    = KeyGenerator.getInstance("CAESAR");

SecureRandom rand = new SecureRandom();
keyGen.initialize(rand);
Key caesarKey = keyGen.generateKey();
System.out.println("The key is " + caesarKey);

Cipher cipher = Cipher.getInstance("CAESAR");
cipher.initEncrypt(caesarKey);

InputStream in = new FileInputStream("plain.txt");
OutputStream out = new CipherOutputStream
    (new FileOutputStream("encrypted.txt"), cipher);
int ch;
while ((ch = in.read()) != -1)
{   out.write((byte)ch);
}
in.close();
out.close();

System.out.println("The plaintext was:");
cipher.initDecrypt(caesarKey);
in = new CipherInputStream
    (new FileInputStream("encrypted.txt"), cipher);
while ((ch = in.read()) != -1)
{   System.out.print((char)ch);
}
in.close();
System.out.println();
    }
}
```

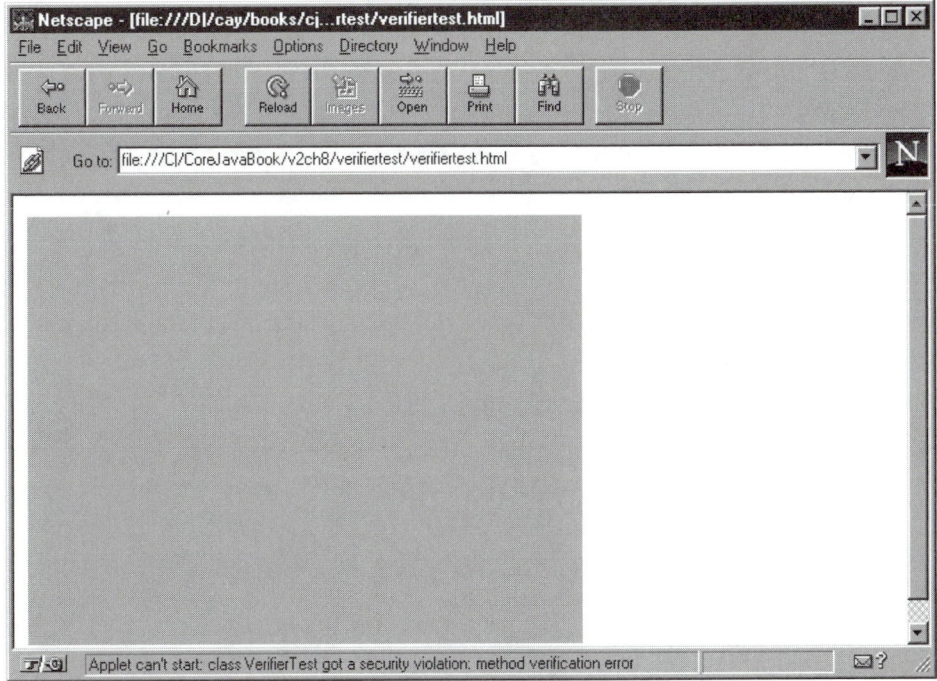

Figure 8-2: Loading a corrupted class file raises a method verification error

Security Managers

Once a class has been loaded into the virtual machine by a class loader or by the default class loading mechanism and checked by the verifier, the third Java security mechanism springs into action: the *security manager*. A security manager is a class that controls whether a specific operation is permitted. Operations checked by a security manager include:

- Whether the current thread can create a new class loader

- Whether the current thread can create a subprocess

- Whether the current thread can halt the virtual machine

- Whether the current thread can load a dynamic link library

- Whether a class can access a member of another class

- Whether the current thread can access a specified package

- Whether the current thread can define classes in a specified package

- Whether the current thread can access or modify system properties

- Whether the current thread can read from or write to a specified file

- Whether the current thread can delete a specified file

- Whether the current thread can accept a socket connection from a specified host and port number

- Whether the current thread can open a socket connection to the specified host and port number

- Whether the current thread can wait for a connection request on a specified local port number

- Whether the current thread can use IP multicast

- Whether the current thread can invoke a `stop`, `suspend`, `resume`, `destroy`, `setPriority/setMaxPriority`, `setName`, or `setDaemon` method of a given thread or thread group

- Whether the current thread can set a socket or stream handler factory

- Whether a class can start a print job

- Whether a class can access the system clipboard

- Whether a class can access the AWT event queue

- Whether the current thread is trusted to bring up a top-level window

The default behavior when running Java applications is that *no* security manager is installed, so all these operations are permitted. The applet viewer, on the other hand, immediately installs a security manager (called `AppletSecurity`) that is quite restrictive. For example, applet code is not granted any unauthorized local file access. Of course, other functions in the ambient execution environment need to have more access privileges than the applet code itself, so the security manager must check who is attempting a particular operation. For example, applets are not allowed to exit the virtual machine, but the applet viewer itself must be able to shut down. Here is the implementation of the `checkExit` method of the `AppletSecurity` class that lets the applet viewer do this.

```
public synchronized void checkExit(int status)
{  if (inClassLoader())
   // current class was loaded by applet class loader
      throw new AppletSecurityException("checkexit",
         String.valueOf(status));
}
```

Here, `inClassLoader` is a method of `SecurityManager` that checks whether *any* of the currently pending calls were made by a class that was loaded by a class loader. If the method returns `false`, then the code that is currently executing is system code and not code that was called from an applet. In that case, the `checkExit` method simply returns. Otherwise, the method throws an `AppletSecurityException`.

The `checkExit` method is called from the `exit` method of the class `Runtime`. Here is the entire code of the `exit` method:

```
public void exit(int status)
{   SecurityManager security = System.getSecurityManager();
    if (security != null)
        security.checkExit(status);
    exitInternal(status);
}
```

Here, `exitInternal` is a *private native* method that actually terminates the virtual machine. There is no other way of terminating the virtual machine, and since the `exitInternal` method is private, it cannot be called from any other class. Thus, any Java code that attempts to exit the virtual machine must go through the `exit` method. That method has been programmed to call the `checkExit` method. If the security manager wishes to disallow exiting, the `checkExit` method throws an exception and `exitInternal` is not called.

Clearly, the integrity of the security policy depends on careful coding. The providers of system services in the standard library must be careful to always consult the security manager before attempting any sensitive operation.

When you run a Java application, the default is that no security manager is running. Your program can install a specific security manager via a call to the static `setSecurityManager` method in the `System` class. Once your program installs a security manager, any attempt to install a second security manager results in a `SecurityException`. This is clearly essential; otherwise, a bad applet could install its own security manager. Thus, while it is possible to have multiple class loaders, a Java program can be governed by only one security manager. It is up to the implementor of that security manager to decide whether to grant all classes the same access or whether to take the origins of the classes into account before deciding what to do.

An Example of a Custom Security Manager

In this section we show you how to build a simple yet complete security manager. We call it the *smut security manager*. It monitors all file access and ensures that you can't open a file if it contains "bad" words (such as *sex, drugs, C++*). We can do this by overriding the `checkRead` method of the security manager class.

Our version of this method opens the file and scans its contents, then grants access to the file only when it didn't find any of the forbidden words. There is just one catch in this scenario. Consider one possible flow of events.

- A method of another class opens a disk file.

- Then, the smut security manager springs into action and uses its `checkRead` method.

But the `checkRead` method must *open the disk file* in order to check its contents, which calls the security manager again! This would result in an infinite regress unless the security manager has a way of finding out in which context it was called. The `getClassContext` method is the way to find out how the method was called. This method returns an array of class objects that gives all the classes whose calls are currently pending. For example, when the security manager is called for the first time, that array is

```
class SmutSecurityManager
class java.io.FileInputStream
class java.io.FileReader
class SecurityManagerTest
. . .
class java.awt.EventDispatchThread
```

The class in the `[0]` index gives the currently executing call. Unfortunately, you only get to see the classes, not the names of the pending methods. When the security manager itself attempts to open the file, it is called again and the `getClassContext` method returns the following array:

```
class SmutSecurityManager
class java.io.FileInputStream
class java.io.FileReader
class SmutSecurityManager
class java.io.FileInputStream
class java.io.FileReader
class SecurityManagerTest
. . .
class java.awt.EventDispatchThread
```

In this case, the security manager should permit the file access. How can we do this? We could test whether

```
getClassContext()[0] == getClassContext()[3]
```

but this approach is fragile. Here's an obvious case of where it can go wrong: Imagine that if the implementation changed, for example, so the `FileReader` constructor calls the security manager directly, then the test would be meaningless because the positions would not be the same in the array. It is far more robust to test whether *any* of the pending calls came from the same security

manager. Here is the entire code for a `checkRead` method that does this:

```
public void checkRead(String file)
{  Class[] cc = getClassContext();
   for (int i = 1; i < cc.length; i++)
       if (getClassContext()[0] == getClassContext()[i]) return;
   BufferedReader in = null;
   try
   {  in = new BufferedReader(new FileReader(file));
      String s;
      while ((s = in.readLine()) != null)
      {  for (int i = 0; i < badWords.length; i++)
         if (s.toLowerCase().indexOf(badWords[i]) != -1)
            throw new SecurityException(file);
      }
      in.close();
   }
   catch(IOException e)
   {  throw new SecurityException();
   }
   finally
   {  if (in != null)
          try { in.close(); } catch (IOException e) {}
   }
}
```

As you can see, we first test whether the read request comes from the same security manager. If not, we open the file and read it line by line. If one of the bad words is found, we throw a security exception. Otherwise, the method simply returns.

Example 8-4 shows a program that puts this security manager to work. The security manager is installed in the main function. (This is the most common place to install a security manager.) When running the program, you can specify a file. The program will load its contents into the text box. However, if the file fails the security check, the program catches the security exception and displays a message instead.

Example 8-4: SecurityManagerTest.java

```
import java.awt.*;
import java.awt.event.*;
import java.io.*;
import java.net.*;
import java.util.*;
import corejava.*;

public class SecurityManagerTest extends CloseableFrame
   implements ActionListener
{  public SecurityManagerTest()
```

```
{   System.setSecurityManager(new SmutSecurityManager());
    MenuBar mbar = new MenuBar();
    Menu m = new Menu("File");
    MenuItem m1 = new MenuItem("Open");
    m1.addActionListener(this);
    m.add(m1);
    MenuItem m2 = new MenuItem("Exit");
    m2.addActionListener(this);
    m.add(m2);
    mbar.add(m);
    setMenuBar(mbar);
    add(fileText, "Center");
}

public void actionPerformed(ActionEvent evt)
{   String arg = evt.getActionCommand();
    if (arg.equals("Open"))
    {   FileDialog d = new FileDialog(this,
            "Open text file", FileDialog.LOAD);
        d.setFile("*.txt");
        d.setDirectory(lastDir);
        d.show();
        String f = d.getFile();
        lastDir = d.getDirectory();
        if (f != null)
        {   filename = lastDir + f;
            loadTextFile();
        }
    }
    else if(arg.equals("Exit")) System.exit(0);
}

public void loadTextFile()
{   try
    {   fileText.setText("");
        BufferedReader in
            = new BufferedReader(new FileReader(filename));
        String s;
        while ((s = in.readLine()) != null)
        fileText.append(s + "\n");
        in.close();
    }
    catch (IOException e)
    {   fileText.append(e + "\n");
    }
    catch (SecurityException e)
    {   fileText.append("I am sorry, but I cannot do that.");
    }
```

```
   }

   public static void main(String[] args)
   {  Frame f = new SecurityManagerTest();
      f.show();
   }

   private TextArea fileText = new TextArea();
   private String filename = null;
   private String lastDir = "";
}

class NullSecurityManager extends SecurityManager
{   public void checkCreateClassLoader() {}
    public void checkAccess(Thread g) {}
    public void checkAccess(ThreadGroup g) {}
    public void checkExit(int status) {}
    public void checkExec(String cmd) {}
    public void checkLink(String lib) {}
    public void checkRead(FileDescriptor fd) {}
    public void checkRead(String file) {}
    public void checkRead(String file, Object context) {}
    public void checkWrite(FileDescriptor fd) {}
    public void checkWrite(String file) {}
    public void checkDelete(String file) {}
    public void checkConnect(String host, int port) {}
    public void checkConnect(String host, int port,
       Object context) {}
    public void checkListen(int port) {}
    public void checkAccept(String host, int port) {}
    public void checkMulticast(InetAddress maddr) {}
    public void checkMulticast(InetAddress maddr, byte ttl) {}
    public void checkPropertiesAccess() {}
    public void checkPropertyAccess(String key) {}
    public void checkPropertyAccess(String key, String def) {}
    public boolean checkTopLevelWindow(Object window)
    { return true; }
    public void checkPrintJobAccess() {}
    public void checkSystemClipboardAccess() {}
    public void checkAwtEventQueueAccess() {}
    public void checkPackageAccess(String pkg) {}
    public void checkPackageDefinition(String pkg) {}
    public void checkSetFactory() {}
    public void checkMemberAccess(Class clazz, int which) {}
    public void checkSecurityAccess(String provider) {}
}
```

```
class SmutSecurityManager extends NullSecurityManager
{  public void checkRead(String file)
   {  Class[] cc = getClassContext();
      for (int i = 1; i < cc.length; i++)
         if (getClassContext()[0] == getClassContext()[i])
            return;
      BufferedReader in = null;
      try
      {  in = new BufferedReader(new FileReader(file));
         String s;
         while ((s = in.readLine()) != null)
         {  for (int i = 0; i < badWords.length; i++)
            if (s.toLowerCase().indexOf(badWords[i]) != -1)
               throw new SecurityException(file);
         }
         in.close();
      }
      catch(IOException e)
      {  throw new SecurityException();
      }
      finally
      {  if (in != null)
            try { in.close(); } catch (IOException e) {}
      }
   }

   public void checkRead(String file, Object context)
   {  checkRead(file);
   }

   private String[] badWords = { "sex", "drugs", "C++" };
}
```

java.lang.System

- void setSecurityManager(SecurityManager s)

  sets the security manager for remainder of this application. If a security manager has already been set and s is not null, throws a SecurityException. If s is null, no action is taken.

- SecurityManager getSecurityManager()

  gets the system security manager; returns null if none is installed.

java.lang.SecurityManager

- `public boolean getInCheck()`

  returns the value of the `inCheck` field. That field is a protected Boolean variable of the `SecurityManager` base class. Security managers should set it to `true` while they carry out a security check.

- `Class[] getClassContext()`

  returns an array of the classes for the currently executing methods. The element at position 0 is the class of the currently running method, the element at position 1 is the class of the caller of the current method, and so on. Only the class names, not the method names, are available.

- `int classDepth(String name)`

  scans the execution stack for the most recent method of the class specified by the (fully qualified) name. Returns the position of that method, or −1 if no method of that class was found.

- `boolean inClass(String name)`

  scans the execution stack for a method of the class specified by the given name; returns `true` if the method exists. Returns `false` if no method of that class is found.

- `Class currentLoadedClass()`

  scans the execution stack for the most recent method of a class loaded by a class loader and returns that class.

- `ClassLoader currentClassLoader()`

  scans the execution stack for the most recent method of a class loaded by a class loader and returns that class loader, or returns `null` if all currently executing methods are methods of system classes.

- `int classLoaderDepth()`

  scans the execution stack for the most recent method of a class loaded by a class loader, and returns the position of that method. Returns −1 if all currently executing methods are methods of system classes.

- `boolean inClassLoader()`

  scans the execution stack for the method of a class loaded with a class loader; returns `true` if such a method exists. Returns `false` if all currently executing methods are methods of system classes.

- `void checkCreateClassLoader()`

  checks whether the current thread can create a class loader.

- void checkAccess(Thread g)

  checks whether the current thread can invoke the stop, suspend, resume, setPriority, setName, and setDaemon methods on the thread g.

- void checkAccess(ThreadGroup g)

  checks whether the current thread can invoke the stop, suspend, resume, destroy, and setMaxPriority methods on the thread group g.

- void checkExit(int status)

  checks whether the current thread can exit the virtual machine with status code status.

- void checkExec(String cmd)

  checks whether the current thread can execute the system command cmd.

- void checkLink(String lib)

  checks whether the current thread can dynamically load the library lib.

- void checkRead(FileDescriptor fd)

- void checkRead(String file)

- void checkWrite(FileDescriptor fd)

- void checkWrite(String file)

- void checkDelete(String file)

  check whether the current thread can read, write, or delete the given file.

- void checkRead(String file, Object context)

  checks whether another thread can read the given file. The other thread must have called getSecurityContext, and the return value of that call is passed as the value of the context parameter.

- void checkConnect(String host, int port)

  checks whether the current thread can connect to the given host at the given port.

- void checkConnect(String host, int port, Object context)

  checks whether another thread can connect to the given host at the given port. The other thread must have called getSecurityContext, and the return value of that call is passed as the context parameter.

- void checkListen(int port)

  checks whether the current thread can listen for a connection to the given local port.

- void checkAccept(String host, int port)

  checks whether the current thread can accept a socket connection from the given host and port.

- void checkSetFactory()

  checks whether the current thread can set the socket or stream handler factory.

- void checkPropertiesAccess()
- void checkPropertyAccess(String key)
- void checkPropertyAccess(String key, String def)

  check whether the current thread can access the system properties, or the system property with the given key.

- void checkSecurityAccess(String key)

  checks whether the current thread can access the security property with the given key.

- boolean checkTopLevelWindow(Object window)

  returns true if the given window can be displayed without a security warning.

- void checkPrintJobAccess()

  checks whether the current thread can access print jobs.

- void checkSystemClipboardAccess()

  checks whether the current thread can access the system clipboard.

- void checkAwtEventQueueAccess()

  checks whether the current thread can access the AWT event queue.

- void checkPackageAccess(String pkg)

  checks whether the current thread can load classes from the given package. This method is called from the loadClass method of some class loaders.

- void checkPackageDefinition(String pkg)

  checks whether the current thread can define new classes that are in the given package. This method is often called from the loadClass method of a custom class loader.

- void checkMemberAccess(Class cl, int member_id)

  checks whether the current thread can access a member of a class. (See Chapter 10 on how to obtain member IDs.)

The Java Security Package

To this point, we have described the security model common to both Java 1.0 and Java 1.1. The class loader, verifier, and security manager mechanisms, when combined, provide enough security to reasonably assure you that when you load applets from anywhere on the Internet, you can run them safely on your local machine. Admittedly, on a few occasions, a very clever person has found a subtle flaw in the implementation of one of these mechanisms. By exploiting such faults, one could have written applets that could break out of the sandbox and theoretically create damage on the local machine.

Sun has actively encouraged the hunt for security bugs. When one is found, Java developers squash it as quickly as possible. (James Gosling said in a speech at the first JavaOne conference that all security bugs are regarded as mission-critical bugs for which Sun will have zero tolerance.)

One way Sun encourages the hunt for new security bugs is to make the source code for the Java Virtual Machine and the security manager available to *all* interested parties. On the surface, this open policy may appear to be poor public relations—it seems that every few weeks, another very clever person finds another subtle security bug, and, to people who don't compare the severity of different security threats, Java's security may look bad. In truth, however, the open policy is a tremendous benefit for Java developers and Java users, and Sun is doing both the right and smart thing. As more and more people understand the security mechanisms and their implementation, it is reasonable to assume that all serious loopholes will be closed.[2]

As we said earlier, applets were what started the Java craze. In practice, people discovered that although they could write animated applets like the famous "nervous text" applet, applets could not do a whole lot of useful stuff in the Java 1.0 security model. For example, because applets under Java 1.0 were so closely supervised, they couldn't do much good on a corporate intranet, even though essentially no risk attaches to downloading an applet from your company's secure intranet. It quickly became clear to Sun that, for applets to become truly useful, it was important for users to be able to assign *different* levels of security, depending on where the applet originated. If an applet comes from a trusted supplier and it has not been tampered with, the user of that applet can then decide whether to give it more privileges.

---

[2] Arguably, it is probably impossible to *prove* that Java is secure because such proof would contradict some known theorems in computer science.

This added control is now possible because of the applet-signing mechanism in Java 1.1. To give more trust to an applet, we need to know two things:

1. Where did the applet come from?

2. Was the code corrupted in transit?

In the past 50 years, mathematicians and computer scientists developed sophisticated algorithms for ensuring the integrity of data and for electronic signatures. The `java.security` package contains implementations of many of these algorithms. Fortunately, you don't need to understand the underlying mathematics[3] to use the algorithms in the Java 1.1 security package. In the next sections, you will see how message digests can detect changes in data files and how digital signatures can prove the identity of the signer.

Message Digests

A message digest is a digital fingerprint of a block of data. For example, the so-called SHA1 (secure hash algorithm #1) condenses any data block, no matter how long, into a sequence of 160 bits (20 bytes). As with real fingerprints, one hopes that no two messages have the same SHA1 fingerprint. Of course, that cannot be true—there are only 2^{160} SHA1 fingerprints, so there must be some messages with the same fingerprint. But 2^{160} is so large that the probability of duplication occurring is negligible. How negligible? According to James Walsh from *True Odds--How Risks Affect Your Everyday Life* [Merritt Publishing, 1996], the chance that you will die from being struck by lightning is about one in 30,000. Now, think of 10 other people, for example, your 10 least favorite managers or professors. The chance that you and *all of them* will die from lighting strikes is about the same as that of a forged message having the same SHA1 fingerprint as the original. (Of course, more than 10 people, none of whom you are likely to know, will die from lightning. But we are talking about the far slimmer chance that *your particular choice* of people will be wiped out.)

A message digest has two essential properties.

1. If one bit or several bits of the data are changed, then the message digest also changes. Of course, there is a very slight possibility that two arbitrary messages have the same fingerprint, but if the messages are similar, then the fingerprints should be able to tell them apart.

2. If a forger has a given message and its fingerprint, that person cannot modify the message by any sequence of steps so that the resulting message has the same fingerprint as the original.

---

[3] One reference for this fascinating topic with lots of code is *Applied Cryptography: Protocols, Algorithms, and Source Code in C*, by Bruce Schneier [John Wiley & Sons, 1995]. For the mathematics behind the code, look at the *Handbook of Applied Cryptography* by Meekness et al. [CRC Press, 1996].

The second property is again a matter of probabilities, of course. Consider the following message by the millionaire father:

> *"Upon my death, my property shall be divided equally among my children; however, my son George shall receive nothing."*

That message has an SHA1 fingerprint of

```
2D 8B 35 F3 BF 49 CD B1 94 04 E0 66 21 2B 5E 57 70 49 E1 7E
```

The distrustful father has deposited the message with one attorney and the fingerprint with another. Now, suppose George can bribe the lawyer holding the message. He wants to change the message so that Bill gets nothing. Of course, that changes the fingerprint to a completely different bit pattern:

```
2A 33 0B 4B B3 FE CC 1C 9D 5C 01 A7 09 51 0B 49 AC 8F 98 92
```

Can George find some other wording that matches the fingerprint? If he had a million computers, each computing a million messages a second, it would take about 100,000 years to find a message he could substitute.

A number of algorithms have been designed to compute these message digests. The two best-known are SHA1, the secure hash algorithm developed by the National Institute of Standards and Technology, and MD5, an algorithm invented by Ronald Rivest of MIT. Both algorithms scramble the bits of a message in ingenious ways. For details about these algorithms, see, for example, *Network and Internetwork Security* by William Stallings [Prentice-Hall, 1995]. Note that recently, subtle regularities have been discovered in MD5, and some cryptographers recommend avoiding it and using SHA1 for that reason. (Both algorithms are easy to compute.)

Java implements both SHA1 and MD5. The `MessageDigest` class is a *factory* for creating objects that encapsulate the fingerprinting algorithms. It has a static method, called `getInstance`, that returns an object of a class that extends the `MessageDigest` class. This means the `MessageDigest` class serves double duty:

- As a factory class
- As the base class for all message digest algorithms

For example, here is how you obtain an object that can compute SHA fingerprints.

```
MessageDigest alg = MessageDigest.getInstance("SHA-1");
```

(To get an object that can compute MD5, use the string `"MD5"` as the argument to `getInstance`.)

After you obtained a `MessageDigest` object, you feed it all the bytes in the message by repeatedly calling the `update` method. For example, the following code passes all bytes in a file to the `alg` object created above to do the fingerprinting:

```
FileInputStream in = new FileInputStream(f);
int ch;

while ((ch = in.read()) != -1)
    alg.update((byte)ch);
```

When you are done, call the `digest` method. This method pads the input—as required by the fingerprinting algorithm—does the computation, and returns the digest as an array of bytes.

```
byte[] hash = currentAlgorithm.digest();
```

The program in Example 8-5 computes a message digest, using either SHA or MD5. You can load the data to be digested from a file, or you can type a message in the text area. Figure 8-3 shows the application.

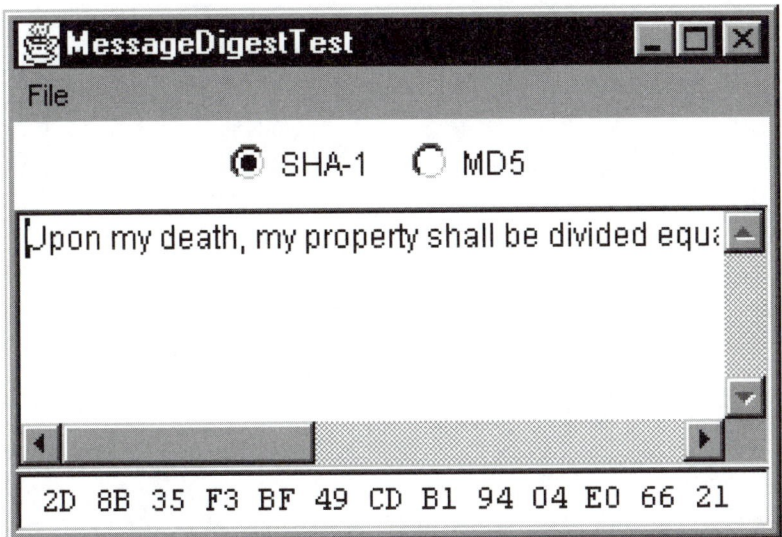

Figure 8-3: Computing a message digest

Example 8-5: MessageDigestTest.java

```
import java.io.*;
import java.security.*;
import java.awt.*;
import java.awt.event.*;
import corejava.*;

public class MessageDigestTest extends CloseableFrame
    implements ActionListener, ItemListener
```

```java
{  public MessageDigestTest()
   {  Panel p = new Panel();

      CheckboxGroup g = new CheckboxGroup();
      addCheckbox(p, "SHA-1", g, true);
      addCheckbox(p, "MD5", g, false);
      add(p, "North");
      add(message, "Center");
      add(digest, "South");
      digest.setFont(new Font("Courier", Font.PLAIN, 12));

      setAlgorithm("SHA-1");

      MenuBar mbar = new MenuBar();
      Menu m = new Menu("File");
      MenuItem m1 = new MenuItem("File digest");
      m1.addActionListener(this);
      m.add(m1);
      MenuItem m2 = new MenuItem("Text area digest");
      m2.addActionListener(this);
      m.add(m2);
      MenuItem m3 = new MenuItem("Exit");
      m3.addActionListener(this);
      m.add(m3);
      mbar.add(m);
      setMenuBar(mbar);
   }

   public void addCheckbox(Panel p, String name,
      CheckboxGroup g, boolean v)
   {  Checkbox c = new Checkbox(name, g, v);
      c.addItemListener(this);
      p.add(c);
   }

   public void itemStateChanged(ItemEvent evt)
   {  if (evt.getStateChange() == ItemEvent.SELECTED)
         setAlgorithm((String)evt.getItem());
   }

   public void setAlgorithm(String alg)
   {  try
      {  currentAlgorithm = MessageDigest.getInstance(alg);
      }
      catch(NoSuchAlgorithmException e)
      {  digest.setText("" + e);
      }
   }
```

```java
public void actionPerformed(ActionEvent evt)
{  String arg = evt.getActionCommand();
   if (arg.equals("File digest"))
   {  FileDialog d = new FileDialog(this,
         "Open text file", FileDialog.LOAD);
      d.setFile("*.txt");
      d.setDirectory(lastDir);
      d.show();
      String f = d.getFile();
      lastDir = d.getDirectory();
      if (f != null)
      {  filename = lastDir + f;
         computeDigest(loadBytes(filename));
      }
   }
   else if (arg.equals("Text area digest"))
   {  String m = message.getText();
      computeDigest(m.getBytes());
   }
   else if(arg.equals("Exit")) System.exit(0);
}

public byte[] loadBytes(String name)
{  FileInputStream in = null;

   try
   {  in = new FileInputStream(name);
      ByteArrayOutputStream buffer
         = new ByteArrayOutputStream();
      int ch;
      while ((ch = in.read()) != -1)
         buffer.write(ch);
      return buffer.toByteArray();
   }
   catch (IOException e)
   {  if (in != null)
      {  try { in.close(); } catch (IOException e2) {}
      }
      return null;
   }
}

public void computeDigest(byte[] b)
{  currentAlgorithm.reset();
   currentAlgorithm.update(b);
   byte[] hash = currentAlgorithm.digest();
   String d = "";
   for (int i = 0; i < hash.length; i++)
```

```
    {   d += new Format("%02X ").form(hash[i] & 0xFF);
        }
        digest.setText(d);
    }

    public static void main(String[] args) throws Exception
    {   Frame f = new MessageDigestTest();
        f.setSize(300, 200);
        f.show();
    }

    private TextArea message = new TextArea();
    private TextField digest = new TextField();
    private String filename = null;
    private String lastDir = "";
    private MessageDigest currentAlgorithm;
}
```

java.security.MessageDigest

- `static MessageDigest getInstance(String algorithm)`

  returns a `MessageDigest` object that implements the specified algorithm. Throws a `NoSuchAlgorithmException` if the algorithm is not provided.

  Parameters: `algorithm`   the name of the algorithm, such as `"SHA-1"` or `"MD5"`

- `void update(byte input)`

- `void update(byte[] input)`

- `void update(byte[] input, int offset, int len)`

  update the digest, using the specified bytes.

- `byte[] digest()`

  completes the hash computation, returns the computed digest, and resets the algorithm object.

- `void reset()`

  resets the digest.

Digital Signatures

In the last section, you saw how to compute a message digest, a fingerprint for the original message. If the message is altered, then the fingerprint of the altered message will not match the fingerprint of the original. If the message and its fingerprint are delivered separately, then the recipient can check whether the message has been tampered with. However, if both the message and the fingerprint were intercepted, it is an easy matter to modify the message and then recompute the fingerprint. After all, the message digest algorithms are publicly known, and they don't require any secret keys. In that case, the recipient of the forged message and the recomputed fingerprint would never know that the message has been altered. In this section, you will see how *digital signatures* can *authenticate* a message. When a message is authenticated, you *know*

- The message came from the claimed sender.

- The message was not altered.

To understand how digital signatures work, we need to explain a little bit behind what is now called *public key cryptography*. Public key cryptography is based on the notion of a *public* key and *private* key. The idea is that you publicize to the world a method of encrypting information (via the public key). However, once data is encrypted, only the person who has the private key can figure out what the original message was. Thus, encrypted messages can be sent over unsecure channels[4]. Many cryptographic algorithms, such as DSA (the Digital Signature Algorithm) and RSA (the encryption algorithm invented by Rivest, Shamir and Adleman), use this idea. The exact structure of the keys and what it means for them to match depend on the algorithm. For example, here is a matching pair of public and private DSA keys:

Public key:

```
p: fca682ce8e12caba26efccf7110e526db078b05edecbcd1eb4a208f3ae16
   17ae01f35b91a47e6df63413c5e12ed0899bcd132acd50d99151bdc43ee7375
   92e17

q: 962eddcc369cba8ebb260ee6b6a126d9346e38c5

g: 678471b27a9cf44ee91a49c5147db1a9aaf244f05a434d6486931d2d1427
   1b9e35030b71fd73da179069b32e2935630e1c2062354d0da20a6c416e50be79
   4ca4

y: c0b6e67b4ac098eb1a32c5f8c4c1f0e7e6fb9d832532e27d0bdab9ca2d2a
   8123ce5a8018b8161a760480fadd040b927281ddb22cb9bc4df596d7de4d1b97
   7d50
```

[4] Kahn remarks in the new edition of his *Codebreakers* that this was the first *new* idea in cryptography in hundreds of years.

Private key:

```
p:  fca682ce8e12caba26efccf7110e526db078b05edecbcd1eb4a208f3ae16
    17ae01f35b91a47e6df63413c5e12ed0899bcd132acd50d99151bdc43ee73759
    2e17

q:  962eddcc369cba8ebb260ee6b6a126d9346e38c5

g:  678471b27a9cf44ee91a49c5147db1a9aaf244f05a434d6486931d2d1427
    1b9e35030b71fd73da179069b32e2935630e1c2062354d0da20a6c416e50be79
    4ca4

x:  146c09f881656cc6c51f27ea6c3a91b85ed1d70a
```

There is a mathematical relationship between these keys, but the exact nature of the relationship is not interesting for practical programming. (If you are interested, you can look it up in *Network and Internetwork Security* by William Stallings [Prentice-Hall, 1995, page 345] or *The Handbook of Cryptography* mentioned earlier.)

The obvious question is how to generate the pair of keys. Usually, this is done by feeding the result of some random process in to a deterministic procedure that returns the key pair to you. Luckily, how to get a random key pair for public key cryptography is not a question anyone but cyptographers and mathematicians need to worry about.

What is implicitly being assumed is that it is impossible to compute the private key from the public key in any reasonable amount of time. (For example, RSA depends on factoring large numbers; this is assumed to be computationally infeasible for the 200+ digit numbers routinely used for strong version of RSA.) This means you can safely place your public key onto your Web page or send it by e-mail. However, you must keep your private key very safe.

One reason for keeping your private key safe is that you can use it to prove who you are—what is particularly neat about public key cryptography is that you can also use it to sign a message. This signature depends on the results of applying the public key and then the private key giving you the original message *regardless of which you do first*.

So, say Joe wants to send his friend Tom a message, and Tom of course wants to know this message came from Joe. What Tom does is use his private key to encrypt something like "I, Joe, wrote this message," Tom, of course, knows Joe's public key. So, since the order is irrelevant, Tom can apply the public key to the message and see if he gets Joe's message or just gibberish. If he gets Joe's message, he can rest assured that Joe sent the message. See Figure 8-4.

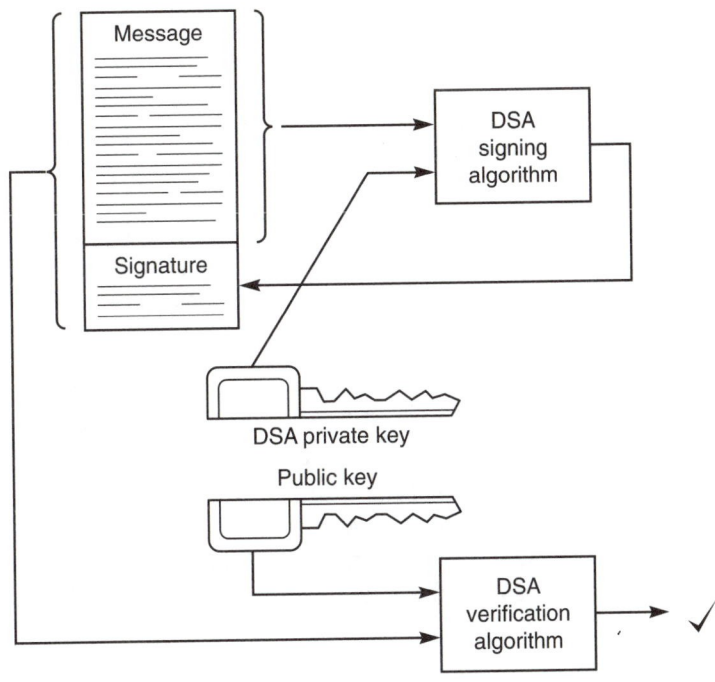

Figure 8-4: Public Key signature exchange using DSA

You can see why security for your private key is all important. If someone steals your private key or if a government can require you to turn it over, then you are hosed. The thief can impersonate you by sending messages that others will believe come from you.

Finally, it may seem difficult to believe that nobody can compute the private key from the public keys, but nobody has ever found an algorithm to do this for DSA or RSA. Except in special cases what is used is essentially a more sophisticated version of brute force", trying lots of the possible private keys and checking if they match. With sufficient key length, a brute-force attack would require more computers than can be built from all the atoms in the solar system crunching away for thousands of years. Most cryptographers believe that keys with a "modulus" of 2,000 bits or more are completely safe from any attack.

The Java security package comes with DSA. If you want to use RSA, you'll need to buy the classes from RSA (www.rsa.com). Let us put the DSA algorithm to work. Actually, there are three algorithms:

1. To generate a key pair

2. To sign a message

3.   To verify a signature

Of course, you generate a key pair only once and then use it for signing and verifying many messages. To generate a new random key pair, make sure you use *truly random* numbers. For example, the regular random number generator in the Random class, seeded by the current date and time, is not random enough. (The jargon says the basic random number generator in java.util is not "cryptographically secure.") For example, supposing the computer clock is accurate to 1/10 of a second; then, there are at most 864,000 seeds per day. If an attacker knows the day a key was issued (which one can often deduce from the expiration date), then it is an easy matter to generate all possible seeds for that day.

The SecureRandom class generates random numbers that are far more secure than those produced by the Random class. You still need to provide a seed to start the number sequence at a random spot. The best method for doing this is to obtain random input from a hardware device such as a white-noise generator. Another reasonable source for random input is to ask the user to type away aimlessly on the keyboard. But each keystroke should contribute only one or two bits to the random seed. Once you gather such random bits in an array of bytes, you pass it to the setSeed method.

```
SecureRandom secrand = new SecureRandom();
byte[] b = new byte[20];
// fill with truly random bits
secrand.setSeed(b);
```

If you don't seed the random number generator, then it will compute its own 20-byte seed by launching threads, putting them to sleep, and measuring the exact time when they are awakened.

NOTE: This is an innovative algorithm that, at this point, is *not* known to be safe. And, in the past, algorithms that relied on timing other components of the computer, such as hard disk access time, were later shown not to be completely random.

Once you seed the generator, you can then draw random bytes with the nextBytes method.

```
byte[] randomBytes = new byte[64];
secrand.nextBytes(randomBytes);
```

Actually, to compute a new DSA key, you don't compute the random numbers yourself. You just pass the random number generator object to the DSA key generation algorithm.

To make a new key pair, you need a KeyPairGenerator object. Just as with the MessageDigest class of the preceding section, the KeyPairGenerator class is

both a factory class and the base class for actual key pair generation algorithms. To get a DSA key pair generator, you call the `getInstance` method with the string "DSA".

```
KeyPairGenerator keygen = KeyPairGenerator.getInstance("DSA");
```

The returned object is actually an object of the class `sun.security.provider.DSAKeyPairGenerator`, which is a subclass of `KeyPairGenerator`.

To generate keys, you must initialize the key generation algorithm object with the key strength and a secure random number generator. Note that the key strength is not the length of the generated keys but the size of one of the building blocks of the key. In the case of DSA, it is the number of bits in the modulus, one of the mathematical quantities that makes up the public and private keys. Suppose you want to generate a key with a modulus of 512 bits:

```
SecureRandom secrand = new SecureRandom();
secrand.setSeed(...);
keygen.initialize(512, secrand);
```

Now you are ready to generate key pairs.

```
KeyPair keys = keygen.generateKeyPair();
KeyPair morekeys = keygen.generateKeyPair();
```

Each key pair has a public and a private key.

```
PublicKey pubkey = keys.getPublic();
PrivateKey privkey = keys.getPrivate();
```

To sign a message, you need a signature algorithm object. You use the `Signature` factory class:

```
Signature signalg = Signature.getInstance("DSA");
```

Signature algorithm objects can be used both to sign and to verify a message. To prepare the object for message signing, use the `initSign` method and pass the private key to the signature algorithm.

```
signalg.initSign(privkey);
```

Now, you use the `update` method to add bytes to the algorithm objects, in the same way as with the message digest algorithm.

```
while ((ch = in.read()) != -1)
    signalg.update((byte)ch);
```

Finally, you can compute the signature with the `sign` method. The signature is returned as an array of bytes.

```
byte[] signature = signalg.sign();
```

The recipient of the message must obtain a DSA signature algorithm object and prepare it for signature verification by calling the `initVerify` method with the public key as parameter.

```
Signature verifyalg = Signature.getInstance("DSA");
verifyalg.initVerify(pubkey);
```

Then, the message must be sent to the algorithm object.

```
while ((ch = in.read()) != -1)
    verifyalg.update((byte)ch);
```

Finally, you can verify the signature.

```
boolean check = verifyalg.verify(signature);
```

If the `verify` method returns `true`, then the signature was a valid signature of the message that was signed with the matching private key. That is, both the sender and the contents of the message have been authenticated.

Example 8-6 demonstrates the key generation, signing, and verification processes.

Example 8-6: SignatureTest.java

```
import java.security.*;

public class SignatureTest
{  public static void main(String[] args)
   {  try
      {  KeyPairGenerator keygen
            = KeyPairGenerator.getInstance("DSA");
         SecureRandom secrand = new SecureRandom();
         keygen.initialize(512, secrand);

         KeyPair keys1 = keygen.generateKeyPair();
         PublicKey pubkey1 = keys1.getPublic();
         PrivateKey privkey1 = keys1.getPrivate();

         KeyPair keys2 = keygen.generateKeyPair();
         PublicKey pubkey2 = keys2.getPublic();
         PrivateKey privkey2 = keys2.getPrivate();

         Signature signalg = Signature.getInstance("DSA");
         signalg.initSign(privkey1);
         String message
            = "Pay authors a bonus of $20,000.";
         signalg.update(message.getBytes());
         byte[] signature = signalg.sign();
         Signature verifyalg = Signature.getInstance("DSA");
         verifyalg.initVerify(pubkey1);
```

```
          verifyalg.update(message.getBytes());
          if (!verifyalg.verify(signature))
              System.out.print("not ");
          System.out.println("signed with private key 1");

          verifyalg.initVerify(pubkey2);
          verifyalg.update(message.getBytes());
          if (!verifyalg.verify(signature))
              System.out.print("not ");
          System.out.println("signed with private key 2");
      }
      catch(Exception e)
      {   System.out.println("Error " + e);
      }
   }
}
```

`java.security.KeyPairGenerator`

- `static KeyPairGenerator getInstance(String algorithm)`

  returns a `KeyPairGenerator` object that implements the specified algorithm. Throws a `NoSuchAlgorithmException` if the algorithm is not provided.

Parameters:	algorithm	the name of the algorithm, such as `"DSA"`

- `void initialize(int strength, SecureRandom random)`

Parameters:	strength	an algorithm-specific measurements, typically, the number of bits of one of the algorithm parameters
	random	the source of random bits for generating keys

- `KeyPair generateKeyPair()`

  generatesa new key pair.

`java.security.KeyPair`

- `Key getPrivate()`

  returns the private key from the key pair.

- `Key getPublic()`

  returns the public key from the key pair.

java.security.Signature

- `static Signature getInstance(String algorithm)`

  returns a `Signature` object that implements the specified algorithm. Throws a `NoSuchAlgorithmException` if the algorithm is not provided.

  Parameters: algorithm   the name of the algorithm, such as `"DSA"`

- `void initSign(PrivateKey publicKey)`

  initializes this object for signing. Throws an `InvalidKeyException` if the key type does not match the algorithm type.

  Parameters: privateKey   the private key of the identity whose signature is being computed

- `void update(byte input)`
- `void update(byte[] input)`
- `void update(byte[] input, int offset, int len)`

  update the message buffer, using the specified bytes.

- `byte[] sign()`

  completes the signature computation and returns the computed signature.

- `void initVerify(PublicKey publicKey)`

  initializes this object for verification. Throws an `InvalidKeyException` if the key type does not match the algorithm type.

  Parameters: publicKey   the public key of the identity to be verified

- `boolean verify(byte[] signature)`

  checks whether the signature is valid.

Authentication

Suppose you get a message from your friend, signed by your friend with his private key, using the method we just showed you. You may already have his public key, or you can easily get it by asking him for a copy or by getting it from your friend's Web page. Then, you can verify that the message was in fact authored by your friend and has not been tampered with. Now, suppose you get a message from a stranger who claims to represent a famous software company, urging you to run the program that is attached to the message. The stranger even sends you a copy of his public key so you can verify that he authored the message. You check that the signature is valid. This proves that the message was signed with the matching private key and that it has not been corrupted.

Be careful: *you still have no idea who wrote the message.* Anyone could have generated a pair of public and private keys, signed the message with the private key, and sent the signed message and the public key to you. The problem of determining the identity of the sender is called the *authentication problem.*

The usual way to solve the authentication problem is simple. Suppose the stranger and you have a common acquaintance whom you both trust. Suppose the stranger meets your acquaintance in person and hands over a disk with the public key. Your acquaintance later meets you, assures you that he met the stranger and that the stranger indeed works for the famous software company, and then gives you the disk (see Figure 8-5). That way, your acquaintance vouches for the authenticity of the stranger.

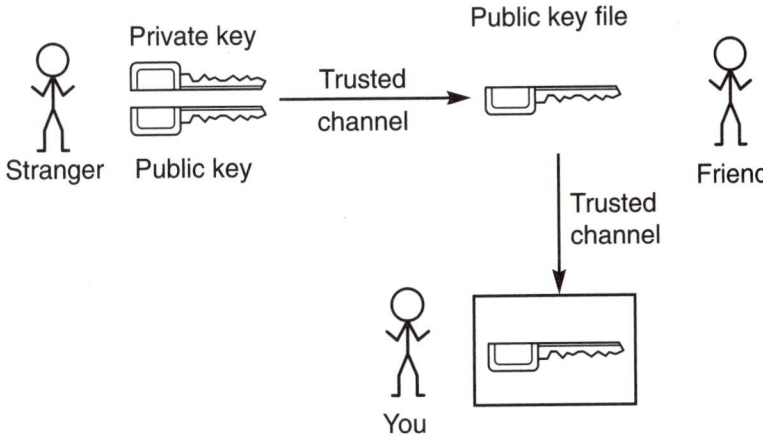

Figure 8-5: Authentication through a trusted intermediary

In fact, your acquaintance does not actually need to meet you. Instead, he can apply his private signature to the stranger's public key file (see Figure 8-6). When you get the public key file, you verify the signature of your acquaintance, and because you trust him, you are confident that he did check the stranger's credentials before applying his signature.

However, you may not have a common acquaintance. Some trust models assume that there is always a chain of "trust"—a chain of mutual acquaintances, so that you trust every member of that chain. In practice, of course, that isn't always true. You may trust your acquaintance, Amy, and you know that Amy trusts Bob, but you don't know Bob and aren't sure if you trust him. Other trust models assume that there is a benevolent big brother in whom we all trust.

Private key   Key file   Private key

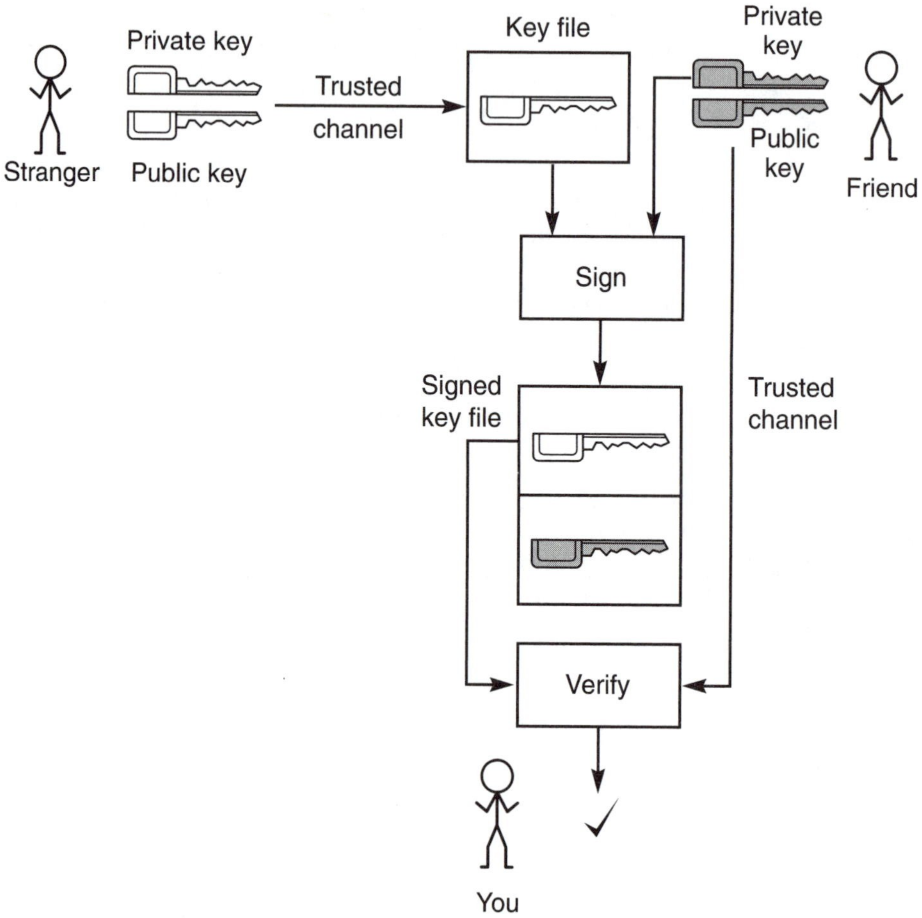

Trusted channel

Stranger   Public key   Public key   Friend

Sign

Signed key file

Trusted channel

Verify

You ✓

Figure 8-6: Authentication through a trusted intermediary's signature

Some companies are working to become such big brothers, such as Verisign, Inc. (www.verisign.com), and, yes, the United States Postal Service.

In real life, people will use some combination of the two approaches. That's why you may be asked to sign someone's public key. Digital signatures may also be signed by one or more groups who will vouch for the authenticity, and you will need to evaluate to what degree you trust the authenticators. You might place a great deal of trust in Verisign, seeing that they went to a great deal of trouble by hiring a CEO with aquiline features and by requiring multiple people with black attache cases to come together into a secure chamber whenever new master keys are to be minted.

However, you should have realistic expectations about what is actually being authenticated. Stratton Sklavos, the CEO of Verisign, does not personally meet every individual who has a public key that is authenticated by Verisign. More likely, that individual just filled out a form on a Web page (see Figure 8-7).

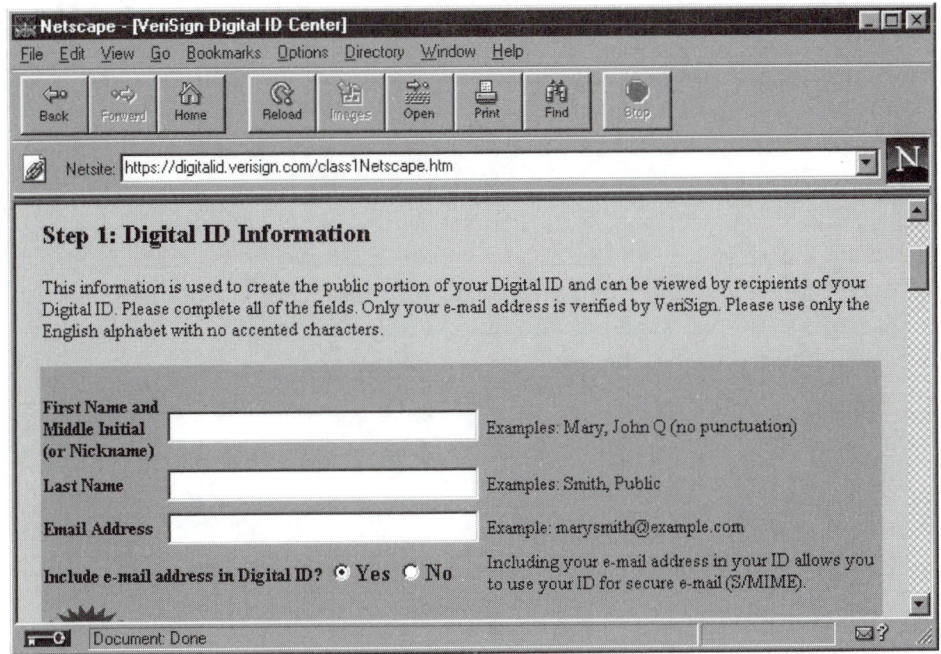

Figure 8-7: Request for a digital ID

Such a form asks the requestor to specify the name, organization, country, and e-mail address. Typically, the key (or instructions on how to fetch the key) is mailed to that e-mail address. Thus, you can be reasonably assured that the e-mail address is genuine, but the requestor could have filled in *any* name and organization. With a "class 1" ID from Verisign, that information is not verified. There are more stringent classes of IDs. With higher classes of IDs, Verisign will require the requestor to appear before a notary public, will check the financial rating of the requestor, and so on. Other authenticators will have different procedures. Thus, when you receive an authenticated message, it is important that you understand what, in fact, is being authenticated.

The Java Authentication Framework

The basic types in the Java authetication framework are the `Principal` interface and the `Identity` class. A *principal* is a real-world entity such as a person, organization, or company. A principal has a name. An *identity* is a principal with a public key. An identity can have *certificates* that authenticate it. Thus, an identity has three important accessor methods:

```
Identity id = new Identity("James Smith");
String name = id.getName();
PublicKey pubkey = id.getKey();
Certificate[] certs = id.certificates();
```

`Certificate` is an interface. A certificate has a *principal*, the identity that is being certified, and a *guarantor*, the identity with which the principal is associated for this certificate. The `encode` and `decode` methods let you write certificates to a stream and read them from a stream. Actual certificate classes must implement these methods. They also must supply other important details, in particular, the claims that the certificate actually certifies.

The name and key of an identity must be unique within its *identity scope*. The `IdentityScope` class represents a collection of identities.

```
IdentityScope departmentScope = new IdentityScope("Java
    Technology group");
. . .
Identity[] identities[] = departmentScope.identities();
```

Conversely, each identity stores its scope.

```
IdentityScope scope = id.getScope();
```

For example, the Java Technology group within Famous Software can be an identity scope. That way, the name "James Smith" in the Java Technology group doesn't conflict with "James Smith" in the Finance department. Of course, there are Java Technology groups and finance departments in many organizations. To keep *those* names safe from conflicts, the `IdentityScope` class extends the `Identity` class, that is, identity scopes themselves have identity scopes. In our example, Famous Software is an identity scope, and it is the scope of the Java Technology group scope. You set the scopes as the second argument of the `Identity` and `IdentityScope` constructors.

```
IdentityScope companyScope = new IdentityScope("Famous
    Software");
IdentityScope departmentScope = new IdentityScope("Java
    Technology group", companyScope);
Identity id = new Identity("James Smith", departmentScope);
```

Note that identity scopes can themselves have keys and certificates.

Each Java Virtual Machine has a *system identity scope*, an object of class
`IdentityScope` (or a subclass), which is available to all Java programs using
that virtual machine. You get the system identity scope by calling the static
`getSystemScope` method:

```
IdentityScope systemScope = IdentityScope.getSystemScope();
```

By default, this is an instance of the class
`sun.security.provider.IdentityDatabase`, a subclass of `IdentityScope`.
You can set another class by editing the `system.scope` entry in the file
`jdk\lib\security\java.security`. Or, you can set another system scope for
your own use with the static `setSystemScope` method, without affecting other
users of the virtual machine. Actually, you won't normally want to replace the
system identity scope. It is easier to use your own identity scope and add it to
the system identity scope.

The last class in the authentication framework that we need to discuss is
`Signer`. A signer is simply an identity with a public and private key pair.

Figure 8-8 shows the relationships between these classes and interfaces.

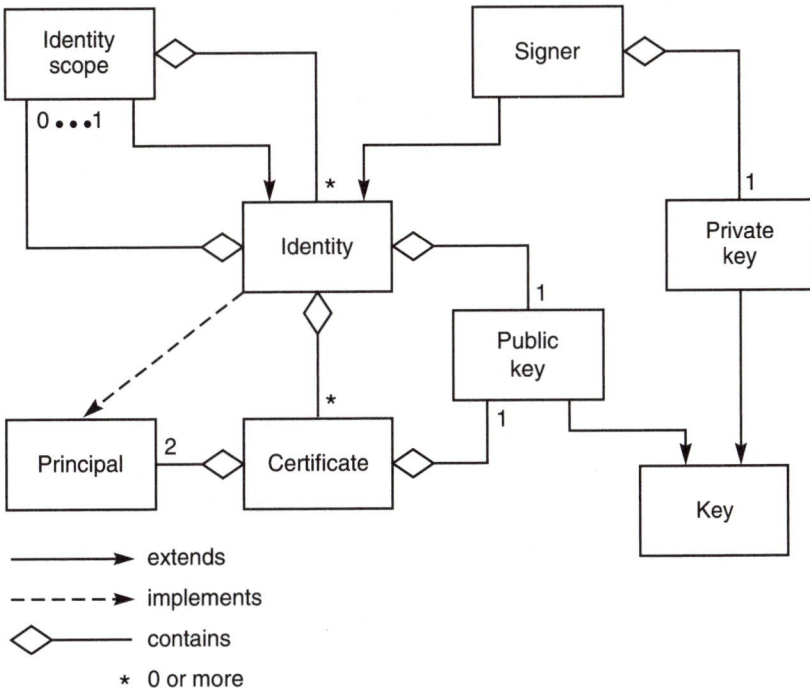

**Figure 8-8: The classes and interfaces in the Java authentication
framework**

Unfortunately, in the current version of Java, no public classes put this framework to use. JavaSoft promises support for certificates for Java 1.2. Java 1.1 supports only signed applets. Therefore, there actually are Java classes for generating, reading, and using certificates. However, these classes are in the private "sun" hierarchy. For example, the class `sun.security.x509.X509Cert` (which implements the `Certificate` interface of the security framework) represents a certificate in the X.509 format.

In the next two sections, we look at the structure of X.509 certificates and the Java tools used to generate them.

java.security.Principal

- `String getName()`

  returns the name of this principal.

java.security.Identity

- `Identity(String name)`

  constructs an identity with the specified name and no scope.

- `Identity(String name, IdentityScope scope)`

  constructs an identity with the specified name and scope. Throws a `KeyManagementException` if there is already an identity with the same name in the scope.

- `void addCertificate(Certificate c)`

  adds a certificate for this identity.

- `void removeCertificate(Certificate c)`

  removes a certificate from this identity.

- `Certificate[] certificates()`

  returns an array of all the certificates for this identity.

- `String getName()`

  returns the name of this identity.

- `void setPublicKey(PublicKey k)`

  sets the public key of this identity.

- `PublicKey getPublicKey()`

  returns the public key of this identity.

- `IdentityScope getScope()`

  returns the identity scope of this identity.

---

java.security.Signer

- `Signer(String name)`

  Constructs a signer with the specified name and no scope.

- `Identity(String name, IdentityScope scope)`

  constructs a signer with the specified name and scope.

- `PrivateKey getPublicKey()`

  returns the private key of this signer.

- `void setKeyPair(KeyPair k)`

  sets the public and private key of this signer.

---

java.security.IdentityScope

- `IdentityScope(String name)`

  constructs a new identity scope with the specified name.

- `IdentityScope(String name, IdentityScope scope)`

  constructs an identity scope with the specified name and scope. Throws a `KeyManagementException` if there is already an identity scope with the same name in the parent scope.

- `static IdentityScope getSystemScope()`

  returns the system identity scope, a scope that is established by the Java Virtual Machine.

- `Identity getIdentity(String name)`

  returns the identity in this scope with the specified name, or `null` if no match is found.

- `Identity getIdentity(Principal principal)`

  returns the identity in this scope with the same name as the specified principal, or `null` if no match is found.

- `Identity getIdentity(PublicKey key)`

  returns the identity in this scope with the specified key, or `null` if no match is found.

- `void addIdentity(Identity id)`

  adds an identity to this scope. Throws a `KeyManagementException` if there is already an identity with the same name in the scope.

- `void removeIdentity(Identity id)`

  removes an identity from this scope. Throws a `KeyManagementException` if the identity could not be found.

- `Enumeration identities()`

  returns an enumeration of all identities in this identity scope.

- `int size()`

  returns the number of identities within this identity scope.

 `java.security.Certificate`

- `Principal getGuarantor()`

  returns the principal who guarantees the authenticity of this certificate. To be useful, this must be a trusted entity, such as a certificate authority.

- `Principal getPrincipal()`

  returns the owner of the key pair that is being guaranteed by this certificate.

- `PublicKey getPublicKey()`

  returns the public key that is being guaranteed by this certificate.

- `void encode(OutputStream stream)`

  encodes this certificate to an output stream in a format that can be read by the `decode` method.

- `void decode(InputStream stream)`

  decodes this certificate from an output stream.

- `String getFormat()`

  returns the name of the encoding format, such as `"X.509"`.

The X.509 Certficate Format

One of the most common formats for signed certificates is the X.509 format. X.509 certificates are widely used by Verisign, Microsoft, JavaSoft, and many other companies, for signing e-mail messages, authenticating program code, and certifying many other kinds of data. The X.509 standard is part of the X.500 series of recommendations for a directory service by the international telephone standards body, the CCITT. In its simplest form, an X.509 certificate contains the following data:

- Version of certificate format

- Serial number of certificate

- Signature algorithm identifier (algorithm ID + parameters of the algorithm used to sign the certificate)

- Name of the signer of the certificate

- Period of validity (begin/end date)

- Name of the identity being certified

- Public key of identity being certified (algorithm ID + parameters of the algorithm + public key value)

- Signature (hash code of all preceding fields, encoded with private key of signer)

Thus, the signer guarantees that a certain identity has a particular public key.

Extensions to the basic X.509 format make it possible for the certificates to contain additional information. For more information on the structure of X.509 certificates, see http://www.ietf.cnri.reston.va.us/ids.by.wg/X.509.html.

The precise structure of X.509 certificates is described in a formal notation, called "abstract syntax notation #1" or ASN.1. Figure 8-9 shows the ASN.1 definition of version 3 of the X.509 format. The exact syntax is not important for us, but, as you can see, ASN.1 gives a precise definition of the structure of a certificate file. The *basic encoding rules,* or BER,describe precisely how to save this structure in a binary file. That is, BER describes how to encode integers, character strings, bit strings, and constructs such as SEQUENCE, CHOICE, and OPTIONAL. (Actually, the BER rules are not unique; there are several ways of specifying some elements. The *distinguished encoding rules* (DER) remove these ambiguities. For a readable description of the BER encoding format, we recommend *A Layman's Guide to a Subset of ASN.1, BER, and DER* by Burton S. Kaliski, Jr., available from http://www.rsa.com/rsalabs/pubs/PKCS/).

```
Certificate  ::=  SEQUENCE  {
        tbsCertificate        TBSCertificate,
        signatureAlgorithm    AlgorithmIdentifier,
        signature             BIT STRING  }

    TBSCertificate  ::=  SEQUENCE  {
        version          [0]  EXPLICIT Version DEFAULT v1,
        serialNumber          CertificateSerialNumber,
        signature             AlgorithmIdentifier,
        issuer                Name,
        validity              Validity,
        subject               Name,
        subjectPublicKeyInfo  SubjectPublicKeyInfo,
        issuerUniqueID   [1]  IMPLICIT UniqueIdentifier OPTIONAL,
                              -- If present, version must be v2
                                    or v3
        subjectUniqueID  [2]  IMPLICIT UniqueIdentifier OPTIONAL,
                              -- If present, version must be v2
                                    or v3
        extensions       [3]  EXPLICIT Extensions OPTIONAL
                              -- If present, version must be v3
        }

    Version  ::=  INTEGER  {  v1(0), v2(1), v3(2)  }

    CertificateSerialNumber  ::=  INTEGER

    Validity ::= SEQUENCE {
        notBefore        CertificateValidityDate,
        notAfter         CertificateValidityDate }

    CertificateValidityDate ::= CHOICE {
        utcTime          UTCTime,
        generalTime      GeneralizedTime }

    UniqueIdentifier  ::=  BIT STRING

    SubjectPublicKeyInfo  ::=  SEQUENCE  {
        algorithm             AlgorithmIdentifier,
        subjectPublicKey      BIT STRING  }

    Extensions  ::=  SEQUENCE OF Extension

    Extension  ::=  SEQUENCE  {
        extnID      OBJECT IDENTIFIER,
        critical    BOOLEAN DEFAULT FALSE,
        extnValue   OCTET STRING  }
```

Figure 8-9: ASN.1 definition of X.509v3

Generating Certificates

The JDK 1.1 comes with the `javakey` program, which is a rudimentary tool to generate and manage a set of certificates. Ultimately, the functionality of this tool will be embedded in other, more user-friendly programs that interact with actual certificate authorities. But right now, we need to use `javakey` to generate sample certificates. We do not discuss all of the `javakey` features—see the JDK documentation for complete information.

The `javakey` program manages a database of identities and signers. By default, that database is called `identitydb.obj`, and it is stored in the Java installation directory (such as `c:\jdk`). You can change that location by adding a line

```
identity.database=database location
```

to the security file `\jdk\lib\security\java.security`. In fact, if you were to use the `javakey`-generated database for any serious purpose, you would need to safeguard this file—it contains the private keys of signers. By the way, the file `identitydb.obj` is a serialized object of type `sun.security.provider.IdentityDatabase`, a class that extends the `IdentityScope` class described previously.

To add new identities and signers to the database, call `javakey` with the `-c` (create identity) or `-cs` (create signer) flag, followed by the name of the principal. In our examples, we use e-mail addresses as names since they are guaranteed to be unique.

```
javakey -cs cay@horstmann.com
javakey -c gcornell@ix.netcom.com
```

To see the state of the database, use the `-ld` (list details) option. The command

```
javakey -ld
```

produces the following output, showing that Gary is stored as an identity and Cay as a signer.

```
gcornell@ix.netcom.com[identitydb.obj][not trusted]
          no public key
          no certificates
          No further information available.


[Signer]cay@horstmann.com[identitydb.obj][not trusted]
          no keys
          no certificates
          No further information available.
```

We discuss the trust level (which by default is "not trusted") in the section on code signing. For `javakey`, the trust level specifies only whether you trust an identity to produce safe code. A signer who is "not trusted" can still sign certificates.

You will see later in this section how to add keys and certificates into the database. You can add further information of your choice by running `javakey` with the `-ii` (input information) command, followed by the name of the principal. Then, type in any information you like. The information can extend over multiple lines. End the input by typing an end-of-file marker (`Ctrl+Z` in Windows, `Ctrl+D` in Unix).

```
javakey -ii cay@horstmann.com
Cay S. Horstmann
http://www.horstmann.com
Ctrl+Z
```

To generate keys, use the `-gk` option. For example,

```
javakey -gk cay@horstmann.com DSA 512
```

creates a new DSA key pair with modulus 512 and stores it in the database.

To make a public key available to others, you generate an X.509 certificate with the `-gc` (generate certificate) command. Unlike the other `javakey` commands that we saw up to now, the "generate certificate" command uses a file, not command-line parameters, to specify the certificate parameters. For example, here is a typical input file to generate a certificate:

```
issuer.name=cay@horstmann.com

subject.name=cay@horstmann.com
subject.real.name=Cay Horstmann
subject.org.unit=San Jose
subject.org=Horstmann Software
subject.country=USA

start.date=1 Jan 1997
end.date=31 Dec 1998
serial.number=1006

out.file=cay.x509
```

Most of the directives are self-explanatory. The X.509 terminology is slightly different from the Java terminology. "Subject" is the principal, the identity that is being certified. "Issuer" is the signer of the certificate. Note that this particular certificate is *self-signed*. There is no independent signer vouching for the information in the certificate.

Place these directives into a file, `cay.dir`, and run `javakey` with the command

```
javakey -gc cay.dir
```

As a result, the certificate is stored in the identity database and in the file named in the `out.file` directive, that is, `cay@horstmann.com.x509`.

To display the contents of a certificate file, use the `-dc` (display certificate) option.

```
javakey -dc cay.x509
```

The command displays the following information:

```
[
   X.509v1 certificate,
   Subject is CN=Cay Horstmann, OU=San Jose, O=Horstmann
      Software, C=USA
   Key:  Sun DSA Public Key
parameters:
p: fca682ce8e12caba26efccf7110e526db078b05edecbcd1eb4a208f3ae1
617ae01f35b91a47e6df63413c5e12ed0899bcd132acd50d99151bdc43ee7375
92e17
q: 962eddcc369cba8ebb260ee6b6a126d9346e38c5
g:
678471b27a9cf44ee91a49c5147db1a9aaf244f05a434d6486931d2d14271b
9e35030b71fd73da179069b32e2935630e1c2062354d0da20a6c416e50be794c
a4

y:
8d2197afb5208432a819982b59ce9e2684caa44ec6fe9195466561d70ab07d
dd9636dc09f5f0da31d729e01a6d9c38853fb41e73d6ad4591771562b07fcf3c
a0
   Validity <Tue Dec 31 16:00:00 PST 1996> until <Wed Dec 30
      16:00:00 PST 1998>
   Issuer is CN=Cay Horstmann, OU=San Jose, O=Horstmann
      Software, C=USA
   Issuer signature used [SHA1withDSA]
   Serial number =      03ee
]
```

As you can see, `javakey` is somewhat confused about the date—it doesn't convert to universal time when it writes the certificate, but it thinks it did when it reads it.

Now, let's use the key to certify the public key of an identity. We want to simulate the following scenario. Gary created his own public/private key pair on his own computer. He forwarded the public key to Cay through a trusted channel so that Cay can sign the certificate. Then, anyone who trusts Cay can use Gary's public key to authenticate information signed by Gary.

Note that Gary is a *signer* in his own identity database, but just an *identity* in Cay's database and the other databases that use his certificate. That is, you really need two computers to try out the simulation. On the second computer, add Gary as a signer, generate keys, and create a self-signed certificate. You will find such a certificate on the CD-ROM. You can import it into your own certificate database with the "import certificate" command:

```
javakey -ic gcornell@ix.netcom.com gary.x509
```

If you run the `javakey -ld` command again, you get the following output.

```
Scope: sun.security.IdentityDatabase, source file:
   D:\JDK\BIN\..\identitydb.obj
gcornell@ix.netcom.com[identitydb.obj][not trusted]
   public key initialized
   certificates:
   certificate 1 for  : CN=Gary Cornell, OU=Department of
      Mathematics, O=University of Connecticut, C=USA
         from : CN=Gary Cornell, OU=Department of Mathematics,
            O=University of Connecticut, C=USA
   No further information available.
[Signer]cay@horstmann.com[identitydb.obj][not trusted]
   public and private keys initialized
   certificates:
   certificate 1 for  : CN=Cay Horstmann, OU=San Jose,
      O=Horstmann Software, C=USA
         from : CN=Cay Horstmann, OU=San Jose, O=Horstmann
            Software, C=USA
Cay S. Horstmann
http://www.horstmann.com
```

That is, the database now contains the public key of Gary. Now, Cay can generate a certificate in which he signs Gary's public key. In this case, the name of the issuer and subject in the certificate file are different.

```
issuer.name=cay@horstmann.com
issuer.cert=1
subject.name=gcornell@ix.netcom.com
subject.real.name=Gary Cornell
subject.org.unit=Department of Mathematics
subject.org=University of Connecticut
subject.country=USA

start.date=1 Jan 1997
end.date=31 Dec 1998
serial.number=1007

out.file=gary-by-cay.x509
```

Since this is not a self-signed certificate, you also need to specify which of the issuer's certificates to use to certify the subject. You need to run `javakey -ld` to find out the numbers that `javakey` assigns to the certificate. In our case, we specify `issuer.cert=1` to indicate that we want to use Cay's first (and only) certificate to sign Gary's certificate.

Cay can then return the signed certificate to Gary via a channel that need not be secure. Anyone who has Cay's public key (through a secure channel) can now verify Gary's certificate.

Note that, currently, javakey supports only version 1 of the X.509 format. You cannot yet import certificates from Verisign or those created with the Microsoft makecert utility.

The program in Example 8-7 checks a certificate for validity. You give the name of the certificate on the command line, such as

```
java CertificateTest gary-by-cay.x509
```

The program then loads the certificate and finds its guarantor. Note that there is no standard Java class yet to describe certificates; the loaded certificate is of type sun.security.x509.X509Cert.

The program then traverses the identity database, as described in the preceding section, and looks at every identity. Unfortunately, the X.509 name of the guarantor differs from the identity name, so we need to look at each certificate and compare its principal's name to that of the guarantor of the loaded certificate. When the names match, we have found a certificate that might have been used to sign the loaded certificate.

We then extract the public key of the database certificate and pass it to the verify method of the loaded certificate. That method is defined in the sun.security.x509.X509Cert class. It checks that the current date falls between the start and end dates of the certificate, and it checks that the DSA signature is valid. If not, it throws an exception.

To test this program, you can do the following experiment. Make sure that the certificate cay.x509 is added in your identity database. Then, run

```
java CertificateTest gary-by-cay.x509
```

The certificate will be verified. We made a copy of that certificate, in a file bad-gary-by-cay.x509, and used Hex Workshop to modify it slightly by changing the name of the organization to "CoreJava State University". If you run

```
java CertificateTest bad-gary-by-cay.x509
```

then the modified certificate will be rejected, as it should be.

NOTE: The current version of the javakey program does not check certificates for validity when importing them. You can import bad certificates into javakey, even when the identity database already contains the guarantor's certificate. Even though it would be an easy matter to check whether the new certificate is valid, javakey does not do this check.

Example 8-7: CertificateTest.java

```java
import java.security.*;
import java.io.*;
import java.util.*;
import corejava.*;

public class CertificateTest
{  public static void main(String[] args) throws Exception
   {  if (args.length != 1)
      {  System.out.println
            ("USAGE: java CertificateTest certificate");
         return;
      }
      sun.security.x509.X509Cert cert
         = new sun.security.x509.X509Cert();
      InputStream in = new FileInputStream(args[0]);
      cert.decode(in);
      in.close();
      System.out.println("Principal is "
         + cert.getPrincipal().getName());
      Principal guarantor = cert.getGuarantor();
      System.out.println("Guarantor is "
         + guarantor.getName());

      // now try to find the guarantor

      IdentityScope identitydb
         = IdentityScope.getSystemScope();

      Enumeration ids = identitydb.identities();
      while (ids.hasMoreElements())
      {  Identity id = (Identity)ids.nextElement();
         Certificate[] c = id.certificates();
         for (int i = 0; i < c.length; i++)
         {  if (c[i].getPrincipal().getName()
               .equals(guarantor.getName()))
            {  PublicKey pubkey = id.getPublicKey();
               try
               {  cert.verify(pubkey);
                  System.out.println("Certificate verified");
                  return;
               }
               catch(SecurityException e)
               {  // verification failed
               }
            }
         }
      }
```

```
    }
        System.out.println("Certificate cannot be verified");
    }
}
```

Code Signing

One of the most important uses of authentication technology is signing executable programs. If you download a program, you are naturally concerned about damage that a program can do. For example, the program could have been infected by a virus. If you knew where the code came from *and* that it had not been tampered with since it left its origin, then your comfort level would be a lot higher than without this knowledge. In fact, if the program was also *written* in Java, so that you have the benefits of the Java language, you can then use this information to make a rational decision about what privileges you will allow that program to have. You might just want it to run in a sandbox as a regular applet, or you might want to grant it a different set of rights and restrictions. For example, if you download a word processing program, you might want to grant it access to your printer and to files in a certain subdirectory. But you may not want to give it the right to make network connections, so that the program can't try to send your files to a third party without your knowledge. Or you may want to be able to monitor access to the network and permit or deny it on a case-by-case basis.

You now know how to implement this sophisticated scheme.

*   First, use authentication to verify the origin of the Java code.

*   Then, run the code with a security manager that enforces the customized security policy that you want to grant the program, depending on its origin.

Signing JAR Files

At this point, the infrastructure for the signing of Java code is just beginning to emerge. The JDK contains a rudimentary tool to manage signatures and certificates, and the HotJava browser is able to interpret them. We describe this mechanism in this section. Then, we speculate how it might be extended in the future.

To sign an applet, you must first place it in a JAR file. For example,

```
jar cvf Calculator.jar CalculatorApplet.class
```

Then, create a directive file such as `applet-by-cay.dir` with the following lines:

```
signer=cay@horstmann.com
cert=1
chain=0
signature.file=SIGNATUR
```

The first line identifies the identity signing the applet. It must be an identity that is stored in the current identity database. The second line (`cert = 1`) identifies the certificate that is to be used (an identity can have multiple certificates). You need to list all certificates with the `javakey -ld` command to find out the certificate number. The third line is a currently unsupported option; later versions of `javakey` will be able to add a chain of certificates to a JAR file. The fourth line gives the file name that is to be used inside the JAR file for the signature and certificate files. The file name must be at most 8 characters, but it does not actually matter what you call it—it is always stored in the directory `META-INF`, away from all other files in the JAR file. We simply always call it `SIGNATUR`.

Now, invoke `javakey` to sign the JAR file, as follows:

```
javakey -gs applet-by-cay.dir Calculator.jar
```

This makes a file: `Calculator.jar.sig`. The only difference between the signed JAR file and the original is that the signed file has two additional files in the `META-INF` directory: the file `SIGNATUR.DSA` that contains the certificate key and the file `SIGNATUR.SF` that contains the signature of the JAR file.

Browsing Signed Applets

At the time of this writing, only beta versions of Netscape and Internet Explorer can execute a Java 1.1 applet or interpret the `javakey` signature. However, the HotJava browser is able to interpret signatures, and it allows the user to adjust the security level according to the level of trust placed in the originator of the code.

If you load into HotJava a Web page that refers to the signed JAR file `Calculator.jar.sig` initially, nothing surprising happens. The calculator program runs normally. However, when you select the menu option Edit | Preferences | Applet Security, then click on Advanced Security, you will see that HotJava has added a new certificate to its certificate list (see Figure 8-10).

NOTE: Currently, the only way to add a certificate to HotJava is to load a signed applet. There is no other way to directly import certificates

Try this yourself—load the `Calculator-sig.html` file from the CD-ROM into HotJava and look at the advanced security page.

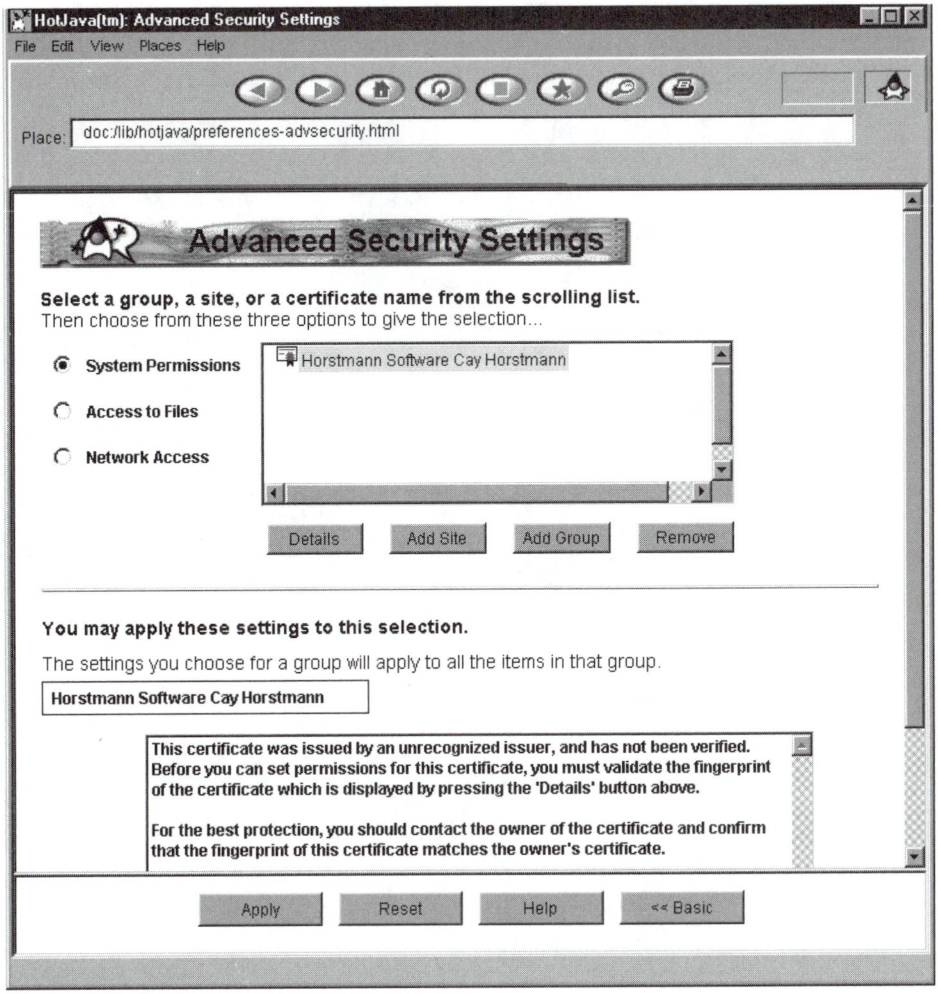

Figure 8-10: The Advanced Security page in HotJava

The text below the certificate states that its issuer is unknown—this makes sense; after all, the certificate is self-signed. Anyone can create a self-signed certificate, and the browser will not trust it any more than it would trust an unsigned applet. HotJava suggests that you contact the owner of the certificate to verify the fingerprint. To see the fingerprint, select the certificate and click on the Detail button (Figure 8-11).

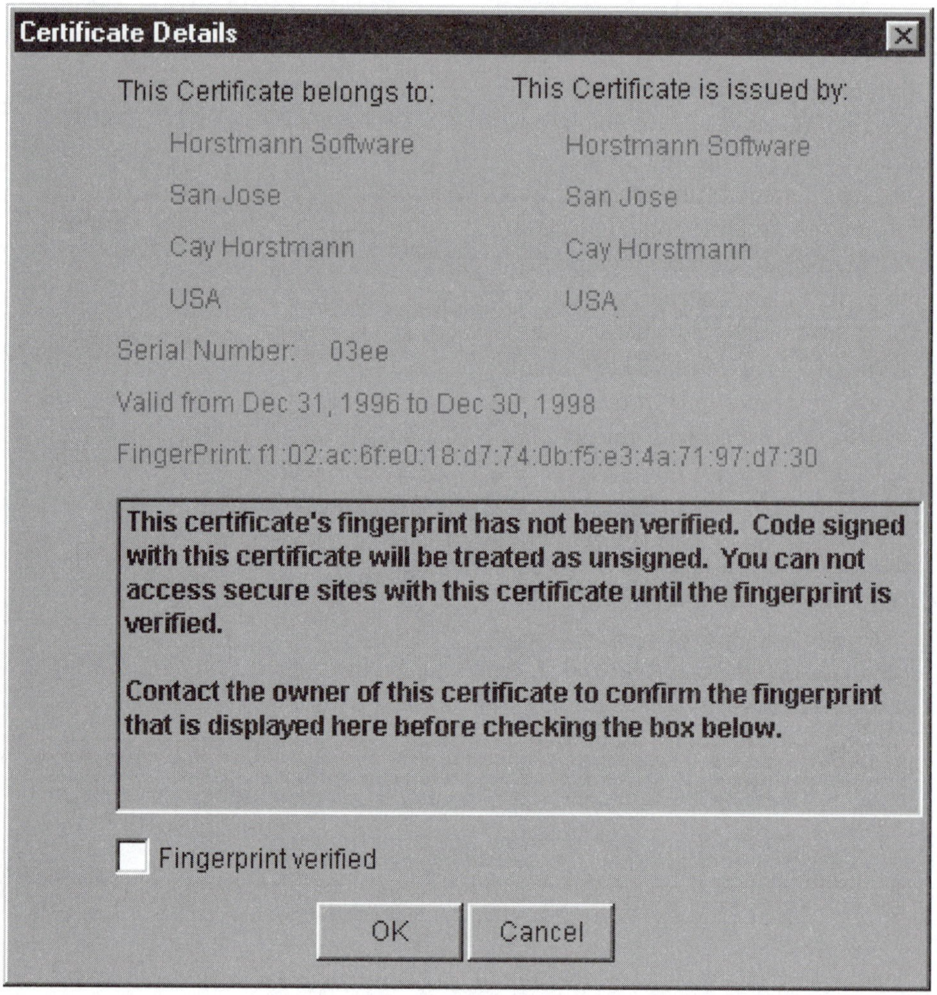

Certificate Details ☒

This Certificate belongs to: This Certificate is issued by:

    Horstmann Software   Horstmann Software

    San Jose   San Jose

    Cay Horstmann   Cay Horstmann

    USA   USA

Serial Number: 03ee

Valid from Dec 31, 1996 to Dec 30, 1998

FingerPrint: f1:02:ac:6f:e0:18:d7:74:0b:f5:e3:4a:71:97:d7:30

> **This certificate's fingerprint has not been verified. Code signed with this certificate will be treated as unsigned. You can not access secure sites with this certificate until the fingerprint is verified.**
>
> **Contact the owner of this certificate to confirm the fingerprint that is displayed here before checking the box below.**

☐ Fingerprint verified

[OK] [Cancel]

Figure 8-11: A Certificate that is imported into HotJava

Verification is a reasonable suggestion. If, when you can reach the owner through a channel you trust, the owner tells you the signature's fingerprint and it matches the one you received, then you can trust the certificate. (There is a small problem—the JDK does not provide a tool to compute the fingerprint of a signature. But if the owner of the certificate has a copy of this book, he or she is in luck. The fingerprint is simply the MD5 message digest of the X.509 file, and it can be computed by loading the file into the `MessageDigestTest` program that you saw previously.) If you accept the fingerprint, HotJava will remember the signature as one that you trust.

Once you've verified the signature, you can then trust that the applet's class files are identical to those that were originally included in the signed JAR file. That is, you know that nobody tinkered with the contents of the JAR file. Can you trust the applet? Not yet. You first need to trust that the certificate owner guarded the private key, so that it is guaranteed that the code in the JAR file really originated with the certificate owner. Finally, and most importantly, before executing the code, you need to believe that the certificate owner is neither malicious nor incompetent. As you can see, trust is a tricky business, and the certificate infrastructure cannot make the decision for you. You have to know how much you trust the author of a program before you run that program. The certificates do have an important benefit: They verify that the trust decision involves only you and the program's creator, that is, that no third parties have tampered with the software.

Trusted Applets

In the last example, we used a self-signed certificate. Of course, it is usually impractical to manually verify certificate fingerprints whenever you run an applet from a new source. This is where signed certificates come in. In our next example, we look at an applet that was signed with the `gary-by-cay` signature. If you have followed through the last example and loaded the `Calculator-sig.html` file into HotJava, then verified the fingerprint of the signature, then you are ready to follow this example as well. Load the file `FileRead-sig.html` from the CD-ROM. The browser goes through the following steps:

1. It sees that the applet is signed with Gary's certificate.

2. It sees that Gary's certificate is signed with Cay's certificate.

3. It sees that it already knows Cay's certificate as trusted.

4. It, therefore, trusts that Gary's certificate is valid.

5. It, therefore, trusts that the applet code has not been tampered with.

Following its default security policy, HotJava now elevates the status of the applet to run under "medium security." The security manager no longer automatically throws an exception when the applet tries to open a file or a network connection. Instead, it pops up a dialog to ask the applet user if the access is permissible (see Figure 8-12).

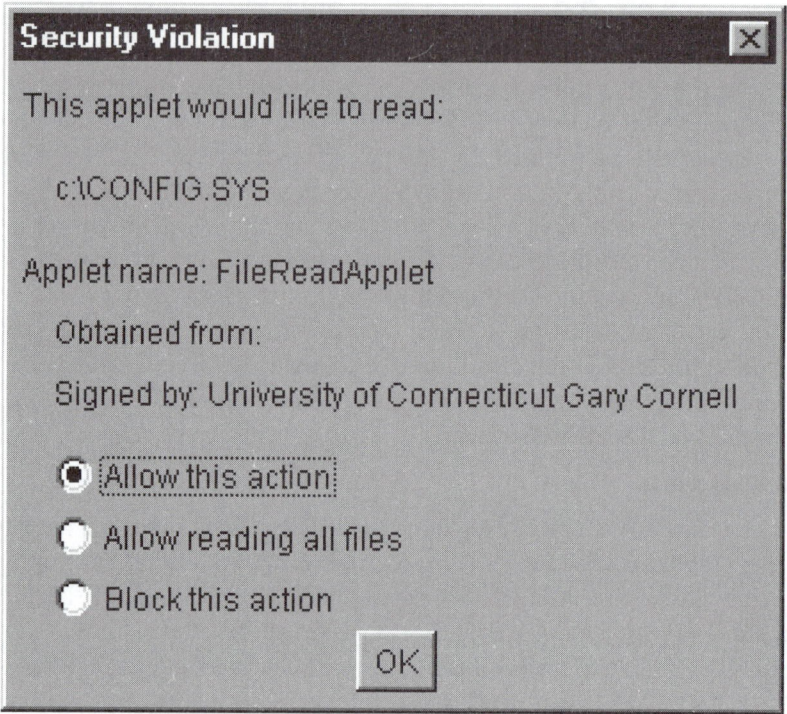

Figure 8-12: HotJava asks whether a signed applet can open a file

You can try this out with the `FileReadApplet`. As you can see from Example 8-8, this applet reads in a file from the local file system, something that is normally verboten for applets. But now that the applet has been signed, the HotJava security manager instead asks the user if the file access is allowed. If you accept, the file will be loaded.

This example shows how signed applets can be more functional than unsigned applets. The HotJava browser has a number of settings to automatically grant more permissions to applets from trusted sources. You can browse the security pages to find out what policies you can set.

Example 8-8: FileReadApplet.java

```java
import java.applet.*;
import java.awt.*;
import java.awt.event.*;
import java.io.*;
import java.net.*;
import java.util.*;
import corejava.*;
```

```
public class FileReadApplet extends Applet
   implements ActionListener
{  public void init()
   {  setLayout(new GridBagLayout());
      GridBagConstraints gbc = new GridBagConstraints();
      gbc.fill = GridBagConstraints.BOTH;
      add(new Label("File name:"), gbc, 0, 0, 1, 1);
      add(fileName, gbc, 1, 0, 1, 1);
      add(openButton, gbc, 2, 0, 1, 1);
      add(fileText, gbc, 0, 1, 3, 1);
      openButton.addActionListener(this);
   }

   public void add(Component c, GridBagConstraints gbc,
      int x, int y, int w, int h)
   {  gbc.gridx = x;
      gbc.gridy = y;
      gbc.gridwidth = w;
      gbc.gridheight = h;
      add(c, gbc);
   }

   public void actionPerformed(ActionEvent evt)
   {  String arg = evt.getActionCommand();
      if (arg.equals("Open"))
      {  try
         {  fileText.setText("");
            BufferedReader in
               = new BufferedReader(new
               FileReader(fileName.getText()));
            String s;
            while ((s = in.readLine()) != null)
            fileText.append(s + "\n");
            in.close();
         }
         catch (IOException e)
         {  fileText.append(e + "\n");
         }
         catch (SecurityException e)
         {  fileText.append
               ("I am sorry, but I cannot do that.");
         }
      }
   }

   private Button openButton = new Button("Open");
   private TextArea fileText = new TextArea(10, 40);
   private TextField fileName = new TextField(30);
}
```

The Future of Applet Signing

As we write this chapter, the mainstream browsers do not yet handle signed applets, and the major programming environments do not yet support applet signing.

Java must support the industry-standard version 3 of the X.509 certificate format, as used by Verisign and other certificate issuers. Publishers and Web sites must be able to easily integrate the applet signing process into their development process. The current `javakey` tool is cumbersome, and the current implementation of the identity database is insecure. And browsers must manage certificates more conveniently. For example, right now it is difficult or impossible to move certificates from one browser to another.

Eventually, the problems of interoperability, security, and convenience will be worked out. At that time, Java will have a terrific security model. Untrusted applets can play in the sandbox. You can run applets that you believe to be trustworthy and be notified whenever the applet does something unexpected. And you can give complete freedom to trusted applets, for example, those from well-established vendors or from the corporate intranet. This model goes way beyond what Microsoft's ActiveX model, which relies solely on signing, can ever do.

Encryption

So far, we have discussed one important cryptographic technique that is implemented in the Java security API, namely, authentication through digital signatures. A second important aspect of security is *encryption*. When information is authenticated, the information itself is plainly visible. The digital signature merely verifies that the information has not been changed. In contrast, when information is encrypted, it is not visible. It can only be decrypted with a matching key.

Authentication is sufficient for code signing—there is no need for hiding the code. But encryption is necessary when applets or applications transfer confidential information, such as credit card numbers and other personal data.

Java has good support for authentication. In particular, the DSA algorithm is very powerful, and it is a widely used standard. Unfortunately, the support for encryption is currently incomplete, for two reasons. Until very recently, all encryption algorithms using highly secure public/private key pairs had been protected by patents. For example, if you want to use the RSA algorithm (named after its inventors, Rivest, Shamir, and Adleman), you need a license from RSA Security Inc., and you would probably need to pay them a substantial fee. (For example, RSA quotes a royalty charge of 3% of your product price,

with an advance of $25,000 if you want to license the JSAFE library, which contains a Java implementation of RSA.) This situation is likely to change soon. In October 1997, the patent for the Diffie-Hellmann algorithm expired, and anyone is now able to use that algorithm freely without having to pay royalties. The second reason for the lack of encryption support in Java is the export restriction imposed by the United States government. It is a crime in the United States to export cryptographic products without an export license. Export licenses are usually granted only for low-grade security (such as 40-bit RC4 keys, which can be broken relatively easily). Recently, higher-grade 128-bit keys were permitted for use by financial institutions overseas. As we write this, there are even efforts by the White House to pass legislation that would make it illegal for any American to use encryption that did not have a back door for law-enforcement agencies. In our opinion, these efforts are ultimately futile and counterproductive. Encryption software, without trapdoors for law enforcement, and with very high grades of security, is widely available over the internet, and the Internet knows no national borders. For example, you can get a free copy of Personal PGP from `http://web.mit.edu/network/pgp-form.html`. However, the patent law and export controls have prevented many companies, including JavaSoft, from offering strong encryption.[5]

Java 1.1 contains no support for encryption. But in February 1997, a specification for Java cryptographic extensions (called JCE) was published. It outlines how cryptographic algorithms will be integrated into the Java security framework. In May, an alpha version of the code was released. It contains an implementation of framework classes and the DES (Data Encryption Standard) algorithm. This is a private-key, freely usable algorithm with a key length of 56 bits.

In this section, we show you how to add a new algorithm to the security framework. As an example, we will simply use the Caesar cipher again. Its patent expired 2,000 years ago, and because key recovery is trivial, we won't be arrested for making the code available overseas. But it is instructive to see the hooks in the security framework that let you add new services.

Ciphers

The Java cryptographic extensions contain a class `Cipher` that is the base class for encryption algorithms. This class, like other security algorithm classes, has two sets of methods: an *application programmer interface* (API) and a *security provider interface* (SPI). Among the API methods are:

---

[5] Ironically, Sun Microsystems will be allowed to sell to foreign customers strong encryption that was developed by a Russian company that Sun hired to create encryption products.

```
void initEncrypt(Key)
void initDecrypt(Key)
byte[] crypt(byte[])
```

These are methods that are called by programmers who use the class for carrying out encryption and decryption. For example, to encrypt a block of memory with the DES algorithm, you use the following code:

```
byte[] input = . . .;
KeyGenerator keyGen = KeyGenerator.getInstance("DES");
keyGen.initialize(new SecureRandom());
Key desKey = keyGen.generateKey();
Cipher cipher = Cipher.getInstance("DES");
cipher.initEncrypt(desKey);
byte[] output = cipher.crypt(input);
```

There are five SPI methods:

```
int engineBlockSize()
int engineOutBufferSize(int inLen, boolean final)
void engineInitEncrypt(Key k)
void engineInitDecrypt(Key k)
int engineUpdate(byte[] in, int inOff, int inLen,
    byte[] out, int outOff)
```

These methods are part of the interface of the `Cipher` class, but they are not meant to be called by the user of the `Cipher` class. For that reason. they are defined as `protected`. Instead, each class that implements a particular cipher, such as the DES class in the JCE library or the `CaesarCipher` class that we will define shortly, needs to override the five methods to implement the particular cryptographic method.

When implementing a new cipher, you must supply three classes:

1. A class that extends `Cipher` and implements the SPI methods

2. A class that implements `Key` and stores the value of an encryption or decryption key

3. A class that extends `KeyGenerator` that can generate random keys for the particular algorithm

In our case, the key is very simple. A key is simply one byte. The code of Example 8-9 shows the implementation of the `CaesarKey` class. Two methods of the key interface, namely, `getFormat` and `getEncoded`, are not of interest for us. These methods are needed if there is a standard format for saving keys for disks. We return `null` to indicate that these keys are not stored.

Example 8-9: CaesarKey.java

```
package corejava;

import java.security.*;

public class CaesarKey implements SecretKey
{   public CaesarKey(byte k)
    {   key = k;
    }
    public String getAlgorithm() { return "CAESAR"; }
    public String getFormat() { return null; }
    public byte[] getEncoded() { return null; }
    public String toString()
    { return "CAESAR key: " + (key & 0xFF); }
    byte getKeyValue() { return key; }

    private byte key;
}
```

The key generator class, shown in Example 8-10, is also simple. It simply generates a random number and uses its lowest byte as the encryption key.

Example 8-10: CaesarKeyGenerator.java

```
package corejava;

import java.security.*;

public class CaesarKeyGenerator extends KeyGenerator
{   public CaesarKeyGenerator() { super("CAESAR"); }
    public void initialize(SecureRandom r) { random = r; }
    public SecretKey generateKey()
    { return new CaesarKey((byte)random.nextInt()); }
    private SecureRandom random;
}
```

The code for the encryption and decryption is implemented in the
CaesarCipher class (see Example 8-11). We need to implement only the SPI
methods; the base class calls them when necessary for encryption and decryption. The engineBlockSize returns the number of bytes per cipher block. In our
case, each byte is encrypted separately, so the block size is 1. In the case of DES,
the block size is 8 bytes. The engineOutBufferSize method returns the number
of bytes required to hold an input block of a certain size.

The `engineInitEncrypt` and `engineInitDecrypt` methods receive a key and store it for use during encryption and decryption. Since the type of the key is the base class `Key`, these methods check that the caller passed in an appropriate key, in this case, a `CaesarKey`. If not, they throw an exception.

The actual encryption is carried out in the `engineUpdate` method. That method receives an array of input bytes and an array to hold the output bytes. When implementing this method, you can rely on valid arguments: the length will always be a multiple of the block size, and there will be sufficient space to hold the output. In our case, the implementation is particularly simple. We simply add or subtract the key, depending on whether the state is ENCRYPT or DECRYPT.

Example 8-11: CaesarCipher.java

```java
package corejava;

import java.security.*;

public class CaesarCipher extends Cipher
{   public CaesarCipher() { super("CAESAR"); }

    protected int engineBlockSize() { return 1; }

    protected int engineOutBufferSize(int inLen, boolean last)
    { return inLen; }

    protected void engineInitEncrypt(Key k)
    {   if (k instanceof CaesarKey)
            key = (CaesarKey)k;
        else throw new IllegalArgumentException
            ("Not a CAESAR key: " + k);
    }

    protected void engineInitDecrypt(Key k)
    {   if (k instanceof CaesarKey)
            key = (CaesarKey)k;
        else throw new IllegalArgumentException
            ("Not a CAESAR key: " + k);
    }

    protected int engineUpdate(byte in[], int inOff, int inLen,
        byte out[], int outOff)
    {   int k = key.getKeyValue();
        if (getState() == Cipher.UNINITIALIZED) return 0;
        if (getState() == Cipher.DECRYPT) k = -k;
        for (int i = 0; i < inLen; i++)
        {   out[i + outOff] = (byte)(in[i + inOff] + k);
```

```
      }
      return inLen;
   }

   CaesarKey key;
}
```

You may wonder why the `engineInitEncrypt` and `engineInitDecrypt` methods do not set the encryption state. However, keep in mind that users of the class call the `initEncrypt` and `initDecrypt` API methods of the `Cipher` base class. These methods set the state and call the engine methods. Thus, the engine methods deal only with those aspects of encryption that are specific to a particular algorithm. That makes life easy for the implementor of a new algorithm. Those parts that are generic to all encryption and decryption processes are carried out by the `Cipher` base class. This class is a good example of an abstract class with several nonabstract, hard-working methods.

`java.security.Cipher`

- `static Cipher getInstance(String algorithm)`

  returns a `Cipher` object that implements the specified algorithm. Throws a `NoSuchAlgorithmException` if the algorithm is not provided. By default, this method returns a block cipher (in ECB mode) with no padding. If you want another mode or padding, you must specify that in the algorithm string.

  Parameters: `algorithm`   the name of the algorithm, such as `"DES"` or `"DES/ECB/PKCS#5"`

- `int getState()`

  returns the current state, one of UNINITIALIZED, ENCRYPT, or DECRYPT.

- `int blockSize()`

  returns the size (in bytes) of a cipher block.

- `void initEncrypt(Key key)`

  initializes this cipher for encryption. If the key is not of the correct type, a `KeyException` is thrown.

- `void initDecrypt(Key key)`

  initializes this cipher for encryption. If the key is not of the correct type, a `KeyException` is thrown.

- `byte[] crypt(byte[] in)`
- `byte[] crypt(byte[] in, int off, int len)`
- `int crypt(byte[] in, int inOff, int inLen, byte[] out, int outOff)`

  encrypts or decrypts the specified data. Note: If the cipher performs padding, you must present it with the *entire* data block. If the number of bytes in the array is not a multiple of the block size, then an `IllegalBlockSizeException` is thrown.

- `int outBufferSize(int inLen)`

  returns the size (in bytes) required to store the output when the input has `inLen` bytes.

- `protected int engineBlockSize()`

  returns the size (in bytes) of a cipher block. This is an SPI method that should be defined by the implementor of a cipher.

- `protected int engineOutBufferSize(int inLen, boolean last)`

  returns the size (in bytes) required to store the output when the input has `inLen` bytes. If `last` is `true`, then the result must take padding into account. This is an SPI method that should be defined by the implementor of a cipher.

Parameters:	`inLen`	size of the input block
	`last`	`true` if this is the last block of the data

- `protected void engineInitEncrypt(Key key)`

  initializes this cipher for encryption. If the key is not of the correct type, a `KeyException` is thrown. This is an SPI method that should be defined by the implementor of a cipher.

- `protected void engineInitDecrypt(Key key)`

  initializes this cipher for encryption. If the key is not of the correct type, a `KeyException` is thrown. This is an SPI method that should be defined by the implementor of a cipher.

- `protected int crypt(byte[] in, int inOff, int inLen, byte[] out, int outOff)`

  encrypts or decrypts the specified data. This method will be called with block-sized chunks of data. This is an SPI method that should be defined by the implementor of a cipher.

`java.security.KeyGenerator`

- `static KeyGenerator getInstance(String algorithm)`

  returns a `KeyGenerator` object that implements the specified algorithm. Throws a `NoSuchAlgorithmException` if the algorithm is not provided.

Parameters:	`algorithm`	the name of the algorithm, such as `"DSA"`

- `void initialize(SecureRandom random)`

Parameters:	`random`	the source of random bits for generating keys

- `SecretKey generateKey()`

  generates a new key.

Padding

In addition to calling the encryption engine methods, the `Cipher` class has to carry out one additional job: padding the size of the text to be encrypted. Consider the DES cipher. It has a block size of 8 bytes. Suppose the last block of a plain text input has less than 8 bytes. Of course, we can fill the remaining bytes with 0, to obtain one final block of 8 bytes, and encrypt it, but during decryption, the result will have several trailing 0 bytes appended to it. Therefore, it will be slightly different from the original input file. That may well be a problem, and a *padding scheme* is needed to avoid it. A commonly used padding scheme is the one described in the Public Key Cryptography Standard (PKCS) #5 by RSA Security, Inc., at (`http://www.rsa.com/rsalabs/pubs/PKCS/html/pkcs-5.html`) In this scheme, the last block is not padded with a pad value of zero, but with a pad value that equals the number of pad bytes. In other words, if L is the last (incomplete) block, then it is padded as follows:

```
L 01                        if length(L) = 7
L 02 02                     if length(L) = 6
L 03 03 03                  if length(L) = 5
. . .
L 07 07 07 07 07 07 07      if length(L) = 1
```

Finally, if the length of the input is actually divisible by 8, then one block

```
08 08 08 08 08 08 08 08
```

is appended to the input and decrypted. During decryption, the very last byte of the input is a count of the padding characters to discard.

In our example, we were lucky—the Caesar cipher required no padding. If padding is required, it is carried out by the `Cipher` methods, *not* by engine

methods. According to the preliminary JCE specification, the `Cipher` class can be instructed to use either no padding or PKCS#5-style padding. To request the latter, you add a mode and padding string to the cipher name, such as

```
Cipher des = Cipher.getInstance("DES/ECB/PKCS#5");
```

Here, the mode ECB refers to "electronic code book" mode, which simply means that each block is encrypted separately. There are three other modes (called CBC, CFB, and OFB) in which the result of encrypting one block influences the encryption of subsequent blocks—see *Network and Internetwork Security* by William Stallings, [Prentice Hall, 1995, pages 58–63] for an explanation of these modes.

Providers

Now that we have implemented the three classes to support the Caesar cipher, we want to make them available to Java programmers in the same way that other algorithms are obtained. That is, a key generator should be obtained as

```
KeyGenerator keyGen = KeyGenerator.getInstance("CAESAR");
```

and the cipher object itself should be obtained as

```
Cipher cipher = Cipher.getInstance("CAESAR");
```

These `getInstance` methods are static methods of the various algorithm classes (such as `Cipher` or, as we saw previously, `Signature`). These methods query the installed *security providers* for algorithms. Therefore, we must implement a provider class, which we call `CoreJavaProvider`—see Example 8-12. It extends the `Provider` base class, which itself extends `Hashtable`. It only has one function, namely, to add algorithm names and the names of the corresponding implementation classes into the hash table. The format is somewhat ad hoc. For example, the call

```
put("Cipher.CAESAR", "corejava.CaesarCipher");
```

means "If the user calls the `getInstance` method of the class `Cipher` with an algorithm name of `"CAESAR"`, then create an object of the class `corejava.CaesarCipher` and return it."

Example 8-12: CoreJavaProvider.java

```
package corejava;
import java.security.*;

public class CoreJavaProvider extends Provider
{  public CoreJavaProvider()
   {  super("COREJAVA", 1.0,
         "CoreJava Security Provider Example");

      put("Cipher.CAESAR",
```

```
        "corejava.CaesarCipher");
    put("KeyGenerator.CAESAR",
        "corejava.CaesarKeyGenerator");
  }
}
```

Once the provider is implemented, it needs to be installed. There are two ways for installing it. You can add a line to the security description file, `\jdk\lib\security\java.security`. By default, there is already a security provider: `sun.security.provider.SUN`. To add a second provider, add the line

```
security.provider.1=corejava.CoreJavaProvider
```

Or, you can dynamically load another security provider with the `addProvider` method of the `Security` class:

```
Security.addProvider(new CoreJavaProvider());
```

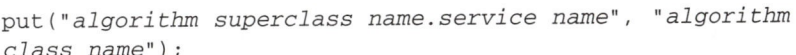

java.security.Provider

- `protected Provider(String name, double version, String info)`

  constructs a new provider object. The provider needs to put all provided algorithms into its superclass hash table, with calls like

  ```
  put("algorithm superclass name.service name", "algorithm
  class name");
  ```

java.security.Security

- `static int addProvider(Provider provider)`

  adds a provider to the set of providers.

- `static void removeProvider(String name)`

  removes the provider with the specified name, or does nothing if no matching provider exists.

- `static Provider[] getProviders()`

  returns the currently installed providers.

- `static Provider getProvider(String name)`

  returns the provider with the specified name, or `null` if no matching provider exists.

- `static String getProperty(String key)`

  gets a security property. By default, security properties are stored in the file `\jdk\lib\java.security`.

- `static void setProperty(String key, String value)`

  sets a security property.

Cipher Streams

The easiest method for encrypting or decrypting data is with the `crypt` method of the `Cipher` class. The call

```
byte[] input = . . .;
byte[] cipher.crypt(input);
```

returns an array of bytes with the encrypted or decrypted input. (Select encryption or decryption by initializing the `cipher` object with either `initEncrypt` or `initDecrypt`.)

However, if the encryption algorithm performs padding, this method *works only if you present it with the entire input you want to encrypt*. The `crypt` method will pad the last bytes when encrypting, and it will interpret the last bytes as padding when decrypting. To encrypt or decrypt a byte at a time, use the `CipherInputStream` and `CipherOutputStream` classes.

These classes are filter streams, as described in Chapter 1. They read from input and decrypt, or write to output and encrypt. They buffer the input and output streams until sufficient bytes are available in the buffer to pass on to the `update` method of the cipher, and they signal to the cipher when the last block has been reached, so that the cipher can carry out padding. All this is transparent to the user. When using these streams, you simply read and write as you would with any other stream. For example, the following code encrypts an input file:

```
Cipher des = Cipher.getInstance("DES/ECB/PKCS#5");
des.initEncrypt(desKey);
InputStream in = new FileInputStream("plain.txt");
OutputStream out = new CipherOutputStream
    (new FileOutputStream("encrypted.txt"), des);
int ch;
while ((ch = in.read()) != -1)
{   out.write((byte)ch);
}
in.close();
out.close();
```

Example 8-13 pulls together all the encryption classes. It loads the Core Java provider. It then generates a random key for the Caesar cipher and encrypts a file, `plain.txt` into a file, `encrypted.txt`. It then decrypts the file and displays it on `System.out`.

We do not distribute the JCE alpha code on the CD-ROM accompanying the book. Instead, the ch8\CipherTest directory contains simplified implementations of the classes Cipher, KeyGenerator, CipherInputStream, and CipherOutputStream that will be added to the java.security package. Only the methods that are needed for the CipherTest example are supplied. In particular, there is no support for padding. You will need these classes if you don't have the JCE libraries installed. If you installed the JCE code, or if you are working with a later version of Java that contains the cryptographic extensions, make sure that the JCE library occurs before "." in your class path, or delete the java\security subdirectory.

Example 8-13: CipherTest.java

```java
import java.security.*;
import java.io.*;
import corejava.*;

public class CipherTest
{   public static void main(String[] args) throws Exception
    {   Security.addProvider(new CoreJavaProvider());

        KeyGenerator keyGen
            = KeyGenerator.getInstance("CAESAR");

        SecureRandom rand = new SecureRandom();
        keyGen.initialize(rand);
        Key caesarKey = keyGen.generateKey();
        System.out.println("The key is " + caesarKey);

        Cipher cipher = Cipher.getInstance("CAESAR");
        cipher.initEncrypt(caesarKey);

        InputStream in = new FileInputStream("plain.txt");
        OutputStream out = new CipherOutputStream
            (new FileOutputStream("encrypted.txt"), cipher);
        int ch;
        while ((ch = in.read()) != -1)
        {   out.write((byte)ch);
        }
        in.close();
        out.close();

        System.out.println("The plaintext was:");
        cipher.initDecrypt(caesarKey);
        in = new CipherInputStream
            (new FileInputStream("encrypted.txt"), cipher);
        while ((ch = in.read()) != -1
```

```
      {   System.out.print((char)ch);
      }
      in.close();
      System.out.println();
   }
}
```

- CipherInputStream(InputStream in, Cipher cipher)

  constructs an input stream that reads data from in and decrypts or encrypts it, using the given cipher.

- int read()

- int read(byte[] b, int off, int len)

  read data from the input stream, which is automatically decrypted or encrypted.

- CipherOutputStream(OutputStream out, Cipher cipher)

  constructs an output stream that writes data to out and encrypts or decrypts it, using the given cipher.

- void write(int ch)

- void write(byte[] b, int off, int len)

  read data from the input stream, which is automatically decrypted or encrypted.

- void flush()

  flushes the cipher buffer and carries out padding, if necessary.

CHAPTER 9

Internationalization

There's a big world out there; hopefully, lots of its inhabitants will be interested in your application or applet. The Internet, after all, effortlessly spans the barriers between countries. On the other hand, when you write your applet in U.S. English, using the ASCII character set, *you* are putting up a barrier. For example, even within countries that can (more or less) function using the ASCII character set, things as basic as dates and numbers are displayed differently. To a German speaker, 3/4/95 means something different than it does to an English speaker. Or, an applet like our retirement calculator from Chapter 10 of Volume 1 could confuse people who do not use the "." to separate the integer and fractional parts of a number. (And, of course, the directions are in English.) Now, it is true that many Internet users are able to read English, but they will certainly be more comfortable with applets or applications that are written in their own language and that present data in the format they are most familiar with. Imagine, for example, that you could write a retirement calculator applet that would change how it displays its results *depending on the location of the machine that is downloading it*. This kind of applet is immediately more valuable—and smart companies will recognize its value.

Java was the first language designed from the ground up to support internationalization. From the beginning, Java had the one essential feature needed for effective internationalization: it used Unicode for all strings. Unicode support makes it easy to write Java programs that manipulate strings in any one of multiple languages.

NOTE: To those who do not own the Unicode specification[1] or who are not familiar with it at all: you can see the two-byte encoding scheme it uses for various character sets by visiting www.unicode.org.

However, there is a lot more to internationalizing programs than just Unicode support since, unfortunately, it is not enough for a programming language to support Unicode. Operating systems and even browsers may not necessarily be Unicode ready. For example, it is almost always necessary to have a translation layer between the character sets and fonts of the host machine and the Unicode-centric Java Virtual Machine. Also, dates, times, currencies—even numbers are formatted differently in different parts of the world. You need an easy way to configure menu and button names, message strings, and keyboard shortcuts for different languages. You need a way to trigger the changes based on information that the ambient machine can report to your program.

None of these issues were addressed in the 1.0 release of Java. The 1.1 release contains fairly extensive support for internationalization, although not all of it is working properly, and not all of it is as easy to use as it should be.

In this chapter, you'll see how to write internationalized Java 1.1 programs. You will see how to localize date and time, numbers and text, and graphical user interfaces, and you'll look at the tools that the JDK and Java 1.1 offer for writing internationalized Java programs. (And, by the way you will see how to write a retirement calculator applet that can change how it displays its results *depending on the location of the machine that is downloading it* (English, German, and Chinese, in our case.)

NOTE: We do not discuss the tools that Java supports for creating new language-specific elements. If you need to build a Brooklyn- or Texas-centric locale, please consult the API documentation.

Locales

When looking at an application that is adapted to an international market, the most obvious difference you notice is the language. This observation is actually a bit too limiting for true internationalization: Countries can share a common language, but you still may need to do some work in order to make computer users of both countries happy[2].

---

[1] The Unicode Standard, Version 2.0, Addison-Wesley, 1996. ISBN 0-201-48345-9.

[2] "We have really everything in common with America nowadays, except, of course, language." Oscar Wilde.

In all cases, menus, button labels, and program messages will need to be translated to the local language; they may also need to be rendered in a different script. There are many more subtle differences, for example, numbers are formatted quite differently in English and in German. The number

```
123,456.78
```

should be displayed as

```
123.456,78
```

to a German user. That is, the role of the decimal point and the decimal comma separator are reversed! There are similar variations in the display of dates. In the United States, dates are somewhat irrationally displayed as month/day/year. Germany uses the more sensible order of day/month/year, whereas in China, the usage is year/month/day. Thus, the date

```
3/22/61
```

should be presented as

```
22.03.1961
```

to a German user. Of course, if the month names are written out explicitly, then the difference in languages becomes apparent. The English

```
March 22, 1961
```

should be presented as

```
22. März 1961
```

in German or

1961年3月22日

in Chinese.

You saw in Volume 1 that the `java.text` class has methods that can format numbers, currencies, and dates. These methods can, in fact, do much more when you give them a parameter that describes the location. To invoke these methods in a non-country-specific way, you only have to supply objects of the `Locale` class. A *locale* describes

- A language

- A location

- Optionally, a variant

For example, in the United States, you use a locale with

> language=English, location=United States.

In Germany, you use a locale with

> language=German, location=Germany.

Switzerland has four official languages (German, French, Italian, and Rhaeto-Romance). A German speaker in Switzerland would want to use a locale with

> language=German, location=Switzerland

This locale would make formatting work similarly to how it would work for the German locale; however, currency values would be expressed in Swiss francs, not German marks, for example.

Variants are, fortunately, rare and are needed only for exceptional or system-dependent situations. For example, the Norwegians are having a hard time agreeing on the spelling of their language (a derivative of Danish). They use two spelling rule sets, a traditional one called Bokmål and a new one called Nynorsk. The traditional spelling would be expressed as a variant

> language=Norwegian, location=Norway, variant=Bokmål

It is also possible to encode platform-dependent information in the variant.

To express the language and location in a concise and standardized manner, Java uses codes that were defined by the International Standards Organization. The language is expressed as a lowercase two-letter code, following ISO-639, and the country code is expressed as an uppercase two-letter code, following ISO-3166. Tables 9-1 and 9-2 show some of the most common codes.

NOTE: For a full list of ISO-639 codes, see, for example, http://www.ics.uci.edu/pub/ietf/http/related/iso639.txt. You can find a full list of the ISO-3166 codes at a number of sites, including http://www.chemie.fu-berlin.de/diverse/doc/ISO_3166.html.

Table 9-1: Common ISO-639 language codes

Language	Code
Chinese	zh
Danish	da
Dutch	nl
English	en
French	fr
Finnish	fi
German	de
Greek	el
Italian	it
Japanese	ja
Korean	ko
Norwegian	no
Portuguese	pt
Spanish	sp
Swedish	sv
Turkish	tr

Table 9-2: Common ISO-3166 country codes

Country	Code
Austria	AT
Belgium	BE
Canada	CA
China	CN
Denmark	DK
Finland	FI
Germany	DE
Great Britain	GB
Greece	GR
Ireland	IE
Italy	IT
Japan	JP
Korea	KR
the Netherlands	NL
Norway	NO
Portugal	PT
Spain	ES
Sweden	SE
Switzerland	CH
Taiwan	TW
Turkey	TR
United States	US

These codes do seem a bit random, especially since some of them are derived from local languages (German = Deutsch = `de`, Chinese = zhongwen = `zh`), but they are, at least, standardized.

To describe a locale, you concatenate the language, country code, and variant (if any) and pass this string to the constructor of the `Locale` class. The variant is optional.

```
Locale germanGermany = new Locale("de", "DE");
Local germanSwitzerland = new Locale("de", "CH");
Locale norwegianNorwayBokmål = new Locale("no", "NO", "B");
```

If you want to specify a locale that describes a language only and not a location, use an empty string as the second argument of the constructor.

```
Locale german = new Locale("de");
```

These kinds of locales can be used only for language-dependent lookups. Since the locales do not specify the location where German is spoken, you cannot use them to determine local currency and date formatting preferences.

For your convenience, Java predefines a number of locale objects:

```
Locale.CANADA
Locale.CANADA_FRENCH
Locale.CHINA
Locale.FRANCE
Locale.GERMANY
Locale.ITALY
Locale.JAPAN
Locale.KOREA
Locale.PRC
Locale.TAIWAN
Locale.UK
Locale.US
```

Java also predefines a number of language locales that specify just a language without a location.

```
Locale.CHINESE
Locale.ENGLISH
Locale.FRENCH
Locale.GERMAN
Locale.ITALIAN
Locale.JAPANESE
Locale.KOREAN
Locale.SIMPLIFIED_CHINESE
Locale.TRADITIONAL_CHINESE
```

Besides constructing a locale or using a predefined one, you have two other methods for obtaining a locale object.

The static `getDefault` method of the `Locale` class gets the default locale as stored by the local operating system. Similarly, in an applet, the `getLocale` method returns the locale of the user viewing the applet. Finally, all locale-dependent utility classes can return an array of the locales they support. For example,

```
Locale[] supportedLocales = DateFormat.getAvailableLocales();
```

returns all arrays that the `DateFormat` class can handle. For example, in Java 1.1, the `DateFormat` class knows how to format dates in Chinese but not in Vietnamese. Therefore, the `getAvailableLocales()` returns the Chinese locales but no Vietnamese ones.

Once you have a locale, what can you do with it? Not much, as it turns out. The only useful methods in the `Locale` class are the ones for identifying the language and country codes. The most important one is `getDisplayName`. It returns a string describing the locale. This string does not contain the cryptic two-letter codes, but it is in a form that can be presented to a user, such as

```
German (Switzerland)
```

Actually, there is a problem here. The display name is issued in the default locale. That may not be appropriate. If your user already selected German as the preferred language, you probably want to present the string in German. You can do just that by giving the German locale as a parameter: The code

```
Locale loc = new Locale("de", "CH");
System.out.println(loc.getDisplayName(Locale.GERMAN));
```

prints out

```
Deutsch (Schweiz)
```

But the real reason you need a `Locale` object is to feed it to locale-aware methods. For example, the `toLowerCase` and `toUpperCase` methods of the `String` class can take an argument of type `Locale` because the rules for forming upper-case letters differ by locale. In France, accents are generally dropped for upper-case letters. But in French-speaking Canada, they are retained. For example, the upper case of "étoile" (star) in France would be "ETOILE," but in Canada it would be "ÉTOILE."

```
String star = "étoile";
String fr = star.toUpperCase(Locale.FRANCE));
  // should return "ETOILE"
String ca = star.toUpperCase(Locale.CANADA_FRENCH));
  // returns "ÉTOILE"
```

Well, not quite: actually, this is the way it is *supposed* to work, but in the version of Java 1.1 that we have, the `toUpperCase` method does not pay attention to the French locale. Still, we hope we have given you an idea of what you *will* be able

to do with a `Locale` object. (Actually, you can give a `Locale` object to many other methods that carry out locale-specific tasks. You will see many examples in the following sections.)

java.util.Locale

- `static Locale getDefault()`

  returns the default locale.

- `static void setDefault(Locale)`

  sets the default locale.

- `String getDisplayName()`

  returns a name describing the locale, expressed in the current locale.

- `String getDisplayName(Locale l)`

  returns a name describing the locale, expressed in the given locale.

- `String getLanguage()`

  returns the language code, a lowercase two-letter ISO-639 code.

- `String getDisplayLanguage()`

  returns the name of the language, expressed in the current locale.

- `String getDisplayLanguage(Locale l)`

  returns the name of the language, expressed in the given locale.

- `String getCountry()`

  returns the country code as an uppercase two-letter ISO-3166 code.

- `String getDisplayCountry()`

  returns the name of the country, expressed in the current locale.

- `String getDisplayCountry(Locale l)`

  returns the name of the country, expressed in the given locale.

- `String getVariant()`

  returns the variant string.

- `String getDisplayVariant()`

  returns the name of the variant, expressed in the current locale.

- `String getDisplayVariant(Locale l)`

  returns the name of the variant, expressed in the given locale.

- `String toString()`

  returns a description of the locale, with the language, country, and variant separated by underscores (e.g., `"de_CH"`).

Numbers and Currencies

We already mentioned how number and currency formatting is highly locale dependent. Java supplies a collection of formatter objects that can format and parse numeric values in the `java.text` class. You go through the following steps to format a number for a particular locale.

1. Get the locale object, as described in the preceding section.

2. Use a "factory method" to obtain a formatter object.

3. Use the formatter object for formatting and parsing.

The factory methods are static methods of the `NumberFormat` class that take a `Locale` argument. There are three factory methods: `getNumberInstance`, `getCurrencyInstance`, and `getPercentInstance`. These objects can format and parse numbers, currency amounts, and percentages, respectively. For example, here is how you can format a currency value in German:

```
Locale loc = new Locale("de", "DE");
NumberFormat currFmt = NumberFormat.getCurrencyInstance(loc);
double amt = 123456.78;
System.out.println(currFmt.format(amt));
```

This code prints

```
123.456,78 DM
```

Note that the currency symbol is DM and that it is placed at the end of the string. Also, note the reversal of decimal points and decimal commas.

Conversely, if you want to read in a number that was entered or stored using the conventions of a certain locale, then you use the `parse` method, which automatically uses the default locale. For example, the following code parses the value that the user typed into a text field. The `parse` method, can deal with decimal points and commas, as well as digits in other typefaces.

```
TextField inputField;
. . .
NumberFormat fmt = NumberFormat.getNumberInstance();
  // get number formatter for default locale
Number input = fmt.parse(inputField.getText().trim());
double x = input.doubleValue();
```

The return type of `parse` is the abstract type `Number`. The returned object is either a `Double` or a `Long` wrapper object, depending on whether the parsed number was a floating-point number. If you don't care about the distinction, you can simply use the `doubleValue` method of the `Number` class to retrieve the wrapped number.

If the number is not in the correct form, the method throws a `ParseException`. For example, leading white space in the string is *not* allowed. (Call `trim` to remove it.) However, any characters that follow the number in the string are simply ignored, so no exception is thrown.

Note that the classes returned by the `getXxxInstance` factory methods are not actually of type `NumberFormat`. The `NumberFormat` type is an abstract class, and the actual formatters belong to one of its subclasses. The factory methods merely know how to locate the object that belongs to a particular locale.

It is quite obvious that it takes effort to produce a formatter object for a particular locale. So, of course, Java 1.1 supports only a limited number of localized formatters—more should follow over time, and you can, of course, write your own.

You can get a list of the currently supported locales with the static `getAvailableLocales` method. That method returns an array of the locales for which number formatter objects can be obtained.

The sample program for this section lets you experiment with number formatters (see Figure 9-1). The list box at the top of the figure contains all locales with number formatters. You can choose between number, currency, and percentage formatters. Each time you make another choice, the number in the text field is reformatted. If you go through a few locales, then you get a good impression of how many ways there are to format a number or currency value. You can also type a different number and click on the Parse button to call the parse method, which tries to parse what you entered. If your input is successfully parsed, then it is passed to `format` and the result is displayed. If parsing fails, then a "Parse error" message is displayed in the text box.

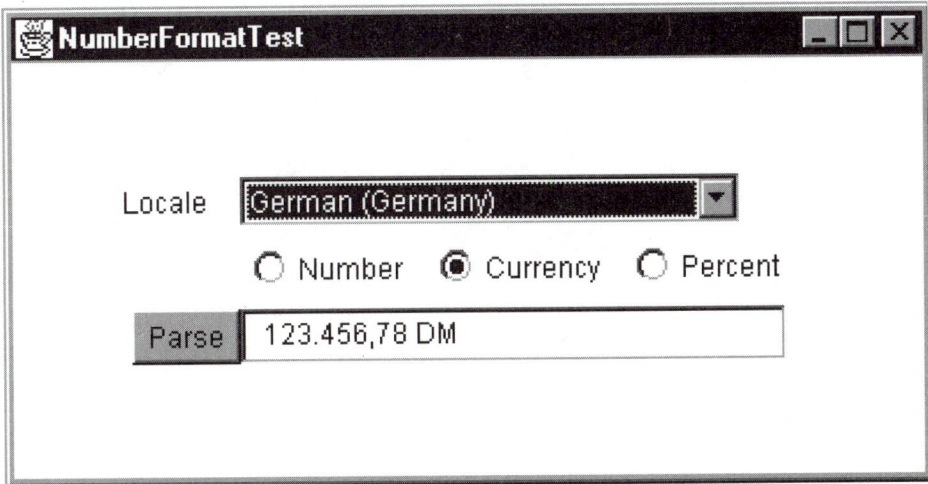

Figure 9-1: The NumberFormatTest program

The code is shown in Example 9-1. It is fairly straightforward. In the constructor, we call NumberFormat.getAvailableLocales. For each locale, we call getDisplayName, and we fill a choice component with the strings it returns. Whenever the user selects another locale or clicks on one of the radio buttons, we create a new formatter object and update the text field. When the user clicks on the Parse button, we call the parse method to do the actual parsing, based on the locale selected.

Example 9-1: NumberFormatTest.java

```
import java.awt.*;
import java.awt.event.*;
import java.text.*;
import java.util.*;
import corejava.*;

public class NumberFormatTest extends CloseableFrame
   implements ActionListener, ItemListener
{  public NumberFormatTest()
   {  Panel p = new Panel();
      addCheckbox(p, "Number", cbGroup, true);
      addCheckbox(p, "Currency", cbGroup, false);
      addCheckbox(p, "Percent", cbGroup, false);

      setLayout(new GridBagLayout());
      GridBagConstraints gbc = new GridBagConstraints();
      gbc.fill = GridBagConstraints.NONE;
```

```java
      gbc.anchor = GridBagConstraints.EAST;
      add(new Label("Locale"), gbc, 0, 0, 1, 1);
      add(p, gbc, 1, 1, 1, 1);
      add(parseButton, gbc, 0, 2, 1, 1);
      gbc.anchor = GridBagConstraints.WEST;
      add(localeChoice, gbc, 1, 0, 1, 1);
      add(numberText, gbc, 1, 2, 1, 1);

      locales = NumberFormat.getAvailableLocales();
      for (int i = 0; i < locales.length; i++)
         localeChoice.add(locales[i].getDisplayName());
      localeChoice.select(
         Locale.getDefault().getDisplayName());
      currentNumber = 123456.78;
      updateDisplay();

      localeChoice.addItemListener(this);
      parseButton.addActionListener(this);
   }

   public void add(Component c, GridBagConstraints gbc,
      int x, int y, int w, int h)
   {  gbc.gridx = x;
      gbc.gridy = y;
      gbc.gridwidth = w;
      gbc.gridheight = h;
      add(c, gbc);
   }

   public void addCheckbox(Panel p, String name,
      CheckboxGroup g, boolean v)
   {  Checkbox c = new Checkbox(name, g, v);
      c.addItemListener(this);
      p.add(c);
   }

   public void actionPerformed(ActionEvent evt)
   {  if (evt.getSource() == parseButton)
      {  String s = numberText.getText();
         try
         {  Number n = currentNumberFormat.parse(s);
            if (n != null)
            {  currentNumber = n.doubleValue();
               updateDisplay();
            }
            else
            {  numberText.setText("Parse error: " + s);
            }
```

```
            }
        catch(ParseException e)
        {   numberText.setText("Parse error: " + s);
        }
    }
}

public void itemStateChanged(ItemEvent evt)
{   if (evt.getStateChange() == ItemEvent.SELECTED)
        updateDisplay();
}

public void updateDisplay()
{   Locale currentLocale = locales[
        localeChoice.getSelectedIndex()];
    currentNumberFormat = null;
    String s = cbGroup.getSelectedCheckbox().getLabel();
    if (s.equals("Number"))
        currentNumberFormat
            = NumberFormat.getNumberInstance(currentLocale);
    else if (s.equals("Currency"))
        currentNumberFormat
            = NumberFormat.getCurrencyInstance(currentLocale);
    else if (s.equals("Percent"))
        currentNumberFormat
            = NumberFormat.getPercentInstance(currentLocale);
    String n = currentNumberFormat.format(currentNumber);
    numberText.setText(n);
}

public static void main(String[] args)
{   Frame f = new NumberFormatTest();
    f.setSize(400, 200);
    f.show();
}

private Locale[] locales;

private double currentNumber;

private Choice localeChoice = new Choice();
private Button parseButton = new Button("Parse");
private TextField numberText = new TextField(30);
private CheckboxGroup cbGroup = new CheckboxGroup();
private NumberFormat currentNumberFormat;
}
```

`java.text.NumberFormat`

- `static Locale[] getAvailableLocales()`

  returns an array of `Locale` objects for which `NumberFormat` formatters are available.

- `static NumberFormat getNumberInstance()`
- `static NumberFormat getNumberInstance(Locale l)`
- `static NumberFormat getCurrencyInstance()`
- `static NumberFormat getCurrencyInstance(Locale l)`
- `static NumberFormat getPercentInstance()`
- `static NumberFormat getPercentInstance(Locale l)`

  return a formatter for numbers, currency amounts, or percentage values for the current locale or for the given locale.

- `String format(double x)`
- `String format(long x)`

  return the string resulting from formatting the given floating-point number or integer.

- `Number parse(String s)`

  parses the given string and returns the number value, as a `Double` if the input string described a floating-point number, and as a `Long` otherwise. The beginning of the string must contain a number; no leading white space is allowed. The number can be followed by other characters, which are ignored. Throws a `ParseException` if parsing was not successful.

- `void setParseIntegerOnly(boolean)/boolean getParseIntegerOnly()`

  sets or gets a flag to indicate whether this formatter should parse only integer values.

- `void setGroupingUsed(boolean)/boolean isGroupingUsed()`

  sets or gets a flag to indicate whether this formatter emits and recognizes decimal separators (such as `100,000`).

- ```
  void setMinimumIntegerDigits(int)/int
  getMinimumIntegerDigits()
  ```
- ```
  void setMaximumIntegerDigits(int)/int
  getMaximumIntegerDigits()
  ```
- ```
  void setMinimumFractionDigits(int)/int
  getMinimumFractionDigits()
  ```
- ```
  void setMaximumFractionDigits(int)/int
  getMaximumFractionDigits()]
  ```

  set or get the maximum or minimum number of digits allowed in the integer or fractional part of a number.

Date and Time

When you are formatting date and time, there are four locale-dependent issues you need to worry about:

- The names of months and weekdays should be presented in the local language.

- There will be local preferences for the order of year, month, and day.

- The Gregorian calendar may not be the local preference for expressing dates.

- The time zone of the location must be taken into account.

The Java `DateFormat` class handles these issues. It is easy to use and quite similar to the `NumberFormat` class. First, you get a locale. You can use the default locale or call the static `getAvailableLocales` method to obtain an array of locales that support date formatting. Then, you call one of the three factory methods:

```
fmt = DateFormat.getDateInstance(dateStyle, loc);
fmt = DateFormat.getTimeInstance(timeStyle, loc);
fmt = DateFormat.getDateTimeInstance(dateStyle, timeStyle,
    loc);
```

To specify the desired style, these factory methods have a parameter which is one of the following constants:

`DateFormat.DEFAULT`
`DateFormat.FULL` (e.g., Thursday, September 18, 1997 8:42:46 o'clock AM PDT for the U.S. locale)
`DateFormat.LONG` (e.g., September 18, 1997 8:42:46 AM PDT for the U.S. locale)
`DateFormat.MEDIUM` (e.g., 18-Sep-97 8:42:46 AM for the U.S. locale)
`DateFormat.SHORT` (e.g., 9/18/97 8:42 AM for the U.S. locale)

The factory method returns a formatting object that you can then use to format dates.

```
Date now = new Date();
String s = fmt.format(now);
```

Just as with the `NumberFormat` class, you can use the `parse` method to parse a date that the user typed. For example, the following code parses the value that the user typed into a text field.

```
TextField inputField;
 . . .
DateFormat fmt = DateFormat.getDateInstance(DateFormat.MEDIUM);
    // get date formatter for default locale
Date input = fmt.parse(inputField.getText().trim());
```

If the number was not typed correctly, this code throws a `ParseException`. Note that leading white space in the string is *not* allowed here, either. You should again call `trim` to remove it. However, any characters that follow the number in the string will again be ignored. Unfortunately, the user must type the date exactly in the expected format. For example, if the format is set to MEDIUM in the U.S. locale, then dates are expected to look like

```
18-Sep-97
```

If the user types

```
September 18, 1997
```

or

```
9/18/97
```

then a parse error results.

A `lenient` flag interprets dates leniently. For example, `February 30, 1999` will be automatically converted to `March 2, 1999`. This seems dangerous, but, unfortunately, it is the default. You should probably turn off this feature. The calendar object that is used to interpret the parsed date will throw an `IllegalArgumentException` when the user enters an invalid day/month/year combination.

Example 9-2 shows the `DateFormat` class in action. You can select a locale and see how the date and time are formatted in different places around the world. If you see question-mark characters in the output, then you don't have the fonts installed for displaying characters in the local language. For example, if you pick a Chinese locale, the date may be expressed as

```
1997?9?19?
```

Figure 9-2 shows the program running under Chinese Windows; as you can see, it correctly displays the output.

You can also experiment with parsing. Type in a date or time, click the Parse lenient checkbox if desired, and click on the Parse date or Parse time button.

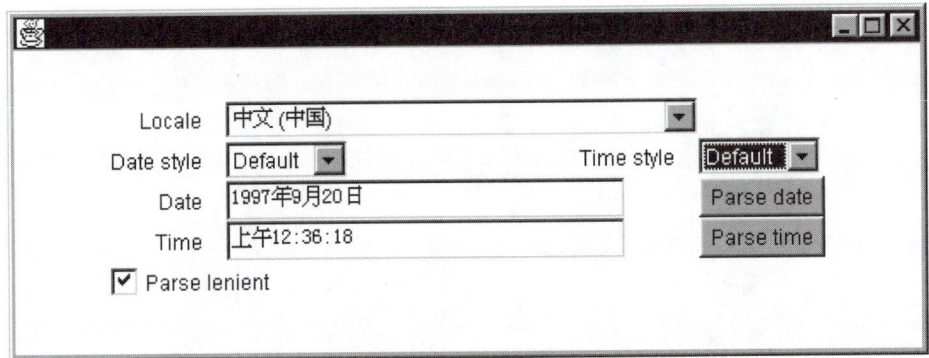

Figure 9-2: The DateFormatTest program running under Chinese Windows

Example 9-2: DateFormatTest.java

```
import java.awt.*;
import java.awt.event.*;
import java.text.*;
import java.util.*;
import corejava.*;

public class DateFormatTest extends CloseableFrame
    implements ActionListener, ItemListener
{  public DateFormatTest()
    {  setLayout(new GridBagLayout());
       GridBagConstraints gbc = new GridBagConstraints();
       gbc.fill = GridBagConstraints.NONE;
       gbc.anchor = GridBagConstraints.EAST;
       add(new Label("Locale"), gbc, 0, 0, 1, 1);
       add(new Label("Date style"), gbc, 0, 1, 1, 1);
       add(new Label("Time style"), gbc, 2, 1, 1, 1);
       add(new Label("Date"), gbc, 0, 2, 1, 1);
       add(new Label("Time"), gbc, 0, 3, 1, 1);
       gbc.anchor = GridBagConstraints.WEST;
       add(localeChoice, gbc, 1, 0, 2, 1);
       add(dateStyleChoice, gbc, 1, 1, 1, 1);
       add(timeStyleChoice, gbc, 3, 1, 1, 1);
       add(dateText, gbc, 1, 2, 2, 1);
       add(dateParseButton, gbc, 3, 2, 1, 1);
```

```
      add(timeText, gbc, 1, 3, 2, 1);
      add(timeParseButton, gbc, 3, 3, 1, 1);
      add(lenientCheckbox, gbc, 0, 4, 2, 1);

      locales = DateFormat.getAvailableLocales();
      for (int i = 0; i < locales.length; i++)
         localeChoice.add(locales[i].getDisplayName());
      localeChoice.select(
         Locale.getDefault().getDisplayName());
      currentDate = new Date();
      currentTime = new Date();
      updateDisplay();

      localeChoice.addItemListener(this);
      dateStyleChoice.addItemListener(this);
      timeStyleChoice.addItemListener(this);
      dateParseButton.addActionListener(this);
      timeParseButton.addActionListener(this);
   }

   public void add(Component c, GridBagConstraints gbc,
      int x, int y, int w, int h)
   {  gbc.gridx = x;
      gbc.gridy = y;
      gbc.gridwidth = w;
      gbc.gridheight = h;
      add(c, gbc);
   }

   public void actionPerformed(ActionEvent evt)
   {  if (evt.getSource() == dateParseButton)
      {  String d = dateText.getText();
         try
         {  currentDateFormat.setLenient
               (lenientCheckbox.getState());
            Date date = currentDateFormat.parse(d);
            currentDate = date;
            updateDisplay();
         }
         catch(ParseException e)
         {  dateText.setText("Parse error: " + d);
         }
         catch(IllegalArgumentException e)
         {  dateText.setText("Argument error: " + d);
         }
      }
      else if (evt.getSource() == timeParseButton)
      {  String t = timeText.getText();
```

```
        try
        {   currentDateFormat.setLenient
                (lenientCheckbox.getState());
            Date date = currentTimeFormat.parse(t);
            currentTime = date;
            updateDisplay();
        }
        catch(ParseException e)
        {   timeText.setText("Parse error: " + t);
        }
        catch(IllegalArgumentException e)
        {   timeText.setText("Argument error: " + t);
        }
    }
}

public void itemStateChanged(ItemEvent evt)
{   if (evt.getSource() instanceof Choice)
    {   if (evt.getStateChange() == ItemEvent.SELECTED)
            updateDisplay();
    }
}

public void updateDisplay()
{   Locale currentLocale = locales[
        localeChoice.getSelectedIndex()];
    int dateStyle = dateStyleChoice.getValue();
    currentDateFormat
        = DateFormat.getDateInstance(dateStyle,
        currentLocale);
    String d = currentDateFormat.format(currentDate);
    dateText.setText(d);
    int timeStyle = timeStyleChoice.getValue();
    currentTimeFormat
        = DateFormat.getTimeInstance(timeStyle,
        currentLocale);
    String t = currentTimeFormat.format(currentTime);
    timeText.setText(t);
}

public static void main(String[] args)
{   Frame f = new DateFormatTest();
    f.setSize(400, 200);
    f.show();
}

private Locale[] locales;
```

```
        private Date currentDate;
        private Date currentTime;
        private DateFormat currentDateFormat;
        private DateFormat currentTimeFormat;

        private Choice localeChoice = new Choice();
        private EnumChoice dateStyleChoice
            = new EnumChoice(DateFormat.class,
                new String[] { "Default", "Full", "Long",
                "Medium", "Short" });
        private EnumChoice timeStyleChoice
            = new EnumChoice(DateFormat.class,
                new String[] { "Default", "Full", "Long",
                "Medium", "Short" });
        private Button dateParseButton = new Button("Parse date");
        private Button timeParseButton = new Button("Parse time");
        private TextField dateText = new TextField(30);
        private TextField timeText = new TextField(30);
        private TextField parseText = new TextField(30);
        private Checkbox lenientCheckbox
            = new Checkbox("Parse lenient", true);
}

class EnumChoice extends Choice
{   public EnumChoice(Class cl, String[] labels)
    {   for (int i = 0; i < labels.length; i++)
        {   String label = labels[i];
            String name = label.toUpperCase().replace(' ', '_');
            int value = 0;
            try
            {   java.lang.reflect.Field f = cl.getField(name);
                value = f.getInt(cl);
            }
            catch(Exception e)
            {   label = "(" + label + ")";
            }
            table.put(label, new Integer(value));
            add(label);
        }
        select(labels[0]);
    }

    public int getValue()
    {   return ((Integer)table.get(getSelectedItem())).intValue();
    }

    private Hashtable table = new Hashtable();
}
```

531

- `static Locale[] getAvailableLocales()`

  returns an array of `Locale` objects for which `DateFormat` formatters are available.

- `static DateFormat getDateInstance(int dateStyle)`
- `static DateFormat getDateInstance(int dateStyle, Locale l)`
- `static DateFormat getTimeInstance(int timeStyle)`
- `static DateFormat getDateTimeInstance(int timeStyle, Locale l)`
- `static DateFormat getDateTimeInstance(int dateStyle, int timeStyle)`
- `static DateFormat getDateTimeInstance(int dateStyle, int timeStyle, Locale l)`

  return a formatter for date, time, or date and time for the default locale or the given locale.

  Parameters: `dateStyle, timeStyle`   one of `DEFAULT`, `FULL`, `LONG`, `MEDIUM`, `SHORT`

- `String format(Date d)`

  returns the string resulting from formatting the given date/time.

- `Date parse(String s)`

  parses the given string and returns the date/time described in it. The beginning of the string must contain a date or time; no leading white space is allowed. The date can be followed by other characters, which are ignored. Throws a `ParseException` if parsing was not successful.

- `void setLenient(boolean)/boolean isLenient()`

  sets or gets a flag to indicate whether parsing should be lenient or strict. In lenient mode, dates such as `February 30, 1999` will be automatically converted to `March 2, 1999`. The default is lenient mode.

- `void setCalendar(Calendar)/Calendar getCalendar()`

  sets or gets the calendar object used for extracting year, month, day, hour, minute, and second from the `Date` object. Use this method if you do not want to use the default calendar for the locale (usually the Gregorian calendar).

- void setTimeZone(TimeZone)/TimeZone getTimeZone()

  sets or gets the time zone object used for formatting the time. Use this method if you do not want to use the default time zone for the locale. The default time zone is the time zone of the default locale, as obtained from the operating system. For the other locales, it is the preferred time zone in the geographical location.

- setNumberFormat(NumberFormat)/NumberFormat getNumberFormat()

  sets or gets the number format used for formatting the numbers used for representing year, month, day, hour, minute, and second.

Text

There are many localization issues to deal with when you display even the simplest text in an internationalized application. In this section, we work on the presentation and manipulation of text strings. For example, the sorting order for strings is clearly locale specific. Obviously, you also need to localize the text itself: directions, labels, and messages will all need to be translated. (Later in this chapter, you'll see how to build *resource bundles*. These let you collect a set of message strings that work for a particular language.)

Collation (Ordering)

Sorting strings in alphabetical order is easy when the strings are made up of only English ASCII characters. You just compare the strings with the compareTo method of the String class. The value of

```
a.compareTo(b)
```

is a negative number if a is lexicographically less than b, 0 if they are identical, and positive otherwise.

Unfortunately, unless all your words are in uppercase English ASCII characters, this method is useless. The problem is that the compareTo method in Java uses the values of the Unicode character to determine the ordering. For example, lowercase characters have a higher Unicode value than do uppercase characters, and accented characters have even higher values. This leads to absurd results; for example, the following five strings are ordered according to Java's compareTo method:

```
America
Zulu
ant
zebra
Ångstrom
```

For dictionary ordering, you want to consider upper case and lower case to be equivalent. To an English speaker, the sample list of words would be ordered as

```
America
Ångstrom
ant
zebra
Zulu
```

However, that order would not be acceptable to a Danish user. In Danish, the letter Å is a different letter than the letter A, and it is collated *after* the letter Z! That is, a Danish user would want the words to be sorted as

```
America
ant
zebra
Zulu
Ångstrom
```

Fortunately, once you are aware of the problem, collation is quite easy in Java.

As always, you start by obtaining a `Locale` object. Then, you call the `getInstance` factory method to obtain a `Collator` object. Finally, you use the `compare` method of the collator, *not* the `compareTo` method of the `String` class, whenever you want to sort strings.

```
Locale loc = . . .;
Collator coll = Collator.getInstance(loc);
if (coll.compare(a, b) < 0) . . .;
```

To show how the `compare` method is used for collation, here is a simple, inefficient insertion sort that is location sensitive:

```
Vector string = . . .;
Vector sortedStrings = new Vector();
for (int i = 0; i < strings.size(); i++)
{   boolean inserted = false;
    String a = (String)strings.elementAt(i);
    for (int j = 0; j < sortedStrings.size()
            && !inserted; j++)
    {   String b = (String)sortedStrings.elementAt(j);
        int d = coll.compare(a, b);
        if (d <= 0)
        {   sortedStrings.insertElementAt(a, j);
            inserted = true;
        }
    }
    if (!inserted) sortedStrings.addElement(a);
}
```

The sample code at the end of this section lets you collate a list of words in all locales that support collation. (As before, you can obtain an array of locales with the `getAvailableLocales` method.) The `compare` method is used to sort a vector of strings with this code.

You can set a collator's *strength* to select how selective it should be. Character differences are classified as *primary, secondary,* and *tertiary*. For example, in English, the difference between "A" and "Z" is considered primary, the difference between "A" and "Å" is secondary, and between "A" and "a" is tertiary.

By setting the collator's strength to `Collator.PRIMARY`, you tell it to pay attention only to primary differences. By setting it to `Collator.SECONDARY`, the collator will take secondary differences into account. That is, two strings will be more likely to be considered different when the strength is set to "secondary." For example,

```
// assuming English locale
String a = "Angstrom";
String b = "Ångstrom";
coll.setStrength(Collator.PRIMARY);
if (coll.compare(a, b) == 0) System.out.print("same");
else System.out.print("different");
// will print "same"
coll.setStrength(Collator.SECONDARY);
if (coll.compare(a, b) == 0) System.out.print("same");
else System.out.print("different");
// will print "different"
```

Table 9-3 shows how a sample set of strings is sorted with the three collation strengths. Note that the strength indicates only whether two strings are considered identical.

Table 9-3: Collation with different strengths

Input	PRIMARY		SECONDARY	TERTIARY
Ant	Angstrom = Ångstrom		Angstrom	Angstrom
ant	Ant = ant		Ångstrom	Ångstrom
Angstrom			Ant = ant	Ant
Ångstrom				ant

Finally, there is one technical setting, the *decomposition mode*. The default, "canonical decomposition," is appropriate for most use. If you choose "no decomposition," then accented characters are not decomposed into their base form + accent. This option is faster, but it gives correct results only when the

input does not contain accented characters. (It never makes sense to sort accented characters by their Unicode values.) Finally, "full decomposition" analyzes Unicode variants, that is, Unicode characters that ought to be considered identical. For example, Japanese displays have two ways of showing English characters, called half-width and full-width. The half-width characters have normal character spacing, whereas the full-width characters are spaced in the same grid as the ideographs. (One could argue that this is a presentation issue and it should not have resulted in different Unicode characters, but we don't make the rules.) With full decomposition, half-width and full-width variants of the same letter are recognized as identical.

It is wasteful to have the collator decompose a string many times. If one string is compared many times against other strings, then you can save the decomposition in a *collation* key object. The `getCollationKey` method returns a `CollationKey` object that you can use for further, faster comparisons. Here is an example:

```
String a = . . .;
CollationKey aKey = coll.getCollationKey(a);
if (aKey.compareTo(coll.getCollationKey(b) == 0) // fast
    comparison
        . . .
```

The program in Example 9-3 lets you experiment with collation order. Type a word into the text field and click on Add to add it to the list of words. Each time you add another word or change the locale, strength, or decomposition mode, the list of words is sorted again. An = sign indicates words that are considered identical (see Figure 9-3).

There are a few interesting points about the code you may want to keep in mind. First, a vector, `strings`, keeps the current collection of input strings. The `sort` method sorts them into a vector, `sortedStrings`. Next, we call the `updateDisplay` method whenever a word is added or a choice has changed, which, in turn, calls `sort` and then sends the sorted strings to the text area. The only mysterious feature about the code is probably the `EnumChoice` class. We used this class to solve the following technical problem. We wanted to fill a choice box with the values `Primary`, `Secondary`, and `Tertiary`, and then automatically convert the user's selection to the integer value `Collation.PRIMARY`, `Collation.SECONDARY` and `Collation.TERTIARY`. To do this, we convert the user's choice to upper case, replace all spaces with underscores, and then use reflection to find the value of the static field with that name. (See Chapter 5 of Volume 1 for more details about reflection.)

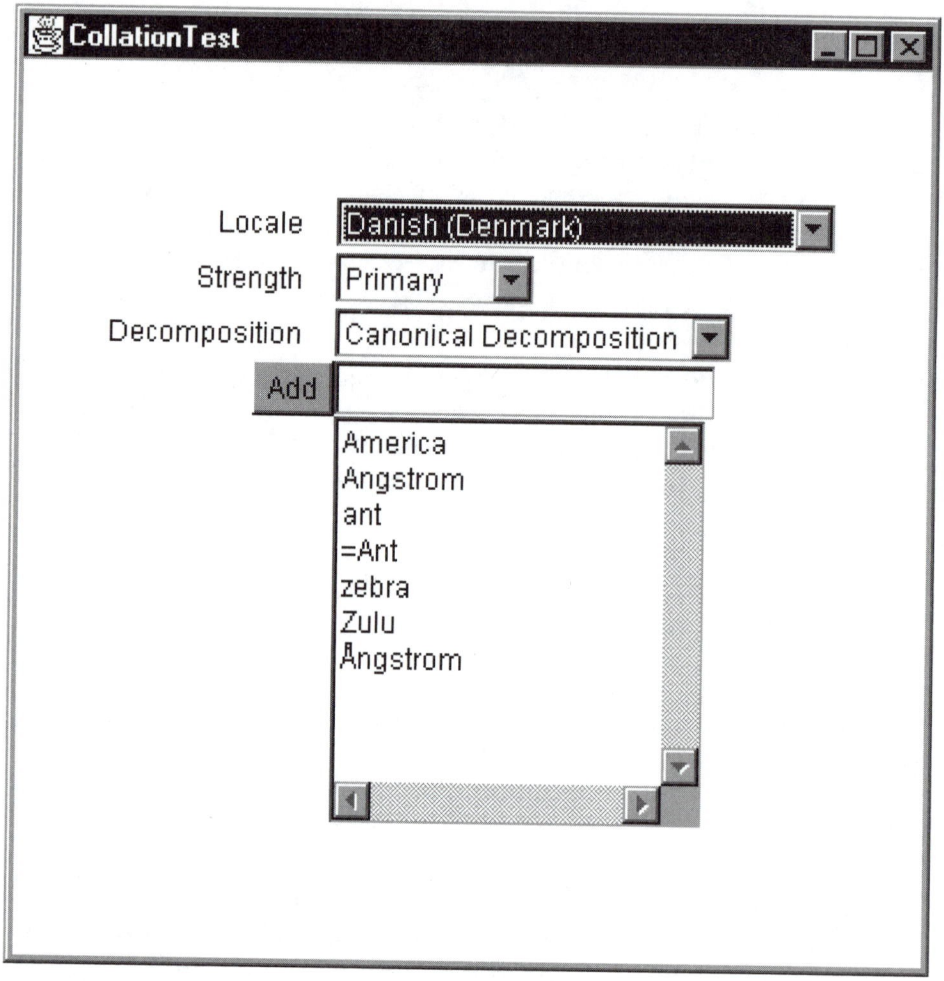

CollationTest

Locale	Danish (Denmark)
Strength	Primary
Decomposition	Canonical Decomposition
Add	

```
America
Angstrom
ant
=Ant
zebra
Zulu
Ångstrom
```

Figure 9-3: The `CollationTest` program

Example 9-3: CollationTest.java

```java
import java.io.*;
import java.awt.*;
import java.awt.event.*;
import java.text.*;
import java.util.*;
import corejava.*;

public class CollationTest extends CloseableFrame
    implements ActionListener, ItemListener
{  public CollationTest()
```

```
{   setLayout(new GridBagLayout());
    GridBagConstraints gbc = new GridBagConstraints();
    gbc.fill = GridBagConstraints.NONE;
    gbc.anchor = GridBagConstraints.EAST;
    add(new Label("Locale"), gbc, 0, 0, 1, 1);
    add(new Label("Strength"), gbc, 0, 1, 1, 1);
    add(new Label("Decomposition"), gbc, 0, 2, 1, 1);
    add(addButton, gbc, 0, 3, 1, 1);
    gbc.anchor = GridBagConstraints.WEST;
    add(localeChoice, gbc, 1, 0, 1, 1);
    add(strengthChoice, gbc, 1, 1, 1, 1);
    add(decompositionChoice, gbc, 1, 2, 1, 1);
    add(newWord, gbc, 1, 3, 1, 1);
    add(sortedWords, gbc, 1, 4, 1, 1);

    locales = Collator.getAvailableLocales();
    for (int i = 0; i < locales.length; i++)
        localeChoice.add(locales[i].getDisplayName());
    localeChoice.select(
        Locale.getDefault().getDisplayName());

    strings.addElement("America");
    strings.addElement("ant");
    strings.addElement("Zulu");
    strings.addElement("zebra");
    strings.addElement("Ångstrom");
    strings.addElement("Angstrom");
    strings.addElement("Ant");
    updateDisplay();

    addButton.addActionListener(this);
    localeChoice.addItemListener(this);
    strengthChoice.addItemListener(this);
    decompositionChoice.addItemListener(this);
}

public void add(Component c, GridBagConstraints gbc,
    int x, int y, int w, int h)
{   gbc.gridx = x;
    gbc.gridy = y;
    gbc.gridwidth = w;
    gbc.gridheight = h;
    add(c, gbc);
}

public void actionPerformed(ActionEvent evt)
{   String arg = evt.getActionCommand();
    if (arg.equals("Add"))
```

```
      {   strings.addElement(newWord.getText());
          updateDisplay();
      }
   }

   public void updateDisplay()
   {   Locale currentLocale = locales[
          localeChoice.getSelectedIndex()];

      currentCollator
         = Collator.getInstance(currentLocale);
      currentCollator.setStrength(strengthChoice.getValue());
      currentCollator.setDecomposition(
         decompositionChoice.getValue());
      sort();
      sortedWords.setText("");
      for (int i = 0; i < sortedStrings.size(); i++)
         sortedWords.append(sortedStrings.elementAt(i) + "\n");
   }

   public void sort()
   {   /* this really should be replaced with a better
         sort algorithm
      */
      sortedStrings = new Vector();
      for (int i = 0; i < strings.size(); i++)
      {   boolean inserted = false;
         String s = (String)strings.elementAt(i);
         for (int j = 0; j < sortedStrings.size()
               && !inserted; j++)
         {   int d = currentCollator.compare(s,
               (String)sortedStrings.elementAt(j));
            if (d < 0)
            {   sortedStrings.insertElementAt(s, j);
               inserted = true;
            }
            else if (d == 0)
            {   sortedStrings.insertElementAt("=" + s, j + 1);
               inserted = true;
            }
         }
         if (!inserted) sortedStrings.addElement(s);
      }
   }

   public void itemStateChanged(ItemEvent evt)
   {   if (evt.getSource() instanceof Choice)
      {   if (evt.getStateChange() == ItemEvent.SELECTED)
```

```
                  updateDisplay();
         }
     }

     public static void main(String[] args)
     {   Frame f = new CollationTest();
         f.setSize(400, 400);
         f.show();
     }

     private Locale[] locales;
     private Vector strings = new Vector();
     private Vector sortedStrings = new Vector();
     private Collator currentCollator;

     private Choice localeChoice = new Choice();
     private EnumChoice strengthChoice
         = new EnumChoice(Collator.class,
            new String[] { "Primary", "Secondary", "Tertiary" });
     private EnumChoice decompositionChoice
         = new EnumChoice(Collator.class,
            new String[] { "Canonical Decomposition",
            "Full Decomposition", "No Decomposition" });
     private TextField newWord = new TextField(20);
     private TextArea sortedWords = new TextArea(10, 20);
     private Button addButton = new Button("Add");
}

class EnumChoice extends Choice
{   public EnumChoice(Class cl, String[] labels)
    {   for (int i = 0; i < labels.length; i++)
        {   String label = labels[i];
            String name = label.toUpperCase().replace(' ', '_');
            int value = 0;
            try
            {   java.lang.reflect.Field f = cl.getField(name);
                value = f.getInt(cl);
            }
            catch(Exception e)
            {   label = "(" + label + ")";
            }
            table.put(label, new Integer(value));
            add(label);
        }
        select(labels[0]);
    }

    public int getValue()
```

```
{  return ((Integer)table.get(getSelectedItem())).intValue();
}

private Hashtable table = new Hashtable();
}
```

java.text.Collator

- static Locale[] getAvailableLocales()

  returns an array of Locale objects for which Collator objects are available.

- static Collator getInstance()
- static Collator getInstance(Locale l)

  return a collator for the default locale or the given locale.

- int compare(String a, String b)

  returns a negative value if a comes before b, 0 if they are considered identical, a positive value otherwise.

- boolean equals(String a, String b)

  returns true if they are considered identical, false otherwise.

- void setStrength(int strength) / int getStrength()

  sets or gets the strength of the collator. Stronger collators tell more words apart. Strength values are Collator.PRIMARY, Collator.SECONDARY, and Collator.TERTIARY.

- void setDecomposition(int decomp) / int getDecompositon()

  sets or gets the decomposition mode of the collator. The more a collator decomposes a string, the more strict it will be in deciding whether two strings ought to be considered identical. Decomposition values are Collator.NO_DECOMPOSITION, Collator.CANONICAL_DECOMPOSITION, and Collator.FULL_DECOMPOSITION.

- CollationKey getCollationKey(String a)

  returns a collation key that contains a decomposition of the characters in a form that can be quickly compared against another collation key.

java.text.CollationKey

- int compareTo(CollationKey b)

  returns a negative value if this key comes before b, 0 if they are considered identical, a positive value otherwise.

Text Boundaries

Consider a "sentence" in an arbitrary language: Where are its "words"? Answering this question sounds trivial, but once you deal with multiple languages, then just as with collation, it isn't as simple as you might think. Actually the situation is even worse than you might think—consider the problem of determining where a *character starts and ends*. If you have a string such as `"Hello"`, then it is trivial to break it up into five individual characters: `H|e|l|l|o`. But accents throw a monkey wrench into this simple model. There are two ways of describing an accented character such as ä, namely, the character ä itself (Unicode `\u00E4`) or the character a followed by a combining diaeresis ¨ (Unicode `\u0308`). That is, the string with four Unicode characters `Ba¨r` is a sequence of three logical characters: `B|a¨|r`. This situation is still relatively easy; it gets much more complex for Asian languages such as the Korean Hangul script.

What about word breaks? Word breaks, of course, are at the beginning and the end of a word. In English, this is simple: sequences of characters are words. For example, the word breaks in

```
The quick, brown fox jump-ed over the lazy dog.
```

are

```
The| |quick|,| |brown| |fox| |jump-ed| |over| |the| |lazy|
    |dog.|
```

(The hyphen in `jump-ed` indicates a soft hyphen.)

Line boundaries are positions where a line can be broken on the screen or in printed text. In English text, this is relatively easy. Lines can be broken before a word or after a hyphen. For example, the line breaks in our sample sentence are

```
The |quick, |brown |fox |jump-|ed |over |the |lazy |dog.|
```

Note that line breaks are the points where a line *can* be broken, not the points where the lines are actually broken.

Determining character, word, and line boundaries is simple for European and Asian ideographic scripts, but it is quite complex for others, such as Devanagari, the script used to write classical Sanskrit and modern Hindi.

Finally, you will want to know about breaks between sentences. In English, for example, sentence breaks occur after periods, exclamation marks, and question marks. Use the `BreakIterator` class to find out where you can break text up into components such as characters, words, lines, and sentences. You would use these classes when writing code for editing, displaying, and printing text.

Luckily, the break iterator class does not blindly break sentences at every period. It knows about the rules for periods inside quotation marks, and about "..." ellipses. For example, the string

```
The quick, brown fox jumped over the lazy "dog." And then
    . . . what happened?
```

is broken into two sentences.

```
The quick, brown fox jumped over the lazy "dog." |And then
    . . . what happened?|
```

Here is an example of how to program with break iterators. As always, you first get a break iterator with a static factory method. You can request one of four iterators to iterate through characters, words, lines, or sentences. Note that once you have a particular iterator object, such as one for sentences, it can iterate only through sentences. More generally, a break iterator can iterate only through the construct for which it was created. For example, the following code lets you analyze individual words:

```
Locale loc = . . .;
BreakIterator wordIter = BreakIterator.getWordInstance(loc);
```

Once you have an iterator, you give it a string to iterate through.

```
String msg = " The quick, brown fox";
wordIter.setText(msg);
```

Then, call the `first` method to get the offset of the first boundary.

```
int f = wordIter.first(); // returns 3
```

In our example, this call to `first` returns a 3—which is the offset of the first space inside the string. You keep calling the `next` method to get the offsets for the next tokens. You know there are no more tokens when a call to `next` returns the constant `BreakIterator.DONE`. For example, here is how you can iterate through the remaining word breaks:

```
int to;
while ((to = currentBreakIterator.next()) !=
    BreakIterator.DONE)
{   // do something with to
}
```

The program in Example 9-4 lets you type text into the text area on the top of the frame. Then, select the way you want to break the text (character, word, line, or sentence). You then see the text boundaries in the text area on the bottom (see Figure 9-4).

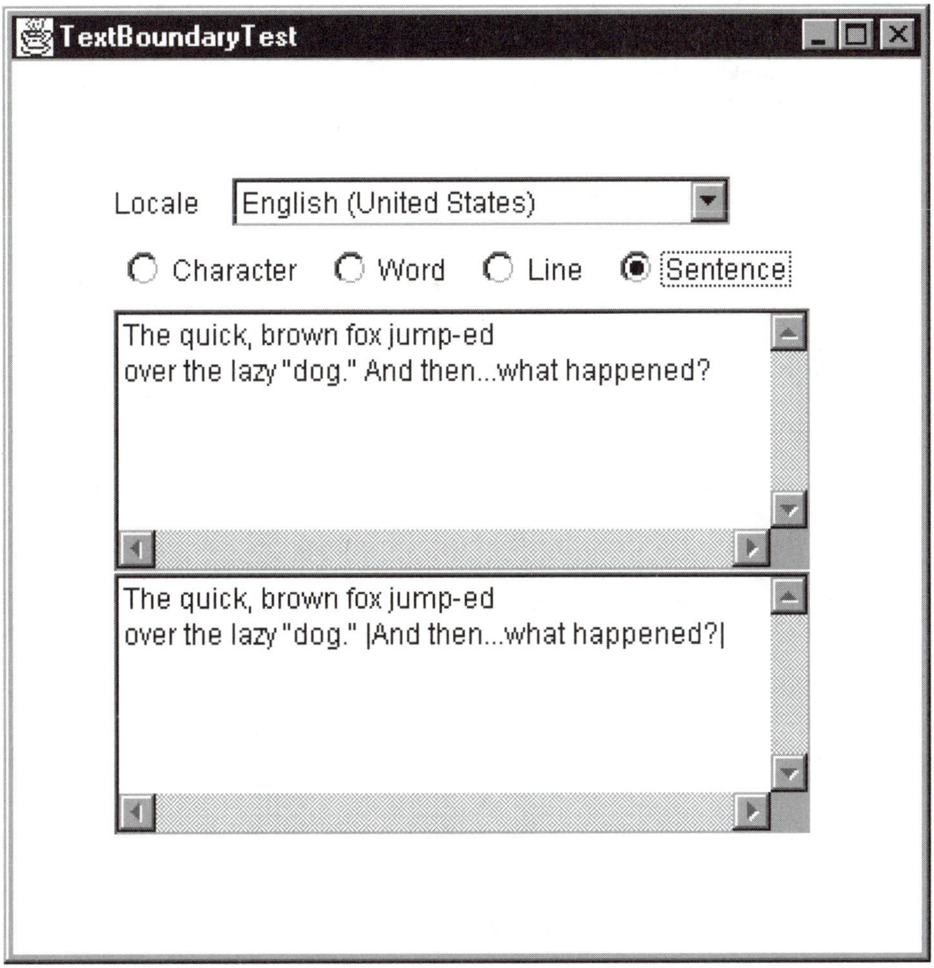

```
┌─────────────────────────────────────────────────────────┐
│ ▓ TextBoundaryTest                               _ □ ✕  │
├─────────────────────────────────────────────────────────┤
│                                                         │
│                                                         │
│     Locale    │English (United States)        ▼│        │
│       ○ Character   ○ Word   ○ Line   ● Sentence        │
│     ┌────────────────────────────────────────────┐     │
│     │The quick, brown fox jump-ed              ▲ │     │
│     │over the lazy "dog." And then...what happened?│     │
│     │                                            │     │
│     │                                            │     │
│     │                                          ▼ │     │
│     │◄                                         ► │     │
│     └────────────────────────────────────────────┘     │
│     ┌────────────────────────────────────────────┐     │
│     │The quick, brown fox jump-ed              ▲ │     │
│     │over the lazy "dog." |And then...what happened?|│   │
│     │                                            │     │
│     │                                            │     │
│     │                                          ▼ │     │
│     │◄                                         ► │     │
│     └────────────────────────────────────────────┘     │
│                                                         │
└─────────────────────────────────────────────────────────┘
```

Figure 9-4: The TextBoundaryTest program

Example 9-4: TextBoundaryTest.java

```
import java.awt.*;
import java.awt.event.*;
import java.text.*;
import java.util.*;
import corejava.*;

public class TextBoundaryTest extends CloseableFrame
   implements ItemListener
{  public TextBoundaryTest()
   {  Panel p = new Panel();
```

```
      addCheckbox(p, "Character", cbGroup, false);
      addCheckbox(p, "Word", cbGroup, false);
      addCheckbox(p, "Line", cbGroup, false);
      addCheckbox(p, "Sentence", cbGroup, true);

      setLayout(new GridBagLayout());
      GridBagConstraints gbc = new GridBagConstraints();
      gbc.fill = GridBagConstraints.NONE;
      gbc.anchor = GridBagConstraints.EAST;
      add(new Label("Locale"), gbc, 0, 0, 1, 1);
      gbc.anchor = GridBagConstraints.WEST;
      add(localeChoice, gbc, 1, 0, 1, 1);
      add(p, gbc, 0, 1, 2, 1);
      add(inputText, gbc, 0, 2, 2, 1);
      add(outputText, gbc, 0, 3, 2, 1);

      localeChoice.addItemListener(this);

      locales = Collator.getAvailableLocales();
      for (int i = 0; i < locales.length; i++)
         localeChoice.add(locales[i].getDisplayName());
      localeChoice.select(
         Locale.getDefault().getDisplayName());

      inputText.setText("The quick, brown fox jump-ed\n"
         + "over the lazy \"dog.\" And then...what happened?");
       updateDisplay();
   }

   public void addCheckbox(Panel p, String name,
      CheckboxGroup g, boolean v)
   {  Checkbox c = new Checkbox(name, g, v);
      c.addItemListener(this);
      p.add(c);
   }

   public void add(Component c, GridBagConstraints gbc,
      int x, int y, int w, int h)
   {  gbc.gridx = x;
      gbc.gridy = y;
      gbc.gridwidth = w;
      gbc.gridheight = h;
      add(c, gbc);
   }

   public void updateDisplay()
   {  Locale currentLocale = locales[
         localeChoice.getSelectedIndex()];
      BreakIterator currentBreakIterator = null;
```

```
      String s = cbGroup.getSelectedCheckbox().getLabel();
      if (s.equals("Character"))
         currentBreakIterator
            = BreakIterator.getCharacterInstance(currentLocale);
      else if (s.equals("Word"))
         currentBreakIterator
            = BreakIterator.getWordInstance(currentLocale);
      else if (s.equals("Line"))
         currentBreakIterator
            = BreakIterator.getLineInstance(currentLocale);
      else if (s.equals("Sentence"))
         currentBreakIterator
            = BreakIterator.getSentenceInstance(currentLocale);

      String text = inputText.getText();
      currentBreakIterator.setText(text);
      outputText.setText("");

      int from = currentBreakIterator.first();
      int to;
      while ((to = currentBreakIterator.next()) !=
         BreakIterator.DONE)
      {  outputText.append(text.substring(from, to) + "|");
         from = to;
      }
      outputText.append(text.substring(from));
   }

   public void itemStateChanged(ItemEvent evt)
   {  if (evt.getStateChange() == ItemEvent.SELECTED)
      {  updateDisplay();
      }
   }

   public static void main(String[] args)
   {  Frame f = new TextBoundaryTest();
      f.setSize(400, 400);
      f.show();
   }

   private Locale[] locales;
   private BreakIterator currentBreakIterator;

   private Choice localeChoice = new Choice();
   private TextArea inputText = new TextArea(6, 40);
   private TextArea outputText = new TextArea(6, 40);
   private CheckboxGroup cbGroup = new CheckboxGroup();
}
```

`java.text.BreakIterator`

- `static Locale[] getAvailableLocales()`

  returns an array of `Locale` objects for which `BreakIterator` objects are available.

- `static BreakIterator getCharInstance()`
- `static BreakIterator getCharInstance(Locale l)`
- `static BreakIterator getWordInstance()`
- `static BreakIterator getWordTimeInstance(Locale l)`
- `static BreakIterator getLineInstance()`
- `static BreakIterator getLineInstance(Locale l)`
- `static BreakIterator getSentenceInstance()`
- `static BreakIterator getSentenceInstance(Locale l)`

  return a break iterator for characters, words, lines, and sentences for the default or the given locale.

- `void setText(String text)/String getText()`

  sets or gets the text to be scanned.

- `void setText(String text)/String getText()`

  sets or gets the text to be scanned.

- `int first()`

  moves the current boundary to the first boundary position in the scanned string and returns the index.

- `int next()`

  moves the current boundary to the next boundary position and returns the index. Returns `BreakIterator.DONE` if the end of the string has been reached.

- `int previous()`

  Move the current boundary to the previous boundary position and return the index. Returns `BreakIterator.DONE` if the beginning of the string has been reached.

- `int last()`

  moves the current boundary to the last boundary position in the scanned string and returns the index.

  `int current()`

  returns the index of the current boundary.

- `int next(int n)`

  moves the current boundary to the nth boundary position from the current one and returns the index. If n is negative, then the position is set closer to the beginning to the string. Returns `BreakIterator.DONE` if the end or beginning of the string has been reached.

- `int following(int pos)`

  moves the current boundary to the first boundary position after offset `pos` in the scanned string and returns the index. The returned value is always larger than `pos` or `BreakIterator.DONE`.

Message Formatting

In the early days of "mail-merge" programs, you had strings like:

```
"On {2}, a {0} destroyed {1} houses and caused {3} of
    damage."
```

where the numbers in braces were placeholders for actual names and values. This technique is actually very convenient for doing certain kinds of internationalization, and Java has a convenience `MessageFormat` class to allow formatting text that has a pattern. The basic way of using this class follows these steps.

1. Write the pattern as a string. You can use up to 10 placeholders `{0}`...`{9}`. You can use each placeholder more than once.

2. Construct a `MessageFormat` object with the pattern string as the constructor parameter.

3. Build an array of objects to substitute for the placeholders. The number inside the braces refers to the index in the array of objects.

4. Call the `format` method with the array of objects as a parameter.

Here is an example of these steps. We first supply the array of objects for the placeholders.

```
String pattern =
    "On {2}, a {0} destroyed {1} houses and caused {3} of
        damage.";
MessageFormat msgFmt = new MessageFormat(pattern);

Object[] msgArgs = {
    "hurricane",
    new Integer(99),
    new GregorianCalendar(1999, 0, 1).getTime(),
    new Double(10E7)
};
String msg = msgFmt.format(msgArgs);
System.out.println(msg);
```

The number of the placeholder refers to the index in the object array. For example, the first placeholder {2} is replaced with msgArgs[2]. Since we need to supply objects, we have to remember to wrap integers and floating-point numbers in their Integer and Double wrappers before passing them. Notice the cumbersome construction of the date that we used. The format method expects an object of type Date, but the Date(int, int, int) constructor is deprecated in favor of the Calendar class. Therefore, we have to create a Calendar object and then call the getTime (sic) method to convert it to a Date object.

This code prints:

```
On 1/1/99 12:00 AM, a hurricane destroyed 99 houses
    and caused 100,000,000 of damage.
```

That is a start, but it is not perfect. We don't want to display the time "12:00 AM," and we want the damage amount printed as a currency value. The way we do this is by supplying an (optional) format for some or all of the placeholders. There are two ways to supply formats:

- By adding them to the pattern string

- By calling the setFormat or setFormats method

Let's do the easy one first. We can set a format for each individual *occurrence* of a placeholder. In our example, we want the first occurrence of a placeholder (which is placeholder {2}) to be formatted as a date, without a time field. And we want the fourth placeholder to be formatted as a currency. Actually, the placeholders are numbered starting at 0, so we actually want to set the formats of placeholders 0 and 3. We will use the formatters that you saw earlier in this chapter, namely, DateFormat.getDateInstance(loc) and NumberFormat.getCurrencyInstance(loc), where loc is the locale we want to use. Conveniently, all formatters have a common base class Format. The setFormat method of the MessageText class receives an integer, the 0-based count of the placeholder to which the format should be applied, and a Format reference.

To build the format we want, we simply set the formats of placeholders 0 and 3 and then call the format method.

```
msgFmt.setFormat(0,
    DateFormat.getDateInstance(DateFormat.LONG, loc));
msgFmt.setFormat(3, NumberFormat.getCurrencyInstance(loc));
String msg = msgFmt.format(msgArgs);
System.out.println(msg);
```

Now, the printout is

```
On January 1, 1999, a hurricane destroyed 99 houses
and caused $100,000,000.00 of damage.
```

Next, rather than setting the formats individually, we can pack them into an array. Use `null` if you don't need any special format.

```
Format argFormats[] =
{  DateFormat.getDateInstance(DateFormat.LONG, loc),
   null,
   null,
   NumberFormat.getCurrencyInstance(loc)
};

msgFmt.setFormats(argFormats);
```

Note that the `msgArgs` and the `argFormats` array entries *do not correspond to one another*. The `msgArgs` indexes correspond to the number inside the `{}` delimiters. The `argFormats` indexes correspond to the position of the `{}` delimiters inside the message string. This arrangement sounds cumbersome, but there is a reason for it. It is possible for the placeholders to be repeated in the string, and each occurrence may require a different format. Therefore, the formats must be indexed by position. For example, if the exact time of the disaster was known, we might use the date object twice, once to extract the day and once to extract the time.

```
String pattern =
    "On {2}, a {0} touched down at {2} and destroyed {1}
        houses.";
MessageFormat msgFmt = new MessageFormat(pattern);

Format argFormats[] =
{  DateFormat.getDateInstance(DateFormat.LONG, loc),
   null,
   DateFormat.getTimeInstance(DateFormat.SHORT, loc),
   null
};
msg.setFormats(argFormats);

Object[] msgArgs = {
    "hurricane",
    new Integer(99),
    new GregorianCalendar(1999, 0, 1, 11, 45, 0).getTime(),
};
String msg = msgFmt.format(msgArgs);
System.out.println(msg);
```

This example code prints:

```
On January 1, 1999, a hurricane touched down
at 11:45 AM and destroyed 99 houses.
```

Note that the placeholder {2} was printed twice, with two different formats!

Rather than setting placeholders dynamically, we can also set them in the message string. For example, here we specify the date and currency formats directly in the message pattern.

```
"On {2,date,long}, a {0} destroyed {1} houses
and caused {3,number,currency} of damage."
```

If you specify formats directly, you don't need to make a call to `setFormat` or `setFormats`. In general, you can make the placeholder index be followed by a type and a style. Separate the index, *type,* and *style* by commas. The type can be any of:

```
number
time
date
choice
```

If the type is `number`, then the style can be:

```
integer
currency
percent
```

or it can be a number format pattern such as `$,##0`. (See Chapter 3 of Volume 1 for a discussion of number format patterns.)

If the type is either `time` or `date`, then the style can be:

```
short
medium
long
full
```

or a date format pattern. (See the documentation of the `SimpleDateFormat` class for more information about the possible formats.)

Choice formats are more complex, and we take them up in the next section.

 `java.text.MessageFormat`

- `MessageFormat(String pattern)`

  constructs a message format object with the specified pattern.

- `void setLocale(Locale loc)/Locale getLocale()`

  sets or gets the locale to be used for the placeholders in the message.

- `void setFormats(Format[] formats)/Format[] getFormats()`

  sets or gets the formats to be used for the placeholders in the message.

- `setFormat(int i, Format format)`

  sets the formats to be used for the i th placeholder in the message.

- `String format(Object[] args)`

  formats the objects by using `args[i]` as input for placeholder `{i}`.

Choice Formats

Let's look closer at the pattern of the preceding section:

```
"On {2}, a {0} destroyed {1} houses and caused {3} of damage."
```

If we replace the disaster placeholder `{0}` with `"earthquake"`, then the sentence is not grammatically correct in English.

```
On January 1, 1999, a earthquake destroyed ...
```

That means what we really want to do is integrate the article "a" into the place-holder:

```
"On {2}, {0} destroyed {1} houses and caused {3} of damage."
```

Then, the `{0}` would be replaced with `"a hurricane"` or `"an earthquake"`. That is especially appropriate if this message needs to be translated into a language where the gender of a word affects the article. For example, in German, the pattern would be

```
"{0} zerstörte am {2} {1} Häuser und richtete einen Schaden von
    {3} an."
```

The placeholder would then be replaced with the grammatically correct combination of article and noun, such as `"Ein Hurrikan"`, `"Eine Naturkatastrophe"`.

Now let us turn to the `{1}` parameter. If the disaster isn't all that catastrophic, then `{1}` might be replaced with the number 1, and the message would read:

```
On January 1, 1999, a mudslide destroyed 1 houses and ...
```

We would ideally like the message to vary according to the placeholder value, so that it can read

```
no houses
one house
2 houses
. . .
```

depending on the placeholder value. The `ChoiceFormat` class was designed to let you do this. A `ChoiceFormat` object is constructed with two arrays:

- An array of *limits*

- An array of *format strings*
  ```
  double[] limits = . . .;
  String[] formatStrings = . . .;
  ```

```
ChoiceFormat choiceFmt = new ChoiceFormat(limits,
    formatStrings);
double input;
String s = choiceFmt.format(input);
```

The `limits` and `formatStrings` arrays must have the same length. The numbers in the `limits` array must be in ascending order. Then, the `format` method checks between which limits the input falls. If

```
limits[i] <= input && input < limits[i + 1]
```

then `formatStrings[i]` is used to format the input. If the input is at least as large as the last limit, then the last format string is used. And, if the input is less than `limits[0]`, then `formatStrings[0]` is used anyway.

For example, consider these limits and format strings:

```
double[] limits = {0, 1, 2};
String[] formatStrings = {"no house", "one house", "many
    houses"};
```

Table 9-4 shows the return values of the call to

```
String selected = choiceFmt.format(input);
```

Table 9-4: String selected by `ChoiceFormat`

input	selected
input < 0	"no houses"
0 <= input && input < 1	"no houses"
1 <= input && input < 2	"one house"
2 <= input	"many houses"

NOTE: This example shows that the designer of the `ChoiceFormat` class was a bit muddleheaded. If you have three strings, you need two limits to separate them. In general, you need *one fewer limit* than you have strings. Thus, the first limit is meaningless, and you can simply set the first and second limit to the same number. For example, the following code works fine:

```
double[] limits = {1, 1, 2};
String[] formatStrings = {"no house", "one house", "many
    houses"};
ChoiceFormat choiceFmt = new ChoiceFormat(limits,
    formatStrings);
```

Of course, in our case, we don't want to return `"many houses"` if the number of houses is 2 or greater. We still want the value to be formatted. Here is the code to format the value:

```
double[] limits = {0, 1, 2};
String[] formatStrings = {"no house", "one house", "{1}
    houses"};
ChoiceFormat choiceFmt = new ChoiceFormat(limits,
    formatStrings);
msgFmt.setFormat(2, choiceFmt);
```

That is, we create the choice format object and set it as the format to use for the third placeholder (because the count is 0-based).

Why do we use `{1}` in the format string? The usage is a little mysterious. When the message format applies the choice format on the placeholder, the choice format returns `"{1} houses"`. That string is then formatted again by the message format, and the answer is spliced into the result. As a rule, you should always feed back the same placeholder that was used to make the choice. Otherwise, you can create weird effects.

You can add formatting information to the returned string, for example,

```
String[] formatStrings
    = {"no house", "one house", "{1, number, integer} houses"};
```

As you saw in the preceding section, it is also possible to express the choice format directly in a format string. When the format type is `choice`, then the next parameter is a list of pairs, each pair consisting of a limit and a format string, separated by a #. The pairs themselves are separated by |. Here is how to express the house format:

```
{1,choice,0#no houses|1#one house|2#{1} houses}
```

Thus, there are three sets of choices:

```
0#no houses
1#one house
2#{1} houses
```

The first one is used if the placeholder value is < 1, the second is used if the value is at least one but < 2, and the third is used if it is at least 2.

NOTE: As previously noted, the first limit is meaningless. But here you can't set the first and second limits to the same value; the format parser complains that

```
1#no houses|1#one house|2#{1} houses
```

is an invalid choice. In this case, you must set the first limit to any number that is strictly less than the second limit.

The syntax would have been a lot clearer if the designer of this class realized that the limits belong *between* the choices, such as

```
no houses|1|one house|2|{1} houses
// not the actual format
```

If we put the choice string inside the original message string, then we get the rather monstrous format instruction:

```
String pattern =
"On {2,date,long}, {0} destroyed {1,choice,0#no houses|1#one
    house|2#{1} houses}
and caused {3,number,currency} of damage.";
```

Or, in German,

```
String pattern =
"{0} zerstörte am {2,date,long} {1,choice,0#kein Haus|1#ein
    Haus|2#{1} Häuser}
und richtete einen Schaden von {3,number,currency} an.";
```

Note that the ordering of the words is different in German, but the array of objects you pass to the format method is the *same*. The order of the placeholders in the format string takes care of the changes in the word ordering.

java.text.ChoiceFormat

- ChoiceFormat(String pattern)

  constructs a choice format from a pattern string containing a | delimited set of pairs, each of which is of the form *limit#formatString*.

- ChoiceFormat(double limits[], String formatStrings[])

  constructs a choice format with the given limits and formats. The limits must be increasing. If input is the value to be formatted, then it is formatted with the formatString[i] where i is the smallest index such that limits[i] <= input. However, all inputs that are less than limits[1] are formatted with formatString[0].

Character Set Conversion

As you know, Java itself is fully Unicode based. However, operating systems typically have their own, homegrown, often incompatible, character encoding, such as ISO 8859-1 (an 8-bit code sometimes called the "ANSI" code) in the United States or BIG5 in Taiwan. So the input that you receive from a user might be in a different encoding system, and the strings that you show to the user must eventually be encoded in a way that the local operating system understands.

Of course, *inside* your program, you should always use Unicode characters. You have to hope that the implementation of the Java Virtual Machine on that platform successfully converts input and output between Unicode and the local character set. For example, if you set a button label, you specify the string in Unicode, and it is up to the Java Virtual Machine to get the button to display your string correctly. Similarly, when you call getText to get user input from a text box, you get the string in Unicode, no matter how the user entered it.

However, *you* need to be careful with text files. Never read a text file one byte at a time! Always use the InputStreamReader or FileReader classes that were described in Chapter 1. These classes automatically convert from a particular character encoding to Unicode. By default, they use the local encoding scheme but as you saw in Chapter 1, you can specify the encoding in the constructor of the InputStreamReader class, for example,

```
InputStreamReader = new InputStreamReader(in, "8859_1");
```

Unfortunately, there is currently no connection between locales and character encodings. For example, if your user has selected the Chinese Traditional locale zh_TW, there is no Java method that tells you that the BIG5 character encoding would be the most appropriate.

When writing text files, you need to decide:

*   Is the output of the text file intended for humans to read or for use with other programs on their local machines?

*   Is the output simply going to be fed into the same or another Java program?

If the output is intended for human consumption or a non-Unicode-enabled program, you'll need to convert it to the local character encoding by using a PrintWriter, as you saw in Chapter 1. Otherwise, just use the writeUTF method of the DataOutputStream to write the string in Unicode Text Format. Then, of course, the Java program reading the file must open it as a DataInputStream and read the string with the readUTF method.

> TIP: In the case of input to a Java program, an even better choice is to use serialization. Then, you never have to worry at all how strings are saved and loaded.

Of course, with both data streams and object streams, the output will not be in human-readable form.

International Issues and Source Files

It is worth keeping in mind that you, the Java programmer, will need to communicate with the Java compiler. And, *you do that with tools on your local system.* For example, you may use the Chinese version of NotePad to write your Java source code files. The resulting source code files are *not portable* because they use the local character encoding (GB or BIG5, depending on which Chinese operating system you use). Only the compiled class files are portable—they will automatically use the UTF encoding for identifiers and strings. That means that even when a Java program is compiling and running, three character encodings are involved:

- Source files: local encoding

- Class files: UTF

- Virtual machine: Unicode

To make your source files portable, restrict yourself to using the plain ASCII encoding. That is, you should change all non-ASCII characters to their equivalent Unicode encodings. For example, rather than using the string `"Häuser"`, use `"H\u0084user"`. The JDK contains a utility, `native2ascii`, that you can use to convert the native character encoding to plain ASCII. This utility simply replaces every non-ASCII character in the input with a `\u` followed by the four hex digits of the Unicode value. To use the `native2ascii` program, simply provide the input and output file names.

```
native2ascii Myfile.java Myfile.temp
```

You can convert the other way with the `-reverse` option:

```
native2ascii -reverse Myfile.java Myfile.temp
```

And you can specify another encoding with the `-encoding` option. The encoding name must be one of the ones listed in the encodings table in Chapter 1.

```
native2ascii -encoding Cp437 Myfile.java Myfile.temp
```

Finally, we strongly recommend that you restrict yourself to plain ASCII class names. Since the name of the class also turns into the name of the *class file,* you are at the mercy of the local file system to handle any non-ASCII coded names—and it will almost certainly not do it right. For example, depressingly enough, Windows 95 uses yet another character encoding, the so-called *Code Page 437* or *original PC* encoding, for its file names. Windows 95 makes a valiant attempt to translate between ANSI and original names, but the Java class loader does not. (NT is much better this way.) For example, if you make a class Bär, then the JDK class loader will complain that it "cannot find class B∑r." There is a reason for this behavior, but you don't want to know. Simply stick to ASCII for your class names until all computers around the world offer consistent support for Unicode.

Resource Bundles

When localizing an application, you'll probably have a dauntingly large number of message strings, button labels, and so on, that all need to be translated. To make this task feasible, you'll want to define the message strings in an external location, usually called a *resource*. The person carrying out the translation can then simply edit the resource files without having to touch the source code of the program.

NOTE: Java resources are not the same as Windows or Macintosh resources. A Windows executable program stores resources such as menus, dialog boxes, icons, and messages in a section separate from the program code. A resource editor can be used to inspect and update these resources without affecting the program code.

Java, unfortunately, does not have a mechanism for storing external resources in class files. Instead, all resource data must be put in a *class*, either as static variables or as return values of method calls. You create a different class for each locale, and then the getBundle method of the ResourceBundle class automatically locates the correct class for your locale.

NOTE: Chapter 10 of Volume 1 describes a concept of file resources, where data files, sounds, and images can be placed in a JAR file. The getResource method of the class Class finds the file, opens it and returns a URL to the resource. Why? When you write a program that needs access to files, it needs to *find* the files. By placing the files into the JAR file, you leave the job of finding the files to the class loader, which already knows how to locate the class files. While this mechanism does not directly support internationalization, it is useful for locating localized property files, and we take advantage of it in the next section.

Locating Resources

When localizing an application, you need to make a set of classes that describe the locale-specific items (such as messages, labels, and so on) for each locale that

you want to support. Each of these classes must extend the class `ResourceBundle`. (You'll see a little later the details involved in designing these kinds of classes.) You also need to use a naming convention for these classes, where the name of the class corresponds to the locale. For example, resources specific for Germany go to the class `ProgramResources_de_DE`, while those that are shared by all German-speaking countries go into `ProgramResources_de`. Taiwan-specific resources go into `ProgramResources_zh_TW`, and any Chinese language strings go into `ProgramResources_zh`. In general, use

```
ProgramResources_language_country
```

for all country-specific resources, and use

```
ProgramResources_language
```

for all language-specific resources. Finally, as a fallback, you can put the US English strings and messages into the class `ProgramResources`, without any suffix. Then, compile all these classes and store them with the other application classes for the project.

Once you have a class for the resource bundle, you load it with the command

```
ResourceBundle currentResources =
    ResourceBundle.getBundle("ProgramResources", currentLocale);
```

The `getBundle` method attempts to load the class that matches the current locale by language, country, and variant. If it is not successful, then the variant, country, and language are dropped in turn. That is, the `getBundle` method tries to load one of the following classes until it is successful.

```
ProgramResources_language_country_variant
ProgramResources_language_country
ProgramResources_language
ProgramResources
```

If all these atttempts are unsuccessful, then the `getBundle` method tries all over again, only this time it uses the default locale instead of the current locale. If even these attempts fail, the method throws a `MissingResourceException`.

Once the `getBundle` method has located a class, say, `ProgramResources_de_DE`, it will still keep looking for `ProgramResources_de` and `ProgramResources`. If these classes exist, they become the *parents* of the `ProgramResources_de_DE` class in a *resource hierarchy*. Later, when looking up a resource, the `getObject` method will search the parents if the lookup was not successful in the current class. That is, if a particular resource was not found in `ProgramResources_de_DE`, then the `ProgramResources_de` and `ProgramResources` will be queried as well.

This is clearly a very useful service and one that would be incredibly tedious to

program by hand. Java's resource mechanism lets you locate the class that is the best match for localization information. It is very easy to add more and more localizations to an existing program: all you have to do is add additional resource classes.

Now that you know how a Java program can locate the correct resource, we show you how to place the language-dependent information into the resource class. Ultimately, it would be nice if you could get tools that even a non-programmer could use to define and modify resources. We hope and expect that developers of integrated Java environments will eventually provide such tools. But right now, creating resources still involves some programming. We take that up next.

Placing Resources into Bundles

In Java, you place resources inside classes that extend the `ResourceBundle` class. Each resource bundle implements a lookup table. When you design a program, you provide a key string for each setting you want to localize, and you use that key string to retrieve the setting.

```
String computeButtonLabel
    = (String)resources.getObject("computeButton");
Color backgroundColor
    = (Color)resources.getObject("backgroundColor");
double[] paperSize
    = (double[])resources.getObject("defaultPaperSize");
```

As you can see, it is quite convenient that a resource bundle can store objects of *any* kind. Not all localized settings are strings!

TIP: You do not need to place all resources for your application into a single bundle. You could have one bundle for button labels, one for error messages, and so on.

For example, you can write the following classes to provide English and German resources.

```
public class ProgramResources_de extends ResourceBundle
{   public static Object getObject(String key)
    if (key.equals("computeButton"))
        return "Rechnen";
    else if (key.equals("backgroundColor")
        return Color.black;
    else if (key.equals("defaultPaperSize")
        return new double[] { 210, 297 };
}
```

```
public class ProgramResources_en_US extends ResourceBundle
{  public static Object getObject(String key)
   if (key.equals("computeButton"))
      return "Compute";
   else if (key.equals("backgroundColor")
      return Color.blue;
   else if (key.equals("defaultPaperSize"))
      return new double[] { 216, 279 };
}
```

NOTE: Everyone on the planet, with the exception of the United States and Canada, uses ISO 216 paper sizes. For more information, see http://www.ft.uni-erlangen.de/~mskuhn/iso-paper.html. According to the U.S. Metric Association (http://lamar.colostate.edu/~hillger), there are only three countries in the world that have not yet officially adopted the metric system, namely, Liberia, Myanmar (Burma), and the United States of America. U.S. businesses that wish to extend their export market further need to go metric. See http://ts.nist.gov/ts/htdocs/200/202/mpo_reso.htm for a useful set of links to information about the metric (SI) system.

Of course, it is extremely tedious to write this kind of code for every resource bundle. The Java standard library provides two convenience classes, `ListResourceBundle` and `PropertyResourceBundle`, to make the job easier.

The `ListResourceBundle` lets you place all your resources into an object array, and then it does the lookup for you. You need to supply the following skeleton:

```
public class ProgramResource_language_country
   extends ListResourceBundle
{  public Object[][] getContents() { return contents;  }
   static final Object[][] contents =
   {  // localization information goes here
   }
}
```

For example,

```
public class ProgramResource_de
   extends ListResourceBundle
{  public Object[][] getContents() { return contents;  }
   static final Object[][] contents =
   {  { "computeButton", "Rechnen" },
      { "backgroundColor", Color.black },
      { "defaultPaperSize", new double[] { 210, 297 } }
   }
}

public class ProgramResource_en_US
   extends ListResourceBundle
```

```
{   public Object[][] getContents() { return contents;   }
    static final Object[][] contents =
    {   { "computeButton", "Compute" },
        { "backgroundColor", Color.blue },
        { "defaultPaperSize", new double[] { 216, 279 } }
    }
}
```

Note that you need not supply the getObject lookup method. Java provides it in the base class ListResourceBundle.

As an alternative, if all your settings are strings, you can use the more convenient PropertyResourceBundle. You place all your strings into a property file, as described in Chapter 11 of Volume 1. This is simply a text file with one key/value pair per line. A typical file would look like this:

```
computeButton=Rechnen
backgroundColor=black
defaultPaperSize=210x297
```

Then, you open a stream to the property file and pass it to the PropertyResourceBundle constructor.

```
InputStream in = . . .; // open property file
PropertyResourceBundle currentResources
    = new PropertyResourceBundle(in);
```

Placing all resources into a text file is enormously attractive. It is much easier for the person performing the localization, especially if he or she is not a Java programmer, to understand a text file than a file with Java code. The downside is that your program must parse strings (such as the paper size "210x297" in the example above.) The best solution is therefore to put the string resources into property files and use a ListResourceBundle for those resource objects that are not strings.

We still have one remaining issue: How can the running Java program locate the file that contains the localized strings? Naturally, that file is best placed with the class files of the application, preferably inside a JAR file. Then, we can use the getResourceAsStream method of the Class class. The method will find the right file and open it.

```
in = Program.class.getResourceAsStream("ProgramProperties_de.
    txt");
PropertyResourceBundle currentResources
    = new PropertyResourceBundle(in);
```

It would be nice if the PropertyResourceBundle class could look for resource text files in the same way that the ResourceBundle class looks for class files. Unfortunately, it does not. Thus, you have to write a class file to accompany

every text file. Fortunately, writing such as class file is completely mechanical. For example, here is the class file that loads `ProgramResources_de.txt`.

```
public class ProgramProperties_de
    extends PropertyResourceBundle
{   ProgramProperties_de() throws IOException
    {   super(ProgramProperties_de.class.getResourceAsStream
            ("ProgramProperties_de.txt"));
    }
}
```

You need to produce two files: the class file and the property file, a text file containing key/value pairs. Place both the class file and property file in the same location in the directory or JAR file.

However, before you actually try to carry out this scheme, be advised that there is a fatal flaw in the current version of Java.

In Java 1.1, the `PropertyResourceBundle` class can read only ISO 8859-1 characters (that is, the 8-bit characters sometimes called the "ANSI" code). Property files are read a byte at a time, with no character code conversion. No other Unicode characters can be specified in a property file.

This flaw (which will eventually be remedied when the `Properties` class is reimplemented to be locale aware) makes the `PropertyResourceBundle` class unsuitable for storing translated messages. You can get away with using it for Western European languages, but it is not a general solution. At this point, we recommend that you use the `ListResourceBundle` and hope for better language and tool support in the near future.

java.util.ResourceBundle

- `static ResourceBundle getBundle(String baseName, Locale loc)`
- `static ResourceBundle getBundle(String baseName)`

  load the resource bundle class with the given name, for the given locale or the default locale, and its parent classes. If the resource bundle classes are located in a package, then the base name must contain the full package name, such as `"intl.ProgramResources"`. The resource bundle classes must be `public` so that the `getBundle` method can access them.

- `Object getObject(String)`

  looks up an object from the resource bundle or its parents.

- `String getString(String)`

  looks up an object from the resource bundle or its parents and casts it as a string.

- `String[] getObject(String)`

  looks up an object from the resource bundle or its parents and casts it as a string array.

- `Enumeration getKeys()`

  returns an enumeration object to enumerate the keys of this resource bundle. It enumerates the keys in the parent bundles as well.

`java.util.PropertyResourceBundle`

- `PropertiesResourceBundle(InputStream in)`

  creates a resource bundle that contains the key/value pairs from the given input stream.

Graphical User Interface Localization

We have spent a lot of time showing you how to localize your applications. Now, we explain how localization requires you to change the kind of code you write. For example, you have to be much more careful how you code your event handlers for user interface events. Consider the following common style of programming:

```
public class MyApplet implements ActionListener
{  public void init()
   {  Button cancelButton = new Button("Cancel");
      cancelButton.addActionListener(this);
      . . .
   }
   public void actionPerformed(ActionEvent evt)
   {  String arg = evt.getActionCommand();
      if (arg.equals("Cancel"))
          doCancel();
      else . . .
   }
   . . .
   private Button cancelButton;
}
```

This example is the standard way to write code, and it works fine as long as you *never* internationalize the interface. Once you do, you are hosed. This code will not work in an internationalized project that adjusts (as it should) the names of

the buttons. When the button name is translated to German, "Cancel" turns into "Abbrechen." Then, the name will need to be updated automatically in both the `init` method and the `actionPerformed` method. This is clearly error prone—it is a well-known corollary to Murphy's theorem in computer science that two entities that are supposed to stay in synch, won't. In this case, if you forget to update one of the occurrences of the string, then the button won't work. There are three ways you can eliminate this potential problem.

1. Use inner classes instead of separate `actionPerformed` procedures.

2. Identify components by their reference, not their label.

3. Use the `name` attribute to identify components.

Let us look at these three strategies one by one.

Rather than having one handler that handles many actions, you can easily define a separate handler for every component. For example,

```
cancelButton = new Button("Cancel");
cancelButton.addActionListener(new ActionListener()
    { public void actionPerformed(ActionEvent e)
        { doCancel(); } } );
```

This code creates an inner class that listens just to the Cancel button. Since the button and its listener are now tightly joined, there is no more code to parse the button label. Hence, there is only one occurrence of the label string to localize.

You may not like inner classes, either because they are confusing to read or because each inner class results in an additional class file. The next choice, therefore, is to make the button into an instance variable and compare its reference against the source of the command.

```
public class MyApplet implements ActionListener
{   public void init()
    {   cancelButton = new Button("Cancel");
        cancelButton.addActionListener(this);
        . . .
    }
    public void actionPerformed(ActionEvent evt)
    {   Object source = evt.getSource();
        if (source == cancelButton)
            doCancel();
        else . . .
    }
    . . .
    private Button cancelButton;
}
```

The disadvantage of this approach is that every user interface element must be stored in an instance variable, and the `actionPerformed` method must have access to the variables.

Finally, you can give any class that inherits from Component (such as the Button class) a *name* property, much as Visual Basic gives each component a name. This name may or may not be distinct from its label in a specific locale, but this is irrelevant; the name property stays constant *regardless* of locale changes. For example, if you give a cancel button the name `"Cancel"`, this is not a visual attribute of the button, it is simply a (text) string associated to the button. (Think of it as a property of the button—see Chapter 6 for more on properties.) When an action event is triggered, you first get the source and then you can find the name attribute of the source.

```java
public class MyApplet implements ActionListener
{   public void init()
    {   Button cancelButton = new Button("Cancel");
        cancelButton.setName("Cancel");
        cancelButton.addActionListener(this);
        . . .
    }
    public void actionPerformed(ActionEvent evt)
    {   Component source = (Component)evt.getSource();
        if (source.getName().equals("Cancel"))
            doCancel();
        else . . .
    }
    . . .
}
```

The possibility of having a name attribute for AWT components was added to Java in version 1.1. At the same time, the Java developers added a second attribute, the current locale, to the Component class. Usually, components do not have their own locale, but they inherit a locale from their parent. Top-level components such as windows and applets have their locales set to the system locale when they are created. You can determine the locale of any component with the getLocale method.

Typically, you use the getLocale method in an applet to tell you the locale of the client computer that executes your code. You can then adapt the behavior of the code to the locale of the user.

java.awt.Component

- void setName(String s)/String getName()

  sets or gets a component name, an arbitrary tag associated with the component.

- Locale getLocale()

  gets the current locale of the component. The current locale is typically inherited from the parent. If the component has not yet been attached to a parent and no locale was set, then an IllegalComponentState exception is thrown.

java.awt.Applet

- Locale getLocale()

  gets the current locale of the applet. The curent locale is determined from the client computer that executes the applet.

Localizing an Applet

In this section, we apply the material from this chapter to localize the retirement calculator from Chapter 10 of Volume 1. The retirement calculator now works in three locales (English, German, and Chinese). Here is what we needed to do.

- The labels, buttons and messages were translated into German and Chinese from the original English. You can find them in the classes RetireResources_de, RetireResources_zh, and RetireResources. (English is used as the fallback.) To generate the Chinese messages, we first typed the file in Chinese Windows 95 and then used the native2ascii utility to convert the characters to Unicode.

- Whenever the locale changed, we reset the labels and reformatted the contents of the text fields.

- The numeric fields handle numbers, currency amounts, and percentages in the local format. This was a tedious change, and we did not implement error-handling in this program. The code would have been a lot simpler if we had access to friendly and locale-aware input field beans.

- The computation field uses a MessageFormat. The format string is stored in the resource bundle of each language. Unfortunately, there is a bug in the version of MessageFormat we had available—it pays no attention to its locale when formatting currencies.

- Just to show that it could be done, we used different colors for the bar graph, depending on the language chosen by the user.

Examples 9-5 through 9-8 show the code. Figures 9-5 and 9-6 show the outputs in German and Chinese. You need to run the Chinese program under Chinese Windows or manually install the Chinese fonts. Otherwise, all Chinese characters show up as "missing character" icons.

> NOTE: This applet was harder to write than a typical localized application because the user can change the locale on the fly. The applet, therefore, had to be prepared to redraw itself whenever the user selects another locale. Normally, you will not need to work so hard. You can simply call `getLocale()` to find the locale of your user's system and then use it for the entire duration of the application.

In sum, while the Java localization mechanism still has some rough edges, it does have one major virtue. Once you have organized your application for localization, it is extremely easy to add more localized versions. You simply provide more resource files, and they will be automatically loaded when a user wants them.

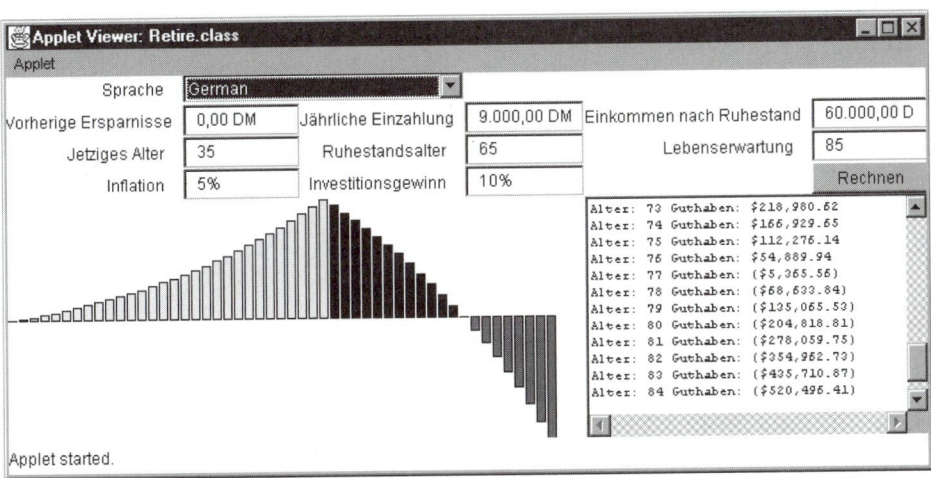

Figure 9-5: The retirement calculator in German

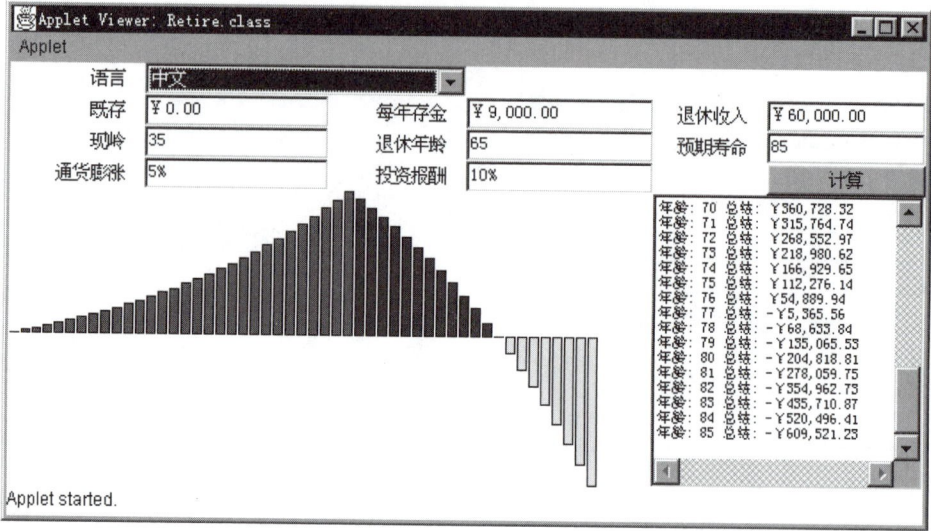

Figure 9-6: The retirement calculator in Chinese

Example 9-5: Retire.java

```java
import java.awt.*;
import java.awt.event.*;
import java.applet.*;
import java.util.*;
import java.text.*;
import java.io.*;
import corejava.*;

public class Retire extends Applet
    implements ActionListener, ItemListener
{  public void init()
    {  GridBagLayout gbl = new GridBagLayout();
       setLayout(gbl);

       GridBagConstraints gbc = new GridBagConstraints();
       gbc.weightx = 100;
       gbc.weighty = 100;

       gbc.fill = GridBagConstraints.NONE;
       gbc.anchor = GridBagConstraints.EAST;
       add(languageLabel, gbc, 0, 0, 1, 1);
       add(savingsLabel, gbc, 0, 1, 1, 1);
       add(contribLabel, gbc, 2, 1, 1, 1);
       add(incomeLabel, gbc, 4, 1, 1, 1);
       add(currentAgeLabel, gbc, 0, 2, 1, 1);
```

```
add(retireAgeLabel, gbc, 2, 2, 1, 1);
add(deathAgeLabel, gbc, 4, 2, 1, 1);
add(inflationPercentLabel, gbc, 0, 3, 1, 1);
add(investPercentLabel, gbc, 2, 3, 1, 1);

gbc.fill = GridBagConstraints.HORIZONTAL;
gbc.anchor = GridBagConstraints.WEST;
add(localeChoice, gbc, 1, 0, 2, 1);
add(savingsField, gbc, 1, 1, 1, 1);
add(contribField, gbc, 3, 1, 1, 1);
add(incomeField, gbc, 5, 1, 1, 1);
add(currentAgeField, gbc, 1, 2, 1, 1);
add(retireAgeField, gbc, 3, 2, 1, 1);
add(deathAgeField, gbc, 5, 2, 1, 1);
add(inflationPercentField, gbc, 1, 3, 1, 1);
add(investPercentField, gbc, 3, 3, 1, 1);

computeButton.setName("computeButton");
computeButton.addActionListener(this);
add(computeButton, gbc, 5, 3, 1, 1);
add(retireCanvas, gbc, 0, 4, 4, 1);
gbc.fill = GridBagConstraints.BOTH;
add(retireText, gbc, 4, 4, 2, 1);
retireText.setEditable(false);
retireText.setFont(new Font("Monospaced", Font.PLAIN, 10));

info.savings = 0;
info.contrib = 9000;
info.income = 60000;
info.currentAge = 35;
info.retireAge = 65;
info.deathAge = 85;
info.investPercent = 0.1;
info.inflationPercent = 0.05;


localeChoice.addItemListener(this);
locales = new Locale[]
    { Locale.US, Locale.CHINA, Locale.GERMANY };
for (int i = 0; i < locales.length; i++)
    localeChoice.add(locales[i].getDisplayLanguage());
localeChoice.select(0);
setCurrentLocale();
}

void updateDisplay()
{  languageLabel.setText(res.getString("language"));
   savingsLabel.setText(res.getString("savings"));
```

```
        contribLabel.setText(res.getString("contrib"));
        incomeLabel.setText(res.getString("income"));
        currentAgeLabel.setText(res.getString("currentAge"));
        retireAgeLabel.setText(res.getString("retireAge"));
        deathAgeLabel.setText(res.getString("deathAge"));
        inflationPercentLabel.setText
            (res.getString("inflationPercent"));
        investPercentLabel.setText
            (res.getString("investPercent"));
        computeButton.setLabel(res.getString("computeButton"));

        doLayout();
    }

    void setCurrentLocale()
    {   currentLocale
            = locales[localeChoice.getSelectedIndex()];
        res = ResourceBundle.getBundle("RetireResources",
            currentLocale);
        currencyFmt
            = NumberFormat.getCurrencyInstance(currentLocale);
        numberFmt
            = NumberFormat.getNumberInstance(currentLocale);
        percentFmt
            = NumberFormat.getPercentInstance(currentLocale);

        updateDisplay();
        updateInfo();
        updateData();
        updateGraph();
    }

    void updateInfo()
    {   savingsField.setText(currencyFmt.format(info.savings));
        contribField.setText(currencyFmt.format(info.contrib));
        incomeField.setText(currencyFmt.format(info.income));
        currentAgeField.setText(numberFmt.format(info.currentAge));
        retireAgeField.setText(numberFmt.format(info.retireAge));
        deathAgeField.setText(numberFmt.format(info.deathAge));
        investPercentField.setText
            (percentFmt.format(info.investPercent));
        inflationPercentField.setText
            (percentFmt.format(info.inflationPercent));
    }

    void updateData()
    {   retireText.setText("");
        MessageFormat retireMsg = new MessageFormat
```

```
        (res.getString("retire"));
    retireMsg.setLocale(getLocale());
    for (int i = info.currentAge; i <= info.deathAge; i++)
    {   Object[] args = { new Integer(i),
            new Double(info.getBalance(i)) };
        retireText.append(retireMsg.format(args) + "\n");
    }

}

void updateGraph()
{   info.colorPre = (Color)res.getObject("colorPre");
    info.colorGain = (Color)res.getObject("colorGain");
    info.colorLoss = (Color)res.getObject("colorLoss");
    retireCanvas.redraw(info);
}

public void add(Component c, GridBagConstraints gbc,
    int x, int y, int w, int h)
{   gbc.gridx = x;
    gbc.gridy = y;
    gbc.gridwidth = w;
    gbc.gridheight = h;
    add(c, gbc);
}

public void itemStateChanged(ItemEvent evt)
{   if (evt.getStateChange() == ItemEvent.SELECTED)
    {   setCurrentLocale();
    }
}

void getInfo() throws ParseException
{   info.savings =
        currencyFmt.parse
        (savingsField.getText()).doubleValue();
    info.contrib =
        currencyFmt.parse
        (contribField.getText()).doubleValue();
    info.income =
        currencyFmt.parse
        (incomeField.getText()).doubleValue();
    info.currentAge =
        (int)numberFmt.parse
        (currentAgeField.getText()).longValue();
    info.retireAge =
        (int)numberFmt.parse
        (retireAgeField.getText()).longValue();
```

```java
    info.deathAge =
        (int)numberFmt.parse
        (deathAgeField.getText()).longValue();
    info.investPercent = percentFmt.parse
        (investPercentField.getText()).doubleValue();
    info.inflationPercent = percentFmt.parse
        (inflationPercentField.getText()).doubleValue();
}

public void actionPerformed(ActionEvent evt)
{   Component source = (Component)evt.getSource();
    if (source.getName().equals("computeButton"))
    {   try
        {   getInfo();
            updateData();
            updateGraph();
        } catch(ParseException e) {}
        updateInfo();
    }
}

private TextField savingsField = new TextField(10);
private TextField contribField = new TextField(10);
private TextField incomeField = new TextField(10);
private TextField currentAgeField = new TextField(4);
private TextField retireAgeField = new TextField(4);
private TextField deathAgeField = new TextField(4);
private TextField inflationPercentField = new TextField(6);
private TextField investPercentField = new TextField(6);
private TextArea retireText = new TextArea(10, 25);
private RetireCanvas retireCanvas = new RetireCanvas();
private Button computeButton = new Button();
private Label languageLabel = new Label();
private Label savingsLabel = new Label();
private Label contribLabel = new Label();
private Label incomeLabel = new Label();
private Label currentAgeLabel = new Label();
private Label retireAgeLabel = new Label();
private Label deathAgeLabel = new Label();
private Label inflationPercentLabel = new Label();
private Label investPercentLabel = new Label();

private RetireInfo info = new RetireInfo();

private Locale[] locales;
private Locale currentLocale;
private Choice localeChoice = new Choice();
private ResourceBundle res;
```

```java
   NumberFormat currencyFmt;
   NumberFormat numberFmt;
   NumberFormat percentFmt;
}

class RetireInfo
{  public double getBalance(int year)
   {  if (year < currentAge) return 0;
      else if (year == currentAge)
      {  age = year;
         balance = savings;
         return balance;
      }
      else if (year == age)
         return balance;
      if (year != age + 1)
         getBalance(year - 1);
      age = year;
      if (age < retireAge)
         balance += contrib;
      else
         balance -= income;
      balance = balance
         * (1 + (investPercent - inflationPercent));
      return balance;
   }

   double savings;
   double contrib;
   double income;
   int currentAge;
   int retireAge;
   int deathAge;
   double inflationPercent;
   double investPercent;

   Color colorPre;
   Color colorGain;
   Color colorLoss;

   private int age;
   private double balance;
}

class RetireCanvas extends Canvas
{  public RetireCanvas()
   {  setSize(400, 200);
   }
```

```java
public void redraw(RetireInfo newInfo)
{  info = newInfo;
   repaint();
}

public void paint(Graphics g)
{  if (info == null) return;

   int minValue = 0;
   int maxValue = 0;
   int i;
   for (i = info.currentAge; i <= info.deathAge; i++)
   {  int v = (int)info.getBalance(i);
      if (minValue > v) minValue = v;
      if (maxValue < v) maxValue = v;
   }
   if (maxValue == minValue) return;

   Dimension d = getSize();
   int barWidth = d.width / (info.deathAge
      - info.currentAge + 1);
   double scale = (double)d.height
      / (maxValue - minValue);

   for (i = info.currentAge; i <= info.deathAge; i++)
   {  int x1 = (i - info.currentAge) * barWidth + 1;
      int y1;
      int v = (int)info.getBalance(i);
      int height;
      int yOrigin = (int)(maxValue * scale);

      if (v >= 0)
      {  y1 = (int)((maxValue - v) * scale);
         height = yOrigin - y1;
      }
      else
      {  y1 = yOrigin;
         height = (int)(-v * scale);
      }

      if (i < info.retireAge)
         g.setColor(info.colorPre);
      else if (v >= 0)
         g.setColor(info.colorGain);
      else
         g.setColor(info.colorLoss);
      g.fillRect(x1, y1, barWidth - 2, height);
      g.setColor(Color.black);
```

```
            g.drawRect(x1, y1, barWidth - 2, height);
        }
    }

    private RetireInfo info = null;
}
```

Example 9-6: RetireResources.java

```java
import java.util.*;
import java.awt.*;

public class RetireResources
    extends java.util.ListResourceBundle
{   public Object[][] getContents() { return contents; }
    static final Object[][] contents =
    {   // BEGIN LOCALIZE
        { "language", "Language" },
        { "computeButton", "Compute" },
        { "savings", "Prior Savings" },
        { "contrib", "Annual Contribution" },
        { "income", "Retirement Income" },
        { "currentAge", "Current Age" },
        { "retireAge", "Retirement Age" },
        { "deathAge", "Life Expectancy" },
        { "inflationPercent", "Inflation" },
        { "investPercent", "Investment Return" },
        { "retire", "Age: {0,number} Balance:
            {1,number,currency}" },
        { "colorPre", Color.blue },
        { "colorGain", Color.white },
        { "colorLoss", Color.red }
        // END LOCALIZE
    };
}
```

Example 9-7: RetireResources_de.java

```java
import java.util.*;
import java.awt.*;

public class RetireResources_de
    extends java.util.ListResourceBundle
{   public Object[][] getContents() { return contents; }
    static final Object[][] contents =
    {   // BEGIN LOCALIZE
        { "language", "Sprache" },
```

```
            { "computeButton", "Rechnen" },
            { "savings", "Vorherige Ersparnisse" },
            { "contrib", "J&hrliche Einzahlung" },
            { "income", "Einkommen nach Ruhestand" },
            { "currentAge", "Jetziges Alter" },
            { "retireAge", "Ruhestandsalter" },
            { "deathAge", "Lebenserwartung" },
            { "inflationPercent", "Inflation" },
            { "investPercent", "Investitionsgewinn" },
            { "retire", "Alter: {0,number} Guthaben:
               {1,number,currency}" },
            { "colorPre", Color.yellow },
            { "colorGain", Color.black },
            { "colorLoss", Color.red }


            // END LOCALIZE
      };
}
```

Example 9-8: RetireResources_zh.java

```
import java.util.*;
import java.awt.*;

public class RetireResources_zh
   extends java.util.ListResourceBundle
{  public Object[][] getContents() { return contents; }
   static final Object[][] contents =
   {  // BEGIN LOCALIZE
       { "language", "\u8bed\u8a00" },
       { "computeButton", "\u8ba1\u7b97" },
       { "savings", "\u65e2\u5b58" },
       { "contrib", "\u6bcf\u5e74\u5b58\u91d1" },
       { "income", "\u9000\u4f11\u6536\u5165" },
       { "currentAge", "\u73b0\u5cad" },
       { "retireAge", "\u9000\u4f11\u5e74\u9f84" },
       { "deathAge", "\u9884\u671f\u5bff\u547d" },
       { "inflationPercent", "\u901a\u8d27\u81a8\u6da8" },
       { "investPercent", "\u6295\u8d44\u62a5\u916c" },
       { "retire",
          "\u5e74\u9f84: {0,number} \u603b\u7ed3:
             {1,number,currency}" },
       { "colorPre", Color.red },
       { "colorGain", Color.blue },
       { "colorLoss", Color.yellow }
```

```
        // END LOCALIZE
   };
}
```

CHAPTER
10

- Calling a C Function from Java

- Numeric Parameters and Return Values

- String Parameters

- Accessing Object Fields

- Accessing Static Fields

- Signatures

- Calling Java Methods

- Arrays

- Error-Handling

- The Invocation API

- A Complete Example: Accessing the Windows Registry

Native Methods

We hope that you are convinced that Java code has a number of advantages over code written in languages like C or C++—even for platform-specific applications. Here, of course, it is not portability that is the issue but rather features like these:

- You are more likely to produce bug-free code using Java than C or C++.

- Multithreading is probably easier to code in Java than in any other language.

- Networking code is a breeze.

Portability is simply a bonus that you may or may not want to take advantage of down the line.

While a "100% Pure Java" solution is nice in principle, realistically, for an application, there are situations where you will want to write (or use) code written in another language. (Such code is usually called *native* code.) There are three obvious reasons why this may be the right choice:

1. You have substantial amounts of tested and debugged code available in that language. Porting the code to Java would be time consuming, and the resulting code would need to be tested and debugged again.

2. Your application requires access to system features or devices, and using Java would be cumbersome, at best, or impossible, at worst.

3. Maximizing the speed of the code is essential. For example, the task may be time critical or it may be code that is used so often that optimizing it has a big payoff. (This is actually the least plausible reason. With just-in-time compilation (JIT), intensive computations coded in Java are not *that* much slower than compiled C code.)

If you are in one of these three situations, it *might* make sense to call the code from Java. Of course, with the usual security manager in place, once you start using native code, you are restricted to applications rather than applets. In particular, the native code library you are calling must exist on the client machine, and it must work with the client machine architecture.

To make calling native methods possible, Java comes with hooks for working with system libraries, and the JDK has a few tools to relieve some (but not all) of the tedium necessary.

NOTE: The language you use for your native code doesn't have to be C or C++; you could use code compiled with a FORTRAN compiler, if you have access to a Java-to-FORTRAN binding, or Visual Basic, if you have access to a Java binding for its types.

Still, keep in mind:

Use native methods and you lose portability.

Even when you distribute your program as an application, you must supply a separate native method library for every platform you wish to support. This means you must also educate your users on how to install these libraries! Also, while users may trust that applets can neither damage data nor steal confidential information, they may not want to extend the same trust to Java code that uses native method libraries. For that reason, many potential users will be reluctant to use Java programs that require native code. Aside from the security issue, native libraries are unlikely to be as safe as Java code, especially if they are written in a language like C or C++ that offers no protection against overwriting memory through invalid pointer usage. It is easy to write native methods that corrupt the Java virtual machine, compromise its security, or trash the operating system.

Thus, we suggest using native code only as a last resort. If you must gain access to a device such as the serial port in a Java program, then you may need to write native code. If you need to access an existing body of code, why not consider native methods as a stopgap measure and eventually port the code to Java? If you are concerned about efficiency, benchmark a Java implementation. In most cases, the speed of Java using a JIT will be sufficient. (Just-in-time compilers and other emerging compiler technologies will soon exist on all platforms that Java has been ported to. They already exist under Windows and Solaris.) A talk at the 1996 JavaOne conference showed this clearly. The implementers of the cryptography library at Sun Microsystems reported that a pure Java implementation of their cryptographic functions was more than adequate. It was true that they were not as fast as a C implementation would have been, but it turned

out not to matter. The Java implementation was far faster than the network I/O. And this turns out to be the real bottleneck.

In summary, there is no point in sacrificing portability for a meaningless speed improvement; don't go native until you determine that you have no other choice.

> NOTE: In this chapter, we describe the so-called Java Native Interface (JNI) binding. An earlier language binding (sometimes called the raw native interface) was used with Java 1.0, and a variation of that earlier binding is still being used by the Microsoft Virtual Machine. JavaSoft has assured developers that the JNI binding described here is a permanent part of Java, and that it needs to be supported by all Java Virtual Machines.

Finally, we use C as our language for native methods in this chapter because C is probably the language most often used for Java native methods. In particular, you'll see how to make the correspondence between Java and C data types, feature names, and function calls. (This correspondence is usually called the C *binding*.)

> C++ NOTE: You can also use C++ instead of C to write native methods. There are a few advantages—type checking is slightly stricter, and accessing the JNI functions is a bit more convenient. However, JNI does not support any direct correspondence between classes in Java and C++. Even when programming with C++, you must access the fields and methods of Java classes through C function calls.

Calling a C Function from Java

Suppose you have a C function that does something you like and, for one reason or another, you don't want to bother reimplementing it in Java. For the sake of illustration, we'll assume it is the useful and venerable `printf` function. You want to be able to call `printf` from your Java programs. Java sensibly uses the keyword `native` for a native method, and you will obviously need to encapsulate the `printf` function in a class. So, you might write something like:

```
public class Printf
{  public native String printf(String s);
}
```

You actually can compile this class but when you go to use it in another program, and call the Java interpreter, then the interpreter will tell you it doesn't know how to find `printf`—reporting an `UnsatisfiedLinkError`. So the trick is to give the run time enough information so that it can link in this class. As you will soon see, under the JDK this requires a three-step process:

1. Generate a C stub for a function that translates between the Java call and the actual C function. The stub does this translation by taking information off the Java stack and passing it to the compiled C function.

2. Create a special shared library and export the stub from it.

3. Use a special Java method, called `System.LoadLibrary.` to tell the Java run time to load the library from Step 2.

We now show you how to carry out these steps for various kinds of examples, starting from a trivial special-case use of `printf` and ending with a realistic example involving the registry function for Windows—examples that are obviously not available directly from Java.

Working with the `printf` Function

Let's start with just about the simplest possible situation using `printf`: calling a native method that prints the message "Hello, Native World." Obviously we are not even tapping into the useful formatting features of `printf`! Still, this is a good way for you to test that your C compiler works as expected before you try implementing more ambitious native methods.

As we mentioned earlier, you first need to declare the native method in a class. The `native` keyword alerts the Java compiler that the method will be defined externally. Of course, native methods will contain no Java code, and the method header is followed immediately by a terminating semicolon. This means, as you saw in the example above, native method declarations look similar to abstract method declarations.

```
class HelloNative
{   public native static void greeting();
    . . .

}
```

In this particular example, note that we also declare the native method as `static`. Native methods can be both static and nonstatic. Note that this method takes no parameters; we do not yet want to deal with parameter passing, not even implicit parameters.

Next, write a corresponding C function. You must name that function *exactly* the way the Java run-time system expects. Here are the rules:

1. Use the full Java method name, such as `HelloNative.greeting`. If the class is in a package, then prepend the package name, such as `corejava.Day.greeting`.

2.   Replace every period with an underscore, and prepend the prefix `Java_`.
     For example, `Java_ HelloNative_greeting` or
     `Java_corejava_Day_greeting`.

3.   If the class name contains characters that are not ASCII letters or digits—
     that is, '`_`', '`$`', or Unicode characters with code > '`\U007F`'—replace
     them with _0*xxxx*, where *xxxx* is the sequence of four hexadecimal digits
     of the character's Unicode value.

> NOTE: If you *overload* native methods, that is, if you provide multiple native methods
> with the same name, then you must append a double underscore followed by the
> encoded argument types. We describe the encoding of the argument types later in
> this chapter. For example, if you have a native method, `greeting`, and another
> native method `greeting(int repeat)`, then the first one is called
> `Java_HelloNative_greeting__`, and the second,
> `Java_HelloNative_greeting__I`.

Actually, nobody does this by hand; instead, you should run the `javah` utility,
which automatically generates the function names. To use `javah` first, compile
the Java file (given in Example 10-3):

```
javac HelloNative.java
```

Next, call the `javah` utility to produce a C header file. The `javah` executable can
be found in the `\jdk\bin` directory.

```
javah -jni HelloNative
```

Using `javah` creates a header file, `HelloNative.h`, as in Example 10-1:

Example 10-1: HelloNative.h

```
/* DO NOT EDIT THIS FILE - it is machine generated */
#include <jni.h>
/* Header for class HelloNative */

#ifndef _Included_HelloNative
#define _Included_HelloNative
#ifdef __cplusplus
extern "C" {
#endif
/*
 * Class:       HelloNative
 * Method:      greeting
 * Signature: ()V
 */
JNIEXPORT void JNICALL Java_HelloNative_greeting
  (JNIEnv *, jclass);
```

```
#ifdef __cplusplus
}
#endif
#endif
```

As you can see, this file contains the declaration of a function Java_HelloNative_greeting. (The strings JNIEXPORT and JNICALL are defined in the header file jni.h. They denote compiler-dependent specifiers for exported functions that come from a dynamically loaded library.)

> NOTE: Be sure to use the -jni flag when running javah. Without that flag, you get the header file for the Java 1.0 binding.

Now, you simply have to copy the function prototype from the header file into the source file and to give the implementation code for the function, as shown in Example 10-2.

Example 10-2: HelloNative.c

```
#include "HelloNative.h"
#include <stdio.h>

JNIEXPORT void JNICALL Java_HelloNative_greeting
  (JNIEnv* env, jclass cl)
{  printf("Hello, Native World!\n");
}
```

In this simple function, we ignore the env and cl arguments. You'll see their use later.

> C++ NOTE: You can use C++ to implement native methods. However, you must then declare the functions that are called from Java as extern "C". For example,
>
> ```
> #include "HelloNative.h"
> #include <stdio.h>
>
> extern "C"
> JNIEXPORT void JNICALL Java_HelloNative_greeting
>     (JNIEnv* env, jclass cl)
> {  printf("Hello, Native World!\n");
> }
> ```

Next, compile the C code into a dynamically loaded library. For example, with the Microsoft C++ compiler under Windows, the command you use is

```
cl -Ic:\jdk\include -Ic:\jdk\include\win32 -LD HelloNative.c
```

```
    -FeHelloNative.dll
```

With the Sun compiler under Solaris, the command to use is

```
cc -G -I/usr/local/java/include -
    I/usr/local/java/include/solaris
        HelloNative.c -o libHelloNative.so
```

(You may need to use different paths to specify the locations of the header files, depending on which directory contains the JDK.)

TIP: If you use the Microsoft C++ compiler to compile DLLs from a DOS shell, first run the batch file

```
    c:\devstudio\vc\bin\vcvars32.bat
```

That batch file properly configures the command-line compiler by setting up the path and the environment variables needed by the compiler.

Finally, we need to add the call to the `System.loadLibrary` method that ensures that Java will load the library prior to the first use of the class. The easiest way to do this is to use a static initialization block in the class that contains the native method, as in Example 10-3:

Example 10-3: HelloNative.java

```
class HelloNative
{   public native static void greeting();
    static
    {   System.loadLibrary("HelloNative");
    }
}
```

Assuming you have followed all the steps given above, you are now ready to run the `HelloNativeTest` application shown in Example 10-4.

Example 10-4: HelloNativeTest.java

```
class HelloNativeTest
{   public static void main(String[] args)
    {   HelloNative.greeting();
    }
}
```

If you compile and run this Java program, the message "Hello, Native World!" is displayed in a terminal window.

Of course, this is not particularly impressive by itself. However, if you keep in mind that this message is generated by the C `printf` command and not by any Java code, you will see that we have taken the first steps toward bridging the gap between Java and C!

`java.lang.System`

- `void loadLibrary(String libname)`

  loads the library with the given name. The library is located in the library search path. The exact method for locating the library is operating-system dependent. Under DOS/Windows, this searches first the current directory, then the directories on the path.

- `void load(String filename)`

  loads the library with the given file name. If the library is not found, then Java throws an `UnsatisfiedLinkError`.

Numeric Parameters and Return Values

When passing numbers between C and Java, you need to understand which C types correspond to which Java types. For example, while C does have data types called `int` and `long`, their implementation is platform dependent. On some platforms, `int`s are 16-bit quantities, and on others they are 32-bit quantities. In Java, of course, an `int` is *always* a 32-bit integer. For that reason, the Java Native Interface defines types `jint`, `jlong`, and so on.

Table 10-1 shows the correspondence between Java and C types.

Table 10-1: Java and C types

Java	C	bytes
boolean	jboolean	1
byte	jbyte	1
char	jchar	2
short	jshort	2
int	jint	4
long	jlong	8
float	jfloat	4
double	jdouble	8

In the header file `jni.h`, these types are declared with `typedef` statements as the equivalent types on the target platform. That header file also defines the constants `JNI_FALSE` = 0 and `JNI_TRUE` = 1.

Using `printf` for Formatting Numbers

Recall that Java has no elegant way for formatted printing of floating-point numbers. (Of course, you can use the `DecimalFormat` class (see Volume 1, Chapter 3) and build custom formats—we just don't think this is as easy as a simple call to `printf`.) Since `printf` is quick, easy, and well known, let's suppose you decide to implement the same functionality via a call to the `printf` function in a native method.

We don't actually recommend this approach the native code needs to be compiled for every target platform. We are using it because it shows off the techniques of passing parameters to a native method and obtaining a return value.

Example 10-5 shows a class called `Printf1` that uses a native method to print a floating-point number with a given field width and precision.

Example 10-5: Printf1.java

```
class Printf1
{   public static native int print(int width,  int
        precision,  double x);
    static
    {   System.loadLibrary("Printf1");
    }
}
```

Notice that when implementing the method in C, we must change all `int` and `double` parameters to `jint` and `jdouble`, as shown in Example 10-6.

Example 10-6: Printf1.c

```
#include "Printf1.h"
#include <stdio.h>

JNIEXPORT jint JNICALL Java_Printf1_print
    (JNIEnv* env, jclass cl, jint width, jint precision, jdouble x)
{   char fmt[30];
    jint ret;
    sprintf(fmt, "%%%d.%df", width, precision);
    ret = printf(fmt, x);
    return ret;
}
```

The function simply assembles a format string `"%w.pf"` in the variable `fmt`, then calls `printf`. It then returns the number of characters it printed.

Example 10-7 shows the test program that demonstrates the `Printf1` class.

Example 10-7: Printf1Test.java

```
class Printf1Test
{  public static void main(String[] args)
   {  int count = Printf1.print(8, 4, 3.14);
      count += Printf1.print(8, 4, (double)count);
      System.out.println();
      for (int i = 0; i < count; i++)
         System.out.print("-");
      System.out.println();
   }
}
```

String Parameters

Next, we want to consider how to transfer strings to and from native methods. As you know, Java strings are sequences of 16-bit Unicode characters; C strings are null-terminated strings of 8-bit characters, so strings in Java and C are quite different. The Java Native Interface has two sets of functions, one that converts Java strings to UTF (Unicode Text Format) and one that converts them to arrays of Unicode characters, that is, to `jchar` arrays. The UTF format was discussed in Chapter 1—recall that ASCII characters are encoded "as is," but all other Unicode characters are encoded as 2-byte or 3-byte sequences.

If your C code already uses Unicode, you'll want to use the second set of conversion functions. On the other hand, if all your Java strings are restricted to ASCII characters, you can use the UTF conversion functions.

A native method with a `String` parameter in its Java declaration actually receives a value of an opaque type called `jstring`. A native method with a Java return value of type `String` must return a value of type `jstring`. JNI functions are used to read and construct these `jstring` objects. For example, the `NewStringUTF` function makes a new `jstring` object out of a `char` array that contains UTF-encoded characters. Unfortunately, JNI functions have a somewhat odd calling convention. Here is a call to the `NewStringUTF` function:

```
JNIEXPORT jstring JNICALL Java_HelloNative_getGreeting
   (JNIEnv* env, jclass cl)
{  jstring jstr;
   char greeting[] = "Hello, Native World\n";
   jstr = (*env)->NewStringUTF(env, greeting);
   return jstr;
}
```

All calls to JNI functions use the `env` pointer that is the first argument of every native method. The `env` pointer is a pointer to a table of function pointers (see

Figure 10-1). Therefore, you must prefix every JNI call with (*env)-> in order to actually dereference the function pointer. Furthermore, you must supply env as the first parameter of every JNI function. This setup is somewhat cumbersome, and it could have easily been made more transparent to C programmers. We suggest that you simply supply the (*env)-> prefix without worrying about the table of function pointers.

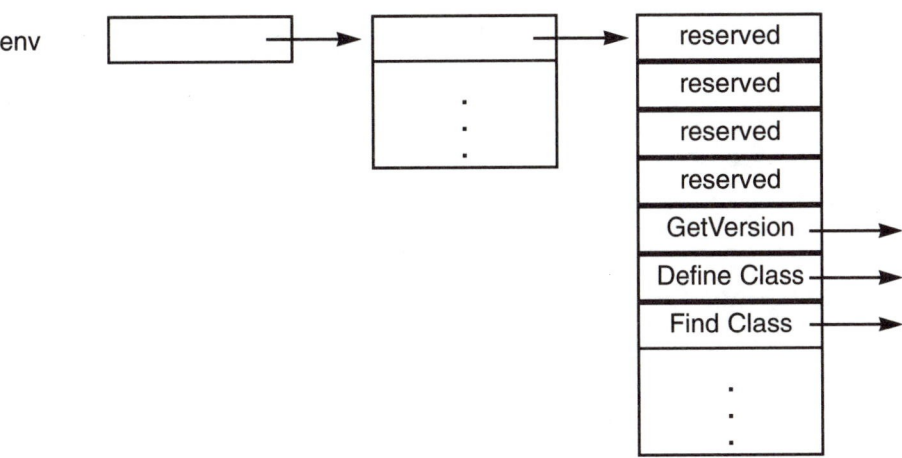

Figure 10-1: The env pointer

C++ NOTE: It is simpler to access JNI functions in C++. The C++ version of the JNIEnv class has inline member functions that take care of the function pointer lookup for you. For example, you can call the NewStringUTF function as

```
jstr = env->NewStringUTF(greeting);
```

Note that you omit the JNIEnv pointer from the paramenter list of the call.

The NewStringUTF function lets you construct a new jstring. To read the contents of an existing jstring object, use the GetStringUTFChars function. This function returns a const jbyte* pointer to the UTF characters that describe the character string. Note that a specific virtual machine is free to use UTF for its internal string representation, so you may get a character pointer into the actual Java string. Since Java strings are meant to be immutable, it is *very* important that you treat the const seriously and do not try to write into this character array. On the other hand, if the virtual machine uses Unicode characters for its internal string representation, then this function call allocates a new memory block that will be filled with the UTF equivalents.

The virtual machine must know when you are finished using the UTF string, so that it can garbage-collect it. (The garbage collector runs in a separate thread, and it can interrupt the execution of native methods.) For that reason, you must call the `ReleaseStringUTFChars` function.

Finally, the `GetStringUTFLength` function returns the number of characters needed for the UTF encoding of the string.

Accessing Java strings from C code

- `jstring NewStringUTF(JNIEnv* env, const char bytes[])`

  returns a new Java string object from an UTF string, or NULL if the string cannot be constructed.

Parameters:	env	the JNI interface pointer
	bytes	the null-terminated UTF string

- `jsize GetStringUTFLength(JNIEnv* env, jstring string)`

  returns the number of characters required for the UTF encoding.

Parameters:	env	the JNI interface pointer
	string	a Java string object

- `const jbyte* GetStringUTFChars(JNIEnv* env, jstring string, jboolean* isCopy)`

  returns a pointer to the UTF encoding of a string, or NULL if the character array cannot be constructed. The pointer is valid until `ReleaseStringUTFChars` is called.

Parameters:	env	the JNI interface pointer
	string	a Java string object
	isCopy	points to a `jboolean` that is filled with JNI_TRUE if a copy is made; with JNI_FALSE otherwise

- `void ReleaseStringUTFChars(JNIEnv* env, jstring string, const jbyte bytes[])`

  informs the virtual machine that the native code no longer needs access to the Java string through `bytes`.

Parameters:	env	the JNI interface pointer
	string	a Java string object
	bytes	a pointer returned by GetStringUTFChars

- `jstring NewString(JNIEnv* env, const jchar chars[], jsize length)`

  returns a new Java string object from a Unicode string, or NULL if the string cannot be constructed.

Parameters:	env	the JNI interface pointer
	chars	the null-terminated UTF string
	length	the number of characters in the string

- `jsize GetStringLength(JNIEnv* env, jstring string)`

  returns the number of characters in the string.

Parameters:	env	the JNI interface pointer
	string	a Java string object

- `const jchar* GetStringChars(JNIEnv* env, jstring string, jboolean* isCopy)`

  returns a pointer to the Unicode encoding of a string, or NULL if the character array cannot be constructed. The pointer is valid until `ReleaseStringChars` is called.

Parameters:	env	the JNI interface pointer
	string	a Java string object
	isCopy	is either NULL or points to a jboolean that is filled with JNI_TRUE if a copy is made; with JNI_FALSE otherwise

- `void ReleaseStringChars(JNIEnv* env, jstring string, const jchar chars[])`

  informs the virtual machine that the native code no longer needs access to the Java string through `chars`.

Parameters:	env	the JNI interface pointer
	string	a Java string object
	chars	a pointer returned by GetStringChars

A Java Equivalent of `sprintf`

Let us put these functions we just described to work and write a Java equivalent of the C function `sprintf`. We would like to call the function as shown in Example 10-8.

Example 10-8: Printf2Test.java

```
class Printf2Test
{  public static void main(String[] args)
   {   double price = 44.95;
       double tax = 7.75;
       double amountDue = price * (1 + tax / 100);

       String s = Printf2.sprint("Amount due = %8.2f",
          amountDue);
       System.out.println(s);
   }
}
```

Example 10-9 shows the class with the native `sprint` method.

Example 10-9: Printf2.java

```
class Printf2
{  public static native String sprint(String format, double x);
   static
   {   System.loadLibrary("Printf2");
   }
}
```

Therefore, the C function that formats a floating-point number has the proto-type

```
JNIEXPORT jstring JNICALL Java_Printf2_sprint
   (JNIEnv* env, jclass cl, jstring format, jdouble x)
```

Example 10-10 shows the code for the C implementation. Note the calls to `GetStringUTFChars` to read the `format` argument, `NewStringUTF` to generate the return value, and `ReleaseStringUTFChars` to inform the virtual machine that access to the string is no longer required.

Example 10-10: Printf2.c

```
#include "Printf2.h"
#include <string.h>
#include <stdlib.h>
#include <float.h>

char* find_format(const char format[])
/**
 * @param format a string containing a printf format specifier
 * (such as "%8.2f"). Substrings "%%" are skipped.
 * @return a pointer to the format specifier (skipping the '%')
```

```
  * or NULL if there wasn't a unique format specifier
  */
{   char* p;
    char* q;
    size_t n;

    p = strchr(format, '%');
    while (p != NULL && *(p + 1) == '%') /* skip %% */
        p = strchr(p + 2, '%');
    if (p == NULL) return NULL;
    /* now check that % is unique */
    p++;
    q = strchr(p, '%');
    while (q != NULL && *(q + 1) == '%') /* skip %% */
        q = strchr(q + 2, '%');
    if (q != NULL) return NULL; /* % not unique */
    q = p + strspn(p, " -0+#"); /* skip past flags */
    q += strspn(q, "0123456789"); /* skip past field width */
    if (*q == '.') { q++; q += strspn(q, "0123456789"); }
        /* skip past precision */
    if (strchr("eEfFgG", *q) == NULL) return NULL;
        /* not a floating point format */
    return p;
}

JNIEXPORT jstring JNICALL Java_Printf2_sprint
   (JNIEnv* env, jclass cl, jstring format, jdouble x)
{   const char* cformat;
    char* fmt;
    jstring ret;

    cformat = (*env)->GetStringUTFChars(env, format, NULL);
    fmt = find_format(cformat);
    if (fmt == NULL)
        ret = format;
    else
    {   char* cret;
        int width = atoi(fmt);
        if (width == 0) width = DBL_DIG + 10;
        cret = (char*)malloc(strlen(cformat) + width);
        sprintf(cret, cformat, x);
        ret = (*env)->NewStringUTF(env, cret);
        free(cret);
    }
    (*env)->ReleaseStringUTFChars(env, format, cformat);
    return ret;
}
```

In this function, we chose to keep the error handling simple. If the format code to print a floating-point number is not of the form %w.pc, where c is one of the characters e, E, f, g, or G, then what we simply do is *not* format the number. You will see later how to make a native method throw an exception.

Accessing Object Fields

All the native methods that you saw so far were static methods with number and string parameters. We next consider native methods that operate on objects. As an exercise, we will implement methods of the Employee class, using native methods. Again, this is not something you would normally want to do, but it does illustrate how to access object fields from a native method when you need to do so. First, consider the raiseSalary method. In Java, the code was simple.

```
public void raiseSalary(double byPercent)
{   salary *= 1 + byPercent / 100;
}
```

Let us rewrite this as a native method. Unlike the previous examples of native methods, this is not a static method. Running javah gives the following prototype.

```
JNIEXPORT void JNICALL Java_Employee_raiseSalary
    (JNIEnv *, jobject, jdouble);
```

Note the second argument. It is no longer of type jclass but of type jobject. In fact, it is the equivalent of the this reference. Static methods obtain a reference to the class, whereas nonstatic methods obtain a reference to the implicit this argument object.

Now we access the salary field of the implicit argument. In the "raw" Java-to-C binding of Java 1.0, this was easy—a programmer could directly access object data fields. However, direct access requires all virtual machines to expose their internal data layout. For that reason, the JNI requires programmers to get and set the values of data fields by calling special JNI functions.

In our case, we need to use the GetDoubleField and SetDoubleField functions because the type of salary is a double. There are other functions— GetIntField/SetIntField, GetObjectField/SetObjectField, and so on—for other field types. The general syntax is:

```
x = (*env)->GetXxxField(env, class, fieldID);
(*env)->GetXxxField(env, class, fieldID, x);
```

Here, class is a value that represents a Java object of type Class, and fieldID is a value of a special type, jfieldID, that denotes the offset of a field in a structure and *Xxx* represents a Java data type (Object, Boolean, byte, and so on). There are two ways for obtaining the *class* object. The GetObjectClass func-

tion returns the class of any object. For example:

```
jclass class_Employee = (*env)->GetObjectClass(env, obj_this);
```

The FindClass function lets you specify the class name as a string (curiously, with / instead of periods as package name separators).

```
jclass class_Day = (*env)->FindClass(env, "corejava/Day");
```

Use the GetFieldID function to obtain the fieldID. You must supply the name of the field and its *signature*, an encoding of its type. For example, here is the code to obtain the field ID of the salary field.

```
jfieldID id_salary = (*env)->GetFieldID(env, class_Employee,
    "salary", "D");
```

The string "D" denotes the type double. You will learn the complete rules for encoding signatures in the next section.

You may be thinking that accessing a data field seems quite convoluted. However, since the designers of the JNI did not want to expose the data fields directly, they had to supply functions for getting and setting field values. To minimize the cost of these functions, computing the field ID from the field name—which is the most expensive step—is factored out into a separate step. That is, if you repeatedly get and set the value of a particular field, you incur only once the cost of computing the field offset. Let us put all the pieces together. The following code reimplements the raiseSalary method as a native method.

```
JNIEXPORT void JNICALL Java_Employee_raiseSalary
   (JNIEnv* env, jobject obj_this, jdouble byPercent)
{  /* get the class */
   jclass class_Employee = (*env)->GetObjectClass(env,
       obj_this);

   /* get the field ID */
   jfieldID id_salary = (*env)->GetFieldID(env, class_Employee,
       "salary", "D");

   /* get the field value */
   jdouble salary = (*env)->GetDoubleField(env, obj_this,
       id_salary);

   salary *= 1 + byPercent / 100;

   /* set the field value */
   (*env)->SetDoubleField(env, obj_this, id_salary, salary);
}
```

Accessing Static Fields

Accessing static fields is similar to accessing nonstatic fields. You use the
`GetStaticFieldID` and `GetStaticXxxField`/`SetStaticXxxField` functions.
They work almost identically to their nonstatic counterpart. There are only two
differences.

- Since you have no object, you must use `FindClass` instead of
  `GetObjectClass` to obtain the class reference.

- You supply the class, not the instance object, when accessing the field.

For example, here is how you can get a reference to `System.out`:

```
/* get the class */
jclass class_System = (*env)->FindClass(env,
    "java/lang/System");

/* get the field ID */
jfieldID id_out = (*env)->GetStaticFieldID(env,
    class_System, "out", "Ljava/io/PrintStream;");

/* get the field value */
jobject obj_out = (*env)->GetStaticObjectField(env,
    class_System, id_out);
```

Accessing object fields

- `jfieldID GetFieldID(JNIEnv *env, jclass cl, const char name[], const char sig[])`

  returns the offset of a field in a class.

Parameters:		
	env	the JNI interface pointer
	cl	the class object
	name	the field name
	sig	the encoded field signature

- `Xxx GetXxxField(JNIEnv *env, jobject obj, jfieldID id)`

  returns the value of a field. The field type *Xxx* is one of `Object`, `Boolean`,
  `Byte`, `Char`, `Short`, `Int`, `Long`, `Float` or `Double`.

Parameters:		
	env	the JNI interface pointer
	obj	the object whose field is being returned
	id	the field offset

- void Set*Xxx*Field(JNIEnv *env, jobject obj, jfieldID id, *Xxx* value)

  sets a field to a new value. The field type *Xxx* is one of Object, Boolean, Byte, Char, Short, Int, Long, Float or Double.

Parameters:	env	the JNI interface pointer
	obj	the object whose field is being set
	id	the field offset
	value	the new field value

- jfieldID GetStaticFieldID(JNIEnv *env, jclass cl, const char name[], const char sig[])

  returns the offset of a static field in a class.

Parameters:	env	the JNI interface pointer
	cl	the class object
	name	the field name
	sig	the encoded field signature

- *Xxx* GetStatic*Xxx*Field(JNIEnv *env, jclass cl, jfieldID id)

  returns the value of a static field. The field type *Xxx* is one of Object, Boolean, Byte, Char, Short, Int, Long, Float or Double.

Parameters:	env	the JNI interface pointer
	cl	the class object whose static field is being set
	id	the field offset

- void Set*Xxx*Field(JNIEnv *env, jclass cl, jfieldID id, *Xxx* value)

  sets a static field to a new value. The field type *Xxx* is one of Object, Boolean, Byte, Char, Short, Int, Long, Float or Double.

Parameters:	env	the JNI interface pointer
	cl	the class object whose static field is being set
	id	the field offset
	value	the new field value

Signatures

To access object fields and call Java methods, learn the rules for "mangling" the names of data types and method signatures. (A method signature describes the parameters and return type of the method.) Here is the encoding scheme:

B	byte
C	char
D	double
F	float
I	int
J	long
L*classname*;	a class type
S	short
V	void
Z	boolean

Note that the semicolon at the end of the L expression is the terminator of the type expression, not a separator between parameters. For example, the constructor

```
Employee(java.lang.String, double, corejava.Day)
```

has a signature

```
"(Ljava/lang/String;DLcorejava/Day;)V"
```

As you can see, there is no separator between the D and Lcorejava/Day;.

Also note that in this encoding scheme, you must use / instead of . to separate the package and class names.

To describe an array type, use a [. For example, an array of strings is

```
[Ljava/lang/String;
```

A float[][] is mangled into

```
[[F
```

For the complete signature of a method, you list the parameter types inside a pair of parentheses and then list the return type. For example, a method receiving two integers and returning an integer is encoded as

```
(II)I
```

The print method that we used in the preceding example has a mangled signature of

```
(Ljava/lang/String;)V
```

That is, the method receives a string and returns void.

TIP: You can use the `javap` command with option `-s` to generate the field signatures from class files. For example, run:

```
javap -s -private Classname
```

You get the following output, displaying the signatures of all fields and methods.

```
public synchronized class Employee extends java.lang.Object
     /* ACC_SUPER bit set */
   {
     private java.lang.String name;
        /*    Ljava/lang/String;    */
     private double salary;
        /*    D    */
     private corejava.Day hireDay;
        /*    Lcorejava/Day;    */
     public Employee(java.lang.String,double,corejava.Day);
        /*    (Ljava/lang/String;DLcorejava/Day;)V    */
     public void print();
        /*    ()V    */
     public void raiseSalary(double);
        /*    (D)V    */
     public int hireYear();
        /*    ()I    */

   }
```

NOTE: There is no rational reason why programmers are forced to use this mangling scheme for describing signatures. The designers of Java could have just as easily written a function that reads Java-style signatures, such as `void(int,java.lang.String)`, and encodes them into whatever internal representation they prefer. Then again, using the mangled signatures lets you partake in the mystique of programming close to the virtual machine.

Calling Java Methods

Of course, Java functions can call C functions—that is, what native methods are for. Can we go the other way and call Java code from C? Why would we want to do this anyway? The answer is that it often happens that a native method needs to request a service from an object that was passed to it. We first show you how to do it for nonstatic methods, and then we show you how to do it for static methods.

Nonstatic Methods

As an example of calling a Java method from native code, let's enhance the Printf class and add a member function that works similarly to the C function fprintf. That is, it should be able to print a string on an arbitrary PrintWriter object.

```
class Printf3
{   public native static void fprint(PrintWriter out,
        String s, double x);
        . . .
}
```

We first assemble the string to be printed into a String object str, as in the sprint method that we already implemented. Then, we call ps.print(s) from the C function that implements the native method.

You can call any Java method from C by using the function call

```
(*env)->CallXxxMethod(env, implicit parameter, methodID,
    explicit parameters)
```

Replace *Xxx* with Void, Int, Object, etc., depending on the return type of the method. Just as you need a fieldID to access a field of an object, you need a method ID to call a method. You obtain a method ID by calling the JNI function GetMethodID and supplying the class, the name of the method, and the method signature.

In our example, we want to obtain the ID of the print method of the PrintWriter class. As you saw in Chapter 1, the PrintWriter class has nine different methods, all called print. For that reason, you must also supply a string describing the parameters and return value of the specific function that you want to use. For example, we want to use void print(java.lang.String). As described in the preceding section, we must now "mangle" the signature into the string "(Ljava/lang/string;)V".

Here is the complete code to make the method call, by:

1.   Obtaining the class of the implicit parameter

2.   Obtaining the method ID

3.   Making the call

```
/* get the class */
class_PrintWriter = (*env)->GetObjectClass(env, out);

/* get the method ID */
id_print = (*env)->GetMethodID(env, class_PrintWriter,
    "print", "(Ljava/lang/String;)V");

/* call the method */
(*env)->CallVoidMethod(env, out, id_print, str);
```

Static Methods

Calling static methods from native methods is similar to calling nonstatic methods. There are two differences.

- You use the `GetStaticMethodID` and `CallStaticXxxMethod` functions.
- You supply a class object, not an implicit parameter object, when invoking the method.

As an example of this, let's make the call to the static method

```
System.getProperty("java.class.path")
```

from a native method. The return value of this call is a string that gives the current class path.

First, we need to find the class to use. Since we have no object of the class `System` readily available, we use `FindClass` rather than `GetObjectClass`.

```
jclass class_System = (*env)->FindClass(env,
"java/lang/System");
```

Next, we need the ID of the static `getProperty` method. The encoded signature of that method is

```
"(Ljava/lang/String;)Ljava/lang/String;"
```

since both the parameter and the return value are a string. Hence, we obtain the method ID as follows:

```
jmethodID id_getProperty = (*env)->GetStaticMethodID(env,
    class_System,
    "getProperty", "(Ljava/lang/String;)Ljava/lang/String;");
```

Finally, we can make the call. Note that the class object is passed to the `CallStaticStringMethod` function.

```
jobject obj_ret = (*env)->CallStaticObjectMethod(env,
    class_System,
    (*env)->NewStringUTF(env, "java.class.path"));
```

The return value of this method is of type `jobject`. If we want to manipulate it as a string, we must cast it to `jstring`:

```
jstring str_ret = (jstring)obj_ret;
```

C++ NOTE: In C, the types `jstring`, `jclass`, as well as the array types that will be introduced later, are all type equivalent to `jobject`. The cast of the preceding example is therefore not strictly necessary in C. But in C++, these types are defined as pointers to "dummy classes" that have the correct inheritance hierarchy. For example, the assignment of a `jstring` to a `jobject` is legal without a cast in C++, but the assignment from a `jobject` to a `jstring` requires a cast.

Constructors

A native method can create a new Java object by invoking its constructor. You invoke the constructor by calling the `NewObject` function.

```
jobject obj_new = (*env)->NewObject(env, class, methodID,
    construction parameters);
```

You obtain the method ID needed for this call from the `GetMethodID` function by specifying the method name as `"<init>"` and the encoded signature of the constructor (with return type `void`). For example, here is how a native method can create a `FileOutputStream` object:

```
const char[] fileName = ". . .";
jstring str_fileName = (*env)->NewStringUTF(env, fileName);
jclass class_FileOutputStream = (*env)->FindClass(env,
    "java/io/FileOutputStream");
jmethodID id_FileOutputStream = (*env)->GetMethodID(env,
    class_FileOutputStream, "<init>", "(Ljava/lang/String;)V");
jobject obj_stream = (*env)->NewObject(env,
    class_FileOutputStream, id_FileOutputStream, str_fileName);
```

Note that the signature of the constructor takes a parameter of type `java.lang.String` and has a return type of `void`.

Alternative Method Invocations

There are several variants of the JNI functions for calling a Java method from native code. These are not as important as the functions that we already discussed, but they are occasionally useful.

The `CallNonvirtualXxxMethod` functions receive an implicit argument, a method ID, a class object of a superclass of the implicit argument, and explicit arguments. The function calls the version of the method in the superclass, bypassing the normal dynamic dispatch mechanism.

All call functions have versions with suffixes "A" and "V" that receive the explicit parameters in an array or a `va_list` (as defined in the C header `stdarg.h`).

Executing Java methods from C code

- `jmethodID GetMethodID(JNIEnv *env, jclass cl, const char name[], const char sig[])`

    returns the offset of a method in a class.

    Parameters: env   the JNI interface pointer

                            cl   the class object

	name	the method name
	sig	the encoded method signature

- void Call*Xxx*Method(JNIEnv *env, jobject obj, jmethodID id, args)

- void Call*Xxx*MethodA(JNIEnv *env, jobject obj, jmethodID id, jvalue args[])

- void Call*Xxx*MethodV(JNIEnv *env, jobject obj, jmethodID id, va_list args)

call a method. The return type *Xxx* is one of Object, Boolean, Byte, Char, Short, Int, Long, Float or Double. The first function has a variable number of arguments—simply append the method parameters after the method ID. The second function receives the method arguments in an array of jvalue, where jvalue is a union defined as

```
typedef union jvalue
{   jboolean z;
    jbyte b;
    jchar c;
    jshort s;
    jint i;
    jlong j;
    jfloat f;
    jdouble d;
    jobject l;
} jvalue;
```

The third function receives the method parameters in a va_list, as defined in the C header stdarg.h.

Parameters:

	env	the JNI interface pointer
	obj	the implicit argument of the method
	id	the method offset
	args	the method arguments

- void CallNonvirtual*Xxx*Method(JNIEnv *env, jobject obj, jclass cl, jmethodID id, args)

- void Call*Xxx*MethodA(JNIEnv *env, jobject obj, jclass cl, jmethodID id, jvalue args[])

- void Call*Xxx*MethodV(JNIEnv *env, jobject obj, jclass cl, jmethodID id, va_list args)

call a method, bypassing dynamic dispatch. The return type xxx is one of Object, Boolean, Byte, Char, Short, Int, Long, Float or Double. The first function has a variable number of arguments—simply append the method parameters after the method ID. The second function receives the method arguments in an array of jvalue. The third function receives the method parameters in a va_list, as defined in the C header stdarg.h.

Parameters:		
	env	the JNI interface pointer
	obj	the implicit argument of the method
	cl	the class whose implementation of the method is to be called
	id	the method offset
	args	the method arguments

- jmethodID GetStaticMethodID(JNIEnv *env, jclass cl, const char name[], const char sig[])

returns the offset of a static method in a class.

Parameters:		
	env	the JNI interface pointer
	cl	the class object
	name	the method name
	sig	the encoded method signature

- void CallStaticXxxMethod(JNIEnv *env, jclass cl, jmethodID id, args)

- void CallStaticXxxMethodA(JNIEnv *env, jclass cl, jmethodID id, jvalue args[])

- void CallStaticXxxMethodV(JNIEnv *env, jclass cl, jmethodID id, va_list args)

call a static method. The return type xxx is one of Object, Boolean, Byte, Char, Short, Int, Long, Float or Double. The first function has a variable number of arguments—simply append the method parameters after the method ID. The second function receives the method arguments in an array of jvalue. The third function receives the method parameters in a va_list, as defined in the C header stdarg.h.

Parameters:		
	env	the JNI interface pointer
	cl	the class of the static method
	id	the method offset
	args	the method arguments

- `jobject NewObject(JNIEnv *env, jclass cl, jmethodID id, args)`
- `jobject NewObjectA(JNIEnv *env, jclass cl, jmethodID id, jvalue args[])`
- `jobject NewObjectV(JNIEnv *env, jclass cl, jmethodID id, va_list args)`

call a constructor. The method ID is obtained from `GetMethodID` with a method name of `"<init>"` and a return type of `void`. The first function has a variable number of arguments—simply append the method parameters after the method ID. The second function receives the method arguments in an array of `jvalue`. The third function receives the method parameters in a `va_list`, as defined in the C header `stdarg.h`.

Parameters:

`env`	the JNI interface pointer
`cl`	the class to be instantiated
`id`	the constructor method offset
`args`	the constructor arguments

Arrays

All Java array types have corresponding C types, as shown in the following table.

Java type	C type
`boolean[]`	`jbooleanArray`
`byte[]`	`jbyteArray`
`char[]`	`jcharArray`
`int[]`	`jintArray`
`short[]`	`jshortArray`
`long[]`	`jlongArray`
`float[]`	`jfloatArray`
`double[]`	`jdoubleArray`
`Object[]`	`jobjectArray`

The type `jarray` denotes a generic array.

C++ NOTE: In C, all these array types are actually type synonyms of `jobject`. In C++, however, they are arranged in the inheritance hierarchy shown in Figure 10-2.

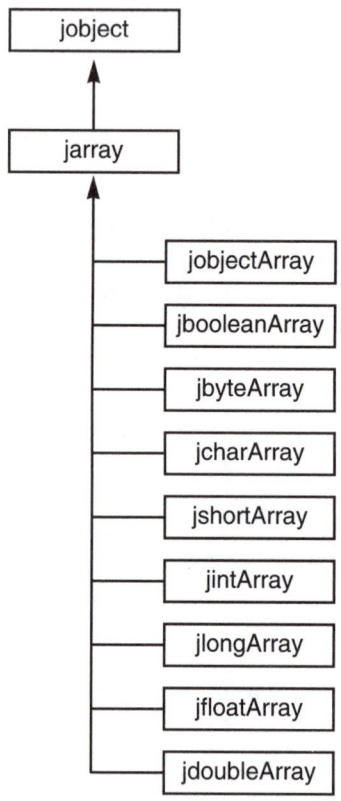

Figure 10-2: Inheritance hierarchy of array types

The GetArrayLength function returns the length of an array.

```
jarray array = ...;
jsize length = (*env)->GetArrayLength(env, array);
```

How you access elements in the array depends on whether the array stores objects or a primitive type (bool, char, or a numeric type). You access elements in an object array with the GetObjectArrayElement and SetObjectArrayElement methods.

```
jobjectArray array = ...;
int i, j;
jobject x = (*env)->GetObjectArray(env, array, i);
(*env)->SetObjectArray(env, array, j, x);
```

While simple, this approach is also clearly inefficient; you want to be able to access array elements directly, especially when doing vector and matrix computations.

The GetXxxArrayElements function returns a C pointer to the starting element of the array. As with ordinary strings, you must remember to call the corresponding ReleaseXxxArrayElements function to tell the virtual machine when you no longer need that pointer. Here, the type Xxx must be a primitive type, that is, not Object. You can then read and write the array elements directly. However, since the pointer *may point to a copy*, any changes that you make are guaranteed to be reflected in the Java array only when you call the corresponding ReleaseXxxArrayElements function!

Here is a code sample that multiplies all elements in an array of double values by a constant. We obtain a C pointer a into the Java array and then access individual elements as a[i].

```
jdoubleArray array_a = ...;
double scaleFactor = ...;
double* a = (*env)->GetDoubleArrayElements(env, array_a, NULL);
for (i = 0; i < (*env)->GetArrayLength(env, array_a); i++)
    a[i] = a[i] * scaleFactor;
(*env)->ReleaseDoubleArrayElements(env, array_a, 0);
```

Whether the virtual machine actually copies the array depends on how it allocates arrays and does its garbage collection. For example, boolean arrays are represented as packed arrays in Sun's Java Virtual Machine, and they need to be copied into unpacked arrays of jboolean values. Some "copying" garbage collectors routinely move objects around and update object references. That strategy is not compatible with "pinning" an array to a particular location because the collector cannot update the pointer values in native code. However, the garbage collector in the current virtual machine supplied with the JDK is not a copying collector, which means that currently non-boolean arrays are not copied.

If you want to access a few elements of a large array, use the GetXxxArrayRegion and SetXxxArrayRegion methods that copy a range of elements from the Java array into a C array and back.

You can create new Java arrays in native methods with the NewXxxArray function. To create a new array of objects, you specify the length, the type of the array elements, and an initial element for all entries (typically, NULL). Here is an example.

```
jclass class_Employee = (*env)->FindClass(env, "Employee");
jobjectArray array_e = (*env)->NewObjectArray(env, 100,
    class_Employee, NULL);
```

Arrays of primitive types are simpler. You just supply the length of the array.

```
jdoubleArray array_d = (*env)->NewDoubleArray(env, 100);
```

The array is then filled with zeroes.

Manipulating Java Arrays in C code

- `jsize GetArrayLength(JNIEnv *env, jarray array)`

  returns the number of elements in the array.

Parameters:	env	the JNI interface pointer
	array	the array object

- `jobject GetObjectArrayElement(JNIEnv *env, jobjectArray array, jsize index)`

  returns the value of an array element.

Parameters:	env	the JNI interface pointer
	array	the array object
	index	the array offset

- `void SetObjectArrayElement(JNIEnv *env, jobjectArray array, jsize index, jobject value)`

  sets an array element to a new value.

Parameters:	env	the JNI interface pointer
	array	the array object
	index	the array offset
	value	the new value

- `Xxx* GetXxxArrayElements(JNIEnv *env, jarray array, jboolean* isCopy)`

  yields a C pointer to the elements of a Java array. The field type Xxx is one of Boolean, Byte, Char, Short, Int, Long, Float or Double. The pointer must be passed to ReleaseXxxArrayElements when it is no longer needed.

Parameters:	env	the JNI interface pointer
	array	the array object
	isCopy	is either NULL or points to a jboolean that is filled with JNI_TRUE if a copy is made; with JNI_FALSE otherwise

- `void ReleaseXxxArrayElements(JNIEnv *env, jarray array, Xxx elems[], jint mode)`

  notifies the virtual machine that a pointer obtained by GetXxxArrayElements is no longer needed.

Parameters:	env	the JNI interface pointer

array	the array object
elems	the pointer to the array elements that is no longer needed
mode	0 = free the `elems` buffer after updating the array elements
	`JNI_COMMIT` = do not free the `elems` buffer after updating the array elements
	`JNI_ABORT` = free the `elems` buffer without updating the array elements

- `void GetXxxArrayRegion(JNIEnv *env, jarray array, jint start, jint length, Xxx elems[])`

copies elements from a Java array to a C array. The field type `Xxx` is one of `Boolean, Byte, Char, Short, Int, Long, Float` or `Double`.

Parameters:	env	the JNI interface pointer
	array	the array object
	start	the starting index
	length	the number of elements to copy
	elems	the C array that holds the elements

- `void SetXxxArrayRegion(JNIEnv *env, jarray array, jint start, jint length, Xxx elems[])`

copies elements from a C array to a Java array. The field type `Xxx` is one of `Boolean, Byte, Char, Short, Int, Long, Float` or `Double`.

Parameters:	env	the JNI interface pointer
	array	the array object
	start	the starting index
	length	the number of elements to copy
	elems	the C array that holds the elements

Error-Handling

Native methods are a significant security risk to Java programs. The C run-time system has no protection against array bounds errors, indirection through bad pointers, and so on. It is particularly important that programmers of native methods handle all error conditions in order to preserve the integrity of Java. In particular, when your native method diagnoses a problem that it cannot handle, then it

should report this problem to the Java Virtual Machine. In Java, you would naturally throw an exception in this situation. However, C has no exceptions. Instead, you must call the `Throw` or `ThrowNew` function in order to create a new exception object. When the native method exits, Java will throw that exception.

To use the `Throw` function, call `NewObject` to create an object of a subtype of `Throwable`. For example, here we allocate an `EOFException` object and throw it.

```
jclass class_EOFException = (*env)->FindClass(env,
    "java/io/EOFException");
jmethodID id_EOFException = (*env)->GetMethodID(env,
    class_EOFException,
    "<init>", "()V"); /* ID of default constructor */
jthrowable obj_exc = (*env)->NewObject(env, class_EOFException,
    id_EOFException);
(*env)->Throw(env, obj_exc);
```

It is usually more convenient to call `ThrowNew`, which constructs an exception object, given a class and an UTF string.

```
(*env)->ThrowNew(env, (*env)->FindClass(env,
    "java/io/EOFException"),
    "Unexpected end of file");
```

Both `Throw` and `ThrowNew` merely *post* the exception; they do not interrupt the control flow of the native method. Only when the method returns is the Java exception thrown by the virtual machine. Therefore, every call to `Throw` and `ThrowNew` should always immediately be followed by a `return` statement.

C++ NOTE: If you implement native methods in C++, you cannot currently throw a Java exception object in your C++ code. In a C++ binding, it would be possible to implement a translation between C++ and Java exceptions—unfortunately, this is not currently implemented. You need to use `SignalError` to throw a Java exception, and you need to make sure that your native methods throw no C++ exceptions.

Normally, native code need not be concerned with catching Java exceptions. However, when a native method calls a Java method, that method might throw an exception. Moreover, a number of the JNI functions throw exceptions as well. For example, `SetObjectArrayElement` throws an `ArrayIndexOutOfBoundsException` if the index is out of bounds and an `ArrayStoreException` if the class of the stored object is not a subclass of the element class of the array. In situations like these, a native method should call the `ExceptionOccurred` method to determine whether an exception has been thrown. The call

```
jthrowable obj_exc = (*env)->ExceptionOccurred(env);
```

returns NULL if no exception is pending, or a reference to the current exception object. Normally, a native method should simply return when an exception has occurred so that the virtual machine can propagate it to the Java code. However, a native method *may* analyze the exception object to determine if it can handle the exception. If it can, then the function

```
(*env)->ExceptionClear(env);
```

must be called to turn off the exception.

In our next example, we implement the fprint native method with the paranoia that is appropriate for a native method. Here are the exceptions that we throw:

- A NullPointerException if the format string is NULL

- An IllegalArgumentException if the format string doesn't contain a % specifier that is appropriate for printing a double

- An OutOfMemoryError if the call to malloc fails

Finally, to demonstrate how to check for an exception when calling a Java method from a native method, we send the string to the stream, a character at a time, and call ExceptionOccurred after each call. Example 10-11 shows the code for the native method. Notice that the native method does not immediately terminate when an exception occurs in the call to PrintWriter.print—it first frees the cstr buffer. When the native method returns, the virtual machine again raises the exception.

Example 10-11: Printf4.c

```c
#include "Printf4.h"
#include <string.h>
#include <stdlib.h>
#include <float.h>

char* find_format(const char format[])
/**
 * @param format a string containing a printf format specifier
 * (such as "%8.2f"). Substrings "%%" are skipped.
 * @return a pointer to the format specifier (skipping the '%')
 * or NULL if there wasn't a unique format specifier
 */
{  char* p;
   char* q;
   size_t n;

   p = strchr(format, '%');
   while (p != NULL && *(p + 1) == '%') /* skip %% */
```

```c
      p = strchr(p + 2, '%');
   if (p == NULL) return NULL;
   /* now check that % is unique */
   p++;
   q = strchr(p, '%');
   while (q != NULL && *(q + 1) == '%') /* skip %% */
      q = strchr(q + 2, '%');
   if (q != NULL) return NULL; /* % not unique */
   q = p + strspn(p, " -0+#"); /* skip past flags */
   q += strspn(q, "0123456789"); /* skip past field width */
   if (*q == '.') { q++; q += strspn(q, "0123456789"); }
      /* skip past precision */
   if (strchr("eEfFgG", *q) == NULL) return NULL;
      /* not a floating point format */
   return p;
}

JNIEXPORT void JNICALL Java_Printf4_fprint
   (JNIEnv* env, jclass cl, jobject out, jstring format,
   jdouble x)
{  const char* cformat;
   char* fmt;
   jclass class_PrintWriter;
   jmethodID id_print;
   char* cstr;
   int width;
   int i;

   if (format == NULL)
   {  (*env)->ThrowNew(env,
         (*env)->FindClass(env,
         "java/lang/NullPointerException"),
         "Printf4.fprint: format is null");
      return;
   }

   cformat = (*env)->GetStringUTFChars(env, format, NULL);
   fmt = find_format(cformat);

   if (fmt == NULL)
   {  (*env)->ThrowNew(env,
         (*env)->FindClass(env,
         "java/lang/IllegalArgumentException"),
         "Printf4.fprint: format is invalid");
      return;
   }
```

```
    width = atoi(fmt);
    if (width == 0) width = DBL_DIG + 10;
    cstr = (char*)malloc(strlen(cformat) + width);

    if (cstr == NULL)
    {   (*env)->ThrowNew(env,
            (*env)->FindClass(env, "java/lang/OutOfMemoryError"),
            "Printf4.fprint: malloc failed");
        return;
    }

    sprintf(cstr, cformat, x);

    (*env)->ReleaseStringUTFChars(env, format, cformat);

    /* now call ps.print(str) */

    /* get the class */
    class_PrintWriter = (*env)->GetObjectClass(env, out);

    /* get the method ID */
    id_print = (*env)->GetMethodID(env, class_PrintWriter,
        "print", "(C)V");

    /* call the method */
    for (i = 0; cstr[i] != 0 && !(*env)->ExceptionOccurred(env);
            i++)
        (*env)->CallVoidMethod(env, out, id_print, cstr[i]);

    free(cstr);
}
```

Example 10-12: Printf4.java

```
import java.io.*;

class Printf4
{   public static native void fprint(PrintWriter ps,
        String format, double x);
    static
    {   System.loadLibrary("Printf4");
    }
}
```

The test program in Example 10-13 demonstrates how the native method will throw an exception when the formatting string is not valid.

Example 10-13: Printf4Test.java

```java
import java.io.*;

class Printf4Test
{  public static void main(String[] args)
   {  double price = 44.95;
      double tax = 7.75;
      double amountDue = price * (1 + tax / 100);
      PrintWriter out = new PrintWriter(System.out);
      Printf4.fprint(out, "Amount due = %%8.2f\n", amountDue);
      out.flush();
   }
}
```

Error handling in C code

- `jint Throw(JNIEnv *env, jthrowable obj)`

  prepares an exception to be thrown upon exiting from the native code. Returns 0 on success, a negative value on failure.

  Parameters: env   the JNI interface pointer

          obj   the exception object to throw

- `jint ThrowNew(JNIEnv *env, jclass clazz, const char msg[])`

  prepares an exception to be thrown upon exiting from the native code. Returns 0 on success, a negative value on failure.

  Parameters: env   the JNI interface pointer

          cl   the class of the exception object to throw

          msg   an UTF string denoting the `String` construction argument of the exception object

- `jthrowable ExceptionOccurred(JNIEnv *env)`

  returns the exception object if an exception is pending, or NULL otherwise.

  Parameters: env   the JNI interface pointer

- `void ExceptionClear(JNIEnv *env)`

  clears any pending exceptions.

  Parameters: env   the JNI interface pointer

The Invocation API

Up to now, we have considered Java programs that made a few C calls, presumably because C was faster or allowed access to functionality that was inaccessible from Java. Suppose you are in the opposite situation. You have a C or C++ program and would like to make a few calls to Java code, perhaps because the Java code is easier to program. Of course, you know how to call the Java methods. But you still need to add the Java Virtual Machine to your program so that the Java code can be interpreted. The so-called *invocation API* is used to embed the Java Virtual Machine into a C or C++ program. Here is the code that you need to initialize a virtual machine.

```
JavaVM *jvm;
JNIEnv *env;
JDK1_1InitArgs vm_args;
vm_args.version = 0x00010001;
JNI_GetDefaultJavaVMInitArgs(&vm_args);
vm_args.classpath = getenv("CLASSPATH");
JNI_CreateJavaVM(&jvm, &env, &vm_args);
```

You need to set up an initialization arguments structure and set the version to Java 1.1. Call `JNI_GetDefaultJavaVMInitArgs` to have the remaining fields in the initialization structure set to their defaults. Then, set the class path and call `JNI_CreateJavaVM` to create the virtual machine. That call fills in a pointer `jvm` to the virtual machine and a pointer `env` to the execution environment.

Once you have set up the Virtual Machine, from that point on, you can call Java methods in he way described in the preceding sections: simply use the `env` pointer in the usual way. You need the `jvm` pointer only to call other functions in the invocation API. Currently, there are only three such functions. The most important one is the function to terminate the virtual machine:

```
(*jvm)->DestroyJavaVM(jvm);
```

The C program in Example 10-14 sets up a virtual machine and then calls the `main` method of the `Welcome` class which was discussed in Chapter 2 of Volume 1.

Example 10-14: InvocationTest.c

```
#include <jni.h>
#include <stdlib.h>

int main()
{   JavaVM *jvm;
    JNIEnv *env;
    JDK1_1InitArgs vm_args;
    jclass cls;
    jmethodID id;
```

```
    vm_args.version = 0x00010001;
    JNI_GetDefaultJavaVMInitArgs(&vm_args);
    vm_args.classpath = getenv("CLASSPATH");

    JNI_CreateJavaVM(&jvm, &env, &vm_args);

    cls = (*env)->FindClass(env, "Welcome");
    id = (*env)->GetStaticMethodID(env, cls, "main",
        "([Ljava/lang/String;)V");
    (*env)->CallStaticVoidMethod(env, cls, id, 100);

    (*jvm)->DestroyJavaVM(jvm);

    return 0;
}
```

To compile this program under Windows, you use the command line

```
cl -Ic:\jdk\include -Ic:\jdk\include\win32 InvocationTest.c
c:\jdk\lib\javai.lib
```

NOTE: When running this program under Windows, make sure that your class path contains c:\jdk\lib**classes.zip**, not just c:\jdk\lib. Otherwise, the class loader will not find the standard Java library.

Suppose you want to deliver this program to your customers. You need to supply the following items:

- Your executable program (InvocationTest.exe)
- The class files of your Java code (Welcome.class)
- The class files of the Java standard library (classes.zip)
- The Java native code library (javai.dll)

Invocation API functions

- jint JNI_GetDefaultJavaVMInitArgs(JDK1_1InitArgs* vm_args)

  fills vm_args with default values. Before calling this function, set vm_args.version to 0x00010001. Returns 0 on success, a negative number on failure.

  Parameters: vm_args   the virtual machine arguments

- jint JNI_CreateJavaVM(JavaVM** p_jvm, JNIEnv** p_env, JDK1_1InitArgs* vm_args)

  initializes the Java Virtual Machine. Before calling this function, set vm_args.version to 0x00010001. You may want to set other fields, such as

the class path. Here is the complete structure:

```
typedef struct
{   jint version; /* Java VM version */
    char **properties; /* System properties. */
    jint checkSource; /* whether to check that Java source
        files are newer than compiled class files. */
    jint nativeStackSize; /* maximum native stack size */
    jint javaStackSize; /* maximum Java stack size. */
    jint minHeapSize; /* initial heap size. */
    jint maxHeapSize; /* maximum heap size. */
    jint verifyMode; /* verify byte codes? 0 = none,
        1 = remotely loaded, 2 = all */
    const char *classpath; /* the class path */
    jint (*vfprintf)(FILE *fp, const char *format, va_list
        args);
        /* VM message printer */
    void (*exit)(jint code); /* VM exit procedure */
    void (*abort)(); /* VM abort procedure */
    jint enableClassGC; /* enable class garbage collection? */
    jint enableVerboseGC; /* display garbage collection
        messages? */
    jint disableAsyncGC; /* disable asynchronous garbage
        collection? */
    jint reserved0; /* Three reserved fields. */
    jint reserved1;
    jint reserved2;
} JDK1_1InitArgs;
```

The function returns 0 if successful, a negative number on failure.

Parameters:	p_jvm	filled with a pointer to the invocation API function table
	p_env	filled with a pointer to the JNI function table
	vm_args	the virtual machine arguments

* `jint DestroyJavaVM(JavaVM* jvm)`

destroys the virtual machine. Returns 0 on success, a negative number on failure. This function must be called through a virtual machine pointer, i.e., `(*jvm)->DestroyJavaVM(jvm)`.

Parameters:	jvm	the virtual machine pointer

A Complete Example: Accessing the Windows Registry

In this section, we describe a full, working example that covers everything we discussed in this chapter: using native methods with strings, arrays, objects, constructor calls, and error handling. What we show you is how to put a Java wrapper around a subset of the ordinary C-based API used to work with the Windows registry. Of course, being a Windows-specific feature, a program using the Windows registry is inherently nonportable. For that reason, the standard Java library has no support for the registry, and it makes sense to use native methods to gain access to it.

An Overview of the Windows Registry

For those who are not familiar with the Windows registry[1], it is a data depository that is accessed by the Windows 95 and NT operating systems, and that is available as a storage area for application programs. In older versions of Windows, the operating system as well as applications used so-called INI files to store configuration parameters. Windows 95 and NT programs are supposed to use the registry, instead. The registry has a number of advantages.

- INI files store data as strings; the registry supports other data types such as integers and byte arrays.

- INI file sections cannot have subsections; the registry supports a complete tree structure.

- Configuration parameters were distributed over many INI files; by placing them into the registry, there is a single point for administration and backup.

Admittedly, the registry is also a single point of failure—if you mess up the registry, your computer may malfunction or even fail to boot! The sample program that we present in this section is safe, but if you plan to make any modifications to it, you should learn how to back up the registry before proceeding. See the book by Petrusha mentioned in the footnote for information on how to back up the Windows registry. (Also, programs like Norton Utilities come with user-friendly programs for registry backup.)

The principal tool for inspecting the registry is the *registry editor*. Because of the potential for error by naive but enthusiastic users, there is no icon for launching the registry editor. Instead, start a DOS shell (or open the Start | Run box) and type `regedit`. Figure 10-3 shows the registry editor in action.

---

[1] A good book is *Inside the Windows 95 Registry* by Ron Petrusha [O'Reilly, 1996].

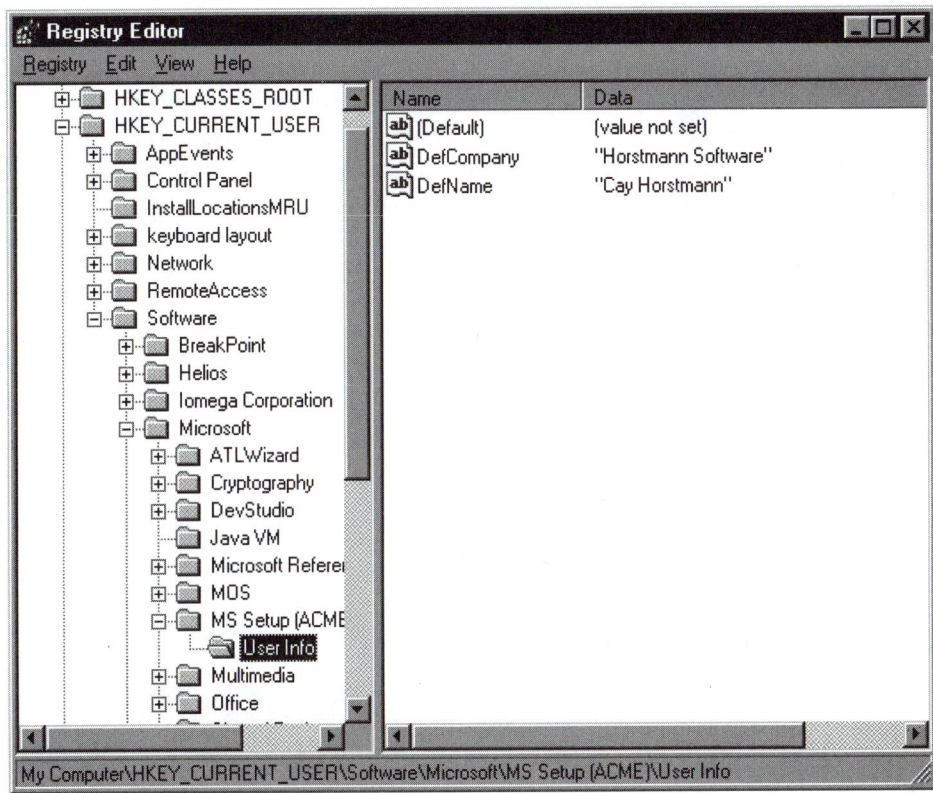

Figure 10-3: The registry editor

The left-hand side shows the keys, which are arranged in a tree structure. Note that each key starts with one of the HKEY nodes like

```
HKEY_CLASSES_ROOT
HKEY_CURRENT_USER
HKEY_LOCAL_MACHINE
. . .
```

The right-hand side shows the name/value pairs that are associated with a particular key. For example, the key

```
HKEY_CURRENT_USER\Software\Microsoft\MS Setup (ACME)\User Info
```

has two name/value pairs, namely,

```
DefCompany="your organization"
DefName="your name"
```

In this case, the values are strings. The values can also be integers or arrays of bytes.

A Java Interface for Accessing the Registry

We will implement a simple interface to access the registry from Java code and then implement this interface with native code. Our interface allows only a few registry operations; to keep the code size down, we omitted other important operations such as adding, deleting, and enumerating keys. (Following our model and the information supplied in Petrusha's book, it would be easy to add the remaining registry API functions.)

Even with the limited subset that we supply, you can

*   Enumerate all names stored in a key

*   Read the value stored with a name

*   Set the value stored with a name

Here is the Java class that encapsulates a registry key:

```
public class Win32RegKey
{   public Win32RegKey(int theRoot, String thePath) { . . . }
    public Enumeration names() { . . . }
    public native Object getValue(String name);
    public native void setValue(String name, Object value);

    public static final int HKEY_CLASSES_ROOT = 0x80000000;
    public static final int HKEY_CURRENT_USER = 0x80000001;
    public static final int HKEY_LOCAL_MACHINE = 0x80000002;
    . . .
}
```

The `names` method returns an enumeration that holds all the names stored with the key. You can get at them with the familiar `hasMoreElements`/`nextElement` methods. The `getValue` method returns an object that is either a string, an `Integer` object, or a byte array. The `value` parameter of the `setValue` method must also be of one of these three types.

Here is a simple function that lists the strings that are stored with the key:

```
HKEY_CURRENT_USER\Software\Microsoft\MS Setup (ACME)\User Info
public static void main(String[] args)
{   Win32RegKey key = new Win32RegKey(
        Win32RegKey.HKEY_CURRENT_USER,
        "Software\\Microsoft\\MS Setup (ACME)\\User Info");

    Enumeration enum = key.names();

    while (enum.hasMoreElements())
    {   String name = (String)enum.nextElement();
        System.out.println(name + " = " + key.getValue(name));
    }
}
```

A typical output of this program is as follows:

```
DefCompany = Horstmann Software
DefUser = Cay Horstmann
```

Implementing the Registry Access Functions as Native Methods

We need to implement three actions:

- Get the value of a key.

- Set the value of a key.

- Iterate through the names of a key.

Fortunately, you have seen essentially all the tools that are required, such as the conversion between Java and C strings and arrays. And you saw how to raise a Java exception in case something goes wrong.

Two issues make these native methods more complex than the preceding examples. The getValue and setValue methods deal with the type Object, which can be one of String, Integer, or byte[]. And the enumeration object needs to *store* the *state* between successive calls to hasMoreElements/nextElement.

Let us first look at the getValue method. The code (which is shown in Example 10-14) goes through the following steps.

1. Open the registry key. To read their values, the registry, API requires that keys be open.

2. Query the type and size of the value that is associated with the name.

3. Read the data into a buffer.

4. If the type is REG_SZ (a string), then call NewStringUTF to create a new string with the value data.

5. If the type is REG_DWORD (a 32-bit integer), then invoke the Integer constructor.

6. If the type is REG_BINARY, then call NewByteArray to create a new byte array and SetByteArrayRegion to copy the value data into the byte array.

7. If the type is none of these, or if there was an error when calling an API function, throw an exception and carefully release all resources that had been acquired up to that point.

8. Close the key and return the object (String, Integer, or byte[]) that had been created.

As you can see, this example illustrates quite nicely how to generate Java objects of different types.

In this native method, it was not difficult to cope with the generic return type. The `jstring`, `jobject`, or `jarray` reference was simply returned as a `jobject`. However, the `setValue` method receives a reference to an `Object`, and it must determine its exact type so it can save it as either a string, integer, or byte array. We can make this determination by querying the class of the `value` object, finding the class references for `java.lang.String`, `java.lang.Integer`, and `byte[]`, and comparing them with the `IsAssignableFrom` function.

If `class1` and `class2` are two class references, then the call

```
(*env)->IsAssignableFrom(env, class1, class2)
```

returns `JNI_TRUE` when `class1` and `class2` are the same class or `class1` is a subclass of `class2`. In either case, references to objects of `class1` can be cast to `class2`. For example, when

```
(*env)->IsAssignableFrom(env,
    (*env)->GetObjectClass(env, value)
    (*env)->FindClass(env, "[B"))
```

is `true`, then we know that `value` is a byte array.

Here is an overview of the code of the `setValue` method.

1. Open the registry key for writing.

2. Find the type of the value to write.

3. If the type is `String`, call `GetStringUTFChars` to get a pointer to the characters. Also, obtain the string length.

4. If the type is `Integer`, call the `intValue` method to get the integer stored in the wrapper object.

5. If the type is `byte[]`, call `GetByteArrayElements` to get a pointer to the bytes. Also, obtain the string length.

6. Pass the data and length to the registry.

7. Close the key. If the type is `String` or `byte[]`, then also release the pointer to the characters or bytes.

Finally, let us turn to the native methods that enumerate keys. These are methods of the `Win32RegKeyNameEnumeration` class (see Example 10-14). When the enumeration process starts, we must open the key. For the duration of the enumeration, we must retain the key handle. That is, the key handle must be stored with the enumeration object. The key handle is of type `DWORD`, a 32-bit quantity, and, hence, can be stored in a Java integer. It is stored in the `hkey` field of the enumeration class. When the enumeration starts, the field is initialized with `SetIntField`. Subsequent calls read the value with `GetIntField`.

TIP: As this example shows using a Java object field to store native-state data is very useful for implementing native methods.

In this example, we store three other data items with the enumeration object. When the enumeration first starts, we can query the registry for the count of name/value pairs and the length of the longest name, which we need so we can allocate C character arrays to hold the names. These values are stored in the count and maxsize fields of the enumeration object. Finally, the index field is initialized with –1 to indicate the start of the enumeration, is set to 0 once the other object fields are initialized, and is incremented after every enumeration step.

Here , we walk through the native methods that support the enumeration. The hasMoreElements method is simple.

1.   Retrieve the index and count fields.

2.   If the index is –1, call the startNameEnumeration function, which opens the key, queries the count and maximum length, and initializes the hkey, count, maxsize and index fields.

3.   Return JNI_TRUE if index is less than count; JNI_FALSE otherwise.

The nextElement method needs to work a little harder.

1.   Retrieve the index and count fields.

2.   If the index is –1, call the startNameEnumeration function, which opens the key, queries the count and maximum length, and initializes the hkey, count, maxsize, and index fields.

3.   If index equals count, throw a NoSuchElementException.

4.   Read the next name from the registry.

5.   Increment index.

6.   If index equals count, close the key.

To compile the program, you must link in the advapi32.lib library. Before compiling, remember to run javah on both Win32RegKey and Win32RegKeyNameEnumeration. The complete command line is

```
cl -Ic:\jdk\include -Ic:\jdk\include\win32 -LD
   Win32RegKey.c advapi32.lib -FeWin32RegKey.dll
```

Example 10-14 shows a program to test our new registry functions. We add three name/value pairs, a string, an integer, and a byte array to the key.

```
HKEY_CURRENT_USER\Software\Microsoft\MS Setup (ACME)\User Info
```

We then enumerate all names of that key and retrieve their values. The program should print out

```
DefName = Cay Horstmann
DefCompany = Horstmann Software
Default user = Bozo the clown
Lucky number = 13
Small primes = 2 3 5 7 11 13
```

Although adding these name/value pairs to that key probably does no harm, you may want to use the registry editor to remove them after running this program.

Example 10-15: Win32RegKey.java

```java
import java.util.*;

public class Win32RegKey
{  public Win32RegKey(int theRoot, String thePath)
   {  root = theRoot;
      path = thePath;
   }
   public Enumeration names()
   {   return new Win32RegKeyNameEnumeration(root, path);
   }
   public native Object getValue(String name);
   public native void setValue(String name, Object value);

   public static final int HKEY_CLASSES_ROOT = 0x80000000;
   public static final int HKEY_CURRENT_USER = 0x80000001;
   public static final int HKEY_LOCAL_MACHINE = 0x80000002;
   public static final int HKEY_USERS = 0x80000003;
   public static final int HKEY_CURRENT_CONFIG = 0x80000005;
   public static final int HKEY_DYN_DATA = 0x80000006;

   private int root;
   private String path;

   static
   {  System.loadLibrary("Win32RegKey");
   }
}

class Win32RegKeyNameEnumeration implements Enumeration
{  Win32RegKeyNameEnumeration(int theRoot, String thePath)
   {  root = theRoot;
      path = thePath;
   }
```

```
    public native Object nextElement();
    public native boolean hasMoreElements();

    private int root;
    private String path;
    private int index = -1;
    private int hkey = 0;
    private int maxsize;
    private int count;
}

class Win32RegKeyException extends RuntimeException
{   public Win32RegKeyException() {}
    public Win32RegKeyException(String why)
    {   super(why);
    }
}
```

Example 10-16: Win32RegKey.c

```c
#include "Win32RegKey.h"
#include "Win32RegKeyNameEnumeration.h"
#include <string.h>
#include <stdlib.h>
#include <windows.h>

JNIEXPORT jobject JNICALL Java_Win32RegKey_getValue
    (JNIEnv* env, jobject this_obj, jstring name)
{   const char* cname;
    jstring path;
    const char* cpath;
    HKEY hkey;
    DWORD type;
    DWORD size;
    jclass this_class;
    jfieldID id_root;
    jfieldID id_path;
    HKEY root;
    jobject ret;
    char* cret;

    /* get the class */
    this_class = (*env)->GetObjectClass(env, this_obj);

    /* get the field IDs */
    id_root = (*env)->GetFieldID(env, this_class, "root", "I");
    id_path = (*env)->GetFieldID(env, this_class, "path",
        "Ljava/lang/String;");
```

```c
/* get the fields */
root = (HKEY)(*env)->GetIntField(env, this_obj, id_root);
path = (jstring)(*env)->GetObjectField(env, this_obj,
    id_path);
cpath = (*env)->GetStringUTFChars(env, path, NULL);

/* open the registry key */
if (RegOpenKeyEx(root, cpath, 0, KEY_READ, &hkey)
    != ERROR_SUCCESS)
{   (*env)->ThrowNew(env,
        (*env)->FindClass(env, "Win32RegKeyException"),
        "Open key failed");
    (*env)->ReleaseStringUTFChars(env, path, cpath);
    return NULL;
}

(*env)->ReleaseStringUTFChars(env, path, cpath);
cname = (*env)->GetStringUTFChars(env, name, NULL);

/* find the type and size of the value */
if (RegQueryValueEx(hkey, cname, NULL, &type, NULL, &size) !=
    ERROR_SUCCESS)
{   (*env)->ThrowNew(env,
        (*env)->FindClass(env, "Win32RegKeyException"),
        "Query value key failed");
    RegCloseKey(hkey);
    (*env)->ReleaseStringUTFChars(env, name, cname);
    return NULL;
}

/* get memory to hold the value */
cret = (char*)malloc(size);

/* read the value */
if (RegQueryValueEx(hkey, cname, NULL, &type, cret, &size) !=
    ERROR_SUCCESS)
{   (*env)->ThrowNew(env,
        (*env)->FindClass(env, "Win32RegKeyException"),
        "Query value key failed");
    free(cret);
    RegCloseKey(hkey);
    (*env)->ReleaseStringUTFChars(env, name, cname);
    return NULL;
}

/* depending on the type, store the value in a string,
    integer or byte array */
if (type == REG_SZ)
```

```
   {  ret = (*env)->NewStringUTF(env, cret);
   }
   else if (type == REG_DWORD)
   {  jclass class_Integer = (*env)->FindClass(env,
          "java/lang/Integer");
      /* get the method ID of the constructor */
      jmethodID id_Integer = (*env)->GetMethodID(env,
          class_Integer, "<init>", "(I)V");
      int value = *(int*)cret;
      /* invoke the constructor */
      ret = (*env)->NewObject(env, class_Integer, id_Integer,
          value);
   }
   else if (type == REG_BINARY)
   {  ret = (*env)->NewByteArray(env, size);
      (*env)->SetByteArrayRegion(env, (jarray)ret, 0, size,
          cret);
   }
   else
   {  (*env)->ThrowNew(env,
          (*env)->FindClass(env, "Win32RegKeyException"),
          "Unsupported value type");
      ret = NULL;
   }

   free(cret);
   RegCloseKey(hkey);
   (*env)->ReleaseStringUTFChars(env, name, cname);

   return ret;
}

JNIEXPORT void JNICALL Java_Win32RegKey_setValue
   (JNIEnv* env, jobject this_obj, jstring name, jobject value)
{  const char* cname;
   jstring path;
   const char* cpath;
   HKEY hkey;
   DWORD type;
   DWORD size;
   jclass this_class;
   jclass class_value;
   jclass class_Integer;
   jfieldID id_root;
   jfieldID id_path;
   HKEY root;
   const char* cvalue;
   int ivalue;
```

```
/* get the class */
this_class = (*env)->GetObjectClass(env, this_obj);

/* get the field IDs */
id_root = (*env)->GetFieldID(env, this_class, "root", "I");
id_path = (*env)->GetFieldID(env, this_class, "path",
    "Ljava/lang/String;");

/* get the fields */
root = (HKEY)(*env)->GetIntField(env, this_obj, id_root);
path = (jstring)(*env)->GetObjectField(env, this_obj,
    id_path);
cpath = (*env)->GetStringUTFChars(env, path, NULL);

/* open the registry key */
if (RegOpenKeyEx(root, cpath, 0, KEY_WRITE, &hkey)
    != ERROR_SUCCESS)
{   (*env)->ThrowNew(env,
        (*env)->FindClass(env, "Win32RegKeyException"),
        "Open key failed");
    (*env)->ReleaseStringUTFChars(env, path, cpath);
    return;
}

(*env)->ReleaseStringUTFChars(env, path, cpath);
cname = (*env)->GetStringUTFChars(env, name, NULL);

class_value = (*env)->GetObjectClass(env, value);
class_Integer = (*env)->FindClass(env, "java/lang/Integer");
/* determine the type of the value object */
if ((*env)->IsAssignableFrom(env, class_value,
    (*env)->FindClass(env, "java/lang/String")))
{   /* it is a string--get a pointer to the characters */
    cvalue = (*env)->GetStringUTFChars(env, (jstring)value,
        NULL);
    type = REG_SZ;
    size = (*env)->GetStringLength(env, (jstring)value) + 1;
}
else if ((*env)->IsAssignableFrom(env, class_value,
    class_Integer))
{   /* it is an integer--call intValue to get the value */
    jmethodID id_intValue = (*env)->GetMethodID(env,
        class_Integer, "intValue", "()I");
    ivalue = (*env)->CallIntMethod(env, value, id_intValue);
    type = REG_DWORD;
    cvalue = (char*)&ivalue;
    size = 4;
}
```

```
    else if ((*env)->IsAssignableFrom(env, class_value,
        (*env)->FindClass(env, "[B")))
    {   /* it is a byte array--get a pointer to the bytes */
        type = REG_BINARY;
        cvalue = (char*)(*env)->GetByteArrayElements(env,
            (jarray)value, NULL);
        size = (*env)->GetArrayLength(env, (jarray)value);
    }
    else
    {   /* we don't know how to handle this type */
        (*env)->ThrowNew(env,
            (*env)->FindClass(env, "Win32RegKeyException"),
            "Unsupported value type");
        RegCloseKey(hkey);
        (*env)->ReleaseStringUTFChars(env, name, cname);
        return;
    }

    /* set the value */
    if (RegSetValueEx(hkey, cname, 0, type, cvalue, size)
        != ERROR_SUCCESS)
    {   (*env)->ThrowNew(env,
            (*env)->FindClass(env, "Win32RegKeyException"),
            "Query value key failed");
    }

    RegCloseKey(hkey);
    (*env)->ReleaseStringUTFChars(env, name, cname);

    /* if the value was a string or byte array, release the
        pointer */
    if (type == REG_SZ)
    {   (*env)->ReleaseStringUTFChars(env, (jstring)value,
            cvalue);
    }
    else if (type == REG_BINARY)
    {   (*env)->ReleaseByteArrayElements(env, (jarray)value,
            (byte*)cvalue, 0);
    }
}

static int startNameEnumeration(JNIEnv* env, jobject this_obj,
    jclass this_class)
/* helper function to start enumeration of names
*/
{   jfieldID id_index;
    jfieldID id_count;
    jfieldID id_root;
```

```c
jfieldID id_path;
jfieldID id_hkey;
jfieldID id_maxsize;

HKEY root;
jstring path;
const char* cpath;
HKEY hkey;
int maxsize = 0;
int count = 0;

/* get the field IDs */
id_root = (*env)->GetFieldID(env, this_class, "root", "I");
id_path = (*env)->GetFieldID(env, this_class, "path",
   "Ljava/lang/String;");
id_hkey = (*env)->GetFieldID(env, this_class, "hkey", "I");
id_maxsize = (*env)->GetFieldID(env, this_class, "maxsize",
   "I");
id_index = (*env)->GetFieldID(env, this_class, "index",
   "I");
id_count = (*env)->GetFieldID(env, this_class, "count",
   "I");

/* get the field values */
root = (HKEY)(*env)->GetIntField(env, this_obj, id_root);
path = (jstring)(*env)->GetObjectField(env, this_obj,
   id_path);
cpath = (*env)->GetStringUTFChars(env, path, NULL);

/* open the registry key */
if (RegOpenKeyEx(root, cpath, 0, KEY_READ, &hkey)
   != ERROR_SUCCESS)
{  (*env)->ThrowNew(env,
      (*env)->FindClass(env, "Win32RegKeyException"),
      "Open key failed");
   (*env)->ReleaseStringUTFChars(env, path, cpath);
   return -1;
}
(*env)->ReleaseStringUTFChars(env, path, cpath);

/* query count and max length of names */
if (RegQueryInfoKey(hkey, NULL, NULL, NULL, NULL,
   NULL, NULL, &count, &maxsize, NULL, NULL, NULL)
   != ERROR_SUCCESS)
{  (*env)->ThrowNew(env,
      (*env)->FindClass(env, "Win32RegKeyException"),
      "Query info key failed");
   return -1;
}
```

```
    /* set the field values */
    (*env)->SetIntField(env, this_obj, id_hkey, (DWORD)hkey);
    (*env)->SetIntField(env, this_obj, id_maxsize, maxsize + 1);
    (*env)->SetIntField(env, this_obj, id_index, 0);
    (*env)->SetIntField(env, this_obj, id_count, count);
    return count;
}

JNIEXPORT jboolean JNICALL
    Java_Win32RegKeyNameEnumeration_hasMoreElements
    (JNIEnv* env, jobject this_obj)
{   jclass this_class;
    jfieldID id_index;
    jfieldID id_count;
    int index;
    int count;
    /* get the class */
    this_class = (*env)->GetObjectClass(env, this_obj);

    /* get the field IDs */
    id_index = (*env)->GetFieldID(env, this_class, "index",
        "I");
    id_count = (*env)->GetFieldID(env, this_class, "count",
        "I");

    index = (*env)->GetIntField(env, this_obj, id_index);
    if (index == -1) /* first time */
    {   count = startNameEnumeration(env, this_obj, this_class);
        index = 0;
    }
    else
        count = (*env)->GetIntField(env, this_obj, id_count);
    return index < count;
}

JNIEXPORT jobject JNICALL
    Java_Win32RegKeyNameEnumeration_nextElement
    (JNIEnv* env, jobject this_obj)
{   jclass this_class;
    jfieldID id_index;
    jfieldID id_hkey;
    jfieldID id_count;
    jfieldID id_maxsize;

    HKEY hkey;
    int index;
    int count;
    int maxsize;
```

```
   char* cret;
   jstring ret;

/* get the class */
 this_class = (*env)->GetObjectClass(env, this_obj);

 /* get the field IDs */
 id_index = (*env)->GetFieldID(env, this_class, "index",
    "I");
 id_count = (*env)->GetFieldID(env, this_class, "count",
    "I");
 id_hkey = (*env)->GetFieldID(env, this_class, "hkey", "I");
 id_maxsize = (*env)->GetFieldID(env, this_class, "maxsize",
    "I");

 index = (*env)->GetIntField(env, this_obj, id_index);
 if (index == -1) /* first time */
 {  count = startNameEnumeration(env, this_obj, this_class);
    index = 0;
 }
 else
    count = (*env)->GetIntField(env, this_obj, id_count);

 if (index >= count) /* already at end */
 {  (*env)->ThrowNew(env,
        (*env)->FindClass(env,
        "java/util/NoSuchElementException"),
        "past end of enumeration");
    return NULL;
 }

 maxsize = (*env)->GetIntField(env, this_obj, id_maxsize);
 hkey = (HKEY)(*env)->GetIntField(env, this_obj, id_hkey);
 cret = (char*)malloc(maxsize);

 /* find the next name */
 if (RegEnumValue(hkey, index, cret, &maxsize, NULL, NULL,
    NULL, NULL) != ERROR_SUCCESS)
 {  (*env)->ThrowNew(env,
        (*env)->FindClass(env, "Win32RegKeyException"),
        "Enum value failed");
    free(cret);
    RegCloseKey(hkey);
    (*env)->SetIntField(env, this_obj, id_index, count);
    return NULL;
 }
```

```
    ret = (*env)->NewStringUTF(env, cret);
    free(cret);

    /* increment index */
    index++;
    (*env)->SetIntField(env, this_obj, id_index, index);

    if (index == count) /* at end */
    {  RegCloseKey(hkey);
    }

    return ret;
}
```

Example 10-17: Win32RegKeyTest.java

```java
import java.util.*;

public class Win32RegKeyTest
{  public static void main(String[] args)
   {  Win32RegKey key = new Win32RegKey(
         Win32RegKey.HKEY_CURRENT_USER,
         "Software\\Microsoft\\MS Setup (ACME)\\User Info");

      key.setValue("Default user", "Bozo the clown");
      key.setValue("Lucky number", new Integer(13));
      key.setValue("Small primes", new byte[]
         { 2, 3, 5, 7, 11 });

      Enumeration enum = key.names();

      while (enum.hasMoreElements())
      {  String name = (String)enum.nextElement();
         System.out.print(name + " = ");

         Object value = key.getValue(name);

         if (value instanceof byte[])
         {  byte[] bvalue = (byte[])value;
            for (int i = 0; i < bvalue.length; i++)
                System.out.print((bvalue[i] & 0xFF) + " ");
         }
         else System.out.print(value);

         System.out.println();
      }
   }
}
```

Type inquiry functions

- `jboolean IsAssignableFrom(JNIEnv *env, jclass cl1, jclass cl2)`

  returns `JNI_TRUE` if objects of the first class can be assigned to objects of the second class; `JNI_FALSE` otherwise. This is the case when the classes are the same, `cl1` is a subclass of `cl2`, or `cl2` represents an interface that is implemented by `cl1` or one of its superclasses.

Parameters:	env	the JNI interface pointer
	cl1, cl2	class references

- `jclass GetSuperClass(JNIEnv *env, jclass cl)`

  returns the superclass of a class. If `cl` represents the class `Object` or an interface, returns `NULL`.

Parameters:	env	the JNI interface pointer
	cl	a class reference

NOTE: Microsoft has a method it calls the *Raw Native Interface* (`http://www.microsoft.com/java`) that is actually fairly close to the method used for calling native functions in the JDK 1.0. As far as we can tell, it has no special virtues; we wouldn't bother with it.

On the other hand, Microsoft and Apple both have announced another approach to calling native methods called *JDirect*. (`www.microsoft.com/java` and `http://applejava.apple.com/MRJGoodies`) Both approaches are based on special virtual machines that handle a lot more of the busy work needed to call native methods than does the standard JVM in the JDK.

In particular, both versions of JDirect would allow you to dispense with the stubs produced by `javah` and to access native methods contained in a DLL without using any C code whatsoever. The JDirect specification is in flux, but it is potentially very interesting. (Keep in mind that using it ties you to using Microsoft's virtual machine or Apple's MRJ.)

For example, Microsoft's version of JDirect essentially makes calling a Windows-based DLL trivial. Based on the current specification, your code for accessing the `Registry` function under JDirect could be as simple as:

```
class Registry
{
/** @dll.import("advapi32") */
private static native int RegCreateKey(int hkey, String
subKey, int result);}
//other registry functions follow


}
```

where the @dll.import will tell Microsoft's JVM to automatically make whatever type conversions need to be made.

Based on the limited information at hand, the Apple version would be something like:

```
import com.apple.NativeObject;
public class MakeBeeps implements NativeObject
{   public native static void SysBeep(short duration);
    private static String[] nativeNames = { "InterfaceLib"
};
}
```

Both of these methods are clearly much simpler than the methods used in the JDK, but whether they will be uniformly adopted by all virtual machines on Windows or on the Apple is exceedingly doubtful. If you use Java as a nice programming language for platform-specific programming, you will find these direct call interfaces quite interesting. If you use Java to write platform-independent code, you will likely pass on them.

Appendix I
Installing the CD-ROM

Contents of the CD-ROM

The CD-ROM has the following directory structure:

```
COREJAVA
WINDOWS
solaris
```

Other operating systems may be added.

The COREJAVA directory contains the sample files for both volumes of Core Java. The WINDOWS directory contains the Java development kit (JDK) for Windows 95/NT and a number of useful shareware programs. The solaris directory contains the JDK for the Solaris operating system.

Installation Directions

Install the JDK

You can skip this step if you already have a Java 1.1 development environment installed.

1. Locate the subdirectory on the CD-ROM that matches your operating system.

2. You will find an installation file for the JDK in a format that is appropriate for your operating system, accompanied by installation instructions. For example, for Windows, this will be an .exe file.

3. Install the JDK files onto your computer, following the procedure that is appropriate for your operating system. We recommend that you place them inside a directory jdk. If you have an older version of the JDK, completely remove it before installing the newer version.

NOTE: If the JDK is installed by a setup program, the setup program usually offers a different default for each version of the JDK, such as jdk1.1.4. We recommend that you change the directory to jdk. However, if you are a Java enthusiast who enjoys collecting different versions of the JDK, go ahead and accept the default.

---

4. Add the jdk\bin directory to the PATH. For example, under Windows 95, place the following line at the *end* of your AUTOEXEC.BAT file:

    ```
    SET PATH=c:\jdk\bin;%PATH%
    ```

> NOTE: If you installed the JDK into another directory such as `jdk1.1.4`, then you need to set the path to `jdk1.1.4\bin`. You need to modify the other instructions as well. We won't mention this again.

5. Add an environment variable `CLASSPATH`. This environment must contain

    -   `jdk\lib\classes.zip`

    -   the current directory (`.`)

    -   `CoreJavaBook` (the directory into which you will install the Core Java examples)

    For example, under Windows, you add the following line to your `AUTOEXEC.BAT` file:

    ```
    SET CLASSPATH=c:\jdk\lib\classes.zip;.;c:\CoreJavaBook
    ```

    If you use the C shell under Unix, place the following command in your `.cshrc` file.

    ```
    setenv CLASSPATH /jdk/lib/classes.zip:.:$home/CoreJavaBook
    ```

6. Check whether there is a separate installation for the Bean Development Kit (BDK) for your operating system on the CD. If so, install the BDK. We recommend that you install it in a directory `bdk`.

7. Log out or reboot your computer.

Install Shareware Software

Skip this step if you do not use Windows 95 or NT.

We include a number of shareware programs on the CD-ROM that you may find useful, including

-   WinZip, our favorite ZIP tool. You can use it to uncompress files in the ZIP, JAR, and TAR formats.

-   TextPad, our favorite ASCII text editor for Windows. This version of TextPad is enhanced to compile and run Java programs. (Look in the Tools menu for the commands.)

-   HexWorkshop, our favorite hex editor. In Volume 2, we show you how to use HexWorkshop to snoop inside class files.

NOTE: Keep in mind that the shareware programs are not free; you are expected to pay its authors if you use the program. We have no connection whatsoever with the authors of these programs. We simply found them very useful and thought you might want to give them a try yourself. If you have trouble installing or using these programs, check out the Web pages of the vendors. We offer no technical support for these products.

To install the software, locate the installation files in the subdirectory of the WINDOWS directory (such as WINDOWS\WINZIP or WINDOWS\TEXTPAD) and run the setup program in that subdirectory.

Install the Core Java Example Files

The CD-ROM contains the source code for all example programs in the book. All files are packed inside a single ZIP archive, corejava.zip.

If you have a ZIP utility such as WinZip (which is supplied on the CD-ROM), you can use it to unzip the files. Otherwise, you need to first install the JDK, as previously described. The JDK program jar can uncompress ZIP files.

Here are the steps to install the Core Java example files:

1. Uncompress the corejava.zip file into the CoreJavaBook directory. You can use WinZip, another ZIP utility, or the jar program that is part of the JDK. If you use jar, do the following:

    *   Make a directory CoreJavaBook.

    *   Copy the corejava.zip file to that directory.

    *   Change to that directory.

    *   Execute the command
        jar xvf corejava.zip.

2. Make sure that the CoreJavaBook directory is on the class path. If you installed the JDK, following our instructions, then the class path will contain the CoreJavaBook directory. Otherwise, you need to add it.

NOTE: Many integrated Java development environments have their own methods for setting the class path. If you use such a product, find out how to tell it to search the CoreJavaBook directory for class files. Consult the documentation of your environment and contact the vendor for assistance if necessary.

The example files are organized as follows:

```
CoreJavaBook
    corejava
    docs
    ch2
        Welcome
        WelcomeApplet
        ImageViewer
    ch3
        FirstSample
        LotteryOdds
        LotteryDrawing
        Mortgage
        MortgageLoop
        Retirement
        SquareRoot
    . . .
    v2ch1
    . . .
```

There is a separate directory for each chapter of this book. Each of these directories has separate subdirectories for example files. For instance, `CoreJavaBook\ch2\ImageViewer` contains the source code and sample images for the image viewer application. (There is no source code for Chapter 1.) The directories for Volume 2 are named `v2ch1`, `v2ch2`, and so on.

NOTE: The `corejava` directory contains a number of useful Java classes we wrote to supplement missing features in the standard Java library. These files are needed for many examples in the book. It is crucial that your `CLASSPATH` environment variable is set to include the `CoreJavaBook` directory so that the programs can find our files, such as `CoreJavaBook\corejava\Format.class` and `CoreJavaBook\corejava\CloseableFrame.class`.

The `docs` directory contains the documentation for the classes in the `corejava` directory. Point your Web browser to `CoreJavaBook\docs\tree.html` for a summary of the utility classes that we supply. Click on the links to get more information about each class.

NOTE: The links—there aren't many—from the Core Java documentation to the JDK documentation do not work because of a limitation of the `javadoc` tool that was used to automatically extract the documentation from the source files.

Testing the Installation

Testing the JDK

Go to the `CoreJavaBook\ch2\Welcome` directory. Then, enter the following commands:

```
javac Welcome.java
java Welcome
```

Or, if you use an integrated development environment, load the file `Welcome.java`, then compile and run the program. There should be no warning or error messages during compilation.

When the program runs, it should write a welcome message in the console window.

Testing the Core Java Utility Package

Go to the `CoreJavaBook\ch7\NotHelloWorld1` directory. Then, enter the following commands:

```
javac NotHelloWorld1.java
java NotHelloWorld1
```

Or, if you use an integrated development environment, load the file `NotHelloWorld1.java`, then compile and run the program. There should be no warning or error messages during compilation.

When the program runs, it should pop up a window with a silly message.

Troubleshooting

Here are some troubleshooting hints in case the installation was not successful.

PATH and CLASSPATH

The single, most common problem we encountered with Java is an incorrect PATH or CLASSPATH environment variable. Check the following:

1.   The `java\bin` directory must be on PATH.

2.   The `java\lib\classes.zip` file and the current directory (that is, the . directory) must be on CLASSPATH.

3.   The `CoreJavaBook` directory must also be on CLASSPATH.

Double-check these settings and reboot your computer if you run into trouble.

Memory Problems

If you have only 16 Mbytes of memory, you may get "insufficient memory" errors from the Java compiler. In that case, close memory hogs like Netscape and Microsoft Exchange. If you have less than 16 Mbytes of memory, you will probably be unable to compile large programs.

NOTE: Only the compiler and applet viewer pig out on memory. Once you compile an application, you should have no trouble running it with the Java interpreter or a browser, even with less than 16 Mbytes of memory.

Case Sensitivity

Java is case sensitive. HTML is sometimes case sensitive. DOS is not case sensitive. This caused us no end of grief, especially since Java can give very bizarre error messages when it messes up because of a spelling error. Always check file names, parameter names, class names, keywords, and so on for capitalization.

Older Browsers

All example programs in this book use Java 1.1. If your browser supports only Java 1.0, you cannot use it to view the applets that are supplied with this book. You can obtain an updated browser or simply use the applet viewer.

About Other Platforms

The setup that we described assumes that your platform has a command-line interface and a way for setting environment variables. That is the case for Windows, Unix, and OS/2, but it is not the case for the Macintosh. Read the information supplied by Sun Microsystems or the vendor of your development environment, and modify the installation instructions accordingly.

Updates and Bug Fixes

The CD-ROM contains several hundred files, and some of them are bound to have minor glitches and inconsistencies. We keep a list of frequently asked questions, a list of typographical errors, and bug fixes on the Web. (The main Web page for the book is `http://www.horstmann.com/corejava.html`.) We very much welcome any reports of typographical errors, example program bugs, and suggestions for improvement.

Before contacting us, please consider the following:

1. Please check the FAQ
   (`http://www.horstmann.com/corejava/faq.html`)
   and list of bug reports
   (`http://www.horstmann.com/corejava/bugs.html`) before mailing us.
   We get many duplicate queries and bug reports.

2. Please, no requests for handholding. Many readers have successfully compiled and executed the programs on the CD-ROM. If you have problems, there is an overwhelming likelihood that the problem is on your end, not because of a flaw with the CD-ROM contents. On the other hand, if we

goofed, and there is a serious problem with the CD-ROM, then there is an overwhelming chance that hundreds of readers complained to us already and that you will find a resolution on the FAQ.

3. We want to support and improve the Core Java book and example files, but we cannot help you with problems with the Java compiler, your development environment, or the shareware programs on the CD-ROM. Please contact the product vendor for assistance in those cases.

4. Finally, when contacting us, please use e-mail only. Please don't be disappointed if we don't answer every query or if we don't get back to you immediately. We do read all e-mail and consider your input to make future editions of this book clearer and more informative.

Index

Exhibit A
Java ™ Development Kit
Version 1.1.x
and
BDK Version 1.0 Combined
Binary Code License

This binary code license (License) contains rights and restrictions associated with use of the accompanying software and documentation ("Software"). Read the License carefully before installing the Software. By installing the Software you agree to the terms and conditions of this License.

1. Limited License Grant. Sun grants to you ("Licensee") a non-exclusive, non-transferable limited license to use the Software without fee for evaluation of the Software and for development of Java TM compatible applets and applications. Licensee may make one archival copy of the Software. Except for the foregoing, Licensee may not re-distribute the Software in whole or in part, either separately or included with a product. Refer to the Java Runtime Environment Version 1.1 binary code license (http://www.javasoft.com/products/JDK/1.1/index.html) for the availability of runtime code which may be distributed with Java compatible applets and applications.

2. Redistribution of Demonstration Files. Sun grants Licensee the right to use, modify and redistribute the Beans example and demonstration code, including the Bean Box ("Demos"), in both source and binary code form provided that (i) Licensee does not utilize the Demos in a manner which is disparaging to Sun; and (ii) Licensee indemnifies and holds Sun harmless from all claims relating to any such use or distribution of the Demos. Such distribution is limited to the source and binary code of the Demos and specifically excludes any rights to modify or distribute any graphical images contained in the Demos.

3. Java Platform Interface. Licensee may not modify the Java Platform Interface ("JPI), identified as classes contained within the "java" package or any subpackages of the "java" package), by creating additional classes within the JPI or otherwise causing the addition to or modification of the classes in the JPI. In the event that Licensee creates any Java-related API and distributes such API to others for applet or application development, Licensee must promptly publish an accurate specification for such API for free use by all developers of Java-based software.

4. Restrictions. Software is confidential copyrighted information of Sun and title to all copies is retained by Sun and/or its licensors. Licensee shall not modify, decompile, disassemble, decrypt, extract, or otherwise reverse engineer Software. Software may not be leased, assigned, or sublicensed, in whole or in part. **Software is not designed or intended for use in on-line control of aircraft, air traffic, aircraft navigation or aircraft communications; or in the design, construction, operation or maintenance of any nuclear facility. Licensee warrants that it will not use or redistribute the Software for such purposes.**

5. Trademarks and Logos. This License does not authorize Licensee to use any Sun name, trademark or logo. Licensee acknowledges that Sun owns the Java trademark and all Java-related trademarks, logos and icons including the Coffee Cup and Duke ("Java Marks") and agrees to: (i) comply with the Java Trademark Guidelines at http://java.com/trademarks.html; (ii) not do anything harmful to or inconsistent with Sun's rights in the Java Marks; and (iii) assist Sun in protecting those rights, including assigning to Sun any rights acquired by Licensee in any Java Mark.

6. Disclaimer of Warranty. Software is provided "AS IS", without a warranty of any kind. ALL EXPRESS OR IMPLIED REPRESENTATIONS AND WARRANTIES, INCLUDING ANY IMPLIED WARRANTY OF MERCHANTABILITY, FITNESS FOR A PARTICULAR PURPOSE OR NON-INFRINGEMENT, ARE HEREBY EXCLUDED.

7. Limitation of Liability. SUN AND ITS LICENSORS SHALL NOT BE LIABLE FOR ANY DAMAGES SUFFERED BY LICENSEE OR ANY THIRD PARTY AS A RESULT OF USING OR DISTRIBUTING SOFTWARE. IN NO EVENT WILL SUN OR ITS LICENSORS BE LIABLE FOR ANY LOST REVENUE, PROFIT OR DATA, OR FOR DIRECT, INDIRECT, SPECIAL, CONSEQUENTIAL, INCIDENTAL OR PUNITIVE DAMAGES, HOWEVER CAUSED AND REGARDLESS OF THE THEORY OF LIABILITY, ARISING OUT OF THE USE OF OR INABILITY TO USE SOFTWARE, EVEN IF SUN HAS BEEN ADVISED OF THE POSSIBILITY OF SUCH DAMAGES.

8. Termination. Licensee may terminate this License at any time by destroying all copies of Software. This License will terminate immediately without notice from Sun if Licensee fails to comply with any provision of this License. Upon such termination, Licensee must destroy all copies of Software.

9. Export Regulations. Software, including technical data, is subject to U.S. export control laws, including the U.S. Export Administration Act and its associated regulation, and may be subject to export or import regulations in other countries. Licensee agrees to comply strictly with all such regulations and acknowledges that it has the responsibility to obtain licenses to export, re-export, or import Software. Software may not be downloaded, or otherwise exported or re-exported (i) into, or to a nation or resident of, Cuba, Iran, North Korea, Libya, Sudan, Syria or any country to which the U. S. has embargoed goods; or (ii) to anyone on the U. S. Treasury Department's list of Specially Designated Nations or the U.S. Commerce Department's Table of Denial Orders.

10. Restricted Rights. Use, duplication or disclosure by the United States government is subject to the restrictions as set forth in the Rights in Technical Data and Computer Software Clauses in DFARS 252.227-7013(c)(1)(ii) and FAR 52.227-19(c)(2) as applicable.

11. Governing Law. Any action related to this License will be governed by California law and controlling U. S. federal law. No choice of law rules of any jurisdiction will apply.

12. Severability. If any of the above provisions are held to be in violation of applicable law, void, or unenforceable in any jurisdiction, then such provisions are herewith waived to the extent necessary for the License to be otherwise enforceable in such jurisdiction. However, if in Sun's opinion deletion of any provisions of the License by operation of this paragraph unreasonably compromises the rights or increases the liabilities of Sun or its licensors, Sun reserves the right to terminate the License and refund the fee paid by Licensee, if any, as Licensee's sole and exclusive remedy.

SUN MICROSYSTEMS PRESS BOOKS
Bringing Sun's Expertise to You!

 **Sun** microsystems

PRENTICE HALL PTR is pleased to publish **SUN MICROSYSTEMS PRESS** books. This year's **SUN MICROSYSTEMS PRESS** catalog has unprecedented breadth and depth, covering not only the inner workings of Sun operating systems, but also guides to intranets, security, Java™, networking, and other topics important to anyone working with these technologies.

CORE JAVA 1.1
Volume 1: Fundamentals
CAY S. HORSTMANN and GARY CORNELL

672 pages; (includes CD-ROM)
ISBN 0-13-766957-7

Now in its third revision, Core Java is still the leading Java book for software developers who want to put Java to work on real problems. Written for experienced programmers with a solid background in languages ranging from Visual Basic to COBOL to C and C++, CORE JAVA 1.1, VOLUME 1 concentrates on the underlying Java 1.1 language along with the fundamentals of using the cross-platform graphics library supplied with the JDK 1.1.

This must-have reference features comprehensive coverage of the essentials for serious programmers:
- Encapsulation
- Classes and methods
- Inheritance
- The Java 1.1 event model
- Data structures
- Exception handling

The accompanying CD is packed with sample programs that demonstrate key language and library features — no toy code! The CD also includes the Windows 95/NT and Solaris™ versions of the JDK 1.1 and shareware versions of WinEdit, WinZip and TextPad for Windows95/NT.

CORE JAVA 1.1
Volume 2: Advanced Features
CAY S. HORSTMANN and GARY CORNELL

750 pages; (includes CD-ROM)
ISBN 0-13-766965-8 .

For programmers already familiar with the core features of the JAVA 1.1 language, VOLUME 2: ADVANCED FEATURES includes detailed and up-to-date explanations of topics such as:
- Streams
- Multithreading
- Network programming
- JDBC, RMI, JavaBeans™
- Distributed objects

The accompanying CD includes useful sample programs (no toy code!), Windows 95/NT and Solaris™ versions of JDK 1.1, and shareware versions of WinEdit, TextPad, and WinZip.

> "Cornell and Horstmann make the details of the powerful and expressive language understandable and they also furnish a conceptual model for its object-oriented foundations."
>
> — GRADY BOOCH

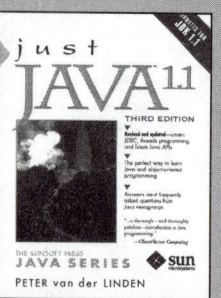

...Also available from Sun Microsystems

CONFIGURATION AND CAPACITY PLANNING FOR SOLARIS SERVERS
BRIAN L. WONG

448 pages; ISBN 0-13-349952-9

A complete reference for planning and configuring Solaris servers for NFS, DBMS, and timesharing environments, featuring coverage of SPARC station 10, SPARC center 2000, SPARC server 1000, and Solaris 2.3.

PANIC!
UNIX System Crash Dump Analysis
CHRIS DRAKE and KIMBERLEY BROWN

480 pages; (includes CD-ROM)
ISBN 0-13-149386-8

UNIX systems crash—it's a fact of life. Until now, little information has been available regarding system crashes. PANIC! is the first book to concentrate solely on system crashes and hangs, explaining what triggers them and what to do when they occur. PANIC! guides you through system crash dump postmortem analysis towards problem resolution. PANIC! presents this highly technical and intricate subject in a friendly, easy style that even the novice UNIX system administrator will find readable, educational, and enjoyable.

TOPICS COVERED INCLUDE:
- What is a panic? What is a hang?
- Header files, symbols, and symbol tables
- A comprehensive tutorial on adb, the absolute debugger
- Introduction to assembly language
- Actual case studies of postmortem analysis

A CD-ROM containing several useful analysis tools—such as adb macros and C tags output from the source trees of two different UNIX systems—is included.

SUN PERFORMANCE AND TUNING:
SPARC and Solaris
ADRIAN COCKCROFT

254 pages; ISBN 0-13-149642-5

This book is an indispensable reference for anyone working with Sun workstations running the Solaris environment. Written for system administrators and software developers, it includes techniques for maximizing system performance through application design, configuration tuning, and system monitoring tools. The book provides detailed performance and configuration information on all SPARC™ machines and peripherals and all operating system releases from SunOS™ 4.1 through Solaris 2.4.

HIGHLIGHTS INCLUDE:
- Performance measurement and analysis techniques
- Uni- and multiprocessor SPARC system architectures and performance
- Hardware components: CPUs, caches, and memory management unit designs
- Kernel algorithms and tuning rules

Second Edition coming early 1998!

WABI 2:
Opening Windows
SCOTT FORDIN and SUSAN NOLIN

383 pages; ISBN 0-13-461617-0

WABI™ 2: OPENING WINDOWS explains the ins and outs of using Wabi software from Sun Microsystems to install, run, and manage Microsoft Windows applications on UNIX systems. Easy step-by-step instructions, illustrations, and charts guide you through each phase of using Wabi—from getting started to managing printers, drives, and COM ports to getting the most from your specific Windows applications.

"...This book could be a lifesaver."

— MILES O'NEAL, *UNIX Review*, January 1996

...Also available from Sun Microsystems

AUTOMATING SOLARIS INSTALLATIONS
A Custom Jumpstart Guide
**PAUL ANTHONY KASPER
and ALAN L. McCLELLAN**

282 pages; (includes a diskette)
ISBN 0-13-312505-X

AUTOMATING SOLARIS INSTALLATIONS describes how to set up "hands-off" Solaris installations for hundreds of SPARC™ and x86 systems. It explains in detail how to configure your site so that when you install Solaris, you simply boot a system and walk away—the software installs automatically! The book also includes a diskette with working shell scripts to automate pre- and post-installation tasks, such as:

- Updating systems with patch releases
- Installing third-party or unbundled software on users' systems
- Saving and restoring system data
- Setting up access to local and remote printers
- Transitioning a system from SunOS™ 4.x to Solaris 2

SOLARIS IMPLEMENTATION
A Guide for System Administrators
GEORGE BECKER, MARY E. S. MORRIS, and KATHY SLATTERY

345 pages; ISBN 0-13-353350-6

Written by expert Sun™ system administrators, this book discusses real world, day-to-day Solaris 2 system administration for both new installations and for migration from an installed Solaris 1 base. It presents tested procedures to help system administrators improve and customize their networks and includes advice on managing heterogeneous Solaris environments. Provides actual sample auto install scripts and disk partitioning schemes used at Sun.

TOPICS COVERED INCLUDE:

- Local and network methods for installing Solaris 2 systems
- Configuring with admintool versus command-line processes
- Building and managing the network, including setting up security
- Managing software packages and patches
- Handling disk utilities and archiving procedures

SOLARIS PORTING GUIDE,
Second Edition
SUNSOFT DEVELOPER ENGINEERING

695 pages; ISBN 0-13-443672-5

Ideal for application programmers and software developers, the SOLARIS PORTING GUIDE provides a comprehensive technical overview of the Solaris 2 operating environment and its related migration strategy.

The Second Edition is current through Solaris 2.4 (for both SPARC and x86 platforms) and provides all the information necessary to migrate from Solaris 1 (SunOS 4.x) to Solaris 2 (SunOS 5.x). Other additions include a discussion of emerging technologies such as the Common Desktop Environment from Sun, hints for application performance tuning, and extensive pointers to further information, including Internet sources.

TOPICS COVERED INCLUDE:

- SPARC and x86 architectural differences
- Migrating from common C to ANSI C
- Building device drivers for SPARC and x86 using DDI/DKI
- Multithreading, real-time processing, and the Sun Common Desktop Environment

"This book is a must for all Solaris 2 system administrators."
— TOM JOLLANDS,
Sun Enterprise Network Systems

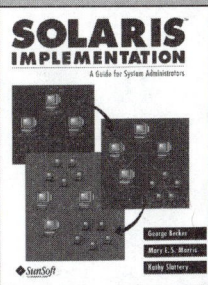

"[This book] deals with daily tasks and should be beneficial to anyone administering Solaris 2.x, whether a veteran or new Solaris user."
— SYS ADMIN,
May/June 1995

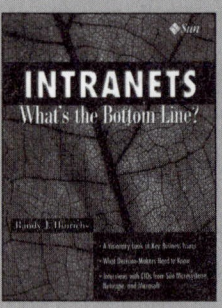

...Also available from Sun Microsystems

NETWORKING THE NEW ENTERPRISE:
The Proof, Not the Hype
HARRIS KERN, RANDY JOHNSON, MICHAEL HAWKINS, and HOWIE LYKE, with WILLIAM KENNEDY and MARK CAPPEL

212 pages; ISBN 0-13-263427-9

NETWORKING THE NEW ENTERPRISE tackles the key information technology questions facing business professionals today—and provides real solutions. The book covers all aspects of network computing, including effective architecture, security, the Intranet, web sites, and the resulting people issues culture shock.

OTHER NETWORKING TOPICS INCLUDE:

- Building a production quality network that supports distributed client/server computing
- Designing a reliable high-speed backbone network
- Centralizing and controlling TCP/IP administration
- Evaluating and selecting key network components

Like RIGHTSIZING THE NEW ENTERPRISE and Managing the New Enterprise, its best-selling companion volumes, NETWORKING THE NEW ENTERPRISE is based on the authors' real-life experiences. It's the expert guide to every strategic networking decision you face. AND THAT'S NO HYPE.

RIGHTSIZING FOR CORPORATE SURVIVAL
An IS Manager's Guide
ROBERT MASSOUDI, ASTRID JULIENNE, BOB MILLRADT, and REED HORNBERGER

250 pages; ISBN 0-13-123126-X

Information systems (IS) managers will find hands-on guidance to developing a rightsizing strategy and plan in this fact-filled reference book. Based upon research conducted through customer visits with multi-national corporations, it details the experiences and insights gained by IS professionals who have implemented systems in distributed, client/server environments. Throughout the book, case studies and "lessons learned" reinforce the discussion and document best practices associated with rightsizing.

"A great reference tool for IS managers planning rightsizing projects."
— G. PHIL CLARK, Kodak Imaging Services